Unity 2018 Cookbook
Third Edition

Over 160 recipes to take your 2D and 3D game
development to the next level

Matt Smith

BIRMINGHAM - MUMBAI

Unity 2018 Cookbook
Third Edition

Contributor: Chico Queiroz
Commissioning Editor: Kunal Chaudhari
Acquisition Editor: Shweta Pant
Content Development Editor: Francis Carneiro
Technical Editor: Ralph Rosario
Copy Editor: Safis Editing
Project Coordinator: Alinka Dias
Proofreader: Safis Editing
Indexer: Aishwarya Gangawane
Graphics: Jason Monteiro
Production Coordinator: Shraddha Falebhai

First published: June 2013
Second edition: October 2015
Third edition: August 2018

Production reference: 1310818

Published by Packt Publishing Ltd.
Livery Place
35 Livery Street
Birmingham
B3 2PB, UK.

ISBN 978-1-78847-190-9

www.packtpub.com

I would like to dedicate this book to my wife Sinéad.

– Matt Smith

`mapt.io`

Mapt is an online digital library that gives you full access to over 5,000 books and videos, as well as industry leading tools to help you plan your personal development and advance your career. For more information, please visit our website.

Why subscribe?

- Spend less time learning and more time coding with practical eBooks and Videos from over 4,000 industry professionals

- Improve your learning with Skill Plans built especially for you

- Get a free eBook or video every month

- Mapt is fully searchable

- Copy and paste, print, and bookmark content

Packt.com

Did you know that Packt offers eBook versions of every book published, with PDF and ePub files available? You can upgrade to the eBook version at `www.packt.com` and as a print book customer, you are entitled to a discount on the eBook copy. Get in touch with us at `customercare@packtpub.com` for more details.

At `www.packt.com`, you can also read a collection of free technical articles, sign up for a range of free newsletters, and receive exclusive discounts and offers on Packt books and eBooks.

Foreword

Not so long ago, developing professional quality games meant licensing an expensive game engine or writing your own from scratch. Then, you needed to hire a small army of developers to use it. Today, game engines like Unity have democratized game development to the point where you can simply download the tools and start making the game of your dreams right away.

Well... kinda. Having a powerful game creation tool is not the same thing as having the technical knowledge and skills to use it effectively.

I've been developing games and game tools professionally for over 15 years. When I first took the plunge into learning Unity development to create the Fungus storytelling tool, I found a huge amount of online documentation, tutorials, and forum answers available for Unity developers. This makes getting started with Unity development relatively easy, but the information can also be quite fragmented. Often, the last piece of the puzzle you need is buried 40 minutes into an hour-long tutorial video or on the 15th page of a forum thread. The hours you spend looking for these nuggets of wisdom is time that would be better spent working on your game.

The beauty of the Unity Cookbooks is that Matt and Chico have distilled this knowledge into a neat collection of easy-to-follow recipes, and they have provided the scripts and complete working projects so that you can put it to use straight away.

In this latest edition for Unity 2018, Matt has updated the recipes from the previous book and added hundreds of new pages to introduce many of the latest Unity features. These include topics such as Shader Graphs, Virtual-Reality projects, 2D and 360-degree Video Players, Cinemachine, in-game geometry building with ProBuilder, and Unity Technologies'2D and 3D GameKits.

Getting started with Unity development is free and easy. When you're ready to take your skills to the next level, this book is an effective way to do just that. It covers a great deal in its hundreds of pages, and if you can master even half of what's here, you'll be well on the way to becoming a great Unity developer!

Chris Gregan

Chief Architect, Romero Games: https://www.romerogames.ie/

Author of Fungus: http://fungusgames.com

Contributors

About the author

Matt Smith is a computing academic at what will soon become the Technological University of Dublin, Ireland.

Matt started computer programming on a brand new ZX80 and submitted two games for his computing O-level exam. After nearly 10 years as a full-time student on a succession of scholarships, he gained several degrees in computing, including a PhD in computational musicology.

In 1985, Matt wrote the lyrics and was in the band whose music appeared on the B-side of the audio cassette carrying the computer game Confusion. Matt is a documentation author for the open source Fungus Unity project.

With his children, he studies and teaches tae kwon do, and all three of them are beginning guitar lessons in 2018.

Many thanks to Chico for all his work on the earlier editions of this cookbook - I look forward to working with you again in the future.

Thanks to my family for all their support. Thanks also to the editors, reviewers, and readers who provided feedback and suggestions. Thanks to my students, who continue to challenge and surprise me with their enthusiasm for multimedia and game development.

Special thanks to Kris for help with the VR recipes and Justin in Limerick for keeping me sane with snooker and golf breaks over the summer.

About the reviewer

Jate Wittayabundit is a Sr Unity developer at WGames based in Toronto, Canada. He loves puzzle games and animation movies. For many years, he has been working as a Sr/lead game developer for many titles, including children's games, such as Dora, Paw Petrol, and such. He was also an author of Unity 3 and 4 Game Development Hotshot, and a technical reviewer for Unity 4.x Cookbook, Packt Publishing. In his spare time, he loves to paint and work on 3D software, such as Zbrush or 3D Studio Max. He also loves painting and drawing.

> *I'd like to thank my family for supporting me. Thanks to everyone at Packt who give me the opportunity, and thanks to all the readers.*

Packt is searching for authors like you

If you're interested in becoming an author for Packt, please visit `authors.packtpub.com` and apply today. We have worked with thousands of developers and tech professionals, just like you, to help them share their insight with the global tech community. You can make a general application, apply for a specific hot topic that we are recruiting an author for, or submit your own idea.

Table of Contents

Preface

Game development is a broad and complex task. It is an interdisciplinary field, covering subjects as diverse as artificial intelligence, character animation, digital painting, and sound editing. All these areas of knowledge can materialize as the production of hundreds (or thousands!) of multimedia and data assets. A special software application—the game engine—is required to consolidate all these assets into a single product. Game engines are specialized pieces of software, which used to belong to an esoteric domain. They were expensive, inflexible, and extremely complicated to use. They were for big studios or hardcore programmers only. Then, along came Unity.

Unity represents the true democratization of game development. It is an engine and multimedia editing environment that is user-friendly and versatile. It has free and Pro versions; the latter includes even more features. Unity offers deployment to many platforms, including the following:

- **Mobile:** Android, iOS, Windows Phone, and BlackBerry
- **Web:** WebGL
- **Desktop:** PC, Mac, and Linux platforms
- **Console:** PS4, PS3, Xbox One, XBox 360, PlayStation Mobile, PlayStation Vita, and Wii U
- **Virtual Reality (VR)/Augmented Reality (AR):** Oculus Rift, Gear VR, Google Daydream, and Microsoft Hololens

Today, Unity is used by a diverse community of developers all around the world. Some are students and hobbyists, but many are commercial organizations, ranging from garage developers to international studios, who use Unity to make a huge number of games—you might have already played some on one platform or another.

This book provides over 170 Unity game development recipes. Some recipes demonstrate Unity application techniques for multimedia features, including working with animations and using preinstalled package systems. Other recipes develop game components with C# scripts, ranging from working with data structures and data file manipulation to artificial intelligence algorithms for computer-controlled characters.

If you want to develop quality games in an organized and straightforward way, and you want to learn how to create useful game components and solve common problems, then both Unity and this book are for you.

Who this book is for

This book is for anyone who wants to explore a wide range of Unity scripting and multimedia features and find ready-to-use solutions for many game features. Programmers can explore multimedia features, and multimedia developers can try their hand at scripting. From intermediate to advanced users, from artists to coders, this book is for you, and everyone in your team! It is intended for everyone who has the basics of using Unity and a little programming knowledge in C#.

What this book covers

Chapter 1, *Displaying Data with Core UI Elements*, is filled with **User Interface** (**UI**) recipes to help you increase the entertainment and enjoyment value of your games through the quality of the visual elements displaying text and data. You'll learn a wide range of UI techniques, including displaying text and images, 3D text effects, and an introduction to displaying text and image dialogues with the free Fungus package.

Chapter 2, *Responding to User Events for Interactive UIs*, teaches you about updating displays (for example basic on timers), and detecting and responding to user input actions, such as mouseovers, while the first chapter introduced code UI for displaying values to the user. Among other things, there are recipes for panels in visual layers, radio buttons and toggle groups, interactive text entry, directional radars, countdown timers, and custom mouse cursors.

Chapter 3, *Inventory UIs*, relates to the many games that involve the player collecting items, such as keys to open doors, ammo for weapons, or choosing from a selection of items, such as from a collection of spells to cast. The recipes in this chapter offer a range of text and graphical solutions for displaying inventory status to the player, including whether they are carrying an item or not, or the maximum number of items they are able to collect.

Chapter 4, *Playing and Manipulating Sounds*, suggests ways to use sound effects and soundtrack music to make your game more interesting. The chapter demonstrates how to manipulate sound during runtime through the use of scripts, Reverb Zones, and the Audio Mixer. It also includes recipes for real-time graphics visualizations of playing sounds and ends with a recipe to create a simple 140 bpm loop manager, with visualizations of each playing loop.

Chapter 5, *Creating Textures, Maps and Materials,* contains recipes that will give you a better understanding of how to use maps and materials with the Physically-Based Shaders, whether you are a game artist or not. It's a great resource for exercising your image editing skills.

Chapter 6, *Shader Graphs and Video Players,* covers two recent visual components that Unity has added: Shader Graphs and the Video Player. Both make it easy to add impressive visuals to your games with little or no programming. Several recipes are presented for each of these features in this chapter.

Chapter 7, *Using Cameras,* presents recipes covering techniques for controlling and enhancing your game's camera(s). It offers solutions to work with both single and multiple cameras, illustrates how to apply Post-Processing effects, such as vignettes and grainy gray-scale CCTVs. The chapter concludes by introducing ways to work with Unity's powerful Cinemachine components.

Chapter 8, *Lights and Effects,* offers a hands-on approach to several of Unity's lighting system features, such as cookie textures, Reflection maps, Lightmaps, Light and Reflection probes, and Procedural Skyboxes. Also, it demonstrates the use of Projectors.

Chapter 9, *2D Animation,* introduces some of Unity's powerful 2D animation and physics features. In this chapter, we will present recipes to help you understand the relationships between the different animation elements in Unity, exploring both the movement of different parts of the body and the use of sprite-sheet image files that contain sequences of sprite frames pictures. In this chapter core, Unity Animation concepts, including Animation State Charts, Transitions, and Trigger events, are also introduced. Finally, 2D games often make use of Tiles and Tilemaps (now features that are part of Unity), and these features, as well as the Unity 3D Gamekit, are all introduced in the recipes of this chapter.

Chapter 10, *3D Animation,* focuses on character animation and demonstrates how to take advantage of Unity's animation system—Mecanim. It covers a range of subjects, from basic character setup to procedural animation and ragdoll physics. It also offers introductions to some of the newer Unity 3D features, such as Probuilder and the Unity 3D Gamekit.

Chapter 11, *Webserver Communication, and Online Version Control*, explores how games running on devices can benefit from communication with other networked applications. In this chapter, a range of recipes are presented, which illustrate how to set up an online, database-driven leaderboard, how to write Unity games that can communicate with such online systems, and ways to protect your games from running on unauthorized servers (to prevent your WebGL games being illegally copied and published on other people's servers. In addition, the recipes illustrate how to structure your projects so that they can be easily backed up using online version control systems such as GitHub, and also how to download projects from online sites to edit and run on our own machine.

Chapter 12, *Controlling and Choosing Positions*, presents a range of recipes for 2D and 3D users and computer-controlled objects and characters, which can lead to games with a richer and more exciting user experience. Examples of these recipes include spawn points, checkpoints, and physics-based approaches, such as applying forces when clicking on objects and firing projectiles into the scene.

Chapter 13, *Navigation Meshes and Agents*, explores ways that Unity's Nav Meshes and Nav Mesh Agents offer for the automation of object and character movement and pathfinding in your games. Objects can follow predefined sequences of waypoints, or be controlled by mouse clicks for point-and-click control. Objects can be made to flock together based on the average location and movement of all members of their flock. Additional recipes illustrate how the "cost" of navigation areas can be defined, simulating hard-to-travel areas such as mud and water. Finally, although much navigation behavior is pre-calculated at Design Time (the "baking" process), a recipe is presented illustrating how movable objects can influence path-finding at runtime through the use of the NavMesh Obstacle component.

Chapter 14, *Design Patterns*, illustrates software design patterns that are reusable, and computer-language independent templates for how to solve common problems. It teaches to avoid reinventing the wheel, learn about tried-and-tested approaches to solving common features for game projects. This chapter introduces several design patterns relevant to games, including the State pattern, the publisher-subscriber pattern, and the model-view-controller pattern.

Chapter 15, *Editor Extensions and Immediate Mode GUI (IMGUI)*, provides several recipes for enhancing design-time work in the Unity Editor. Editor Extensions are scripting and multimedia components, which allow working with custom text, UI presentation of the game parameters, data in the Inspector and Scene panels, and custom menus and menu items. These can facilitate workflow improvements, allowing game developers to achieve their goals quicker and easier. Some of the recipes in this chapter include menu items, interactive panels with persistent storage, registering actions for the Undo system, deactivating menu items, progress bars, and ways to create new GameObjects based on prefabs.

To get the most out of this book

All you need is a copy of Unity 2018, which can be downloaded for free from http://www.unity3d.com.
If you wish to create your own image files, for the recipes in the *Creating Maps and Materials*, for example, you will also need an image editor, such as Adobe Photoshop, which can be found at http://www.photoshop.com, or GIMP, which is free and can be found at http://www.gimp.org.

Download the example code files

You'll find the recipes assets and completed Unity projects for each chapter at: https://github.com/PacktPublishing/Unity-2018-Cookbook-Third-Edition.

You can either download these files as Zip archives or use free Git software to download (clone) these files. These GitHub repositories will be updated with any improvements.

We also have other code bundles from our rich catalog of books and videos available at https://github.com/PacktPublishing/. Check them out!

Download the color images

We also provide a PDF file that has color images of the screenshots/diagrams used in this book. You can download it here: https://www.packtpub.com/sites/default/files/downloads/Unity2018CookbookThirdEdition_ColorImages.pdf.

Conventions used

There are a number of text conventions used throughout this book.

`CodeInText`: Indicates code words in text, database table names, folder names, filenames, file extensions, pathnames, dummy URLs, user input, and Twitter handles. Here is an example: "Import file `arrowCursor.png` into your Unity project."

A block of code is set as follows:

```
using UnityEngine;
using UnityEngine.UI;

[RequireComponent(typeof(PlayerInventoryTotal))]
public class PlayerInventoryDisplay : MonoBehaviour {
    public Text starText;
    public void OnChangeStarTotal(int numStars) {
        string starMessage = "total stars = " + numStars;
        starText.text = starMessage;
    }
}
```

Bold: Indicates a new term, an important word, or words that you see onscreen. For example, words in menus or dialog boxes appear in the text like this. Here is an example: "Select **System info** from the **Administration** panel."

Warnings or important notes appear like this.

Tips and tricks appear like this.

Get in touch

Feedback from our readers is always welcome.

General feedback: If you have questions about any aspect of this book, mention the book title in the subject of your message and email us at `customercare@packtpub.com`.

Errata: Although we have taken every care to ensure the accuracy of our content, mistakes do happen. If you have found a mistake in this book, we would be grateful if you would report this to us. Please visit `www.packt.com/submit-errata`, selecting your book, clicking on the Errata Submission Form link, and entering the details.

Piracy: If you come across any illegal copies of our works in any form on the Internet, we would be grateful if you would provide us with the location address or website name. Please contact us at copyright@packt.com with a link to the material.

If you are interested in becoming an author: If there is a topic that you have expertise in and you are interested in either writing or contributing to a book, please visit authors.packtpub.com.

Reviews

Please leave a review. Once you have read and used this book, why not leave a review on the site that you purchased it from? Potential readers can then see and use your unbiased opinion to make purchase decisions, we at Packt can understand what you think about our products, and our authors can see your feedback on their book. Thank you!

For more information about Packt, please visit packt.com.

Displaying Data with Core UI Elements

1

In this chapter, we will cover:

- Displaying a "Hello World" UI text message
- Displaying a digital clock
- Displaying a digital countdown timer
- Creating a message that fades away
- Displaying a perspective 3D Text Mesh
- Creating sophisticated text with TextMeshPro
- Displaying an image
- Creating UIs with the Fungus open source dialog system
- Creating a Fungus character dialog with images

Introduction

A key element contributing to the entertainment and enjoyment of most games is the quality of the visual experience, and an important part of this is the **User Interface (UI)**. UI elements involve ways for the user to interact with the game (such as buttons, cursors, and text boxes), as well as ways for the game to present up-to-date information to the user (such as the time remaining, current health, score, lives left, or location of enemies). This chapter is filled with UI recipes to give you a range of examples and ideas for creating game UIs.

The big picture

Every game is different, and so this chapter attempts to fulfill two key roles. The first aim is to provide step-by-step instructions on how to create a range of the Unity 2018 basic UI elements and, where appropriate, associate them with game variables in code. The second aim is to provide a rich illustration of how UI elements can be used for a variety of purposes so that you can get good ideas about how to make the Unity UI set of controls deliver the particular visual experience and interactions for the games that you are developing.

The basic UI elements can provide static images and text to just make the screen look more interesting. By using scripts, we can change the content of these images and text objects, so that the players' numeric scores can be updated, or we can show stickmen images to indicate how many lives the player has left. Other UI elements are interactive, allowing users to click on buttons, choose options, enter text, and so on. More sophisticated kinds of UI can involve collecting and calculating data about the game (such as percentage time remaining or enemy hit damage; or the positions and types of key GameObjects in the scene, and their relationship to the location and orientation of the player), and then displaying these values in a natural, graphical way (such as progress bars or radar screens).

Core GameObjects, components, and concepts relating to Unity UI development include:

- **Canvas**: Every UI element is a child to a **Canvas**. There can be multiple **Canvas** GameObjects in a single scene. If a **Canvas** is not already present, then one will automatically be created when a new UI GameObject is created, with that UI object as the child to the new **Canvas** GameObject.
- **EventSystem**: An **EventSystem** GameObject is required to manage the interaction events for UI controls. One will automatically be created with the first UI element. Unity generally only allows one **EventSystem** in any Scene (some proposed code for multiple event systems can be found at `https://bitbucket.org/Unity-Technologies/ui/pull-requests/18/support-for-multiple-concurrent-event/diff`)
- **Visual UI controls**: The visible UI controls themselves include **Button, Image, Text,** and **Toggle.**

- **The Rect Transform component**: UI GameObjects can exist in a different space from that of the 2D and 3D scenes, which cameras render. Therefore, UI GameObjects all have the special **Rect Transform** component, which has some different properties to the scene's GameObject Transform component (with its straightforward X/Y/Z position, rotation, and scale properties). Associated with **Rect Transforms** are pivot points (reference points for scaling, resizing, and rotations) and anchor points.

The following diagram shows the four main categories of UI controls, each in a **Canvas** GameObject and interacting via an **EventSystem** GameObject. UI Controls can have their own Canvas, or several UI controls can be in the same **Canvas**. The four categories are: **static** (display-only) and **interactive UI** controls, **non-visible** components (such as ones to group a set of mutually exclusive radio buttons), and **C# script** classes to manage UI-control behavior through logic written in the program code. Note that UI controls that are not a child or descendant of a Canvas will not work properly, and interactive UI controls will not work properly if the **EventSystem** is missing. Both the **Canvas** and **EventSystem** GameObjects are automatically added to the Hierarchy as soon as the first UI GameObject is added to a scene:

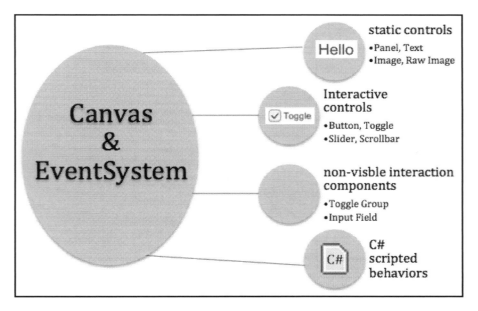

Rect Transforms for UI GameObjects represent a rectangular area rather than a single point, which is the case for scene GameObject Transforms. **Rect Transforms** describe how a UI element should be positioned and sized relative to its parent. Rect Transforms have a width and height that can be changed without affecting the local scale of the component. When the scale is changed for the **Rect Transform** of a UI element, this will also scale font sizes and borders on sliced images, and so on. If all four anchors are at the same point, resizing the Canvas will not stretch the Rect Transform. It will only affect its position. In this case, we'll see the **Pos X** and **Pos Y** properties, and the **Width** and **Height** of the rectangle. However, if the anchors are not all at the same point, Canvas resizing will result in stretching the element's rectangle. So instead of the Width, we'll see the values for Left and Right—the position of the horizontal sides of the rectangle to the sides of the **Canvas,** where the Width will depend on the actual Canvas width (and the same for Top/Bottom/Height).

Unity provides a set of preset values for pivots and anchors, making the most common values very quick and easy to assign to an element's **Rect Transform**. The following screenshot shows the 3 x 3 grid that allows you quick choices about the left, right, top, bottom, middle, horizontal, and vertical values. Also, the extra column on the right offers horizontal stretch presets, and the extra row at the bottom offers vertical stretch presets. Using the *Shift+Alt* keys sets the pivot and anchors when a preset is clicked:

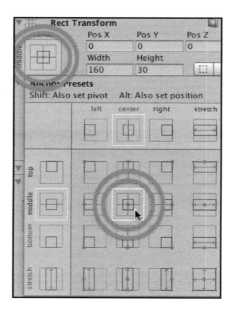

The Unity manual provides a very good introduction to the **Rect Transform**. In addition, Ray Wenderlich's two-part Unity UI web tutorial also presents a helpful overview of the Rect Transform, pivots, and anchors. Both parts of Wenderlich's tutorial make great use of animated GIFs to illustrate the effect of different values for pivots and anchors:

- `http://docs.unity3d.com/Manual/UIBasicLayout.html`
- `http://www.raywenderlich.com/78675/unity-new-gui-part-1`

There are three **Canvas** render modes:

- **Screen Space: Overlay**: In this mode, the UI elements are displayed without any reference to any camera (there is no need for any **Camera** in the scene). The UI elements are presented in front of (overlaying) any sort of camera display of the scene contents.
- **Screen Space: Camera**: In this mode, the **Canvas** is treated as a flat plane in the frustum (viewing space) of a **Camera** scene – where this plane is always facing the camera. So, any scene objects in front of this plane will be rendered in front of the UI elements on the **Canvas**. The **Canvas** is automatically resized if the screen size, resolution, or camera settings are changed.
- **World Space**: In this mode, the **Canvas** acts as a flat plane in the frustum (viewing space) of a **Camera** scene – but the plane is not made to always face the **Camera**. How the **Canvas** appears is just as with any other objects in the scene, relative to where (if anywhere) in the camera's viewing frustum the **Canvas** plane is located and oriented.

In this chapter, we have focused on the **Screen Space:Overlay** mode. But all these recipes can be used with the other two modes as well.

Be creative! This chapter aims to act as a launching pad of ideas, techniques, and reusable C# scripts for your own projects. Get to know the range of Unity UI elements, and try to work smart. Often, a UI element exists with most of the components that you may need for something in your game, but you may need to adapt it somehow. An example of this can be seen in the recipe that makes a UI Slider non-interactive, instead using it to display a red-green progress bar for the status of a countdown timer. See this in the *Displaying a countdown timer graphically with a UI Slider* recipe.

Many of these recipes involve C# script classes that make use of the Unity scene-start event sequence of `Awake()` to all game objects, `Start()` to all GameObjects, then `Update()` every frame to every GameObject. Therefore, you'll see many recipes in this chapter (and the whole book) where we cache references to GameObject components in the `Awake()` method, and then make use of these components in `Start()` and other methods, once the scene is up and running.

Displaying a "Hello World" UI text message

The first traditional problem to be solved with a new computing technology is to display the **Hello World** message. In this recipe, you'll learn to create a simple UI Text object with this message, in large white text with a selected font, in the center of the screen:

Hello World

Getting ready

For this recipe, we have prepared the font that you need in a folder named `Fonts` in the `01_01` folder.

How to do it...

To display a **Hello World** text message, follow these steps:

1. Create a new **Unity 2D project**.
2. Import the provided `Fonts` folder.
3. In the **Hierarchy** panel, add a **UI | Text GameObject** to the scene—choose menu: **GameObject | UI | Text**. Name this GameObject `Text-hello`.

 Using the **Create** menu : Alternatively, use the **Create** menu immediately below the **Hierarchy** tab, choosing menu: **Create | UI | Text**.

4. Ensure that your new `Text-hello` GameObject is selected in the
   Hierarchy panel.

   Now, in the Inspector, ensure the following properties are set:

   - Text set to read `Hello World`
   - Font set to `Xolonium-Bold`
   - Font size as per your requirements (large—this depends on your
     screen—try `50` or `100`)
   - Alignment set to horizontal and vertical center
   - `Horizontal` and `Vertical Overflow` set to `Overflow`
   - **Color** set to white

The following screenshot shows the **Inspector** panel with these settings:

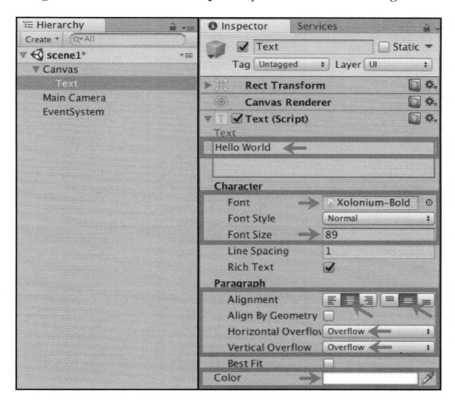

5. In the **Rect Transform**, click on the **Anchor Presets** square icon, which should result in several rows and columns of preset position squares appearing. Hold down *Shift+Alt* and click on the center one (middlerow and center column).

The screenshot of the **Rect Transform** in the *Introduction* highlights the middle-center preset needed for this recipe.

6. Your **Hello World** text will now appear, centered nicely in the **Game panel**.

How it works...

You have added a new `Text-hello` GameObject to a scene. A parent Canvas and **UI EventSystem** will also have been automatically created.

You set the text content and presentation properties and used the Rect Transform anchor presets to ensure that whatever way the screen is resized, the text will stay horizontally and vertically centered.

There's more...

Here are some more details you don't want to miss.

Styling substrings with Rich Text

Each separate **UI Text** component can have its own color, size, boldness styling, and so on. However, if you wish to quickly add some highlighting style to part of a string to be displayed to the user, the following are examples of some of the HTML-style markups that are available without the need to create separate UI Text objects:

- Embolden text with the "b" markup: I am `<b>bold</b>`
- Italicize text with the "i" markup: I am `<i>italic</i>`
- Set the text color with hex values or a color name: I am `<color=green>green text </color>`, but I am `<color=#FF0000>red</color>`

Learn more from the Unity online manual's Rich Text page at http://docs.unity3d.com/Manual/StyledText.html.

Displaying a digital clock

Whether it is the real-world time, or an in-game countdown clock, many games are enhanced by some form of clock or timer display. The most straightforward type of clock to display is a string composed of the integers for hours, minutes, and seconds, which is what we'll create in this recipe.

The following screenshot shows the kind of clock we will be creating in this recipe:

```
15:09:06
```

Getting ready

For this recipe, we have prepared the font that you need in a folder named Fonts in the 01_01 folder.

How to do it...

To create a digital clock, follow these steps:

1. Create a new **Unity 2D project**.
2. Import the provided Fonts folder.
3. In the **Hierarchy** panel, add a **UI | Text** game object to the scene named **Text-clock**.
4. Ensure that the Text-clock GameObject is selected in the **Hierarchy** panel. Now, in **Inspector**, ensure that the following properties are set:

   - Text set to read as time goes here (this placeholder text will be replaced by the time when the scene is running)
   - Font type set to Xolonium Bold
   - Font Size set to 20

- **Alignment** set to horizontal and vertical center
- **Horizontal** and **Vertical Overflow** settings set to Overflow
- Color set to white

5. In the **Rect Transform**, click on the **Anchor Presets** square icon, which will result in the appearance of several rows and columns of preset position squares. Hold down *Shift+Alt* and click on the top and center column rows.

6. Create a folder named _Scripts and create a C# script class called ClockDigital in this new folder:

```
using UnityEngine;
using System.Collections;
using UnityEngine.UI;
using System;

public class ClockDigital : MonoBehaviour {
  private Text textClock;

  void Awake (){
    textClock = GetComponent<Text>();
  }

  void Update (){
    DateTime time = DateTime.Now;
    string hour = LeadingZero( time.Hour );
    string minute = LeadingZero( time.Minute );
    string second = LeadingZero( time.Second );

    textClock.text = hour + ":" + minute + ":" +
  second;
  }

  string LeadingZero (int n){
    return n.ToString().PadLeft(2, '0');
  }
}
```

Underscore prefix so items appear first in sequence

Since scripts and scenes are things that are most often accessed, prefixing their folder names with an underscore character, _as _Scenes and _Scripts, means they are always at the top in the Project panel.

Although the preceding code is useful for illustrating how to access the time component of a `DateTime` object individually, the `Format(...)` method of the `String` class can be used to format a `DateTime` object all in a single statement, for example, the preceding could be written more succinctly in a single statement:
`String.Format("HH:mm:ss", DateTime.Now)`
For more examples,
see `http://www.csharp-examples.net/string-format-datetime/`.

7. Ensure the `Text-clock` GameObject is selected in the **Hierarchy** panel.

8. In the **Inspector** panel, add an instance of the `ClockDigital` script class as a component by clicking the **Add Component** button, selecting **Scripts**, and choosing the `Clock Digital` script class:

Add script components through drag and drop

Script components can also be added to GameObjects via drag and drop. For example, with the `Text-clock` GameObject selected in the **Hierarchy** panel, drag your `ClockDigital` script onto it to add an instance of this script class as a component to the `Text-clock` GameObject.

9. When you run the scene, you will now see a digital clock that shows hours, minutes, and seconds at the top-center part of the screen.

How it works...

You added a Text GameObject to a scene. You added an instance of the ClockDigital C# script class to that GameObject.

Notice that as well as the standard two C# packages (UnityEngine and System.Collections) that are written by default for every new script, you have added the using statements for two more C# script packages, UnityEngine.UI and System. The **UI package** is needed, since our code uses the UI Text object; and the System package is needed, since it contains the DateTime class that we need to access the clock on the computer where our game is running.

There is one variable, textClock, which will be a reference to the Text component, whose text content we wish to update in each frame with the current time in hours, minutes, and seconds.

The Awake() method (executed when the scene begins) sets the textClock variable to be a reference to the Text component in the GameObject, to which our scripted object has been added. Storing a reference to a component in this way is referred to as caching—it means that code executed later does not need to repeat the computationally-expensive task of searching the GameObject hierarchy for a component of a particular type.

Note that an alternative approach would be to make textClock a public variable. This will allow us to assign it via drag and drop in the Inspector panel.

The Update() method is executed in every frame. The current time is stored in the time variable, and strings are created by adding leading zeros to the number values for the hours, minutes, and seconds properties of variable time.

This method finally updates the text property (that is, the letters and numbers that the user sees) to be a string, concatenating the hours, minutes, and seconds with colon separator characters.

The LeadingZero(...) method takes as input an integer and returns a string of this number with leading zeros added to the left, if the value was less than 10.

There's more...

There are some details you don't want to miss.

The Unity tutorial for animating an analog clock

Unity has published a nice tutorial on how to create 3D objects, and animate them through a C# script to display an analog clock, at `https://unity3d.com/learn/tutorials/modules/beginner/scripting/simple-cloc k`.

Displaying a digital countdown timer

This recipe will show you how to display a digital countdown clock, as shown here:

`Countdown seconds remaining = 25`

Getting ready

This recipe adapts the previous one. So, make a copy of the project for the previous recipe, and work on this copy.

For this recipe, we have prepared the script that you need in a folder named `_Scripts` in the `01_03` folder.

How to do it...

To create a digital countdown timer, follow these steps:

1. Import the provided `_Scripts` folder.
2. In the Inspector panel, remove the scripted component, `ClockDigital`, from the `Text-clock` GameObject.
3. In the Inspector panel, add an instance of the `CountdownTimer` script class as a component by clicking the `Add Component` button, selecting **Scripts,** and choosing the `CountdownTimer` script class.

4. Create a `DigitalCountdown` C# script class that contains the following code, and add an instance as a scripted component to the `Text-clock` GameObject:

```csharp
using UnityEngine;
using UnityEngine.UI;

public class DigitalCountdown : MonoBehaviour {
    private Text textClock;
    private CountdownTimer countdownTimer;

    void Awake() {
        textClock = GetComponent<Text>();
        countdownTimer = GetComponent<CountdownTimer>();
    }
    void Start() {
        countdownTimer.ResetTimer( 30 );
    }

    void Update () {
        int timeRemaining =
countdownTimer.GetSecondsRemaining();
        string message = TimerMessage(timeRemaining);
        textClock.text = message;
    }

    private string TimerMessage(int secondsLeft) {
        if (secondsLeft <= 0){
            return "countdown has finished";
        } else {
            return "Countdown seconds remaining = " +
secondsLeft;
        }
    }
}
```

5. When you run the **Scene,** you will now see a digital clock counting down from 30. When the countdown reaches zero, the message countdown has finished will be displayed.

Automatically add components with `[RequireComponent(...)]`

The `DigitalCountdown` script class requires the same GameObject to also have an instance of the `CountdownTimer` script class. Rather than having to manually attach an instance of a require script, you can use the `[RequireComponent(...)]` C# attribute immediately before the class declaration statement. This will result in Unity automatically attaching an instance of the required script class.

For example, by writing the following, Unity will add an instance of `CountdownTimer` as soon as an instance of the `DigitalCountdown` script class has been added as a component of a GameObject:

```
using UnityEngine;
using UnityEngine.UI;

[RequireComponent (typeof (CountdownTimer))]
public class DigitalCountdown : MonoBehaviour {
```

Learn more from the Unity documentation at https://docs.unity3d.com/ScriptReference/RequireComponent.html.

How it works...

You have added instances of the `DigitalCountdown` and `CountdownTimer` C# script classes to your scene's UI Text GameObject.

The `Awake()` method caches references to the Text and `CountdownTimer` components in the `countdownTimer` and `textClock` variables. The `textClock` variable will be a reference to the **UI Text** component, whose text content we wish to update in each frame with a time-remaining message (or a timer-complete message).

The `Start()` method calls the countdown timer object's `CountdownTimerReset(...)` method, passing an initial value of 30 seconds.

The `Update()` method is executed in every frame. This method retrieves the countdown timer seconds remaining and stores this value as an integer (whole number) in the `timeRemaining` variable. This value is passed as a parameter to the `TimerMessage()` method, and the resulting message is stored in the string (text) variable message. This method finally updates the text property (that is, the letters and numbers that the user sees) of the `textClock` UI Text GameObject to equal to the string message about the remaining seconds.

The `TimerMessage()` method takes an integer as input, and if the value is zero or less, a message stating the timer has finished is returned. Otherwise (if greater than zero seconds remain) a message stating the number of remaining seconds is returned.

Creating a message that fades away

Sometimes, we want a message to display just for a certain time, and then fade away and disappear.

Getting ready

This recipe adapts the previous one. So, make a copy of the project for the that recipe, and work on this copy.

How to do it...

To display a text message that fades away, follow these steps:

1. In the **Inspector** panel, remove the scripted component, `DigitalCountdown`, from the `Text-clock` GameObject.

2. Create a C# script class, `FadeAway`, that contains the following code, and add an instance as a scripted component to the `Text-hello` GameObject:

```
using UnityEngine;
using UnityEngine.UI;

[RequireComponent (typeof (CountdownTimer))]
public class FadeAway : MonoBehaviour {
    private CountdownTimer countdownTimer;
    private Text textUI;

    void Awake () {
```

```
        textUI = GetComponent<Text>();
        countdownTimer = GetComponent<CountdownTimer>();
    }

    void Start(){
        countdownTimer.ResetTimer( 5 );
    }

    void Update () {
        float alphaRemaining =
        countdownTimer.GetProportionTimeRemaining();
        print (alphaRemaining);
        Color c = textUI.color;
        c.a = alphaRemaining;
        textUI.color = c;
    }
}
```

3. When you run the **Scene,** you will now see that the message on the screen slowly fades away, disappearing after five seconds.

How it works...

You added an instance of the FadeAway scripted class to the Text-hello GameObject. Due to the RequireComponent(...) attribute, an instance of the CountdownTimer script class was also **automatically** added.

The Awake() method caches references to the Text and CountdownTimer components in the countdownTimer and textUI variables.

The Start() method reset the countdown timer to start counting down from five seconds.

The Update() method (executed every frame) retrieves the proportion of time remaining in our timer by calling the GetProportionTimeRemaining() method. This method returns a value between 0.0 and 1.0, which also happens to be the range of values for the alpha (transparency) property of the color property of a UI Text game object.

Flexible range of `0.0-1.0`

 It is often a good idea to represent proportions as values between 0.0 and 1.0. Either this will be just the value we want for something, or we can multiply the maximum value by our decimal proportion, and we get the appropriate value. For example, if we wanted the number of degrees of a circle for a given `0.0-0.1` proportion, we just multiply by the maximum of 360, and so on.

The `Update()` method then retrieves the current color of the text being displayed (via `textUI.color`), updates its alpha property, and resets the text object to have this updated color value. The result is that each frame in the text object's transparency represents the current value of the proportion of the timer remaining until it fades to fully transparent when the timer gets to zero.

Displaying a perspective 3D Text Mesh

Unity provides an alternative way to display text in 3D via the Text Mesh component. While this is really suitable for a text-in-the-scene kind of situation (such as billboards, road signs, and generally wording on the side of 3D objects that might be seen close up), it is quick to create and is another way of creating interesting menus or instruction scenes.

In this recipe, you'll learn how to create a scrolling 3D text, simulating the famous opening credits of the movie Star Wars, which looks something like this:

Getting ready

For this recipe, we have prepared the fonts that you need in a folder named `Fonts`, and the text file that you need in a folder named `Text`, in the `01_07` folder.

How to do it...

To display perspective 3D text, follow these steps:

1. Create a new Unity 3D project (this ensures that we start off with a **Perspective** camera, suitable for the 3D effect we want to create).

 If you need to mix 2D and 3D scenes in your project, you can always manually set any camera's **Camera Projection** property to **Perspective** or **Orthographic** via the **Inspector** panel.

2. In the **Hierarchy** panel, select the **Main Camera** item, and, in the **Inspector** panel, set its properties as follows: Camera Clear Flags to solid color, **Field of View** to 150, and **Background** color to black.

3. Import the provided `Fonts` and `Text` folders.

4. In the **Hierarchy** panel, add a **UI | Text** game object to the scene—choose menu: **GameObject | UI | Text**. Name this GameObject as Text-star-wars.

5. Set UI Text Text-star-wars Text Content to Star Wars (with each word on a new line). Then, set its **Font** to `Xolonium Bold`, its **Font Size** to 50, and its **Color** to White. Use the anchor presets in Rect Transform to position this UI Text object at the top-center of the screen. Set **Vertical Overflow** to `Overflow`. Set Alignment Horizontal to center (leaving Alignment Vertical as top).

6. In the **Hierarchy** panel, add a 3D Text game object to the scene – choose menu: **GameObject | 3D Object | 3D Text**. Name this GameObject Text-crawler.

7. In the Inspector panel, set the **Transform** properties for the Text-crawler GameObject as follows: **Position** (100, -250, 0), **Rotation** (15, 0, 0).

8. In the Inspector panel, set the **Text Mesh** properties for the `Text-crawler` GameObject as follows:
   - Paste the content of the provided text file, `star_wars.txt`, into Text.

- Set **Offset Z** = –20, **Line Spacing** = 1, and **Anchor** = Middle center
- Set **Font Size** = 200, **Font** = SourceSansPro-BoldIt

9. When the **Scene** is made to run, the Star Wars story text will now appear nicely squashed in 3D perspective on the screen.

How it works...

You have simulated the opening screen of Star Wars, with a flat UI Text object title at the top of the screen, and 3D Text Mesh with settings that appear to be disappearing into the horizon with 3D perspective "squashing."

There's more...

There are some details you don't want to miss.

We have to make this text crawl like it does in the movie

With a few lines of code, we can make this text scroll in the horizon just as it does in the movie. Add the following C# script class, ScrollZ, as a component to the Text-crawler GameObject:

```
using UnityEngine; using System.Collections; public class ScrollZ :
MonoBehaviour { public float scrollSpeed = 20; void Update () {
Vector3 pos = transform.position; Vector3 localVectorUp =
transform.TransformDirection(0,1,0); pos += localVectorUp *
scrollSpeed * Time.deltaTime; transform.position = pos; } }
```

In each frame via the Update() method, the position of the 3D text object is moved in the direction of this GameObject's local up-direction.

Where to learn more

Learn more about 3D Text and Text Meshes in the Unity online manual at `http://docs.unity3d.com/Manual/class-TextMesh.html`.

 An alternative way of achieving perspective text like this would be to use a Canvas with the World Space render mode.

Creating sophisticated text with TextMeshPro

In 2017, Unity purchased the **TextMeshPro Asset Store** product, with a view to integrate it into Unity as a free core feature. **TextMeshPro** uses a **Signed Distance Field (SDF)** rendering method, resulting in clear and sharply-drawn characters at any point size and resolution. Therefore, you will need SDF fonts to work with this resource.

Getting ready

At the time of writing, **TextMeshpro** is a free **Asset Store** download and **Unity Essentials Beta**, so the first step is still to import it via the asset store. By the time you read this, you'll probably find **TextMeshPro** as a standard GameObject type that you can create in the Scene panel, with no downloading required. So, if required, open the **Asset Store** panel, search for **TextMeshPro,** and import this free asset package.

For this recipe, we have prepared the fonts that you need in a folder named Fonts & Materials in the `01_08` folder.

How to do it...

To display a text message with sophisticated **TextMeshPro** visual styling, follow these steps:

1. Create a new **Unity 3D** project.

2. Add a new UI **TextMeshPro Text** GameObject in the scene – choose menu: **GameObject | UI | TextMeshPro – text**. Name this GameObject Text-sophisticated.

 TextMeshPro GameObjects do not have to be part of the UI Canvas. You can add a **TextMeshPro** GameObject to the Scene directly by choosing the Scene panel menu **Create | 3D Object | TextMeshPro – text**.

3. Ensure that your new **Text-sophisticated** GameObject is selected in the **Hierarchy** panel. In the Inspector for the Rect Transform, click on the **Anchor Presets** square icon, hold down *Shift + Alt*, and click on the top and stretch rows.

4. Ensure the following properties are set:
   Font Settings:
   - **Font Asset** set to `Anton SDF`
   - **Material Preset** set to `Anton SDF – Outline`
   - **Font** size `200`
   - **Alignment** set to horizontal center

5. **Face:**
   - **Color** set to `white`
   - **Dilate** set to `0`

6. **Outline:**
   - **Color** set to `Red`
   - **Thickness** set to `0.1`

7. **Underlay (shadow):**
   - **Offset X** set to `1`
   - **Offset Y** set to `−1`
   - **Dilate** set to `1`

The following screenshot shows the **Inspector** panel with these settings:

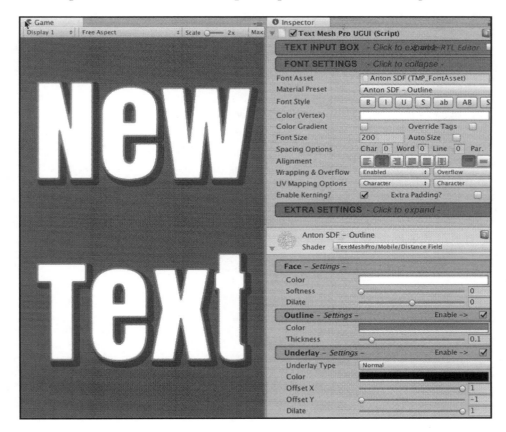

8. The **Text-sophisticated** GameObject will now appear as very large, with a white inner, red outline, and a drop shadow to the lower right.

How it works...

You have added a new **UI TextMeshPro Text** GameObject to a scene. You chose one of the SDF fonts, and an outline material preset. You then adjusted settings for the face (inner part of each character), outline, and drop shadow (Underlay).

There are hundreds of settings for a **TextMeshPro** component, and therefore much experimentation may be required to achieve a particular effect.

There's more...

Here are some more details you don't want to miss.

Rich Text substrings for colors, effects, and sprites

TextMeshPro offers over 30 HTML-style markups to substrings. The following code illustrates some, including the following:

```
<sprite=5> inline sprite graphics

<smallcaps>...</smallcaps> small-caps and colors

<#ffa000>...</color> substring colors
```

One powerful markup is the `<page>` tag, this allows a single set of text to be made interactive and presented to the user as a sequence of pages.

Learn more from the online manual **Rich Text** page at `http://digitalnativestudios.com/textmeshpro/docs/rich-text/`.

Displaying an image

There are many cases where we wish to display an image onscreen, including logos, maps, icons, and splash graphics. In this recipe, we will display an image centered at the top of the screen.

The following screenshot shows Unity displaying an image:

Getting ready

For this recipe, we have prepared the image that you need in a folder named `Images` in the `01_07` folder.

How to do it...

To display an image, follow these steps:

1. Create a new Unity 2D project.
2. Set the Game panel to a 400 x 300 size. Do this by first displaying the **Game** panel, and then creating a new **Resolution** in the drop-down menu at the top of the panel. Click the plus symbol at the bottom of this menu, setting **Label = Chapter 2, Width = 400**, and **Height = 300.** Click **OK** and the **Game** panel should be set to this new resolution:

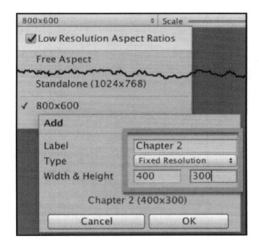

 Alternatively, you can set the default **Game** panel resolution through menu **Edit** | **Project Settings** | **Player** and then the Resolution and Presentation width and height in the Inspector (having turned off the Full Screen option).

3. Import the provided `Images` folder. In the **Inspector** tab, ensure that the `unity_logo` image has the **Texture Type** set to **Default**. If it has some other type, then choose **Default** from the drop-down list, and click on the **Apply** button.
4. In the **Hierarchy** panel, add a **UI** | **RawImage** GameObject named `RawImage-logo` to the scene.

5. Ensure that the `RawImage-logo` GameObject is selected in the **Hierarchy** panel. In the **Inspector** for the **RawImage (Script)** component, click the file viewer circle icon at the right side of the **Texture** property, and select **image unity_logo**, as shown in the following screenshot:

 An alternative way of assigning this Texture is to drag the unity_logo image from your **Project** folder (Images) into the **Raw Image (Script)** public property **Texture.**

6. Click on the **Set Native Size** button to resize the image so it is no longer stretched and distorted.
7. In **Rect Transform,** click on the **Anchor Presets** square icon, which will result in several rows and columns of preset position squares appearing. Hold down *Shift + Alt* and click on the top row and the center column.
8. The image will now be positioned neatly at the top of the **Game** panel, and will be horizontally centered.

How it works...

You have ensured that an image has the **Texture Type** set to **Default.** You added a **UI RawImage** control to the scene. The **RawImage** control has been made to display the `unity_logo` image file.

The image has been positioned at the top-center of the **Game** panel.

There's more...

There are some details you don't want to miss:

Working with 2D Sprites and UI Image components

If you simply wish to display non-animated images, then Texture images and **UI RawImage** controls are the way to go. However, if you want more options on how an image should be displayed (such as tiling, and animation), the UI Image control should be used instead. This control needs image files to be imported as the **Sprite (2D and UI)** type.

Once an image file has been dragged into the UI Image control's **Sprite** property, additional properties will be available, such as **Image Type**, and options to preserve the aspect ratio.

If you wish to prevent the distortion and stretching of a UI Sprite GameObject, then in the Inspector panel, check the **Preserve Aspect** option, in its **Image (Script)** component.

See also

An example of tiling a Sprite image can be found in the *Revealing icons for multiple object pickups by changing the size of a tiled image* recipe in `Chapter 3`, *Inventory UIs*.

Creating UIs with the Fungus open source dialog system

Rather than constructing your own UI and interactions from scratch each time, there are plenty of UI and dialogue systems available for Unity. One powerful, free, and open source dialog system is called Fungus, which uses a visual flowcharting approach to dialog design.

In this recipe, we'll create a very simple, one-sentence dialogue, to illustrate the basics of Fungus. The following screenshot shows the Fungus-generated dialog for the sentence **How are you today?**:

How to do it...

To create a one-sentence dialog using **Fungus**, follow these steps:

1. Create a new Unity 2D project.
2. Open the **Asset Store** panel, search for **Fungus,** and Import this free asset package (search for Fungus and free).
3. Create a new **Fungus** Flowchart GameObject by choosing menu: **Tools** | **Fungus** | **Create** | **Flowchart.**
4. Display and dock the Fungus Flowchart window panel by choosing menu: **Tools** | **Fungus** | **Flowchart Window.**
5. There will be one block in the **Flowchart Window**. Click on this block to select it (a green border appears around the block to indicate that it is selected). In the **Inspector** panel, change the **Block Name** of this block to Start:

6. **Each Block** in a **Flowchart** follows a sequence of commands. So in the **Inspector,** we are now going to create a sequence of (Say) commands to display two sentences to the user when the game runs.
7. Ensure that the **Start** block is still selected in the **Flowchart** panel. Click on the plus (+) button at the bottom section of the **Inspector** panel to display the menu of **Commands,** and select the **Narrative** | Say **command:**

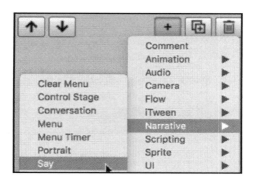

8. Since we only have one command for this block, that command will automatically be selected (highlighted green) in the top part of the **Inspector.** The bottom half of the Inspector presents the properties for the currently-selected **Command,** as shown in the following screenshot. In the bottom half of the Inspector, for the **Story Text** property, enter the text of the question that you wish to be presented to the user, which is **How are you today?**:

9. Create another **Say Command**, and type the following for its **Story Text** property: **Very well thank you**.

10. When you run the game, the user will first be presented with the **How are you today?** text (hearing a clicking noise as each letter is typed on screen). After the user clicks on the **continue** triangle button (at the bottom-right part of the dialog window), they will be presented with the second sentence: **Very well thank you.**

How it works...

You have created a new Unity project, and imported the **Fungus** asset package, which contains the **Fungus Unity** menus, windows, and commands, and also the example projects.

You have added a **Fungus Flowchart** to your scene with a single **Block** that you have named **Start.** Your block starts to execute when the game begins (since the default for the first block is to be executed upon receiving the Game Started event).

In the **Start** block, you added a sequence of two **Say Commands**. Each command presents a sentence to the user, and then waits for the continue button to be clicked before proceeding to the next **Command.**

As can be seen, the **Fungus** system handles the work of creating a nicely-presented panel to the user, displaying the desired text and continue button. **Fungus** offers many more features, including menus, animations, and control of sounds and music, the details of which can be found in the next recipe, and by exploring their provided example projects, and their websites:

- http://fungusgames.com/
- https://github.com/FungusGames/Fungus

Creating a Fungus character dialog with images

The **Fungus** dialog system introduced in the previous recipe supports multiple characters, whose dialogs can be highlighted through their names, colors, sound effects, and even portrait images. In this recipe, we'll create a two-character dialog between Sherlock Holmes and Watson to illustrate the system:

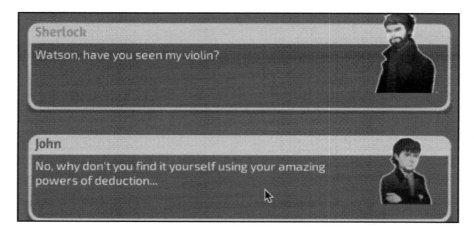

How to do it...

To create a character dialog with portrait images using Fungus, follow these steps:

1. Create a new Unity 2D project.

2. Open the **Asset Store** panel, and **Import** the **Fungus** dialogue asset package (this includes the **Fungus** Examples, whose images we'll use for the two characters).

3. Create a new **Fungus Flowchart** GameObject by choosing menu: **Tools** | **Fungus** | **Create** | **Flowchart.**

4. Display and dock the **Fungus Flowchart** window panel by choosing menu: **Tools** | **Fungus** | **Flowchart Window.**

5. Change the name of the only **Block** in the **Flowchart** to The case of the missing violin.

6. Create a new Character by choosing menu: **Tools** | **Fungus** | **Create** | **Character.**

7. You should now see a new **Character** GameObject in the **Hierarchy.**

8. With GameObject **Character** 1 – Sherlock selected in the **Project** panel, edit its properties in the Inspector:

    *   Rename this GameObject **Character** 1 – **Sherlock.**

    *   In its **Character(Script)** component, set the **Name Text** to **Sherlock** and the **Name Color** to green.

    *   In the **Inspector,** click the **Add Portrait** button (the plus sign "+"), to get a "slot" into which to add a portrait image.

    *   Drag the appropriate image into your new portrait image slot (in this screenshot, we used the "confident" image from the Sherlock example project: **Fungus Examples** | **Sherlock** | **Portraits** | **Sherlock):**

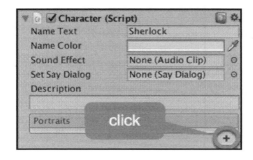

9. Repeat steps 6-8 above to create a second character, John, using **Name Color** = blue, and **Portrait Image** = annoyed.

10. Select your **Block** in the **Fungus Flowchart**, so you can add some **Commands** to be executed.

11. Create a **Say** command, for **Character 1 - Sherlock**, saying **Watson, have you seen my violin?** and choose the **confident** portrait (since this is the only one we added to the character):

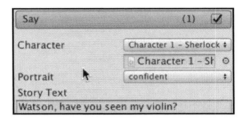

12. Add a second **Say** command, this time for **Character 2 – John**, saying **No, why don't you find it yourself using your amazing powers of deduction..** and choose the **annoyed** portrait:

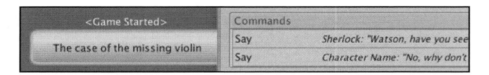

13. Run the scene you should see a sequence of statements, clearly showing who is saying both with (colored) name text **AND** the portrait image you selected for each Say command (after Sherlock's text has finished appearing, click the box to start John's sentence).

How it works...

You have created a new Unity project with the **Fungus** asset package.

You have added a **Fungus Flowchart** to your scene, and also added two characters (each with a text color and a portrait image).

For the **Block** in the **Flowchart,** you added to **Say** commands, stating which character was saying each sentence, and which portrait to use (if you had added more portrait images, you could select different images to indicate the emotion of the character speaking).

There's more...

There are some details you don't want to miss.

Data-driven conversations

Fungus offers a data-driven approach to conversations. The character and portrait (and facing direction, and movement onto-off the stage, and so on) can be defined through text in a simple format, using the Say command's **Narrative | Conversation** option. This recipe's conversation with portrait images can be declared with just two lines of text in a **Conversation:**

```
Sherlock confident: Watson, have you seen my violin?
John annoyed: No, why don't you find it yourself using your amazing
powers of deduction...
```

Learn more about the Fungus conversation system on their documentation pages: http://fungusdocs.snozbot.com/conversation_system.html.

2
Responding to User Events for Interactive UIs

In this chapter, we will cover the following:

- Creating UI Buttons to move between scenes
- Animating button properties on mouse-over
- Organizing image panels and changing panel depths via buttons
- Displaying the value of an interactive UI Slider
- Displaying a countdown timer graphically with a UI Slider
- Setting custom mouse cursors for 2D and 3D GameObjects
- Setting custom mouse cursors for UI controls
- Interactive text entry with an Input Field
- Toggles and radio buttons via Toggle Groups
- Creating text and image icon UI Dropdown menus
- Displaying a radar to indicate the relative locations of objects

Introduction

Almost all the recipes in this chapter involve different interactive UI controls. Although there are different kinds of interactive UI controls, the basic way to work with them, and have scripted actions respond to user actions, is all based on the same idea: events triggering the execution of object method functions.

Then, for fun, and an example of a very different kind of UI, the final recipe demonstrates how to add to your game a sophisticated real-time communication of the relative positions of objects in the scene (that is, a radar!).

The big picture

The UI can be used for three main purposes:

1. To display **static (unchanging) values**, such as the name or logo image of the game, or word labels such as Level and Score, that tell us what the numbers next to them indicate (recipes for these can be found in the `Chapter 1`, *Displaying Data with Core UI Elements*).

2. To display **values that change due to our scripts**, such as timers, scores, or the distance from our Player character to some other object (an example of this is the radar recipe at the end of this chapter).

3. **Interactive** UI controls, whose purpose is to allow the Player to communicate with the game scripts via their mouse or touchscreen. These are the ones we'll look at in detail in this chapter.

The core concept for working with Unity Interactive UI controls is the *registration of an object's public method to be informed when a particular event occurs*. For example, we can add a UI Dropdown to a scene named DropDown 1, and then write a `MyScript` script class containing a `NewValueAction()` public method to do some action. But nothing will happen until we do two things:

1. We need to add an *instance of the script class as a component* on a GameObject in the scene (which we'll name `go1` for our example – although we can also add the script instance to the UI GameObject itself if we choose to).

2. In the UI Dropdown's properties, we need to *register the GameObject's public method* of its script component to respond to the `On Value Changed` event messages:

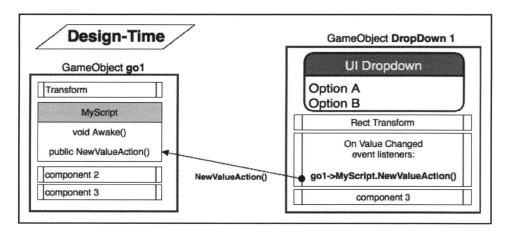

The NewValueAction() public method of the MyScript script will typically retrieve the value selected by the user in the Dropdown and do something with it – for example, confirm it to the user, change the music volume, or change the game difficulty. The NewValueAction() method will be invoked (executed) each time GameObject go1 receives the NewValueAction() message. In the DropDown 1's properties, we need to register GameObject go1's scripted component MyScript's NewValueAction() public method as an event listener for On Value Changed events. We need to do all this at **Design-Time** (that is, in the Unity editor before running the scene):

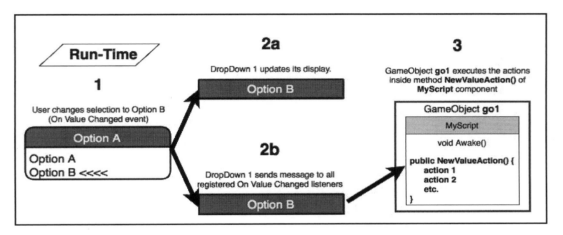

At **runtime** (when the scene in the built application is running), if the user changes the value in the drop-down menu of UI Dropdown GameObject DropDown 1 (step 1 in the diagram), this will generate an On Value Changed event. DropDown 1 will update its display on screen, to show the user the newly-selected value (step 2a). It will also send messages to all the GameObject components registered as listeners to **On Value Changed** events (step 2b). In our example, this will lead to the NewValueAction() method in GameObject go1's scripted component being executed (step 3).

Registering public object methods is a very common way to handle events such as user interaction or web communications, which may occur in different orders, may never occur, or may happen several times in a short period. Several software Design Patterns describe ways to work with these event setups, such as the *Observer Pattern* and the *Publisher-Subscriber* pattern (we'll learn more about this pattern in `Chapter 16`, *Design Patterns*).

Core GameObjects, components, and concepts relating to interactive Unity UI development include:

- **Visual UI controls**: The visible UI controls themselves include Button, Image, Text, and Toggle. These are the UI controls the user sees on the screen, and uses their mouse/touchscreen to interact with. These are the GameObjects that maintain a list of object-methods that have subscribed to user-interaction events.
- **Interaction UI controls**: These are non-visible components that are added to GameObjects; examples include Input Field and Toggle Group.
- **Panel**: UI objects can be grouped together (logically and physically) with UI Panels. Panels can play several roles, including providing a GameObject parent in the Hierarchy for a related group of controls. They can provide a visual background image to graphically relate controls on the screen, and they can also have scripted resize and drag interactions added, if desired.
- **Sibling Depth**: The bottom-to-top display order (what appears on the top of what) for a UI element is determined initially by their sequence in the Hierarchy. At **Design-Time**, this can be manually set by dragging GameObjects into the desired sequence in the Hierarchy. At **Run-Time**, we can send messages to the Rect Transforms of GameObjects to dynamically change their Hierarchy position (and therefore, the display order), as the game or user interaction demands. This is illustrated in the *Organizing images inside panels and changing panel depths via buttons* recipe.

Often, a UI element exists with most of the components that you may need for something in your game, but you may need to adapt it somehow. An example of this can be seen in the recipe that makes a UI Slider non-interactive, instead using it to display a red-green progress bar for the status of a countdown timer. See this in the *Displaying a countdown timer graphically with a UI Slider* recipe.

Creating UI Buttons to move between scenes

As well as scenes where the player plays the game, most games will have menu screens, which display to the user messages about instructions, high scores, the level they have reached so far, and so on. Unity provides UI Buttons to offer users a simple way to indicate their choices.

In this recipe, we'll create a very simple game consisting of two screens, each with a button to load the other one, as illustrated in the screenshot:

How to do it...

To create a button-navigable multi-scene game, follow these steps:

1. Create a new Unity 2D project.
2. Save the current (empty) scene, in a new folder, _Scenes, naming the scene **page1**.
3. Add a **UI Text** object positioned at the top center of the scene, containing large white text that says **Main Menu (page 1)**.
4. Add a **UI Button** to the scene positioned in the middle-center of the screen. In the **Hierarchy**, click on the show children triangle to display the **Text** child of this GameObject button. Select the **Text** GameObject, and in the **Inspector** for the **Text** property of the **Text (Script)** component, enter the text **goto page 2**:

5. Create a second scene, named **page2**, with UI Text = **Instructions (page 2)**, and a **UI Button** with the goto page 1 text. You can either repeat the preceding steps, or you can duplicate the **page1** scene file, naming the duplicate **page2**, and edit the UI Text and UI Button Text appropriately

6. Add both scenes to the Build, which is the set of scenes that will end up in the actual application built by Unity. To add the scene1 to the Build, open scene page1, then choose menu: **File | Build Settings...** then click on the **Add Current** button so that the **page1** scene becomes the first scene on the list of Scenes in the Build. Now open scene **page2** and repeat the process, so both scenes have been added to the Build.

 We cannot tell Unity to load a scene that has not been added to the list of scenes in the build. This makes sense since when an application is built we should never try to open a scene that isn't included as part of that application.

7. Ensure you have scene **page1** open.

8. Create a C# script class, SceneLoader, in a new folder, _Scripts, containing the following code, and add an instance as a scripted component to the **Main Camera**:

```
using UnityEngine;
using UnityEngine.SceneManagement;

public class SceneLoader : MonoBehaviour {
    public void LoadOnClick(int sceneIndex) {
        SceneManager.LoadScene(sceneIndex);
    }
}
```

9. Select the **Button** in the **Hierarchy** and click on the plus sign (**+**) button at the bottom of the **Button (Script)** component, in the **Inspector** view, to create a new OnClick event handler for this button (that is, an action to perform when the button is clicked).

10. Drag the **Main Camera** from the **Hierarchy** over the Object slot immediately below the menu saying **Runtime Only**. This means that when the Button receives an OnClick event, we can call a public method from a scripted object inside the **Main Camera**.

11. Select the `LoadOnClick` method from the **SceneLoader** drop-down list (initially showing **No Function**). Type **1** (the index of the scene we want to be loaded when this button is clicked) in the text box, below the method's drop-down menu. This integer, **1**, will be passed to the method when the button receives an `OnClick` event message, as shown here:

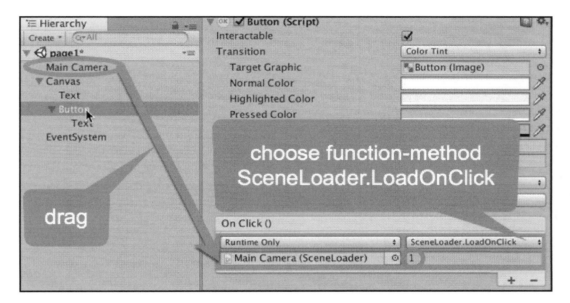

12. Save the current scene (**page1**).
13. Open **page2** and follow the same steps to make the **page2** button load **page1**. That is, add an instance of the `SceneLoader` script class to the main camera, then add an `OnClick` event action to the button, which calls `LoadOnClick`, and passes the integer **0,** so scene **page1** is loaded.
14. Save scene **page2**.
15. When you run the page1 scene, you will be presented with your **Main Menu** text and a button, which when clicked, makes the game load the **page2** scene. On scene page2, you'll have a button to take you back to **page1**.

How it works...

You have created two scenes, and added both of these scenes to the game's build. You added a UI Button, and some UI Text to each scene.

 Note, the Build sequence of scenes is actually a scripted array, which count from 0, then 1, and so on, so page1 has index 0, and page2 has index 1.

When a UI Button is added to the Hierarchy panel, a child UI Text object is also automatically created, and the content of the Text property of this UI Text child is the text that the user sees on the button.

You created a script class, and added an instance as a component to the **Main Camera**. In fact, it didn't really matter where this script instance was added, as long as it was in one of the GameObjects of the scene. This is necessary since the `OnClick` event action of a button can only execute a method (function) of a component in a GameObject in the scene.

For the button of each scene, you then added a new `OnClick` event action, which invokes (executes) the `LoadOnClick` method of the SceneLoader scripted component in the Main Camera. This method inputs the integer index of the scene in the project's Build settings, so that the button on the **page1** scene gives integer 1 as the scene to be loaded, and the button for **page2** gives integer 0.

There's more...

There are some details you don't want to miss.

Color tint when mouse pointer is over the button

There are several ways in which we can visually inform the user that the button is interactive when they move their mouse cursor over it. The simplest is to add a **Color Tint** that will appear when the mouse is over the button – this is the default **Transition**. With the **Button** selected in the **Hierarchy**, choose a tint color (for example, red), for the **Highlighted Color** property of the Button (Script) component, in the **Inspector** tab:

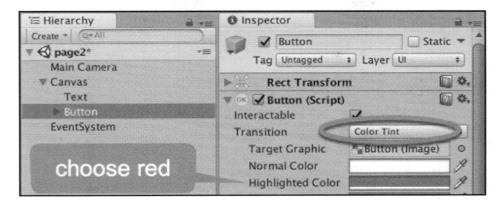

Another form of visual Transition to inform the user of an active button is Sprite Swap. In this case, properties for different images for Targeted/Highlighted/Pressed/Disabled are available in the **Inspector** panel. The default Targeted Graphic is the built-in Unity **Button (Image)** – this is the grey rounded rectangle default when GameObject buttons are created. Dragging in a very different-looking image for the **Highlighted** Sprite is an effective alternative to set a Color Tint. We have provided a `rainbow.png` image with the project for this recipe that can be used for the Button mouse over Highlighted Sprite. The screenshot shows the button with this rainbow background image:

Animating button properties on mouse-over

At the end of the previous recipe, we illustrated two ways to visually communicate buttons to users. The **Animation** of button properties can be a highly effective, and visually interesting, way to reinforce to the user that the item their mouse is currently over is a clickable, active button. One common animation effect is for a button to get larger when the mouse is over it, and then it shrinks back to its original size when the mouse pointer is moved away. Animation effects are achieved by choosing the **Animation** option for the Transition property of a `Button` GameObject, and by creating an animation controller with triggers for the Normal, Highlighted, Pressed, and Disabled states.

How to do it...

To animate a button for enlargement when the mouse is over it (the **Highlighted** state), do the following:

1. Create a new Unity 2D project.
2. Create a **UI Button**.
3. In the **Inspector Button (Script)** component, set the **Transition** property to **Animation**.
4. Click the **Auto Generate Animation** button (just below the **Disabled Trigger** property) for the **Button (Script)** component:

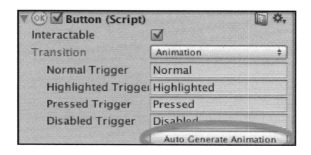

5. Save the new controller (in new folder Animations), naming it **button-animation-controller**.
6. Ensure that the **Button** GameObject is selected in the Hierarchy. In the Animation panel, select the **Highlighted** clip from the drop-down menu:

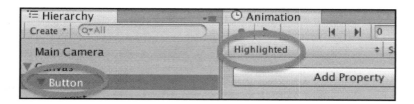

7. In the **Animation** panel, click on the red record circle button, and then click on the **Add Property** button, choosing to record changes to the **Rect Transform | Scale** property.

8. Two keyframes will have been created. Delete the second one at 1 : 00 (since we don't want a "bouncing" button):

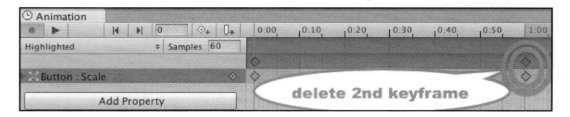

9. Select the frame at 1 : 00 by clicking one of the diamonds (both turn blue when selected), then press the *Backspace/Delete* key.
10. Select the first keyframe at 0 : 00 (the only one now!). In the Inspector, set the X and Y scale properties of the **Rect Transform** component to (1 . 2, 1 . 2).
11. Click on the red record circle button for the second time to end the recording of the animation changes.
12. Save and run your scene, and you will see that the button smoothly animates to get larger when the mouse is over it, and then smoothly returns to its original size when the mouse has moved away.

How it works...

You have created a button, and set its **Transition** mode to **Animation**. This makes Unity require an Animation Controller with four states: **Normal**, **Highlighted**, **Pressed**, and **Disabled**. You then made Unity automatically create an Animation Controller with these four states.

Then, you edited the Animation for the Highlighted (mouse-over) state, deleting the second keyframe, and making the only keyframe a version of the Button made larger to a scale of 1.2.

When the mouse is not over the Button, it's unchanged and Normal state settings are used. When the mouse moves over the Button, the Animation Controller smoothly in-betweens the settings of the Button to become those of its Highlighted state (that is, bigger). When the mouse is moved away from the Button, the Animation Controller smoothly in-betweens the settings of the Button to become those of its Normal state (that is, its original size).

The following web pages offer video and web-based tutorials on UI animations:

The Unity button transitions tutorial is available at `http://unity3d.com/learn/tutorials/modules/beginner/ui/ui-transitions`.

Ray Wenderlich's great tutorial (part 2), including the button animations, is available at `http://www.raywenderlich.com/79031/unity-new-gui-tutorial-part-2`.

Organizing image panels and changing panel depths via buttons

UI Panels are provided by Unity to allow UI controls to be grouped and moved together, and also to visually group elements with an Image background (if desired). The sibling depth is what determines which UI elements will appear above or below others. We can see the sibling depth explicitly in the Hierarchy, since the top-to-bottom sequence of UI GameObjects in the Hierarchy sets the sibling depth. So, the first item has a depth of 1, the second has a depth of 2, and so on. The UI GameObjects with larger sibling depths (further down the Hierarchy and so drawn later) appear above the UI GameObjects with lower sibling depths.

In this recipe, we'll create three UI Panels, each showing a different playing card image. We'll also add four triangle arrangement buttons to change the display order (move to bottom, move to top, move up one, and move down one):

Getting ready

For this recipe, we have prepared the images that you need in a folder named Images in the 02_03 folder.

How to do it...

To create the UI Panels whose layering can be changed by clicking buttons, follow these steps:

1. Create a new Unity 2D project.

2. Create a new **UI Panel** GameObject named **Panel-jack-diamonds**. Do the following to this Panel:

    - For the **Image (Script)** component, drag the `jack_of_diamonds` playing card image asset file from the **Project** panel into the **Source Image** property. Select the **Color** property and increase the **Alpha** value to 255 (so this background image of the panel is no longer partly transparent).

    - For the **Rect Transform** property, position it in the middle-center part of the screen, and size it with **Width** = 200 and **Height** = 300.

3. Create a **UI Button** named **Button-move-to-front**. In the **Hierarchy**, child this button to **Panel-jack-diamonds**. Delete the **Text** child GameObject of this button (since we'll use an icon to indicate what this button does).

4. With the **Button-move-to-front** GameObject selected in the **Hierarchy**, do the following in the Inspector:

    - In the **Rect Transform**, position the button top-center of the player card image so that it can be seen at the top of the playing card. Size the image to **Width** = 16 and **Height** = 16. Move the icon image down slightly, by setting **Pos Y** = -5 (to ensure we can see the horizontal bar above the triangle).

    - For the **Source Image** property of the **Image (Script)** component, select the arrangement triangle icon image:
      icon_move_to_front.

    - Add an **OnClick** event handler by clicking on the plus sign (+) at the bottom of the **Button (Script)** component.

    - Drag **Panel-jack-diamonds** from the **Hierarchy** over to the **Object** slot (immediately below the menu saying **Runtime Only**).

- Select the `RectTransform.SetAsLastSibling` method from the drop-down function list (initially showing **No Function**):

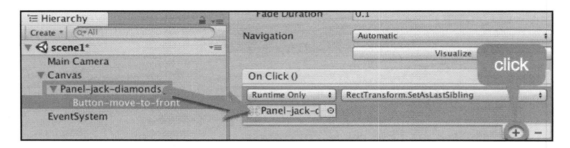

5. Repeat step 2; create a second Panel named **Panel-2-diamonds** with its own **move-to-front** button, and **Source Image** of `2_of_diamonds`. Move and position this new panel slightly to the right of **Panel-jack-diamonds**, allowing both the **move-to-front** buttons to be seen.

6. Save your **Scene** and run the game. You will be able to click the **move-to-front** button on either of the cards to move that card's panel to the front. If you run the game with the Game panel not maximized, you'll actually see the panels changing order in the list of the children of the **Canvas** in the **Hierarchy**.

How it works...

You have created two **UI Panels**, each panel contains a background **Image** of a playing card and a **UI Button** whose action will make its parent panel move to the front. You set the **Alpha** (transparency) setting of the background image's **Color** to `255` (no transparency).

You added an `OnClick` event action to the button of each **UI Panel**. The action sends a `SetAsLastSibling` message to the **Button's Panel** parent. When the **OnClick** message is received, the clicked **Panel** is moved to the bottom (end) of the sequence of GameObjects in the **Canvas**, and therefore this **Panel** is drawn last of the **Canvas** objects, and so appears visually in front of all other GameObjects.

The button's action illustrates how the **OnClick** function does not have to be the calling of a public method of a scripted component of an object, but it can be sending a message to one of the non-scripted components of the targeted GameObject. In this recipe, we send the **SetAsLastSibling** message to the **Rect Transform** of the Panel where the Button is located.

There's more...

There are some details you don't want to miss.

Moving up or down by just one position, using scripted methods

While the **Rect Transform** offers a useful SetAsLastSibling (move to front) and SetAsFirstSibling (move to back), and even SetSiblingIndex (if we knew exactly what position in the sequence to type in), there isn't a built-in way to make an element move up or down just one position in the sequence of GameObjects in the **Hierarchy**. However, we can write two straightforward methods in C# to do this, and we can add buttons to call these methods, providing full control of the top-to-bottom arrangement of the UI controls on the screen. To implement four buttons (move-to-front/move-to-back/up one/down one), do the following:

1. Create a C# script class called ArrangeActions, containing the following code, and add an instance as a scripted component to each of your **Panels**:

```
using UnityEngine;

public class ArrangeActions : MonoBehaviour {
   private RectTransform panelRectTransform;

   void Awake() {
        panelRectTransform = GetComponent<RectTransform>();
   }

   public void MoveDownOne() {
        int currentSiblingIndex =
panelRectTransform.GetSiblingIndex();
        panelRectTransform.SetSiblingIndex(
currentSiblingIndex - 1 );
    }
   public void MoveUpOne() {
        int currentSiblingIndex =
panelRectTransform.GetSiblingIndex();
        panelRectTransform.SetSiblingIndex(
currentSiblingIndex + 1 );
    }
}
```

2. Add a second **UI Button** to each card panel, this time using the arrangement triangle icon image called `icon_move_to_front`, and set the **OnClick** event function for these buttons to `SetAsFirstSibling`.

3. Add two further **UI Buttons** to each card panel with the up and down triangle icon images: `icon_down_one` and `icon_up_one`. Set the **OnClick** event-handler function for the down-one buttons to call the `MoveDownOne()` method, and set the functions for the up-one buttons to call the `MoveUpOne()` method.

4. Copy one of the **UI Panels** to create a third card (this time showing the Ace of diamonds). Arrange the three cards so that you can see all four buttons for at least two of the cards, even when those cards are at the bottom (see the screenshot at the beginning of this recipe).

5. Save the **Scene** and run your game. You will now have full control over the layering of the three card panels.

Note, we should avoid *negative* sibling depths, so we should probably test for the currentSiblingIndex value before subtracting 1:
```
if(currentSiblingIndex > 0)
        panelRectTransform.SetSiblingIndex(
currentSiblingIndex - 1 );
```

Displaying the value of an interactive UI Slider

This recipe illustrates how to create an interactive **UI Slider**, and execute a C# method each time the user changes the **UI Slider** value:

How to do it...

To create a **UI Slider** and display its value on the screen, follow these steps:

1. Create a new 2D project.

2. Add a **UI Text** GameObject to the scene with a **Font** size of 30 and placeholder text, such as **slider value here** (this text will be replaced with the slider value when the scene starts). Set **Horizontal-** and **Vertical-Overflow** to **Overflow**.

3. In the **Hierarchy** add a **UI Slider** GameObject to the scene – choose menu: **GameObject | UI | Slider**.

4. In the **Inspector**, modify the settings for the position of the **UI Slider** GameObject's **Rect Transform** to the top-middle part of the screen.

5. In the **Inspector**, modify settings for **Position** of the **UI Text's Rect Transform** to just below the slider (top, middle, then **Pos Y** = −30).

6. In the **Inspector**, set the **UI Slider's Min Value** to 0, the **Max Value** to 20, and check the **Whole Numbers** checkbox:

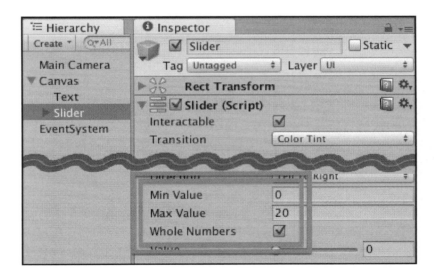

7. Create a C# script class called `SliderValueToText`, containing the following code, and add an instance as a scripted component to the **Text** GameObject:

```
using UnityEngine;
using UnityEngine.UI;
```

```
public class SliderValueToText : MonoBehaviour {
    public Slider sliderUI;
    private Text textSliderValue;

    void Awake() {
        textSliderValue = GetComponent<Text>();
    }

    void Start() {
        ShowSliderValue();
    }

    public void ShowSliderValue () {
        string sliderMessage = "Slider value = " +
sliderUI.value;
        textSliderValue.text = sliderMessage;
    }
}
```

8. Ensure that the **Text** GameObject is selected in the **Hierarchy**. Then, in the **Inspector**, drag the **Slider** GameObject into the public **Slider UI** variable slot for the **Slider Value To Text (Script)** scripted component:

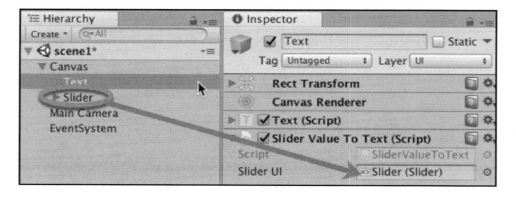

9. Ensure that the **Slider** GameObject is selected in the **Hierarchy**. Then, in the **Inspector**, drag the **Text** GameObject into the public **None (Object)** slot for the **Slider (Script)** scripted component, in the section for **On Value Changed (Single)** - as shown in the screenshot:

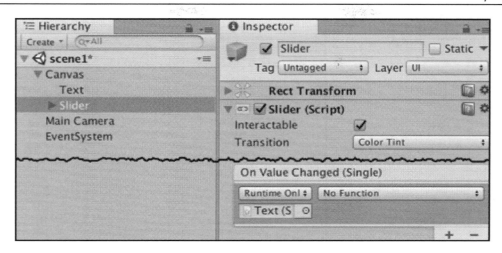

Registering an object to receive UI event messages

You have now told Unity to which object a message should be sent each time the slider is changed.

10. From the drop-down menu, select **SliderValueToText** and the ShowSliderValue() method, as shown in the following screenshot. This means that each time the slider is updated, the ShowSliderValue() method, in the scripted object, in the **Text** GameObject will be executed:

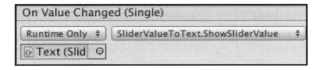

11. When you run the **Scene**, you will now see a **UI Slider**. Below it, you will see a text message in the form Slider value = <n>.

12. Each time the **UI Slider** is moved, the text value shown will be (almost) instantly updated. The values should range from 0 (the leftmost of the slider) to 20 (the rightmost of the slider).

How it works...

You created a **UI Slider** GameObject, and set it to be whole numbers in the range of 0 ... 20.

You have added an instance of the SliderValueToText C# script class to the **UI Text** GameObject.

The Awake() method caches references to the Text component in the textSliderValue variable.

The Start() method invokes the ShowSliderValue() method, so that the display is correct when the scene begins (that is, the initial slider value is displayed).

The ShowSliderValue() method gets the value of the slider and then updates the text displayed to be a message in the form of Slider value = <n>.

You added the ShowSliderValue() method of the **SliderValueToText** scripted component to the **Slider** GameObject's list of **On Value Changed** event listeners. So, each time the slider value changes, it sends a message to call the ShowSliderValue() method, and so the new value is updated on the screen.

Displaying a countdown timer graphically with a UI Slider

There are many cases where we wish to inform the player of the proportion of time remaining, or at the completion of some value at a point in time, for example, a loading progress bar, the time or health remaining compared to the starting maximum, or how much the player has filled up their water bottle from the fountain of youth. In this recipe, we'll illustrate how to remove the interactive "handle" of a **UI Slider**, and change the size and color of its components to provide us with an easy-to-use, general purpose progress/proportion bar. In this recipe, we'll use our modified **UI Slider** to graphically present to the user how much time remains for a countdown timer:

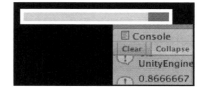

Getting ready

For this recipe, we have prepared the script and images that you need in the folders named _Scripts and Images in the 02_05 folder.

How to do it...

To create a digital countdown timer with a graphical display, follow these steps:

1. Create a new 2D project.
2. Import the **CountdownTimer** script and the red_square and green_square images to this project.
3. Add a **UI Text** GameObject to the scene with a **Font** size of 30 and placeholder text such as **UI Slider** value here (this text will be replaced with the slider value when the scene starts). Set **Horizontal-** and **Vertical-Overflow** to **Overflow**.
4. In the **Hierarchy**, add a **Slider** GameObject to the scene – choose menu: GameObject | UI | Slider.
5. In the **Inspector**, modify the settings for the **Position** of the **Slider** GameObject's **Rect Transform** to the top-middle part of the screen.
6. Ensure that the **Slider** GameObject is selected in the **Hierarchy**.
7. Deactivate the **Handle Slide Area** child GameObject (by unchecking it)
8. You'll see the "drag circle" disappear in the **Game** panel (the user will not be dragging the slider, since we want this slider to be display-only):

9. Select the **Background** child:
   - Drag the `red_square` image into the **Source Image** property of the **Image (Script)** component in the **Inspector**

10. Select the Fill child of the Fill Area child:
   - Drag the `green_square` image into the **Source Image** property of the **Image (Script)** component in the **Inspector**

11. Select the **Fill Area** child:
   - In the **Rect Transform** component, use the **Anchors** preset position of left-middle
   - Set **Width** to 155 and **Height** to 12:

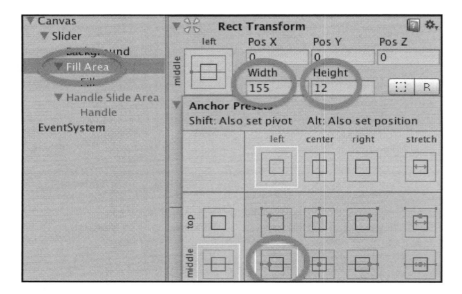

12. Create a C# script class called `SliderTimerDisplay` that contains the following code, and add an instance as a scripted component to the **Slider** GameObject:

```csharp
using UnityEngine;
using UnityEngine.UI;

[RequireComponent(typeof(CountdownTimer))]
public class SliderTimerDisplay : MonoBehaviour {
    private CountdownTimer countdownTimer;
    private Slider sliderUI;

    void Awake() {
```

```
            countdownTimer = GetComponent<CountdownTimer>();
            sliderUI = GetComponent<Slider>();
    }

    void Start() {
            SetupSlider();
            countdownTimer.ResetTimer( 30 );
    }

    void Update () {
            sliderUI.value =
countdownTimer.GetProportionTimeRemaining();
            print (countdownTimer.GetProportionTimeRemaining());
    }

    private void SetupSlider () {
            sliderUI.minValue = 0;
            sliderUI.maxValue = 1;
            sliderUI.wholeNumbers = false;
    }
}
```

Run your game and you will see the slider move with each second, revealing more and more of the red background to indicate the time remaining.

How it works...

You hid the **Handle Slide Area** child so that the **UI Slider** is for display only, and cannot be interacted with by the user. The **Background** color of the **UI Slider** was set to red, so that, as the counter goes down, more and more red is revealed – warning the user that the time is running out.

The **Fill** of the **UI Slider** was set to green, so that the proportion remaining is displayed in green – the more green displayed, the greater the value of the slider/timer.

An instance of the provided **CountdownTimer** script class was automatically added as a component to the Slider via [RequireComponent (...)].

The Awake() method caches references to the **CountdownTimer** and **Slider** components in the countdownTimer and sliderUI variables.

The Start() method calls the SetupSlider() method and then resets the countdown timer to start counting down from 30 seconds.

The `SetupSlider()` method sets up this slider for float (decimal) values between `0.0` and `1.0`.

In each frame, the `Update()` method sets the slider value to the float returned by calling the `GetProportionRemaining()` method from the running timer. At runtime, Unity adjusts the proportion of red/green displayed in the Slider to match the slider's value.

Setting custom mouse cursors for 2D and 3D GameObjects

Cursor icons are often used to indicate the nature of the interaction that can be done with the mouse. Zooming, for instance, might be illustrated by a magnifying glass; shooting, on the other hand, is usually represented by a stylized target. In this recipe, we will learn how to implement custom mouse cursor icons to better illustrate your gameplay – or just to escape the Windows, macOS, and Linux default UI:

Getting ready

For this recipe, we have prepared the folders that you'll need in the `02_06` folder.

How to do it...

To make a custom cursor appear when the mouse is over a GameObject, follow these steps:

1. Create a new Unity 2D project.
2. Import the provided folder, called `Images`. Select the `unity_logo` image in the **Project** panel, and in the **Inspector** change the **Texture** Type to **Sprite (2D and UI)**. This is because we'll use this image for a **2D Sprite** GameObject, and it requires this **Texture Type** (it won't work with the **Default** type).

3. Add a **2D Object | Sprite** GameObject to the scene. Name this **New Sprite**, if this wasn't the default name when created.

   - In the **Inspector**, set the **Sprite** property of the **Sprite Renderer** component to the unity_logo image. In the GameObjects **Transform** component, set the scaling to (3, 3, 3), and if necessary, reposition the **Sprite** to be centered in the **Game** panel when the **Scene** runs.
   - Add to the **Sprite** GameObject a Physics 2D | Box Collider. This is needed for this GameObject to receive OnMouseEnter and OnMouseExit event messages.

4. Import the provided folder called IconsCursors. Select all three images in the **Project** panel, and in the **Inspector**, change the **Texture Type** to **Cursor**. This will allow us to use these images as mouse cursors without any errors occurring.

5. Create a C# script class called CustomCursorPointer, containing the following code, and add an instance as a scripted component to the **New Sprite** GameObject:

```
using UnityEngine;
using System.Collections;

public class CustomCursorPointer : MonoBehaviour {
  public Texture2D cursorTexture2D;
  private CursorMode cursorMode = CursorMode.Auto;
  private Vector2 hotSpot = Vector2.zero;

  public void OnMouseEnter() {
    SetCustomCursor(cursorTexture2D);
  }

  public void OnMouseExit() {
    SetCustomCursor(null);
  }

  private void SetCustomCursor(Texture2D curText){
    Cursor.SetCursor(curText, hotSpot, cursorMode);
  }
}
```

Event methods `OnMouseEnter()` and `OnMouseExit()` have been deliberately declared as public. This will allow these methods to also be called from UI GameObjects when they receive the `OnPointerEnterExit` events.

6. With the **New Sprite** item selected in the **Hierarchy**, drag the `CursorTarget` image into the public **Cursor Texture 2D** variable slot in the **Inspector** for the **Customer Cursor Pointer (Script)** component.
7. Save and run the current **Scene**. When the mouse pointer moves over the Unity logo sprite, it will change to the custom **CursorTarget** image that you chose.

How it works...

You created a **Sprite** GameObject and assigned it the Unity logo image. You imported some cursor images, and set their **Texture Type** to **Cursor**, so they could be used to change the image for the user's mouse pointer. You added a **Box Collider** to the sprite GameObject so that it would receive `OnMouseEnter` and `OnMouseExit` event messages.

You created the **CustomCursorPointer** script class, and added an instance-object of this class to the sprite GameObject – this script tells Unity to change the mouse pointer when an `OnMouseEnter` message is received, that is, when the user's mouse pointer moves over the part of the screen where the Unity logo sprite image is being rendered. When an `OnMouseExit` event is received (the users mouse pointer is no longer over the cube part of the screen), the system is told to go back to the operating system's default cursor. This event should be received within a few milliseconds of the user's mouse exiting from the collider.

Finally, you selected the image `CursorTarget` to be the custom mouse-pointer cursor image the user sees when the mouse is over the Unity logo image.

Setting custom mouse cursors for UI controls

The previous recipe demonstrated how to change the mouse pointer for 2D and 3D GameObjects receiving OnMouseEnter and OnMouseExit events. Unity UI controls do not receive OnMouseEnter and OnMouseExit events. Instead, UI controls can be made to respond to PointerEnter and PointerExit events if we add a special **Event Trigger** component to the UI GameObject. In this recipe, we'll change the mouse pointer to a custom magnifying glass cursor when it moves over a **UI Button** GameObject:

Getting ready

For this recipe, we'll use the same asset files as for the previous recipe, and its CustomCursorPointer C# script class, all of which can be found in the 02_07 folder.

How to do it...

To set a custom mouse pointer when the mouse moves over a UI control GameObject, do the following:

1. Create a new Unity 2D project.
2. Import the provided IconsCursors folder. Select all three images in the **Project** panel, and in the **Inspector** change the **Texture Type** to **Cursor**. This will allow us to use these images as mouse cursors without any errors occurring.
3. Import the provided _Scripts folder, containing the CustomCursorPointer C# script class.
4. Add a **UI Button** GameObject to the scene, leaving this named as **Button**.

5. Add an instance of the `CustomCursorPointer` C# script class to the **Button** GameObject.

6. With the **Button** GameObject selected in the **Hierarchy**, drag the `CursorZoom` image into the public **Cursor Texture 2D** variable slot in the **Inspector** for the **Customer Cursor Pointer (Script)** component.

7. In the **Inspector**, add an **Event Triggers** component to GameObject **Button**. Choose menu: **Add Component | Event | Event Trigger**.

8. Add a **PointerEnter** event to your **Event Trigger** component, click on the plus (+) button to add an event handler slot, and drag GameObject **Button** into the **Object** slot.

9. From the **Function** drop-down menu, choose **CustomCursorPointer** and then choose the `OnMouseEnter` method:

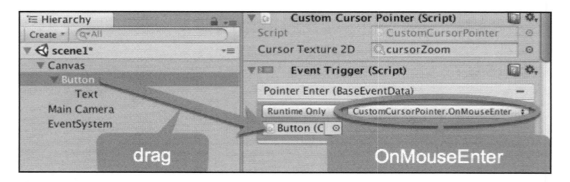

10. Add a **Pointer Exit** event to your **Event Trigger** component, and make it call the `OnMouseExit()` method from **CustomCursorPointer** when this event is received.

11. Save and run the current **Scene**. When the mouse pointer moves over the **UI Button**, it will change to the custom **CursorZoom** image that you chose.

How it works...

You have imported some cursor images, and set their **Texture Type** to **Cursor**, so they could be used to change the image for the user's mouse pointer. You also created a **UI Button** GameObject and added to it an **Event Triggers** component.

You added an instance of the `CustomCursorPointer` C# script class to the **Button** GameObject, and selected the magnifying-glass-style `CursorZoom` image.

You created a **PointerEnter** event, and linked it to invoke the OnMouseEnter method of the instance of the CustomCursorPointer script in the **Button** GameObject (which changes the mouse pointer image to the custom mouse cursor).

You created a **PointerExit** event, and linked it to invoke the OnMouseExit method of the instance of the CustomCursorPointer C# script class to the **Button** GameObject (which resets the mouse cursor back to the system default).

Essentially, you have redirected **PointerEnter/Exit** events to invoke the **OnMouseEnter/Exit** methods of the CustomCursorPointer C# script class so we can manage custom cursors for 2D, 3D, and UI GameObjects with the same scripting methods.

Interactive text entry with an Input Field

While often we just wish to display non-interactive text messages to the user, there are times (such as name entry for high scores) where we want the user to be able to enter text or numbers into our game. Unity provides the UI Input Field component for this purpose. In this recipe, we'll create an Input Field that prompts the user to enter their name:

Having interactive text on the screen isn't of much use unless we can *retrieve* the text entered to use in our game logic, and we may need to know each time the user changes the text content and act accordingly. This recipe adds an event-handler C# script that detects each time the user has completed editing the text, and updates an extra message on screen confirming the newly-entered content.

How to do it...

To create an interactive text input box to the user, follow these steps:

1. Create a new Unity 2D project.
2. In the **Inspector**, change the background of the **Main Camera** to solid white.

3. Add a **UI Input Field** to the **Scene**. Position this to the top-center of the screen.

4. Add a **UI Text** GameObject to the scene, naming it **Text-prompt**. Position this to the left of **Input Field**. Change the **Text** property of this GameObject to **Name:**.

5. Create a new **UI Text** GameObject named **Text-display**. Position this to the right of the **Input Text** control, and color its text red.

6. Delete all of the content of the **Text** property of this new GameObject (so initially the user won't see any text on screen for this GameObject).

7. Add an instance of the `DisplayChangedTextContent` C# script class to the **Text-display** GameObject:

```csharp
using UnityEngine;
using UnityEngine.UI;

public class DisplayChangedTextContent : MonoBehaviour {
    public InputField inputField;
    private Text textDisplay;

    void Awake() {
        textDisplay = GetComponent<Text>();
    }

    public void DisplayNewValue () {
        textDisplay.text = "last entry = '" + inputField.text
+ "'";
    }
}
```

8. With **Text-display** selected in the **Hierarchy**, from the **Project** panel drag the **Input Field** GameObject into the public **Input Field** variable of the **Display Changed Content (Script)** component:

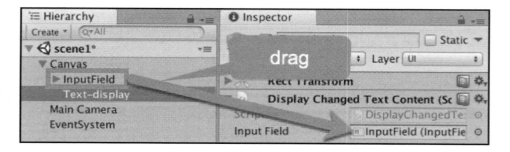

9. With **Input Field** selected in the **Hierarchy**, add an **End Edit (String)** event to the list of event handlers for the **Input Field (Script)** component. Click on the plus (+) button to add an event-handler slot, and drag the **Text-display** GameObject into the **Object** slot.

10. From the **Function** drop-down menu, choose **DisplayChangedTextContent** and then choose the `DisplayNewValue` method.

11. Save and run the **Scene**. Each time the user types in new text and then presses Tab or Enter, the End Edit event will fire, and you'll see a new content text message displayed in red on the screen.

How it works...

The core of interactive text input in Unity is the responsibility of the **Input Field** component. This needs a reference to a **UI Text** GameObject. To make it easier to see where the text can be typed, **Text Input** (as do Buttons) include a default rounded rectangle image, with a white background.

There are usually three **Text** GameObjects involved with the user text input:

- The static prompt text, in our recipe, displaying to the user the text **Name:**
- The faint placeholder text, reminding users where and what they should type.
- The editable text object (with the font and color settings) that is actually displayed to the user, showing the characters as they type.

You created an **Input Field** GameObject, which automatically provides two child **Text** GameObjects, named **Placeholder** and **Text**. These represent the faint placeholder text, and the editable text, which you renamed **Text-input**. You then added a third **Text** GameObject, **Text-prompt**, containing text **Name:**.

The built-in scripting that is part of **Input Field** components does lots of work for us. At runtime, a **Text-Input** Input Caret GameObject is created – displaying the blinking vertical line to inform the user where their next letter will be typed. When there is no text content, the faint placeholder text will be displayed. As soon as any characters have been typed, the placeholder will be hidden and the characters typed will appear in black text. Then, if all the characters are deleted, the placeholder will appear again.

You then added a red fourth **Text** GameObject **Text-display**, to confirm to the user what they last entered in the **Input Field**. You created the `DisplayChangedTextContent` C# script class, and added an instance as a component of the **Text-display** GameObject. You linked the **Input Field** GameObject to the **Input Field** public variable of the scripted component (so the script can access the text content entered by the user).

You registered an **End Edit** event handler of the **Input Field**, so that each time the user finished editing text (by pressing *Enter*), the `DisplayNewValue()` method of your `DisplayChangedTextContent` scripted object is invoked (executed), and the red text content of **Text-display** updated to tell the user what the newly edited text contained.

There's more...

There are some details you don't want to miss.

Limiting the type of content that can be typed

The **Content Type** of the **Input Field (Script)**, can be set (restricted) to several specific types of text input, including email addresses, integer or decimal numbers only, or the password text (where an asterisk is displayed for each entered character). Learn more about Input Fields on the Unity Manual page:
`https://docs.unity3d.com/Manual/script-InputField.html`.

Toggles and radio buttons via Toggle Groups

Users make choices, and often, these choices have *one of two* options (for example, sound on or off), or sometimes *one of several* possibilities (for example, difficulty level as easy/medium/hard). Unity **UI Toggles** allows users to turn options on and off; and when combined with **Toggle Groups**, they restrict choices to one of the group of items. In this recipe, we'll first explore the basic Toggle, and a script to respond to a change in values. Then, we'll extend the example to illustrate **Toggle Groups**, and styling these with round images to make them look more like traditional radio buttons.

The screenshot shows how the button's status changes are logged in the **Console** panel when the scene is running:

Getting ready

For this recipe, we have prepared the images that you'll need in a folder named UI Demo Textures in the 02_09 folder.

How to do it...

To display an on/off UI Toggle to the user, follow these steps:

1. Create a new Unity 2D project.
2. In the **Inspector**, change the Background color of the **Main Camera** to white.
3. Add **UI Toggle** to the scene.
4. For the **Label** child of the **Toggle** GameObject, set the **Text** property to **First Class**.
5. Add an instance of the C# script class called ToggleChangeManager to the **Toggle** GameObject:

```
using UnityEngine;
using UnityEngine.UI;

public class ToggleChangeManager : MonoBehaviour {
    private Toggle toggle;

    void Awake () {
        toggle = GetComponent<Toggle>();
    }

    public void PrintNewToggleValue() {
        bool status = toggle.isOn;
        print ("toggle status = " + status);
```

```
        }
    }
```

6. With the **Toggle** GameObject selected, add an **On Value Changed** event to the list of event handlers for the **Toggle (Script)** component, click on the plus (**+**) button to add an event-handler slot, and drag **Toggle** into the **Object** slot.

7. From the **Function** drop-down menu, choose **ToggleChangeManager** and then choose the `PrintNewToggleValue` method.

8. Save and run the **Scene**. Each time you check or uncheck the **Toggle** GameObject, the **On Value Changed** event will fire, and you'll see a new text message printed into the **Console** window by our script, stating the new Boolean true/false value of the **Toggle**.

How it works...

When you create a Unity **UI Toggle** GameObject, it comes with several child GameObjects automatically – **Background**, **Checkmark**, and the text **Label**. Unless we need to style the look of a **Toggle** in a special way, all that is needed is simply to edit the text **Label** so that the user knows what option or feature this **Toggle** is going to turn on/off.

The `Awake()` method of the `ToggleChangeManager` C# class caches a reference to the **Toggle** component in the GameObject where the script instance is located. When the game is running, each time the user clicks on the **Toggle** to change its value, an **On Value Changed** event is fired. We then register the `PrintNewToggleValue()` method, which is to be executed when such an event occurs. This method retrieves, and then prints out to the **Console** panel, the new Boolean true/false value of the **Toggle**.

There's more...

There are some details that you don't want to miss.

Adding more Toggles and a Toggle Group to implement mutually-exclusive radio buttons

Unity **UI Toggles** are also the base components if we wish to implement a group of mutually-exclusive options in the style of *radio buttons*. We need to group related radio button **UI Toggles** together, so when one turns on, all the others in the group turn off.

We also need to change the visual look if we want to adhere to the usual style of radio buttons as circles, rather than the square **UI Toggle** default images:

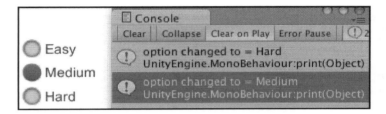

To create a group of related toggles in the visual style of radio buttons, do the following to the project you just created:

1. Import the UI Demo Textures folder into the project.
2. Remove the C# script class ToggleChangeManager component from the **Toggle** GameObject.
3. Rename the **Toggle** GameObject as **Toggle-easy**.
4. Select the **Canvas** GameObject, and in the **Inspector** add a UI | **Toggle Group** component.
5. With the **Toggle-easy** GameObject selected, in the **Inspector** drag the **Canvas** GameObject into the **Toggle Group** property of the **Toggle (Script)** component.
6. Change the **Label** text to **Easy**, and tag this GameObject with a new tag called Easy.
7. Select the **Background** child GameObject of **Toggle-easy**, and in the Image (Script) component, drag the UIToggleBG image into the **Source Image** property (a circle outline).

8. Ensure that the **Is On** property of the **Toggle (Script)** component is checked, and then select the **Checkmark** child GameObject of **Toggle-easy**. In the **Image (Script)** component, drag the `UIToggleButton` image into the **Source Image** property (a filled circle).

Of the three choices (easy, medium, and hard) that we'll offer to the user, we'll set the easy option to be the one that is supposed to be initially selected. Therefore, we need its Is On property to be checked, which will lead to its checkmark image being displayed.

To make these Toggles look more like radio buttons, the background of each is set to the circle outline image of `UIToggleBG`, and the checkmark (which displays the Toggles that are on) is filled with the circle image called `UIToggleButton`.

9. Duplicate the **Toggle-easy** GameObject, naming the copy **Toggle-medium**. Set its **Rect Transform** property **Pos Y** to -25 (so, this copy is positioned below the easy option), and uncheck the **Is On** property of the **Toggle (Script)** component. Tag this copy with a new tag called `Medium`.

10. Duplicate the **Toggle-medium** GameObject, naming the copy **Toggle-hard**. Set its **Rect Transform** property **Pos Y** to -50 (so this copy is positioned below the medium option). Tag this copy with a new tag called `Hard`.

11. Add an instance of the `RadioButtonManager` C# script class to the **Canvas** GameObject:

```
using UnityEngine;
using System.Collections;
using UnityEngine.UI;

public class RadioButtonManager : MonoBehaviour {
  private string currentDifficulty = "Easy";

  public void PrintNewGroupValue(Toggle sender){
    // only take notice from Toggle just switched to On
    if(sender.isOn){
      currentDifficulty = sender.tag;
      print ("option changed to = " + currentDifficulty);
    }
  }
}
```

12. Select the **Toggle-easy** GameObject in the **Project** panel. Now do the following:

    - Since we based this on the **First Class** toggle, there is already an **On Value Changed** event to the list of event handlers for the **Toggle (Script)** component. Drag the **Canvas** GameObject in the target object slot (under the drop-down showing **Runtime Only**).
    - From the **Function** drop-down menu, choose **RadioButtonManager,** and then choose the `PrintNewGroupValue` method.
    - In the **Toggle** parameter slot, which is initially **None (Toggle)**, drag the **Toggle-easy** GameObject. Your **On Value Changed** settings in the Inspector should look as shown in the following screenshot:

13. Do the same for the **Toggle-medium** and **Toggle-hard** GameObjects – so each Toggle object calls the `PrintNewGroupValue(...)` method of a C# scripted component called `RadioButtonManager` in the **Canvas** GameObject, passing itself as a parameter.

14. Save and run the **Scene**. Each time you check one of the three radio buttons, the **On Value Changed** event will fire, and you'll see a new text message printed into the **Console** window by our script, stating the tag of whichever **Toggle** (radio button) was just set to true (**Is On**).

By adding a **Toggle Group** component to the **Canvas**, and having each **Toggle** GameObject link to it, the three radio buttons can tell the **Toggle Group** when they have been selected, and the other member of the group are then deselected. If you had several groups of radio buttons in the same scene, one strategy is to add the **Toggle Group** component to one of the **Toggles**, and have all the others link to that one.

We store the current radio button value (the last one switched On) in the currentDifficulty class property. Since variables declared outside a method are remembered, we could, for example, add a public method, such as `GetCurrentDifficulty()`, which could tell other scripted objects the current value, regardless of how long it's been since the user last changed their option.

Creating text and image icon UI Dropdown menus

In the previous recipe, we created radio-style buttons with a **Toggle Group**, to present the user with a choice of one of many options. Another way to offer a range of choices is with a drop-down menu. Unity provides the **UI Dropdown** control for such menus. In this recipe, we'll offer the user a drop-down choice for the suit of a deck of cards (hearts, clubs, diamonds, or spades).

Note, the **UI Dropdown** created by default includes a scrollable area, in case there isn't space for all the options. We'll learn how to remove the GameObjects and components, to reduce complexity when such a feature is not required.

Then we'll learn how to add icon images with each menu option, as shown in the screenshot:

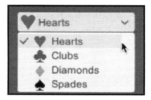

Getting ready

For this recipe, we have prepared the image that you need in a folder named Images in the 02_10 folder.

How to do it...

To create a **UI Dropdown** control GameObject, follow these steps:

1. Create a new Unity 2D project.
2. Add **UI Dropdown** to the scene.

3. In the **Inspector**, for the **Dropdown (Script)** component, change the list of **Options** from **Option A, Option B,** and **Option C** to **Hearts, Clubs, Diamonds,** and **Spades**. You'll need to click the plus (+) button to add space for the fourth option of **Spades**.

4. Add an instance of the C# script class called `DropdownManager` to the **Dropdown** GameObject:

```
using UnityEngine;
using UnityEngine.UI;

public class DropdownManager : MonoBehaviour  {
    private Dropdown dropdown;

    private void Awake() {
        dropdown = GetComponent<Dropdown>();
    }

    public void PrintNewValue() {
        int currentValue = dropdown.value;
        print ("option changed to = " + currentValue);
    }
}
```

5. With the **Dropdown** GameObject selected, add an **On Value Changed** event to the list of event handlers for the **Dropdown (Script)** component, click on the plus (**+**) button to add an event-handler slot, and drag **Dropdown** into the **Object** slot.

6. From the **Function** drop-down menu, choose **DropdownManager** and then choose the `PrintNewValue` method.

7. Save and run the **Scene**. Each time you change the **Dropdown**, the **On Value Changed** event will fire, and you'll see a new text message printed into the **Console** window by our script, stating the **Integer** index of the chosen **Dropdown** value (0 for the first item, 1 for the second item and so on):

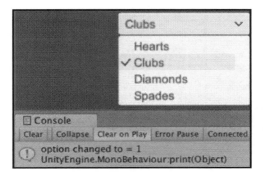

8. Select the **Template** child GameObject of the **Dropdown** in the **Project** panel, and in its **Rect Transform** reduce its height to 50. When you run the **Scene**, you should see a scrollable area, since not all options fit within the **Template's** height:

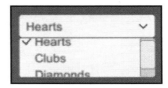

9. Delete the **Scrollbar** child of the **Template** GameObject, and remove the **Scroll Rect (Script)** component of the **Template** GameObject. When you run the **Scene** now, you'll only see the first two options (**Hearts** and **Clubs**), with no way to access the other two options. When you are sure your **Template's** height is sufficient for all its options, you can safely remove these scrollable options to simplify the GameObjects in your scene.

How it works...

When you create a Unity **UI DropDown** GameObject, it comes with several components and child GameObjects automatically – **Label**, **Arrow**, and **Template** (and **ViewPort** and **Scrollbar**, and so on). **Dropdowns** work by duplicating the **Template** GameObject for each of the **Options** listed in the **Dropdown (Script)** component. Both **Text** and **Sprite** image values can be given for each option. The properties of the **Template** GameObject are used to control the visual style and behavior of the **Dropdown's** thousands of possible settings.

You first replaced the default options (**Option A, Option B**, and so on) in the **Dropdown (Script)** component. You then created a C# script class, DropdownManager, that when attached to your **Dropdown**, and having its PrintNewValue method registered for **On Value Changed** events, means that we can see the **Integer** index of the option each time the user changes their choice. Item index values start counting at zero (as with many computing items), so 0 for the first item, 1 for the second item, and so on.

Since the default **Dropdown** GameObject created includes a **Scroll Rect (Script)** component and a **Scrollbar** child GameObject, when you reduced the height of the **Template**, you could still scroll through the options. You then removed these items so that your **Dropdown** had no scrolling feature anymore.

There's more...

There are some details you don't want to miss.

Adding images to a Dropdown control

There are two pairs of items Unity uses to manage how **Text** and **Images** are displayed:

- The **Caption Text** and **Image** GameObjects are used to control how the currently-selected item for the **Dropdown** is displayed – the part of the **Dropdown** we always see, whether the **Dropdown** is being interacted with or not.
- The **Item Text** and **Image** GameObjects are part of the **Template** GameObject, and they define how each option is displayed as a row when the **Dropdown** menu items are being displayed – the rows displayed when the user is actively working with the **Dropdown** GameObject.

So we have to add an **Image** in two places (**Caption** and **Template** Item), in order to get a **Dropdown** working fully with image icons for each option.

To add a **Sprite** image with each **Text** item in the **Dropdown**, do the following:

1. Import the provided Images folder.
2. In the **Inspector**, for the **Dropdown (Script)** component, for each item in the list of **Options Hearts**, **Clubs**, **Diamonds**, and **Spades**, drag the associated **Sprite** image from the card_suits folder in the **Project** panel (hearts.png for **Hearts**, and so on).
3. Add a **UI Image** in the **Project** panel, and child this **Image** to the **Dropdown** GameObject.
4. Drag the hearts.png Image from the **Project** panel into the **Source Image** property of the **Image (Script)** for the **Image** GameObject. Size this Image to 25 x 25 in the **Rect Transform**, and drag it over the letter "**H**" in "**Hearts**" in the **Label** GameObject.
5. Move the **Label** GameObject to the right of the hearts image.
6. With **Dropdown** Selected in the **Project** panel, drag the **Image** GameObject into the **Caption Image** property of the **Dropdown (Script)** component.
7. Enable the **Template** GameObject (usually it is disabled).

8. Duplicate the **Image** GameObject child of **Dropdown**, and name the copy **Item Image**. Child this **Image** in between the **Item Background** and **Item Checkmark** GameObjects that are in **Dropdown-Template-Content-Item** (the **Item Image** needs to appear below the white **Item Background Image**, otherwise it will be covered by the background and not be visible).

9. Since items in the **Dropdown** are slightly smaller, resize Item Image to be 20 x 20 in its **Rect Transform**.

10. Position **Item Image** over the "O" of "Option A" of **Item Text**, and then move **Item Text** to the right so that the icon and text are not on top of each other.

11. With **Dropdown** Selected in the **Project** panel, drag the **Item Image** GameObject into the **Item Image** property of the **Dropdown (Script)** component:

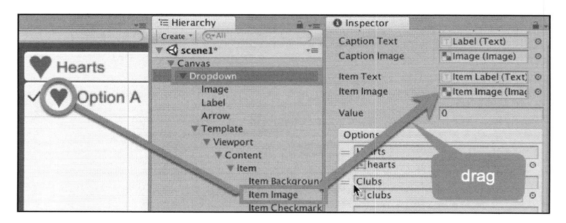

12. Disable the **Template** GameObject, then run the scene to see your **Dropdown** with icon images for each menu option.

 Unity UI Dropdowns are powerful interface components – learn more about these controls from the Unity Manual at https://docs.unity3d.com/Manual/script-Dropdown.html.

Displaying a radar to indicate the relative locations of objects

A radar displays the locations of other objects relative to the player, usually based on a circular display, where the center represents the player, and each graphical blip indicates how far away and what relative direction objects are to the player. Sophisticated radar displays will display different categories of objects with different colored or shaped blip icons.

In the screenshot, we can see two red square blips, indicating the relative position of the two red cube GameObjects tagged Cube near the player, and a yellow circle blip indicating the relative position of the yellow sphere GameObject tagged Sphere. The green circle radar background image gives the impression of an aircraft control tower radar or something similar:

Getting ready

For this recipe, we have prepared the images that you need in a folder named Images in 02_11.

How to do it...

To create a radar to show the relative positions of the objects, follow these steps:

1. Create a new 3D project, with a textured **Terrain**. Import the **Environment** standard asset package contents, by choosing menu: **Assets | Import Package | Environment**.

    1. Create a terrain by navigating to the **Create | 3D Object | Terrain** menu.

    2. Size the **Terrain** 20 x 20, positioned at (-10, 0, -10) - so that its center is at (0, 0, 0):

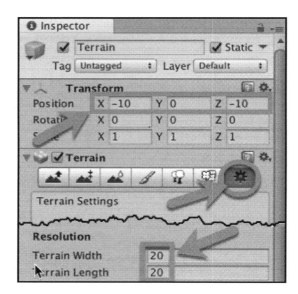

3. Texture paint your **Terrain** with the **SandAlbedo** option, as shown in the screenshot. You need to select the **Paintbrush** tool in the **Terrain** component, then click the **Edit Textures** button, and select the **SandAlbedo** texture from the imported **Environment** assets:

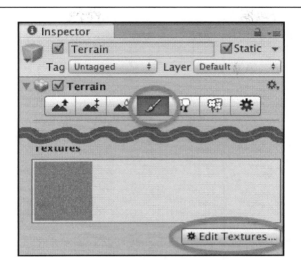

2. Import the provided folder Images.

3. Create a 3D Cube GameObject at **Position** (2, 0.5, 2). Create a Tag Cube and tag this GameObject with this new tag. Texture this GameObject with the red image called icon32_square_yellow, by dragging image icon32_square_yellow from the **Project** panel over this GameObject in the **Hierarchy** panel.

4. Duplicate the **cube** GameObject, and move this new cube to **Position** (6, 0.5, 2).

5. Create a 3D Sphere GameObject at Position (0, 0.5, 4). Create a Tag with the name Sphere and tag this GameObject with this new tag. Texture this GameObject with the red image called icon32_square_yellow.

6. Import the **Characters** standard asset package into your project.

7. From the Standard Assets folder in the **Project** panel, drag the prefab ThirdPersonController into the **Scene** and position it at (0, 1, 0).

8. Tag this **ThirdPersonController** GameObject as Player (selecting this built-in tag means that the camera we'll add will automatically track this player object, without us having to manually set the target for the camera).

9. Remove the **Main Camera** GameObject.

10. Import the **Cameras** standard asset package into your project.

11. From the Standard Assets folder in the **Project** panel, drag the prefab Multi-PurposeCameraRig into the **Scene**.

12. In the **Hierarchy** panel, add a **UI | RawImage** GameObject to the scene named **RawImage-radar**.

13. Ensure that the **RawImage-radar** GameObject is selected in the **Hierarchy** panel. From the `Images` folder in the **Project** panel, drag the `radarBackground` image into the **Raw Image (Script)** public property **Texture**.

14. In **Rect Transform**, position **RawImage-radar** at the top-left using the **Anchor Presets** item. Then set both width and height to 200 pixels.

15. Create a new **UI RawImage** named **RawImage-blip**. Assign it the `yellowCircleBlackBorder` Texture image file from the **Project** panel. In the **Project** panel, create a new empty prefab asset file named `blip-sphere`, and drag the **RawImage-blip** GameObject into this prefab to store all its properties.

16. Set the texture of GameObject **RawImage-blip** to `redSquareBlackBorder` from the **Project** panel. In the **Project** panel, create a new empty prefab asset file named `blip-cube`, and drag the **RawImage-blip** GameObject into this prefab to store all its properties.

17. Delete the **RawImage-blip** GameObject from the **Hierarchy**.

18. Create a C# script class called `Radar`, containing the following code, and add an instance as a scripted component to the **RawImage-radar** GameObject:

```
using UnityEngine;
using UnityEngine.UI;

public class Radar : MonoBehaviour {
    public float insideRadarDistance = 20;
    public float blipSizePercentage = 5;
    public GameObject rawImageBlipCube;
    public GameObject rawImageBlipSphere;
    private RawImage rawImageRadarBackground;
    private Transform playerTransform;
    private float radarWidth;
    private float radarHeight;
    private float blipHeight;
    private float blipWidth;

    void Start() {
        rawImageRadarBackground = GetComponent<RawImage>();
        playerTransform =
GameObject.FindGameObjectWithTag("Player").transform;
        radarWidth =
rawImageRadarBackground.rectTransform.rect.width;
        radarHeight =
rawImageRadarBackground.rectTransform.rect.height;
```

```
            blipHeight = radarHeight * blipSizePercentage / 100;
            blipWidth = radarWidth * blipSizePercentage / 100;
      }

      void Update() {
            RemoveAllBlips();
            FindAndDisplayBlipsForTag("Cube", rawImageBlipCube);
            FindAndDisplayBlipsForTag("Sphere",
rawImageBlipSphere);
      }

      private void FindAndDisplayBlipsForTag(string tag,
GameObject prefabBlip) {
            Vector3 playerPos = playerTransform.position;
            GameObject[] targets =
GameObject.FindGameObjectsWithTag(tag);
            foreach (GameObject target in targets) {
                  Vector3 targetPos = target.transform.position;
                  float distanceToTarget =
Vector3.Distance(targetPos, playerPos);
                  if ((distanceToTarget <= insideRadarDistance))
                   CalculateBlipPositionAndDrawBlip (playerPos,
targetPos, prefabBlip);
            }
      }

       private void CalculateBlipPositionAndDrawBlip (Vector3
playerPos, Vector3 targetPos, GameObject prefabBlip) {
            Vector3 normalisedTargetPosition =
NormaizedPosition(playerPos, targetPos);
            Vector2 blipPosition =
CalculateBlipPosition(normalisedTargetPosition);
            DrawBlip(blipPosition, prefabBlip);
      }

      private void RemoveAllBlips() {
            GameObject[] blips =
GameObject.FindGameObjectsWithTag("Blip");
            foreach (GameObject blip in blips)
                  Destroy(blip);
      }

      private Vector3 NormaizedPosition(Vector3 playerPos,
Vector3 targetPos) {
            float normalisedyTargetX = (targetPos.x -
playerPos.x) / insideRadarDistance;
            float normalisedyTargetZ = (targetPos.z -
playerPos.z) / insideRadarDistance;
```

```
            return new Vector3(normalisedyTargetX, 0,
normalisedyTargetZ);
    }

    private Vector2 CalculateBlipPosition(Vector3 targetPos) {
            float angleToTarget = Mathf.Atan2(targetPos.x,
targetPos.z) * Mathf.Rad2Deg;
            float anglePlayer = playerTransform.eulerAngles.y;
            float angleRadarDegrees = angleToTarget - anglePlayer
- 90;
            float normalizedDistanceToTarget =
targetPos.magnitude;
            float angleRadians = angleRadarDegrees *
Mathf.Deg2Rad;
            float blipX = normalizedDistanceToTarget *
Mathf.Cos(angleRadians);
            float blipY = normalizedDistanceToTarget *
Mathf.Sin(angleRadians);
            blipX *= radarWidth / 2;
            blipY *= radarHeight / 2;
            blipX += radarWidth / 2;
            blipY += radarHeight / 2;
            return new Vector2(blipX, blipY);
    }

    private void DrawBlip(Vector2 pos, GameObject blipPrefab) {
            GameObject blipGO =
(GameObject)Instantiate(blipPrefab);
            blipGO.transform.SetParent(transform.parent);
            RectTransform rt =
blipGO.GetComponent<RectTransform>();
rt.SetInsetAndSizeFromParentEdge(RectTransform.Edge.Left,
pos.x, blipWidth);
rt.SetInsetAndSizeFromParentEdge(RectTransform.Edge.Top,
pos.y, blipHeight);
    }
}
```

Run your game. You will see two red squares and one yellow circle on the radar, showing the relative positions of the red cubes and yellow sphere. If you move too far away, the blips will disappear.

How it works...

A radar background is displayed on the screen. The center of this circular image represents the position of the player's character. You have created two prefabs; one for red square images to represent each red cube found within the radar distance, and one for yellow circles to represent yellow sphere GameObjects.

The `Radar` C# script class has been added to the radar **UI Image** GameObject. This class defines four public variables:

- **insideRadarDistance**: This value defines the maximum distance in the scene that an object may be from the player to still be included on the radar (objects further than this distance will not be displayed on the radar).
- **blipSizePercentage**: This public variable allows the developer to decide how large each blip will be, as a proportion of the radar's image.
- **rawImageBlipCube** and **rawImageBlipSphere**: These are references to the prefab UI RawImages that are to be used to visually indicate the relative distance and position of cubes and spheres on the radar.

Since there is a lot happening in the code for this recipe, each method will be described in its own section.

The Start() method

The `Start()` method first caches a reference to the **Raw Image** of the radar background image. Then it caches a reference to the **Transform** component of the player's character (tagged as `Player`). This allows the scripted object to know about the position of the Player's character in each frame. Next, the width and height of the radar image are cached – so, the relative positions for blips can be calculated, based on the size of this background radar image. Finally, the size of each blip (`blipWidth` and `blipHeight`) is calculated, using the `blipSizePercentage` public variable.

The Update() method

The `Update()` method calls the `RemoveAllBlips()` method, which removes any old **RawImage** UI GameObjects of cubes and spheres that might currently be displayed. If we didn't remove old blips before creating the new ones, then you'd see "tails" behind each blip as new ones are created in different positions – which could actually be an interesting effect.

Next, the `FindAndDisplayBlipsForTag(...)` method is called twice. First, for the objects tagged `Cube`, to be represented on the radar with the `rawImageBlipCube` prefab and then again for objects tagged `Sphere`, to be represented on the radar with the `rawImageBlipSphere` prefab. As you might expect, most of the hard work for the radar is to be performed by the `FindAndDisplayBlipsForTag(...)` method.

 This code is a simple approach to creating a radar. It is very inefficient to make repeated calls to `FindGameObjectWithTag("Blip")` for every frame from the `Update()` method. In a real game, it would be much better to cache all created blips in something such as a `List` or `ArrayList`, and then simply loop through that list each time.

The FindAndDisplayBlipsForTag(...) method

This method inputs two parameters: the string tag for the objects to be searched for, and a reference to the `RawImage` prefab to be displayed on the radar for any such tagged objects within the range.

First, the current position of the player's character is retrieved from the cached player **Transform** variable. Next, an array is constructed, referring to all GameObjects in the scene that have the provided tag. This array of GameObjects is looped through, and for each GameObject, the following actions are performed:

- The position of the target GameObject is retrieved.
- The distance from this target position to the player's position is calculated.
- If this distance is within the range (less than or equal to `insideRadarDistance`), then the `CalculateBlipPositionAndDrawBlip(...)` method is called.

The CalculateBlipPositionAndDrawBlip (...) method

This method inputs three parameters: the position of the player, the position of the target, and a reference to the prefab of the blip to be drawn.

Three steps are now required to get the blip for this object to appear on the radar:

1. The normalized position of the target is calculated by calling `NormalizedPosition(...)`
2. The position of the blip on the radar is calculated from this normalized position by calling `CalculateBlipPosition(...)`
3. The `RawImage` blip is displayed by calling `DrawBlip(...)` and passing the blip position and the reference to the RawImage prefab that is to be created there

The NormalisedPosition(...) method

The `NormalizedPosition(...)` method inputs the player's character position and the target GameObject position. It has the goal of outputting the relative position of the target to the player, returning a **Vector3** object with a triplet of X, Y, and Z values. Note that since the radar is only 2D, we ignore the Y-value of target GameObjects. So, the Y-value of the **Vector3** object returned by this method will always be 0. So, for example, if a target was at exactly the same location as the player, the returned X, Y, Z **Vector3** object would be (0, 0, 0).

Since we know that the target GameObject is no further from the player's character than `insideRadarDistance`, we can calculate a value in the $-1 \ldots 0 \ldots +1$ range for the X and Z axis by finding the distance on each axis from the target to the player, and then dividing it by `insideRadarDistance`. An X-value of -1 means that the target is fully to the left of the player (at a distance that is equal to insideRadarDistance), and $+1$ means it is fully to the right. A value of 0 means that the target has the same X position as the player's character. Likewise, for $-1 \ldots 0 \ldots +1$ values in the Z-axis (this axis represents how far, in front or behind us an object, is located, which will be mapped to the vertical axis in our radar).

Finally, this method constructs and returns a new **Vector3** object, with the calculated X and Z normalized values, and a Y-value of zero.

The normalized position

A normalized value is one that has been simplified in some way, so the context has been abstracted away. In this recipe, what we are interested in is where an object is relative to the player. So, our normal form is to get a value of the X and Z position of a target in the −1 to +1 range for each axis. Since we are only considering GameObject within our insideRadarDistance value, we can map these normalized target positions directly onto the location of the radar image in our UI.

The CalculateBlipPosition(...) method

First, we calculate angleToTarget: the angle from (0, 0, 0) to our normalized target position.

Next, we calculate anglePlayer: the angle the player's character is facing. This recipe makes use of the yaw angle of the rotation, which is the rotation about the Y-axis, that is, the direction that a character controller is facing. This can be found in the Y component of a GameObject's eulerAngles component of its transform. You can imagine looking from above and down at the character controller, and see what direction they are facing – this is what we are trying to display graphically with the radar.

Our desired radar angle (the angleRadarDegrees variable) is calculated by subtracting the player's direction angle from the angle between the target and player, since a radar displays the relative angle from the direction that the player is facing, to the target object. In mathematics, an angle of zero indicates an east direction. To correct this, we need to also subtract 90 degrees from the angle.

The angle is then converted into radians, since this is required for the Unity trigonometry methods. We then multiply the Sin() and Cos() results by our normalized distances to calculate the X and Y values, respectively (see the following diagram):

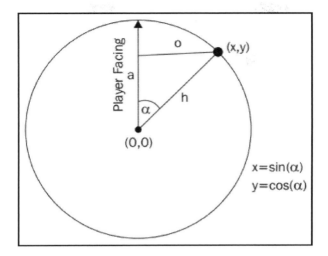

 In this figure, alpha is the angle between player and target object, "a" is the adjacent side, "h" is the hypotenuse, and "o" is the side opposite the angle.

Our final position values need to be expressed as pixel lengths, relative to the center of the radar. So, we multiply our `blipX` and `blipY` values by half the width and the height of the radar; note that we multiply only with half the width, since these values are relative to the center of the radar. We then add half the width and height of the radar image to the blipX/Y values. So, these values are now positioned relative to the center.

Finally, a new **Vector2** object is created and returned, passing back these final calculated X and Y pixel values for the position of our blip icon.

The DrawBlip() method

The `DrawBlip()` method takes the input parameters of the position of the blip (as a **Vector2** X, Y pair), and the reference to the **RawImage** prefab to be created at that location on the radar.

A new GameObject is created (Instantiated) from the prefab, and is parented to the **radar** GameObject (of which the scripted object is also a component). A reference is retrieved from the **Rect Transform** of the new **RawImage** GameObject that has been created for the blip. Calls to the Unity **RectTransform** method SetInsetAndSizeFromParentEdge(...) result in the blip GameObject being positioned at the provided horizontal and vertical locations over the radar image, regardless of where in the Game panel the background radar image has been located.

There's more...

There are some details you don't want to miss.

Adapt for object heights and opaque obstacles

This radar script scans 360 degrees all around the player, and only considers straight line distances in the X-Z plane. So, the distances in this radar are not affected by any height difference between the player and target GameObjects. The script can be adapted to ignore targets whose height is more than some threshold different to the player's height.

Also, as presented, this recipe radar sees through *everything*, even if there are obstacles between the player and the target. The recipe can be extended to not show obscured targets through the use of the Ray Casting techniques. See the Unity scripting reference for more details about ray-casting: http://docs.unity3d.com/ScriptReference/Physics.Raycast.html.

3

Inventory UIs

In this chapter, we will cover the following topics:

- Creating a simple 2-D mini-game - SpaceGirl
- Displaying single object pickups with carrying and not-carrying text
- Displaying single object pickups with carrying and not-carrying icons
- Displaying multiple pickups of the same object with multiple status icons
- Using panels to visually outline the inventory UI area and individual items
- Creating a C# inventory slot display UI scripted component
- Generalizing multiple icon displays using UI Grid Layout Groups (with scrollbars!)
- Displaying multiple pickups of different objects as a list of text via a dynamic `List<>` of scripted PickUp objects
- Displaying multiple pickups of different objects as text totals via a dynamic `Dictionary<>` of PickUp objects and enum pickup types

Introduction

Many games involve the player collecting items or choosing from a selection of items. Examples are collecting keys to open doors, collecting ammo for weapons, and choosing from a collection of spells to cast.

The recipes in this chapter provide a range of solutions for displaying to the player whether they are carrying an item or not, whether they are allowed more than one of an item, and how many they have.

The big picture

The two parts of software design for implementing inventories relate to, first, how we choose to represent the data about inventory items (that is, the data types and structures to store the data) and, second, how we choose to display information about inventory items to the player (the UI).

Also, whilst not strictly inventory items, player properties such as lives left, health, and time remaining can also be designed around the same concepts that we present in this chapter.

We need to first think about the nature of different inventory items for any particular game:

- Single items:
    - Examples: the only key for a level, our suit of magic armor
    - Data type: `bool` (Boolean – `true`/`false`)
    - UI: nothing (if not carried) or text/image to show being carried
        - Or perhaps, if we wish to highlight to the player that there is an **option** to carry this item, then we could display a text `string` saying `no key`/`key`, or two images, one showing an empty key outline and the second showing a full-color key.

- Continuous item:
    - Examples: time left, health, shield strength
    - Data type: `float` (for example, 0.00-1.00) or `int` (Integer) scale
      (for example, 0% to 100%)
    - UI: text number or image progress bar/pie chart

- Two or more of same item
    - Examples: lives left, or number of arrows or bullets left
    - Data type: `int` (Integer – whole numbers)
    - UI: text count or images

- Collection of related items
    - Examples: keys of different colors to open correspondingly colored doors, potions of different strength with different titles
    - Data structure: a `struct` or `class` for the general item type (for example, class `Key` (color/cost/doorOpenTagString), stored as an array or `List<>`
    - UI: text list or list/grid arrangement of icons
- Collection of different items
    - Examples: keys, potions, weapons, tools, all in the same inventory system
    - Data structure: `List<>` or `Dictionary<>` or array of objects, which can be instances of different class for each item type

Each of the preceding representations and UI display methods are illustrated by the recipes in this chapter. In addition, in the chapter we'll learn how to create and use custom **Sorting Layers** in order to have complete control over which objects appear on top of or below other objects – something that is pretty important when scene content can contain background images, pickups, player characters, and so on.

These recipes demonstrate a range of C# data representations for inventory items and a range of Unity UI interface components for displaying the status and contents of player inventories at runtime. Inventory UI needs good quality graphical assets for a high-quality result. Some sources of assets that you might wish to explore include the following sites:

- The graphics for our SpaceGirl mini-game are from Space Cute art by Daniel Cook; he generously publishes lots of 2D art for game developers to use:
    - `http://www.lostgarden.com/`
    - `http://www.lostgarden.com/search?q=planet+cute`
- Sethbyrd-lots of fun 2D graphics:
    - `http://www.sethbyrd.com/`
- Royalty-free art for 2D games:
    - `http://www.gameart2d.com/freebies.html`

Creating a simple 2D mini-game – SpaceGirl

This recipe shows how to create the 2D Space Girl mini-game, on which all the recipes of this chapter are based.

Getting ready

For this recipe, we have prepared the images you need in a folder named Sprites in the 03_01 folder. We have also provided the completed game as a Unity package in this folder, named Simple2DGame_SpaceGirl.

How to do it...

To create the simple 2D Space Girl mini-game, follow these steps:

1. Create a new, empty 2D project.
2. Import the supplied folder Sprites into your project.
3. Since it's a 2D project, each sprite image should be of type **Sprite (2D and UI)**. Check this by selecting the sprite in the **Project** panel, then, in the **Inspector**, check property **Texture** Type. If you need to change the type, change it from this drop-down menu, then click the **Apply** button.
4. Set the Unity Player screen size to 800 x 600: choose this resolution from the drop-down menu on the Game panel. If 800 x 600 isn't an offered resolution, the click the plus sign + button and create this as a new resolution for the panel.
5. Display the **Tags** and **Layers** properties for the current Unity project. Choose menu **Edit | Project Settings | Tags and Layers**. Alternatively, if you are already editing a GameObject, then you can select the **Add Layer...** menu from the Layer drop-down menu at the top of the Inspector panel, next to the Static true/false toggle.

6. Use the expand/contract triangle tools to contract **Tags and Layers,** and to expand **Sorting Layers**. Use the plus sign + button to add two new sorting layers, as shown in the screenshot: first, add one named `Background`, and next, add one named `Foreground`. The sequence is important since Unity will draw items in layers
further down this list on top of items earlier in the list. You can rearrange the layer sequence by clicking and dragging the position control: the wide equals sign (=) icon to the left of the word Layer in each row:

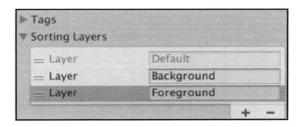

7. Drag the `background_blue` sprite from the Project panel (in the `Sprites` folder) into either the **Game** or **Hierarchy** panel to create a GameObject for the current scene. Set the `Position` of this GameObject to (0,0,0). It should completely cover the Game panel (at resolution `800 x 600`).

8. Set the **Sorting Layer** of GameObject background-blue to **Background** (in the **Sprite Renderer** component):

9. Drag sprite star from the **Project** panel (in the `Sprites` folder) into either the **Game** or **Hierarchy** panel to create a GameObject for the current scene:

- Create a new tag, **Star**, and assign this tag to GameObject star (tags are created in the same way we created sorting layers).
- Set the **Sorting Layer** of GameObject star to Foreground (in the Sprite Renderer component).
- Add to GameObject star a **Box Collider 2D** (**Add Component | Physics 2D | Box Collider 2D**) and check **Is Trigger**, as shown in the screenshot:

10. Drag the girl1 sprite from the **Project** panel (in the `Sprites` folder) into either the **Game** or **Hierarchy** panel to create a GameObject for the player's character in the current scene. Rename this GameObject `player-girl1`.

11. Set the Sorting Layer of GameObject `player-girl1` to Foreground.

12. Add a **Physics | Box Collider 2D** component to GameObject `player-girl1`.

13. Add a **Physics 2D | Rigid Body 2D** component to GameObject `player-girl1`. Set its Gravity Scale to zero (so it isn't falling down the screen due to simulated gravity), as shown in the screenshot:

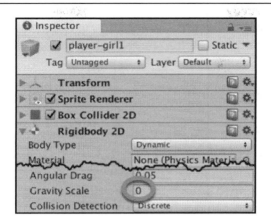

14. Create a new folder for your scripts named _Scripts.

15. Create the following C# Script PlayerMove (in the _Scripts folder) and add an instance as a component to GameObject **player-girl1** in the **Hierarchy**:

```csharp
using UnityEngine;
using System.Collections;

public class PlayerMove : MonoBehaviour {
  public float speed = 10;
  private Rigidbody2D rigidBody2D;
  private Vector2 newVelocity;

void Awake(){
rigidBody2D = GetComponent<Rigidbody2D>();
}

void Update() {
  float xMove = Input.GetAxis("Horizontal");
  float yMove = Input.GetAxis("Vertical");

  float xSpeed = xMove * speed;
  float ySpeed = yMove * speed;

  newVelocity = new Vector2(xSpeed, ySpeed);
}

void FixedUpdate() {
  rigidBody2D.velocity = newVelocity;
}

}
```

16. Save the scene (name it Main Scene and save it into a new folder named _Scenes).

How it works...

You have created a player character in the scene using the girl1 sprite, and added a scripted component instance of class `PlayerMove`. You have also created a star GameObject (a pickup), tagged Star and with a 2D box collider that will trigger a collision when the player's character hits it. When you run the game, the `player-girl1` character should move around using W A S D, the arrow keys, or joystick. There is a `newVelocity` variable, which is updated each frame in the `Update()` method based on the inputs. This `Vector2` value is then applied in the `FixedUpdate()` method to become the new velocity for the GameObject.

Unity maps user inputs such as key presses, arrow keys, and game controller controls to its `Input` class. Two special properties of the Input class are the Horizontal and Vertical axes – accessed via the `Input.GetAxis("Horizontal")` and `Input.GetAxis("Vertical")` methods.

Managing your input mapping: You can manage the mapping from different user input methods (keys, mouse, controllers, and so on) to the axes through menu: **Edit | Project Settings | Input**

Currently, nothing will happen if the `player-SpaceGirl` character hits a star because that has yet to be scripted.

You have added a background (GameObject background-blue) to the scene, which will be behind everything since it is in the rearmost sorting layer, **Background**. Items you want to appear in front of the background (the player character and the star, so far) are placed on the **Foreground** sorting layer.

We can learn more about Unity tags and layers at `http://docs.unity3d.com/Manual/class-TagManager.html`.

Displaying single object pickups with carrying and not-carrying text

Often the simplest inventory situation is to display text to tell players whether they are carrying a single item (or not). We'll add the ability to detect collisions with GameObject tagged **Star** to the SpaceGirl mini-game, and display an on-screen message stating whether a star has been collected or not:

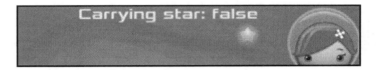

At the end of the recipe, in the *There's more...* section, we'll learn to adapt this recipe to maintain an **Integer** total of how many stars have been collected, for a version of the game with lots of stars to collect.

Getting ready

For this recipe, we have prepared a folder named Fonts in the 03_02 folder.

This recipe assumes that you are starting with the Simple2Dgame_SpaceGirl project that was set up from the first recipe in this chapter. So, make a copy of that project, and work on this copy.

How to do it...

To display text to inform the user about the status of carrying a single object pickup, follow these steps:

1. Start with a new copy of the Simple2Dgame_SpaceGirl mini-game.
2. Add a UI Text object (**Create** | **UI** | **Text**). Rename it Text-carrying-star. Change its text to Carrying star: false.
3. Import the provided Fonts folder into your project.

4. In the **Inspector** panel, set the font of Text-carrying-star to **Xolonium-Bold**, and set its color to yellow. Center the text horizontally and vertically, set its **Height** to 50, and set the **Font Size** to 32.

5. Edit its Rect Transform, and while holding down *Shift + Alt* (to set pivot and position), choose the top-stretch box:

6. Your text should now be positioned at the middle top of the **Game** panel, and its width should stretch to match that of the whole panel, as shown in the screenshot in the introduction to this recipe.

7. Create the following C# script class PlayerInventory in the _Scripts folder:

```
using UnityEngine;

public class PlayerInventory : MonoBehaviour {
    private PlayerInventoryDisplay playerInventoryDisplay;
    private bool carryingStar = false;

    void Awake() {
        playerInventoryDisplay =
GetComponent<PlayerInventoryDisplay>();
    }
```

```
    void Start() {
            playerInventoryDisplay.OnChangeCarryingStar(
carryingStar);
    }

    void OnTriggerEnter2D(Collider2D hit) {
            if (hit.CompareTag("Star")) {
                carryingStar = true;
                playerInventoryDisplay.OnChangeCarryingStar(
carryingStar);
                Destroy(hit.gameObject);
            }
    }
}
```

8. Create the following C# script class PlayerInventoryDisplay in the _Scripts folder:

```
using UnityEngine;
using UnityEngine.UI;

[RequireComponent(typeof(PlayerInventory))]
public class PlayerInventoryDisplay : MonoBehaviour  {
    public Text starText;
    public void OnChangeCarryingStar(bool carryingStar) {
            string starMessage = "no star :-(";
            if(carryingStar)
                starMessage = "Carrying star :-)";
            starText.text = starMessage;
    }
}
```

9. Add an instance of script-class PlayerInventoryDisplay to the **player-SpaceGirl** GameObject in the **Hierarchy**.

 Note, since the PlayerInventoryDisplay class contains RequireComponent(), then an instance of script class PlayerInventory will be automatically added to GameObject player-SpaceGirl.

10. From the **Hierarchy** view, select the `player-SpaceGirl` GameObject. Then, from the **Inspector**, access the **Player Inventory Display (Script)** component and populate the **Star Text** public field with GameObject **Text-carrying-star**, as shown in the screenshot.

11. When you play the scene, after moving the character into the star, the star should disappear, and the onscreen **UI Text** message should change to **Carrying star :-)**:

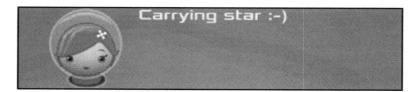

How it works...

You created a **UI Text** GameObject Text-carrying-star to display to the player a text message stating whether or not a star is being carried. You created two script classes, and an instance of each was added as a component to the player's `player-SpaceGirl` character GameObject:

- Script-class `PlayerInventory` detects player-star collisions, updates internal variables saying whether a star is carried, and asks for the UI display to be updated each time a collision is detected.

- Script-class `PlayerInventoryDisplay` handles the communication to the user by updating the text message displayed by the **Text-carrying-star** UI Text GameObject.

A game design pattern (best practice approach) called the **Model-View-Controller pattern** (**MVC**) separates the code that updates the UI from the code that changes player and game variables such as score and inventory item lists. Although this recipe has only one variable and one method for updating the UI, well-structured game architectures scale up to cope with more complex games, so it is often worth the effort of a little more code and an extra script class, even at this game-beginning stage, if we want our final game architecture to be well structured and maintainable.

One additional advantage of this design pattern is that the method in which the information is communicated to the user via the UI can be changed (for example, from text to an icon – see the next recipe!), without any change to the code in script class `PlayerInventory`.

The PlayerInventory script class

The `playerInventoryDisplay` variable is a reference to an instance object of class `PlayerInventoryDisplay`.

The bool variable carryingStar represents whether or not the player is carrying the star at any point in time; it is initialized to **false**.

Method `Awake()` caches a reference to the sibling component `playerInventoryDisplay`.

When the scene begins, via the `Start()` method, we call the `OnChangeCarryingStar(...)` method of script component `playerInventoryDisplay`, passing in the initial value of `carryingStar` (which is false). This ensures that we are not relying on text typed into the **UI Text** object Text-carrying-star at **Design-Time**, so that the UI seen by the user is always set by our **Run-Time** methods. This avoids problems where the words to be displayed to the user are changed in code and not in the **Inspector** panel – which leads to a mismatch between the onscreen text when the scene first runs and after it has been updated from a script.

A golden rule in Unity game design is to avoid duplicating content in more than one place, and, therefore, we avoid having to maintain two or more copies of the same content. Each duplicate is an opportunity for maintenance issues when some, but not all, copies of a value are changed.

Maximizing use of prefabs is another example of this principle in action. This is also know as the DRY principal – don't repeat yourself.

Each time the player's character collides with any object that has its Is **Trigger** set to true, an OnTriggerEnter2D() event message is sent to both objects involved in the collision. The OnTriggerEnter2D() message is passed as a parameter that is a reference to the Collider2D component inside the object just collided with.

Our player's OnTriggerEnter2D() method tests the tag string of the object collided with to see whether it has the **Star** value. Since the GameObject star we created has its trigger set, and has the tag **Star**, the if statement inside this method will detect a collision with the star and complete the following three actions:

- The Boolean (flag) variable carryingStar is set to true
- The method **OnChangeCarryingStar(...)** of script component **playerInventoryDisplay** is called, passing in the updated value of **carryingStar**
- The GameObject just collided with is destroyed – that is, the star

Boolean variables are often referred to as flags.
The use of a bool (true/false) variable to represent whether some feature of the game state is true or false is very common. Programmers often refer to these variables as flags. So, programmers might refer to the carryingStar variable as the star-carrying flag.

The PlayerInventoryDisplay script class

The public `Text` variable `starText` is a reference to the **UI Text** object Text-carrying-star. Its value has been set via drag-and-drop at design time.

The `OnChangeCarryingStar`(carryingStar) method updates the text property of starText with the value of string variable `starMessage`. This method takes an input bool argument `carryingStar`. The default value of string `starMessage` tells the user that the player is not carrying the star, but an if statement tests the value of `carryingStar`, and, if that is true, then the message is changed to inform the player that they are carrying the star.

There's more...

Here are some details you won't want to miss.

Collecting multiple items and display total number carried

Often there are pickups that the player can collect more than one of. In such situations, we can use an Integer to represent the total number collected, and use a UI Text object to display this total to the user. Let's modify the recipe to allow SpaceGirl to collect lots of stars!

To convert this recipe to one that shows the total number of stars collected, do the following:

1. Make three or four more copies of the **star** GameObject and spread them around the scene. This gives the player several stars to collect rather than just one.

Use keyboard shortcut *Ctrl* + *D* (Windows) or *CMD* + *D* (Mac) to quickly duplicate GameObjects.

2. Change the contents of the C# script class PlayerInventory to contain the following:

```
using UnityEngine;
public class PlayerInventory : MonoBehaviour {
   private PlayerInventoryDisplay playerInventoryDisplay;
   private int totalStars = 0;

   void Awake() {
         playerInventoryDisplay =
GetComponent<PlayerInventoryDisplay>();
   }

   void Start() {
         playerInventoryDisplay.OnChangeStarTotal(totalStars);
   }

   void OnTriggerEnter2D(Collider2D hit) {
         if (hit.CompareTag("Star")) {
            totalStars++;
playerInventoryDisplay.OnChangeCarryingStar(totalStars);
            Destroy(hit.gameObject);
         }
   }
}
```

3. Change the contents of C# script class PlayerInventoryDisplay to contain the following:

```
using UnityEngine;
using UnityEngine.UI;

[RequireComponent(typeof(PlayerInventoryTotal))]
public class PlayerInventoryDisplay : MonoBehaviour {
   public Text starText;
   public void OnChangeStarTotal(int numStars) {
         string starMessage = "total stars = " + numStars;
         starText.text = starMessage;
   }
}
```

As you can see, in `PlayerInventory` we now increment totalStars by 1 each time a star GameObject is collided with. In `PlayerInventoryDisplay` we display on screen a simple text message of "total stars = " followed by the integer total received by the method `OnChangeStarTotal(...)./`

Now when you run the game you should see the total stars start at zero, and increase by 1 each time the player's character hits a star.

Alternative – combining all the responsibilities into a single script

The separation of the player inventory (what they are carrying) and how to display the inventory to the user is an example of a game design pattern (best practice approach) called the **Model-View-Controller** (**MVC**) whereby we separate the code that updates the UI from the code that changes player and game variables such as score and inventory item lists. Although this recipe has only one variable and one method to update the UI, well-structured game architectures scale up to cope with more complex games, so it is often worth the effort of a little more code and an extra script class, even at this game's development, if we want our final game architecture to be well structured and maintainable.

However, for *very simple games* we may choose to combine both status and display of that status in a single script class. For an example of this approach for this recipe, remove script components `PlayerInventory` and `PlayerInventoryDisplay` and create the following C# script class `PlayerInventoryCombined` and add an instance to GameObject `player-SpaceGirl` in the **Hierarchy**:

```
using UnityEngine.UI;
public class PlayerInventoryCombined : MonoBehaviour {
    public Text starText;
    private bool carryingStar = false;

    void Start() {
        UpdateStarText();
    }

    void OnTriggerEnter2D(Collider2D hit) {
        if (hit.CompareTag("Star")){
            carryingStar = true;
            UpdateStarText();
            Destroy(hit.gameObject);
        }
    }
```

```
private void UpdateStarText() {
    string starMessage = "no star :-(";
    if (carryingStar)
        starMessage = "Carrying star :-)";
    starText.text = starMessage;
}
}
```

There is no difference in the experience of the player, and the change is simply in the architectural structure of our game code.

Displaying single object pickups with carrying and not-carrying icons

Graphic icons are an effective way to inform the player that they are carrying an item. In this recipe, if no star is being carried, a gray-filled icon in a blocked-off circle is displayed in the top-left of the screen:

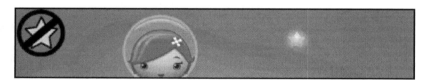

Then, after a star has been picked up, a yellow-filled star icon is displayed. In many cases, icons are clearer (they don't require reading and thinking about) and can also be smaller onscreen than text messages that indicate player status and inventory items.

This recipe also illustrates the benefits of the MVC design pattern described in the previous recipe – we are changing how to communicate to the user (using the **View** via icons rather than text), but we can use, with no changes required, script class PlayerInventory (the **Model-Controller**), which detects player-star collisions and maintains the Boolean flag that tells us whether a star is being carried or not.

Getting ready

This recipe assumes that you are starting with the Simple2Dgame_SpaceGirl project set up in the first recipe in this chapter.

For this recipe, we have prepared a folder named _Scripts in the 03_03 folder.

How to do it...

To toggle carrying and not-carrying icons for a single object pickup, follow these steps:

1. Start with a new copy of the Simple2Dgame_SpaceGirl mini-game.
2. Import the _Scripts folder from the provided files (this contains a copy of the script class PlayerInventory from the previous recipe, which we can use unchanged for this recipe).
3. Add to the scene a **UI Image** object (**Create | UI | Image**). Rename it Image-star-icon.
   - With Image-star-icon selected in the **Hierarchy**, drag the icon_nostar_100 sprite (in the Sprites folder) from the **Project** panel into the **Source Image** field in the **Inspector** (in the Image (Script) component).
4. Click on the **Set Native Size** button for the **Image** component. This will resize the **UI Image** to fit the physical pixel width and height of the icon_nostar_100 sprite file:

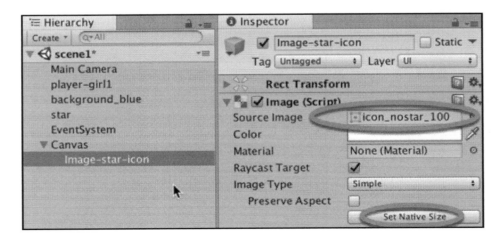

5. Position the image icon at the top and left of the Game panel, in Rect Transform. Choose the top-left box component while holding down *SHIFT* and *ALT* (to set pivot and position).

6. Create the following C# Script class PlayerInventoryDisplay and add an instance to GameObject player-SpaceGirl in the Hierarchy:

```
using UnityEngine;
using UnityEngine.UI;

[RequireComponent(typeof(PlayerInventory))]
public class PlayerInventoryDisplay : MonoBehaviour  {
   public Image imageStarGO;
   public Sprite iconNoStar;
   public Sprite iconStar;

   public void OnChangeCarryingStar(bool carryingStar) {
      if (carryingStar)
         imageStarGO.sprite = iconStar;
      else
         imageStarGO.sprite = iconNoStar;
   }
}
```

7. From the Hierarchy view, select the GameObject player-SpaceGirl. Then, from the Inspector, access the PlayerInventoryDisplay (Script) component and populate the Star Image public field with UI Image object Image-star-icon.

8. Populate the Icon No Star public field from the Project panel with the icon_nostar_100 sprite, and then populate the Icon Star public field from the Project panel with the icon_star_100 sprite, as shown in the screenshot:

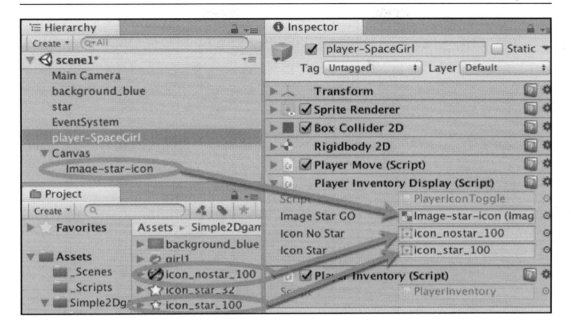

9. Play the scene. You should see the no star icon (a gray-filled icon in a blocked-off circle) in the top left until you pick up the star, at which point it will change to show the carrying star icon (yellow-filled star).

How it works...

In the script class `PlayerInventoryDisplay` the Image variable `imageStarGO` is a reference to the UI Image object `Image-star-icon`. The sprite variables `iconStar` and `iconNoStar` are references to the Sprite files in the Project panel - the sprites to tell the player whether or not a star is being carried.

Each time method `OnChangeCarryingStar(carryingStar)` is invoked by the `PlayerInventory` object, this method uses an `if` statement to set the **UI Image** to the sprite that corresponds to the value of the bool argument received.

Displaying multiple pickups of the same object with multiple status icons

If there is a small, fixed total number of an item to be collected rather than text totals, an effective UI approach is to display placeholder icons (empty or grayed out pictures) to show the user how many of the item remain to be collected, and each time an item is picked up, a placeholder icon is replaced by a full color collected icon.

In this recipe, we use gray-filled star icons as the placeholders and yellow-filled star icons to indicate each collected star, as shown in the screenshot:

Getting ready

This recipe assumes that you are starting with the `Simple2Dgame_SpaceGirl` project set up in the first recipe in this chapter.

How to do it...

To display multiple inventory icons for multiple pickups of same type of object, follow these steps:

1. Start with a new copy of the `Simple2Dgame_SpaceGirl` mini-game.
2. Create C# Script class `PlayerInventory` in the _Scripts folder:

```
using UnityEngine;

public class PlayerInventory : MonoBehaviour {
    private PlayerInventoryDisplay playerInventoryDisplay;
    private int totalStars = 0;

    void Awake() {
        playerInventoryDisplay =
GetComponent<PlayerInventoryDisplay>();
```

```
        }

        void Start() {
            playerInventoryDisplay.OnChangeStarTotal(totalStars);
        }

        void OnTriggerEnter2D(Collider2D hit) {
            if (hit.CompareTag("Star")) {
                totalStars++;
playerInventoryDisplay.OnChangeCarryingStar(totalStars);
                Destroy(hit.gameObject);
            }
        }
}
```

3. Select the GameObject **star** in the **Hierarchy** panel and make three more copies of this GameObject. There are now four **star** GameObjects in the scene. Move these new **star** GameObjects to different parts of the screen.

4. Add the following C# Script `PlayerInventoryDisplay` to the GameObject `player-SpaceGirl` in the **Hierarchy**:

```
using UnityEngine;
using System.Collections;
using UnityEngine.UI;

public class PlayerInventoryDisplay : MonoBehaviour {
    public Image[] starPlaceholders;
    public Sprite iconStarYellow;
    public Sprite iconStarGrey;

    public void OnChangeStarTotal(int starTotal){
        for (int i = 0;i < starPlaceholders.Length; ++i){
            if (i < starTotal)
                starPlaceholders[i].sprite = iconStarYellow;
            else
                starPlaceholders[i].sprite = iconStarGrey;
        }
    }
}
```

5. Select the Canvas in the Hierarchy panel and add a new UI Image object (**Create** | **UI** | **Image**). Rename it Image-star0.

6. Select Image-star0 in the Hierarchy panel.

7. From the Project panel, drag the sprite `icon_star_grey_100` (in the Sprites folder) into the Source Image field in the Inspector for the Image (Script) component.

8. Click on the Set Native Size button for this for the Image (Script) component. This will resize the UI Image to fit the physical pixel width and height of sprite file `icon_star_grey_100`.

9. Now we will position our icon at the top-left of the Game panel. Edit the UI Image's Rect Transform component, and while holding down *Shift + Alt* (to set pivot and position), choose the top-left box. The UI Image should now be positioned at the top left of the Game panel.

10. Make three more copies of **Image-star0** in the Hierarchy panel, naming them **Image-star1**, **Image-star2**, and **Image-star3**.

11. In the Inspector panel, change the **Pos X** position (in the Rect Transform component) of **Image-star1** to 100, of **Image-star2** to 200, and of **Image-star3** to 300:

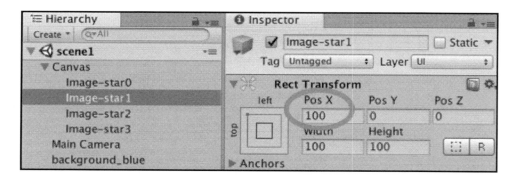

12. In the **Hierarchy**, select the GameObject **player-SpaceGirl**. Then, from the **Inspector**, access the **Player Inventory Display** (Script) component and set the Size property of the public field **Star Placeholders** to 4.

13. Next, populate the **Element 0/1/2/3** array values of public field **Star Placeholders** with **UI Image** objects **Image-star0/1/2/3**.

14. Now, populate the Icon **Star Yellow** and **Icon Star Grey** public fields from the Project panel with sprite `icon_star_100` and `icon_star_grey_100`, as shown in the screenshot:

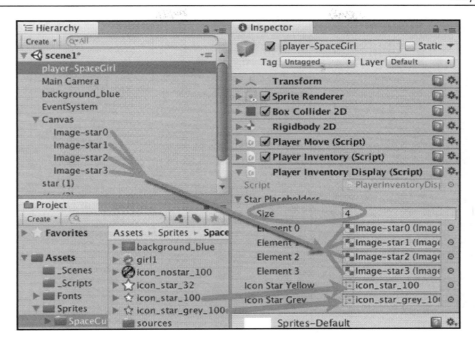

15. Now, when you play the scene, you should see the sequence of four gray placeholder star icons initially, and each time you collide with a star, the next icon at the top should turn yellow.

How it works...

Four **UI Image** objects **Image-star0/1/2/3** have been created at the top of the screen — initialized with the gray placeholder icon. The gray and yellow icon sprite files have been resized to be 100 x 100 pixels, making their horizontal arrangement positioning at design time easier, since their positions are (0,0), (100,0), (200,0), and (300,0). In a more complicated game screen, or one where real estate is precious, the actual size of the icons would probably be smaller – a decision to be made by the game graphic designer.

In script class PlayerInventory, the int variable totalStars represents how many stars have been collected so far; it is initialized to zero. The variable playerInventoryDisplay is a reference to the scripted component that manages our inventory display – this variable is cached before the scene begins in the Awake() method.

The `Start()` method that runs at the beginning of the scene, calls the `OnChangeStarTotal(...)` method of the `PlayerInventoryDisplay` component to ensure that the icons on screen are displayed to match the starting value of totalStars.

In the `OnTriggerEnter2D()` method, the totalStars counter is incremented by 1 each time the player's character hits an object tagged **Star**. As well as destroying the hit GameObject, the `OnChangeStarTotal(...)` method of the `PlayerInventoryDisplay` component is called, passing the new star total integer.

The `OnChangeStarTotal(...)` method of script class `PlayerInventoryDisplay` has references to the four **UI Images**, and loops through each item in the array of Image references, setting the given number of images to yellow, and the remaining to gray. This method is public, allowing it to be called from an instance of script class `PlayerInventory`.

There's more...

Here are some details you don't want to miss:

Revealing icons for multiple object pickups by changing the size of a tiled image

Another approach that could be taken to show increasing numbers of images is to make use of tiled images. The same visual effect as in the previous recipe can also be achieved by making use of a tiled gray star image of width 400 (showing four copies of the gray star icon), behind a tiled yellow star image, whose width is 100 times the number of stars collected.

If the yellow-starred image is less wide that the gray starred imaged beneath then we'll see gray stars for any remaining locations. For example, if we are carrying 3 stars, we'll make the width of the yellow-starred image 3 x 100 = 300 pixels wide. This will show 3 yellow stars and reveal 100 pixels, that is, 1 gray star, from the gray starred image beneath it.

To display grey and yellow star icons for multiple object pickups using tiled images, let's adapt our recipe to illustrate this technique by following these steps:

1. In the **Hierarchy** panel, delete the entire **Canvas** GameObject (and therefore delete all four **UI Images**).

2. Add to your scene a new **UI Image** object (**Create | UI | Image**). Rename the GameObject **Image-stars-gray**.

3. Ensure **Image-stars-gray** is selected in the **Hierarchy**. From the **Project** panel, drag sprite `icon_star_grey_100` (in the Sprites folder) into the **Source Image** field in the **Inspector** (in the **Image (Script)** component).

4. Click on the **Set Native Size** button for this for the Image (Script) component. This will resize the **UI Image** to fit the physical pixel width and height of sprite file `icon_star_grey_100`.

5. Now position the icon at the **top** and **left** of the screen. Edit the **UI Image's** **Rect Transform** component, and while holding down *Shift + Alt* (to set pivot and position), choose the **top-left** box. The UI Image should now be positioned at the top left of the **Game** panel.

6. In the **Inspector** panel, change the **Width** (in the Rect Transform component) of **Image-stars-grey** to 400. Also, set the **Image Type** (in the **Image (Script)** component) to **Tiled**, as shown in the following screenshot:

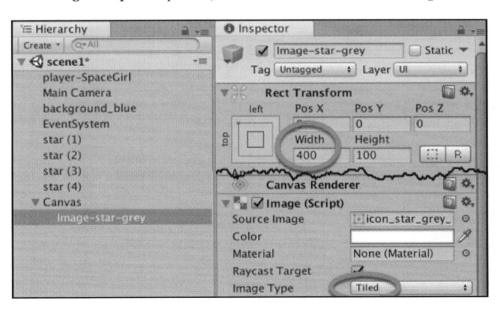

For a simple game like this, we are choosing simplicity over memory efficiency. You'll see a notice suggesting using an advanced texture with Wrap mode repeat and a cleared packing tag. While more memory efficient, it's more complicated to do for small, simple tiling such as in this recipe.

7. Make a copy of **Image-stars-grey** in the **Hierarchy** panel, naming the copy **Image-stars-yellow**.

8. With **Image-stars-yellow** selected in Hierarchy panel, from the **Project** panel, drag the sprite `icon_star_100` (in the `Sprites` folder) into the **Source Image** field in the Inspector (in the **Image (Script)** component).

9. Set the width of **Image-stars-yellow** to 0 (in the **Rect Transform** component). So, now we have the yellow stars tiled image above the grey tiled image, but since its width is zero, we don't see any of the yellow stars yet.

10. Replace the existing C# script `PlayerInventoryDisplay` with the following code:

```
using UnityEngine;
using UnityEngine.UI;

[RequireComponent(typeof(PlayerInventory))]
public class PlayerInventoryDisplay : MonoBehaviour {
    public Image iconStarsYellow;

    public void OnChangeStarTotal(int starTotal) {
        float newWidth = 100 * starTotal;
iconStarsYellow.rectTransform.SetSizeWithCurrentAnchors(
RectTransform.Axis.Horizontal, newWidth );
    }
}
```

11. From the **Hierarchy** view, select the GameObject **player-SpaceGirl**. Then, from the **Inspector**, access the **Player Inventory Display (Script)** component and populate the Icons Stars Yellow public field with UI Image object **Image-stars-yellow**.

UI Image **Image-stars-gray** is a tiled image, wide enough (`400px`) for the gray sprite `icon_star_grey_100` to be shown four times. UI Image **Image-stars-yellow** is a tiled image, above the grey one, initially with width set to zero, so no yellow stars can be seen.

Each time a star is picked up, a call is made from the `PlayerInventory` scripted object to the `OnChangeStarTotal()` method of the script component `PlayerInventoryDisplay`, passing the new integer number of stars collected. By multiplying this by the width of the yellow sprite image (100 px), we get the correct width to set for **UI Image Image-stars-yellow** so that the corresponding number of yellow stars will now be seen by the user. Any stars that remain to be collected will still be seen as the grey stars that are not yet covered up.

The actual task of changing the width of UI Image **Image-stars-yellow** is completed by calling the `SetSizeWithCurrentAnchors(...)` method. The first parameter is the axis, so we pass the constant `RectTransform.Axis.Horizontal` so that it will be the width that is changed. The second parameter is the new size for that axis, so we pass a value that is 100 times the number of stars collected so far (the variable `newWidth`).

Using panels to visually outline the inventory UI area and individual items

We see four kinds of objects when playing a game:

- GameObjects that have some visual elements, such as 2D and 3D objects.
- UI elements located in **World Space**, so they appear next to GameObjects in the scene.
- UI elements located in **Screen Space - Camera**, so they appear at a fixed distance from the camera (but can be obscured by GameObjects closer to the camera than these UI elements).
- UI elements located in **Screen Space - Overlay**. These always appear above the other three kinds of visual element, and are perfect for **Head Up Display (HUD)** elements, such as inventories.

Sometimes we want to visually make it clear which elements are part of the UI HUD and which are visual objects in the scene. Unity **UI Panels** with an opaque or translucent background image are a simple and effective way to achieve this.

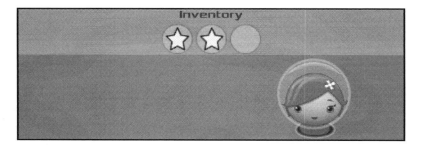

Panels can also be used to display locations (slots) with shaped or colored backgrounds indicating where items may be placed, or how many may be collected. As shown in the screenshot, in this recipe we'll create a panel with some title text, and three inventory slots, two of which will be filled with star icons, communicating to the player that there is one more star that could be collected/carried.

Getting ready

This recipe assumes that you are starting with the Simple2Dgame_SpaceGirl project set up in the first recipe in this chapter. The font you need can be found in the 03_02 folder.

How to do it...

To use panels to visually outline the inventory area and individual items, follow these steps:

1. Start with a new copy of the Simple2Dgame_SpaceGirl mini-game.
2. In the **Hierarchy** panel, create a **UI Panel (Create | UI | Panel)** and rename it **Panel-background**.
3. Let's now position **Panel-background** at the top of the Game panel, stretching the horizontal width of the canvas. Edit the UI **Image's Rect Transform** component, and while holding down *Shift + Alt* (to set pivot and position), choose the **top-stretch** box.

4. The panel will still be taking up the whole game window. Now, in the **Inspector**, change the **Height** (in the **Rect Transform** component) of **Panel-background** to 100.

5. Add a UI Text object (**Create | UI | Text**), rename it **Text-inventory**. For its Text (Script) component, change the text to Inventory.

6. In the Hierarchy panel, child **UI Text** object **Text-inventory** to panel **Panel-background**.

7. In the **Inspector panel**, also set the font of Text-inventory to Xolonium-Bold (the Fonts folder). Center the text horizontally, for Alignment choose vertical center, set its **Height** to 50, and set the **Font Size** to 23.

8. Edit the **Rect Transform** of **Text-inventory**, and while holding down *Shift + Alt* (to set pivot and position), choose the **top-stretch** box. The text should now be positioned at the **top-center** of the UI Panel object **Panel-background**, and its width should stretch to match that of the whole panel.

9. The text should now be positioned at the **top-center** of the UI Panel object **Panel-background** and its width should stretch to match that of the whole panel.

10. Create a new UI Panel (**Create | UI | Panel**) and rename it **Panel-inventory-slot**.

11. Edit the Rect Transform of Panel-inventory-slot, and while holding down *Shift + Alt* (to set pivot and position), choose the **top-center** box. Set both the Width and Height to 70, and the **Pos Y** to -30. See the following screenshot:

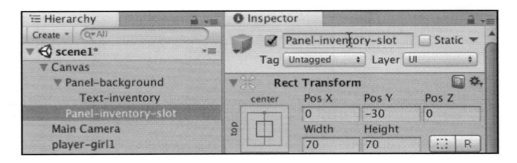

12. Ensure GameObject **Panel-inventory**-slot is selected in the Hierarchy. In the **Image (Script)** component change the Source Image from the **UI Panel** default of Background to the circular **Knob** image (this is one of the built-in images that come as part of the Unity UI system). As shown in the following screenshot, you should now see a circle centered below the title text in our inventory HUD rectangle. This circle visually tells the user that there is space in the inventory for an item to be collected:

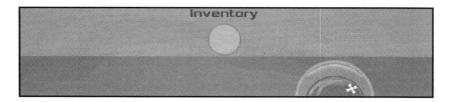

13. Imagine the player has collected a star. Let's now add (inside our inventory slot circle panel) a yellow star icon image. Add to the scene a UI Image object (**Create | UI | Image**). Rename it Image-icon. Child GameObject **Image-icon** to the panel **Panel-inventory-slot**.

Child GameObjects can be hidden making the GameObject **inactive**. By creating a new **UI Image** GameObject for our star icon, and adding it as a child of our **Panel-inventory-slot** GameObject, we can now display the star icon when the **Image** is enabled and hide it by making it inactive. This is a general approach, which means as long as we have a reference to the **Image** GameObject, we don't have to do extra work swapping images as we had to do in some of the previous recipes. This means we can begin to write more general-purpose code that will work with different inventory panels for keys, stars, money, and so on.

14. With Image-icon selected in the **Hierarchy**, drag the sprite icon_star_100 (in the Sprites folder) from the **Project** panel into the **Source Image** field in the Inspector (in the **Image (Script)** component).

15. Edit the **Rect Transform** of **Image-icon**, and while holding down *Shift + Alt* (to set pivot and position), choose the stretch-stretch box. The star icon should now be stretched the perfect size to fit inside the 70x70 parent panel, so we see a star inside the circle.

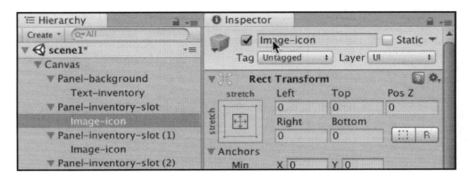

16. Save and run the scene and play the game. You should see a clearly defined rectangle at the top of the screen, with the title text **Inventory**. Inside the inventory rectangular area you can see a circular slot, currently showing a star.

17. Let's display 3 slots to the player. First, change the **Pos X** horizontal position of panel **Panel-inventory-slot** to **-70**. This moves it left of center, making space for the next one, and allowing us to center the three slots when we've finished.

18. Duplicate panel **Panel-inventory-slot**, renaming (if necessary) the copy to panel **Panel-inventory-slot (1)**. Set the **Pos X** of this copy to 0.

19. Duplicate panel **Panel-inventory-slot** again, renaming (if necessary) the copy to panel **Panel-inventory-slot (2)**. Set the **Pos X** of this copy to **70**. Now select the child Image-star-icon of this third panel and make it inactive (at the top of the **Inspector** uncheck its active checkbox, to the left of the GameObject name) . The star for this panel should now be hidden, and only the circle background of the slot's panel is visible.

How it works...

We have created one simple panel (**Panel-background**) with title UI Text as a child GameObject at the top of the game canvas, which shows a grayish background rectangle and the title text Inventory. This indicates to the player that this part of the screen is where the inventory HUD will be displayed.

To illustrate how this might be used to indicate a player carrying stars, we added a smaller panel for one slot in the inventory with a circular background image, and in that added a star icon a child GameObject. We then duplicated the slot panel two more times, positioning them 70 pixels apart. We then disabled (make inactive) the star icon of the third slot, so that the an empty slot circle is shown.

Our scene presents to the user a display indicating two out of a possible three stars are being carried. This recipe is a good start for a more general-purpose approach to creating inventory UIs in Unity, and we'll build from it in some of the following recipes in this chapter.

We'll learn how to limit the player's movement to prevent their character moving into the rectangle of HUD items like this in `Chapter 12`, *Controlling and Choosing Positions*.

Creating a C# inventory slot UI display scripted component

In the previous recipe, we started to work with UI panels and images to create a more general-purpose GameObject for displaying inventory slots, and images to indicate what is stored in them. In this recipe, we look at taking things a little further with the graphics, and also create a C# script class to work with each inventory slot object.

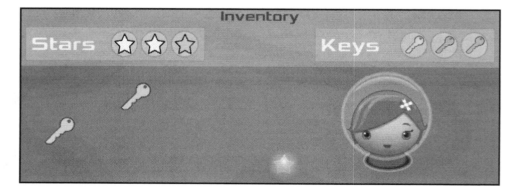

As we can see in the screenshot, in this recipe we'll create the UI (and scripts) for an inventory that has three locations for stars, and three more for keys, using colored and gray icons to indicate how many have been collected.

Getting ready

This recipe adapts the previous one. So, make a copy of the project for the previous recipe and work on this copy.

For this recipe, we have prepared a folder named _Scripts in the 03_06 folder.

How to do it...

To create a C# inventory slot display script component, follow these steps:

1. Import the _Scripts folder from the provided files (this contains a copy of the script class PlayerInventory from one of the previous recipes, which we can use unchanged for this recipe).

2. Delete two of the three inventory slot GameObjects: **Panel-inventory-slot (1)** and **(2)**. So, only Panel-inventory-slot remains.

3. First we'll create a panel for three star slots. In the **Hierarchy** panel, create a UI Panel (**Create | UI | Panel**) and rename it **Panel-stars**.

4. We'll now position **Panel-stars** at the top-left of the **Game** panel, and make it fit within the left side of our general inventory rectangle. Edit the UI **Image's Rect Transform** component, and while holding down *SHIFT* and *ALT* (to set pivot and position), choose the **top-left** box. Now set the **Height** to **60** and the **Width** to **300**. We'll now nudge this away from the top-left corner by setting **Pos X** to 10 and **Pos Y** to -30.

5. Add a **UI Text** object (**Create | UI | Text**) and rename it **Text-title**. For its **Text (Script)** component, change the text to Stars. Child this UI Text object to the panel Panel-stars.

6. Edit the **Rect Transform** of **Text-title**, and while holding down *Shift + Alt* (to set pivot and position), choose the left-middle box. The text should now be positioned at the **left-middle** of the **UI Panel** object **Panel-stars**.

7. In the **Inspector** panel, also set the font of **Text-title** to **Xolonium-Bold** (the Fonts folder). Center the text horizontally, **center-align** the text vertically, set its **Height** to 50, and set the **Font Size** to 32. Choose a **yellow** text color. Set **Vertical-overflow** to Overflow, and set **Alignment** vertical to center. We'll now nudge this away from the very left edge by setting **Pos X** to **10**.

8. Child the existing GameObject **Panel-inventory-slot** to **Panel-stars**. Edit its **Rect Transform**, and while holding down *Shift + Alt* (to set pivot and position), choose the left-middle box.

9. Resize **Panel-inventory-slot** to **Width** and **Height** 50 x 50 pixels. Set its **Pos X** to 140. It should now appear to the right of the yellow Stars text:

10. Rename GameObject **Image-icon** as **Image-icon-grey**. Then duplicate this GameObject, naming the copy **Image-icon-color**. Both should be child GameObjects of **Panel-inventory-slot**. In the Hierarchy the sequence should be that the first child is **Image-icon-grey** and the second child is **Image-icon-color**. If this isn't the order, then swap them.

11. Select **Image-icon-grey**, and drag the sprite icon_star_grey_100 (in the Sprites folder) from the **Project** panel into the **Source Image** field in the **Inspector** (in the **Image (Script)** component). Now, if you disable GameObject **Image-icon-color** you should see the grey star icon inside the slot panel circle.

12. Create the following C# Script PickupUI (in the _Scripts folder) and add an instance as a component to GameObject of **Panel-inventory-slot** in the **Hierarchy**:

```
using UnityEngine;
using System.Collections;

public class PickupUI : MonoBehaviour {
    public GameObject iconColor;
    public GameObject iconGrey;

    void Awake() {
        DisplayEmpty();
    }

    public void DisplayColorIcon() {
        iconColor.SetActive(true);
        iconGrey.SetActive(false);
    }
```

```
        public void DisplayGreyIcon() {
            iconColor.SetActive(false);
            iconGrey.SetActive(true);
        }

        public void DisplayEmpty() {
            iconColor.SetActive(false);
            iconGrey.SetActive(false);
        }
    }
```

13. Select **Panel-inventory-slot** in the **Hierarchy**. In the Inspector, for the **Pickup UI (Script)** component, populate the **Icon Color** public field by dragging **Image-icon-color** from the Hierarchy. Likewise, populate the Icon Grey public field by dragging **Image-icon-grey** from the Hierarchy. Now the scripted component **PickupUI** in **Panel-inventory-slot** has references to the colored and grey icons for this inventory slot GameObject.

14. Duplicate GameObject **Panel-inventory-slot** and for the new duplicate GameObject set its **Pos X** to 190.

15. Duplicate GameObject **Panel-inventory-slot** second time and for the new duplicate GameObject, set its **Pos X** to 240. You should now see all three star inventory icons lined up nicely spaced to the right of the yellow **Stars** title text:

16. Add the following C# Script **PlayerInventoryDisplay** to the GameObject **player-SpaceGirl** in the **Hierarchy**:

```
using UnityEngine;
using System.Collections;
using UnityEngine.UI;

[RequireComponent(typeof(PlayerInventory))]
public class PlayerInventoryDisplay : MonoBehaviour  {
    public PickupUI[] slots = new PickupUI[1];
    public void OnChangeStarTotal(int starTotal) {
        int numInventorySlots = slots.Length;
        for(int i = 0; i < numInventorySlots; i++){
            PickupUI slot = slots[i];
            if(i < starTotal)
                slot.DisplayColorIcon();
```

```
                    else
                        slot.DisplayGreyIcon();
                }
            }
        }
```

17. From the **Hierarchy**, select the GameObject **player-SpaceGirl**. Then do the following in the **Inspector** for the **Player Inventory Display (Script)** component:

- Set the **Size** of public array **slots** to 3.
- Populate the **Element 0** public field with the **GameObject Panel-inventory-slot**.
- Populate the **Element 1** public field with the **GameObject Panel-inventory-slot (1)**.
- Populate the **Element 2** public field with the **GameObject Panel-inventory-slot (2)**:

18. Finally, make two more copies of GameObject **star** in the scene and move them around. So, there are now three GameObjects tagged **Star** for the player to collect.

19. When you run the game and the player's character hits each **star** GameObject, it should be removed from the scene, and the next free inventory star icon should change from grey to yellow.

How it works...

We have created a panel (**Panel-stars**) in which to display the large title text Stars and three inventory slot panels to show how many stars can be collected, and how many have been collected at any point in the game. Each star panel-slot is a **UI Panel** with a circular Knob background image, and then two children, one showing a grey icon image and a second showing a colored icon image. When the colored icon image GameObject is disabled it will be hidden, and so reveal the grey icon. When both colored and grey images are disabled, then an empty circle will be shown, which could, perhaps, be used to indicate to the user that a general-purpose location is empty and available in the inventory.

The script class `PickupUI` has two public variables that are references to the grey and colored icon for the GameObject it relates to. Before the scene starts (method `Awake()`), the script hides the grey and colored icons and displays an empty circle. This script class declares three public methods (public so that they can be invoked from another scripted object when the game is running). These methods hide/reveal the appropriate icons to display the related inventory panel UI object as either empty, grey, or colored. The methods are clearly named `DisplayEmpty()`, `DisplayGreyIcon()`, and `DisplayColorIcon()`.

The script class `PlayerInventory` maintains an integer total `starTotal` of how many stars have been collected (initialized to zero). Each time the player character collides with an object, then if that object is tagged Star, the method `AddStar()` is invoked. This method increments the total and sends a message passing the new total to method `OnChangeStarTotal(...)` of its sibling scripted component `PlayerInventoryDisplay`.

The script-class `PlayerInventoryDisplay` has a public array of references to **PickupUI** objects, and the single public method `OnChangeStarTotal(...)`. This method loops through its array of **PickupUI** scripted objects, setting them to display color icons while the loop counter is less than the number of stars carried, and thereafter setting them to display grey icons. This results in the color icons being displayed to match the number of stars being carried.

Note: It might seem that we could make our code simpler by assuming that slots are always displaying grey (no star) and just changing one slot to yellow each time a yellow star is picked up. But this would lead to problems if something happens in the game (for example, hitting a black hole or being shot by an alien) that makes us drop one or more stars. The C# script class PlayerInventoryDisplay makes no assumptions about which slots may or may not have been displayed grey or yellow or empty previously. Each time it is called, it ensures that an appropriate number of yellow stars are displayed, and all other slots are displayed with grey stars.

The UI Panel GameObjects slots for the three stars have a PickupUI scripted component added, and each is linked to its grey and colored icons.

Several star GameObjects are added to the scene (all tagged Star). The array of PickupUI object references in the `PlayerInventoryDisplay` scripted component in GameObject player-SpaceGirl is populated with references to the PickupUI scripted components in the three the UI Panels for each star.

There's more...

Here are some details you won't want to miss.

Modifying the game for a second inventory panel for keys

We have created a great display panel for the collection of star objects. Now we can reuse that work, to create a second panel to display the collection of key objects in the game.

To modify the game to make a second inventory panel for key collection, do the following:

1. Duplicate GameObject **Panel-stars**, naming the copy **Panel-keys**.
2. With Panel-keys selected in the Hierarchy, do the following:
    - Change the **Text (Script)** of child **Text-title** from **Stars** to **Keys**.
    - In the **Rect Transform**, choose top-right, set **Pos X** to -10 (to move away from the right edge) and **Pos Y** to -30 (to vertically align with Panel-keys).

- For each Image-icon-grey GameObject that is a child of all three panel-inventory-slots, change the **Image (Script)** Source Image to: **icon_key_grey_100**.
- For each Image-icon-color GameObject that is a child of all three panel-inventory-slots, change the **Image (Script)** Source Image to: **icon_key_green_100**.
- For all of the **Image-icon-grey** GameObjects and the Image-icon-color GameObjects that are children of all three panel-inventory-slots, in the **Rect Transform** set the Scale to (**0.75, 0.75, 1**). This is to make the key images fit fully inside the background panel circle images.

3. Remove from GameObject **player-SpaceGirl** script components: **PlayerInventory** and **PlayerInventoryDisplay**.
4. Create the following C# Script PlayerInventoryKeys in the _Scripts folder:

```
using UnityEngine;

public class PlayerInventoryKeys : MonoBehaviour {
    private int starTotal = 0;
    private int keyTotal = 0;
    private PlayerInventoryDisplayKeys playerInventoryDisplay;

    void Awake() {
        playerInventoryDisplay =
GetComponent<PlayerInventoryDisplayKeys>();
    }

    void Start() {
        playerInventoryDisplay.OnChangeStarTotal(starTotal);
        playerInventoryDisplay.OnChangeKeyTotal(keyTotal);
    }

    void OnTriggerEnter2D(Collider2D hit) {
        if(hit.CompareTag("Star")){
            AddStar();
            Destroy(hit.gameObject);
        }

        if(hit.CompareTag("Key")){
            AddKey();
            Destroy(hit.gameObject);
        }
    }
```

```
        private void AddStar() {
                starTotal++;
                playerInventoryDisplay.OnChangeStarTotal(starTotal);
        }

        private void AddKey() {
                keyTotal++;
                playerInventoryDisplay.OnChangeKeyTotal(keyTotal);
        }
}
```

5. Add the following C# script PlayerInventoryDisplayKeys to
   GameObject **player-SpaceGirl** in the **Hierarchy**:

```
using UnityEngine;

[RequireComponent(typeof(PlayerInventoryKeys))]
public class PlayerInventoryDisplayKeys : MonoBehaviour  {
    public PickupUI[] slotsStars = new PickupUI[1];
    public PickupUI[] slotsKeys = new PickupUI[1];

    public void OnChangeStarTotal(int starTotal) {
            int numInventorySlots = slotsStars.Length;
            for(int i = 0; i < numInventorySlots; i++){
                    PickupUI slot = slotsStars[i];
                    if(i < starTotal)
                            slot.DisplayColorIcon();
                    else
                            slot.DisplayGreyIcon();
            }
    }

    public void OnChangeKeyTotal(int keyTotal) {
            int numInventorySlots = slotsKeys.Length;
            for(int i = 0; i < numInventorySlots; i++){
                    PickupUI slot = slotsKeys[i];
                    if(i < keyTotal)
                            slot.DisplayColorIcon();
                    else
                            slot.DisplayGreyIcon();
            }
    }
}
```

6. With the GameObject **player-SpaceGirl** selected in the **Hierarchy**, for its **PlayerInventoryDisplayKeys** scripted component, set both **slotsKeys** and **slotsStars** to 3 (making the size of each of these arrays 3). Then drag the corresponding inventory-slot GameObjects from the Hierarchy to populate these arrays.

7. Create a new GameObject **key** by dragging a copy of the sprite image **icon-key-green-100** from the **Project** panel into the scene. Then add a **Box Collider** component (**Physics 2D**) and tick its **Is Trigger** setting. In its **Sprite Renderer** component, set the Sorting Layer to Foreground. Create a new **Tag: Key**, and add this tag to this GameObject.

8. Make two duplicates of GameObject key, moving them to different locations in the scene (so the player can see all three stars and all three keys).

As you can see, we have duplicated and adjusted the visual UI Panel and components of for star carrying inventory to give us a second one for key carrying inventory. Likewise, we have added code to detect collisions with objects tagged Key, and added to the inventory display script to update the UI Panel for keys when notified that a change has occurred in the number of keys being carried.

Using UI Grid Layout Groups to automatically populate a panel

The recipes in this chapter up to this point have been hand-crafted for each situation. While this is fine, more general and automated approaches to inventory UIs can sometimes save time and effort but still achieve visual and usability results of equal quality.

There can be a lot of dragging slots from the **Hierarchy** panel into arrays, such as in the previous recipe for the scripted component `PlayerInventoryDisplay`. This takes a bit of work (and mistakes might be made when dragging items in the wrong order or the same item twice). Also, if we change the number of slots, then we may have to do this all over again or try to remember to drag more slots if we increase the number. A better way of doing things is to make the first task of the script class `PlayerInventoryDisplay` when the scene begins to create at **Run-Time** as many as required of the panels for grey-color star (or key or whatever) icon GameObjects as children of Panel-slot-grid, and then populate the array of the display scripted component at the same time.

In this recipe, we will begin to explore a more engineered approach to inventory UIs by exploiting the automated sizing and layouts offered by Unity's Grid Layout Group component. Some enhancements at the end of this recipe include adding an interactive scrollbar, as show in the screenshot.

Getting ready

This recipe adapts the previous one. So, make a copy of the project for the previous recipe, and work on this copy.

How to do it...

To automatically populate a panel using UI Grid Layout Groups to follow these steps:

1. Create a new folder named Prefabs. In this folder, create a new empty prefab named panel-inventory-slot.
2. From the **Hierarchy** panel, drag the GameObject **Panel-inventory-slot** into your new empty prefab named panel-inventory-slot. This prefab should now turn blue, showing it is populated.
3. In the **Hierarchy** panel, delete the three GameObjects **Panel-inventory-slot** / **(1)** / **(2)**.
4. Un-child Text-title from Panel-stars. Set the **Pos-X** position of **Panel-stars**. To 130 - so that the panel is now to the right of the text Stars.

5. With the panel Panel-stars selected in the Hierarchy panel, add a grid layout group component (**Add Component | Layout | Grid Layout Group**). Set **Cell Size** to 50 x 50 and Spacing to 5 x 5. Also, set the **Child Alignment** to **Middle Center** (so our icons will have even spacing at the far left and right), as shown in the following screenshot:

6. Replace the C# script `PlayerInventoryDisplay` in GameObject **player-SpaceGirl** with the following code:

```
using UnityEngine;
using System.Collections;
using UnityEngine.UI;

[RequireComponent(typeof(PlayerInventory))]
public class PlayerInventoryDisplay : MonoBehaviour  {
    const int NUM_INVENTORY_SLOTS = 5;
    public GameObject panelSlotGrid;
    public GameObject starSlotPrefab;
    private PickupUI[] slots = new
PickupUI[NUM_INVENTORY_SLOTS];

    void Awake() {
        float width = 50 + (NUM_INVENTORY_SLOTS * 50);
panelSlotGrid.GetComponent<RectTransform>().SetSizeWithCurrent
Anchors( RectTransform.Axis.Horizontal, width );

        for(int i=0; i < NUM_INVENTORY_SLOTS; i++){
            GameObject starSlotGO = (GameObject)
```

```
                      Instantiate(starSlotPrefab);
       starSlotGO.transform.SetParent(panelSlotGrid.transform);
                      starSlotGO.transform.localScale = new
Vector3(1,1,1);
                      slots[i] = starSlotGO.GetComponent<PickupUI>();
             }
       }

    public void OnChangeStarTotal(int starTotal) {
          for(int i = 0; i < NUM_INVENTORY_SLOTS; i++){
                PickupUI slot = slots[i];
                if(i < starTotal)
                      slot.DisplayColorIcon();
                else
                      slot.DisplayGreyIcon();
          }
       }
    }
```

7. Ensure GameObject **player-girl1** is selected in the **Hierarchy.** Then drag from the **Project** panel GameObject **Panel-stars** into the **Player Inventory Display (Script)** variable **Panel-slot-grid**, in the **Inspector**.

8. With GameObject **player-girl1** selected in the **Hierarchy**, drag from the **Project** panel prefab **panel-inventory-slot** into **Player Inventory Display (Script)** the variable **Star Slot Prefab**, in the **Inspector**. Steps 7 and 8 are illustrated in this screenshot:

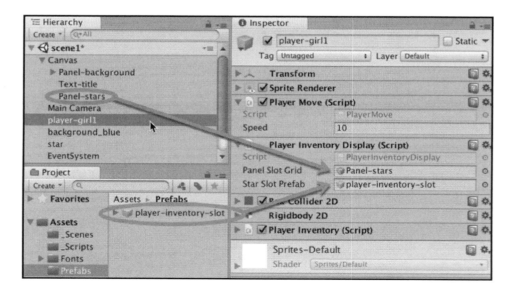

9. Edit the script class `PlayerInventoryDisplay` to set the constant `NUM_INVENTORY_SLOTS` to have 10 or 15 slots. So some can only be seen when using the horizontal scroll bar.

10. Save the scene and play the game. As you pick up stars, you should see more of the grey stars change to yellow in the inventory display.

How it works...

We took one of the panels that contained the **Knob** circle background, and children GameObjects of grey and colored star images, and used it to create a **Prefab panel-inventory-slot**. We then removed the star panel GameObjects from the scene since our script class PlayerInventoryDisplay will create as many of these as needed when the scene begins. This approach saves a lot of drag and dropping, saving **Design-Time** effort, and eliminating one possible source of sequence/object reference errors when the design of a scene is changed.

The C# script class `PlayerInventoryDisplay` has two properties:

- A constant integer (`NUM_INVENTORY_SLOTS`) defining the number of slots in our inventory, which for this game we set to 5.
- A (`slots`) array of references to `PickupUI` scripted components. Each of these will become a reference to the scripted component in each of the five `Panel-inventory-slot` GameObjects in our `Panel-stars`.

The `Awake()` method is used to create instances of the prefab in `PlayerInventoryDispay` so that we know this will be executed before the `Start()` method in `PlayerInventory` since no `Start()` method is executed in a scene until all `Awake()` methods for all GameObjects in the scene have been completed. The `Awake()` method first calculates the width of the **Panel-stars** (50 + (50 * number of inventory slots)). Next, the panel is resized to have that width, using the `SetSizeWithCurrentAnchors()` method. Then a loop runs for the number of slots in the inventory, each time creating a new star slot GameObject from the prefab, childing the new GameObject to **Panel-stars**, and adding a reference to the icon slot GameObject in array slots. When the `OnChangeStarTotal(...)` method is passed the number of stars we are carrying, it loops through each of the five slots. While the current slot is less than our star total, a yellow star is displayed by the calling of the `DisplayYellow()` method of the current slot (PickupUI scripted component). Once the loop counter is equal to or larger than our star total, then all remaining slots are made to display a grey star via the method `DisplayGrey()`.

Our player character GameObject, player-girl1, has a very simple basic `PlayerInventory` script. This just detects collisions with objects tagged Star, and when this happens, it removes the star GameObject collided with and calls its `AddStar()` method of its `playerInventoryModel` scripted component. Each time the `AddStar()` method is called, it increments (adds 1) to the total umber of stars being carried, and then calls the `OnChangeStarTotal(...)` method of the scripted component `playerInventoryDisplay`. Also, when the scene starts, an initial call is made to the `OnChangeStarTotal(...)` method so that the UI display for the inventory is set up to show that we are initially carrying no stars.

The public array has been made private and no longer needs to be populated through manual drag-and-drop. When you run the game, it will play just the same as before, with the population of the array of images in our inventory grid panel now automated. The `Awake()` method creates new instances of the prefab (as many as defined by constant `NUM_INVENTORY_SLOTS`) and immediately childed them to Panel-slot-grid. Since we have a grid layout group component, their placement is automatically neat and tidy in our panel.

 The scale property of the transform component of GameObjects is reset when a GameObject changes its parent (to keep the child size to relative to the parent size). So, it is a good idea to always reset the local scale of GameObjects to (1,1,1) immediately after they have been childed to another GameObject. We do this in the for loop of starSlotGO immediately following the `SetParent(...)` statement.

There's more...

Here are some details you won't want to miss.

Automatically infer number of inventory slots based on number of GameObjects tagged Star

Rather than having to manually change Integer constant `NUM_INVENTORY_SLOTS` in the script class **PlayerInventoryDisplay** to match the number of GameObjects created in the scene for the player to collect, let's have our script count how many GameObjects are tagged **Star**, and use this to size and populate our array of references to inventory UI panel slots.

We just need to change from a constant to a variable for our array size, and set that variable before anything else in our `Awake()` method. The statement `GameObject.FindGameObjectsWithTag("Star")` gets an array of references to all GameObjects with tag Star, and its length is the array size we want:

1. Replace the C# Script `PlayerInventoryDisplay` in the GameObject **player-SpaceGirl** with the following code:

```
using UnityEngine;
using System.Collections;
using UnityEngine.UI;

[RequireComponent(typeof(PlayerInventory))]
public class PlayerInventoryDisplay : MonoBehaviour  {
    private int numInventorySlots;
    private PickupUI[] slots;
    public GameObject panelSlotGrid;
    public GameObject starSlotPrefab;

    void Awake() {
        GameObject[] gameObjectsTaggedStar =
GameObject.FindGameObjectsWithTag("Star");
        numInventorySlots = gameObjectsTaggedStar.Length;
        slots = new PickupUI[numInventorySlots];
        float width = 50 + (numInventorySlots * 50);
panelSlotGrid.GetComponent<RectTransform>().SetSizeWithCurrent
Anchors( RectTransform.Axis.Horizontal, width);

        for(int i=0; i < numInventorySlots; i++){
            GameObject starSlotGO = (GameObject)
            Instantiate(starSlotPrefab);
starSlotGO.transform.SetParent(panelSlotGrid.transform);
            starSlotGO.transform.localScale = new
Vector3(1,1,1);
            slots[i] = starSlotGO.GetComponent<PickupUI>();
        }
    }

    public void OnChangeStarTotal(int starTotal) {
        for(int i = 0; i < numInventorySlots; i++){
            PickupUI slot = slots[i];
            if(i < starTotal)
                slot.DisplayColorIcon();
            else
                slot.DisplayGreyIcon();
        }
```

```
        }
    }
```

2. Add or remove some of the duplicates of GameObject **star** so the total is no longer 5.

3. Run the scene. You should see the size and contents of **Panel-star** change to match the number of GameObjects tagged **Star** when the scene begins.

Add a horizontal scrollbar to the inventory slot display

How could we cope with many inventory slots, more than fit in the space provided? One solution is to add a scroll bar so that the user can scroll left and right, viewing five at a time, say, as shown in the following screenshot.

Let's add a horizontal scroll bar to our game. This can be achieved without any C# code changes, all through the Unity 5 UI system.

To implement a horizontal scrollbar for our inventory display, we need to do the following:

1. Increase the height of Panel-background to 110 pixels.

2. In the **Inspector p**anel, set the **Child Alignment** property of component **Grid Layout Group (Script)** of Panel-slot-grid to Upper Left. Then, move this panel to the right a little so that the inventory icons are centered on screen.

3. Add a **UI Panel** to the **Canvas** and name it Panel-scroll-container, and tint it red by setting the Color property of its **Image (Script)** component to red.

4. In the **Hierarchy** panel, drag Panel-slot-grid so that it is now childed to Panel-scroll-container.

5. Size and position Panel-scroll-container so that it is just behind our Panel-slot-grid. Set its **Rect Transform** to top-left, **Pos X** to 130, **Pos Y** to -30, **Width** to 300 and **Height** to 60. So, you should now see a red rectangle behind the `Panel-slot-grid` inventory panel.

6. Add a **UI Mask** to `Panel-scroll-container` so now you should only be able to see the parts of `Panel-slot-grid` that fit within the rectangle of this red-tinted panel.

One workflow is to to temporarily set this mask component as inactive so that you can see and work on the unseen parts of Panel-slot-grid if required.

7. Add a **UI Scrollbar** to the **Canvas** and name it Scrollbar-horizontal. Move it to be just below the red-tinted `Panel-scroll-container`, and resize it to be the same width as shown in the following screenshot:

8. Add a UI **Scroll Rect** component to Panel-scroll-container. Uncheck the **Vertical** property of this **Scroll Rect** component.

9. In the **Inspector** panel, drag **Scrolbar-horizontal** to the Horizontal Scrollbar property of the Scroll Rect component of **Panel-scroll-container**.

10. In the **Inspector** panel, drag **Panel-slot-grid** to the **Content** property of the **Scroll Rect** component of Panel-scroll-container, as shown in the following screenshot:

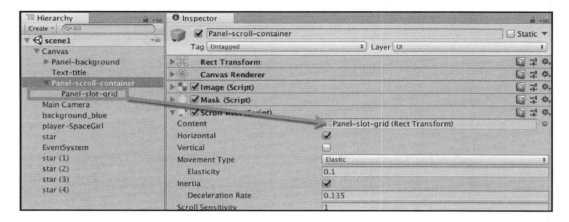

11. Now, ensure the mask component of **Panel-scroll-container** is set as active so that we don't see the overflow of **Panel-slot-grid** and uncheck this mask components option to **Show Mask Graphic** (so that we don't see the red rectangle any more).

You should now have a working scrollable inventory system.

Automatically changing the grid cell size based on the number of slots in the inventory

Consider a situation where we wish to change the number of slots. An alternative to using something like scrollbars is to change the cell size in the **Grid Layout Group** component. We can automate this through code so that the cell size is changed to ensure that NUM_INVENTORY_SLOTS will fit along the width of our panel at the top of the canvas.

To implement the automated resizing of the **Grid Layout Group** cell size for this recipe, we need to do the following:

- Comment-out the third statement in method `Awake()`:

```
//
panelSlotGrid.GetComponent<RectTransform>().SetSizeWithCurrent
Anchors(
// RectTransform.Axis.Horizontal, width);
```

- Add the following method Start() to the C# Script PlayerInventoryDisplay in GameObject player-SpaceGirl with the following code:

```
void Start() {
  float panelWidth =
panelSlotGrid.GetComponent<RectTransform>().rect.width;
  print ("slotGrid.GetComponent<RectTransform>().rect = " +
panelSlotGrid.GetComponent<RectTransform>().rect);
  GridLayoutGroup gridLayoutGroup =
panelSlotGrid.GetComponent<GridLayoutGroup>();
  float xCellSize = panelWidth / NUM_INVENTORY_SLOTS;
  xCellSize -= gridLayoutGroup.spacing.x;
  gridLayoutGroup.cellSize = new Vector2(xCellSize,
xCellSize);
}
```

We write our code in the `Start()` method, rather than adding to code in the Awake() method, to ensure that the `RectTransform` of GameObject Panel-slot-grid has finished sizing (in this recipe, it stretches based on the width of the Game panel). While we can't know the sequence in which **Hierarchy** GameObjects are created when a scene begins, we can rely on the Unity behavior that every GameObject sends the `Awake()` message, and only after all corresponding `Awake()` methods have finished executing all objects, and then sends the Start() message. So, any code in the `Start()` method can safely assume that every GameObject has been initialized.

The screenshot above shows the value of NUM_INVENTORY_SLOTS having been changed to 15, and the cell size, having been corresponding, changed, so that all 15 now fit horizontally in our panel. Note that the spacing between cells is subtracted from the calculated available with divided by the number of slots (xCellSize -= gridLayoutGroup.spacing.x) since that spacing is needed between each item displayed as well.

Displaying multiple pickups of different objects as a list of text via a dynamic List<> of scripted PickUp objects

When working with different kinds of pickups, one approach is to use a C# List to maintain a flexible-length data structure of the items currently in the inventory. In this recipe, we will show you how, each time an item is picked up, a new object is added to such a List collection. An iteration through the List is how the text display of items is generated each time the inventory changes. We introduce a very simple PickUp script class, demonstrating how information about a pickup can be stored in a scripted component, extracted upon collision, and stored in our List.

Getting ready

This recipe assumes that you are starting with the Simple2Dgame_SpaceGirl project we set up in the first recipe in this chapter. The font you need can be found in the 03_02 folder.

How to do it...

To display inventory total text for multiple pickups of different object types, follow these steps:

1. Start with a new copy of the `Simple2Dgame_SpaceGirl mini-game`.

2. Edit the tags, changing Star to Pickup. Ensure that the star GameObject now has the **Pickup** tag.

3. Add the following C# Script **PickUp** to the GameObject star in the Hierarchy:

```
using UnityEngine;
using System.Collections;

public class PickUp : MonoBehaviour {
    public string description;
}
```

4. In the Inspector, change the description property of component Pick Up (Script) of GameObject star to the text `star`:

5. Select the GameObject star in the Hierarchy panel and make a copy of this GameObject, renaming the copy heart.

6. In the Inspector, change the description property of component `Pick Up` (Script) of GameObject heart to the text heart. Also, drag the health heart image from the Project panel (in the Sprites folder) into the Sprite property of GameObject heart. The player should now see the heart image on screen for this pickup item.

7. Select the GameObject star in the **Hierarchy** panel and make a copy of this GameObject, renaming the copy key.

8. In the Inspector, change the description property of component Pick Up (Script) of GameObject key to the text key. Also, drag the `icon_key_green_100` image from the Project panel (in the Sprites folder) into the Sprite property of GameObject key. The player should now see the key image on screen for this pickup item.

9. Make another one or two copies of each pickup GameObject and arrange them around the screen, so there are two or three each of star, heart, and key pickup GameObjects.

10. Create the following C# Script `PlayerInventory` in the _Scripts folder.

```
using UnityEngine;
using System.Collections;
using UnityEngine.UI;
using System.Collections.Generic;

public class PlayerInventory : MonoBehaviour {
    private PlayerInventoryDisplay playerInventoryDisplay;
    private List<PickUp> inventory = new List<PickUp>();

    void Awake() {
        playerInventoryDisplay =
GetComponent<PlayerInventoryDisplay>();
    }

    void Start() {
        playerInventoryDisplay.OnChangeInventory(inventory);
    }

    void OnTriggerEnter2D(Collider2D hit) {
        if(hit.CompareTag("Pickup")){
            PickUp item = hit.GetComponent<PickUp>();
            inventory.Add( item );
playerInventoryDisplay.OnChangeInventory(inventory);
            Destroy(hit.gameObject);
        }
    }
}
```

11. Add a UI Text object (**Create | UI | Text**). Rename it Text-inventory-list. Change its text to **the quick brown fox jumped over the lazy dog the quick brown fox jumped over the lazy dog,** or another long list of nonsense words, to test the overflow settings you'll change in the next step.

12. In the Text (Script) component, ensure that **Horizontal Overflow** is set to Wrap, and set **Vertical Overflow** to **Overflow**. This will ensure that the text will wrap onto a second or third line (if needed) and not be hidden if there are lots of pickups.

13. In the **Inspector** panel, set its font to **Xolonium-Bold** (folder Fonts) and set its color to yellow. For the **Alignment** property, center the text horizontally and ensure that the text is top aligned vertically, set the **Font Size** to 28, and choose a yellow text Color.

14. Edit its **Rect Transform** and set its **Height** to 50. Then, while holding down *Shift + Alt* (to set pivot and position), choose the top-stretch box. The text should now be positioned at the middle top of the **Game** panel, and its width should stretch to match that of the whole panel.

15. Your text should now appear at the top of the game panel.

16. Add the following C# Script `PlayerInventoryDisplay` to GameObject **player-girl1** in the **Hierarchy**:

```csharp
using UnityEngine;
using System.Collections;
using UnityEngine.UI;
using System.Collections.Generic;

[RequireComponent(typeof(PlayerInventory))]
public class PlayerInventoryDisplay : MonoBehaviour {
    public Text inventoryText;

    public void OnChangeInventory(List<PickUp> inventory) {
        // (1) clear existing display
        inventoryText.text = "";

        // (2) build up new set of items
        string newInventoryText = "carrying: ";
        int numItems = inventory.Count;
        for(int i = 0; i < numItems; i++){
            string description = inventory[i].description;
            newInventoryText += " [" + description+ "]";
        }

        // if no items in List then set string to message
saying inventory is empty
        if(numItems < 1)
```

```
                    newInventoryText = "(empty inventory)";

            // (3) update screen display
            inventoryText.text = newInventoryText;
        }
    }
```

17. From the **Hierarchy**, select the GameObject **player-girl1**. Then, from the **Inspector**, access the **Player Inventory Display (Script)** component and populate the **Inventory Text** public field with the **UI Text** object **Text-inventory-lis**t.

18. Play the game. Each time you pick up a star or key or heart, the updated list of what you are carrying should be displayed in the form **carrying [key] [heart]**.

How it works...k

In the script class `PlayerInventory`, the variable inventory is a C# List<>. This is a flexible data structure that can be sorted, searched, and dynamically (at runtime, when the game is being played) have items added to and removed from it. The `<PickUp>` in pointy brackets means that variable inventory will contain a list of `PickUp` objects. For this recipe, our `PickUp` class just has a single field, a string description, but we'll add more sophisticated data items in `PickUp` classes in later recipes. This variable inventory is initialized to be a new, empty C# List of `PickUp` objects.

Before the scene starts, the `Awake()` method of script class Player caches a reference to the `PlayerInventoryDisplay` scripted component.

When the scene starts the `Start()` method invokes the `OnChangeInventory(...)` method of the `PlayerInventoryDisplay` scripted component. This is so the text displayed to the user at the beginning of the scene corresponds to the initial value of the variable inventory (which might, for some games, not be empty. For example, a player might start a game with some money, or a basic weapon, or a map).

When the `OnTriggerEnter2D(...)` method detects collisions with items tagged Pickup, the `PickUp` object component of the item hit is added to our inventory list. A call is also made to the `OnChangeInventory(...)` method of `playerInventoryDisplay` to update out inventory display to the player, passing the updated inventory List as a parameter.

The script class `playerInventoryDisplay` has a public variable, linked to the UI Text object **Text-inventory-list**. The `OnChangeInventory(...)` method first sets the UI text to empty, and then loops through the inventory list, building up a string of each items description in square brackets (**[key]**, **[heart]**, and so on). If there were no items in the list, then the string is set to the text (empty inventory). Finally, the text property of the **UI Text object Text-inventory-list** is set to the value of this string representation of what is inside the variable inventory.

There's more...

Here are some details you won't want to miss.

Order items in the inventory list alphabetically

It would be nice to alphabetically sort the words in the inventory list, both for neatness and consistency (so, in a game, if we pick up a key and a heart, it will look the same regardless of the order they are picked up in), but also so that items of the same type will be listed together so that we can easily see how many of each item we are carrying.

To implement alphabetical sorting of the items in the inventory list, we need to do the following:

1. Add the following C# code to the beginning of method `OnChangeInventory(...)` in the script class `PlayerInventoryDisplay`:

```
public void OnChangeInventory(List<PickUp> inventory){
    inventory.Sort(
        delegate(PickUp p1, PickUp p2){
            return p1.description.CompareTo(p2.description);
        }
    );

    // rest of the method as before ...
}
```

2. You should now see all the items listed in alphabetic sequence.

This C# code takes advantage of the C# List.Sort(...) method, a feature of collections whereby each item can be compared to the next, and they are swapped if in the wrong order (if the CompareTo(...) methods returns false). Learn more at `https://msdn.microsoft.com/en-us/library/3da4abas(v=vs.1 10).aspx`.

Displaying multiple pickups of different objects as text totals via a dynamic Dictionary<> of PickUp objects and enum pickup types

While the previous recipe worked fine, any old text might have been typed into the description for a pickup or perhaps mistyped (**star**, **Sstar**, **starr**, and so on). A much better way of restricting game properties to one of a predefined (enumerated) list of possible values is to use C# enums. As well as removing the chance of mistyping a string, it also means that we can write code to appropriately deal with the predefined set of possible values. In this recipe, we will improve our general purpose `PickUp` class by introducing three possible pickup types (Star, Heart, and Key), and write inventory display code that counts the number of each type of pickup being carried and displays these totals via a **UI Text** object on screen. We also switch from using a **List** to using a **Dictionary**, since the Dictionary data structure is designed specifically for key-value pairs, perfect for associating a numeric total with an enumerated pickup type.

In this recipe, we will also manage the additional complexity by separating the controller (user collection event) logic from the stored inventory data, by introducing an inventory manager scripted class. Our player controller is then simplified to just two methods (Awake, getting a reference to the inventory manager, and `OnTriggerEnter2D`, responding to collisions by communicating with the inventory manager).

Getting ready

This recipe adapts the previous one. So, make a copy of the project for the previous recipe, and work on this copy.

How to do it...

To display multiple pickups of different objects as text totals via a dynamic Dictionary, follow these steps:

1. Replace the content of the script class `PickUp` with the following code:

```
using UnityEngine;

public class PickUp : MonoBehaviour {
    public enum PickUpType {
        Star, Key, Heart
    }

    public PickUpType type;
}
```

2. Remove the instance of the script class `PlayerInventory` from the GameObject `player-SpaceGirl`.

3. Create a new C# script class `PlayerController` containing the following code, and add an instance as a component to GameObject `player-girl1`:

```
using UnityEngine;

public class PlayerController : MonoBehaviour {
    private InventoryManager inventoryManager;

    void Awake() {
        inventoryManager = GetComponent<InventoryManager>();
    }

    void OnTriggerEnter2D(Collider2D hit) {
        if(hit.CompareTag("Pickup")){

PickUp item = hit.GetComponent<PickUp> ();

            inventoryManager.Add(item);
            Destroy(hit.gameObject);
        }
    }
```

}

4. Replace the content of script class `PlayerInventoryDisplay` with the following code:

```
using UnityEngine;
using UnityEngine.UI;
using System.Collections.Generic;

[RequireComponent(typeof(PlayerController))]
[RequireComponent(typeof(InventoryManager))]
public class PlayerInventoryDisplay : MonoBehaviour {
    public Text inventoryText;

    public void OnChangeInventory(Dictionary<PickUp.PickUpType,
int> inventory) {
        inventoryText.text = "";
        string newInventoryText = "carrying: ";

        foreach (var item in inventory) {
            int itemTotal = item.Value;
            string description = item.Key.ToString();
            newInventoryText += " [ " + description + " " +
itemTotal + " ]";
        }

        int numItems = inventory.Count;
        if (numItems < 1)
            newInventoryText = "(empty inventory)";

        inventoryText.text = newInventoryText;
    }
}
```

5. Add an instance of the following C# Script `InventoryManager` to the GameObject `player-SpaceGirl` in the Hierarchy:

```
using UnityEngine;
using System.Collections.Generic;

public class InventoryManager : MonoBehaviour {
    private PlayerInventoryDisplay playerInventoryDisplay;
    private Dictionary<PickUp.PickUpType, int> items = new
Dictionary<PickUp.PickUpType, int>();

    void Awake() {
        playerInventoryDisplay =
GetComponent<PlayerInventoryDisplay>();
```

```
            }

            void Start() {
                  playerInventoryDisplay.OnChangeInventory(items);
            }

            public void Add(PickUp pickup) {
                  PickUp.PickUpType type = pickup.type;
                  int oldTotal = 0;

                  if(items.TryGetValue(type, out oldTotal))
                        items[type] = oldTotal + 1;
                  else
                        items.Add (type, 1);

                  playerInventoryDisplay.OnChangeInventory(items);
            }
      }
```

6. In the **Hierarchy** (or **Scene**) panel, select *each pickup* GameObject in turn, and choose from the drop-down menu its corresponding **Type** in the **Inspector** panel. As you can see, public variables that are of an enum type are automatically restricted to the set of possible values as a combo-box drop-down menu in the **Inspector** panel.

7. Play the game. First, you should see a message on screen stating the inventory is empty, and then as you pick up one or more items of each pickup type, you'll see text totals of each type you have collected.

How it works...

Each pickup GameObject in the scene has a scripted component of the class PickUp. The PickUp object for each Pickup GameObject has a single property, a pickup type, which has to be one of the enumerated set of Star, Key, or Heart. The use of an enumerated type means that the value has to be one of these three listed values, so there can be no misspelling/mistyping errors that could have happened with a general text string type, as in the previous recipe.

Previously, the script class PlayerInventory script had two sets of responsibilities:

- Maintain the internal record of items being carried
- Detect collisions, update the state, and ask the display class to inform the player visually of the changed items being carried

In this recipe, we separate these two set of responsibilities into separate script classes:

- The script class InventoryManager will maintain the internal record of items being carried (and ask the display class to inform the player visually each time there is a change to the items being carried).
- The script class Player will detect collisions, and ask the InventoryManager to update what is being carried.

The addition of this extra software layer both separates the player collision detection behavior from how the inventory is internally stored, and also prevents any single script class from becoming too complex by attempting to handle too many different responsibilities. This recipe is an example of the low coupling of the **Model-View-Controller** (**MVC**) design pattern. We have designed our code to not rely on or make too many assumptions about other parts of the game so that the likelihood of a change in some other part of our game breaking our inventory display code is reduced. The display (view) is separated from the logical representation of what we are carrying (inventory manager model), and changes to the model are made by public methods called from the player (controller).

The Player script class gets a reference to the InventoryManager component via its Awake() method, and each time the player's character collides with a pickup GameObject, it calls the Add(...) method of the inventory manager, passing the PickUp object of the object collided with.

In the script class `InventoryManager`, the inventory being carried by the player is being represented by a C# **Dictionary**. A Dictionary is made up of a sequence of *key-value pairs*, where the key is one of the possible `PickUp.PickUpType` enumerated **values**, and the value is an integer total of how many of that type of pickup is being carried. The Dictionary is declared stating what type will be used for a key, and then what type (or script class) will be stored as the value for that key. Here is the statement declaring our Dictionary variable items:

```
items = new Dictionary<PickUp.PickUpType, int>()
```

C# dictionaries provide a `TryGetValue(...)` method, which receives parameters of a key and is passed a reference to a variable the same data type as the value for the Dictionary. When the `Add(...)` method of the inventory manager is called, the type of the PickUp object is tested to see if a total for this type is already in Dictionary items. If an item total is found inside the Dictionary for the given type, then the value for this item in the Dictionary is incremented. If no entry is found for the given type, then a new element is added to the Dictionary with a total of 1.

TryGetValue call-by-reference parameter

Note the use of the C# `out` keyword before the parameter `oldTotal` in this statement:
`items.TryGetValue(type, out oldTotal)`
indicates that a reference to the actual variable oldTotal is being passed to method `TryGetValue(...)`, not just a copy of its value. This means that the method can change the value of the variable.

The method returns true if an entry is found in the Dictionary for the given type, and if so, sets the value of oldTotal to the value against this key.

The last action of the `Add(...)` method is to call the `OnChangeInventory(...)` method of the `PlayerInventoryDisplay` scripted component of the player GameObject to update the text totals displayed on screen.

The method `OnChangeInventory(...)` of the script class `PlayerInventoryDisplay` first initializes the string variable `newInventoryText`, and then iterates through each item in the Dictionary, appending to `newInventoryText` a string of the type name and total for the current item. Finally, the text property of the UI Text object is updated with the completed text inside `newInventoryText`, showing the pickup totals to the player.

Learn more about using C# lists and dictionaries in Unity in the Unity Technologies tutorial

at `https://unity3d.com/learn/tutorials/modules/intermediate/scripting/lists-and-dictionaries`.

4
Playing and Manipulating Sounds

In this chapter, we will cover the following topics:

- Playing different one-off sound effects with a single AudioSource
- Playing and controlling different sounds each with their own AudioSource
- Creating just-in-time AudioSource components at runtime through C# scripting
- Delaying before playing a sound
- Preventing an Audio Clip from restarting if it is already playing
- Waiting for audio to finish playing before auto-destructing an object
- Creating a metronome through the precise scheduling of sounds with dspTime
- Matching the audio pitch to the animation speed
- Simulating acoustic environments with Reverb Zones
- Adding volume control with Audio Mixers
- Making a dynamic soundtrack with Snapshots
- Balancing in-game audio with Ducking
- Audio visualization from sample spectral data
- Synchronizing simultaneous and sequential music to create a simple 140 bpm music-loop manager

Introduction

Sound is a very important part of the gaming experience. In fact, it can't be stressed enough how crucial it is to the player's immersion in a virtual environment. Just think of the engine running in your favorite racing game, the distant urban buzz in a simulator game, or the creeping noises in horror games. Think of how these sounds transport you into the game.

The big picture

Before getting on with the recipes, let's first review how the different sound features work in Unity. A project with audio needs one or more audio files, which are called **AudioClips** in Unity, and these sit in your **Project** folders. At the time of writing, Unity 2017 supports four audio file formats: `.wav`, `.ogg`, `.mp3`, and `.aif`. Files in these types are re-encoded when Unity builds for a target platform. It also supports tracker modules in four formats: .xm, **.mod**, **.it**, and **.s3m**.

A scene or prefab GameObject can have an **AudioSource** component – which can be linked to an **AudioClip** sound file at Design-Time, or through scripting at Run-Time. At any time in a scene, there is one active **AudioListener** component inside a GameObject. When you create a new scene, there is one added automatically for you in the *Main Camera*. One can think of an **AudioListener** as a simulated digital '"ear," since the sounds Unity plays are based on the relationship between playing **AudioSources** and the active **AudioListener**.

Simple sounds, such as pickup effects and background soundtrack music, can be defined as as **2D sound**. However, Unity supports **3D sounds**, which means that the location and distance between playing **AudioSources** and the active **AudioListener** determine the way the sound is perceived in terms of loudness and the left/right balance.

You can also engineer synchronized sound playing and scheduling through `AudioSettings.dspTime` – a value based on the samples in the audio system, so it is much more precise than the `Time.time` value. Also, `dspTime` will pause/suspend with the scene, so no logic is required for rescheduling when using `dspTime`. Several recipes in this chapter illustrate this approach.

In recent years, Unity has added a powerful new feature to game audio: the **AudioMixer**. The **AudioMixer** radically changes the way in which sound elements can be experienced by players and worked with by game developers. It allows us to mix and arrange audio pretty much in the same way that musicians and producers do in their **Digital Audio Workstations (D.A.W.)**, such as **GarageBand** or **ProTools**. It allows you to route **AudioSource** clips into specific channels that can have their volumes individually adjusted and processed by customized effects and filters. You can work with multiple **AudioMixers**, send a mixer's output to a parent mixer, and save mix preferences as **Snapshots**. Also, you can access mixer parameters from scripting. The following figure represents the main Unity audio mixing concepts and their relationships:

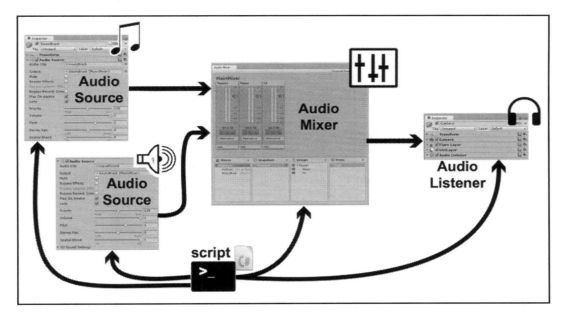

The figure above represents the main Unity audio mixing concepts and their relationships:

Taking advantage of the new **AudioMixer** feature in many example projects, this chapter is filled with recipes that will hopefully help you implement a better and more efficient sound design for your projects, augmenting the player's sense of immersion, transporting them into the game environment, and even improving the gameplay.

Future audio features

The recipes demonstrate both scripted and Unity audio system approaches to managing audio and introducing dynamic effects at runtime. Games can become much more engaging when the audio environment of effects and music can subtly change based on the context of what is happening in the game – whether you chose effects such as reverb zones, ducking to de-emphasize some sounds for a while, or allow the user to control the audio volumes.

Finally, what is possible with special audio is now getting even more interesting, with the introduction of Ambisonic Audio when playing 3D VR games – allowing rich audio experiences based on whether sounds are above or below the listener, as well as their distance from an audio source. Some reference sources for ambisonic audio include:

- Wikipedia offers some history of ambisonics: `https://en.wikipedia.org/wiki/Ambisonics`.
- Learn about Unity and ambisonic audio in the Unity docs: `https://docs.unity3d.com/Manual/AmbisonicAudio.html`.
- Google's reference pages about special audio and ambisonics: `https://developers.google.com/vr/concepts/spatial-audio`.
- Occulus reference pages about special audio and ambisonics: `https://developer.oculus.com/downloads/package/oculus-ambisonics-starter-pack/`.
- Robert Hernadez has published a great article at Medium.com disambiguating how to record and edit ambisonic audio: `https://medium.com/@webjournalist/spatial-audio-how-to-hear-in-vr-10914a41f4ca`.

Playing different one-off sound effects with a single AudioSource component

The basics of playing a sound are very straightforward in Unity (adding an **AudioSource** component to a GameObject and linking it to an **AudioClip** sound file). For simple sound effects such as short, one-off plays of pickup confirmation noises, it's useful to have a single **AudioSource** component and reuse it to play different sound effects – which is what we'll do in this recipe.

Getting ready

Try this with any short audio clip that is less than one second in duration. We have included some classic Pacman game sound clips inside the `04_01` folder.

How to do it...

To play multiple sounds using the same **AudioSource** component, do the following:

1. Create a new Unity 2D project and import the sound clip files.
2. Create a C# script class, `PlaySounds`, in a new folder, `_Scripts`, containing the following code, and add an instance as a scripted component to the **Main Camera**:

```csharp
using UnityEngine;

[RequireComponent(typeof(AudioSource))]
public class PlaySounds : MonoBehaviour
{
    public AudioClip clipEatCherry;
    public AudioClip clipExtraLife;

    private AudioSource audioAudioSource;

    void Awake() {
        audioAudioSource = GetComponent<AudioSource>();
    }

    void Update() {
        if (Input.GetKey(KeyCode.UpArrow))
            audioAudioSource.PlayOneShot(clipEatCherry);

        if (Input.GetKey(KeyCode.DownArrow))
            audioAudioSource.PlayOneShot(clipExtraLife);
    }
}
```

3. Ensure that the **MainCamera** GameObject is selected in the **Hierarchy**. Then, in the **Inspector** panel, drag the **Pacman Eating Cherry** sound clip from the **Project** panel into the public **Pacman Eating Cherry AudioClip** variable in the PlaySounds (Script) scripted component. Repeat this procedure for the **Pacman Extra Life** sound clip. These steps are illustrated in the screenshot:

4. Run the scene, and press the *UP* and *DOWN* arrow keys to play the different sound effects.

How it works...

You have created a C# script class, PlaySounds. The script class includes a RequireComponent attribute declaring that any GameObject containing a scripted object component of this class must have a sibling AudioSource component (and one will be automatically added if such a component does not exist when the scripted component is added).

The PlaySounds script class has two public **AudioClip** properties: Pacman Eating Cherry and Pacman Extra Life. At **Design-Time**, we associated **AudioClip** sound files from the **Project** panel with these public properties.

At runtime, the Update() method is executed in every frame. This method checks for the *UP* and *DOWN* array keys being pressed, and if so, plays the Eat Cherry or Extra Life sounds correspondingly – sending the **AudioSource** component a PlayOneShot() message with the appropriate **AudioClip** sound file link.

NOTE: Cannot pause/interrogate sounds played with **PlayOneShot**

While great for short, one-off sound effects, a limitation of the PlayOneShot() method is that you cannot then interrogate the status of the playing sound (has it finished, at what point is it playing, and so on). Nor can you pause/restart a sound played with PlayOneShot(). For such detailed control of sounds, each sound needs its own AudioSource component.

Learn more about the PlayOneShot() method in the Unity documentation: https://docs.unity3d.com/ScriptReference/AudioSource.PlayOneShot.html.

There's more...

There are some details that you don't want to miss.

Play a sound at a static point in 3D world space

Similar to PlayOneShot() is the PlayClipAtPoint() **AudioSource** method. This allows you to play a sound clip for an **AudioSource** created at a specific point in 3D World Space. Note that this is a static class method – so that you don't need an **AudioSource** component to use this method – an **AudioSource** component is created (at the location you give), and will exist as long as the **AudioClip** sound is playing. The **AudioSource** component will automatically be removed by Unity once the sound has finished playing. All you need is a Vector3 (x,y,z) position object, and a reference to the **AudioClip** file to be played:

```
Vector3 location = new Vector3(10, 10, 10);
AudioSource.PlayClipAtPoint(soundClipToPlay, location);
```

Playing and controlling different sounds each with their own AudioSource component

While the approach in the previous recipe (using `PlayOneShot(...)` with a single **AudioSource**) is fine for one-off sound effects, when further control may be required over a playing sound, each sound will needs to be played in its own **AudioSource** component. In this recipe, we'll create two separate **AudioSource** components and pause/resume each with different arrow keys.

Getting ready

Try this with two audio clips that are several seconds long. We have included two free music clips inside folder `04_02`.

How to do it...

To play different sounds each with their own AudioSouce component, do the following:

1. Create a new Unity 2D project and import the sound clip files.
2. Create a GameObject in the scene containing an **AudioSource** component linked to the **186772__dafawe__medieval AudioClip**. This can be done in a single step by dragging the music clip from the **Project** panel into either the **Hierarchy** or **Scene** panels. Rename this new GameObject to **music1_medieval**.
3. Repeat the previous step to create another GameObject named **music2_arcade**, containing an **AudioSource** linked to **251461__joshuaempyre__arcade-music-loop**.
4. For both AudioSources created, uncheck the Play Awake property – so these sounds do not begin playing as soon as the scene is loaded.
5. Create an empty GameObject named **Manager**.

6. Create a C# script class, MusicManager, in a new folder, _Scripts, containing the following code, and add an instance as a scripted component to the Manager GameObject:

```
using UnityEngine;

public class MusicManager : MonoBehaviour  {
    public AudioSource audioSourceMedieval;
    public AudioSource audioSourceArcade;

    void Update() {
        if (Input.GetKey(KeyCode.RightArrow)){
            if (audioSourceMedieval.time > 0)
                audioSourceMedieval.UnPause();
            else
                audioSourceMedieval.Play();
        }

        if (Input.GetKey(KeyCode.LeftArrow))
            audioSourceMedieval.Pause();
        if (Input.GetKey(KeyCode.UpArrow)){
            if (audioSourceArcade.time > 0)
                audioSourceArcade.UnPause();
            else
                audioSourceArcade.Play();
        }

        if (Input.GetKey(KeyCode.DownArrow))
            audioSourceArcade.Pause();
    }
}
```

7. Ensure that the **Manager** GameObject is selected in the **Hierarchy**. In the **Inspector** panel, drag the **music1_medieval GameObject** from the Scene panel into the public **Audio Source Medieval AudioSourc**e variable in the MusicManager (Script) scripted component. Repeat this procedure, dragging GameObject **music2_arcade** into the public **Audio Source Arcade** variable.

8. Run the scene, and press the *UP* and *DOWN* arrow keys to start/resume and pause the medieval sound clip. Press the *RIGHT* and *LEFT* arrow keys to start/resume and pause the arcade sound clip.

How it works...

You created a C# script class, MusicManager, and added an instance of this class as a component to the Manager GameObject. You also created two **GameObjects**, named **music1_medieval** and **music2_arcade**, in the scene, each containing an **AudioSource** component linked to a different music clip.

The script class has two public **AudioSource** properties: Music Medieval and Music Arcade. At **Design-Time**, we associated the **AudioSource** components of **GameObjects music1_medieval and music2_arcade** with these public properties.

At Run-Time, the Update() method is executed in every frame. This method checks for the *UP/DOWN/RIGHT/LEFT* array keys being pressed. If the *UP* arrow key is detected, the medieval music audio source is sent a Play() or UnPause() message. The Play() message is sent if the clip is not already playing (its time property is zero). If the DOWN arrow key is pressed, the medieval music audio source is sent a Pause() message.

The arcade music clip is controlled in a corresponding way through detection of the RIGHT/LEFT array keys.

Each **AudioClip** sound file being associated with its own **AudioSource** component allows simultaneous playing, and managing of each sound independently.

Creating just-in-time AudioSource components at runtime through C# scripting

In the previous recipe, for each sound clip we wanted to manage, in the scene we had to manually create **GameObjects** with **AudioSource** components at Design-Time. However, using C# scripting, we can create our own **GameObjects** that contain **AudioSources** at **Run-Time**, just when they are needed. This method is similar to the built-in **AudioSource PlayClipAtPoint()** method, but the created **AudioSource** component is completely under our programmatic control – although we then have to be responsible for destroying this component when it is no longer needed.

This code was inspired by some of the code posted in 2011 in the online **Unity Answers** forum by user Bunny83. Unity has a great online community helping each other and posting interesting ways of adding features to games. Learn more about that post at `http://answers.unity3d.com/questions/123772/playoneshot-r eturns-false-for-isplaying.html`

Getting ready

This recipe adapts the previous one. So, make a copy of the project for the previous recipe, and work on this copy.

How to do it...

To create just-in-time AudioSource components at run time through C# scripting do the following:

1. Delete the **music1_medieval** and **music-loop** GameObjects from the scene – we'll be creating these at **Run-Time** in this recipe!

2. Refactor the `MusicManager` C# script class to read as follows (note that the `Update()` method is unchanged):

```
using UnityEngine;

public class MusicManager : MonoBehaviour {
    public AudioClip clipMedieval;
    public AudioClip clipArcade;

    private AudioSource audioSourceMedieval;
    private AudioSource audioSourceArcade;

    void Awake() {
        audioSourceMedieval = CreateAudioSource(clipMedieval,
true);
        audioSourceArcade = CreateAudioSource(clipArcade,
false);
    }

    private AudioSource CreateAudioSource(AudioClip audioClip,
bool startPlayingImmediately) {
        GameObject audioSourceGO = new GameObject();
            audioSourceGO.transform.parent = transform;
```

```
                    audioSourceGO.transform.position = transform.position;
                    AudioSource newAudioSource =
            audioSourceGO.AddComponent<AudioSource>() as AudioSource;
                    newAudioSource.clip = audioClip;
                    if(startPlayingImmediately)
                        newAudioSource.Play();

                    return newAudioSource;
            }

        void Update(){
            if (Input.GetKey(KeyCode.RightArrow)){
                if (audioSourceMedieval.time > 0)
                    audioSourceMedieval.UnPause();
                else
                    audioSourceMedieval.Play();
            }

            if (Input.GetKey(KeyCode.LeftArrow))
                audioSourceMedieval.Pause();
            if (Input.GetKey(KeyCode.UpArrow)){
                if (audioSourceArcade.time > 0)
                    audioSourceArcade.UnPause();
                else
                    audioSourceArcade.Play();
            }

            if (Input.GetKey(KeyCode.DownArrow))
                audioSourceArcade.Pause();
        }
    }
```

3. Ensure that the MainCamera **GameObject** is selected in the **Hierarchy**. In the Inspector panel, drag the **AudioClip 186772__dafawe__medieval** sound clip from the Project panel into the public **Clip Medieval AudioClip** variable in the MusicManager (Script) scripted component. Repeat this procedure with **AudioClip 251461__joshuaempyre__arcade-music-loop** for the **Clip Arcade** variable.

4. Run the scene, and press the *UP* and *DOWN* arrow keys to start/resume and pause the medieval sound clip. Press the *RIGHT* and *LEFT* arrow keys to start/resume and pause the arcade sound clip.

How it works...

The key feature of this recipe is the new `CreateAudioSource(...)` method. This method takes input as a reference to a sound clip file and a Boolean true/false value as to whether the sound should start playing immediately. The method does the following:

- Creates a new **GameObject** (with the same parent, and at the same location as the **GameObject** doing the creating)
- Adds a new **AudioSource** component to the new **GameObject**
- Sets the audio clip of the new AudioSource component to the provided AudioClip parameter
- If the Boolean parameter was true, the **AudioSource** component is immediately sent a `Play()` message to start it playing the sound clip
- A reference to the AudioSource component is returned

The rest of the `MusicManager` script class is very similar to that in the previous recipe. There are two public `AudioClip` variables, `clipMedieval` and `clipArcade`, which are set through drag-and-drop at **Design-Time** to link to the sound clip files in **Sounds Project** folder.

The `audioSourceMedieval` and `audioSourceArcade` AudioSource variables are now private. These values are set up in the `Awake()` method, by calling and storing values returned by the `CreateAudioSource(...)` method with the **clipMedieval** and `clipArcade` AudioClip variables.

To illustrate how the Boolean parameter works, the medieval music **AudioSource** is created to play immediately, while the arcade music won't start playing until the *UP* arrow key is pressed. Playing/Resuming/Pausing the two audio clips is just the same as in the previous recipe – via the arrow-key detection logic in the (unchanged) `Update()` method.

There's more...

There are some details that you don't want to miss.

Adding the CreateAudioSource(...) method as an extension to the MonoBehavior class

Since the `CreateAudioSource(...)` method is a general-purpose method that could be used by many different game script classes, it doesn't naturally sit within the `MusicManager` class. The best place for general-purpose generative methods such as this is to add them as static (class) methods to the component class they work with – in this case it would be great if we could add this method to `MonoBehavior` class itself – so any scripted component could create **AudioSource** GameObjects on the fly.

All we have to do is create a class (usually named `ExtensionMethods`) with a static method, as follows:

```
using UnityEngine;

public static class ExtensionMethods {
    public static AudioSource CreateAudioSource(this MonoBehaviour
parent, AudioClip audioClip, bool startPlayingImmediately)
    {
        GameObject audioSourceGO = new GameObject("music-player");
        audioSourceGO.transform.parent = parent.transform;
        audioSourceGO.transform.position = parent.transform.position;
        AudioSource newAudioSource =
audioSourceGO.AddComponent<AudioSource>() as AudioSource;
        newAudioSource.clip = audioClip;

        if (startPlayingImmediately)
            newAudioSource.Play();

        return newAudioSource;
    }
}
```

As we can see, we add an extra first parameter to the extension method, stating which class we are adding this method to. Since we have added this to the `MonoBehavior` class, we can now use this method in our scripted classes as if it were built-in. So our `Awake()` method in our `MusicManager` class looks as follows:

```
void Awake() {
    audioSourceMedieval = this.CreateAudioSource(clipMedieval, true);
    audioSourceArcade = this.CreateAudioSource(clipArcade, false);
}
```

That's it – we can now remove the method from our `MusicManager` class and use this method in any of our `MonoBehavior` scripted classes.

Delaying before playing a sound

Sometimes we don't want to play a sound immediately, but after a short delay. For example, we might want to wait a second or two before playing a sound to indicate the slightly delayed onset of a poison drunk or having walked into a spell that weakens the player. For such cases, **AudioSource** offers the `PlayDelayed(...)` method. This recipe illustrates a simple approach for such cases where we do not wish to immediately start playing a sound.

Getting ready

Try this with two audio clips that are several seconds long. We have included two free music clips inside the `04_04` folder.

How to do it...

To schedule a sound to play after a given delay, do the following:

1. Create a new Unity 2D project and import the sound clip files.
2. Create a **GameObject** in the scene containing an **AudioSource** component linked to the **Pacman Opening Song AudioClip**. This can be done in a single step by dragging the music clip from the Project panel into either the **Hierarchy** or **Scene** panels.
3. Repeat the previous step to create another **GameObject**, containing an **AudioSource** linked to the **Pacman Dies** clip.
4. For both **AudioSources** created, uncheck the Play Awake property – so these sounds do not begin playing as soon as the scene is loaded.
5. Create a **UI Button** named **Button-music** on the screen, changing its text to **Play Music Immediately**.
6. Create a **UI Button** named **Button-dies** on the screen, changing its text to **Play Dies Sound After 1 second**.

7. Create an empty **GameObject** named **SoundManager**.

8. Create a C# script class, DelayedSoundManager, in a new folder, _Scripts, containing the following code, and add an instance as a scripted component to the **SoundManager GameObject**:

```
using UnityEngine;

public class DelayedSoundManager : MonoBehaviour {
    public AudioSource audioSourcePacmandMusic;
    public AudioSource audioSourceDies;

    public void ACTION_PlayMusicNow() {
        audioSourcePacmandMusic.Play();
    }

    public void ACTION_PlayDiesSoundAfterDelay() {
        float delay = 1.0F;
        audioSourceDies.PlayDelayed(delay);
    }
}
```

9. With the **Button-music GameObject** selected in the Hierarchy panel, create a new on-click event-handler, dragging the **SoundsManager GameObject** into the **Object** slot, and selecting the **ACTION_PlayMusicNow()** method.

10. With the **Button-dies** GameObject selected in the Hierarchy panel, create a new on-click event-handler, dragging the **SoundsManager** GameObject into the **Object** slot, and selecting the **ACTION_PlayDiesSoundAfterDelay()** method.

How it works...

You add two **GameObjects** to the scene, containing AudioSources linked to music and dying sound clips. You created a C# script class, DelayedSoundManager, and added an instance to an empty **GameObject**. You associated the two AudioSources in your **GameObjects** with the two public variables in your scripted component.

You created two buttons:

- **Button-music**, with a click action to invoke the DelayedSoundManager.ACTION_PlayMusicNow() method
- **Button-dies**, with a click action to invoke the DelayedSoundManager.PlayDiesSoundAfterDelay() method.

The `DelayedSoundManager.ACTION_PlayMusicNow()` method immediately sends a Play() message to the audio source linked to the **Pacman Opening Song AudioClip**. However, the `DelayedSoundManager.PlayDiesSoundAfterDelay()` method sends a PlayDelayed(...) message to the audio source linked to the **Pacman Dies AudioClip**, passing a value of 1.0, making Unity wait 1 second before playing the sound clip.

Preventing an Audio Clip from restarting if it is already playing

In a game, there may be several different events that cause a particular sound effect to start playing. If the sound is already playing, then in almost all cases, we won't wish to restart the sound. This recipe includes a test, so that an Audio Source component is only sent a `Play()` message if it is currently not playing.

Getting ready

Try this with any audio clip that is one second or longer in duration. We have included the engineSound audio clip inside the `04_05` folder.

How to do it...

To prevent an **AudioClip** from restarting, follow these steps:

1. Create a new Unity 2D project and import the sound clip file.
2. Create a GameObject in the scene containing an **AudioSource** component linked to the `AudioClip engineSound`. This can be done in a single step by dragging the music clip from the Project panel into either the Hierarchy or Scene panels.
3. Uncheck the Play Awake property for the **AudioSource** component of the engineSound GameObject – so this sound does not begin playing as soon as the scene is loaded.
4. Create a UI button named **Button-play-sound**, changing its text to **Play Sound**. Position the button in the center of the screen by setting its Rect **Transform** property position to middle-center.

5. Create a C# script class, `WaitToFinishBeforePlaying`, in a new folder, `_Scripts`, containing the following code, and add an instance as a scripted component to the **Main Camera** GameObject:

```
using UnityEngine;
using UnityEngine.UI;

public class WaitToFinishBeforePlaying : MonoBehaviour  {
    public AudioSource audioSource;
    public Text buttonText;

    void Update() {
        string statusMessage = "Play sound";
        if(audioSource.isPlaying )
            statusMessage = "(sound playing)";

        buttonText.text = statusMessage;
    }

    public void ACTION_PlaySoundIfNotPlaying() {
        if( !audioSource.isPlaying )
            audioSource.Play();
    }
}
```

6. With **Main Camera** selected in the **Hierarchy** panel, drag **engineSound** into the Inspector panel for the public Audio Source variable, and drag the **Text** child of **Button-play-sound** for the public **ButtonText**.

7. With **Button-play-sound** selected in the Hierarchy panel, create a new on-click event-handler, dragging the **Main Camera** into the **Object** slot, and selecting the `ACTION_PlaySoundIfNotPlaying()` function.

How it works...

Audio Source components have a public readable property, **isPlaying**, which is a Boolean true/false flag, indicating whether the sound is currently playing. In this recipe, the text of the button is set to display Play Sound when the sound is not playing, and (sound playing) when it is. When the button is clicked, the `ACTION_PlaySoundIfNotPlaying()` method is called. This method uses an `if` statement, ensuring that a `Play()` message is only sent to the Audio Source component if its **isPlaying** is false, and updates the button's text as appropriate.

See also

The *Waiting for the audio to finish playing before auto-destructing an object* recipe in this chapter.

Waiting for the audio to finish playing before auto-destructing an object

An event may occur (such as an object pickup or the killing of an enemy) that we wish to notify to the player of by playing an audio clip, and an associated visual object (such as an explosion particle system, or a temporary object in the location of the event). However, as soon as the clip has finished playing, we will want the visual object to be removed from the scene. This recipe provides a simple way to link the ending of a playing audio clip with the automatic destruction of its containing object.

Getting ready

Try this with any audio clip that is a second or more in duration. We have included the engineSound audio clip inside the 04_06 folder.

How to do it...

To wait for audio to finish playing before destroying its parent GameObject, follow these steps:

1. Create a new Unity 2D project and import the sound clip file.
2. Create a GameObject in the scene containing an **AudioSource** component linked to the **AudioClip engineSound**. This can be done in a single step by dragging the music clip from the Project panel into either the **Hierarchy** or **Scene** panels. Rename this the **AudioObject** GameObject.
3. Uncheck the **Play Awake** property for the AudioSource component of the **GameObject engineSound** – so this sound does not begin playing as soon as the scene is loaded.

4. Create a C# script class, `AudioDestructBehaviour`, in a new folder, `_Scripts`, containing the following code, and add an instance as a scripted component to the **AudioObject** GameObject:

```csharp
using UnityEngine;
using UnityEngine;

public class AudioDestructBehaviour : MonoBehaviour {
    private AudioSource audioSource;

    void Awake() {
        audioSource = GetComponent<AudioSource>();
    }

    private void Update() {
        if( !audioSource.isPlaying )
            Destroy(gameObject);
    }
}
```

5. In the **Inspector** panel, disable (uncheck) the `AudioDestructBehaviour` scripted component of **AudioObject** (when needed, it will be re-enabled via C# code):

6. Create a C# script class, `ButtonActions`, in the `_Scripts` folder, containing the following code, and add an instance as a scripted component to the **Main Camera** GameObject:

```csharp
using UnityEngine;

public class ButtonActions : MonoBehaviour {
    public AudioSource audioSource;

    public AudioDestructBehaviour audioDestructScriptedObject;
```

```
public void ACTION_PlaySound() {
    if( !audioSource.isPlaying )
        audioSource.Play();
}

public void ACTION_DestroyAfterSoundStops(){
    audioDestructScriptedObject.enabled = true;
}
}
```

7. With **Main Camera** selected in the **Hierarchy** panel, drag **AudioObject** into the **Inspector** panel for the public **Audio Source** variable.

8. With **Main Camera** selected in the **Hierarchy** panel, drag **AudioObject** into the **Inspector** panel for the public **Audio Destruct Scripted Object** variable.

9. Create a UI button named **Button-play-sound**, changing its text to **Play** Sound. Position the button in the center of the screen by setting its **Rect Transform** property to **middle-center**.

10. With **Button-play-sound** selected in the **Hierarchy** panel, create a new on-click event-handler, dragging the **Main Camera** into the **Object** slot, and selecting the ACTION_PlaySound() function.

11. Create a second UI button named **Button-destroy-when-finished-playing**, changing its text to **Destroy When Sound Finished**. Position the button in the center of the screen (just below the other button) by setting its **Rect Transform** property to **middle-center** and then drag the button down a little.

12. With **Button-destroy-when-finished-playing** selected in the **Hierarchy** panel, create a new on-click event-handler, dragging the **Main Camera** into the **Object** slot, and selecting the ACTION_ DestroyAfterSoundStops() function.

13. Run the scene. Clicking the **Play Sound** button will play the engine sound each time. However, once the **Destroy When Sound Finished** button has been clicked, as soon as the engineSound finished playing, you'll see the **AudioObject** GameObject disappear from the **Hierarchy** panel, since the GameObject has destroyed itself.

How it works...

You created a ButtonActions script class and added an instance as a component to the **Main Camera GameObject**. This has two public variables, one to an **AudioSource** and one to an instance of the AudioDestructBehaviour scripted component.

The GameObject named **AudioObject** contains an **AudioSource** component, which stores and manages the playing of the audio clip. **AudioObject** also contains a scripted component, which is an instance of the `AudioDestructBehaviour` class. This script is initially disabled. When enabled, every frame in this object (via its `Update()` method) tests whether the audio source is playing (`!audio.isPlaying`). As soon as the audio is found to be not playing, the GameObject is destroyed.

There are two UI buttons created. The **Button-play-sound** button calls the `ACTION_PlaySound()` method of the scripted component in **Main Camera**. This method will start playing the audio clip, if it is not already playing.

The second button, **Button-destroy-when-finished-playing**, calls the `ACTION_DestoryAfterSoundStops()` method of the scripted component in Main Camera. This method enables the **AudioDestructBehaviour** scripted component in the **AudioObject** GameObject – so that the **AudioObject GameObject** will be destroyed, once its **AudioSource** sound has finished playing.

See also

The *Preventing an Audio Clip from restarting if it is already playing* recipe in this chapter.

Creating a metronome through the precise scheduling of sounds with dspTime

In cases where we need precise scheduling of when sounds play, we should use the `AudioSource.PlayScheduled(...)` method. This method uses the `AudioSettings.dspTime` value, which is highly accurate based on the playing of music data through the Unity audio system. Another advantage of the `dspTime` value is that is it independent of the graphical rendering frame rate:

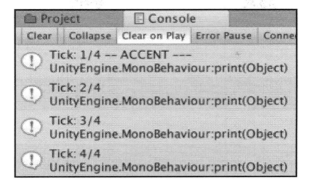

Note that the `dspTime` value is automatically frozen when a game is paused or suspended – so music scheduled using this approach will pause and resume flawlessly along with the scene gameplay. In this recipe, we'll create a metronome by precisely scheduling when two different sounds will play. Note that this recipe is based on some examples from the Unity documentation for the `AudioSource.PlayScheduled(...)` method: `https://docs.unity3d.com/ScriptReference/AudioSource.PlayScheduled.html`.

Getting ready

For this recipe, we have provided two metronome sound clips inside the `04_07` folder.

How to do it...

To schedule a sound to play after a given delay, do the following:

1. Create a new Unity 2D project and import the provided sound clip files.
2. Create a GameObject in the scene containing an **AudioSource** component linked to the **metronome_tick AudioClip**. This can be done in a single step by dragging the music clip from the Project panel into either the **Hierarchy** or **Scene** panels.
3. Repeat the previous step to create another GameObject, containing an **AudioSource** linked to the **metronome_tick_accent** clip.

4. For both **AudioSources** created, uncheck the **Play Awake** property – so these sounds do not begin playing as soon as the scene is loaded.
5. Create an empty GameObject named **MetronomeManager**.
6. Create a C# script class, Metronome, in a new folder, _Scripts, containing the following code, and add an instance as a scripted component to the **MetronomeManager** GameObject:

```csharp
using UnityEngine;

public class Metronome : MonoBehaviour {
    public AudioSource audioSourceTickBasic;
    public AudioSource audioSourceTickAccent;

    public double bpm = 140.0F;
    public int beatsPerMeasure = 4;

    private double nextTickTime = 0.0F;
    private int beatCount;
    private double beatDuration;

    void Start() {
        beatDuration = 60.0F / bpm;
        beatCount = beatsPerMeasure; // so about to do a beat
        double startTick = AudioSettings.dspTime;
        nextTickTime = startTick;
    }

    void Update() {
        if (IsNearlyTimeForNextTick())
            BeatAction();
    }

    private bool IsNearlyTimeForNextTick() {
        float lookAhead = 0.1F;
        if ((AudioSettings.dspTime + lookAhead) >=
nextTickTime)
            return true;
        else
            return false;
    }

    private void BeatAction() {
        beatCount++;
        string accentMessage = "";

        if (beatCount > beatsPerMeasure)
            accentMessage = AccentBeatAction();
```

```
        else
            audioSourceTickBasic.PlayScheduled(nextTickTime);

        nextTickTime += beatDuration;
        print("Tick: " + beatCount + "/" + signatureHi +
accentMessage);
    }

    private string AccentBeatAction() {
        audioSourceTickAccent.PlayScheduled(nextTickTime);
        beatCount = 1;
        return " -- ACCENT ---";
    }
}
```

7. Select the MetronomeManager GameObject in the Hierarchy. Drag **metronome_tick** from the Hierarchy into the **Inspector Audio Source Tick Basic** public variable, for the Metronome (Script) component.

8. Drag **metronome_tick_accent** from the Hierarchy into the Inspector **Audio Source Tick Accent** public variable, for the **Metronome (Script)** component:

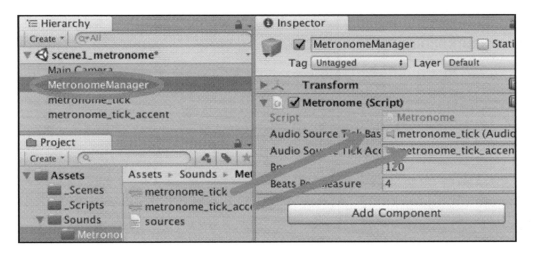

9. Play the scene. You will see (in the Console) and hear the regular metronome sounds, with the first beat of each count playing the accented (and louder) sound.

10. Try changing the **Bpm** (beats per minute) setting, to speed up or slow down the metronome. Or change the number of **Beats Per Measure**, to count up to 3, 4, or 6 beats between each accented beat.

How it works...

You add to the scene two GameIObjects, containing AudioSources linked to music clips for a basic and an accented metronome "tick." You created a Metronome C# script class and added an instance to an empty GameObject. You associated the two AudioSources in your GameObjects with the two public variables in your scripted component.

The Start() method calculates the duration of each beat (based on bpm), initializes the beat count (so the first beat is an accented beat), and then sets nextTickTime, the time for the next tick to the current dspTime.

The IsNearlyTimeForNextTick() method returns a Boolean true/false value indicating if it is nearly time to schedule the next tick. The value returned is based on whether the current dspTime is within 1/10th of a second of the value of nextTickTime. If so, then true is returned.

The Update() method is a single if statement. If it's nearly time for the next beat, the BeatAction() method is invoked.

The BeatAction() method does the following:

- Adds 1 to the number of beats
- Initializes the accentMessage string to be empty (the default)
- IF:
  the next beat should be 1 (the accent), AccentBeatAction() and the string returned are stored in accentMessage
- ELSE (if not accent next beat):
  the basic beat sound is scheduled
- The next beat time is calculated (current beat time + duration of each beat)
- It displays the beat count message in Console (including the string for any accent message)

The AccentBeatAction() method does three things: it schedules the accented beat sound, it resets the beat count to 1, and it returns a string to be shown with the beat message (with text to indicate an accent beat is next: -- ACCENT ---).

There's more...

There are some details that you don't want to miss.

Creating just-in-time AudioSource GameObjects for the basic and accented beats

We can reduce the Design-Time work for the metronome by making use of the Extension method presented in the *Creating just-in-time AudioSource components at runtime through C# scripting* recipe.

First, copy the `ExtensionMethods.cs` C# script class into your metronome project. Next, delete the two GameObjects in the scene containing **AudioSource** components, and instead declare two public variables for each `AudioClip ()`. Finally, we just need to write an `Awake()` method that will create the required GameObjects in the scene containing **AudioSource** basic on the **AudioClip** variables (and making the basic beat quieter than the accented one):

```
void Awake() {
    audioSourceTickBasic = this.CreateAudioSource(clipTickBasic,
false);
    audioSourceTickBasic.volume = 0.5F;

    audioSourceTickAccent = this.CreateAudioSource(clipTickAccent,
false);
    audioSourceTickAccent.volume = 1.00F;
}
```

Creating beat sounds through data rather than AudioClips

The Unity documentation about `dspTime` provides an interesting approach to creating the basic and accented beats for a metronome – though editing the audio data samples themselves. Check out their scripted metronome at `https://docs.unity3d.com/ScriptReference/AudioSettings-dspTime.html`.

Matching the audio pitch to the animation speed

Many artifacts sound higher in pitch when accelerated and lower when slowed down. Car engines, fan coolers, a record player... the list goes on. If you want to simulate this kind of sound effect in an animated object that can have its speed changed dynamically, follow this recipe.

Getting ready

For this recipe, you'll need an animated 3D object and an audio clip. Please use the animatedRocket.fbx and engineSound.wav files, available in the 04_08 folder.

How to do it...

To change the pitch of an audio clip according to the speed of an animated object, please follow these steps:

1. Create a new Unity 3D project.
2. Create a new **Models** folder in the **Project** panel, and into this import the provided **animatedRocket.fbx** file.
3. Create a new Sounds folder in the **Project** panel, and into this Import the provided audio clip, **engineSound.wav**.
4. Select the **animatedRocket** file in the Project panel. In the Inspector for **animatedRocket** Import Settings, click the **Animations** button. In **Animations** select (the only) Take 001 clip, and make sure to check the Loop Time option. Click on the Apply button to save the changes. See the screenshot for these settings:

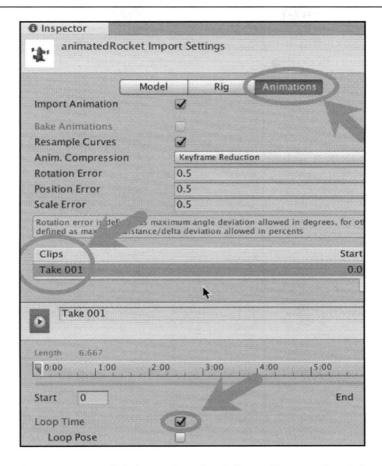

The reason we didn't need to check **Loop Pose** option is because our animation already loops in a seamless fashion. If it didn't, we could have checked that option to automatically create a seamless transition from the last to the first frame of the animation.

5. Add an instance of `animatedRocket` as a GameObject in the scene by dragging it from the **Project** panel into the Scene or **Hierarchy** panel.
6. Add an AudioSource component to the engineSound GameObject.

7. With **engineSound** selected in the **Hierarchy**, drag the **engineSound AudioClip** file from the **Project** panel into the **Inspector** for the **Audio Clip** parameter of the Audio Source component. Ensure the **Loop** option is checked, and the **Play On Awake** option is unchecked:

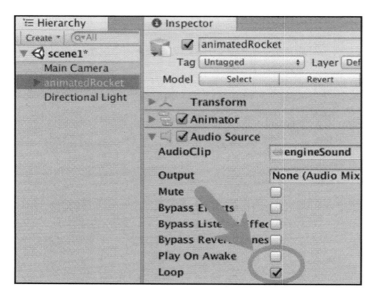

8. Create an **Animator Controller** for our model. Select the **Models** folder in the Project panel, and use the Create menu to create a new **Animator** Controller file named **Rocket Controller**.

9. Double-click the **Rocket Controller** file in the Project panel to open the **Animator** panel. Create a new state by choosing menu option: Create **State | Empty** (as shown in the screenshot):

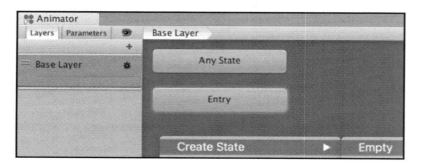

10. Rename this new state spin (in its **Inspector** properties), and set Take 001 as its motion in the Motion field:

11. Select **animatedRocket** in the **Hierarchy** panel. Drag Rocket Controller from the `Models` folder in the Project panel into the Controller parameter for the Animator component in the **Inspector**. Ensure that the **Apply Root Motion** option is unchecked in the **Inspector**:

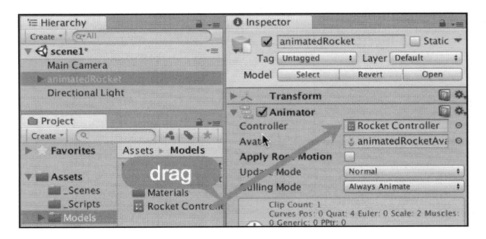

12. Create a C# script class, `ChangePitch`, in the `_Scripts` folder, containing the following code, and add an instance as a scripted component to the `animatedRocket` GameObject:

```csharp
using UnityEngine;

public class ChangePitch : MonoBehaviour{
    public float acceleration = 0.05f;
    public float minSpeed = 0.0f;
    public float maxSpeed = 2.0f;
    public float animationSoundRatio = 1.0f;

    private float speed = 0.0f;
    private Animator animator;
    private AudioSource audioSource;

    private void Awake() {
        animator = GetComponent<Animator>();
        audioSource = GetComponent<AudioSource>();
    }

    void Start() {
        speed = animator.speed;
        AccelerateRocket (0);
    }

    void Update() {
        if (Input.GetKey (KeyCode.Alpha1))
            AccelerateRocket(acceleration);
        if (Input.GetKey (KeyCode.Alpha2))
            AccelerateRocket(-acceleration);
    }

    public void AccelerateRocket(float acceleration) {
        speed += acceleration;
        speed = Mathf.Clamp(speed,minSpeed,maxSpeed);
        animator.speed = speed;
        float soundPitch = animator.speed *
animationSoundRatio;
        audioSource.pitch = Mathf.Abs(soundPitch);
    }
}
```

13. Play the scene and change the animation speed by pressing number key 1 (accelerate) and 2 (decelerate) on your keyboard. The audio pitch will change accordingly.

How it works...

You created a C# script class, **ChangePitch**, and added an instance to the **animatedRocket** GameObject. It declares several variables, the most important of which is `acceleration`.

It's `Awake()` method caches references to the Animator and **AudioSource** sibling components. The `Start()` method sets the initial speed from the **Animator**, and calls the `AccelerateRocket(...)` method, passing 0 to calculate the resulting pitch for the Audio Source.

In each frame, the Update() method tests for keyboard keys 1 and 2. When detected, they call the `AccelerateRocket(...)` method, passing a positive or negative value of acceleration as appropriate.

The `AccelerateRocket(...)` method increments variable speed with the received argument. The `Mathf.Clamp()` command limits the new speed value between the minimum and maximum speed. Then, it changes the **Animator** speed and **Audio Source** pitch according to the new speed absolute (positive) value. The value is then clamped a second time to avoid negative numbers. If you wish to reverse the animation, check out the code files in the solution provided for this recipe.

Please note that setting the animation speed, and therefore the sound pitch, to 0 will cause the sound to stop, making it clear that stopping the object's animation also prevents the engine sound from playing.

There's more...

Here is some information on how to fine-tune and customize this recipe.

Changing the Animation/Sound Ratio

If you want the audio clip pitch to be more or less affected by the animation speed, change the value of the public Animation/Sound Ratio parameter in the Inspector.

Accessing the function from other scripts

The `AccelerateRocket(...)` function was made public so that it can be accessed from other scripts. As an example, we have included the `ExternalChangePitch.cs` script in the `_Scripts` folder. To illustrate how the **ChangePitch** scripted component can be controlled form another script, do the following:

1. Attach this script to the **Main Camera** GameObject. Drag the **animatedRocket** GameObject from the Hierarchy into the public **Change Pitch Scripted Component** variable.
2. Run the scene.
3. Use the *UP* and *DOWN* arrow keys to control the animation speed (and sound pitch).

Allowing reverse animation (negative speeds!)

In the Animator panel, create a new Float parameter, **Speed**, initialized to 1.0. With state spin selected in the **Animator** panel, check the **Speed Parameter Multiplier** option and choose the **Speed** parameter. In the Inspector, set **Min Speed** to -2, to allow negative speeds for animations.

In the **ChangePitch** C# script, replace the **AccelerateRocket** method with the following:

```
public void AccelerateRocket(float acceleration) {
    speed += acceleration;
    speed = Mathf.Clamp(speed, minSpeed, maxSpeed);

    animator.SetFloat("Speed", speed);
    float soundPitch = speed * animationSoundRatio;
    audioSource.pitch = Mathf.Abs(soundPitch);
}
```

Now when you use key 1 (accelerate) and 2 (decelerate), you can actually decelerate to zero and then continue to reverse the animation.

Simulating acoustic environments with Reverb Zones

Once you have created your level's geometry and the scene is looking just the way you want it to, you might want your sound effects to correspond to that look. Sound behaves differently depending upon the environment in which it is projected, so it can be a good idea to make it reverberate accordingly. In this recipe, we will address this acoustic effect by using Reverb Zones.

Getting ready

For this recipe, we have prepared the ReverbZone.unitypackage file, containing a basic level named **reverbScene** and a prefab, Signal. The package can be found in the 04_09 folder.

How to do it...

Follow these steps to simulate the sonic landscape of a tunnel:

1. Create a new Unity 3D project.
2. Import the provided **Unity** package, **ReverbZone**, into your project.
3. From the Project panel, open **reverbScene** – it's in the _Scenes folder in the ReverbZones folder. This scene gives you a tunnel, and a controllable character (*W A S D* keys and *Shift* to run).

4. From the Project panel, drag the Signal prefab into the Hierarchy – it's in the _Prefabs folder in the ReverbZones folder. This will add a sound-emitting object to the scene. Place it in the center of the tunnel:

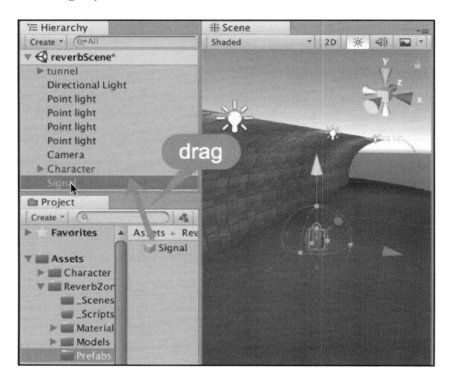

5. Make five copies of the **Signal** GameObject and distribute them throughout the tunnel (leaving a copy just outside each entrance):

6. In the Hierarchy panel, use the **Create menu** | **Audio** | **Audio Reverb Zone** to add a **Reverb Zone** to the scene. Then place this new GameObjct in the center of the tunnel.

Use menu GameObject | Move To View if there is already a GameObject where you want to position another one. Since our Signal GameObject is in the middle of the tunnel, we can double-click that GameObject, then single-click Reverb Zone and move to view – to move the Reverb Zone object to the same location.

7. Select the **Reverb Zone** GameObject. In the Inspector panel, change the **Reverb Zone** component parameters to these values: **Min Distance** = 6, **Max Distance** = 18, and **Preset** = StoneCorridor:

8. Play the scene. As you walk through the tunnel, you will hear the audio reverberate when inside the Reverb Zone area.

How it works...

Once positioned, the Audio Reverb Zone applies an audio filter to all audio sources within its radius.

There's more...

Here are more options for you to try.

Attaching the Audio Reverb Zone component to Audio Sources

Instead of creating an Audio Reverb Zone GameObject, you can attach it to the sound-emitting object (in our case, Signal) as a component through the **Component | Audio | Audio Reverb Zone** menu. In such cases, the Reverb Zone will be individually set up around its parent GameObject.

Making your own Reverb settings

Unity comes with several **Reverb Presets**. We have used **StoneCorridor**, but your scene can ask for something less intense (such as Room) or more radical (such as Psychotic). If these presets still won't be able to recreate the effect that you have in mind, change it to User and edit its parameters as you wish.

Adding volume control with Audio Mixers

Sound-volume adjustment can be a very important feature, especially if your game is a standalone. After all, it can be very frustrating for players to have to access the **Operating System** volume control. In this recipe, we will use the Audio Mixer feature to create independent volume controls for Music and Sound FX.

Getting ready

For this recipe, we have provided a Unity package named
`VolumeControl.unitypackage,` containing an initial scene featuring soundtrack
music and sound effects. The file is available inside the `04_10` folder.

How to do it...

To add volume control sliders to your scene, follow these steps:

1. Create a new Unity 3D project.
2. Import the provided **Unity** package, **Volume**, into your project.
3. Open the **Volume** scene from **Project** panel folder, **VolumeControl |**
   `_Scenes.`
4. Play the scene and walk toward the semitransparent green wall in the
   tunnel, using the *W A S D* keys (press *Shift* to run). You will be able to
   listen to:
     - A looping music soundtrack
     - Bells ringing
     - A robotic speech whenever the character collides with the wall
5. In the **Project** panel, use the Create menu to add an **Audio Mixer** file.
   Rename this new file MainMixer.
6. Double-click MainMixer to open the **Audio Mixer** panel.

7. In the the **Audio Mixer** panel **Groups** section, highlight **Master** and click the + (plus) sign to add a child to the **Master** group. Name this child **Music**. Repeat these actions to add a second child of **Master** named FX:

8. In the the Audio Mixer panel Mixers section, highlight MainMixer and click the + (plus) sign to add a new item to the Mixers group. Rename this MusicMixer (you may need to rename this via the Project panel, since you've created a new Audio Mixer file through this process).

9. Drag MusicMixer onto MainMixer (child it), and select Music as its output in the pop-up dialog window.

10. In the the **Audio Mixer** panel Mixers section, highlight **MainMixer** and click the + (plus) sign to add a new item to the **Mixers** group. Name this **FxMixer**.

11. Child (drag) **FxMixer** onto **MainMixer**, and select Fx as its output in the pop-up dialog window.

12. Select MusicMixer. Select its Master group and add a child named Soundtrack.

13. Select **FxMixer** and add two children to its **Master** group: one named Speech, and another named Bells:

14. Select the **DialogueTrigger** GameObject in the **Hierarchy**. In the **Inspector**, change its **Audio Source** component Output track to **FxMixer | Speech**:

15. Select the **Soundtrack** GameObject in the **Hierarchy**. In the **Inspector**, change its Audio Source component **Output** track to **MusicMixer | Soundtrack**.

16. Select **Signal** from the `Prefabs` folder in the **Project** panel. In the **Inspector**, change its Audio Source component Output track to FxMixer | Bells.

17. Select **MainMixer** in the **Audio Mixer** panel, and select its **Master** track. In the **Inspector** panel, right-click on Volume in the **Attenuation** component. From the pop-up-context menu, select **Expose Volume** (of Master) to script:

18. Repeat the operation to expose the **Volume** to scripts for both the **Music** and FX Groups.

19. At the top-right of the **Audio Mixer** panel, you should see **Exposed Parameters** (three). Click the drop-down icon, and rename them as follows: **MyExposedParam** to OverallVolume; **MyExposedParam1** to **MusicVolume**, and **MyExposedParam2** to FxVolume. Note the sequence of the three parameters may not match the order you added them, so double-check that the greyed-out track names on the right correspond correctly:

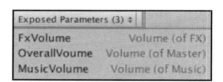

20. In the **Hierarchy** panel, use the **Create** drop-down menu to add a **UI Panel** to the scene (menu: **Create | UI | Panel**). Unity will automatically add a Canvas parent for this panel.

21. In the **Hierarchy** panel, create a UI Slider to the scene (menu: **Create | UI | Slider**). Make it a child of the **Panel** object. Rename this slider as **Slider-overall**. Set the slider's Min Value to 0.000025 (or $2.5e-05$).

22. Duplicate it and rename the new copy to Slider-music. In the **Inspector** panel, **Rect Transform** component, change its **Pos Y** parameter to -40.

23. Duplicate Slider-music and rename the new copy to **Slider-fx**. Change its **Pos Y** parameter to -70:

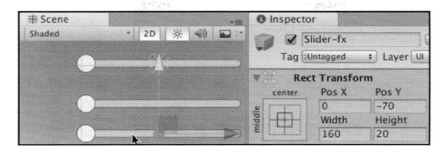

24. Create a C# script class, **VolumeControl**, in the _Scripts folder, containing the following code, and add an instance as a scripted component to the **Main Camera** GameObject:

```csharp
using UnityEngine;
using UnityEngine.Audio;

public class VolumeControl : MonoBehaviour {
    public GameObject panel;
    public AudioMixer myMixer;
    private bool isPaused = false;

    void Start(){
        panel.SetActive(false);

        ON_CHANGE_OverallVol(0.01F);
        ON_CHANGE_MusicVol(0.01F);
        ON_CHANGE_FxVol(0.01F);
    }

    void Update() {
        if (Input.GetKeyUp (KeyCode.Escape)) {
            panel.SetActive(!panel.activeInHierarchy);

            if(isPaused)
                Time.timeScale = 1.0f;
            else
                Time.timeScale = 0.0f;

            isPaused = !isPaused;
        }
    }

    public void ON_CHANGE_OverallVol(float vol) {
        myMixer.SetFloat("OverallVolume", Mathf.Log10(vol) *
20f);
    }
```

```
public void ON_CHANGE_MusicVol(float vol) {
        myMixer.SetFloat ("MusicVolume", Mathf.Log10(vol) *
20f);
    }

public void ON_CHANGE_FxVol(float vol) {
        myMixer.SetFloat ("FxVolume", Mathf.Log10(vol) *
20f);
    }
}
```

25. With **Main Camera** selected in the **Hierarchy** panel, drag the **Panel** GameObject into the Inspector for the public Panel variable.

26. With **Main Camera** selected in the **Hierarchy** panel, drag **MainMixer** from the Project panel into the **Inspector** for the public My Mixer variable.

27. Select the **OverallSlider** component. Below the **On Value Changed** list, click the + sign to add an action. From the **Hierarchy** panel, drag Main Camera into the Object slot and using the drop-down menu, choose **VolumeControl | ON_CHANGE_OverallVol** option. For testing purposes, change the appropriate selector from Runtime Only to Editor and Runtime.

28. Repeat the previous step with MusicSlider and FxSlider, but this time, choose the **ON_CHANGE_MusicVol** and **ON_CHANGE_FxVol** options, respectively, from the drop-down menu.

29. Play the scene. You will be able to access the sliders when pressing *ESCAPE* on your keyboard and adjust volume settings from there.

How it works...

The **Audio Mixer** feature works in a similar fashion to **Digital Audio Workstations**, such as **Logic** and **Sonar**. Through Audio Mixers you can organize and manage audio elements by routing them into specific groups that can have individual audio tracks you can tweak, allowing adjustments in volume level and sound effects.

By organizing and routing our audio clips into two groups (Music and FX), we established MainMixer as a unified controller for volume. Then, we used the Audio Mixer to expose the volume levels for each track of **MainMixer**, making them accessible to our script.

Also, we have set up a basic UI featuring three sliders that, when in use, will pass their float values (between 0.000025 and 1) as arguments to three specific functions in our script: **ON_CHANGE_MusicVol, ON_CHANGE_FxVol,** and **ON_CHANGE_OverallVol**. These functions, on their turn, use the SetFloat command to effectively change the volume levels at runtime. However, before passing on the new volume levels, the script converts linear values (between 0.000025 and 1) to the decibel levels that are used by the Audio Mixer. This conversion is calculated through the $\log(x) * 20$ mathematical function.

For a full explanation on issues regarding the conversion of linear values to decibel levels and vice-versa, check out Aaron Brown's excellent article at `http://www.playdotsound.com/portfolio-item/ decibel-db-to-float-value-calculator-making-sense-of- linear-values-in-audio-tools/`.

If one of the sliders seems not to work, double-check that the name of the first parameter to `SetFloat(...)` matches the exposed parameter in the **AudioMixer** – any spelling difference will mean the on-change function will not change values in the **Audio Mixer**. For example, if the named exposed parameter was wrongly named **"OveralVolume"** (missing an "l"), this statement in response to a slider change would not work due to the spelling mismatch:

```
myMixer.SetFloat ("OverallVolume ", Mathf.Log10(vol) * 20f);
```

The `VolumeControl` script includes code to enable and disable the UI and the **EventSystem**, depending upon whether the player hits the *ESCAPE* key to activate/deactivate the volume-control sliders.

Since our VolumeControl script sets the maximum volume level for the music and Fx tracks, you should not manually change any of the track volumes of the MainMixer at Design-Time. For general adjustments, use the secondary MusicMixer and FxMixer mixers.

There's more...

Here is some extra information on Audio Mixers.

Playing with Audio Production

There are many creative uses for exposed parameters. We can, for instance, add effects such as **Distortion**, **Flange**, and **Chorus** to audio channels, allowing users to operate virtual sound tables/mixing boards.

See also

The *Making a dynamic soundtrack with Snapshots* recipe in this chapter.
The *Balancing the in-game audio with Ducking* in this chapter.

Making a dynamic soundtrack with Snapshots

Dynamic soundtracks are the ones that change according to what is happening to the player in the game, musically reflecting that place or moment of the character's adventure. In this recipe, we will implement a soundtrack that changes twice; the first time when entering a tunnel, and the second time when coming out of it. To achieve this, we will use the **Snapshot** feature of the **Audio Mixer**.

Snapshots are a way of saving the state of your **Audio Mixer**, keeping your preferences for volume levels, audio effects, and more. We can access these states through C# scripting, creating transitions between mixes, and by bringing up the desired sonic ambience for each moment of the player's journey.

Getting ready

For this recipe, we have prepared a basic game level, contained inside the Unity package named `DynamicSoundtrack`, and two soundtrack audio clips in the `.ogg` format: `Theme01_Percussion` and `Theme01_Synths`. All these files can be found in the `04_11` folder.

How to do it...

To make a dynamic soundtrack, follow these steps:

1. Create a new Unity 3D project.
2. Import the provided Unity package, **DynamicSoundtrack**, and the two .ogg files into your project.
3. Open the **Dynamic** scene from **Project** panel folder, **DynamicSoundtrack |** **_Scenes**.
4. In the Project panel, use the **Create** menu to add an **Audio Mixer** file. Rename this new file Mixer-music. Double-click it to open the **Audio Mixer** panel.
5. In the the **Audio Mixer** panel **Groups** section, highlight **Master** and click the + (plus) sign to add a child to the **Master** group. Name this child **Percussion**. Repeat these actions to add a second child of **Master**, named Synths:

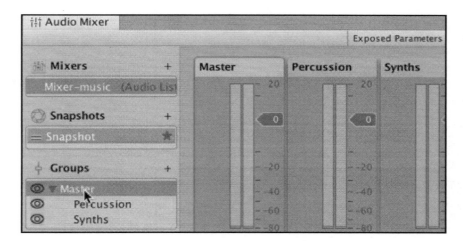

6. From the **Hierarchy** view, create a new **Empty** GameObject. Name it Music.
7. Create a GameObject in the scene containing an **AudioSource** component linked to the **Theme01_Percussion AudioClip**. This can be done in a single step by dragging the music clip from the Project panel into either the **Hierarchy** or Scene panels. Child this new GameObject to the **Music** GameObject in the **Hierarchy**.

8. Ensure the **Theme01_Percussion** GameObject is selected in the **Hierarchy**. In the Inspector for the **AudioSource** component, change its Output to Percussion (**MusicMixer**), make sure the **Play On Awake** option is checked, check the **Loop** option, and make sure its **Spatial Blend** is set to 2D:

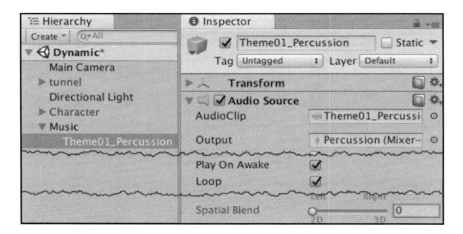

9. Repeat the previous two steps for the **Theme01_Synths AudioClip** – setting the **Output** to Synths (**MusicMixer**).

10. Open the **Audio Mixer** and play the scene. We will now use the mixer to set the soundtrack for the start of the scene. With the scene playing, click on the **Edit** in Play Mode button, as shown in the screenshot, at the top of the **Audio Mixer**. Drop the volume on the **Synths** track down to **-30 dB**:

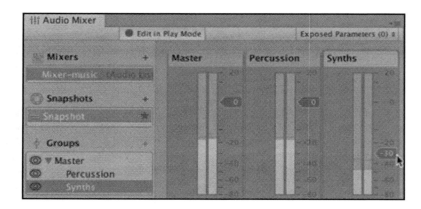

11. Select the Percussion track. Click the **Add..** button for **Attenuation**, and add a **High-pass** effect. From the **Inspector** view, change the **Cutoff** frequency of the **High-pass** effect to **544.00 Hz**:

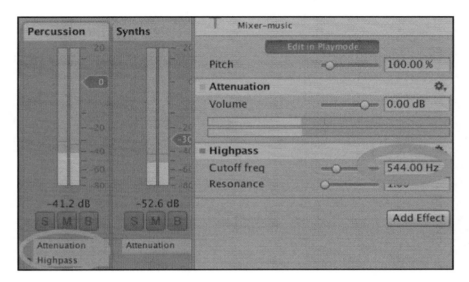

12. Every change, so far, has been assigned to the current Snapshot. From the Snaphots view, right-click on the current Snapshot and rename it to Start. Click the + (plus) sign to make a copy of the current snapshot, rename this copy Tunnel:

13. Select the **Tunnel** snapshot and select the **High-pass** effect of the **Percussion** group. In the **Inspector**, set property **Cutoff frequency** of **10.00** Hz:

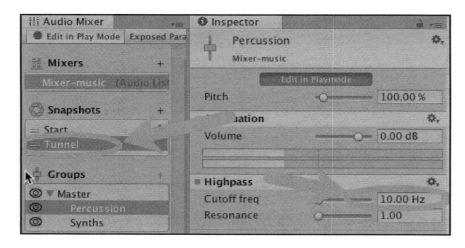

14. Switch between the **Tunnel** and Start snapshots. You'll be able to hear the difference.
15. Duplicate the **Tunnel** snapshot, rename it **OtherSide**, and select it.
16. Raise the volume of the **Synths** track up to 0 dB.
17. Now that we have our three **Snapshots**, it's time to create triggers to make transitions among them.
18. Stop running the scene (so changes to the **Hierarchy** will be stored in the scene).
19. In the **Hierarchy**, create a **Cube** GameObject (menu: **Create** | **3D Object** | **Cube**). Name it **Cube-tunnel-trigger**.
20. In the Inspector, access the Cube-tunnel-trigger GameObject's Box Collider component and check the **Is Trigger** option. Uncheck its **Mesh Renderer** component. Adjust its size and position to the scene tunnel's interior. You may find Scene Wireframe view useful for the cube collider positioning:

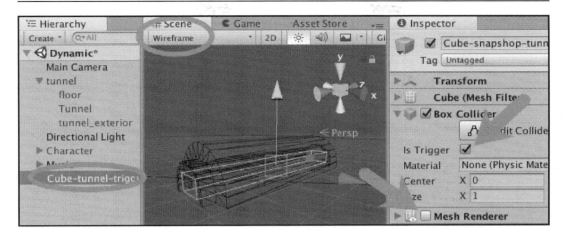

21. Make two copies of cube **Cube-tunnel-trigger** and rename them to cube **Cube-start-trigger** and cube **Cube-otherside-trigger**. Adjust their size and position, so that they occupy the areas before the tunnel's entrance (where the character is) and after its exit:

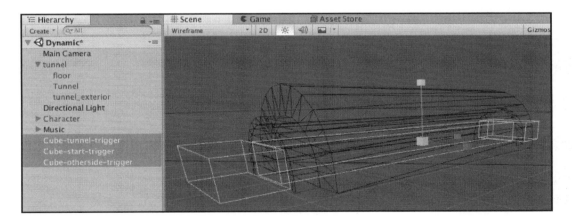

22. Create a C# script class, SnapshotTrigger, in the **_Scripts folder**, containing the following code:

```
using UnityEngine;
using UnityEngine.Audio;

public class SnapshotTrigger : MonoBehaviour {
    public AudioMixerSnapshot snapshot;
    public float crossfade;
```

```
       private void OnTriggerEnter(Collider other) {
            snapshot.TransitionTo (crossfade);
       }
}
```

23. Add an instance of SnapshotTrigger to all three trigger cubes (**Cube-tunnel-trigger**, **Cube-start-trigger**, and **Cube-otherside-trigger**).

24. Select **Cube-tunnel-trigger**. From the **Inspector** for the **Snapshot Trigger (Script)** component, set Snapshot to **Tunnel**, and **Crossfade** as 2:

25. Make changes to **Cube-start-trigger** and **Cube-otherside-trigger** by setting their **Snapshots** to **Start** and **OtherSide**, respectively – also with **Crossfade** as 2.

26. Test the scene. The background music will change as the character moves from the starting point, through the tunnel, and out the other side.

How it works...

The Snapshot feature allows you to save **Audio Mixer** states (including all volume levels and every filter setting) so that you can change those mixing preferences at **Run-Time**, making the audio design more suitable for specific locations or gameplay settings. For this recipe, we have created three **Snapshots** for different moments in the player's journey:

- Before entering the tunnel
- Inside the tunnel
- Outside the tunnel

We have used the **Highpass** filter to make the initial **Snapshot** less intense. We have also turned the Synths track volume up to emphasize the open environment outside the tunnel. Our aim is for the changes in the audio mix to help set the right mood for the game.

To activate our snapshots, we have placed **trigger** colliders, featuring our **Snapshot Trigger** scripted component in which we set the desired Snapshot and the time in seconds, that it takes to make the transition (a crossfade) between the previous Snapshot and the next. In fact, the function in our script is really this straightforward – the line of `snapshot.TransitionTo (crossfade)` code simply starts a transition lasting `crossfade` seconds to the desired Snapshot.

There's more...

Here is some information on how to fine-tune and customize this recipe.

Reducing the need for multiple audio clips

You might have noticed how different the `Theme01_Percussion` audio clip sounds when the **Cutoff frequency** of the **High-pass** filter is set as `10.00 Hz`. This is because the high-pass filter, as its name suggests, cuts off lower frequencies of the audio signal. In this case, it attenuated the bass drum down to inaudible levels while keeping the shakers audible. The opposite effect can be achieved through the **Lowpass** filter. A major benefit is
the opportunity to have two separate tracks in the same audio clip.

Dealing with audio file formats and compression rates

To avoid a loss of audio quality, you should import your sound clips using the appropriate file format, depending upon your target platform. If you are not sure which format to use, check out Unity's documentation on the subject at `http://docs.unity3d.com/Manual/AudioFiles.html`.

Applying Snapshots to background noise

Although we have applied Snapshots to our music soundtrack, background noise can also benefit immensely. If your character travels across places that are significantly different, transitioning from open spaces to indoor environments, you should consider applying snapshots to your environment audio mix. Be careful, however, to create separate **Audio Mixers** for Music and Environment – unless you don't mind having musical and ambient
sound tied to the same Snapshot.

Getting creative with effects

In this recipe, we have mentioned the **High-pass and Low-pass** filters. However, there are many effects that can make audio clips sound radically different. Experiment! Try applying effects such as **Distortion**, **Flange**, and **Chorus**. In fact, we encourage you to try every effect, playing with their settings. The creative use of these effects can bring out different expressions to a single audio clip.

See also

The *Adding volume control with Audio Mixers* recipe in this chapter.

The *Balancing soundtrack volume with Ducking* recipe in this chapter.

Balancing in-game audio with Ducking

As much as the background music can be important in establishing the right atmosphere, there will be times when other audio clips should be emphasized, and the music volume turned down for the duration of that clip. This effect is known as **Ducking**. Maybe you will need it for dramatic effect (simulating hearing loss after an explosion took place), or maybe you want to make sure that the player listens to a specific bit of information presented as an audio speed sound clip. In this recipe, we will learn how to emphasize a piece of dialog by ducking the audio whenever a specific sound message is played. For that effect, we will use the **Audio Mixer** to send information between tracks.

Getting ready

For this recipe, we have provided the `soundtrack.mp3` audio clip and a Unity package named Ducking.unitypackage, containing an initial scene. All these files are available inside the `04_12` folder.

How to do it...

To apply Audio Ducking to your soundtrack, follow these steps:

1. Create a new **Unity 3D** project.
2. Import the provided **Unity** package, **Ducking,** and the `soundtrack.mp3` file into your project.
3. Open the Ducking scene from **Project** panel folder, **Ducking** | _Scenes.
4. Enter Run-Time by playing the scene and walk toward the semitransparent green wall in the tunnel, using the *W, A, S,* and *D* keys (by pressing *Shift* to run). You will hear the robotDucking speech audio clip play as the character collides with the green wall ("This your captain speaking ..."). Then stop the scene playing to return to Design-Time.
5. Create a **GameObject** in the scene containing an **AudioSource** component linked to the soundtrack **AudioClip**. This can be done in a single step by dragging the music clip from the **Project** panel into either the **Hierarchy** or **Scene** panels.

6. Ensure the GameObject soundtrack is selected in the **Hierarchy**. In the **Inspector** for the **Audio Source** component, make sure the Play On Awake option is checked, check the Loop option, and make sure its **Spatial Blend** is set to 2D (if necessary, see screenshot in the previous recipe for same action on the percussion GameObject).

7. Play the scene again. The soundtrack music should be playing. Then stop the scene playing to return to **Design-Time**.

8. In the **Project** panel, use the **Create** menu to add an **Audio Mixer** file. Rename this new file **MainMixer**.

9. Double-click **MainMixer** to open the **Audio Mixer** panel.

10. In the the **Audio Mixer** panel Groups section, highlight **Master** and click the + (plus) sign to add a child to the **Master** group. Name this child Music. Repeat these actions to add a second child of Master, named FX. Add a third child to the **Master** group, named Input:

11. In the Audio Mixers view, add a new **Mixer** by clicking the + (plus) sign to add a new **Mixer** to the project. Name it **MusicMixer**. Drag it into the **MainMixer** (to become its child) and select the **Music** group as its Output:

12. Repeat the previous step to add another child of **MainMixer**, named **FxMixer**, to the project, selecting the FX group as the output.

13. Select **MusicMixer**. Select its **Master** group and add a child named Soundtrack:

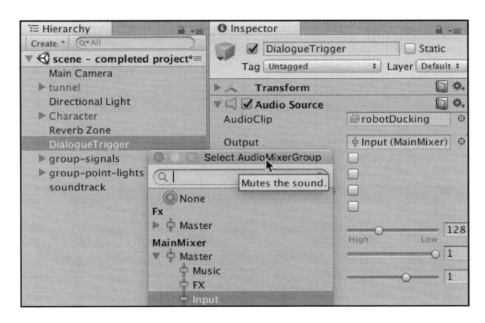

14. Select **FxMixer** and add a child named **Bells**.

15. From the **Hierarchy** view, select the **DialogueTrigger GameObject**. In the **Inspector**, change the Output track to **MainMixer | Input**, for the **Audio Source** component:

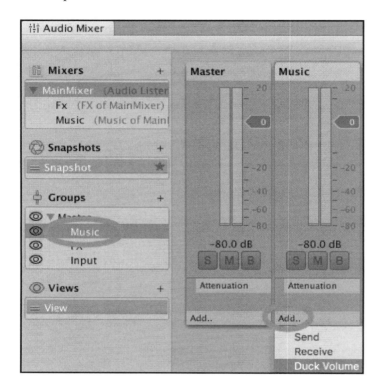

16. Select the **Soundtrack** GameObject. In the **Inspector** for the **Audio Source** component, change its Output track to **MusicMixer | Soundtrack**.

17. From the **Ducking | Prefabs** folder in the Project panel, select the Signal prefab. In the Inspector, set its **Audio Source** component **Output** to **FxMixer | Bells**.

18. Open the **Audio Mixer** window. Choose **MainMixer**, select the Music track controller, right-click on **Attenuation**, and using the context menu, add the **Duck Volume** effect:

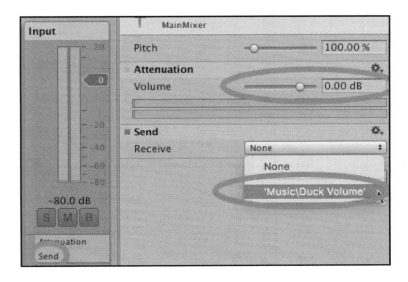

19. Select the **Input** track, right-click on **Attenuation**, and using the context menu, add **Send**.

20. With the **Input** track still selected, go to the **Inspector** view and change the Receive setting in **Send** to **Music\Duck** Volume and its **Send** level to 0.00 db.

21. Select the **Music** track. From the Inspector view, change the settings on the **Duck Volume** as follows: **Threshold**: -40.00 db, **Ratio**: 300.00%, **Attack Time**: 100.00 ms, **Release Time**: 200.00 ms:

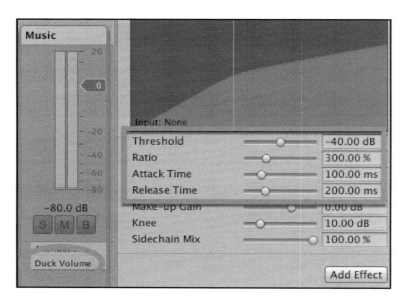

22. Test the scene again. Entering the trigger object will cause the soundtrack volume to drop considerably, recovering the original volume in two seconds.

How it works...

In this recipe, we have created, in addition to Music and Sound FX, a group named Input, to which we have routed the audio clip that triggers the Duck Volume effect attached to our music track. The Duck Volume effect changes the track's volume whenever it receives an input that is louder than indicated in its Threshold setting. In our case, we have sent the Input track as input, and adjusted the settings so the volume will be reduced as soon as 0.1 seconds after the input had been received, turning back to its original value of 2 seconds after the input has ceased. The amount of volume reduction was determined by our Ratio of 300.00%. Playing around with the setting values will give you a better idea of how each parameter affects the final result. Also, make sure to visualize the graphic as the trigger sound is played. You will be able to see how the Input sound passes the threshold, triggering the effect.

The tracks are organized so that the other sound clips (other than speech) will not affect the volume of the music – but every music clip will be affected by audio clips sent to the input track.

See also

The *Adding volume control with Audio Mixers* recipe in this chapter.

The *Making a dynamic soundtrack with Snapshots* recipe in this chapter.

Audio visualization from sample spectral data

The Unity audio systems allows us to access the music data – via the AudioSource.GetSpectrumData(...) method. This gives us the opportunity to use that data to present Run-Time visualization of the overall sound being heard (from the **AudioListener**), or the individual sound being played by individual **AudioSources**.

The screenshot shows lines drawn using a sample script provided by Unity (https://docs.unity3d.com/ScriptReference/AudioSource.GetSpectrumData.html):

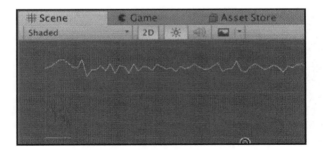

However, in that sample code, their use of `Debug.DrawLine()` only appears in the Scene panel when running the game in the Unity Editor (not for final builds), and so cannot be seen by the game player. In this recipe, we'll take that same spectral data, and use it to create a **Run-Time** audio spectral visualization in the Game panel. We'll do this by creating a row of 512 small cubes, and then changing their heights each frame based on 512 audio data samples for the playing **AudioSource** component.

Getting ready

For this recipe, we have provided several 140 bmp sampled free music clips inside the `04_13` folder.

How to do it...

To schedule a sound to play after a given delay, do the following:

1. Create a new 3D project and import the provided sound clip files.
2. In the **Inspector**, set the Background of the **Main Camera** to black.
3. Set the **Main Camera Transform Position** to (224, 50, -200).
4. Set the **Main Camera Camera** component to have these settings: **Projection = Perspective, Field of View 60, and Clipping Planes 0.3 - 300.**
5. Add **DirectionalLight** to the scene.
6. Add a new empty GameObject named visualizer to the scene. Add an **AudioSource** component to this GameObject, and set its **AudioClip** to one of the 140 bmp loops provided.
7. Create a C# script class, **SpectrumCubes**, in a new folder, _Scripts, containing the following code, and add an instance as a scripted component to the visualizer GameObject:

```csharp
using UnityEngine;

public class SpectrumCubes : MonoBehaviour
{
    const int NUM_SAMPLES = 512;
    public Color displayColor;
    public float multiplier = 5000;
    public float startY;
    public float maxHeight = 50;
    private AudioSource audioSource;
    private float[] spectrum = new float[NUM_SAMPLES];
```

```
    private GameObject[] cubes = new GameObject[NUM_SAMPLES];

    void Awake() {
        audioSource = GetComponent<AudioSource>();
        CreateCubes();
    }

    void Update() {
        audioSource.GetSpectrumData(spectrum, 0,
FFTWindow.BlackmanHarris);
        UpdateCubeHeights();
    }

    private void UpdateCubeHeights() {
        for (int i = 0; i < NUM_SAMPLES; i++)
        {
            Vector3 oldScale = cubes[i].transform.localScale;
            Vector3 scaler = new Vector3(oldScale.x,
HeightFromSample(spectrum[i]), oldScale.z);
            cubes[i].transform.localScale = scaler;
            Vector3 oldPosition = cubes[i].transform.position;
            float newY = startY +
cubes[i].transform.localScale.y / 2;
            Vector3 newPosition = new Vector3(oldPosition.x,
newY, oldPosition.z);
            cubes[i].transform.position = newPosition;
        }
    }

    private float HeightFromSample(float sample) {
        float height = 2 + (sample * multiplier);
        return Mathf.Clamp(height, 0, maxHeight);
    }

    private void CreateCubes() {
        for (int i = 0; i < NUM_SAMPLES; i++) {
            GameObject cube =
GameObject.CreatePrimitive(PrimitiveType.Cube);
            cube.transform.parent = transform;
            cube.name = "SampleCube" + i;

            Renderer cubeRenderer =
cube.GetComponent<Renderer>();
            cubeRenderer.material = new
Material(Shader.Find("Specular"));
            cubeRenderer.sharedMaterial.color = displayColor;

            float x = 0.9f * i;
```

```
                                float y = startY;
                                float z = 0;
                                cube.transform.position = new Vector3(x, y, z);

                                cubes[i] = cube;
                        }
                }
        }
```

8. With the visualizer GameObject selected in the **Hierarchy**, click to choose a visualization color from the **Inspector Display Color** public variable for the **SpectrumCubes** (Script) component.

9. Run the scene – you should see the cubes jump up and down, presenting a Run-Time visualization of the sound data spectrum for the playing sound.

How it works...

You created a C# script class, SpectrumCubes. You created a GameObject with an **AudioSource** component, and an instance of your scripted class. All the work is done by the methods in the SpectrumCues C# script class, so each of these is explained in the following sections.

The void Awake() method

This method caches references to the sibling **AudioSource** component, and then invokes the CreateCubes() method.

The void CreateCubes() method

This method loops for the number of samples (default is 512), to create a 3D Cube GameObject, in a row along the X-axis. Each Cube is created with the name "Cube<i>" (where "i" is from 0 to 511) and then parented to the visualizer GameObject (since the scripted method is running in this GameObject). Each cube then has the color of its renderer set to the value of the public displayColor parameter. The cube is then positioned on the X-axis according to the loop number, at the value of the public startY parameter (so multiple visualizations can be at different parts of the screen), and Z = 0. Finally, a reference to the new cube GameObject is stored in the cubes[] array.

The void Update() method

Each frame in this method updates the values inside the spectrum[] array through a call to GetSpectrumData(...). In our example, the FFTWindow.BlackmanHarris frequency window technique is used. Then the UpdateCubeHeights() method is invoked.

The void UpdateCubeHeights() method

This method loops for each cube to set its height to a scaled value of its corresponding audio data value in the spectrum[] array. The cube has its Y-value scaled by the value returned by the HeightFromSample(spectrum[i]) method. The cube is then moved up (its transform position is set) from the value of startY by half its height – so that all the scaling appears upwards (rather than up and down) – this is to have a flat line along the base of our spectrum of cubes.

The float HeightFromSample(float) method

Method HeightFromSample(float) does a simple calculation (sample value times public parameter multiplier), plus minimum value of two added to it. The value returned from the function is this result, limited to the maxHeight public parameter (via the Mathf.Clamp(...) method).

There's more...

There are some details that you don't want to miss.

Adding visualizations to a second AudioSource

The script has been written to be easy to have multiple visualizations in a scene. So to create a second visualizer for a second **AudioClip** in the scene, do the following:

1. Duplicate the **visualizer** GameObject.
2. Drag a different AudioClip from the **Project** panel into the **Audio Source** component of your new GameObject.

3. Set the Start **Y** public parameter in the **Inspector** to 60 (so the new row of cubes will be above the original row).

4. In the **Inspector**, choose a different **Display Color** public variable for the **SpectrumCubes (Script)** component:

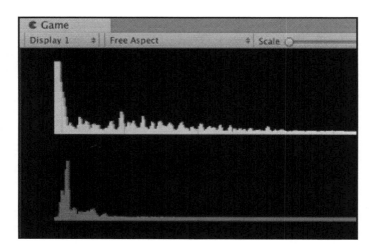

Try out different FFT (Fast Fourier Transform) window types

There are several different approaches to frequency analysis of audio data, our recipe currently uses the `FFTWindow.BlackmanHarris` version. Learn (and try out!) some of the others from the Unity `FFTWindow` documentation page: https://docs.unity3d.com/ScriptReference/FFTWindow.html.

Synchronizing simultaneous and sequential music to create a simple 140 bpm music-loop manager

The *Creating a metronome through the precise scheduling of sounds with* dspTime recipe demonstrated how to create a metronome by scheduling when sounds play using the AudioSource.PlayScheduled(...) method and the AudioSettings.dspTime value. Another situation when we need to precisely schedule audio start times is to ensure a smooth transition from one music track to another, or to ensure simultaneous music tracks play in time together.

In this recipe, we'll create a simple 4-track 140 bpm music manager that starts playing a new sound after a fixed time – the result of which is that the tracks fit together perfectly, and those that overlap do so in synchronicity:

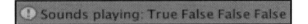

Getting ready

For this recipe, we have provided several 140 bmp sampled free music clips inside the 04_14 folder.

How to do it...

To create a music-loop manager, do the following:

1. Create a new Unity 3D project and import the provided sound clip files.
2. Create four GameObjects in the scene containing an **AudioSource** component linked to different **AudioClip** loops from the 140 bpm files provided. This can be done in a single step by dragging the music clip from the **Project** panel into either the **Hierarchy** or Scene panels.

3. In the Inspector, uncheck the **Play On Awake** parameter for all four **AudioSource** components (so they don't start playing until we tell them to).
4. Add a new empty **GameObject** named **musicScheduler** to the scene.
5. Create a C# script class, **LoopScheduler**, in a new folder, _Scripts, containing the following code, and add an instance as a scripted component to the **musicScheduler** GameObject:

```csharp
using UnityEngine;

public class LoopScheduler : MonoBehaviour {
    public float bpm = 140.0F;
    public int numBeatsPerSegment = 16;
    public AudioSource[] audioSources = new AudioSource[4];
    private double nextEventTime;
    private int nextLoopIndex = 0;
    private int numLoops;
    private float numSecondsPerMinute = 60F;
    private float timeBetweenPlays;

    void Start() {
        numLoops = audioSources.Length;
timeBetweenPlays = numSecondsPerMinute / bpm *
numBeatsPerSegment;
        nextEventTime = AudioSettings.dspTime;
    }

    void Update() {
        double lookAhead = AudioSettings.dspTime + 1.0F;
        if (lookAhead > nextEventTime)
            StartNextLoop();

        PrintLoopPlayingStatus();
    }

    private void StartNextLoop() {
audioSources[nextLoopIndex].PlayScheduled(nextEventTime);
        nextEventTime += timeBetweenPlays;

        nextLoopIndex++;
        if (nextLoopIndex >= numLoops)
            nextLoopIndex = 0;
    }

    private void PrintLoopPlayingStatus(){
        string statusMessage = "Sounds playing: ";
        int i = 0;
```

```
while (i < numLoops) {
    statusMessage += audioSources[i].isPlaying + " ";
    i++;
}

print(statusMessage);
    }
}
```

6. With the **musicScheduler** GameObject selected in the **Hierarchy**, drag each of the music loop GameObjects into the four available slots for the **AudioSources** public array variable in the **Loop Scheduler (Script)** component:

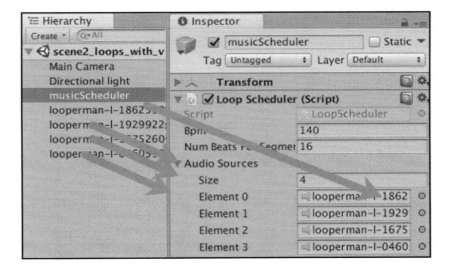

7. Run the scene – each clips should start in turn after the same time delay. If you chose one or two longer clips, they will continue playing while the next clip begins – all overlapping perfectly since they are all 140 bpm sound clips.

How it works...

You added four **GameObjects** to the scene, containing **AudioSources** linked to 140 bpm music clips. You created a C# script class, `LoopScheduler`, and added an instance to an empty **GameObject**. You associated the four **AudioSources** in your **GameObjects** with the four slots in the public **AudioSource** array variable in your scripted component.

The numbers of music clips you use can easily be changed by changing the size of the public array variable.

The `Start()` method counts the length of the array to set the `numLoops` variable. It then calculates the number of seconds to delay before starting each clip (this is fixed according to the beats-per-minute and beats-per-measure). Finally, it sets the current time to be the time to start the first loop.

The `Update()` method decides whether it's time to schedule the next loop, by testing whether the current time plus a 1-second look-ahead, is past the time to start the next loop. If so, the `StartNextLoop()` method is invoked. Regardless of whether we have started the next loop, the `PrintLoopPlayingStatus()` method to display to the user which loops are playing or not is printed to the Console.

The `PrintLoopPlayingStatus()` method loops for each **AudioSource** reference in the array, creating a string of trues and falses to be then printed out.

The `StartNextLoop()` method sends a `PlayScheduled(...)` message to the next `AudioSource` to be played, passing the `nextEventTime` value. It then adds the time between plays for the next event time. The next value of the loop index is then calculated (add one, if past the end of the array, then reset to 0 again).

There's more...

There are some details that you don't want to miss.

Adding visualizations to the four playing loops

It's great fun to watch the visualization of the loop sounds as they play together. To add visualizations to the four AudioSources, all you have to do is:

1. Import the **SpectrumCubes.cs** C# script file from the previous recipe into this project.

2. Set the **Main Camera Transform Position** to (**224, 50, -200**).

3. Set the **Main Camera Camera component** to have these settings: Projection = Perspective, Field of View 60, and Clipping Planes 0.3 - 300.

4. Add a **Directional Light GameObject** to the scene.

5. For each of the four **GameObjects** containing your **AudioSources**, add an instance of the **SpectrumCubes** script class.

6. In the **Inspector** for the **Spectrum Cubes (Script)** component, change the **displayColors** for each **AudioSource GameObject**.

7. Set the startY values of **Spectrum Cubes (Script)** components for the four **GameObjects** to be -50, 0, 50, 100. For most screen sizes, this should allow you too see all four visualization spectrums:

Creating Textures, Maps, and Materials

5

In this chapter, we will cover:

- Creating a basic material with Standard Shader (Specular setup)
- Adapting a basic material from Specular setup to Metallic
- Applying Normal maps to a Material
- Adding Transparency and Emission maps to a material
- Highlighting materials at mouse-over
- Adding Detail maps to a material
- Fading the transparency of a material

Introduction

There is a close relationship between **Textures**, **Materials**, and **Shaders**, and their relationships are important:

- Textures are two-dimensional images. The surface of 2D and 3D objects in Unity games are defined by meshes. The **Texture** images are mapped onto meshes by **Materials** – each point (vertex) on a mesh has to be mapped to some value in the **Texture**. A **Texture** may indicate colors, but may indicate bumps/wrinkles or transparency – all of which can contribute to determining what is finally rendered for the user to see.

- **Materials** specify which **Shader** should be used to render the images onto the meshes, plus values for the **Shader's** parameters (such as which textures/parts of a texture map, colors, other values). Learn more at the Unity documentation page about Materials:
  https://docs.unity3d.com/Manual/Materials.html.

- **Shaders** define the method to render an object. **Shaders** can use multiple textures for more sophisticated results, and specify which parameters may be customized in the Material Inspector. At the end of the day, **Shaders** are code and mathematics, but Unity provides a set of **Shaders** for us. We can also use the new **Shader Graph** package, which allows the creation of sophisticated **Shaders** using a visual, drag-and-drop graphing interface. In addition, custom shaders can be written in the **ShaderLab** language.

Unity offers physically-based Shaders. **Physically-Based Rendering** (**PBR**) is a technique that simulates the appearance of **Materials** based on how the light reacts with that **Material** (more specifically, the matter from which that material is made) in the real world. Such a technique allows for more realistic and consistent materials. So, your creations in Unity should look better than ever. Creating **Materials** in Unity has also become more efficient now. Once you have chosen between the available workflows (**Metallic** or **Specular** setup; we'll get back to that later), there is no longer a need to browse the drop-down menus in search of specific features, as Unity optimizes the shader for the created **Material**, removing unnecessary code for unused properties once the material has been set up and the texture maps have been assigned.

Creating and saving texture maps

The visual aspects of a material can be modified through the use of textures. In order to create and edit image files, you will need an image editor, such as Adobe Photoshop (the industry standard, and has its native format supported by Unity) or GIMP. In order to follow the recipes in this chapter, it's strongly recommended that you have access to a few pieces of software such as these.

When saving **Texture Maps**, especially the ones that have an **Alpha Channel**, you might want to choose an adequate file format. PSD, Photoshop's native format, is practical for preserving the original artwork in many layers. The PNG format is also a great option, but please note that Photoshop doesn't handle PNG's **Alpha Channel** independently of the transparency, possibly compromising the material's appearance. Also, PNG files don't support layers. For this chapter, we will often use the TIF format for three main reasons:

- It's open to those not using Photoshop
- It uses layers
- It preserves the **Alpha Channel** information

The file size is significantly greater than in PSDs and PNGs, so feel free to save your work as PSDs (if you have Photoshop) or PNGs (if you don't need layers and, if using Photoshop, **Alpha Channels**).

Finally, a word of advice: although it's possible to manually create **Texture Maps** for our materials by using the traditional image-editing software, new tools such as Allegorthmic's Substance Painter and Bitmap2Material make this work much more efficient, complete, and intuitive, complementing the traditional **Texture**-making process or replacing it altogether. These tools provide Texture work support in a similar way to what zBrush and Mudbox did for 3D modeling. For design professionals, we strongly recommend at least trying such tools. Note, however, that products from Allegorithmic won't make use of Unity's Standard Shader, relying on the substance files (which are natively supported by Unity).

The big picture

To understand the **Standard Shaders**, it's a good idea to know the workflows, their properties, and how they affect the material's appearance. There are, however, many possible ways to work with **Materials** – texture map requirements, for instance, might change from engine to engine, or from one tool to another. Presently, Unity supports two different workflows: one based on **Specular**, and another based on Metallic values. Although both workflows share similar properties (such as **Normal**, **Height**, **Occlusion**, and **Emission**), they differ in the way the diffuse color and reflectance properties are set up.

Standard Shader (Specular workflow)

Unity's Standard **Shader** (**Specular** setup) uses **Albedo** and **Specular/Smoothness** maps, combining them to create some of the material's aspect – mainly its color and reflectance qualities. The following shows the difference between the **Albedo** and **Smoothness** maps:

- **Albedo**: This is the material's diffused color. Plainly and simply, this is how you usually describe the appearance of the **Material** (the British flag is red, white and blue; Ferrari's logo is a black horse in a yellow setting; some sunglasses' lenses are semi-transparent gradients). This description, however, can be deceptive. Purely metallic objects (such as aluminum, chrome, and gold) should have black as their diffuse color. Their colors, as we perceive them, have originated from their specular channel. Non-metallic objects (plastic, wood, and even painted or rusted metal), on the other hand, have very distinct diffuse colors. **Texture Maps** for the **Albedo** property feature RGB channels for colors and (optionally) an Alpha Channel for transparency.

- **Specular/Smoothness**: This refers to the shininess of the material. **Texture** maps make use of RGB channels for specular color (which inform hue and intensity), and **Alpha Channel** for smoothness/gloss (dark values for less shiny surfaces and blurred reflections; light/white values for shiny, mirror-like appearance). It is important to note that non-metallic objects feature neutral, very dark specular colors (with plastic, for instance, you should work with a grey value around 59). Metallic objects, on the other hand, feature very light values, and are also a bit yellowish in hue.

To illustrate such concepts, we have created a battery object, featuring brushed metal caps and a plastic body. Observe how each map contributes to the final result:

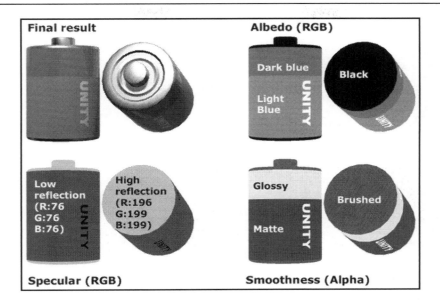

Standard Shader (Metallic workflow)

Unity's default **Standard Shader** combines **Albedo** and **Metallic/Glossiness** maps to create the color and reflectance qualities of the material. The following are the differences:

- **Albedo**: As in the **Specular** workflow, this is the **Material's** diffuse color; how you would describe the **Material**. However, **Albedo** maps for the Metallic workflow should be configured in a slightly different way than ones for **Specular** workflow. This time around, the perceived diffuse color of metallic materials (grey for iron, yellow/orange for golden, and so on) have to be present in the Albedo map. Again, Albedo maps feature RGB channels for the colors and (optionally) an Alpha Channel for transparency.

- **Metallic/Smoothness**: This refers to how metallic the **Material** looks. **Metallic Texture Maps** make use of the Red channel for the **Metallic** value (black for non-metallic and white for metallic **Materials** that are not painted or rusted) and the **Alpha Channel** for smoothness (in a similar way to the **Specular** workflow). Please note that **Metallic** maps do not include any information on hue, and in these cases the yellow-ish nature of the metallic gloss should be applied to the **Albedo** map.

To reproduce the battery that illustrated the **Specular** workflow by using the Metallic workflow, maps would have to be recreated as follows:

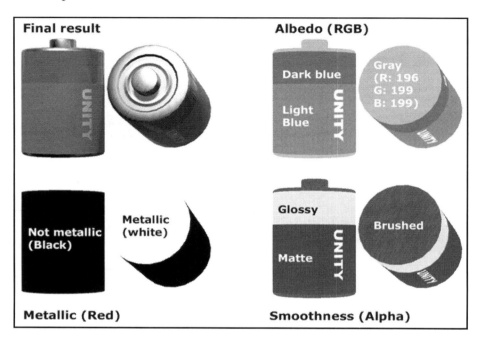

You might have noticed that we've used white to convey a metallic object. Technically, since only the Red channel is relevant, we could have used red (R: 255, G: 0, B: 0), yellow (R: 255, G: 255, B: 0), or, for that matter, any color that has a red value of 255.

The Unity documentation pages provide two very useful charts giving examples of common properties for the **Standard Shader Metallic** and **Specular** workflows (`https://docs.unity3d.com/Manual/StandardShaderMaterialCharts.html`):

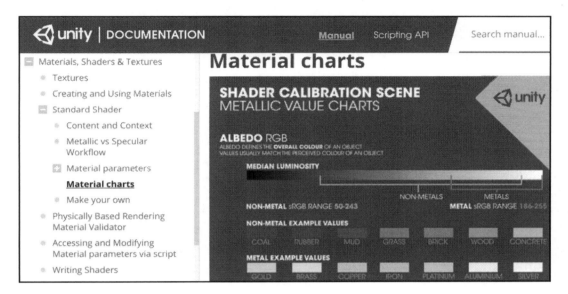

Other material properties

It's also worth mentioning that Unity's **Standard Shaders** support other maps such as:

- **Normal Maps**: The normal map adds detailed bumpiness into the **Material**, simulating a more complex geometry. For instance, the internal ring on the positive (top) node of the battery that illustrated shader workflows is not modeled in the 3D object's geometry, but rather created through a simple **Normal Map**.
- **Occlusion Maps**: A greyscale map is used to simulate the dark sections of an object under ambient light. Usually, it is used to emphasize joints, creases, and other details of geometry.
- **Height Maps**: These add a displacement effect, giving the impression of depth without the need for complex geometry.
- **Emission Maps**: These add color emitted by the **Material**, as if self-illuminated, such as fluorescent surfaces or LCDs. **Texture** maps for Emission maps feature RGB channels for color.

Resources

Physically-Based Rendering (**PBR**) is a complex (and current) topic, so it's a good idea to study it a bit by familiarizing yourself with the tools and concepts behind it. To help you with this task, we have included a non-exhaustive list of resources that you should take a look at.

Unity samples and documentation

Before you start, it might be a good idea to read Unity's documentation on **Textures**, **Materials**, and **Shaders**. They can be found online:

- https://docs.unity3d.com/Manual/Textures.html
- https://docs.unity3d.com/Manual/Materials.html
- https://docs.unity3d.com/Manual/shader-StandardShader.html

This chapter covers a number of techniques used to create, often manually and sometimes automatically, texture maps that are capable of giving distinctive features to materials. Hopefully, you will become confident working with Unity's **Physically-Based Shading**, which is capable of understanding differences between available workflows, is aware of the role of each material property, and is ready to make better-looking materials for your games. We have also explored ways of changing the properties of materials during runtime by accessing an object's **Material** via script.

Unity has put together a great resource for those looking for some pointers regarding how to set up maps for a variety of materials:

- The **Shader Calibration Scene**, which can be downloaded (for free) from the Unity Asset Store. It is a fantastic collection, featuring sample materials (both **Metallic** and **Specular** setup) for wood, metal, rubber, plastic, glass, skin, mud, and much more:
https://assetstore.unity.com/packages/essentials/tutorial-project s/shader-calibration-scene-25422.

References

Here's a list of interesting, detailed material on **Physically-Based Rendering** (within and outside Unity):

- For a deep understanding of **Physically-Based Rendering,** we recommend you to take a look at The Comprehensive PBR Guide, written by Wes McDermott from Allegorithmic. Allegorithmic's guide takes an in-depth look at the practical and theoretical aspects of PBR, including a great analysis of possible workflows. The guide is freely available in two volumes at `http://www.allegorithmic.com/pbr-guide`.
- Mastering Physically Based Shading in Unity 5 by Renaldas Zioma (Unity), Erland Körner (Unity), and Wes McDermott (Allegorithmic), is available at `http://www.slideshare.net/RenaldasZioma/unite2014-mastering-physically-based-shading-in-unity-5`. This is a detailed presentation about using PBS in Unity. Originally presented at the Unite 2014 conference, it contains some out-of-date information, but it is still worth taking a look at.
- Physically Based Shading in Unity 5 by Aras Pranckevičius, from Unity, is available at `http://aras-p.info/texts/talks.html`. Slides and notes from a presentation on the subject are given at the GDC.
- Tutorial: Physically Based Rendering, And You Can Too! by Joe "EarthQuake" Wilson is available at `http://www.marmoset.co/toolbag/learn/pbr-practice`. It is a great overview from the makers of Marmoset Toolbag and Skyshop.
- Polycount PBR Wiki, available at http://wiki.polycount.com/wiki/PBR, is a list of resources compiled by the Polycount community.
- Lots of general 3D graphics articles and tutorials from Jeremy Brin of Pixar: `http://3drender.com/`.

Tools

This is a new generation of texturing software for you to check out, in case you haven't yet:

- Substance Painter is a 3D painting application from Allegorithmic. It is available at `http://www.allegorithmic.com/products/substance-painter`. Again, it's worth mentioning that Allegorithmic products won't make use of Unity's Standard Shader, relying instead on substance files that are natively supported by Unity.
- Bitmap2Material creates full-featured materials (including normal maps and specular maps) from a single bitmap image. Also, it is from Allegorithmic, and it is available at `http://www.allegorithmic.com/products/bitmap2material`.
- Quixel DDO is a plugin for creating PBR-ready textures in Adobe Photoshop. From Quixel, it is available at `http://www.quixel.se/ddo`.
- Quixel NDO is a plugin for creating Normal maps in Adobe Photoshop. From Quixel, it is available at `http://www.quixel.se/ndo`.
- Mari is a 3D painting tool from The Foundry. It is available at `http://www.thefoundry.co.uk/products/mari/`.
- CrazyBump is a standalone tool for Windows and Mac, which is available at `http://www.crazybump.com`.
- The GIMP normalmap plugin, available for Windows only, is available at `http://code.google.com/p/gimp-normalmap/`.
- NVIDIA Texture Tools for Adobe Photoshop, available for Windows only, is available at `http://developer.nvidia.com/nvidia-texture-tools-adobe-photoshop`.
- The **NormalMap Online** free online tool, developed by Christian Petry, can be used to generate **Normal** maps, regardless of your computers **Operating System**. This tool can be accessed at `http://cpetry.github.io/NormalMap-Online/`.

Additional reading

Two new Unity features relating to **Materials** and **Textures** are the **Shader Graph** tool, and the **Video Player** component. Learn more about these in their own chapter: *Shader* Graphs and *Video Players.*

Creating a basic material with Standard Shader (Specular setup)

In this recipe, we will learn how to create a basic **Material** using the new **Standard Shader** (**Specular Setup**), an **Albedo** map, and a **Specular/Smoothness** map. The **Material** will feature both metallic and non-metallic parts, with various smoothness levels.

Getting ready

Two files have been prepared to support this recipe: a 3D model (in FBX format) of a battery, and an UVW template texture (in PNG format) to guide us when creating the diffuse texture map. 3D models and UVW templates can be made with 3D modeling software, such as 3DS MAX, Maya, or Blender. All necessary files are available in the 05_01 folder.

How to do it...

To create a basic material, follow these steps:

1. Create a new Unity 3D project and import the **battery.fbx** and **uvw_template.png** files to your project.

2. Place the battery model in the scene by dragging it from the Assets folder, in the **Project** panel, to the **Hierarchy** panel. Select it on the **Hierarchy** panel and make sure, via the Transform component on the **Inspector** panel, that it is positioned at X: 0, Y: 0, Z: 0.

3. Let's create a **Specular/Smoothness** map for our object. Open the image file called **uvw_template.png** in your image editor (we'll use Adobe Photoshop to illustrate the next steps). Note that the image file has only a single layer, mostly transparent, containing the UVW mapping templates that we will use as guidelines for our specular map.

4. Create a new layer and place it beneath the one with the guidelines. Fill the new layer with dark gray (R: 56, G: 56, B: 56). The guidelines will be visible at the top of the solid black fill:

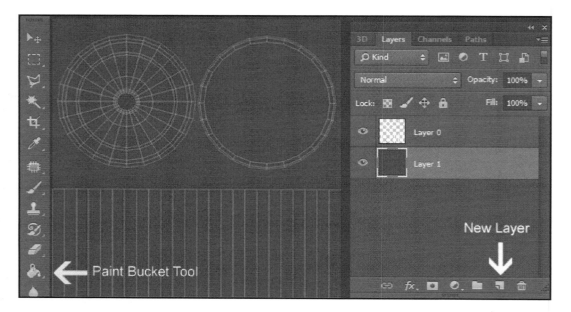

5. Create a new layer and select the upper section of the image (the one with the circles). Fill that area with a slightly-hued light gray (R: 196, G: 199, B: 199):

The RGB values for our specular map are not arbitrary: **Physically-Based Shading** takes out most of the guesswork from the mapping process, replacing it with the research for references. In our case, we have used colors based on the reflectance values of iron (the slightly-hued light gray) and plastic (the dark gray). Check out the chapter's conclusion for a list of references.

6. Use the text elements in white to add a brand, size, and positive/negative indicators to the battery body. Then, hide the guidelines layer:

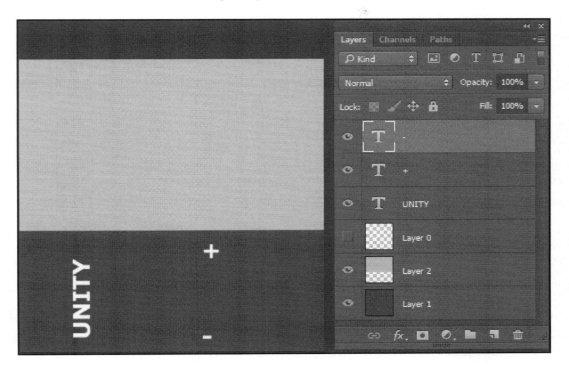

7. Select all your layers and organize them into a group (in Photoshop, this can be done by clicking on the drop-down menu in the **Layers** window and navigating to **Window | New Group from Layers...**). Name the new group **Specular**:

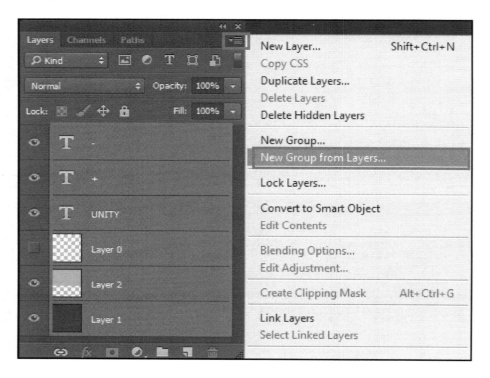

8. Duplicate the **Specular** group (in the **Layers** window, right-click on the group's name and select **Duplicate Group...**). Name the duplicated group **Smoothness**.

9. Hide the **Smoothness** group. Expand the **Specular** group and hide all text layers:

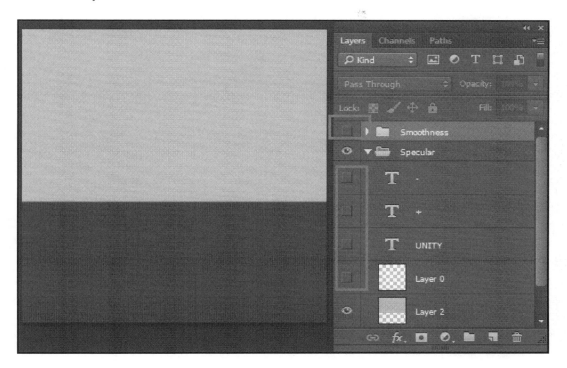

10. Unhide the **Smoothness** group, and hide the **Specular** group. Select the dark gray layer. Make an area selection around the upper region of the battery body, and fill it with light gray (R: 220, G: 220, B: 220). Rescale and rearrange the **Text** layers if needed:

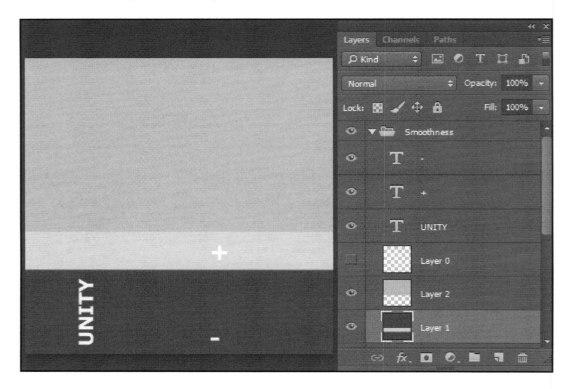

11. Duplicate the layer that contains the gray fill for the upper section of the image (the one that went over the circles).

12. To add a brushed quality to this material, add a **Noise** filter to the duplicated layer (in Photoshop, this can be done by navigating to **Filter | Noise | Add Noise...**). Use 50% as the Amount and set Monochromatic to true. Then, apply a Motion Blur filter (Filter | Blur | Motion Blur...) using 30 pixels as the **Distance**.

13. Duplicate the **Smoothness** group. Select the duplicated group and merge it into a single layer (on the **Layers** window, right-click on the group's name and select Merge Group).

14. Select the merged layer, use the *Ctrl + a* key combination to select the entire image, and copy it using the *Ctrl + c* keys:

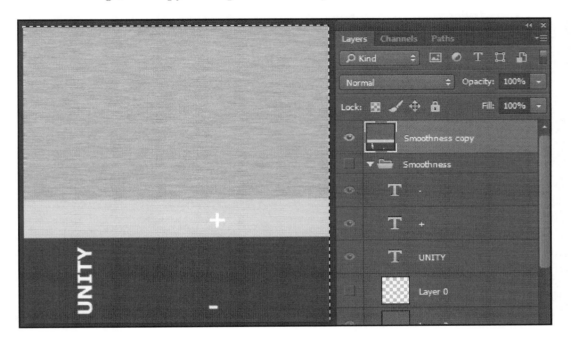

15. Hide the merged layer and the **Smoothness** group. Unhide the **Specular** group.

16. In your image editor, access the image channels window (in Photoshop, this can be done by navigating to **Window | Channels**). Create a **New Channel**. This will be our Alpha Channel.

17. Paste the image that you previously copied (from the merged layer) in to the **Alpha Channel**. Set all channels as visible:

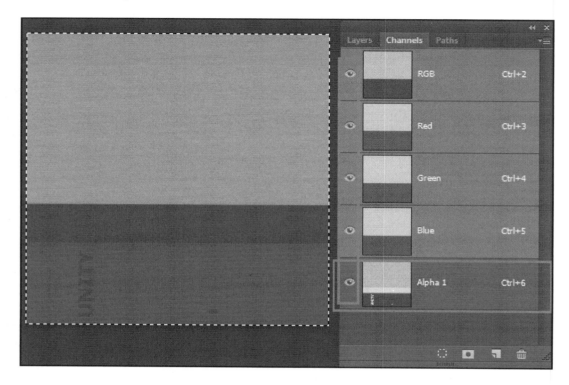

18. Save your image in the project's `Assets` folder as Battery_specular, either in Photoshop format (PSD) or TIF format.
19. Let's work on the Albedo map. Save a copy of **Battery_specular** as **Battery_albedo**. From the **Channels** window, delete the **Alpha Channel**.

20. From the **Layers** window, hide the **Smoothness** copy merged layer, and unhide the **Smoothness** group. Expand the **Smoothness** group, and hide the layer where the Noise filter was applied:

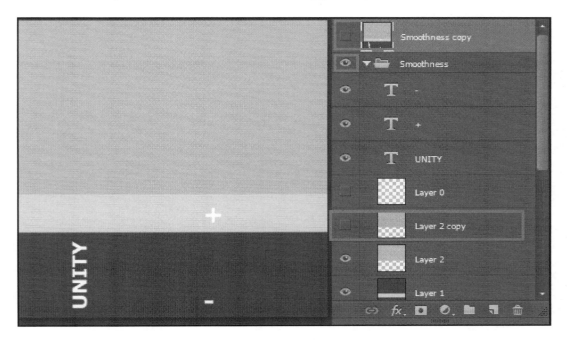

21. Change the color of the upper rectangle to black. Change the light gray area to dark red (R: 204, G: 0, B: 0), and the dark gray to red (R: 255, G: 0, B: 0). Rename the group Albedo and save the file:

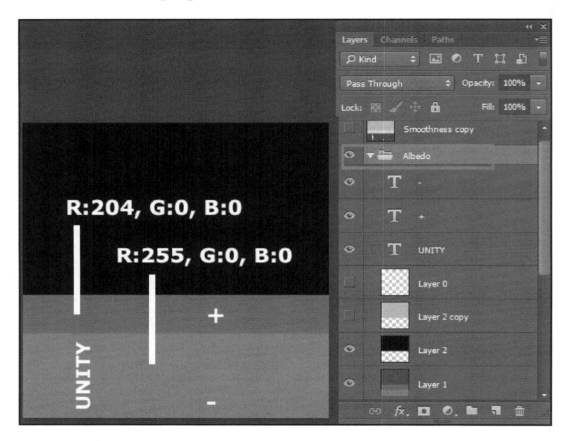

22. Go back to Unity and make sure that both files were imported. From the **Project** panel, create a new **Material** (menu: **Create | Material**). Name it **Battery_MAT**.

23. Select **Battery_MAT**. From the Inspector panel, change the **Shader** to **Standard (Specular setup)**, make sure that the rendering mode is set to **Opaque**, and that the **Smoothness slider** is at the maximum value of 1:

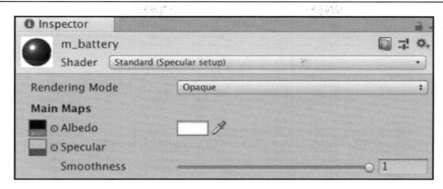

24. Set **Battery_specular** as the **Specular** map, and **Battery_albedo** as the **Albedo** map for **Battery_MAT**.

25. Drag the **Battery_MAT** Material from the **Project** project and drop it into the **battery** object in the Hierarchy:

How it works...

Ultimately, the visual aspect of the battery is a combination of three properties of its material: **Specular**, **Smoothness**, and **Albedo**.

To compose the dark red part of the plastic body, for instance, we have mixed the following:

- **The Specular map (RGB)**: Very dark grey specularity (for non-metallic appearance)
- **The Smoothness (the Alpha Channel of the Specular map)**: Light gray (for a glossy aspect)
- **The Albedo map**: Dark red (for a dark-red color)

The light red portion, on the other hand, combines the following:

- **The Specular map (RGB)**: That same dark grey specular
- **The Smoothness (the Alpha Channel of the Specular map)**: Dark gray (for a matte aspect)
- **The Albedo map**: Red (for a red color)

Finally, the brushed metal used for the top and bottom covers combines the following:

- **The Specular map (RGB)**: Light grey (for a metallic aspect)
- **The Smoothness (the Alpha Channel of the Specular map)**: A blurred grey noise pattern (for a brushed aspect)
- **The Albedo map**: Black (for a red color)

Regarding how the image layers are structured, it's good practice to organize your layers into groups named after the property that they are related to. As texture maps get more diversified, it can be a good idea to keep a file that contains all the maps for quick reference and consistency.

There's more...

The following are some things you should have in mind when working with Albedo maps.

Setting the texture type for an image file

Since image files can be used for several purposes within Unity (**Texture Maps**, UI textures, cursors, and more), it's a good idea to check whether the right **Texture Type** is assigned to your file. This can be done by selecting the image file in the **Project** panel, and in the **Inspector** panel by using the drop-down menu to select the right **Texture Type** (in this case, Texture). Please note that other settings can be adjusted, such as **Wrap Mode, Filter Mode,** and **Maximum Size**. This last parameter is very useful if you want to keep your Texture maps small in size for your game, while still being able to edit them in full size.

Combining the map with color

When editing a **Material**, the color picker to the right of the **Albedo** map slot, on the **Inspector** panel, can be used to select the **Material's** color, in case there is no **Texture** map. If a **Texture** map is being used, the selected color will be multiplied to the image, allowing variations on the **Material's** color hue.

Adapting a basic material from Specular setup to Metallic

For a better understanding of the differences between **Metallic** and **Specular** workflows, we will modify the **Albedo** and **Specular/Smoothness** maps that are used on a Specular setup Material, in order to adapt them to the Metallic workflow. The material to be generated will feature both metallic and non-metallic parts, with various smoothness levels.

Getting ready

This recipe builds on the previous one, so make a copy of that project and use the copy for this recipe.

How to do it...

To create a basic Material using the Metallic workflow, follow these steps:

1. From the **Project** panel, select the **battery_prefab** element. From the Inspector, access its **Material** (named **Battery_MAT**) and change its **Shader** to **Standard** (as opposed to its current shader – **Standard (Specular setup)**):

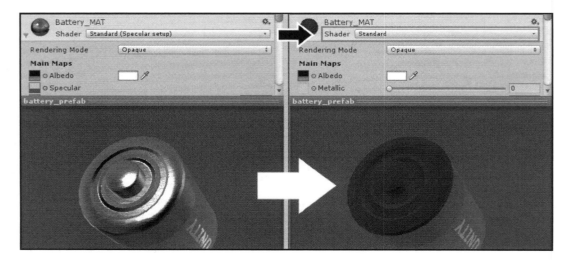

2. In the **Project** panel, find the **Battery_specular** map and rename it **Battery_metallic**. Open it in your image editor (we'll use Adobe Photoshop to illustrate the following steps).

3. Find the layer group named Specular and rename it Metallic. Fill the light gray layer (named **Layer 2**, in the **Metallic** group) with white (R: 255, G: 255, B: 255), and the dark gray layer (named **Layer 1**, in the **Metallic** group) with black (R: 0, G: 0, B: 0). Save the file:

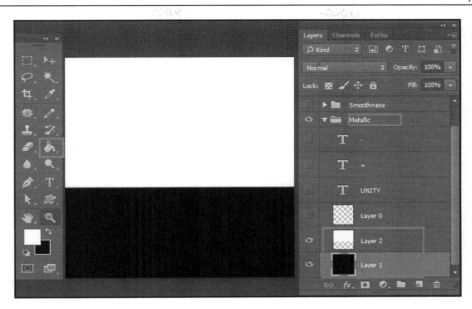

4. Go back to Unity. From the **Inspector**, set the **modified Battery_metallic** map as the **Metallic** map of the **Battery_MAT** material. Also, set **None** as the Albedo map for that **Material**. This will give you an idea of how the **Material** is coming along:

5. Let's adjust the **Albedo** texture map. From the **Project** panel, locate the **Battery_albedo** map and open it in your image editor. Use the **Paint Bucket** tool to fill the black area of **Layer 2**, in the **Albedo** group, with light gray (R: 196, G: 199, B: 199). Save the file:

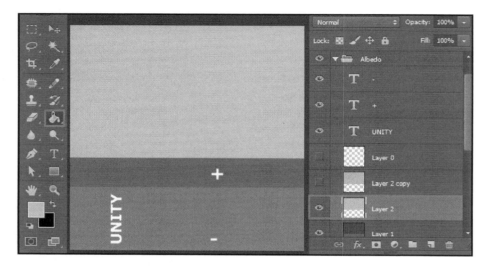

6. Go back to Unity. From the **Inspector**, set the modified **Battery_albedo** map as the Albedo map of the **Battery_MAT** material.

7. Your **Material** is ready, combining visual properties based on the different maps that you have edited and assigned:

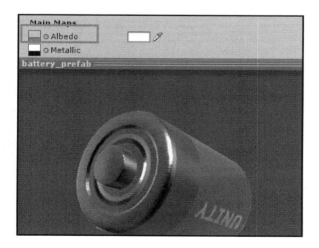

How it works...

The visual aspect of the battery is a combination of three properties of its material: Metallic, Smoothness, and Albedo.

To compose the dark-red part of the plastic body, for instance, we have mixed the following:

- **The Metallic map (RGB)**: Black (for a non-metallic appearance)
- **The Smoothness (the Alpha Channel of a Metallic map)**: Light gray (for a glossy appearance)
- **The Albedo map**: Dark red (for a dark-red color)

The light-red portion, on the other hand, combines the following:

- **The Metallic map (RGB)**: Black
- **The Smoothness (the Alpha Channel of the Metallic map)**: Dark gray (for a matte appearance)
- **The Albedo map**: Red (for a red color)

Finally, the brushed metal used for the top and bottom covers combines the following:

- **The Metallic map (RGB)**: White (for a metallic aspect)
- **The Smoothness (the Alpha Channel of the Metallic map)**: Blurred grey noise pattern (for a brushed appearance);
- **The Albedo map**: Light grey (for an iron-like appearance)

Remember to organize your layers into groups named after the property that they are related to.

Applying Normal maps to a Material

Normal Maps are generally used to simulate complex geometry that would be too expensive, in terms of computer processing, to be actually represented by the 3D polygons during the game's runtime. To oversimplify: **Normal Maps** fake complex geometry on low-definition 3D meshes. These maps can be generated either by projecting high-definition 3D meshes onto low-poly ones (a technique usually referred to as baking), or, as will be the case for this recipe, from another **Texture** map:

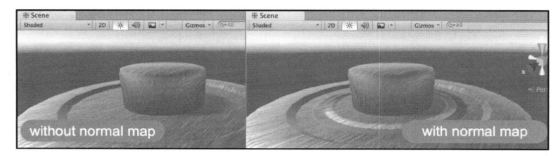

Getting ready

For this recipe, we will prepare two **Texture** maps: the **Heightmap** and the **Normal** map. The former will be made from simple shapes in an image editor. The latter will be automatically processed from the Heightmap. Although there are a number of tools that can be used to generate **Normal** maps, we will use the free, online NormalMap tool: `http://cpetry.github.io/NormalMap-Online/`.

To help you with this recipe, we've provided an FBX 3D model of the battery (**battery.fbx**), and its **Albedo** and **Specular Textures** (**Battery_albedo.tif and Battery_specular.tif**).

We've also included the UVW template texture (in PNG format) to guide you when creating the diffuse **Texture** map. All the files are in the `05_03` folder.

How to do it...

To apply a **Normal Map** to a **Material**, follow these steps:

1. Import **battery.fbx** and its **Albedo** and **Specular Textures** to your project.

2. Add an instance of your 3D model in the Scene by dragging asset **battery** from the Project panel into the Scene (or Hierarchy) panel.

3. In the **Project** panel, select model asset **battery**. In the **Inspector**, click the **Materials** button and then click **Extract Materials...** You should now have a **Material** asset file in the **Project** panel named **BatteryMaterial**.

4. Select **BatteryMaterial**, and change the **Shader** to **Standard (Specular setup)**. Drag the **Battery_albedo Texture** from the **Project** panel into the **Albedo Texture** slot in the **Inspector**. Drag the **Battery_specular Texture** from the **Project** panel into the **Specular Texture** slot.

5. After comparing the **battery** model in your project with some reference photos, inform yourself about the features that should be reproduced by the Normal map: (A) a bumpy ring at the top, and (B) some circular creases at the bottom:

6. In an image editor, open **uvw_template.png**. Create a new layer, fill it with grey (RGB: 128), and position it below the pre-existing layer:

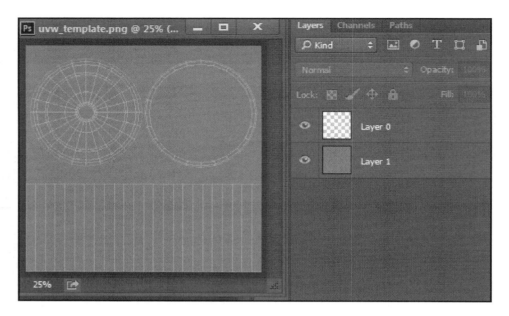

7. On a separate layer, draw a white circle centered on the battery's top. Then, on another layer, draw a black circle, centered on the battery's bottom:

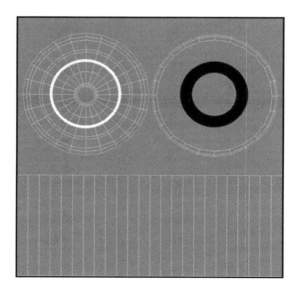

8. If you have used vector shapes to make the circles, rasterize their layers (in Adobe Photoshop, right-click on the layer's name and select the **Rasterize Layer** option from the context menu).

9. Blur the white circle (in Photoshop, this can be done by navigating to **Filter | Blur | Gaussian Blur...**). Use 4,0 pixels as the **Radius**.

10. Hide the UVW template layer and save the image as Battery_height.png.

11. If you want to convert the Heightmap directly from Unity, import it into your project. Select it from the Project panel and, from the Inspector panel, change its Texture Type to Normal map. Check the **Create** from Grayscale option, adjust **Bumpiness** and **Filtering** as you like, and click on **Apply** to save the changes:

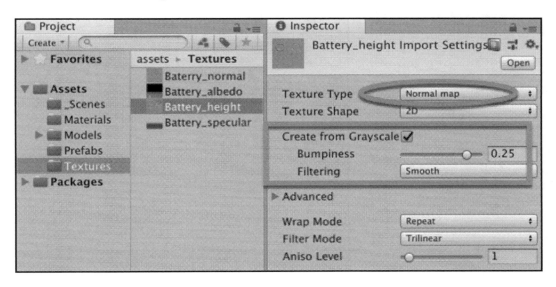

12. To convert your **Heightmap** externally, go
to `http://cpetry.github.io/NormalMap-Online/`. Drag the
Battery_height.png file to the appropriate image slot. Feel free to play with
the **Strength, Level,** and **Blur/Sharp** parameters:

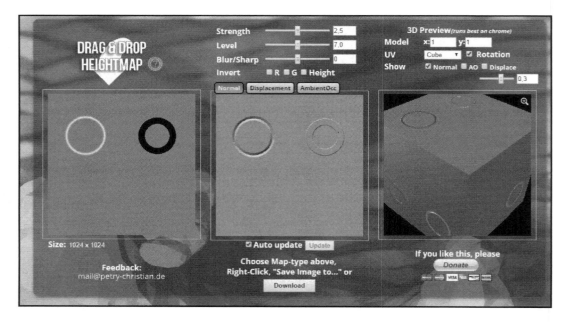

13. Save the resulting **Normal** map as **Battery_normal.jpg** and add it to your
Unity project.
14. In Unity, select **Battery_normal** from the **Project** panel. Then, in the
Inspector, change its **Texture Type** to **Normal**, leaving the Create from
Grayscale box unchecked. Click on Apply to save the changes.

15. In the **Project** panel, select the **BatteryMaterial** asset. In the Inspector for the **Material** component, assign **Battery_normal** to the **Normal Map** slot. To adjust its intensity and direction, change its value to -0.35:

How it works...

The Normal Map was calculated from the grey values on the **Heightmap**, where the lighter tones were interpreted as recesses (applied to the top of the battery), and the darker tones as bulges (applied to the bottom). Since the desired output was actually the opposite, it was necessary to adjust the **Normal Map** to a negative value (**-0.35**). Another possible solution to the issue would have been to redraw the **Heightmap** and switch the colors for the white and black circles.

Adding Transparency and Emission maps to a material

The **Emission** property can be used to simulate a variety of self-illuminated objects, from the LEDs of mobile displays to futuristic Tron suits. **Transparency**, on the other hand, can make the diffuse color of a **Material** more or less visible. In this recipe, you will learn how to configure these properties to produce a toy's cardboard packaging that features a partially-transparent plastic case, cutouts (totally transparent), and glow-in-the-dark text:

Getting ready

For this recipe, we have prepared two files in the 05_04 folder:

- **package.fbx**: A 3D object of a package (FBX format)
- **card_diffuse_start.png**: The diffused texture map for the packaging (PNG format)

Also provided are the two final, image-edited files you'll create in the project:

- **card_diffuse.png**: The **Albedo** texture map for the packaging with cutouts (PNG format)
- **card_emission.png**: The **Emission Texture** map for the emission glow text (PNG format)

How to do it...

To add transparency and color emission maps to materials, follow these steps:

1. Import the provided files.
2. Duplicate the **card_diffuse_start Texture**, naming the **copy card_diffuse**.
3. From the **Project** panel, drag the FBX model **package** into the **Hierarchy** to create a GameObject in the **Scene**.
4. Create a new **Material named m_card**. Choose **Project** menu: **Create | Material**. Drag the **card_diffuse Texture** into the **Albedo** property of **m_card**.
5. In the **Hierarchy**, select **PackageCard** (child of package), and assign it your new **m_card** Material.
6. Create a new **Material** named **m_plastic**. Choose **Project** menu: **Create | Material**. Change its **Rendering Mode** to **Transparent**. Use the Diffuse color picker to change the color's RGB values to 56/56/56, and **Alpha** to 25. Change the **Smoothness** level to 0.9:

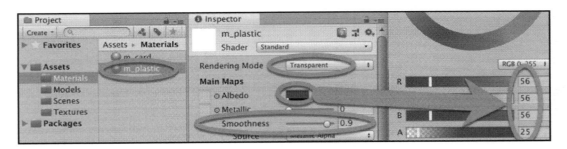

7. In the **Hierarchy**, select **PackagePlastic** (child of package), and assign it your new **m_plastic Material**. The plastic portion of the 3D model should now appear partially transparent, as if made of plastic.

8. To create the cutouts around the package and hang hole, we need to first prepare the diffuse image in an image editor (such as Photoshop). Open the **card_diffuse Texture** in your image editor.

9. We will add transparency to the image by deleting the white areas around the package (and the hang hole). Make a selection of those areas (in Photoshop, this can be done with the **Magic Wand Tool**).

10. Make sure you unlock the **Background** layer by clicking on the lock icon, to the left of the layer's name:

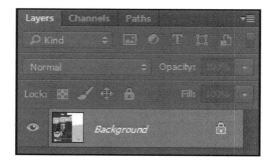

11. Delete the previously-made selection (this can be done in Photoshop by pressing the Delete key). The background of the image should be transparent:

12. Save your file in your image editor, and return to Unity.

13. Select the **m_card Material** in the Project panel. In the Inspector, change its **Rendering Mode** to **Cutout**, and adjust its **Alpha Cutoff** to 0.9:

Choosing **Cutout** means that your material can be either invisible or fully visible, not allowing for semi-transparency. The **Alpha Cutoff** is used to get rid of unwanted pixels around the transparent borders.

14. Let's work on the **Emission** map for the bright lettering. From the **Assets** folder, duplicate the **card_diffuse.png Texture**, rename it **card_emission.png**, and open it in your image editor.

15. Select all the characters from the Ms. Laser inscription and the green star (in Photoshop, this can be done with the **Magic Wand** tool, keeping the *Shift* key pressed while selecting multiple areas).

16. Copy and paste your selection into a new layer. Then, select it and apply a Noise filter to it (in Photoshop, this can be done by navigating to **Filter | Noise | Add Noise...**). Use 50% as the value.

17. Create a new layer and, using a tool such as the **Paint Bucket**, fill it with black (R: 0, G: 0, B: 0). Place this black layer beneath the one with the colored elements.

18. Flatten your image (in Photoshop this can be done by navigating to **Layer |
    Flatten Image**):

19. Save your file in your image editor, and return to Unity.
20. Select the **m_card Material** in the **Project** panel. Check the **Emission**
    property – three new properties should appear:
    - **A Texture slot**: Set this to Texture **card_emission** (drag asset file
      from the Project panel)
    - **A Color slot**: Set this to white (R: 255; G: 255; B: 255)
    - **A Global Illumination drop-down menu**: Ensure this is set to
      Baked (so that its glow won't be added to the Lightmaps or
      influence the illumination in Real-Time):

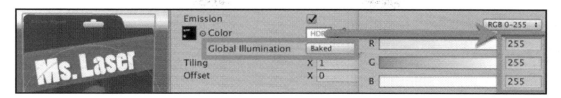

How it works...

Unity is able to read four channels of a texture map: R (Red), G (Green), B (Blue), and A (Alpha). When set to **Transparent** or **Cutout**, the **Alpha Channel** of the diffuse texture map sets the transparency of the material according to each pixel's brightness level (the Cutout mode will not render semi-transparency – only fully visible or invisible pixels).

We didn't add an **Alpha Channel** – this is because Photoshop exports the PNG's Alpha map based on its transparency. To help you visualize the Alpha map, the provided folder also contains the **package_diffuse.tif** (TIF format) Texture file; an image file featuring an **Alpha** map that works in exactly the same way as the PNG file that we have generated:

Regarding the **Emission** texture map, Unity assigns its RGB colors to the Material, combining them with the appropriate color selection slot, and allows adjustments to the intensity of that Emission.

There's more...

Let's look at a little more information on **Transparency** and **Emission**.

Using texture maps with the Transparent Mode

Please note that you can use a bitmap texture for the **Diffuse** map in the **Transparent** render mode. In this case, RGB values will be interpreted as the Diffuse color, while the Alpha will be used to determine that pixel's transparency (in this case, semi-transparent materials are allowed).

Avoiding issues with the semi-transparent objects

You might have noticed that the plastic case was made from two objects (**PackagePlastic** and **innerPlastic**). This was done to avoid z-sorting problems, where faces are rendered in front of other geometry when they should be behind it. Having multiple meshes instead of a single one allows these faces to be correctly sorted for rendering. **Materials** in the **Cutout** mode are not affected by this problem, though.

Emitting light over other objects

The Emission value can be used to calculate the **Material's** light projection over other objects when using Lightmaps.

Highlighting materials at mouse-over

Changing the color of an object at runtime can be a very effective way of letting players know that they can interact with it. This is very useful in a number of game genres, such as puzzles and point-and-click adventures, and it can also be used to create 3D user interfaces.

How to do it...

To highlight a material at mouse-over, follow these steps:

1. Create a new 3D project.

2. Create **3D Cube** in the scene (Hierarchy menu: **Create | 3D Object | Cube**).

3. In the Project panel, create a new **Material** aaset named **m_cube**. Set its **Albedo Color** to red.

4. In the **Hierarchy**, select the **Cube** GameObject, and assign it the **m_cube Material** (drag the asset from the Project panel).

5. Create a new C# script-class named **MouseOverHighlighter**, and add an instance object as a component to the **Cube**:

```
using UnityEngine;

public class MouseOverHighlighter : MonoBehaviour {
public Color mouseOverColor = Color.yellow;

private Material originalMaterial;
private Material mouseOverMaterial;
private MeshRenderer meshRenderer;

void Start() {
    meshRenderer = GetComponent<MeshRenderer>();
    originalMaterial = meshRenderer.material;
    mouseOverMaterial = new
    Material(meshRenderer.sharedMaterial);
    mouseOverMaterial.color = mouseOverColor;
}

void OnMouseOver() {
    meshRenderer.material = mouseOverMaterial;
}

void OnMouseExit() {
    meshRenderer.material = originalMaterial;
}
}
```

6. With the **Cube** selected, in the **Mouse Over Highlighter (Script)** component in the Inspector, you'll see the mouse-over color is yellow. You may wish to change this.

7. Test the scene. The **Cube** will be highlighted red when the mouse is over it (and green when clicked on).

How it works...

The Start() method does four things:

- Stores a reference to the **MeshRenderer** component in the meshRenderer variable
- Stores a reference to the original Material of the GameObject in the originalMaterial variable
- Creates a new Material named mouseOverMaterial
- Sets the color of mouseOverMaterial to the color in the **mouseOverColor** public variable

The cube is automatically sent the mouse enter/exit events as the user moves the mouse pointer over and away from the part of the screen where the cube is visible. Our code adds a behavior to the cube when these events are detected.

When the OnMouseOver message is received, the method with that name is invoked, and the GameObject's material is set to mouseOverMaterial.
When the OnMouseExit message is received, the GameObject's material is returned to originalMaterial.

The material property of the Renderer is a copy of the

If the Material of a GameObject is shared by several objects, we must be careful when changing Material properties to only change those we want to. If we wish to only change values for a particular GameObject, use the .material property of Renderer – since a separate clone is created if more than one object uses the same Material. If we want all GameObjects using the same Material to be affected by changes, use the .sharedMaterial property of Renderer. Since there was only one GameObject in this recipe, either could have been used.
Read more
at https://docs.unity3d.com/ScriptReference/Renderer-materi al.html

There's more...

Here are some ways to enhance this recipe.

Collider needed for custom meshes

We created a primitive 3D Cube – this automatically has a Box Collider component. If you were to use the preceding script with a custom 3D mesh object, ensure the GameObject has a **Physics | Collider** component, so that it will respond to mouse events.

Mouse Down/Up events – for clicking color

We can extend our code to also display a different color when an object is clicked on (mouse down/up events).

Do the following:

1. Remove the scripted `MouseOverHighlighter` from the Cube `GameObject`.

2. Create a new C# script-class named `MouseOverDownHighlighter`, and add an instance object as a component to the Cube:

```
using UnityEngine;

public class MouseOverDownHighlighter : MonoBehaviour {
    public Color mouseOverColor = Color.yellow;
    public Color mouseDownColor = Color.green;

    private Material originalMaterial;
    private Material mouseOverMaterial;
    private Material mouseDownMaterial;
    private MeshRenderer meshRenderer;

    private bool mouseOver = false;

    void Start() {
        meshRenderer = GetComponent<MeshRenderer>();
        originalMaterial = meshRenderer.sharedMaterial;
        mouseOverMaterial =
NewMaterialWithColor(mouseOverColor);
        mouseDownMaterial =
NewMaterialWithColor(mouseDownColor);
```

```
        }

        void OnMouseEnter() {
            mouseOver = true;
            meshRenderer.sharedMaterial = mouseOverMaterial;
        }

        void OnMouseDown() {
            meshRenderer.sharedMaterial = mouseDownMaterial;
        }

        void OnMouseUp() {
            if (mouseOver)
                OnMouseEnter();
            else
                OnMouseExit();
        }

        void OnMouseExit() {
            mouseOver = false;
            meshRenderer.sharedMaterial = originalMaterial;
        }

        private Material NewMaterialWithColor(Color newColor) {
            Material material = new
  Material(meshRenderer.sharedMaterial);
            material.color = newColor;

            return material;
        }
    }
```

3. There are two public Colors: one for mouse-over and one for mouse-down (click) highlighting.
4. Run the Scene. You should now see different highlight colors when the mouse pointer is over the Cube, and when you click the mouse button when the mouse pointer is over the Cube.

Since we are creating two new Materials, the reusable `NewMaterialWithColor(...)` C# method is included above, to simplify the content of the `Start()` method. A Boolean (true/false) variable has been introduced, so that the correct behavior occurs after the mouse button is released, depending on whether the mouse pointer is still over the object (`mouseOver = true`) or has moved away from the object (`mouseOver = false`).

Adding Detail maps to a material

When creating a large object, there is not only the desire to **Texture** it as a whole, but also to add details that can make it look better when viewed up close. To overcome the need for large, memory-hogging, highly-detailed texture maps, the use of Detail maps can make a real difference.

In this recipe, we will add **Detail maps** to a rocket toy by applying a **Detail mask** and a **Detail Normal** map. In our case, we want to add a textured quality (and a stripe pattern) to the green plastic, except in the region where there is a battery compartment and the toy's logo:

Getting ready

For this recipe, we have prepared three files in the 05_06 folder:

- **rocketToy.fbx**: A 3D object of a package (FBX format)
- **ship_diffuse.png**: The diffused texture map for the rocket ship toy (PNG format)
- **ship_height.png**: The heightmap to be used to create a normal map (PNG format)

Also provided are the four final, image-edited files you'll create in the project:

- **detail_diffuse.png**: The Albedo texture map for the packaging with cutouts (PNG format)
- **detail_height.png**: The greyscale gradient circle – for the dimpled surface detail effect (PNG format)
- **ship_mask.tif**: The detail mask – indicating how much the text and battery holder appear raised up (TIF format)
- **ship_mask2.tif**: The detail mask – where the Alpha for the battery holder is greater, so no dimples will appear from `detail_height` (TIF format)

How to do it...

To add the Detail maps to your object, follow these steps:

1. Import the provided files.
2. In the **Project** panel, select the **rocketToy** model asset. In the **Inspector**, click the `Materials` button and then click **Extract Materials...** Extract the model's Materials into a new folder named `Materials`. You should now have five Materials for each part of the rocketToy model (`MAT_base/end/level1/2/3`):

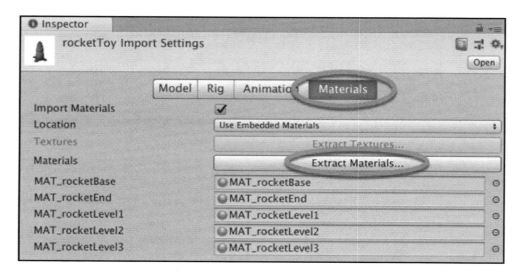

3. Select **Material MAT_rocketLevel1,** and change the **Shader** to **Standard** (**Specular setup**). Drag the `ship_diffuse` Texture from the Project panel into the **Albedo** Texture slot in the Inspector properties for **MAT_rocketLevel1.**

4. Drag the `rocketToy` model asset from the **Project** panel into the **Scene** panel (or Hierarchy) to add an instance of the model as a `GameObject` in the Scene. You should be able to see the image of the text of the toy's logo ("Rocket") and the battery compartment in level 1 (above the base).

5. Duplicate the **ship_diffuse** Texture, naming the copy **ship_mask.**

6. Open **ship_mask** in your image editor. Select all the solid green pixels around the logo and battery compartment (in Photoshop, this can be done with the Magic Wand tool, keeping the *Shift* key pressed while selecting multiple areas):

7. Keeping your selection active, access the image **Channels** window (in Photoshop, this can be done by navigating to **Window | Channels**). Click on **New Channel**. This will be our **Alpha Channel**:

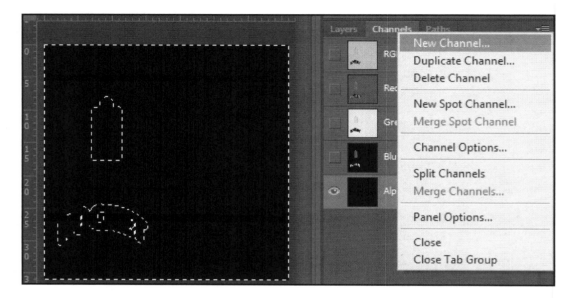

8. Hide the **Red, Green**, and **Blue** channels. Select the Alpha Channel and paint the selection white. Select the area of the battery compartment and paint it grey (R, G, and B: 100):

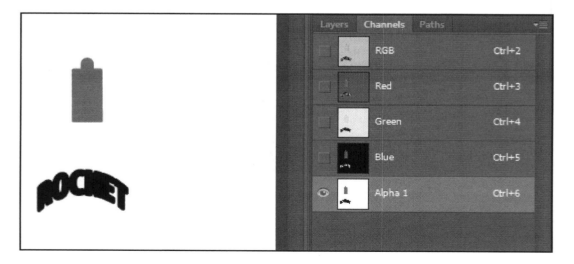

9. Save it in the TIF format as **ship_mask.tif**, in the Assets folder. Make sure that you include **Alpha Channels**:

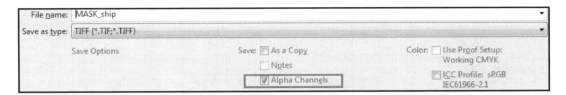

10. Now that we have the mask, let's create a diffuse map for our detail. In your image editor, create a new image with the following dimensions: width: 64, and height: 64:

11. Fill the new image with grey (R, G, and B: 128). Use shapes or rectangular fills to create a dark grey (R, G, and B: 100) horizontal line that is about 16 pixels tall:

12. Save the image as detail_diff.png in the Assets folder.

13. Create a new 64 x 64 image. Use a Gradient tool to create a black and white Radial Gradient (in Photoshop, this can be done with the Gradient Tool in Radial mode):

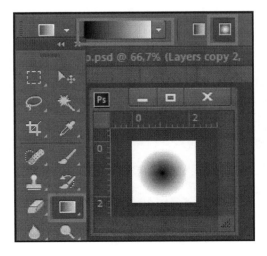

14. Save the image as **detail_height.png** in the `Assets` folder. Return to the Unity editor.

15. From the `Assets` folder, select **detail_height**. In the **Inspector**, change its **Texture** Type to **Normal** map, check the Create from **Grayscale** option, adjust Bumpiness to 0.25, and set **Filtering** to smooth. Click on **Apply** to save the changes:

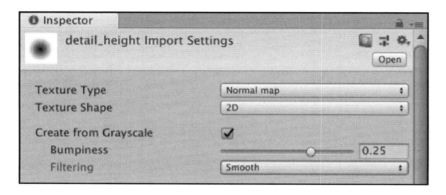

16. Do the same for the **ship_height** Texture – in the **Inspector**, change its **Texture** Type to Normal map, check the **Create** from **Grayscale** option, adjust **Bumpiness** to 0.25, and set Filtering to smooth. Click on **Apply** to save the changes.

17. Select the `MAT_rocketLevel1` Material and view its properties in the **Inspector**. Set the following properties:
    - Assign the **ship_height** Texture to the **Normal** Map slot, and set its **intensity** to 0.3.
    - Assign the **ship_mask** Texture to the **Detail Mask** slot.
    - Assign the **detail_diff** Texture to Secondary Maps | Detail **Albedo x 2**.
    - Assign the **detail_height** Texture as **Secondary Maps** | **Normal Map**, and set its **intensity** to 0.6.

18. In the Secondary Maps section, change the Tiling values as follows:
    - Set **Tiling X** to 200 and **Y** to 50.
    - Set **UV Set** to **UV1**.

Until we set **UV Set** to **UV1**, you might have noticed that the pattern was not seamless. This was because we were using the same **UV Set** from our Diffuse Texture. However, the object has been assigned to two different UV channels (back when it was being modelled). While UV channel 1 contains the mapping for our Diffuse map, UV channel 2 uses a basic cylindrical mapping. We need to change the **Secondary Maps** section's UV Set from **UV0** to **UV1**.

19. The **Detail map** for your Material is ready:

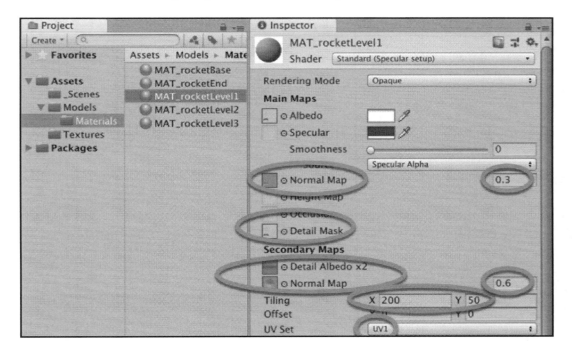

How it works...

When in use, Secondary Maps are blended onto the Material's primary Diffuse and Normal maps – that's why our object is green even after the Diffuse Detail is applied: the grey tones are superimposed on the original Diffuse Texture. By using a Detail Mask, the artist defines which areas of the object should be affected by Secondary Maps. This is great for customization, and also for creating nuances (such as the semi-bumped battery compartment in our example).

Another helpful feature is the possibility of using a separate UV channel for Details maps and Tiling. Besides adding variation to Texture mapping, this allows us to paint the details that can be perceived even at a very close distance by dramatically enhancing the visual quality of our objects.

Fading the transparency of a material

A feature of many games is for objects to fade away to invisible, or appear gradually from invisible to fully visible. Unity provides the special Rendering Mode of Fade for exactly this purpose.

In this recipe, we will create an object that, once clicked, fades out and disappears. We'll also look at how to enahnce the code, to take account of the GameObject's own initial alpha value, to self-destruct when fading has finished and so on.

How to do it...

Follow these steps:

1. Create a new **3D Sphere**, named **Sphere-Game**. Choose menu: **3D Object | Sphere**.
2. Select **Sphere-Game** and ensure it has a Collider (if you are using a custom 3D object, you might have to add a collider through menu: Add **Component | Physics | Box (or Mesh)** Collider).
3. Create a new Material named **m_fade**.
4. With the **m_fade Material** selected, change its **Rendering Mode** to **Fade** in the Inspector:

The **Fade** rendering mode is specifically designed for situations such as this. Other rendering modes, such as Transparent, will turn the Albedo color transparent, but not the specular highlights nor the reflections, in which case the object will still be visible.

5. Apply the **m_fade Material** to **Sphere-Game** by dragging it from the Project panel into the Sphere-Game GameObject.

6. Create a new C# script-class named FadeAway and add an instance object as a component to **Sphere-Game**:

```
using UnityEngine;
    public class FadeObject: MonoBehaviour {
        public float fadeDurationSeconds = 1.0f;
        public float alphaStart = 1.0f;
        public float alphaEnd = 0.0f;
        private float startTime;
        private MeshRenderer meshRenderer;
        private Color fadeColor;
        private bool isFading = false;

        void Start () {
            meshRenderer = GetComponent<MeshRenderer>();
            fadeColor = meshRenderer.material.color;
            UpdateMaterialAlpha(alphaStart);
        }

        void Update() {
            if (isFading)
                FadeAlpha();
        }

        void OnMouseUp() {
            StartFading();
        }

        private void StartFading()
        {
            startTime = Time.time;
            isFading = true;
        }

        private void FadeAlpha()
        {
            float timeFading = Time.time - startTime;
            float fadePercentage = timeFading /
            fadeDurationSeconds;
            float alpha = Mathf.Lerp(alphaStart, alphaEnd,
            fadePercentage);
            UpdateMaterialAlpha(alpha);

            if (fadePercentage >= 1)
                isFading = false;
```

```
        }

        private void UpdateMaterialAlpha(float newAlpha) {
            fadeColor.a = newAlpha;
            meshRenderer.material.color = fadeColor;
        }
    }
```

7. Play your **Scene** and click on the **Sphere** to see it fade away and self-destruct.

How it works...

The opaqueness of the material using a transparent **Shader** is determined by the **alpha** value of its main **color**. This recipe is based around changing the Alpha value of the **Color** of the **MeshRenderer**.

There are three public variables:

- `fadeDurationSeconds`: The time in seconds we want our fading to take
- `alphaStart`: The initial alpha (transparency) we want the GameObject to start with (1 = fully visible, 0 = invisible)
- `alphaEnd`: The alpha value we want to fade the GameObject into

The `UpdateMaterialAlpha(...)` method updates the alpha value of the GameObject's Color object with the given value by updating the alpha value of the `fadeColor` Color variable, and then forcing the MeshRenderer Material to update its Color value to match those in fadeColor.

When the Scene begins, the `Start()` method caches a reference to the MeshRenderer component (the `meshRenderer` variable), and also the Color object of the Material of the MeshRenderer (the `fadeColor` variable). Finally, the GameObject's alpha is set to match the value of variable alphaStart, by invoking the `UpdateMaterialAlpha(...)` method.

The OnMouseUp() method is invoked when the user clicks the **GameObject** with their mouse. This invokes the StartFading() method.

 The actions to start fading weren't simply put in this method, since we may also wish to start fading due to some other events (such as keyboard clicks, a timer hitting some value, or an NPC changing into some mode such as dying). So we separate the logic that detects that event that we are interested has taken place, with the actions we wish to perform, in this case to start the fading process.

The StartFading() method records the current **Time**, since we need that to know when to finish fading (time when we started fading + fadeDurationSeconds). Also the isFading Boolean flag is set to true, so logic elsewhere relating to fading will know it's time to do things.

The Update() method, called each frame, tests whether the isFading flag is **true**. If it is, the FadeAlpha() method is invoked for each frame.

The FadeAlpha() method is where the majority of our alpha-fading logic is based:

- timeFading is calculated: The time since we started fading
- fadePercentage is calculated: How far we are from start (0) to finish (1) of our fading
- alpha is calculated: The appropriate alpha value for our fade percentage, using the Lerp(...) method to choose an intermedia value based on a 0..1 percentage
- The UpdateMaterialAlpha(...) method with the new alpha value
- If fading has finished (fadePercentage >= 1), we set the isFading Boolean flag to false to indicate this

There's more...

Here are some ways to enhance our fading features.

Start with keypress and fade in from invisible

The preceding code can fade in from invisible (`alphaStart` = 0) to fully visible (`alphaEnd` = 1). However, if we can't see the object initially, then it's a bit much to ask the player to click an invisible Sphere! So let's add code to the `Update()` method (checked each frame) to detect when the *F* key is pressed, as an alternative way to start our fading process:

```
void Update()
 {
 if (Input.GetKeyDown(KeyCode.F))
 StartFading();

 if (isFading)
 FadeAlpha();
 }
```

Destroy object when fading complete

If fading to invisible is how a GameObject communicates to the player that it is leaving the scene (completed/dying), then we may want that GameObject to be Destroyed after the fading process is completed. Let's add this feature to our code.

Do the following:

1. Add a new public Boolean variable to our script (default to false):

   ```
   public bool destroyWhenFadingComplete = true;
   ```

2. Add a new `EndFade()` method, which sets `isFading` to `false`, and then tests whether the public `destroyWhenFadingComplete` variable was set to true, and if so, Destroys the GameObject:

   ```
   private void EndFade() {
           isFading = false;

           if(destroyWhenFadingComplete)
               Destroy (gameObject);
       }
   ```

3. Refactor the `FadeAlpha()` method so that it invokes `EndFade()` when the fading is completed (`fadeProgress >= fadeDurationSeconds`):

```
private void FadeAlpha()
{
    float fadeProgress = Time.time - startTime;
    float alpha = Mathf.Lerp(alphaStart, alphaEnd, fadeProgress
        / fadeDurationSeconds);
    UpdateMaterialAlpha(alpha);

    if (fadeProgress >= fadeDurationSeconds)
        EndFade();
}
```

Using GameObect's alpha as our starting alpha value

It may be that the game designer has set the alpha value of a GameObject in the Inspector to the initial value they want. So let's enhance our code to allow this to be indicated by checking a public Boolean flag variable in the **Inspector**, and adding code to read and use the GameObject's alpha if that option is chosen.

Do the following:

1. In the **Inspector**, click the **Color picker** for the Material **Albedo**, and set the Alpha value to something other than 255 (for example, set to 32, which is mostly transparent):

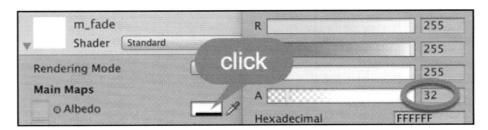

2. Add a new public Boolean variable to our script (default to false):

```
public bool useMaterialAlpha = false;
```

3. Add logic to the `Start()` method so that if this flag is true, we use the alpha value of the Color read from the GameObject's Material as the Scene begins (`fadeColor.a`):

```
void Start () {
        meshRenderer = GetComponent<MeshRenderer>();

        // set object material's original color as fadeColor
        fadeColor = meshRenderer.material.color;

        // IF using material's original alpha value, THEN use
            //material's alpha value for alphaStart
        if (useMaterialAlpha)
            alphaStart = fadeColor.a;

        // start object's alpha at our alphaStart value
        UpdateMaterialAlpha(alphaStart);
}
```

Using a coroutine for our fading loop

Where possible, we should avoid adding code in the `Update()` method, since this is invoked every frame, and so can reduce the performance of our games, especially if many objects have scripted components with `Update()` methods, all testing flags every frame.

One very effective solution is to invoke a coroutine when we want some actions performed over several frames, since a coroutine can perform some actions, then yield control back to the rest of the Scene, and then resume its actions from the point it left off previously, and so on until its logic is completed.

Do the following:

1. Remove the `Update()` method.
2. Add a new using statement at the top of the script class, since coroutines return an `IEnumerator` value, which is part of the `System.Collections` package:

```
using System.Collections;
```

3. Add a new method:

```
private IEnumerator FadeFunction() {
        while (isFading)
        {
            yield return new WaitForEndOfFrame();
            FadeAlpha();
        }
}
```

4. Refactor the `StartFading()` method, so that is starts our coroutine:

```
private void StartFading() {
        startTime = Time.time;
        isFading = true;
        StartCoroutine(FadeFunction());
}
```

That's it – once the coroutine has been started, it will be called each frame until it completes its logic, temporarily suspending its execution each time a yield statement is executed.

6
Shader Graphs and Video Players

In this chapter, we will cover the following topics:

- Playing videos by manually adding a VideoPlayer component to a GameObject
- Using scripting to control video playback on scene textures
- Using scripting to play a sequence of videos back-to-back
- Creating and using a simple Shader Graph
- Using a Shader Graph to create a color glow effect
- Toggling a Shader Graph color glow effect through C# code

Introduction

Two powerful recent additions to Unity have been the Video Player component (and API), and the Shader Graph tool. Between them, they offer easier and more configurable ways to work with visual content in games. For example, they help with the loading and playing of videos on different visible objects, and provide a comprehensive way for non-shader programmers to construct sophisticated shader transformations using a visual graphing approach.

The big picture

The two core new Unity features discussed in this chapter are **Shader Graphs** and the **Video Player**. Each has its own section below.

The new Shader Graph tool

In 2018, Unity published details about the exciting new **Shader Graph** feature. **Shader Graph** is a tool that allows **visual** building of shaders, by creating and connecting inputs and output of nodes. Currently, it only works with the Lightweight Scriptable Render Pipeline, but should eventually work with many pipelines.

Unity's **Scriptable Render Pipeline** allow different, and customizable, rendering pipelines, that can be efficiently targeted for specific projects and hardware settings (for example, exploiting GPUs in powerful desktop computers, or reducing performance requirements for less powerful mobile devices).

Some great **Shader Graph** features include the following:

- An instant, visual preview of each node in the graph, so that you can see how different nodes are contributing to the final **Master** output node.
- Properties can be publicly exposed in the graph (via the **Blackboard**), so that they become customizable values in the **Inspector** for the **Material** using the **Shader Graph**.
- Publicly exposed properties can also be accessed and changed via scripts.
- The output of one node can become one of the inputs to another node, so a sophisticated shader can be created from many combined, simple component nodes:

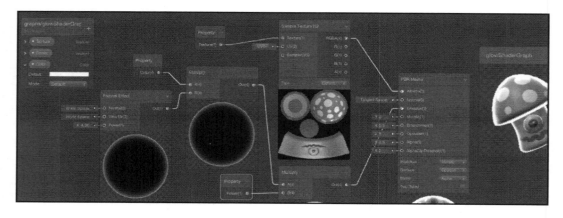

This screenshot illustrates how Shader Graphs are composed of a graph of connected nodes, where the output of one node becomes the input to another node. Node input/outputs can be numeric values, Textures, noise, Boolean true/false values, Colors etc.

Shader Graph files are created in the **Project** panel, and can be selected as a graph shader in the Shader property of a **Material**.

Several recipes are presented in this chapter to introduce some of the powerful **Shader Graph** features and workflow.

Playing videos with the new Video Player

In 2017, Unity replaced the old `MovieTexture` with the VideoPlayer component (as well as the associated VideoClip asset file type). Playing videos is as simple as manually adding a VideoPlayer component in the Inspector to a GameObject at design time, and associating a VideoClip asset file from the Project panel, or providing the URL of a online resource.

Videos can be played on the camera's far plane (appearing behind the scene content), or near plane (appearing in front of content – often with semi-transparency). Video content can also be directed to a `RenderTexture` asset, which can then (via a Material) be displayed on a 2D or 3D object in the scene. The internal texture used by a VideoPlayer can also be mapped to a texture on screen – such as UI Raw Image.

Scripting can be used to manage video playback for single and arrays (sequence) of video clips. Several recipes are presented in this chapter to introduce these different ways to work with the VideoPlayer.

Online references materials

The following are useful sources of information for the topics of this chapter.

Shader Graph online resources

Unity documentation and third-party articles about the Shader Graphs can be found online at the following links:

- The Shader Graph blog introduction: `https://blogs.unity3d.com/2018/02/27/introduction-to-shader-graph-build-your-shaders-with-a-visual-editor/`
- The Unity Shader Graph overview: `https://unity3d.com/shader-graph`
- The Unity GitHub Shader Graph wiki: `https://github.com/Unity-Technologies/ShaderGraph/wiki`
- The Shader Graph example library on GitHub: `https://github.com/UnityTechnologies/ShaderGraph_ExampleLibrary`

- Great video tutorial of Shader Graph from Unity Technology's Andy Tough at GDC 2018: `https://www.youtube.com/watch?v=NsWNRLD-FEI`
- Unity's manual page about the Scriptable Render Pipeline: `https://docs.unity3d.com/Manual/ScriptableRenderPipeline.html`

Video Player online resources

Unity documentation and third-party articles about the Video Player can be found online at the following links:

- The Unity Video Player manual page: `https://docs.unity3d.com/Manual/class-VideoPlayer.html`
- The Unity Scripting reference for the VideoPlayer class: `https://docs.unity3d.com/ScriptReference/Video.VideoPlayer.html`
- Creative Chris' blog post about the Video Player: `https://creativechris.me/2017/02/07/unitys-new-video-playback-component/`

Playing videos by manually adding a VideoPlayer component to a GameObject

TV sets, projectors, monitors.... If you want complex animated materials in your level, you can play video files as texture maps. In this recipe, we will learn how to add and use VideoPlayer components on the main camera.

Getting ready

If you need a video file so that you can follow this recipe, please use the `videoTexture.mov` file included in the `13_01` folder.

How to do it...

To place videos manually with a VideoPlayer component, follow these steps:

1. Import the provided `videoTexture.mov` file.
2. Add a 3D Cube to the scene by choosing menu: **GameObject | 3D Object | Cube**.

3. Select the Main Camera GameObject, and in the Inspector, add a Video Player component by clicking **Add Component**, and choosing **Video | Video Player**. Unity will have noticed that we are adding the Video Player component to a camera, and so should have set up the default properties correctly for us:

   - **Play On Awake** (Checked)
   - **Wait For First Frame** (Checked)
   - **Render Mode: Camera Far Plane**
   - **Camera: Main Camera (Camera)**

4. Drag the video clip asset file videoTexture from the Project panel into the Video Clip property slot in the Inspector, like so:

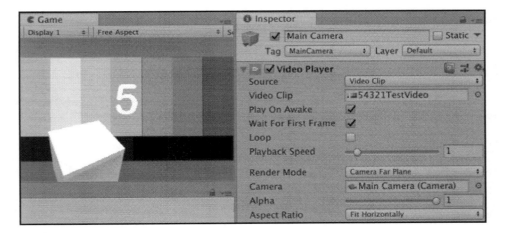

5. Test your scene. You should be able to see the movie being played behind the scene content.

6. You can choose whether to stretch the video content by changing the **Aspect Ratio** property in the Inspector (for example, you can change it to Stretch in order to fill in the complete background of the screen).

How it works...

We gave the Video Player component a reference to a Video Clip asset file. Since we added the Video Player component to a Camera (the Main Camera, in this example), it automatically chose the Camera Far Play Render Mode linked to the Main Camera.

The default setting is Play On Awake, so as soon as the first frame has loaded (since Wait For First Frame is also checked by default), the video will start playing. The video is displayed behind all main camera content (the far plane). Because of this, we see our 3D Cube in the scene, with the video playing in the background.

There's more...

Here are some additional ways to work with the Video Player component.

Semi-transparent video and Camera Near Plane

Sometimes, we may want to play a video so that it's the user's main focus, but allow them to see scene objects in the background.

To achieve this with the Video Player component, we just need to make two changes:

1. Change the Render Mode to Near Camera Plane (so that the video content is played in front of the scene content).
2. To allow the user to partially see through the video, we need to make the Video Player semi-transparent. Change its Alpha property to 0.5.

Now, when you run the scene, you'll see the video playing in front of scene content, but now you will be able to see the 3D cube in the background.

Audio issues and AudioSource solution

At the time of writing this book, there seem to be issues with the Direct option for Audio Output Mode audio playback for some non-Apple systems. One solution is to add an AudioSource component to the same GameObject that has the VideoPlayer component, and to set the Audio Output Mode to AudioSource.

Using scripting to control video playback on scene textures

While the last recipe demonstrated how we can plan videos using the Video Player component that's set up at design time, much more is possible when controlling video playback through scripting.

In this recipe, we'll using scripting to play/pause the playback of a video rendered onto a 3D cube:

Getting ready

If you need a video file to follow this recipe, please use the videoTexture.mov file included in the 13_01 folder.

How to do it...

To use scripting to control video playback, follow these steps:

1. Import the provided videoTexture.mov file.
2. Create a 3D cube by choosing menu: **Create | 3D | Cube**.

3. Create a C# script class named `PlayPauseMainTexture`, and attach an instance object as a component to your 3D cube GameObject:

```
using UnityEngine;
    using UnityEngine.Video;

    [RequireComponent(typeof(VideoPlayer))]
    [RequireComponent(typeof(AudioSource))]

    public class PlayPauseMainTexture : MonoBehaviour {
        public VideoClip videoClip;

        private VideoPlayer videoPlayer;
        private AudioSource audioSource;

        void Start() {
            videoPlayer = GetComponent<VideoPlayer>();
            audioSource = GetComponent<AudioSource>();

            videoPlayer.playOnAwake = false;
            audioSource.playOnAwake = false;

            videoPlayer.source = VideoSource.VideoClip;
            videoPlayer.clip = videoClip;

            videoPlayer.audioOutputMode =
VideoAudioOutputMode.AudioSource;
            videoPlayer.SetTargetAudioSource(0, audioSource);

            videoPlayer.renderMode =
VideoRenderMode.MaterialOverride;
            videoPlayer.targetMaterialRenderer =
GetComponent<Renderer>();
            videoPlayer.targetMaterialProperty = "_MainTex";
        }

        void Update() {
            if (Input.GetButtonDown("Jump"))
                PlayPause();
        }

        private void PlayPause() {
            if (videoPlayer.isPlaying)
                    videoPlayer.Pause();
            else
                videoPlayer.Play();
        }
    }
```

4. Ensure that your 3D cube is selected in the **Project** panel. Then, drag the Video Clip asset file `videoTexture` from the **Project** panel into the Video Clip property slot of the `PlayPauseMainTexture` component (script) in the Inspector.

5. Run your scene. Pressing the spacebar should play/pause playback of the video on the surfaces of the 3D cube. You should also hear the beeping audio for video.

How it works...

We added the instance object of our scripted class to the 3D cube, and dragged a reference to a Video Clip asset file to the public slot. In our code, we are telling the VideoPlayer component to override the Material of the object it is a component of (in this case, the 3D cube) so that the Video Player will render (display) onto the main texture of the 3D cube:

```
videoPlayer.renderMode = VideoRenderMode.MaterialOverride;
videoPlayer.targetMaterialRenderer = GetComponent&lt;Renderer&gt;();
videoPlayer.targetMaterialProperty = "_MainTex";
```

The basics to using scripting and the VideoPlayer is as follows. As well as defining and setting up where the Video Player will render, we also need to do the following each time:

1. Create or get references to the VideoPlayer and AudioSource components (we will automatically have both components for this recipe since we have the `RequireComponent(...)` script instructions immediately before our class declaration):

```
videoPlayer = GetComponent&lt;VideoPlayer&gt;();
audioSource = GetComponent&lt;AudioSource&gt;();
```

2. Set their Play On Awake to `true/false`:

```
videoPlayer.playOnAwake = false;
audioSource.playOnAwake = false;
```

3. Define where the Video Player will find a reference to the Video Clip to play:

```
videoPlayer.source = VideoSource.VideoClip;
videoPlayer.clip = videoClip;
```

4. Define the audio settings (so that you can output to the AudioSource component):

```
videoPlayer.audioOutputMode =
VideoAudioOutputMode.AudioSource;
 videoPlayer.SetTargetAudioSource(0, audioSource);
```

There's more...

Here are some additional ways to work with Video Player scripting.

Ensuring that a movie's prepared before playing it with the prepareCompleted event

In the preceding recipe, the movie has time to prepare since the game waits until we press the jumo/space key. If we are using scripting to set up a Video Player for a video clip, we need to do some initial work before the video is ready to play. Unity provides the `prepareCompleted` event, which allows us to register a method to be invoked once a VideoPlayer is ready to play.

Do the following:

1. Add a UI Raw Image to the scene by choosing menu: **Create | UI | Raw Image**.
2. Create a new empty GameObject named video-object.
3. Create a C# script class named `PrepareCompleted`, and attach an instance object as a component to GameObject's video-object:

```
using UnityEngine;
 using UnityEngine.UI;
 using UnityEngine.Video;

public class PrepareCompleted: MonoBehaviour {
    public RawImage image;
    public VideoClip videoClip;

    private VideoPlayer videoPlayer;
    private AudioSource audioSource;

    void Start() {
        SetupVideoAudioPlayers();
        videoPlayer.prepareCompleted +=
```

```
PlayVideoWhenPrepared;
        videoPlayer.Prepare();
        Debug.Log("A - PREPARING");
    }

    private void SetupVideoAudioPlayers() {
        videoPlayer =
gameObject.AddComponent&lt;VideoPlayer&gt;();
        audioSource =
gameObject.AddComponent&lt;AudioSource&gt;();

        videoPlayer.playOnAwake = false;
        audioSource.playOnAwake = false;

        videoPlayer.source = VideoSource.VideoClip;
        videoPlayer.clip = videoClip;

        videoPlayer.audioOutputMode =
VideoAudioOutputMode.AudioSource;
        videoPlayer.SetTargetAudioSource(0, audioSource);
    }

    private void PlayVideoWhenPrepared(VideoPlayer
theVideoPlayer) {
        Debug.Log("B - IS PREPARED");

        image.texture = theVideoPlayer.texture;

        Debug.Log("C - PLAYING");
        theVideoPlayer.Play();
    }
}
```

4. Ensure that video-object is selected in the **Project** panel. Now, drag the Raw Image from the Hierarchy into the Raw Image slot. Then, drag the Video Clip asset file `videoTexture` from the Project panel into the Video Clip property slot of the `PrepareCompleted` component (script) in the Inspector.

5. Test your scene. You should be able to see the movie being played behind the scene content.

You can see that, in the `Start()` method, we first register a method named `PlayVideoWhenPrepared` with the `videoPlayer.prepareCompleted` event, before invoking the `Prepare()` method of the `videoPlayer` component:

```
videoPlayer.prepareCompleted += PlayVideoWhenPrepared;
  videoPlayer.Prepare();
```

The `PlayVideoWhenPrepared(...)` method has to accept a parameter as a reference to a VideoPlayer object. We first directly assign the VideoPlayer's texture property to the Raw Image's texture. Then, we send the `Play()` message.

 Directly working with the VideoPlayer texture works for this example, but usually setting up a separate Render Texture is more reliable and flexible - see the following subsection for how to do this.

You can track progress of clip preparation and so on through the Log messages in the **Console** panel.

Outputting video playback to a Render Texture asset

A flexible way to work with Video Players is to output their playback to a Render Texture asset file. A Material can be created to get input from the Render Texture, and GameObjects using that Material will display the video. Also, some GameObjects can directly have the Render Texture assigned as their texture.

Do the following:

1. In the **Project** panel, create a new Render Texture asset file named `myRenderTexture` (menu: **Create | Render Texture**).
2. Select the UI Raw Image in the Hierarchy, and assign its Raw Image (Script) texture property to the `myRenderTexture` asset file.
3. In the Project panel, create a new Material asset file named `m_video`. For this Material, in the Inspector, set its Albedo Texture property to `myRenderTexture` (drag it from the **Project** panel into the Inspector).
4. Create a new 3D capsule in the scene, and assign it the Material m_video.
5. Edit the C# script class `PrepareCompleted` by replacing the public `rawImage` variable with a public `renderTexture` variable:

```
public VideoClip videoClip;
```

```
public RenderTexture renderTexture;
```

6. Edit the C# script class `PrepareCompleted` by adding the following statements at the end of the `SetupVideoAudioPlayers()` method to output video to `RenderTexture`:

```
videoPlayer.renderMode = VideoRenderMode.RenderTexture;
 videoPlayer.targetTexture = renderTexture;
```

7. Edit the C# script class PrepareCompleted in the `PlayVideoWhenPrepared()` method. Remove the statement that directly assigns the VideoPlayer's texture property to the Raw Image's Texture:

```
private void PlayVideoWhenPrepared(VideoPlayer
theVideoPlayer) {
     Debug.Log("B - IS PREPARED");

     // Play video
     Debug.Log("C - PLAYING");
     theVideoPlayer.Play();
 }
```

8. Ensure that the GameObject video-object is selected in the **Project** panel. Now, drag the `myRenderTexture` asset from the Project panel into the Render Texture public property of the Prepare Completed (Script) in the Inspector.

9. Run the scene. You should now see the video playing both in the UI Raw Image and also rendered over the 3D Capsule object:

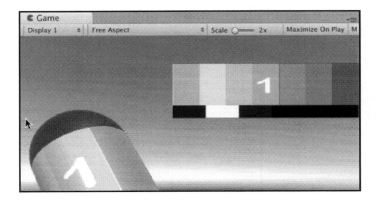

Ensuring that the movie is prepared before playing with coroutines

Many Unity programmers are very used to working with coroutines, so instead of using the `prepareCompleted` event, we can rewrite the preceding script by using a coroutine.

Do the following:

1. Remove the `PlayVideoWhenPrepared()` method.
2. Add a new using statement at the top of the script (so that we can refer to IEnumerator interface):

   ```
   using System.Collections;
   ```

3. Replace the existing `Start()` method with the following:

   ```
   private IEnumerator Start() {
       SetupVideoAudioPlayers();
       videoPlayer.Prepare();

       while (!videoPlayer.isPrepared)
           yield return null;

       videoPlayer.Play();
   }
   ```

As we can see, our `Start()` method has become a coroutine (returning an IEnumerator), which means that it can yield control back to Unity during its execution. In the next frame, it will resume execution at that same statement.

There is a while loop that will continue running until the isPrepared property is true for VideoPlayer. So, each frame of Unity will return to this while loop, and if the VideoPlayer is still not prepared, it enters the loop again and yields execution until the next frame. When VideoPlayer isPrepared is finally true, the loop condition is false, so the statement after the loop is executed (`videoPLayer.Play()`), and the method finally completes its execution.

For a single video, there is little to choose from between the `isPrepared` event and the preceding coroutine. However, for a sequence of videos, the use of the `isPrepared` and `loopPointReached` events helps us make much simpler logic for preparing and then waiting to play the next video in a sequence (see the next recipe for more information).

Downloading an online video (rather than a clip)

Rather than dragging an existing Video Clip asset file to specify which video to play, the Video Player can also download Video Clips from an online source. We need to assign a string URL to the Video Player's URL property.

Do the following:

1. Declare a public array of strings, in which one or more URLs can be defined:

```
public string[] urls = {
"http://mirrors.standaloneinstaller.com/video-sample/grb_2.mov
",
"http://mirrors.standaloneinstaller.com/video-sample/lion-samp
le.mov"
    };
```

2. Declare a new method that returns one URL string, randomly chosen from the array:

```
public string RandomUrl(string[] urls)
  {
      int index = Random.Range(0, urls.Length);
      return urls[index];
  }
```

3. Finally, in the `SetupVideoAudioPlayers()` method, we need to get the random URL string, and assign it to the Video Player's `url` property:

```
private void SetupVideoAudioPlayers()
  {
      ... as before

      // assign video clip
      string randomUrl = RandomUrl(urls);
      videoPlayer.url = randomUrl;

      ... as before
  }
```

Using scripting to play a sequence of videos back-to-back

One of the advantages of scripting is that it allows us to easily work with multiple items through loops and arrays, and so on. In this recipe, we'll work with an array of Video Clip assets and use scripting to play them back-to-back (one starts as soon as the previous clip finishes), illustrating the use of the isPrepared and loopPointReached events to avoid complicated loops and coroutines.

Getting ready

If you need video files in order to follow this recipe, please use the videoTexture.mov file included in the 13_01 folder.

 NOTE: The Standalone Installer website provides a good online source of test videos: http://standaloneinstaller.com/blog/big-list-of-sample-videos-for-testers-124.html.

How to do it...

To play a sequence of videos using scripting, follow these steps:

1. Import the provided videoTexture.mov file, and perhaps a second video clip, so that we can have a sequence of two different videos to test (although you can run the same one twice if you wish).
2. In the Project panel, create a new Render Texture asset file named myRenderTexture (menu: **Create | Render Texture**).
3. Add a UI Raw Image to the scene by choosing menu: **Create | UI | Raw Image**.
4. Select the UI Raw Image in the Hierarchy, and assign its Raw Image (Script) Texture property to the myRenderTexture asset file.
5. In the Project panel, create a new Material asset file named m_video. For this Material, in the Inspector, set its Albedo Texture property to myRenderTexture (drag it from the Project panel into the Inspector).
6. Create a 3D cube by choosing menu: **Create | 3D | Cube**. Assign the m_video Material to your 3D cube.
7. Create a new empty GameObject named video-object.

8. Create a C# script class named VideoSequenceRenderTexture, and attach an instance object as a component to the GameObject's video-object:

```csharp
using UnityEngine;
 using UnityEngine.Video;

 public class VideoSequenceRenderTexture : MonoBehaviour {
     public RenderTexture renderTexture;
     public VideoClip[] videoClips;

     private VideoPlayer[] videoPlayers;
     private int currentVideoIndex;

     void Start() {
         SetupObjectArrays();
         currentVideoIndex = 0;
         videoPlayers[currentVideoIndex].prepareCompleted
 += PlayNextVideo;
         videoPlayers[currentVideoIndex].Prepare();
         Debug.Log("A - PREPARING video: " +
 currentVideoIndex);
         }

         private void SetupObjectArrays() {
             videoPlayers = new
 VideoPlayer[videoClips.Length];
             for (int i = 0; i < videoClips.Length; i++)
                 SetupVideoAudioPlayers(i);
         }

         private void PlayNextVideo(VideoPlayer
 theVideoPlayer) {
             VideoPlayer currentVideoPlayer =
 videoPlayers[currentVideoIndex];

             Debug.Log("B - PLAYING Index: " +
 currentVideoIndex);
             currentVideoPlayer.Play();

             currentVideoIndex++;
             bool someVideosLeft = currentVideoIndex <
 videoPlayers.Length;

             if (someVideosLeft) {
                 VideoPlayer nextVideoPlayer =
 videoPlayers[currentVideoIndex];
                 nextVideoPlayer.Prepare();
                 Debug.Log("A - PREPARING video: " +
```

```
currentVideoIndex);
                    currentVideoPlayer.loopPointReached +=
PlayNextVideo;
            } else {
                Debug.Log("(no videos left)");
            }
        }

        private void SetupVideoAudioPlayers(int i) {
            string newGameObjectName = "videoPlayer_" + i;
            GameObject containerGo = new
GameObject(newGameObjectName);
            containerGo.transform.SetParent(transform);
            containerGo.transform.SetParent(transform);

            VideoPlayer videoPlayer =
containerGo.AddComponent<VideoPlayer>();
            AudioSource audioSource =
containerGo.AddComponent<AudioSource>();

            videoPlayers[i] = videoPlayer;

            videoPlayer.playOnAwake = false;
            audioSource.playOnAwake = false;

            videoPlayer.source = VideoSource.VideoClip;
            videoPlayer.clip = videoClips[i];

            videoPlayer.audioOutputMode =
VideoAudioOutputMode.AudioSource;
            videoPlayer.SetTargetAudioSource(0, audioSource);

            videoPlayer.renderMode =
VideoRenderMode.RenderTexture;
            videoPlayer.targetTexture = renderTexture;
        }
    }
```

9. Ensure that the GameObject video-object is selected in the Project panel. Now, drag the myRenderTexture asset from the Project panel into the Render Texture public property of the PrepareCompleted (Script) in the Inspector. For the Video Clips property, set the size to 2 – you should now see two video clip elements (elements 0 and 1). From the Project panel, drag in a video clip to each slot.

10. Run the scene. You should now see the first video clip playing both for the UI Raw Image and the 3D cube surface. Once the the first video clip has finished playing, the second video clip should immediately start playing.

 You can track the progress of clip preparation and so on through the Log messages in the Console panel.

How it works...

This script class makes the Video Player objects output their videos to Render Texture's asset file, myRenderTexture. This is used by both 3D cube and the UI Raw Image for their surface display.

The videoClips variable is a public array of video clip references.

The instance object of the C# script class VideoSequenceRenderTexture was added as a component to GameObject's video-object. This script will create child GameObjects of GameObject video-object, each containing a VideoPlayer and AudioSource component, ready to play each of the video clips assigned in the public array's videoClips variables.

The SetupObjectArrays() method initializes videoPlayers to be an array the same length as videoClips. It then loops for each item, invoking SetupVideoAudioPlayers(...) by passing the current integer index.

The SetupVideoAudioPlayers(...) method creates a new child GameObject for GameObject's video-object, and adds VideoPlayer and AudioSource components to that GameObject. It sets the Video Player clip property to the corresponding element in the public videoClips array variable. It also adds a reference to the new VideoPlayer component to the appropriate location in the videoPlayers array. It then sets the Video Player to output audio to the new AudioSource component, and to output its video to the renderTexture public variable.

The Start() method does the following:

- It invokes SetupObjectArrays()
- It sets the currentVideoIndex variable to 0 (for the first item in the arrays)

- It registers `PlayNextVideo` method for the prepareCompleted event of the first videoPlayers object (currentVideoIndex = 0)
- It invokes the `Prepare()` method for the videoPlayers object (currentVideoIndex = 0)
- Finally, it logs a debug message stating that the item is preparing

The `PlayNextVideo(...)` method does the following:

- It gets a reference to the Video Player element of the videoPlayers array that corresponds to the currentVideoIndex variable

 This method ignores the reference to the videoPlayer argument it receives – this parameter is required in the method declaration since it is the required signature to allow this method to register for the prepareCompleted and loopPointReached events.

- It sends a `Play()` message to the current Video Player
- It then increments the value of currentVideoIndex, and tests whether there are any remaining video clips in the array
- If there are remaining clips, then it gets a reference to the next clip, and sends it a `Prepare()` message; also the currently playing Video Player has its loopPointReached event registered for the PlayNextVideo method (If there are no videos left, then a simple debug log message is printed and the method ends)

The clever bit is when the currently playing Video Player has its loopPointReached event registered for the PlayNextVideo method. The loopPointReached event occurs when a video clip has finished playing, and will start to look again (if its loop property is true). What we are doing with this script is say that when the current Video Player video clip has finished, the `PlayNextVideo(...)` method should be invoked again – once again using the value of currentVideoIndex to send a `Play()` message to the next Video Player, and then testing for any remaining Video Players, and so on until the end of the array has been reached.

This is a good example of conditions (if statements) being used with events, rather than coroutine while loops. As long as you're happy with how methods can be registered with C# events, then this approach allows our code to be less complex by avoiding loops and coroutine yield null statements.

In the following screenshot, we can see how our video-object GameObject, at runtime, ends up with videoPlayer_<n> child GameObjects – one for each element in the array. This allows one VideoPlayer to be playing while the next is preparing, and so on:

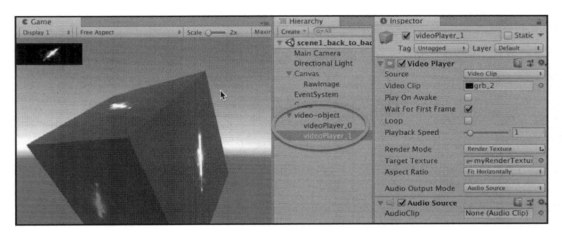

Creating and using a simple Shader Graph

The new Shader Graph feature in Unity 2018 is a powerful and exciting feature, opening up shader creation and editing to everyone, without any need for complex mathematics or coding skills. In this recipe, we'll create a simple Shader Graph to generate a checkerboard pattern, and create a Material that uses that shader, and apply it to a 3D cube. The end result will be as follows:

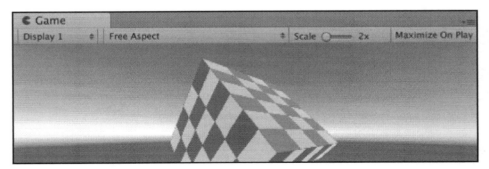

How to do it...

To create and use a simple Shader Graph, follow these steps:

1. First, we need to set up the Lightweight Rendering Pipeline. Use the Package Manager to import the Lightweight Rendering Pipeline package.

2. In the Project panel, create a new Lightweight Pipeline Asset file named myLightweightAsset. Choose menu: **Create | Rendering | Lightweight Pipeline Asset**.

3. In the Inspector, display the project's graphics settings by choosing menu: **Edit | Project Settings | Graphics**. Then, drag myLightweightAsset from the Project panel into the Scriptable Render Pipeline Settings property:

4. Use the Package Manager to import the Shader Graph package.

5. In the Project panel, create a new Physically-Based Rendering (PBR) Shader Graph, named myShaderGraph. Choose menu: **Create | Shader | PBR Graph**.

6. In the Project panel, create a new Material named m_cube. Choose menu: **Create | Material**.

7. With the m_cube selected, in the Inspector, set its Shader property to myShaderGraph. For the Material's Shader property, choose menu: **graphs | myShaderGraph**:

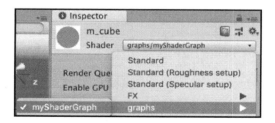

8. Add a 3D cube to the scene (menu: **GameObject | 3D Object | Cube**). Set the Material for this 3D Cube to m_Cube.

9. In the Project panel, double click myShaderGraph to open the Shader Graph editing panel. A new PRB Shader Graph will open with three components: (1) the BlackBoard (for publically exposing parameters); (2) the Master PRB node; (3) the output previewer node:

It is easiest, when editing a Shader Graph, to maximize the Shader Graph panel.

10. Right-click the output previewer, and select Cube:

You can zoom and rotate the preview mesh. You can also choose a custom mesh from within your project, allowing a preview of the Shader Graph on the intended destination's 3D object.

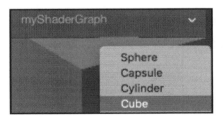

11. Let's flood the shader with a red color. Choose red from the color picker for the top property of the PRB Master node Albedo.

12. Create a new graph node by right-clicking the mouse and choosing menu: **Create Node | Procedural | Checkerboard**. You'll see the checkerboard patter in the preview for this node. Set the X property to 2, and the Y property to 3.

13. Now, drag a link from the checkerboard note output Out(3), to the Emission (3) input for the PRB Master node. You should now see a red/pink checkerboard patter in the PBR Master node preview, and you'll also see the following output applied to the Cube mesh in the output previewer node:

14. You must save the changes to your Shader Graph before you can see them applied to the scene. Click the Save Asset button on the top-left of the Shader Graph panel.

15. Save and run your scene. You should see a red/pink checkerboard 3D cube being displayed.

How it works...

You enabled the Lightweight Rending Pipeline by installing the package, creating an asset, and choosing that asset for the Project's Scriptable Rending Pipeline Graphics property.

You then created a new Shader Graph asset file, and a new Material that uses your shader.

Your Shader Graph feeds a procedurally generated checkerboard into the Emission property of the PBR Master output node, and also tints the output by choosing a red Color value for the Albedo property. You saved the changes to your Shader Graph asset so that they will be available when the scene runs.

Creating a glow effect with Shader Graph

In the previous recipe, a simple Shader Graph was created by using a Material for a primitive 3D Cube mesh. In this recipe, we'll take things further, creating a Shader Graph that applies a parameterized glow effect to a 3D object. The end result will look as follows:

Getting ready

This recipe builds on the previous one, so make a copy of that project and use the copy for this recipe.

How to do it...

To create a glow effect with a Shader Graph, follow these steps:

1. In the Project panel, create a new Physically-Based Rendering (PBR) Shader Graph, named glowShaderGraph. Choose menu: **Create | Shader | PBR Graph**.
2. In the Project panel, create a new Material named m_glow. Choose menu: **Create | Material**.
3. 3. With the m_glow selected, in the Inspector, set its Shader property to glowShaderGraph. For the Material's Shader property, choose menu: **graphs | glowShaderGraph**.

4. We now need a 3D mesh object in the scene that uses m_glow. While we could just use a 3D Cube again, it's more fun to add a low-polygon textured character to the scene. For this recipe, we've used the free Unity Asset Store character pack **Fantasy Mushroom Mon(ster)** from **AmusedArt**. Once the package has been added, drag the Mushroom Monster Prefab into the scene from Project panel folder: **amusedART | Mushroom Monster | Prefab**:

5. In the **Project** panel, double click **glowShaderGraph** to open the **Shader Graph** editing panel.

6. Right-click the output previewer, select **Custom Mesh**, and choose **MushroomMon** from the selection dialog.

7. Add a new **Texture** exposed property to your **Shader Graph** by creating a new property texture in the **Shader Graph Blackboard**. Click the plus + button and choose property type **Texture**.

8. In the **Blackboard**, change the **Default** value of the property **Texture** from **None** to **Mushroom Green**.

9. To use a publically exposed **Blackboard** property in our **Shader Graph**, we need to drag a reference to the property from the **Blackboard** into the **Graph** area. Drag the **Blackboard** property Texture into the **Graph** area. You should see a new node with the title **Property**, and value **Texture (T)**:

10. There is no **Texture** input to the **Master PDB Node**, so we need to add a converter node that can take (sample) data from a **2D Texture** image, and turn it into RBG values that can be sent to the Albedo input of the **PBR Master Node**. Create a new **Sample Texture 2D** node in your **Shader Graph** by right-clicking the mouse, then choose menu: **Create Node | Input | Texture | Sample Texture 2D**.

11. Now, let's send the **Texture Mushroom Green** into the **Master PRB Node** via the **Sample Texture 2D** converter node. Link the **Texture (T)** output from the Property node to the **Texture (T)** input of the **Sample Texture 2D** node. You should now see the **Mushroom Green Texture** image appear in the 2D rectangular preview at the bottom of the **Sample Texture 2D node**.

12. Next, link the **RGBA (4)** output of the **Sample Texture 2D** node to the **Albedo (3)** input of the Master PRB node (Unity will intelligently just ignore the 4th **Alpha (A)** values). You should now see the **Mushroom Green Texture** image appear in the preview at the bottom of the **Master PRB** node. You should also see the **Mushroom Green Texture** being applied to the **3D Mushroom Monster Mesh** in the **Shader Graph** output previewer node:

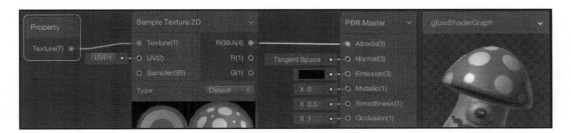

13. One way to create a glow effect is by applying a **Fresnel Effect**. Create a new **Fresnel Effect** node in our **Shader Graph**. Link the **Out (3)** output from the **Fresnel Effect** node to the **Emission (3)** input of the **PRB Master** node. You should now see a brighter glow outline effect in the **Shader Graph** output previewer node.

Augustin-Jean Fresnel (1788-1827) studied and documented how an object's reflection depends on the viewing angle – for example, looking straight down into still water, there is little sunlight reflected and we can see into the water clearly. But if our eyes are closer to the level of the water (for example, if we are swimming), then much more light is reflected by the water. Simulating this effect in a digital shader is a way to make the edges of an object lighter, since light is glancing off the edges of the object and reflected to our game camera.

14. Let's tint our **Fresnel Effect** by combining it with a publicly exposed **Color** property, which can be set by game designers either in the Inspector or through C# code.

15. First, delete the link from the **Out (3)** output from the **Fresnel Effect** node to the **Emission (3)** input of the **PBR Master** node.

16. Add a new **Color** exposed property to your **Shader Graph** by creating a new property **Color** in the **Shader Graph Blackboard**. Click the plus **+** button and choose the **Color** property type.

17. In the **Blackboard**, set the **Default** value of the Color property to red (using the Color picker).

18. Drag the Blackboard's **Color** property into the **Graph** area. You should see a new node with the title **Property** and a value of **Color(4)**.

19. Create a new **Multiply** node in your **Shader Graph** by right-clicking the mouse and then choosing menu: **Create Node | Math | Basic | Multiply**.

The mathematical Multiply node is an easy way to combine values from two nodes, which are then to be passed to a single input of a third node.

20. Let's combine the **Color** and **Fresnel Effect** by making both inputs to the **Multiply** node. Link the **Color (4)** output from the **Property (Color)** node to the **A (4)** input of the **Multiply** node. Next, link the **Out (3)** output from the **Fresnel Effect** node to the **B (4)** input of the **Multiply** node. Finally, link the **Out (3)** output from the **Fresnel Effect** node to the **Emission (3)** input of the **PRB Master** node. You should now see a red tinted glow outline effect in the **Shader Graph** output previewer node: The overview screenshot below shows these node connections completed for our Shader Graph

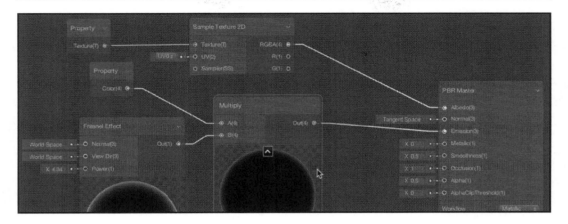

21. Save your updated **Shader Graph** by clicking the **Save Asset** button at the top-right of the **Shader Graph** panel.

22. Save and run your Scene. You should see a red glow around the character.

23. In the **Project** panel, locate the **Material** that your 3D GameObject uses (for the Green Mushroom Monster, it is folder: **Project | amusedART | Mushroom_Monster | Materials | MusroomMonGreen**). The publicly exposed properties of the **Shader Graph Blackboard** should appear in the **Inspector** as customizable properties. Change the **Color** property to blue. Run the scene again. The glow effect around the 3D GameObject should now be blue:

How it works...

You created a new **Shader Graph**, which has several connected nodes. The output(s) of one node become the input(s) of another node.

You created publicly exposed properties for **Color** and **Texture** using the **Shader Graph Blackboard**, and introduced those properties as inputs in your Graph.

You used a Sample Texture 2D node to convert the **2D Texture** image into RBG values suitable for the **Albedo** input for the **PBR Master** node.

You created a **Fresnel Effect** node, and combined this, via a **Multiply** node, with the publicly exposed **Color** property, sending the output into the **Emission** input of the **PRB Master** node.

You then learned how to change the publicly exposed property for **Color** in the Inspector via the Material's properties.

Toggling a Shader Graph color glow effect through C# code

Effects such as the glow effect from the previous recipe are often features we wish to toggle on and off under different circumstances. The effect could be turned on or off during a game to visually communicate the status of a GameObject—for example, an *angry* character might glow red, while a *happy* monster might glow green, and so on.

We'll add to the previous recipe to create a new publicly exposed **Shader Graph Blackboard** property named **Power**, and write code that can be used to set this value to zero or five in order to turn the glow effect on and off. We'll also access the **Color** property so that we're able to set what color the glow effect displays.

Getting ready

This recipe builds on the previous one, so make a copy of that project and use the copy for this recipe.

How to do it...

To toggle the glow effect from the Shader Graph, follow these steps:

1. First, delete the link from the **Out (3)** output from the Multiply node to the **Emission (3)** input of the **PBR Master** node. We are doing this because the output of this **Multiply** node will become an input for a second **Multiple** node that we are about to create.
2. Create a new **Multiply** node in your **Shader Graph** by right-clicking the mouse and then choosing menu: **Create Node | Math | Basic | Multiply**.

3. Link the **Out (4)** output from the original **Multiply** node to the **A (4)** input of your new **Multiply** node. Also, link the **Out (3)** output from the new **Multiply** node to the **Emission (3)** input of the **PBR Master** node.

4. Add a new `float` (decimal number), exposed to the **Power** property, to your **Shader Graph** by creating a new property in the **Shader Graph Blackboard**. Click the plus **+** button and choose property type `Vector 1`, and rename this `Power`.

5. In the **Blackboard**, set the Default value of the **Power** property to 5. Also, set the display **Mode** to **Slider** with the values of Min 0 and Max 5.

6. Drag the **Blackboard Power** property into the **Graph** area. You should see a new node with the title **Property**, and a value of **Power(1)**.

7. Finally, link the **Power(1)** output from Property node (Power) to the B (4) input of the new Multiply node:

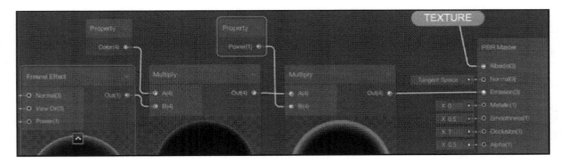

8. Save your updated **Shader Graph** by clicking the **Save Asset** button at the top-right of the **Shader Graph** panel.

9. Create a new C# script class named `GlowManager` containing the following:

```
using UnityEngine;

public class GlowManager : MonoBehaviour {
    private string powerId = "Vector1_AA07C639";
    private string colorId = "Color_466BE55E";

    void Update () {
        if (Input.GetKeyDown("0"))
GetComponent&lt;Renderer&gt;().material.SetFloat(powerId, 0);

        if (Input.GetKeyDown("1"))
            SetGlowColor(Color.red);

        if (Input.GetKeyDown("2"))
```

```
                      SetGlowColor(Color.blue);
        }

        private void SetGlowColor(Color c) {
GetComponent&lt;Renderer&gt;().material.SetFloat(powerId, 5);
GetComponent&lt;Renderer&gt;().material.SetColor(colorId, c);
        }
    }
```

10. Select **Shader Graph glowShaderGraph** in the **Project** panel, and view its properties in the **Inspector**:

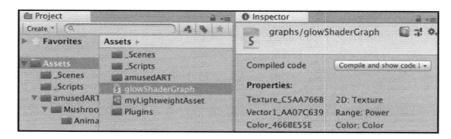

11. Find the internal IDs of the publicly exposed properties Power and Color – they will be something like Vector1_AA07C639 and Color_466BE55E. Copy these IDs into C# script statements by setting the ID strings:

```
private string powerId = "Vector1_AA07C639";
private string colorId = "Color_466BE55E";
```

At the time of writing this book, the current version of **Shader Graph** doesn't provide a convenient way to access exposed properties using the names chosen in the Shader Graph Blackboard, hence the need to look up the internal ID needed for the material.SetFloat(powerId, power) statement when changing the value. It is likely that Unity will soon update the **Shader Graph** scripting API to make this action more straightforward.

12. In the **Hierarchy**, locate the component of your 3D GameObject that contains the **Mesh Renderer** component (for our **Mushroom Monster** example, this is the **Mushroom Mon** child of the **Mushroom Monster** GameObject). Add an instance object of the `GlowManager` script class as a component to this **GameObject**.

13. Save and run your **Scene**. Pressing the *1* key should turn on the red glow effect, pressing the *2* key should turn on the blue glow effect, and pressing the *0* key should turn off the glow effect.

How it works...

You created a new **Power** exposed property for your **Shader Graph** that combined with the **Fresnel** color effect so that a value of **zero** will turn off the effect. You looked up the internal IDs of the **Power** and **Color** exposed properties, and updated the C# script so that it can update these properties.

The scriptclass checks for the 0/1/2 keys, and correspondingly turns the effect off/to a red glow/to a blue glow.

By combining publicly exposed properties with code, you are able to change **Shader Graph** values at runtime through events detected by code.

There's more...

Here are some ways to take your **Shader Graph** features even further.

Using Sine Time to create a pulsating glow effect

You could make the glow effect *pulse* by creating a **Time** node, and linking the Sine **Time (1)** output to the **Fresnel Effect** input **Power (1)**. As the Sine Time value changes between - 1/0/+1, it will influence how strong the **Fresnel Effect** is, changing the brightness of the glow effect.

Using the Compile and Show Code button as another way to find exposed property IDs

When you are viewing the properties of a **Shader Graph** asset in the **Inspector**, you'll see a button entitled **Compile and Show Code**. If you click this, you'll then see a generated **ShaderLab** code file in your script editor.

It isn't the actual code used by Unity, but it provides a good idea of the code that is generated from your **Shader Graph**. The internal IDs for your publicly exposed **Blackboard** properties are listed in the Properties section, which is at the beginning of the generated code:

```
Shader "graphs/glowShaderGraph" {
    Properties {

    [NoScaleOffset]  Texture_C5AA766B ("Texture", 2D) = "white" { }
    Vector1_AA07C639 ("Power", Range(0.000,5.000)) = 5.000

    Color_466BE55E ("Color", Color) = (1.000,0.000,0.038368,0.000)
    }

    etc.
```

7 Using Cameras

In this chapter, we will cover the following recipes:

- Creating the basic scene for this chapter
- Creating a picture-in-picture effect
- Switching between multiple cameras
- Making textures from screen content
- Zooming a telescopic camera
- Displaying a minimap
- Creating an in-game surveillance camera
- Working with Unity's multi-purpose camera rig
- Using Cinemachine ClearShot to switch cameras to keep the player in shot
- Letting the player switch to a Cinemachine FreeLook camera

Introduction

As developers, we should never forget to pay attention to **Cameras**. After all, they are the windows through which our players see our games. In this chapter, we will take a look at interesting ways of using **Cameras** that enhance the player's experience.

The big picture

A **Scene** can contain multiple **Cameras**. Often, we have one **Main Camera** (we're given one by default with a new **Scene**). For **First-Person** viewpoint games, we control the position and rotation of the **Camera** directly, since it acts as our eyes. In **Third-Personal** viewpoint games, our main **Camera** follows an animated 3D character (usually from above/behind/over the shoulder), and may slowly and smoothly change its position and rotation as if a person were holding the **Camera** and moving to keep us in view.

Perspective **Cameras** have a triangular pyramid-shaped volume of space in front of them, called a **frustrum**. Objects inside this space are projected onto a plane, which determines what we see from the **Camera**. We can control this volume of space by specifying the clipping planes and the field of view. The clipping planes define the minimum and maximum distance objects have to be between to be considered viewable. The field of view is decided by how wide or narrow the pyramid shape is:

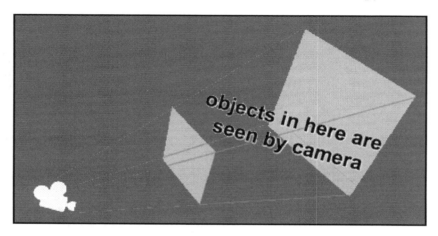

Cameras can be customized in many ways:

- They can exclude objects on specific layers from rendering
- They can be set to render in Orthographic mode (that is, without perspective)
- They can have their **Field of View** (**FOV**) manipulated to simulate a wide- or narrow-angle lenses
- They can be rendered on top of other cameras or within specific areas of the screen (viewports)
- They can be rendered into Textures files

The list goes on. The following screenshot illustrates several of these **Camera** features. The same Scene has a perspective Camera, outputting to a viewport taking up the entire **Game** screen (from 0,0 to 1,1). On top of this is a second viewport for an Orthographic **Camera**, showing a 2D top-down view of the same Scene's contents. This viewport is just the top-left quarter of the screen (0, 0.5) to (0.5, 1.0). The "ghost" character is on a layer that is ignored (culled) by the second **Orthographic Camera**:

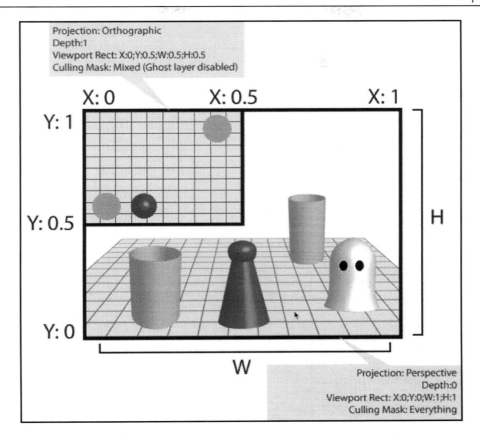

Projection: Orthographic
Depth:1
Viewport Rect: X:0;Y:0.5;W:0.5;H:0.5
Culling Mask: Mixed (Ghost layer disabled)

X: 0   X: 0.5   X: 1

Y: 1

Y: 0.5

H

Y: 0

W

Projection: Perspective
Depth:0
Viewport Rect: X:0;Y:0;W:1;H:1
Culling Mask: Everything

Cameras have a **depth** property. This is used by Unity to determine in what sequence **Cameras** are rendered. Unity renders **Cameras** starting with the lowest depth number, and working up to the highest. This is needed to ensure that **Cameras** that are not rendered to fill the whole screen are rendered after **Cameras** that are. You'll see this illustrated in several recipes, including the picture-in-picture recipe.

Cinemachine

Developed by Adam Myhill, and now available free as a Unity Package, **Cinemachine** is a powerful automated system for camera control. It offers much to Unity developers, both for **Run-Time** in-game camera control and also cinematic creation for cut scenes or complete animated films. We end this chapter with examples of how to add some **Run-Time** camera controls to your games using **Cinemachine**.

At the core of Cinemachine is the concept of a set of Virtual Cameras in a Scene and a Cinemachine Brain component, which decides which virtual camera's properties should be used to control the Scene's **Main Camera**.

Learn more about the history and development of Cinemachine at http://www.cinemachineimagery.com/.

Creating the basic scene for this chapter

All the recipes in this chapter start off with the same basic scene, featuring a 3D maze, some objects, and a keyboard-controllable 3D character. In this recipe, you'll create a project with such a scene, which can be duplicated and adapted for each recipe that follows.

Getting ready

For this recipe, we have prepared a Unity package named CamerasChapter.unity, containing all the resources needed for this chapter. The package can be found in the 06_01 folder.

How to do it...

To create the basic scene for this chapter, just follow these steps:

1. Create a new 3D project.
2. Import the CamerasChapter package into your Unity Project.
3. In the **Project** panel, you'll find three Prefabs in the `Prefabs` folder (`maze-floor-walls`, `maze-objects`, `character-MsLazer`). Create GameObjects for each of these three Prefabs by dragging the Prefabs from the Project panel into the Hierarchy or **Scene** panels.
4. You should now have a maze with a floor, some walls, some **Sphere** objects, a green respawn point, and the keyboard-controllable character-MsLazer 3D character.
5. Let's attach the Scene's **Main Camera** to the character, so that you'll see this Third Person Controller character all the time as you move it around the maze. Child the Main Camera to `character-MsLazer`.
6. In the **Inspector**, set the Main Camera Position to (0, 3, -5), and Rotation to (5, 0, 0).
7. Now, as you use the arrow keys to move the character around the maze, the **Main Camera** should move and rotate automatically with the character, and you should be able to see the back of the character at all times.
8. Save and run the Scene. As you move the character, the **Main Camera** should move around with the character.

How it works...

By cloning Prefabs, you have added a maze and some objects to an empty **Scene**. You have also added a keyboard-controller character to the **Scene**.

By childing the **Main Camera** to the character GameObject, the **Main Camera** maintains the same position and rotation relative to the character at all times. Therefore, as the character moves so does the **Main Camera,** giving a simple, over-the-shoulder type viewpoint for the game action.

Creating a picture-in-picture effect

Having more than one viewport displayed can be useful in many situations. For example, you may want to show simultaneous events going on in different locations, or you may want to have a separate window for hot-seat multiplayer games:

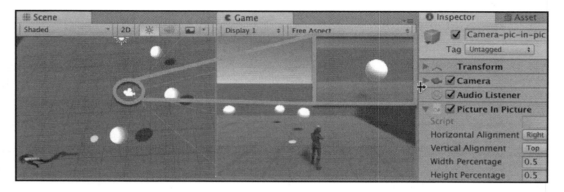

Getting ready

This recipe adds to the scene created in the first recipe of this chapter, so make a copy of that project folder and do your work for this recipe with that copy.

How to do it...

To create a picture-in-picture display, just follow these steps:

1. Add a new **Camera** to the scene named `Camera-pic-in-pic`. Choose menu: **Create | Camera**.

2. In the **Inspector**, for the `Camera` component, set the Depth property to `1`.

3. Uncheck or remove the camera's **Audio Listener** component, since there should only be one active **Audio Listener** in a Scene.

4. Create a new C# script-class named `PictureInPicture`, and add an instance-object as a component to the **Camera-pic-in-pic** GameObject:

```
using UnityEngine;
public class PictureInPicture : MonoBehaviour {
    public enum HorizontalAlignment {
        Left, Center, Right
    };
```

```
public enum VerticalAlignment {
    Top, Center, Bottom
};

public HorizontalAlignment horizontalAlignment =
HorizontalAlignment.Left;
public VerticalAlignment verticalAlignment =
VerticalAlignment.Top;
public float widthPercentage = 0.5f;
public float heightPercentage = 0.5f;
private Camera camera;

void Start(){
    camera = GetComponent<Camera>();
}

void Update() {
    Vector2 origin = CalcOrigin();
    Vector2 size = new Vector2(widthPercentage,
heightPercentage);
    Rect newCameraRect = new Rect(origin, size);
    camera.rect = newCameraRect;
}


private Vector2 CalcOrigin() {
    float originX = 0;
    float originY = 0;

    switch (horizontalAlignment) {
        case HorizontalAlignment.Right:
            originX = 1 - widthPercentage;
            break;

        case HorizontalAlignment.Center:
            originX = 0.5f - (0.5f *
widthPercentage);
            break;

        case HorizontalAlignment.Left:
        default:
            originX = 0;
            break;
    }

    switch (verticalAlignment) {
        case VerticalAlignment.Top:
            originY = 1 - heightPercentage;
```

```
                                    break;

                    case VerticalAlignment.Center:
                            originY = 0.5f - (0.5f *
       heightPercentage);
                            break;

                    case VerticalAlignment.Bottom:
                    default:
                            originY = 0;
                            break;
            }

            return  new Vector2(originX, originY);
        }
    }
```

5. In the **Inspector**, change some of the **Picture In Picture (Script)** parameters: choose top and right for vertical and horizontal alignment. Choose 0.25 for vertical and horizontal percentage.

6. Play your **Scene**. In the **Game** panel, your picture-in-picture Camera's viewport should be visible in the top-left corner of the screen, taking up a quarter (25%) of the screen.

How it works...

In this example, you added a second **Camera** in order to display the scene from a different point of view.

The default **Main Camera** has the default depth of 0. You set the depth for our **Camera-pic-in-pic** to 1, so the **Main Camera** is rendered first, covering the whole Game window, and then our second Camera (picture-in-picture) is rendered last, on top of the Main Camera rendering.

The Picture In Picture script changes the camera's **Normalized Viewport Rect**, thus resizing and positioning the viewport according to the user's preferences. The four values of **Vertical** and **Horizontal Alignment**, plus width and height percentage, are used to create a rectangle in the (0,0) - (1.0, 1.0) **normalized** coordinates of the the Game panel. The rect property of the **Camera** is set to the new rectangle calculated.

There's more...

The following are some aspects of your picture-in-picture that you could change.

Changing the size and location of the picture-in-picture viewport on the screen

You can change the **size** of the picture-in-picture rectangle by setting the horizontal and vertical percentage values.

The **Vertical Alignment** and **Horizontal Alignment** options can be used to change the viewport's vertical and horizontal alignment. Use them to place it where you wish, such as top-left, bottom-right, center-center, and so on.

Adding further contols for depth-of-field and aspect-ratio

You can add additional public variables to the code, and corresponding **Camera** adjustments, for **field-of-view, aspect ratio**, and so on:

```
[Range(20f, 150f)]
public float verticalFieldOfView = 90f;

[Range(0.25f, 2f)]
public float ascectRatio = 1f;

void Update()
{
    Vector2 origin = CalcOrigin();
    Vector2 size = new Vector2(widthPercentage,
heightPercentage);
    Rect newCameraRect = new Rect(origin, size);
    camera.rect = newCameraRect;
    camera.fieldOfView = verticalFieldOfView;
    camera.aspect = ascectRatio;
}
```

The camera field-of-view is how much of the world the camera captures; often, we think of this as how wide or narrow our view is. Learn more at https://en.wikipedia.org/wiki/Field_of_view and https://docs.unity3d.com/ScriptReference/Camera-fieldOfView.html.

Camera aspect ratio is the relationship of the width to the height of the rectangle. It is calculated as the width divided by the height. Learn more at `https://docs.unity3d.com/ScriptReference/Camera-aspect.html` and `https://en.wikipedia.org/wiki/Aspect_ratio_(image)`.

Manually changing Camera viewport properties in the Inspector

Once you are happy working with the normalized viewport coordinate system of (0,0) to (1.0, 1.0), you can manually edit **Camera Viewport** settings for the **Camera** component directly in the **Inspector**, without having to use any C# script-classes:

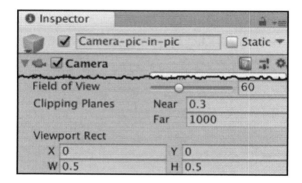

See also

The *Displaying a minimap* recipe in this chapter.

Switching between multiple cameras

Choosing from a variety of cameras is a common feature in many genres: racing, sports, tycoon/strategy, and many others. In this recipe, you will learn how to give players the ability to choose from many cameras by using their keyboards.

Getting ready

This recipe adds to the scene created in the first recipe of this chapter, so make a copy of that project folder and do your work for this recipe with that copy.

How to do it...

To implement switchable cameras, follow these steps:

1. Create a new **Camera** in the Scene named **Camera-1** (**Create | Camera**). Set its position to (0, 0, 0). Set the **Tag** for this **Camera** to be **MainCamera**.

2. Duplicate **Camera-1**, naming the copy **Camera-2**. Set its **Position** to (0, 0, -15), and its **Rotation** to (20, 0, 0).

3. Disable the **Camera** and **AudioListener** components for both **Camera-1** and **Camera-2**.

4. Create an empty **GameObject** named switchboard (**Create | Create Empty**).

5. Create a new C# script-class named CameraSwitch containing the following, and add an object-instance as a component to the **switchboard** GameObject:

```
using UnityEngine;
public class CameraSwitch : MonoBehaviour  {
        public Camera[] cameras = new Camera[3];
        public bool changeAudioListener = true;

        void  Update() {
            if (Input.GetKeyDown("0")) {
                EnableCamera(cameras[0], true);
                EnableCamera(cameras[1], false);
                EnableCamera(cameras[2], false);
            }

            if (Input.GetKeyDown("1")) {
                EnableCamera(cameras[0], false);
                EnableCamera(cameras[1], true);
                EnableCamera(cameras[2], false);
            }

            if (Input.GetKeyDown("2")) {
                EnableCamera(cameras[0], false);
                EnableCamera(cameras[1], false);
```

```
                          EnableCamera(cameras[2], true);
                  }
          }

          private void EnableCamera(Camera cam, bool
      enabledStatus) {
                  cam.enabled = enabledStatus;

              if(changeAudioListener)
                    cam.GetComponent<AudioListener>().enabled =
      enabledStatus;
                  }
          }
```

6. Ensure the **switchboard** GameObject is selected in the **Hierarchy**. In the **Inspector** for the **Camera Switch (Script)** component, set the size of the **Cameras** array to 3. Then, drag and populate the **Camera** slots with the cameras from the scene, including the **Main Camera** and the child of the **MsLazer** character:

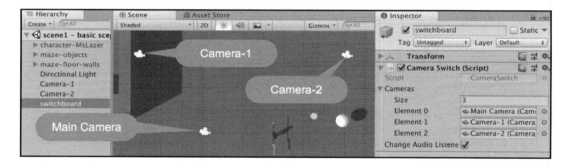

7. Save and Play the scene. Pressing keys *0*, *1*, and *2* should switch between each of the three **Cameras**.

How it works...

Each frame, a test is made for each of the three shortcut key presses (0, 1, or 2). If one of those keys has been pressed, then the corresponding **Camera** is enabled, and the other two **Cameras** are disabled.

If the public Boolean property changeAudioListener has been checked, then the AudioListener inside the selected Camera is enabled and the AudioListeners in the other two Cameras are disabled.

There's more...

Here are some ideas about how you could try adapting this recipe.

Using a single-enabled camera

A different approach to the problem would be keeping all secondary cameras disabled and assigning their position and rotation to the **Main Camera** via a script-class (you would need to make a copy of the **Main Camera** and add it to the list, in case you wanted to save its **Transform** settings). This is similar to the virtual **Camera** properties applied to the **Main Camera** approach that the Cinemachine package implements (see the last two recipes in this chapter to learn more about Cinemachine).

See also

The Creating an in-game surveillance camera recipe in this chapter.

Making textures from screen content

If you want your game or player to take in-game snapshots and apply them as textures, this recipe will show you how. This can be very useful if you plan to implement an in-game photo gallery or display a snapshot of a key moment at the end of a level (racing games and stunt simulations use this feature a lot). For this particular example, we will take a snapshot of a framed region of the screen and print it in the top-right corner of the display:

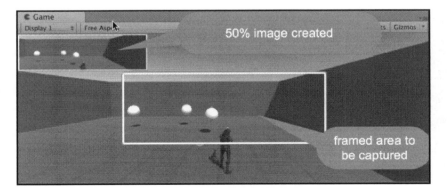

Getting ready

This recipe adds to the scene created in the first recipe of this chapter, so make a copy of that project folder and do your work for this recipe with that copy.

How to do it...

To create textures from screen content, follow these steps:

1. In the **Hierarchy**, create a new **UI Image** named **Image-frame** by choosing the following from the **Hierarchy** panel menu: **Create | UI | Image**. Since this is the first UI GameObject to be created in this Scene, new **Canvas** and EventSystem GameObjects should be created automatically, and the **Image-frame** UI should be a child of the Canvas GameObject.

2. From the **Inspector** panel, find the **Image (Script)** component of the frame GameObject and set InputFieldBackground as its **Source Image**. Also, uncheck the **Fill Center** option.

 Sprite InputFieldBackground comes bundled with Unity, and it's already sliced for resizing purposes.

3. Set the **Anchors** for **Image-frame** to: **Min** (0.25), (0.25); **Max** (0.75), (0.750).

4. Zero the Position (**Left**: 0, **Top**: 0, **Pos Z**: 0) and Size (**Width**: 0, **Height**: 0).

5. The **Image-frame** GameObject should appear in the center of the screen, taking up half the screen:

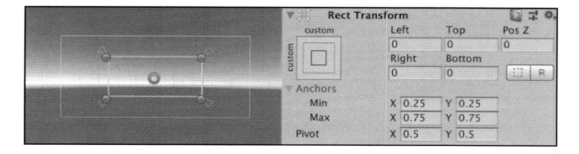

6. In the **Hierarchy**, create a new **UI Raw Image** named **RawImage-Photo** by choosing the following from the **Hierarchy** panel menu: **Create | UI | RawImage**. Ensure its **Texture** is **None** for its **Raw Image (Script)** component.

7. In the **Inspector,** now disable the entire **RawImage-Photo** GameObject.

8. Set the **Width** and **Height** to 1. Set the Anchors for **RawImage-Photo** to: **Min** (0), (1); **Max** (0), (1).

9. Set the **Pivot** to (0, 1). And zero the Position by setting **Left** to 0, **Top** to 0, and **Z** to 0.

10. Create a new C# script-class named `TextureFromCamera,` and add an instance-object as a component to the **Main Camera** GameObject (child of `MsLazer`):

```csharp
using UnityEngine;
 using UnityEngine.UI;
 using System.Collections;

public class TextureFromCamera : MonoBehaviour {
    public GameObject imageFrame;
    public GameObject rawImagePhoto;
    public float ratio = 0.25f;

    void  LateUpdate ()  {
        if (Input.GetKeyUp(KeyCode.Mouse0))
        {
            rawImagePhoto.SetActive (false);
            StartCoroutine(CaptureScreen());
            rawImagePhoto.SetActive (true);
        }
    }

    IEnumerator CaptureScreen () {
        RectTransform frameTransform =
imageFrame.GetComponent<RectTransform> ();
        Rect framing = frameTransform.rect;
        Vector2 pivot = frameTransform.pivot;
        Vector2 origin = frameTransform.anchorMin;
        origin.x *= Screen.width;
        origin.y *= Screen.height;
        float xOffset = pivot.x * framing.width;
        origin.x += xOffset;
        float yOffset = pivot.y * framing.height;
        origin.y += yOffset;
        framing.x += origin.x;
        framing.y += origin.y;
```

```
                      Texture2D texture = new
        Texture2D((int)framing.width, (int)framing.height);

                      yield return new WaitForEndOfFrame();
                      texture.ReadPixels(framing, 0, 0);
                      texture.Apply();
                      Vector3 photoScale = new Vector3 (framing.width *
        ratio, framing.height * ratio, 1);
                      rawImagePhoto.GetComponent<RectTransform>
        ().localScale = photoScale;
                      rawImagePhoto.GetComponent<RawImage>().texture =
        texture;
                  }
              }
```

11. In the **Inspector,** find the **Screen Texture** component and populate the **Raw Image Photo** field with **GameObjectRawImage-Photo;** and the **Image Frame** field with the **Image-frame** GameObject.

12. Play the **Scene**. Each time you click the mouse, you'll take a snapshot of the screen within the rectangular frame, and the snapshop should be displayed in the top-left of the screen.

How it works...

First, we created a UI frame from which to take a snapshot, and a **UI Raw Image** at the top-left of the screen, onto which to apply the snapshot textures.

Each frame, the `LateUpdate()` method of C# script-class `TextureFromCamera` is executed. Each time this happens a test is made to see whether the mouse button has been clicked. If it has, then the UI Raw Image is disabled (so previous snapshots don't appear in new snapshots) and the `CaptureScreen()` coroutine method is invoked.

 We use `LateUpdate()` here to ensure all rendering has been completed before we capture the image.

Coroutine `CaptureScreen()` calculates a `Rect` area, copies screen pixels from that area, and applies them to a texture to be displayed by the **UI Raw Image** element, which is also resized to fit the texture.

The size of the `Rect` is calculated from the screen's dimensions and the frame's **Rect Transform** settings, particularly its **Pivot**, **Anchors**, **Width**, and **Height**. The screen pixels are then captured by the `ReadPixels()` command and applied to the texture, which is then applied to the **Raw Image** photo, which is itself resized to fit the desired ratio between the photo size and the original pixels.

The `CaptureScreen()` method is a coroutine, which allows it to wait until the end of a frame (`yield return new WaitForEndOfFrame()`), before attempting to capture a copy of the image from the **Camera**.

There's more...

Apart from displaying the texture as a UI element, you can use it in other ways.

Applying your texture to a material

You can apply your texture to an existing object's material by adding a line similar to `GameObject.Find("MyObject").renderer.material.mainTexture=` texture to the end of the `CaptureScreen` method.

Using your texture as a screenshot

You can encode your texture as a PNG image file and save it. This is explored in the Unity documentation pages about encoding PNG images:
`https://docs.unity3d.com/ScriptReference/ImageConversion.EncodeToPNG.html`.

See also

The Saving screenshots from the game recipe in `Chapter 10`, *Working with External Resource Files and Devices*, Saving and Loading Data Files.

Zooming a telescopic camera

In this recipe, we will create a telescopic camera that zooms in whenever the left mouse button is pressed.

Getting ready...

This recipe adds to the scene created in the first recipe of this chapter, so make a copy of that project folder and do your work for this recipe with that copy.

How to do it...

To create a telescopic camera, follow these steps:

1. Create a new C# script-class named `TelescopicView`, and add an instance-object as a component to the **Main Camera** (child of `MsLazer`):

```csharp
using UnityEngine;

public class TelescopicView : MonoBehaviour {
    public float zoom = 2.0f;
    public float speedIn = 100.0f;
    public float speedOut = 100.0f;
    private float initFov;
    private float currFov;
    private float minFov;
    private float addFov;

    void Start() {
        initFov = Camera.main.fieldOfView;
        minFov = initFov / zoom;
    }

    void Update() {
        if (Input.GetKey(KeyCode.Mouse0))
            ZoomView();
        else
            ZoomOut();
    }

    void ZoomView(){
        currFov = Camera.main.fieldOfView;
        addFov = speedIn * Time.deltaTime;

        if (Mathf.Abs(currFov - minFov) < 0.5f)
            currFov = minFov;
        else if (currFov - addFov >= minFov)
            currFov -= addFov;

        Camera.main.fieldOfView = currFov;
    }
```

```
void ZoomOut () {
    currFov = Camera.main.fieldOfView;
    addFov = speedOut * Time.deltaTime;

    if (Mathf.Abs(currFov - initFov) < 0.5f)
        currFov = initFov;
    else if (currFov + addFov <= initFov)
        currFov += addFov;

    Camera.main.fieldOfView = currFov;
  }
}
```

2. Play the level. You should see an animated zooming effect when you click and hold the right mouse button.

How it works...

The zooming effect is actually caused by changes to the value of the camera's **Field Of View (FOV)** property; small values result in closer views of a smaller area, while larger values enlarge the FOV.

The `TelescopicView` script-class changes the camera's field of view by reducing it whenever the left mouse button is pressed. It also adds to the FOV value when the right mouse button is not being held, until it reaches its original value.

The zoom limit of the FOV can be deduced from the `minFov = initFov / zoom` code. This means that the minimum value of the FOV is equal to its original value divided by the zoom amount. For instance, if our **Camera** originally features an FOV of 60, and we set the **Telescopic View Zoom** amount to `2.0`, the minimum FOV allowed will be 60/2 = 30.

There's more...

There are some details that you don't want to miss.

Adding a vignette effect when you zoom

Often in games, a visual vignette effect is applied at the same time as camera zooming. Vignetting is when the edges of an image are made less bright or more blurred (often in an oval or circular shape). It used to be an unintended (and often unwanted) effect of older cameras and lenses, but can be purposely applied in games to help the player focus on the content at the center of the screen, and to add a more intense atmosphere at a certain point in the game:

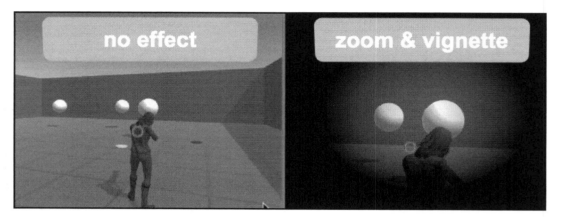

To add a vignette effect, do the following:

1. Open the **Asset Store** panel, then download and import the free **Post-Processing Stack** assets published by Unity Technologies.
2. In the **Inspector**, select the **Main Camera** GameObject (child of **MsLazer**). Then, add a **Post-Processing Behaviour** component. Go to **Add Component | Effects | Post-Processing Behaviour**.
3. In the **Project** panel, create a new **Post-Processing Profile** file named my-vignette by choosing the following from the **Project** panel menu: **Create | Post-Processing Profile**.
4. With the my-vignette file selected in the Project panel, in the Inspector, check the my-vignette effect and click it once to reveal its properties. Set its properties as follows:
     - Center: (X: 0.5, Y: 0.5)
     - Intensity: 0.75
     - Smoothness: 0.5
     - Roundness: 1

5. With the **Main Camera** selected in the **Inspector,** drag the `my-vignette` file from the **Project** panel into the **Inspector** to populate the **Profile** property of the **Post-Processing Behaviour** component.

6. You should now see the dark, fuzzy vignetting circular effect around the edges of the **Game** panel camera view.

7. In the **Inspector,** select the **Main Camera** and disable its **Post-Processing Behaviour** component (uncheck the box for this component in the **Inspector).** We'll be enabling this effect in the script only when the zoom effect is switched on.

8. Add a new using statement at the top of the `TelescopicView` script-class:

   ```
   using UnityEngine.PostProcessing;
   ```

9. Add a new private variable to the `TelescopicView` script-class:

   ```
   private PostProcessingBehaviour postProcessingBehaviour;
   ```

10. Add a statement to get and store a reference to the **Post-Processing Behaviour** component at the end of the `Start()` method in the `TelescopicView` script-class:

    ```
    void Start() {
        initFov = Camera.main.fieldOfView;
        minFov = initFov / zoom;
        postProcessingBehaviour =
    GetComponent<PostProcessingBehaviour>();
        }
    ```

11. Add statements in the `Update()` method of script-class `TelescopicView`, to enable the **Post-Processing Behaviour** when the mouse key is pressed and disable it when not pressed:

```
void Update() {
    if (Input.GetKey(KeyCode.Mouse0)) {
        postProcessingBehaviour.enabled = true;
        ZoomView();
    }
    else {
        ZoomOut();
        postProcessingBehaviour.enabled = false;
    }
}
```

12. Play the **Scene**. You should see an animated vignette effect, in addition to the zooming, when the mouse button is clicked and held.

Learn more about the Vignette effect and the **Post-processing Stack** in the Unity documentation:

- `https://docs.unity3d.com/Manual/PostProcessing-Vignette.html`
- `https://docs.unity3d.com/Manual/PostProcessing-Stack.html`

Going further with version 2 of the Unity Post Processing Stack

At the time of printing, Unity have published an experimental version 2 of their Post Processing Stack.

To add a vignette effect, do the following:

1. Select the **Main Camera** in the **Inspector** (child of `MsLazer`). In the **Inspector,** create a new **Layer** named `PostProcessing,` and set the **Layer** of the **Main Camera** to **PostProcessing**.
2. Download the ZIP from the Unity GitHub account at `https://github.com/Unity-Technologies/PostProcessing.`
3. Then, unzip the folder into your project's **Assets** folder.
4. Add a **Post-Process Layer** component to the **Main Camera**. Do this in the **Inspector** by clicking **Add Component | Rendering | Post Process Layer**. Set the **Layer** property of this component to **Post Processing**.
5. Now, add a **Post-process Volume Component** by clicking **Add Component | Rendering | Post Process Volume**. Check the Is **Global** property. Create a **New profile** (click the **New button**). Then, click the **Add Effect...** button and choose Vignette from the drop-down menu.
6. Add a using statement at the top of the `TelescopicView` script-class:

    ```
    using UnityEngine.Rendering.PostProcessing;
    ```

7. Add two more properties to the `TelescopicView` script-class:

    ```
    private Vignette vignetteEffect;
     public float vMax = 1f;
    ```

8. Add the following statements to the end of the `Start()` method of script-class `TelescopicView`, in order to get a reference to the Vignette effect in the **Post-Processing Volume** component:

```
void Start() {
        initFov = Camera.main.fieldOfView;
        minFov = initFov / zoom;

        PostProcessVolume volume =
GetComponent<PostProcessVolume>();
        volume.profile.TryGetSettings<Vignette>(out
vignetteEffect);
    }
```

9. Add the following statements to the end of the `Update()` method of script-class `TelescopicView`, in order to update the vignette settings:

```
void Update()
    {
        if (Input.GetKey(KeyCode.Mouse0))
            ZoomView();
        else
            ZoomOut();

        float currDistance = currFov - initFov;
        float totalDistance = minFov - initFov;
        float vMultiplier = currDistance / totalDistance;

        float vAmount = vMax * vMultiplier;
        vAmount = Mathf.Clamp(vAmount, 0, vMax);
        vignetteEffect.intensity.Override(vAmount);
    }
```

10. Play the **Scene**. You should see an animated vignette effect, in addition to the zooming, when the mouse button is clicked and held.

Learn more about this new version at the following locations:

- The project Wiki:
  https://github.com/Unity-Technologies/PostProcessing/wiki
- Unity GitHub account from which to download it:
  https://github.com/Unity-Technologies/PostProcessing
- This article about scripting with the Post Processing Stack v2 by Juan Sebastian Munoz Arango:
  http://www.pencilsquaregames.com/changing-parameters-through-scripting-on-unitys-post-processing-stack-v2/

Displaying a minimap

In many games, a broader view of the scene can be invaluable for navigation and information. Minimaps are great for giving players that extra perspective that they may need when in first- or third-person mode. In this recipe, we'll first create a simple square minimap that appears at the top-right of the screen; then, you'll learn how to make it circular and add a rotating compass effect:

Getting ready...

This recipe adds to the scene created in the first recipe of this chapter, so make a copy of that project folder and do your work for this recipe with that copy.

How to do it...

To create a minimap, follow these steps:

1. From the **Hierarchy** panel, create a new UI Panel object (**Create | UI | Panel**) named `Panel-miniMap`. Since this is the first UI GameObject to be created in this **Scene**, new Canvas and `EventSystem` GameObjects should be created automatically, and the UI Panel should be a child of the Canvas GameObject.

2. With the `Panel-miniMap` GameObject selected in the **Inspector,** do the following:
    - In the Rect Transform, set the alignment to top-right (click the top-right box while holding down the Shift and Alt keys)
    - In the Rect Transform, set **Width** to `128` and **Height** to `128`

3. We'll create a **Render Texture** file to which our minimap Camera will copy its view. In the **Project** panel, create a new **Render Texture** and name it `RenderTextureMap`. In the **Inspector,** ensure its **Size** is set to **256 x 256**.

4. In the **Inspector,** select GameObject Panel-minimap and add a new child UI Raw Image named `RawImage-TextureMap` (**Create | UI | Raw Image**).

5. For the UI `RawImage-TextureMap` GameObject, populate the **Source Image** field with the `RenderTextureMap` image. This means when our minimap Camera updates its view to the **Render Texture**, what the **Camera** sees will be automatically displayed in this UI Raw Image.

6. After ensuring UI Raw `Image-RenderTextureMap` is a child of `Panel-minimap,` make it fill the whole panel by choosing **Stretch** for both the vertical and horizontal axes in the Rect Transform (while holding down the Shift and Alt keys):

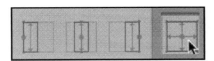

7. From the **Hierarchy** panel, create a new Camera **(Create | Camera)** and rename it `Camera-minimap`. Uncheck (or remove) the camera's **Audio Listener** component, since there should only be one active **Audio Listener** in a **Scene**.

8. In the Hierarchy child `Camera-minimap` to the `character-MsLazer` character. Then, in the **Inspector,** set its properties as follows:
    - **Position:** `(0, 10, 0)`
    - **Rotation:** `(90, 0, 0)`
    - **Clear Flags: Depth Only**
    - **Projection: Orthographic**
    - **Camera: Size: 5 (default)**
    - **Depth: 1 (or higher)**
    - **Target Texture: RenderTextureMap**

9. Play the **Scene**. You should be able to see the square-shaped minimap functioning in the top-right corner of the screen:

How it works...

The main element of the minimap is a UI Raw Image element (RawImage-TextureMap), displaying the contents of the Render Texture file named RenderTextureMap.

You created a second Camera in the Scene (Camera-minimap), and set its Target Texture to the RenderTextureMap file; this means that the view seen by the Camera updates the contents of RenderTextureMap each frame, which in turn is then displayed to the user in UI RawImage-TextureMap.

Camera-minimap is an orthographic camera that follows the player's character from a top-down viewpoint. You removed/disabled the AudioListener component in this new Camera, since there should only be one active AudioListener in a **Scene,** and there is already one in the default **Main Camera** GameObject.

You childed this new Camera to character-MsLazer, so it moves with the character. You positioned it 10 units above the character (Y = 10), and you made it point downwards towards the character (X-rotation of 90 degrees).

There's more...

If you want to experiment more with your minimap, read on.

Using a UI Mask to make the minimap circular in shape

One way to make the minimap stand out in the UI is to make it circular. We can do this easily by adding a UI Mask based on a circle:

A good way to make the minimap stand out in the UI is to present it as a circular shape, do the following:

1. In the **Project** panel, select the **circleMask** file in the Textures folder, and in the **Inspector** ensure the **Texture Type** is **Sprite (2D and UI)**.

 To change a Texture type to **Sprite (2D and UI)**, select the file in the **Project** panel, then in the **Inspector** change its **Texture Type** to **Sprite (2D and UI)** and click on **Apply** to confirm the changes.

2. Ensure the `Panel-miniMap` GameObject is selected in the **Hierarchy**. In the **Inspector** for the **Image (Script)** component, populate the **Source Image** field with the **circleMask** texture, click the **Color** property, and set the **Alpha** value to `255`:

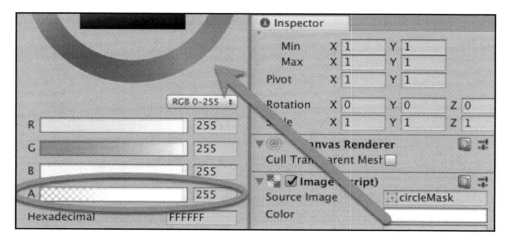

3. Now, add a **Mask** component to `Panel-miniMap` in the **Inspector,** by choosing menu: **Add Component | UI | Mask**. Uncheck the **Show Mask Graphic** property (it will become invisible).

The circle image serves as a mask for the minimap, so that only images inside the `circleMask` area will be displayed, resulting in a circular minimap.

Hiding player character image at center of minimap and showing triangle marker

With most minimaps, the center of the minimap is the location of the player's character, so we don't need to show the player's character in the minimap. Let's create a **Layer** named `Player` and place `character-MsLazer` onto that **Layer.** We can then improve efficiency and reduce visual clutter by creating a **Culling Mask** that ignores the **Player Layer**. We can display a simple **2D Sprite** in the center of our minimap, pointing upwards, to indicate that our player is always facing upwards relative to what is displayed in the minimap:

1. Create a new **User Layer** named `Player`.

2. Select the `character-MsLaser` GameObject (the player's character) in the Hierarchy, and set the **Layer** property to **Player** (click **Yes** in the **Change Children** popup dialog).

3. With `Camera-minimap` selected in the **Hierarchy,** in the **Inspector** for the **Culling Mask** property of the **Camera,** deselect **Layer Player.** This property should now say **Mixed...,** which means that GameObjects on the **Player Layer** will be ignored by our our `Camera-minimap`.

4. Let's add a triangle marker 2D image at the center of the **Panel.** Create a new UI Image as a child of `Panel-minimap;` rename this `Image-marker`. In the **Inspector,** set the **Source Image** property to **Texture** asset file `triangleMarker`. Click the **Set Native Size button.**

5. Run the **Scene.** Rather than the top-down view of the player's character, you should now see a triangle at the center of the minimap (always pointing upwards):

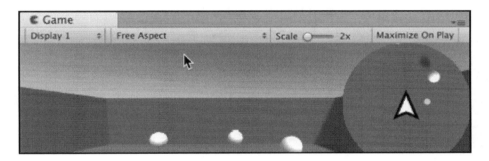

Rather than just having a triangle image in the center representing the player, you can create, for example, colored 3D objects that in Orthographic projection look like circles, squares, and so on by using **Layers** further. This involves having a **Layer** for objects to be displayed in the minimap, and another **Layer** (such as **Player)** that will be ignored by the minimap Camera. The Knights Of Unity have published a short tutorial that explains just how to do this kind of thing:

http://blog.theknightsofunity.com/implementing-minimap-unity/.

Rotating a compass-style image

Sometimes we want a compass-style image around our minimaps, so we can see any differences between the current bearing (forward direction) of our player's character and the direction we were originally facing.

To add a rotating compass-style image around our minimap, do the following:

1. Let's add a compass-style circular image at the center of the Panel (with the letter **N** pointing upwards). To do this, create a new UI Image as a child of **Panel-minimap;** rename this **Image-compass.** In the **Inspector,** set the **Source Image** property to Texture compass.

2. Ensure both **Image-compass** and **Image-marker** appear below **RawImage-TextureMap** in the **Hierarchy** of the children of the `Panel-minimap` GameObject; this ensures the triangle marker and compass circle images are drawn after the Camera texture (that is, on top of the Camera's view image):

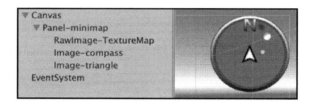

3. Create a C# script-class MiniMap, and add an `instance-object` as a component to `Camera-minimap`:

```csharp
using UnityEngine;

public class MiniMap : MonoBehaviour {
    public GameObject mapUI;
    private Transform target;

    void Start() {
        target =
GameObject.FindGameObjectWithTag("Player").transform;
    }

    void Update() {
        Vector3 compassAngle = new Vector3();
        compassAngle.z = target.transform.eulerAngles.y;
        mapUI.transform.eulerAngles = compassAngle;
    }
}
```

4. Play the Scene. You should be able to see the minimap functioning in the top-right corner of the screen. As you rotate the player character's orientation, you'll see the "N" north indicator in the circle around the minimap rotate too (but in the opposite direction).

Every frame, the compass UI Image is rotated to match the rotation of the player's 3D character in the Scene.

Making the range of the map larger or smaller

Since our Camera-minimap is Orthographic, changing the height of the **Camera** above the character will make no difference (since distance doesn't change how objects are projected onto an Orthographic camera). However, changing the **Size** property of the **Camera** component in the **Inspector** will control how large or small an area of the world is projected to the **Camera.**

Try increasing the size to 20, and your minimap will show much more of the surrounding maze around your character:

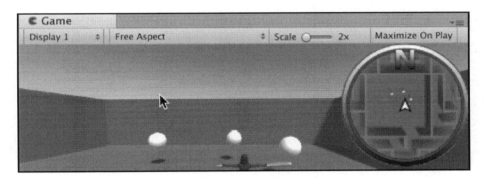

 When increasing the range of the minimap, you may wish to make the triangle marker Image in the center of the minimap smaller. You can do this easily by centering its Rect Transform, then setting a smaller Width and Height (such as 16 x 16).

Adapting your minimap to other styles

You can easily modify this recipe to make a top-down or isometric view of a racing game circuit map. In the **Inspector,** unchild the Camera-minimap GameObject; this will prevent it from following any of the **Scene** characters.

Creating an in-game surveillance Camera

In the previous recipe, we rendered the output from our minimap **Camera** to a **Render Texture**, and displayed the contents of that image in a **UI Raw Image**. Another example of when we may wish to capture and output the view of a **Camera** at runtime is to simulate an in-game surveillance **Camera,** such as a **Closed-Circuit Television** (CCTV) system. In this recipe, we will make use of a **Render Texture** to create an in-game surveillance camera that transmits its video to a 3D monitor elsewhere in the **Scene**:

Getting ready

This recipe adds to the scene created in the first recipe of this chapter, so make a copy of that project folder and do your work for this recipe with that copy.

For this recipe, we have also prepared two 3D models (FBX files) needed for the monitor and cctv-camera objects. These 3D model files can be found in the 06_07 folder.

How to do it...

To create an in-game surveillance **Camera,** just follow these steps:

1. Import the monitor and `cctv-camera` models into your Unity Project.

2. Create clones of the monitor and `cctv-camera` models by dragging them from the **Project** panel into the Hierarchy panel.

3. In the **Inspector,** set the following properties for the monitor GameObject:
   - **Position:** (-3, 0, 6)
   - **Rotation:** (0, 180, 0)
   - **Scale:** (1, 1, 1)

4. In the **Inspector,** set the following properties for the `cctv-camera` GameObject:
   - **Position:** (-6, 0, 1)
   - **Rotation:** (0, 90, 0)

5. From the **Project** panel, create a new **Render Texture** file and rename it `screenRenderTexture`. In the **Inspector,** change its **Size** to **512 x 512.**

6. Add a new **Camera** to the scene (menu: **Create | Camera**) named `Camera-surveillance`. Child this new GameObject to `cctv-camera`. Uncheck (or remove) the camera's **Audio Listener** component, since there should only be one active **Audio Listener** in a Scene.

7. In the **Inspector,** set the following properties for the `Camera-surveillance` GameObject:
   - **Position:** (0, 2, 0)
   - **Rotation:** (0, 0, 0)
   - **Clipping Planes: Near:** 0.6
   - **Target Texture:** `screenRenderTexture`.

8. Create a new **Material** named `m_renderTexture`, and set its **Albedo Texture** to `screenRenderTexture`.

9. In the **Hierarchy,** find the screen child of the monitor GameObject and set its **Mesh Renderer Material** to `m_renderTexture`.

10. Play your **Scene**. You should be able to see your actions in front of the `cctc-camera` displayed in real time on the monitor's screen:

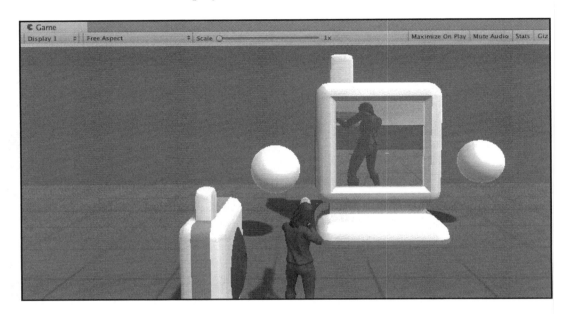

How it works...

We achieved the final result by using the surveillance camera as a source for the **Render Texture** applied to the screen. The camera was made a child of the camera's 3D model for easier relocation. Also, its **Near Clipping** plane was readjusted in order to avoid displaying parts of the camera's 3D model geometry, and its **Audio Source** component was disabled so that it wouldn't clash with the main camera's component.

Finally, our **Render Texture** was applied to the material of the monitor GameObject.

There's more...

If you want to experiment more with your minimap, read on.

Using Post-Processing to add a grainy, grayscale effect to the CCTV

A great effect to add for in-game TV systems is grainy (visual noise) grayscale **Post-Processing.** This adds the feel of cheap, old-style CCTV systems, such as might be used for a security system, and to add some kind of menacing film noir effect:

To add a vignette effect, do the following:

1. Open the **Asset Store** panel, then download and import the free **Post-Processing Stack** assets published by Unity Technologies.

2. In the **Project** panel, create a new **Post-Processing** Profile file by going to **Create | Post-Processing** Profile. Name this new profile `film-noir`.

3. In the **Hierarchy,** select the `Camera-surveillance` child of the `cctv-camera` GameObject. Add a **Post-Processing Behaviour** component to this **Camera,** by chosing menu: **Add Component | Effects | Post-Processing** Behaviour.

4. Drag the `film-noir` file from the **Project** panel into the **Inspector** to populate the **Profile** property of the **Post-Processing Behaviour** component.

5. In the **Inspector,** set the following properties for the **Post-Processing Profile** film-noir file:
   - Check the **Color Grading** option, and set **Basic: Saturation to zero**
   - Check the **Grain** option, uncheck **Colored,** and set the maximum values for **Intensity (1), Luminescence Contribution (1),** and **Size (3).**

6. Run the **Scene.**

By processing the image generated from the **Camera,** the image in the monitor should now be an old-style grainy, grayscale video feed from cctv-camera. The image is made grayscale, since color saturation is zero, and a grainy effect has also been applied.

Working with Unity's multi-purpose camera rig

Unity provides some **Camera** rigs, which can make setting up scenes much faster and help to test out ideas. In this recipe, you'll use a 3rd Person Character and the multi-purpose camera rig from the default Unity asset packages to quickly create a scene with a camera that automatically follows a character as it moves, smoothing rotating behind the character as the character changes direction:

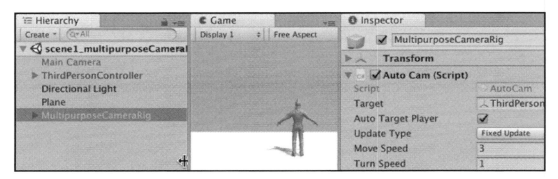

How to do it...

To work with Unity's multi-purpose camera rig, just follow these steps:

1. Create a new Unity 3D scene.
2. Import the **Characters** and **Cameras Asset Packages**: use menu: **Assets | Import Package ... | Cameras & Characters**.
3. You should now have a `Standard Assets` folder in your **Project** panel, containing the `Cameras` and `Characters` folders (and possibly some others, such as `CrossPlatformInput`, `Editor`, and so on).
4. Create a 3D Plane in your **Scene.**
5. Add a clone of the `ThirdPersonController` Prefab to your Scene. Do this by dragging the `ThirdPersonController` Prefab from the `Standard Assets | Characters | ThirdPersonController | Prefabs` folder into the **Scene.**
6. With GameObject `ThirdPersonController` selected in the **Hierarchy,** in the **Inspector** tag this GameObject with the **Player** tag.
7. Add a clone of the `MultipurposeCameraRig` Prefab to your Scene. Do this by dragging the `MultipurposeCameraRig` Prefab from the `Standard Assets | Cameras | Prefabs` folder into the Scene.
8. Disable the **Main** Camera GameObject.
9. Run the **Scene.** As you move the character around the **Scene,** the **Camera** should smoothly follow behind.

How it works...

You added a `ThirdPersonController` to the Scene and tagged it **Player.** You added a `MultipurposeCameraRig` to the **Scene.** The code attached to the camera rig automatically looks for a target GameObject tagged Player, and positions itself to follow from above and behind this GameObject.

You can adjust the speed at which the camera follows and turns by changing the public properties for the `MultipurposeCameraRig` in its **Inspector** component **Auto Cam (Script).**

Using Cinemachine ClearShot to switch cameras to keep the player in shot

A new feature of Unity is the `Cinemachine` set of components:

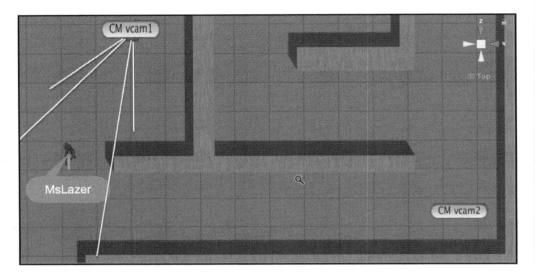

Getting ready

This recipe adds to the scene created in the first recipe of this chapter, so make a copy of that project folder and do your work for this recipe with that copy.

How to do it...

To use **Cinemachine ClearShot** to switch cameras to keep the player in shot, just follow these steps:

1. Open the scene provided, containing a 3D maze and `character-MsLazer`.
2. Un-child the **Main Camera** from `character-MsLazer`, since we need this camera free for `Cinemachine` to take control of it.
3. Install the `Cinemachine` package using the Unity Package Manager (to get the most up-to-date version).

4. Add a **Cinemachine ClearShot** camera GameObject to the scene (menu: **Cinemachine | Ceate ClearShot Camera).** You should see a new GameObject in the Hierarchy named CM Clearshot 1. Set the position of this new GameObject to (0,0,0).

5. CM Clearshot 1 should have a child GameObject, Cinemachine Virtual Camera CM vcam 1. Set the position of this virtual camera, CM vcam 1, to (10, 4, -10).

6. You will also see that a Cinemachine Brain component has been added to the **Main Camera,** and in the **Hierarchy** you'll see the Cinemacine Brain icon next to the **Main Camera** name (half gray cog, half red camera):

7. Locate the `mixamorig:neck` GameObject in the Hierarchy inside character-MsLazer. We'll use this part of `character-MsLazer` to be the part that our `Cinemachine` cameras will use to orient towards.

8. Select **CM Clearshot 1**, and in the **Inspector** populate the **Look At** property of the **Cinemachine ClearShot** component with a reference to the `mixamorig:neck` GameObject (drag the GameObject from Hierarchy into the property in the **Inspector**):

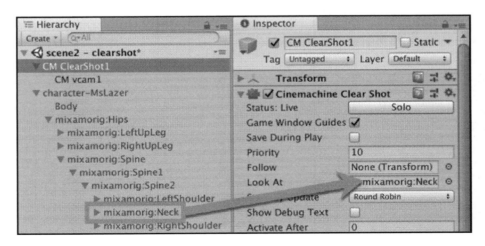

9. Run the **Scene.** As you move `character-MsLazer` around the scene, the Main Camera (controlled by the `Cinemachein` Brain) should rotate to always look at the character. However, sometimes a wall obscures the view.

10. Create a second child Virtual Camera by selecting CM Clearshot 1 in the Hierarchy, and then in the Inspector, click the + button for the **Virtual Camera Children** property of the `Cinemachine` Clear Shot component. You should see a new virtual camera child named CM vcam 2 has been created. Set the **Position** of CM vcam 2 to (27, 4, -18).

11. Run the **Scene.** Initially, CM vcam 1 has the best shot, and so this camera's position will be used to direct the **Main Camera.** However, if you move `character-MsLazer` along the corridor towards CM vcam 2, `Cinemachine` will then switch control to CM vcam 2.

How it works...

A Cinemachine Brain component was added to the **Scene.** This takes control of the **Main Camera** and uses properties of one or more **Virtual Cinemachine Camera** to decide what properties to apply to the **Main Camera.** You added a **Cinemachine ClearShot** GameObject, whose purpose is to tell the **Cinemachine Brain** which of its **Virtual Camera** children has the best shot.

You set the **Look At** property of the `ClearShot` component to the neck component of `character-MsLazer`; the position of this GameObject is used by the `ClearShot` component to rank each **Virtual Camera's** quality of shot.

There's more...

We've only just touched the surface of what **Cinemachine** has to offer. Here are some suggestions for how to learn more.

Unity Cinemachine tutorials

In the learn section of the Unity website, you'll find many video tutorials introducing the different animation features of Unity. There is a special category for **Cinemachine** tutorials, which provide a great overview of the features and uses of Cinemachine: `https://unity3d.com/learn/tutorials/s/animation`.

Will Goldstone's ClearShot turtorial

This recipe was inspired by Will Goldstone's ClearShot tutorial, available on YouTube: https://www.youtube.com/watch?v=kLcdrDljakA.

Adam Myhill's Cinemachine blog posts

Adam Myhill's blog posts (he is the creator of **Cinemachine**) have lots of information and video links about many different Cinemachine features: https://blogs.unity3d.com/2017/08/25/community-stories-cinemachine-and-tim eline/.

Read the installed Cinemachine documentation

Later versions of **Cinemachine (2.1+)** have documentation installed with the package. Display the **Cinemachine** About panel **(Menu: Cinemachine | About),** then click the **Documentation** button:

You can also find the documentation online at https://docs.unity3d.com/Packages/com.unity.cinemachine@2.1/manual/inde x.html.

Letting the player switch to a Cinemachine FreeLook camera

It's always good to give players choices and control in their game experience. In this recipe, we'll set up a mouse-controllable **Cinemachine FreeLook** camera and let the player switch to it.

Getting ready

This recipe adds to the previous one, so make a copy of that project folder and do your work for this recipe with that copy.

How to do it...

To explore Cinemachine, just follow these steps:

1. Ensure the **Default Blend** property of the **Cinemachine Brain** component in the **Main Camera** is set to Ease In Out. This means we'll have a smooth transition when switching between cameras.

2. Add a **Cinemachine FreeLook** camera GameObject to the scene (menu: **Cinemachine | Ceate FreeLook Camera**). You should see a new GameObject in the **Hierarchy** named CM FreeLook 1. Set the **Priority** property of the **Cinemachine Free Look (Script)** component to zero.

3. Locate the mixamorig:neck GameObject in the **Hierarchy** inside **MsLazer**. We'll use this part of the **MsLazer** character to be the part that our **Cinemachine** cameras will use to orient towards and follow at a steady distance.

4. Select **CM FreeLook 1**, and in the **Inspector** populate the **Look At** and **Follow** properties of the **Cinemachine Free Look (Script)** component with a reference to the mixamorig:neck GameObject (drag the GameObject from Hierarchy into the properties in the **Inspector**).

5. Create a new FreeLookSwitcher C# Script-class containing the following code, and add an instance-object as a component to the **CM FreeLook 1** GameObject:

```
using UnityEngine;
 using Cinemachine;
```

```
public class FreeLookSwitcher : MonoBehaviour {
    private CinemachineFreeLook cinemachineFreeLook;

    private void Start() {
        cinemachineFreeLook =
GetComponent<CinemachineFreeLook>();
    }

    void Update () {
        if (Input.GetKeyDown("1"))
            cinemachineFreeLook.Priority = 99;

        if (Input.GetKeyDown("2"))
            cinemachineFreeLook.Priority = 0;
    }
}
```

6. Run the **Scene.** When moving around the maze, initially the **Cinemachine ClearShot** cameras will be chosen by the **Cinemachine** Brain. But, pressing the *1* key will make it switch to the **FreeLook** camera following the player's character. Pressing *2* will switch back to the **ClearShot** cameras.

How it works...

You added a **FreeLook Cinemachine** GameObject, but with a priority of zero, so it will be ignored initially. When the *1* key is pressed, the script increases the **Priority** to 99 (much higher than the default 10 of the **ClearShot** cameras), so then the **Cinemachine** Brain will make the **FreeLook** virtual camera control the **Main Camera.** Pressing the *2* key reduces the **FreeLook** component's **Priority** back to **zero,** so the **ClearShot** cameras will be used again.

There should be a smooth transition from **FreeLook** to **ClearShot** and back again, since you set the **Default Blend** property of the **Cinemachine Brain** component in the **Main Camera** to **Ease In Out.**

8
Lights and Effects

In this chapter, we will cover the following topics:

- Directional Light with a cookie Texture to simulate a cloudy day
- Creating and applying a cookie Texture to a spotlight
- Adding a custom reflection map to a scene
- Creating a laser aim with a projector
- Enhancing the laser aim with a line renderer
- Setting up an environment with Procedural Skybox and Directional Light
- Reflecting surrounding objects with reflection probes
- Using material emission to bake light from a glowing lamp onto scene objects
- Lighting a scene with lightmaps and light probes

Introduction

Whether you're trying to make a better-looking game or you want to add interesting features, lights and effects can boost your project and help you deliver a higher quality product. Modern game engines, including Unity, use complex mathematics and physical modelling of how light from light sources interacts with objects in a **Scene**.

For visually realistic virtual game **Scenes**, the game engine must model sources of light, how light falls directly from those sources onto surfaces, and also how light then indirectly bounces from those surfaces to other objects in the scene, and again onto other objects and so on. For rich, complex **Scenes** containing many objects and light sources, it would be impossible to calculate everything from scratch every frame, so pre-computation needs to take place to model these light source and surface interactions.

In this chapter, we will look at the creative ways of using lights and effects, and also take a look at some of Unity's key **Lighting** features, such as **Procedural Skyboxes**, **Reflection** emissive **Materials**, **Probes**, **Light Probes**, custom **Reflection Sources**, and **Global Illumination** (**GI**).

The big picture

There are many ways of creating light sources in Unity. Here's a quick overview of the most common methods.

Lights

Lights are placed into the scene as GameObjects, featuring a **Light** component. They can function in **Realtime**, **Baked**, or **Mixed** modes. Among the other properties, they can have their **Range**, **Color**, **Intensity**, and **Shadow Type** set by the user. There are four types of lights:

- **Directional Light**: This is normally used to simulate the sunlight
- **Spot Light**: This works like a cone-shaped spot light
- **Point Light**: This is a bulb-like, omnidirectional light
- **Area Light**: This baked-only light type is emitted in all directions from a rectangle-shaped entity, allowing for a smooth, realistic shading

The following screenshot illustrates different types of lights, with their scene panel icons:

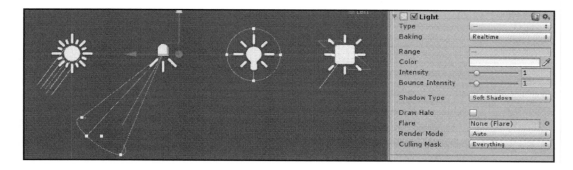

Environment lighting

Unity's **Environment Lighting** is often achieved through the combination of a **Skybox Material** and sunlight defined by the scene's **Directional Light**. Such a combination creates an ambient light that is integrated into the scene's environment, and which can be set as real-time or baked into **Lightmaps**.

Ambient lighting doesn't come from any locational source, as it exists evenly throughout the scene. Ambient light can be used to influence the overall brightness of a scene:

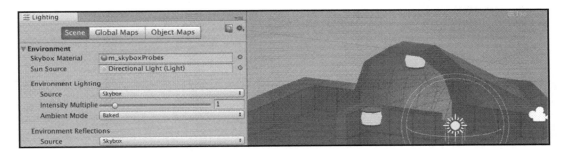

Emissive materials

When applied to static objects, materials featuring the **Emission** colors or maps will cast light over surfaces nearby, in both **Real-Time** and **Baked** modes, as shown in the following screenshot:

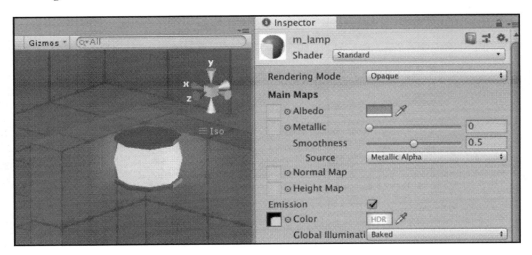

Projector

As its name suggests, a **Projector** can be used to simulate projected lights and shadows, basically by projecting a material and its **Texture** map onto the other objects:

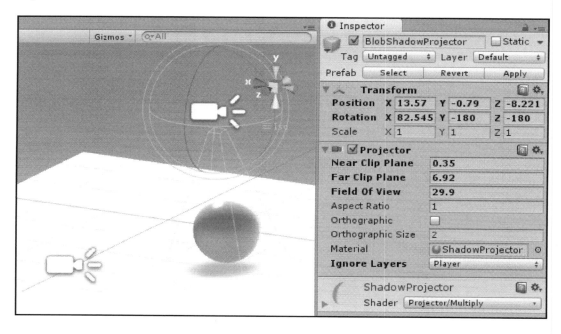

Lightmaps

Lightmaps are basically **Texture** maps generated from the **Scene's** lighting information and applied to the scene's static objects in order to avoid the use of processing-intensive **Real-Time** lighting.

Pre-computation of lighting in a **Scene** is known as **Lightmap** *Baking. Static –* immovable – parts of the scene (lights and other objects) can have their lighting "baked" (pre-computed), before the game is run. Then, during **Run-Time**, game performance is improved, since the pre-calculated **Lightmaps** can be used rather than having to re-calculate each frame at **Run-Time** (although this does require more memory to store the pre-computations).

Unity offers two lightmappers, Enlighten, and more recently the Progressive lightmapper. Enlighten can work well for Precomputed real-time Global Illumination (ambient lighting). The Progressive lightmapper is recommended for **Baked Lightmaps**.

Light probes

Light Probes are a way of sampling the **Scene's** illumination at specific points in order to have it applied onto dynamic objects without the use of **Real-Time** lighting. *Moving* (dynamic) objects can use **Light Probes** so that their lighting changes in relation to where the baked light sources are located in the **Scene**.

The Lighting settings window

The **Lighting** window, (menu: **Window** I **Rendering** I **Lighting Settings**), is the hub for setting and adjusting the scene's illumination features, such as **Lightmaps**, **Global Illumination**, **Fog**, and much more:

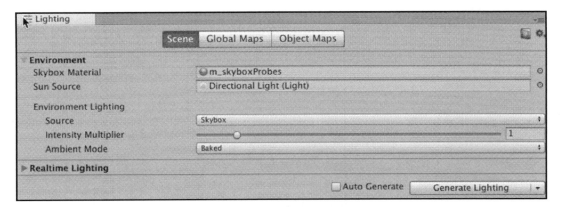

The Light Explorer panel

When working with **Lights** and **Lighting**, a useful tool in Unity is the **Lighting Explorer** panel, which allows editing and viewing the properties of all of the lights in the current scene. The **Lighting Explorer** panel lists all **Lights** in a single panel, making it easy to work with each individually, or change the settings of several at the same time. It can be a great time-saving tool when working with scenes involving lots of **Light** Game Objects.

To display the Light Explorer panel, choose the following menu: **Window** | **Rendering** | **Light Explorer**:

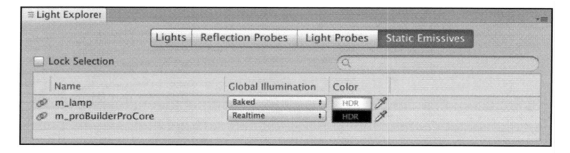

Cucoloris cookies

Lights can have a cookie **Texture** applied. **Cookies** are **Textures** used to cast shadows or silhouettes in a **Scene**. They are produced by using the cookie **Texture** as a mask between the light source and the surfaces being rendered. Their name, and usage, comes from the use of physical devices called cucoloris (nicknamed cookies) used in theatre and movie production, to give the shadow effects implying environments such as moving clouds, the bars of a prison window, or the sunlight broken up by a jungle leaf canopy.

Color space (Gamma and Linear)

Unity now offers a choice of two **Color spaces**: **Gamma** (the default) and **Linear**. You can select your desired **Color Space** via the following menu: **Edit** | **Project Settings** | **Player**. While **Linear** space has significant advantages, it isn't supported by all hardware (especially mobile systems), so which you choose will depend on which platform you are deploying for.

Further resources

This chapter aims to present you with some of Unity's lighting features, and offer a few tricks with lights and effects. As you work through the recipes in this chapter, you may wish to learn more about this chapter's topics from some of these sources:

- The Unity lighting manual entry:
  https://docs.unity3d.com/Manual/Lighting.html

- Unity's **Global Illumination** (GI) pages:
  - `https://docs.unity3d.com/Manual/GIIntro.html`
  - `http://docs.unity3d.com/Manual/GlobalIllumination.html`
- Unity's information about cookie **Textures** can be found at their manual page: `https://docs.unity3d.com/Manual/Cookies.html`
- Another source about Unity and cookie **Textures** is the *CgProgramming WikiBook* for Unity: `https://en.wikibooks.org/wiki/Cg_Programming/Unity/Cookies`
- Unity manual about choosing a color space: `https://unity3d.com/learn/tutorials/topics/graphics/choosing-color-space`
- Unity manual about the **Lighting Explorer** panel: `https://docs.unity3d.com/Manual/LightingExplorer.html`
- About **Linear** and **Gamma** lighting workflows: `https://docs.unity3d.com/Manual/LinearRendering-LinearOrGammaWorkflow.html`
- LMHPoly article on 7 tips for better Unity Lighting: `https://lmhpoly.com/7-tips-for-better-lighting-in-unity/`

Directional Light with cookie Texture to simulate a cloudy day

As can be seen in many first-person shooters and survival horror games, lights and shadows can add a great deal of realism to a **Scene**, helping to create the right atmosphere for the game immensely. In this recipe, we will create a cloudy outdoor environment using cookie **Textures**. **Cookie Textures** work as masks for lights. It functions by adjusting the intensity of the light projection to the cookie texture's alpha channel. This allows for a silhouette effect (just think of the bat signal) or, as in this particular case, subtle variations that give a filtered quality to the lighting.

Getting ready

If you don't have access to an image editor, or prefer to skip the **Texture** map elaboration in order to focus on the implementation, we have provided the prepared cookie image file **cloudCookie.tga**, inside the `07_01` folder.

How to do it...

To simulate a cloudy outdoor environment, follow these steps:

1. In your image editor, create a new 512 x 512 pixel image.
2. Using black as the foreground color and white as the background color, apply the **Clouds** filter – in Photoshop, choose the following menu: **Filter | Render | Clouds**:

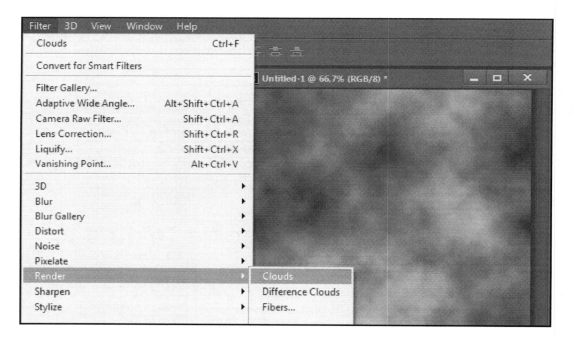

 Learning about the Alpha channel is useful, but you could get the same result without it. Skip steps 3 to 7, save your image as cloudCookie.png and, when changing texture type in step 9, leave Alpha from Greyscale checked.

3. Select your entire image and copy it.
4. Open the Channels window (in Photoshop, this can be done choosing the following menu: **Window | Channels**.
5. There should be three channels: **Red**, **Green**, and **Blue**. Create a new channel. This will be the **Alpha** channel.
6. In the **Channels** window, select the **Alpha** 1 channel and paste your image into it:

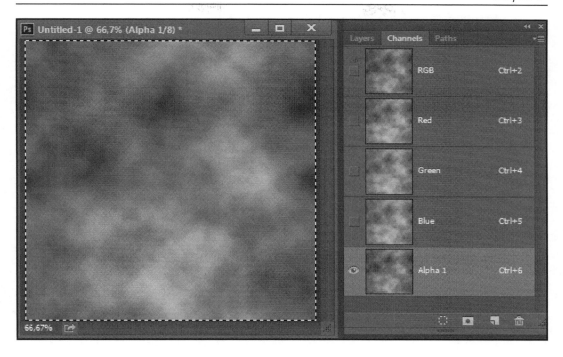

7. Save your image file as **cloudCookie.PSD** or TGA.

8. Import your image file to Unity and select it in the **Project** panel.

9. From the **Inspector**, change its **Texture Type** to **Cookie** and its **Light Type** to Directional. Then, click on **Apply**, as follows:

10. Let's add a light to our scene. Since we want to simulate sunlight, the best option is to create a **Directional Light**. Choose the **Hierarchy** menu: **Create | Light | Directional Light**.

11. We will need a surface to actually see the lighting effect. You can either add a 3D plane to your scene (menu: **GameObject** | **3D Object** | **Plane**), or create a 3D Terrain (menu: **GameObject** | **3D Object** | **Terrain**).

12. In the Inspector, reset the light's **Transform Position** to (0, 0, 0) and its **Rotation** to (90, 0, 0).

13. In the **Cookie** field, select the **cloudCookie** texture that you imported earlier. Change the **Cookie Size** field to 15, or a value that you feel is more appropriate for the **Scene's** dimensions. Set the **Shadow Type** as **No Shadows**:

14. Create a new C# script class named **ShadowMover**, and add an instance object as a component to the **Directional Light**:

```
public class ShadowMover : MonoBehaviour {
        public float windSpeedX = 2;
        public float windSpeedZ = 2;

        private float lightCookieSize;
        private Vector3 startPosition;
        private float limitX;
        private float limitZ;
        private Vector3 windMovement;

        void Start() {
            startPosition = transform.position;
            lightCookieSize =
GetComponent<Light>().cookieSize;
            limitX = Mathf.Abs(startPosition.x) +
lightCookieSize;
            limitZ = Mathf.Abs(startPosition.z) +
lightCookieSize;
            windMovement = new Vector3(windSpeedX, 0,
```

```
            windSpeedZ);
                }

            void Update() {
                Vector3 position = transform.position +
(Time.deltaTime
                    * windMovement);
                position.x = WrapValue(position.x, limitX,
                startPosition.x);
                position.z = WrapValue(position.z, limitZ,
                startPosition.z);
                transform.position = position;
            }

            private float WrapValue(float n, float limit, float
            startValue) {
                float absoluteValue = Mathf.Abs(n);
                if (absoluteValue > limit)
                    return startValue;
                else
                    return n;
            }
        }
```

15. Select the **Directional Light**. In the Inspector, change the parameters **Wind Speed X** and Wind Speed Z to different values.

16. Play your scene. The shadows will now be moving.

How it works...

The script class offers two public values for the X- and Z- speeds of movement (simulating wind).

When the scene starts, first, the initial position of the Directional Light is stored. Then, the size of the cookie is read from the sibling Light component, and used to calculate maximum X and Z values. Finally, a **Vector3** is created, for the amount to move our light by in seconds, based on the X and Z window speeds (Y is zero, since we don't need to move the Directional Light in the Y axis).

The WrapValue(...) method is defined, which returns a value. If the positive value of the first parameter exceeds the second parameter (the limit), then the third parameter (the initial value) is returned. Otherwise, the value of the first parameter is returned. This allows is to ensure that if a value (for example, our X or Z coordinate) goes beyond a limit, we can "wrap" it back to its start value.

The `Update()` method is executed in each frame. The next position for the light is calculated (current position plus the current frame's proportion of the wind speed per second vector). The X and Z values of this new position are set using our `WrapValue(...)` method, so we know that their limit values are not exceeded. Finally, the position of the light is set to this new position, `Vector3`.

> The reason we are not enabling shadows is because the light angle for the X axis must be 90 degrees (or there will be a noticeable gap when the light resets to the original position). If you want dynamic shadows in your scene, please add a second **Directional Light**.

Creating and applying a cookie texture to a spotlight

Cookie Textures can work well with Unity **Spotlight**s to simulate shadows coming from projectors, windows, and so on. An example of this would be for the bars of a prison window.

In this recipe, we'll create and apply a cookie **Texture** suitable to use with Unity **Spotlights**:

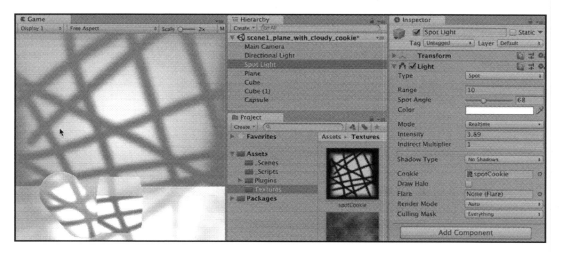

Getting ready

If you don't have access to an image editor, or prefer to skip the **Texture** map elaboration in order to focus on the implementation, we have provided the prepared cookie image file called **spotCookie.tif** inside the 07_02 folder.

How to do it...

To create and apply a cookie texture to a spotlight, follow these steps:

1. In your image editor, create a new **512 x 512** greyscale pixel image.
2. Ensure that the border is completely black by setting the brush tool color to black and drawing around the four edges of the image. Then, draw some criss-crossed lines. Save your image, naming it **spotCookie**:

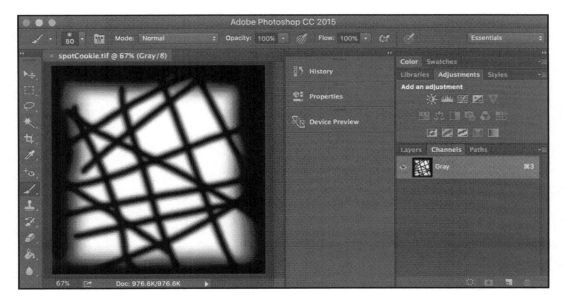

3. Import your image file to Unity and select it in the **Project** panel.

4. From the Inspector, change its **Texture Type** to **Cookie** and its **Light Type** to Spotlight, and set the **Alpha Source** to **From Grayscale**. Then, click on **Apply**, as follows:

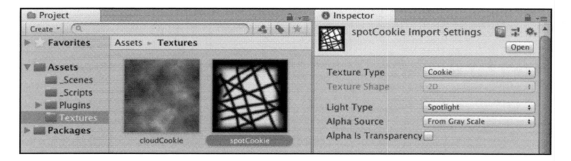

5. Create a scene containing the following:
   - A flat **3D Terrain** or **Plane** as our ground
   - A **3D Cube** or **Plane**, stretched to act as a wall
   - Two or three other 3D objects in front of the wall

6. Position the **Main Camera** to be showing the 3D objects in front of the "wall".

7. Now, add a **Spotlight** to the scene by choosing the following menu: **Create | Light | Spotlight**.

8. Orient the **Spotlight** to be pointing in the direction of the **Main Camera** – you'll probably have to rotate the Y value by 180 degrees.

9. Set **Shadow Type** to **No Shadows**, and drag your **spotCookie Texture** from the Project panel into the **Cookie** slot.

10. Play your **Scene**. You should now see the spotlight casting shadows as if a light had been shone through a grid of planks of wood or metal.

How it works...

We created a greyscale Texture for use with Unity **Spotlights** – that's completely black around the edges – so that light does not "bleed" around the edge of our **Spotlight** emission. The black lines in the Texture are used by Unity to create shadows in the light emitted from the **Spotligh**, creating the effect that there are some straight beams of wood or metal through which the **Spotlight** is being shone.

You can learn more about creating **Spotlight** cookies in Unity at the Unity tutorial page: `http://docs.unity3d.com/Manual/HOWTO-LightCookie.html`.

Adding a custom Reflection map to a scene

Unity's Standard Shader gets its reflection from the scene's Reflection Source, as configured in the scene section of the Lighting window. The level of reflectiveness for each Material is defined by its Metallic value or Specular value, depending on which Shader is being used. This approach can be a real time-saver, allowing you to quickly assign the same reflection map to every object in the scene. It also helps keep the overall look of the scene coherent and cohesive. In this recipe, we will learn how to take advantage of the **Reflection Source** feature:

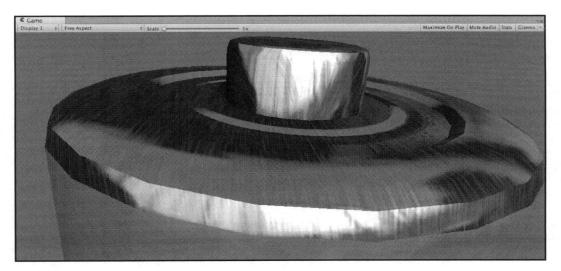

Getting ready

For this recipe, we will prepare a Reflection Cubemap, which is basically the environment to be projected as a reflection onto the material. It can be made from either six or, as shown in this recipe, a single image file.

To help us with this recipe, we have provided a Unity package (**batteryPrefab.unitypackage**), containing a prefab made of a 3D object and a basic Material (using a TIFF as a Diffuse map), and also a JPG file to be used as the reflection map. All of these files are inside the 07_03 folder.

How to do it...

To add Reflectiveness and Specularity to a material, follow these steps:

1. Import the **batteryPrefab.unitypackage** package into a new project. Then, select the battery_prefab object from the Assets folder, in the **Project** panel.

2. From the Inspector, expand the **Material** component and observe the asset preview window. Thanks to the **Specular** map, the material already features a reflective look. However, it looks as if it is reflecting the scene's default **Skybox**, as shown in the following screenshot:

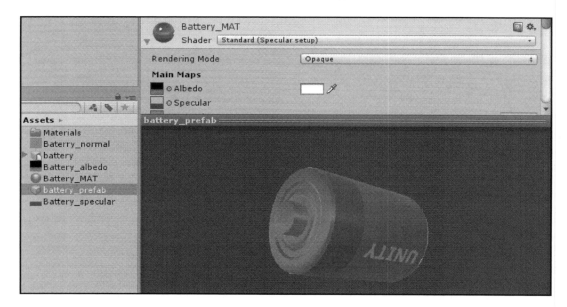

3. Import the **CustomReflection.jpg** image file. Ensure that this asset is selected in the Project panel.

4. In the Inspector for its **Import Settings**, set the following properties:
   - **Texture Type**: Default
   - **Texture Shape**: Cube
   - **Mapping**: Latitude-Longitude Layout (Cylindrical)
   - **Convolution Type**: None
   - **Fixup Edge Seams**: Checked
   - **Filter Mode**: Trilinear
   - Now, click on the **Apply** button, as follows:

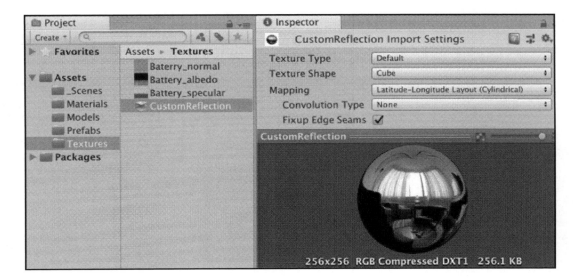

5. Let's replace the scene's Skybox with our newly created Cubemap as the Reflection map for our scene (menu: **Window | Rendering | Lighting Settings**).

6. Select the **Scene** section and use the drop-down menu to change the **Reflection Source** to **Custom**. Finally, assign the newly created **CustomReflection** texture as the Cubemap, as follows:

7. Check out the new reflections on the **battery_prefab** object.

How it works...

The material's specular map provides a reflective look, including the intensity and smoothness of the reflection. However, the image you see in the refection itself is given by the **Cubemap** that we created.

There's more...

Reflection Cubemaps can be achieved in many ways and have different mapping properties.

Mapping coordinates

The **Cylindrical** mapping that we applied was well-suited for the photograph that we used. However, depending on how the reflection image is generated, a **Cubic**- or **Spheremap**-based mapping can be more appropriate. Also, note that the **Fixup Edge** Seams option will try to make the image seamless.

Sharp reflections

You might have noticed that the reflection is somewhat blurry compared to the original image; this is because we have ticked the **Glossy Reflections** box. To get a sharper-looking reflection, deselect this option; in this case, you can also leave the **Filter Mode** option as **default (Bilinear)**.

Maximum size

At 512 x 512 pixels, our reflection map will probably run fine on lower-end machines. However, if the quality of the reflection map is not very important in your game's context, and the original image dimensions are big (say, 4,096 x 4,096), you might want to change the texture's **Max Size** from the **Import Settings** menu to a lower number.

Creating a laser aim with a projector

Although using UI elements, such as a cross-hair, is a valid way to allow players to aim, replacing (or combining) it with a projected laser dot might be a more interesting approach. In this recipe, we will use a light projector to implement this concept:

Getting ready

To help us with this recipe, in the 07_04 folder, we've provided a Unity package (**laserAssets.unitypackage**) containing a sample scene featuring a character holding a laser pointer, and also a texture map named **LineTexture**.

How to do it...

To create a laser dot aim with a Projector, follow these steps:

1. Start a new 3D project.
2. We'll be importing the **Projectors** components from the **Unity Standard Assets**. If you didn't install the **Standard Assets** when you installed Unity, go the the **Asset Store** and install the free **Standard Assets** now.
3. Import `laserAssets.unitypackage` into a new project. Then, open the scene named **basic_scene_MsLaser**. This is a basic scene, featuring a player character in a maze, with standard arrow keys or WASD movement.
4. Import the **Projectors** contents from the Effects Unity Standard Assets package folder:

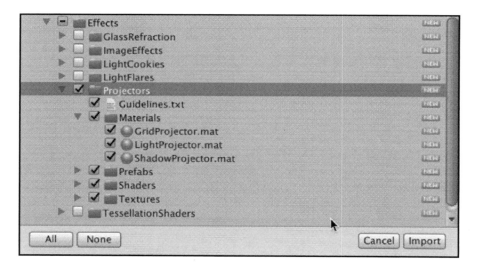

5. From the **Inspector**, locate the **ProjectorLight** shader (inside the **Assets | Standard Assets | Effects | Projectors | Shaders** folder). Duplicate the file and name the new copy as **ProjectorLaser**.
6. Open **ProjectorLaser**. From the first line of the code, change Shader `"Projector/Light"` to Shader `"Projector/Laser"`. Then, locate `Blend DstColor One` and change it to `Blend One One`. Save and close the file:

```
Shader "Projector/Laser" {
    Properties {
        _Color ("Main Color", Color) = (1,1,1,1)
        _ShadowTex ("Cookie", 2D) = "" {}
        _FalloffTex ("FallOff", 2D) = "" {}
    }

    Subshader {
        Tags {"Queue"="Transparent"}
        Pass {
            ZWrite Off
            ColorMask RGB
            Blend One One
            Offset -1, -1
```

The reason for editing the shader for the laser was to make it stronger by changing its blend type to Additive. Shader programming is a complex subject, which is beyond the scope of this book. However, if you want to learn more about it, check out Unity's documentation on the subject, which is available at `http://docs.unity3d.com/Manual/SL-Reference.html`, and also the book called *Unity Shaders and Effects Cookbook*, published by Packt.

7. Create a new material called **m_laser**. In the Inspector, change its **Shader** to **Projector/Laser**.
8. Locate the **Falloff Texture** in the **Project** panel (inside **Effects** | **Projectors** | **Textures**).
9. Open it in your image editor and, except for the first and last columns column of pixels, which should be black, paint everything white. Save the changed image file as **Falloff_laser** and go back to Unity:

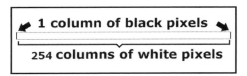

10. Select the **m_laser** asset in the **Project** panel. In the Inspector, set the **Main Color** to red (RGB: 255, 0, 0). Then, from the texture slots, drag **Texture Light** into the Cookie slot, and **Texture Falloff_laser** into the Falloff slot (these **Textures** are inside your imported folder, **Effects | Projectors | Textures**):

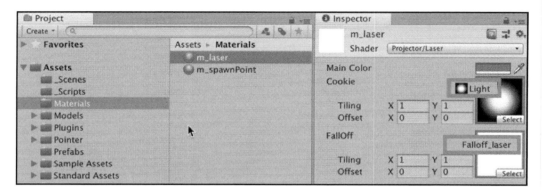

11. From the **Hierarchy**, find and select the **pointerPrefab** object (**MsLaser | mixamorig:Hips | mixamorig:Spine | mixamorig:Spine1 | mixamorig:Spine2 | mixamorig:RightShoulder | mixamorig:RightArm | mixamorig:RightForeArm | mixamorig:RightHand | pointerPrefab**). Then, create a new child GameObject (menu: **Create | Create Empty Child**). Rename this new child **laserProjector**:

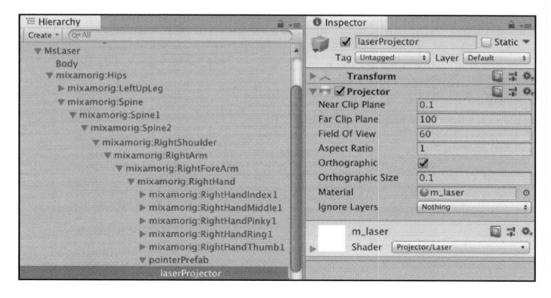

12. Select the **laserProjector** object. Then, from the **Inspector**, click the **Add Component** button and navigate to **Effects | Projector**. Then, from the new **Projector** component, set the **Orthographic** option as true and set **Orthographic Size** as 0.1. Finally, select **m_laser** from the **Material** slot.
13. Run the scene. You will be able to see the laser aim dot.

How it works...

In this recipe, the size of the aim dot has been exaggerated. Should you need a more realistic thickness for your laser pointer, change the **Orthographic Size** of the **Projector** component to something smaller, like 0.025.

The laser aim effect was achieved by using a **Projector**. A **Projector** can be used to simulate light, shadows, and more, and is a component that projects a **Material** (and its **Texture**) onto other game objects. By attaching a projector to the **laserPointer** object, we have ensured that it will face the right direction at all times. To get the desired, vibrant look, we edited the projector **Material's Shader** code, making it brighter.

There's more...

Here are some ways to enhance this recipe.

Limiting the range of the laser with Raycast hit to limit the far clip plane

Our laser target should highlight the first object it hits – it shouldn't go through all of the objects ahead of it. The project's **far clip plane** defined the distance at which the projector stops. We can use a simple script to fire a Raycast, and use the distance to the first object it hits as a guide for setting this far clip plane:

```
using UnityEngine;

public class LaserAim : MonoBehaviour  {
    private Projector projector;
    private float margin = 0.5f;

    void Start () {
        projector = GetComponent<Projector> ();
    }
```

```
                void Update ()  {
                    RaycastHit hit;
                    Vector3 forward =
                    transform.TransformDirection(Vector3.forward);

                    if (Physics.Raycast(transform.position, forward, out
    hit))
                        projector.farClipPlane = hit.distance + margin;
                }
            }
```

If the **Raycast** hits an object, we set the **Projector far clip plane** to that distance, plus a little margin if 0.5 Unity units (for example, it might be a curved surface).

We scripted a way to prevent projections from going through objects, by setting its **far clip plane** on approximately the same level of the first object that is receiving the projection. The line of code that is responsible for this action is as follows:

```
    projector.farClipPlane = hit.distance + margin
```

Further reading

Learn more about projectors from the Unity manual page:
https://docs.unity3d.com/Manual/class-Projector.html.

Enhancing the laser aim with a Line Renderer

Let's improve the previous recipe by displaying a laser beam from the character's laser gun to the projected laser target. We'll implement the laser beam through scripting a **Line Renderer**, which is being redrawn each frame:

Getting ready

This recipe is based on the previous one, so make a copy of that project and work with its copy. You'll also need a **Texture** for the beam color; one is provided in the 07_05 folder called **beam.psd**.

How to do it...

To enhance the laser aim with a **Line Renderer**, follow these steps:

1. Our **Line Renderer** will need a **Material** to work with. Create a new Material named **m_beam**.

2. In the **Inspector**, set the **Shader** of the **m_beam** to **Particles/Additive**. Also, set its Tint Color to red (**RGB**: 255; 0; 0).

3. Import the beam image file. Then, set it as the **Particle Texture** for the **m_beam**, as follows:

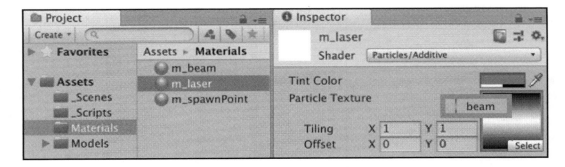

4. Create a new C# script class named **LaserBeam**, and add an instance object as a component to the Game Object's Laser Projector:

```
public class LaserBeam : MonoBehaviour  {
    public float lineWidth = 0.2f;
    public Color regularColor = new Color (0.15f, 0, 0, 1);
    public Material beamMaterial;

    private Vector3 lineEnd;
    private LineRenderer line;

    void Start () {
        line = gameObject.AddComponent<LineRenderer>();
        line.material = beamMaterial;
```

```
            line.material.SetColor("_TintColor", regularColor);
            line.SetVertexCount(2);
            line.SetWidth(lineWidth, lineWidth);
    }

    void Update () {
        RaycastHit hit;
        Vector3 forward =
        transform.TransformDirection(Vector3.forward);

        if (Physics.Raycast (transform.position, forward, out
hit))
            lineEnd =  hit.point;
        else
            lineEnd = transform.position + forward * 10f;

        line.SetPosition(0, transform.position);
        line.SetPosition(1, lineEnd);
    }
}
```

5. Select the **LaserProjector** Game Object. From the **Inspector**, find the Laser Beam (Script) component and drag the **m_beam** Material from the Project panel into the Beam Material.

6. Play the scene. The red laser beam should be shining in a line from the laser gun to the first object hit by the beam.

How it works...

The laser aim effect was achieved by using a dynamic **Line Renderer**, which created and updated each frame through code.

In this recipe, the width of the laser beam has been exaggerated. Should you need a more realistic thickness for your beam, change the **Line Width** field of the **Laser Beam (Script)** component to 0.05. Also, remember to make the beam more opaque by setting the **Regular Color** of the **Laser Beam** component brighter. You'll probably want to match the size of the laser aim Projector, too, so set the **Orthographic Size** of the **Projector** component to something smaller, such as 0.025.

Regarding the **Line Renderer**, we have opted to create it dynamically, via code, instead of manually adding the component to the game object.

There's more...

Here are some ways to enhance this recipe.

Changing the beam color when the Fire key is held down

It's always good to provide the player with audio or visual feedback when they do something. So, when the player presses the *Fire* button (for example, the mouse button) let's change the color of the beam. Do the following:

1. Add a new public variable for the fire beam color:

   ```
   public Color firingColor = new Color (0.31f, 0, 0, 1);
   ```

2. Add a new method to set up changing a color (using a Sine wave value):

   ```
   private void SetupColor() {
           float lerpSpeed = Mathf.Sin (Time.time * 10f);
           lerpSpeed = Mathf.Abs(lerpSpeed);
           Color lerpColor = Color.Lerp(regularColor,
   firingColor,
           lerpSpeed);
           line.material.SetColor("_TintColor", lerpColor);
       }
   ```

3. Add statements at the end of the Update() method to detect when the Fire button is pressed/released to trigger a color change:

   ```
   void Update ()   {
           // ... (as before)

           if(Input.GetButton("Fire1"))
               SetupColor();

           if(Input.GetButtonUp("Fire1"))
               line.material.SetColor("_TintColor",
   regularColor);
       }
   ```

Setting up an environment with Procedural Skybox and Directional Light

Besides the traditional six-sided and Cubemap Skyboxes, Unity also features a third type of skybox: the Procedural Skybox. Easy to create and set up, the Procedural Skybox can be used in conjunction with a Directional Light to provide Environment Lighting in your scene. In this recipe, we will learn about the different parameters of the Procedural Skybox:

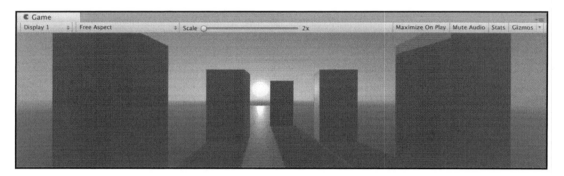

How to do it...

To set up **Environment Lighting** using the **Procedural Skybox** and **Directional Light**, follow these steps:

1. Create a new **Scene** inside a Unity project. Observe that a new scene already includes two objects: the **Main Camera** and a **Directional Light**.

2. In the scene, create a **3D Plane** named **Plane-ground**; positioned at (0, 0, 0) and scaled to (20, 20, 20).

3. Add some **3D Cubes** to your scene, like so:

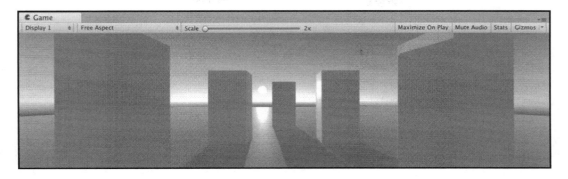

4. Create a new **Material** asset file named **m_skybox**. In the Inspector, change the **Shader** from **Standard** to Skybox/Procedural.

5. Open the Lighting window (**Window | Rendering | Lighting Settings**), and access the scene section. In the Environment Lighting subsection, populate the Skybox slot with the m_skybox Material, and the Sun slot with the scene's default Directional Light. Ensure that the real-time Global Illumination option is checked (from **real-time Lighting**), and that the Environment Ambient Mode is set to real-time.

6. From the **Project** panel, select **m_skybox**. Then, from the Inspector, set the Sun Size as 0.05 and the Atmosphere Thickness as 1.4. Experiment by changing the Sky Tint color to RGB: 148; 128; 128, and the Ground color to a value that resembles the scene cube floor's color (such as RGB: 202; 202; 202). If you feel that the scene is too bright, try bringing the Exposure level down to 0.85, as follows:

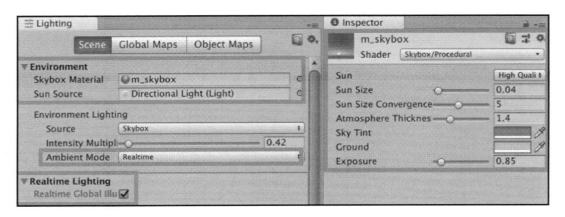

7. Select the Directional Light and change its Rotation to 5, 170, 0. Also ensure that its Light Mode setting is real-time (not baked or Mixed).

8. Run the scene – it should resemble a dawning environment.

How it works...

Ultimately, the appearance of Unity's native Procedural Skyboxes depends on the five parameters that make them up:

- Sun size: The size of the bright yellow sun that is drawn onto the Skybox is located according to the Directional Light's Rotation on the X and Y axes.

- Atmosphere Thickness: This simulates how dense the atmosphere is for this Skybox. Lower values (less than 1.0) are good for simulating the outer space settings. Moderate values (around 1.0) are suitable for earth-based environments. Values that are slightly above 1.0 can be useful when simulating air pollution and other dramatic settings. Exaggerated values (for example, more than 2.0) can help to illustrate extreme conditions or even alien settings.

- Sky Tint: This is the color that is used to tint the Skybox. It is useful for fine-tuning or creating stylized environments.

- Ground: This is the color of the ground. It can really affect the Global Illumination of the scene. So, choose a value that is close to the level's terrain and/or geometry (or a neutral one).

- Exposure: This determines the amount of light that gets in the Skybox. The higher levels simulate overexposure, while the lower values simulate underexposure.

It is important to note that the Skybox appearance will respond to the scene's Directional Light, playing the role of the sun. In this case, rotating the light around its X axis can create dawn and sunset scenarios, whereas rotating it around its Y axis will change the position of the sun, changing the cardinal points of the scene.

Also, regarding the Environment Lighting, note that although we have used the Skybox as the Ambient Source, we could have chosen a Gradient or a single color instead, in which case the scene's illumination wouldn't be attached to the Skybox's appearance.

Finally, also regarding the Environment Lighting, please note that we have set the Ambient GI to real-time. The reason for this was to allow the real-time changes in the GI, promoted by the rotating Directional Light. In case we didn't need these changes at runtime, we could have chosen the baked alternative.

There's more...

Here are some ways to enhance this recipe.

Setting and rising the sun through scripted rotation of Directional Light

Let's make things even more interesting by using code to change the rotation of the Directional Light. This will give a dynamic rising/setting sun effect as our scene runs.

Ceate a new C# script class named RotateLight, and add an instance object as a component to the Directional Light Game Object:

```
using UnityEngine;
    using System.Collections;
    public class RotateLight : MonoBehaviour {
      public float speed = -1.0f;
      void Update () {
        transform.Rotate(Vector3.right * speed *
Time.deltaTime);
      }
    }
```

Now, when you run the scene, you will see the sun rising/setting and the lighting colors changing accordingly.

Adding a sun flare

Let's add a sun flare effect to our scene.

For this step, you will need to import **Unity's Standard Assets** Effects package, which you should have installed when you installed Unity, but you can also add it to an individual project via the Unity Asset Store.

1. Import the Light Flares contents from the Effects Unity Standard Assets package folder.

2. Select the **Directional** Light. In the **Inspector**, for the Light component, populate the Flare slot with the sun flare (from the project panel, the **Effects | Light Flares | Flares** folder).

3. From the scene section of the Lighting window, find the **Other Settings** subsection. Then, set **Flare Fade Speed** to **1** and **Flare Strength** to **0.46**, as follows:

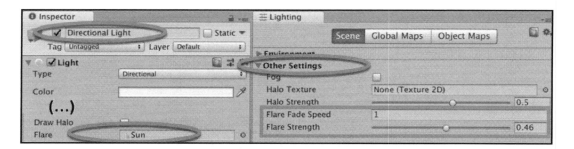

4. Play the scene. A sun flare effect should have been applied to the scene's lighting.

Reflecting surrounding objects with Reflection Probes

If you want your scene's environment to be reflected by Game Objects by featuring reflective Materials (such as the ones with high Metallic or Specular levels), then you can achieve such an effect by using Reflection Probes. They allow for real-time, baked, or even Custom reflections through the use of Cubemaps.

real-time reflections can be expensive in terms of processing; in which case, you should favor baked reflections, unless it's really necessary to display dynamic objects being reflected (mirror-like objects, for instance). Still, there are some ways real-time reflections can be optimized. In this recipe, we will test three different configurations for reflection probes:

- real-time reflections (constantly updated)
- real-time reflections (updated on-demand via scripting)
- baked reflections (from the editor)

Getting ready

For this recipe, we have prepared a basic scene, featuring three sets of reflective objects: one is constantly moving, one is static, and one moves whenever it is interacted with. The reflectionProbes.unitypackage package that is containing the scene can be found inside the 07_07 folder.

How to do it...

To reflect the surrounding objects using the Reflection Probes, follow these steps:

1. Import the Unity package reflectionProbes.unitypackage. Then, open the scene named reflective_objects. This is a basic scene featuring three sets of reflective objects.

2. Ensure that the Quality setting for the project has enabled real-time Reflection Probes. Do this by choosing menu: **Edit** | **Project Settings** | **Quality**, and ensuring that the real-time Reflection Probes option is checked for the quality setting you wish to use.

3. Play the scene. Observe that one of the systems is dynamic, one is static, and one rotates randomly, whenever a key is pressed.

4. Stop the scene.

5. First, let's create a constantly updated real-time Reflection Probe for the scene (menu: **Create** | **Light** | **Reflection Probe**). Name it ReflectionProbe-real-time.

6. Make ReflectionProbe-real-time a child of the Game Object System 1 real-time | MainSphere. Then, in the Inspector, set its Transform Position to (0, 0, 0):

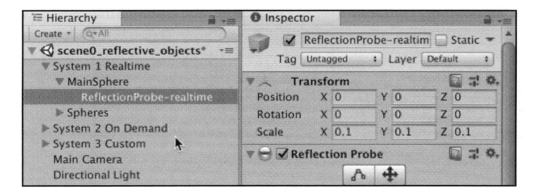

7. In the Inspector, find the Reflection Probe component. Set the Type as real-time, Refresh Mode as Every Frame, and Time Slicing as No time slicing, as follows:

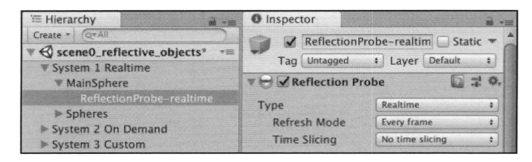

8. Play the scene. The reflections on System 1 real-time will now be updated in real-time. Stop the scene.

9. Observe that the only object displaying the real-time reflections is System 1 real-time | MainSphere. The reason for this is the size of the box of the Reflection Probe. From the Reflection Probe component, change its size to (25, 10, 25). Note that the small red spheres are now affected as well. However, it is important to note that all objects display the same reflection. Since our Reflection Probe's origin is placed at the same location as the MainSphere, all reflective objects will display reflections from that point of view:

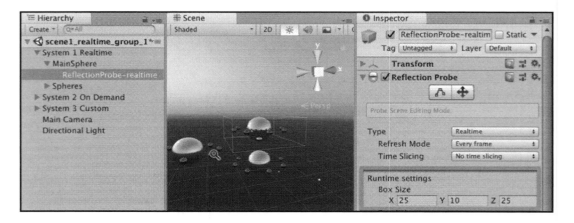

10. If you want to eliminate the reflection from the reflective objects within the Reflection Probe, such as the small red spheres, select the objects and, from the Mesh Renderer component, set Reflection Probes as Off, as shown in the following screenshot:

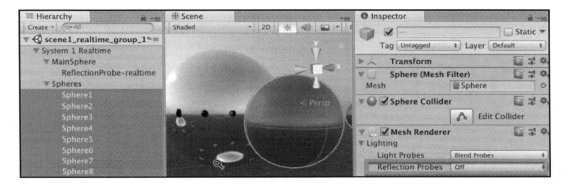

11. Add a new Reflection Probe to the scene. This time, name it ReflectionProbe-onDemand and make it a child of the System 2 On Demand | MainSphere GameObject. Then, in the Inspector, change its transform position to (0,0,0).

12. Now, go to the Reflection Probe component. Set Type as real-time, Refresh Mode as Via scripting, and Time Slicing as Individual faces, as shown in the following screenshot:

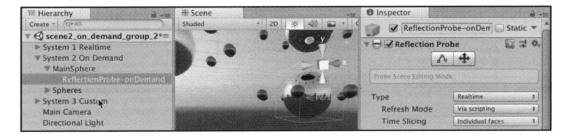

13. Create a new C# script class named UpdateProbe, and add an instance object as a component to GameObject ReflectionProbe-onDemand:

```
using UnityEngine;
using System.Collections;

public class UpdateProbe : MonoBehaviour {
    private ReflectionProbe probe;
```

```
      void Awake () {
         probe = GetComponent<ReflectionProbe> ();
         probe.RenderProbe();
      }

      public void RefreshProbe(){
         probe.RenderProbe();
      }
   }
```

14. Now, find the script class named RandomRotation, which is attached to the System 2 On Demand | Spheres object, and replace it with the following:

```
using UnityEngine;

public class RandomRotation : MonoBehaviour {
   private GameObject probe;
   private UpdateProbe updateProbe;

   void Awake() {
      probe = GameObject.Find("ReflectionProbe-onDemand");
      updateProbe = probe.GetComponent<UpdateProbe>();
   }

   void Update () {
      if (Input.anyKeyDown) {
         Vector3 newRotation = transform.eulerAngles;
         newRotation.y = Random.Range(0F, 360F);
         transform.eulerAngles = newRotation;
         updateProbe.RefreshProbe();
      }
   }
}
```

15. Save the script and test your scene. Observe how the Reflection Probe is updated whenever a key is pressed.

16. Stop the scene. Add a third Reflection Probe to the scene. Name it ReflectionProbe-custom and make it a child of the System 3 On Custom | MainSphere GameObject. Then, from the Inspector, change its Transform Position to (0,0,0).

17. Go to the Reflection Probe component. Set Type as Custom and click on the Bake button, as follows:

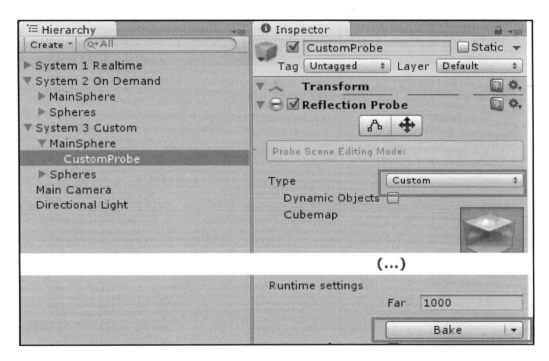

18. A **Save File** dialog window will show up. Save the file as **ReflectionProbe-custom-reflectionHDR.exr**.

19. Observe that the reflection map does not include the reflection of red spheres on it. To change this, you have two options: set the **System 3 On Custom | Spheres GameObject** (and all its children) as **Reflection Probe Static**, like so:

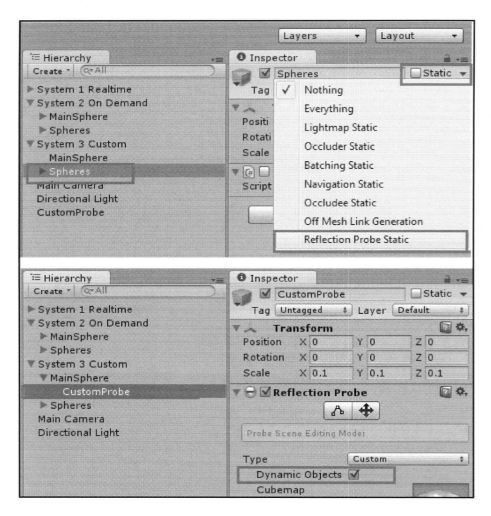

20. Or check the **Dynamic Objects** option **Reflection Probe** component of the **ReflectionProbe-custom** GameObject. Note that with this option, you will also see a reflection of the other two large spheres and their belt of red spheres in the reflection on the **MainSphere** of **System 3 Custom**.

21. Select GameObject **ReflectionProbe-custom**, and click the **Bake** button again. You should now see the reflection of red spheres on it.

22. If you want your reflection **Cubemap** to be dynamically baked while you edit your scene, you can set the **Reflection Probe** Type to baked, open the Lighting window (menu: **Window | Rendering | Lighting Settings**), access the scene section, and check the **Auto Generate** option, as follows:

 This mode won't include dynamic objects in the reflection, so be sure to set **System 3 Custom | Spheres** and **System 3 Custom | MainSphere** as **Reflection Probe Static**.

How it works...

The Reflection Probes element acts like omnidirectional cameras that render **Cubemaps** and applies them onto the objects within their constraints. When creating Reflection Probes, it's important to be aware of how the different types work:

- **Real-time Reflection Probes**: **Cubemaps** are updated at runtime. The real-time Reflection Probes have three different Refresh Modes: On Awake (Cubemap is baked once, right before the scene starts); Every frame (Cubemap is constantly updated); Via scripting (Cubemap is updated whenever the RenderProbe function is used). Since Cubemaps feature six sides, the Reflection Probes features Time Slicing, so each side can be updated independently. There are three different types of Time Slicing: All Faces at Once (renders all faces at once and calculates mipmaps over 6 frames. It updates the probe in 9 frames); Individual Faces (each face is rendered over a number of frames. It updates the probe in 14 frames. The results can be a bit inaccurate, but it is the least expensive solution in terms of frame rate impact); No Time Slicing (the Probe is rendered and mipmaps are calculated in one frame. It provides high accuracy, but it also the most expensive in terms of frame rate).

- **baked**: **Cubemaps** are baked when editing the screen. Cubemaps can be either manually or automatically updated, depending on whether the Auto Generation option is checked (it can be found at the Scene section of the Lighting Settings window).
- **Custom**: The **Custom Reflection Probes** can be either manually baked from the scene (and even include Dynamic objects), or created from a premade Cubemap.

There's more...

There are a number of additional settings that can be tweaked, such as Importance, Intensity, Box Projection, Resolution, HDR (Hight Dynamic Range), and so on. For a complete view on each of these settings, we strongly recommend that you read Unity's documentation on the subject, which is available at `http://docs.unity3d.com/Manual/class-ReflectionProbe.html`.

Using Material Emission to bake light from a glowing lamp onto scene objects

As well as Lights, other objects can also emit light if their Materials have Emmision properties (such as a Texture, and/or tint color). In this recipe we'll create a lamp that glows green via its Emission Texture. The lamp and other 3D objects in the scene will be baked in order to create a pre-computed Lightmap for the scene:

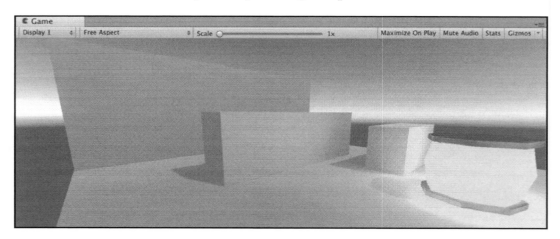

Getting ready

For this recipe, we have provided a 3D lamp model (**lamp**), as well as a green Texture (lamp_emission) in the `lamp.unitypackage` Unity package in the `07_08` folder .

How to do it...

To create a glowing lamp using Material Emission, follow these steps:

1. Create a new 3D Project. You should start with a basic **scene** containing a Main Camera and a Directional Light.

2. Import the Unity package `lamp.unitypackage` containing the 3D lamp model (lamp), as well as a green Texture (lamp_emission).

3. With the 3D model asset lamp selected in the Project panel, in the Inspector, check its Generate Lightmap UVs option, and click on the Apply button to confirm the changes:

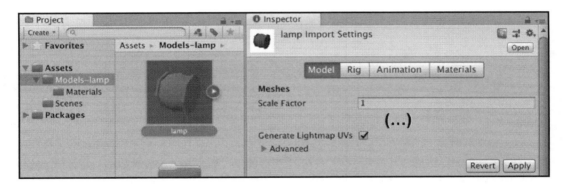

4. In the **Project** panel, select Material **m_lamp**. Check the Emission option, and then assign Texture **lamp_emission** to its **Emission Color** property. Set the Global Illumination drop-down menu to baked. This will make the lamp object emit a green light that will be baked into the Lightmap:

5. Also, for **Material m_lamp**, click the **HDR color** box, and increase the intensity of this light emitting Material to 1 or 2 (this is a value you may wish to play with and "tweak" in order to get your desired settings for a scene):

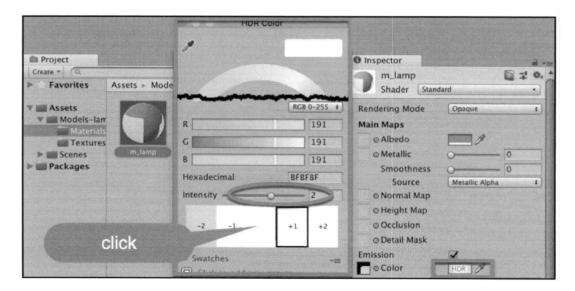

6. Add some 3D GameObjects to create a simple 3D scene containing a 3D Plane (the ground) and three 3D cubes. Position and scale the 3D cubes so that there is large one at the back of the **3D Plane**, a medium sized one in the middle, and a small one in the front.

7. Now, drag an instance of the 3D **lamp** model from the **Project** panel into the scene, placing it near the front-most 3D cube:

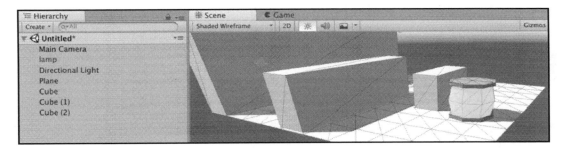

8. You may need to adjust the **Main Camera** position and rotation so that you can see the lamp and the three 3D cubes sitting on the 3D Plane.

9. Baked lighting only works for static objects, so, with the exception of the **Main Camera**, select everything in the **Hierarchy** and check the **Static** option at the top-right of the **Inspector** panel:

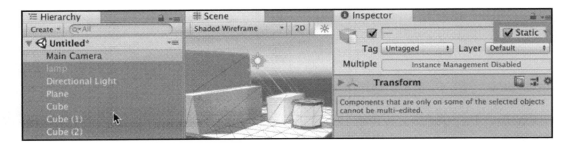

10. Now, select the **Directional Light** in the **Hierarchy** and change its **Light Mode** drop-down menu property to baked:

11. We can now assign the **Directional Light** as an **Environmental Lighting Sun source**. Open the **Lighting Settings** window (choose menu: **Window | Rendering | Lighting Settings**), and drag the **Directional Light** from the **Hierarchy** into the Sun slot for the scene **Environment** properties. Also, set the **Environment Lighting Ambient Mode** drop-down menu to baked. In the **Debug Settings**, uncheck **Auto Generate** and click the **Generate Lighting** button to "bake" the **Ambient** light and green lamp emission light into the **Scene**:

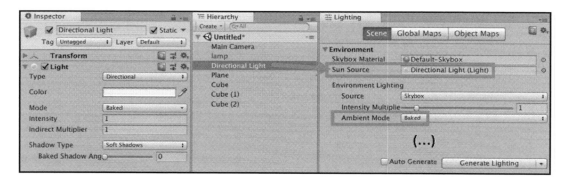

12. For a few seconds (depending on the speed of your computer and the complexity of the scene), you'll see a progess bar of the **Lightmap** baking process at the bottom-right of the Unity Editor application window:

13. Play your **Scene**. You should see how the **Scene** objects are lit both by the **Directional Light**, and by the green Texture emitted from the lamp.

14. Change the rotation of the **Directional Light**, and try setting its **Light Intensity** and **Indirect Multiplier** to 0.5. Also, play with the HDR intensity of the **Material m_lamp**, and re-bake the Lightmap to make the lamp emission more emphasized (and the **Directional Light** play a lessor role).

How it works...

You have added an emissive **Material** to a GameObject (the lamp), and baked a **Lightmap** based on the static objects in the **Scene** (which include the lamp, the **Directional Light**, and the 3D Plane and cubes). The environment's **Global Illumination** ambient lighting is sourced from the **Directional Light** settings.

Lightmaps are basically **Texture** maps including scene lights/shadows, global illumination, indirect illumination, and objects featuring the **Emissive Materials**. They can be generated automatically or on demand by Unity's lighting engine. However, there are some points that you should pay attention to, such as the following:

- Set all the non-moving objects and lights to be baked as Static
- Set the game lights as **Baked**
- Set the scene's **Ambient GI** as **Baked**
- Set the **Global Illumination** option of the emissive materials as baked
- **Generate Light UVs** for all 3D meshes (specially the imported ones)
- Either build the **Lightmaps** manually from the **Lighting Settings** window, or check the **Auto Generate** option

Lighting a simple scene with Lightmaps and Light Probes

Lightmaps are a great alternative to real-time lighting, as they can provide the desired look to an environment without being processor-intensive. There is one downside, though – since there is no way of baking **Lightmaps** onto the dynamic objects, the lighting of the important elements of the game (such as player characters themselves) can look artificial, failing to match the intensity of the surrounding area. The solution? **Light Probes**.

Light Probes work by sampling the light intensity over the location that they are placed at. Dynamic objects, once **Light Probe**-enabled, will be lit according to the interpolation of the nearest probes around them:

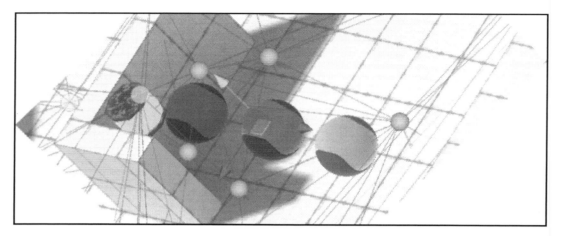

Getting ready

For this recipe, we have prepared a basic Unity package (**rollerballLevel.unitypackage**), including a game environment containing emissive lamps (from the previous recipe!), and Game Objects, making a suitable level for a **RollerBall** game. The Game Objects are static, and the Directional Light and **Emissive** Material are set to baked, so the scene has been set up as a baked **Lightmapped** scene.

The **rollerBallLevel.unitypackage** package, containing the scene, can be found inside the 07_09 folder. You'll also find the two PNG images you need to create the RollerBall Material (**RollerBallAlbedo.png** and **RollerBallSpecularGloss.png**).

The geometry for this scene was created using ProBuilder, an extension developed by ProCore, which is now free as part of Unity 2018. ProBuilder is a fantastic level design tool that speeds up the design process considerably for both simple and complex level design. You can learn more at http://www.procore3d. com and https://blogs.unity3d.com/2018/02/15/probuilder-joins-unity-offering-integrated-in-editor-advanced-level-design/.

How to do it...

To reflect the surrounding objects using the Reflection Probes, follow these steps:

1. Import **rollerBallLevel.unitypackage** into a new project. Then, open the scene named **scene0_level_baked**. The scene features a basic environment, with a Directional Light and some green emissive lamps.

2. Import Standard Assets into your project. We need three packages, as follows:

   - **Cameras**
   - **Characters** (we need the RollerBall, so you can uncheck **FirstPersonCharacter** and **ThirdPersonCharacter** when importing)
   - **Effects** (we just need the **Projectors** assets, so you can uncheck all other folders apart from that one when importing)

3. Drag the **RollerBall** prefab from the **Project** panel (**Standard Assets** | **Characters** | **RollerBall** | **Prefabs**) into the scene.

4. Drag the **FreeLookCameraRig** prefab from the **Project** panel (**Standard Assets** | **Cameras** | **Prefabs**) into the scene. If this does not automatically target the **RollerBall** character, then drag the **RollerBall** Game Object from the **Hierarchy** into the **Free Look Cam (Script) Target** slot in the **Inspector**.

5. Let's add a little color to our **RollerBall** by creating and applying a new **Material** for this GameObject. Create a new **Material** **m_rollerballColor** with a **Specular** setup. Set the **Albedo Texture** to **RollerBallAlbedo** and its tint to 127/127/127. Set the **Specular** Texture to **RollerBallSpecularGloss**.

6. Select Game Object **RollerBall** in the **Hierarchy**. Apply the **m_rollerballColor Material** to the **RollerBall** Game Object. This should now be a two-colored ball.

7. We now need to ensure that the **RollerBall** GameObject will be dynamically affected by **Light Probes**, so with Game Object **RollerBall** still selected in the **Hierarchy**, for the **Mesh Renderer** component for the **Light Probes** option, choose the **Blend Probes** option from the drop-down menu:

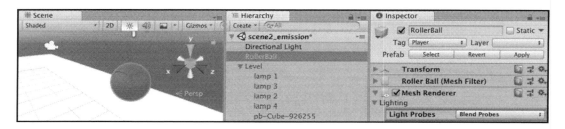

8. Now, we need to create the **Light Probes** for the scene. Choose the Hierarchy menu: **Create | Light | Light Probe Group**. This will give you a basic group of eight Light Probes, arranged in pairs to form a cubic volume.

 It is important to note that even if you are working on a level that is flat, you shouldn't place all your probes on the same level, as Light Probe Groups will form a volume in order for the interpolation to be calculated correctly.

9. To facilitate the manipulation of the probes, type **Probe** into the search field of the **Hierarchy** panel. This will isolate the newly created **Light Probe Group**, making it the only editable object on the scene:

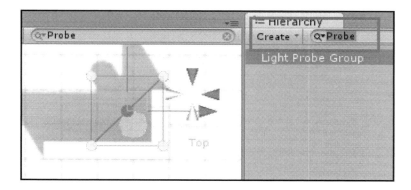

10. Change your viewport layout to **4 Split** by choosing **Window | Layouts | 4 Split**. Then, set viewports as **Top**, **Front**, **Right**, and **Persp**. Optionally, change **Top**, **Front**, and **Right** views to **Wireframe** mode. Finally, make sure that they are set to **Orthographic** view, as shown in the following screenshot. This will make it easier for you to position the **Light Probes**:

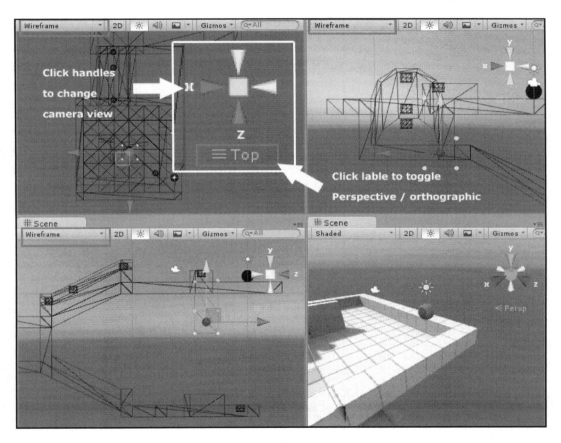

11. Position the initial **Light Probes** at the corners of the top room of the level. To move the **Probes** around, simply click and drag them, as follows:

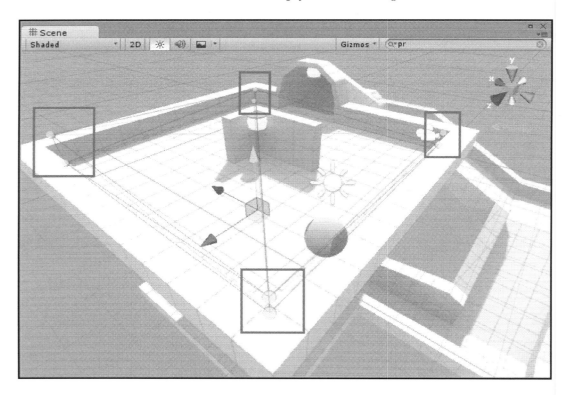

12. Select the four probes to the left side of the tunnel's entrance. Then, duplicate them (use the *Ctrl/Cmd + D* keys). Finally, drag the new probes slightly to the right, to a point that they are no longer over the shadow that is projected by the wall, as follows:

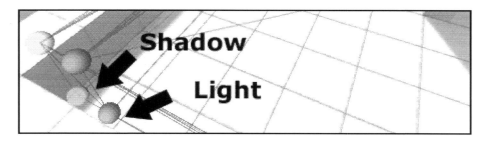

13. Repeat the last step, this time duplicating the probes next to the tunnel's entrance and bringing them inward toward the group. To delete the selected probes, either use the respective button on the **Light Probe Group** component, or use the *Ctrl/Cmd + Backspace* keys:

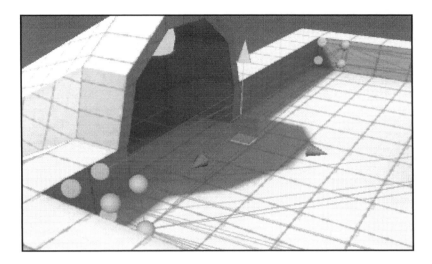

14. Duplicate and reposition the four probes that are nearest to the tunnel, repeating the operation five times and conforming each duplicate set to the shadow projected by the tunnel:

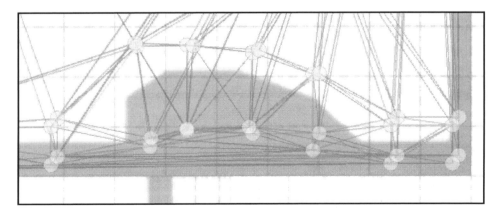

15. Use the **Add Probe** button to place the three probes over well-lit areas of the scene:

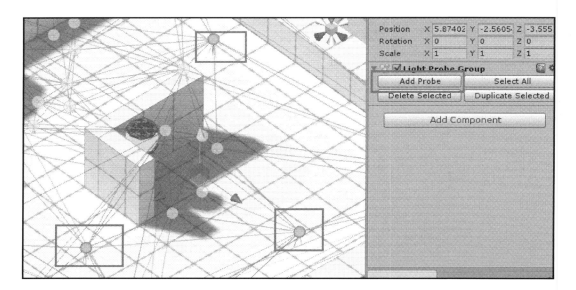

16. Now, add **Light Probes** within the shadow that is projected by the L-shaped wall:

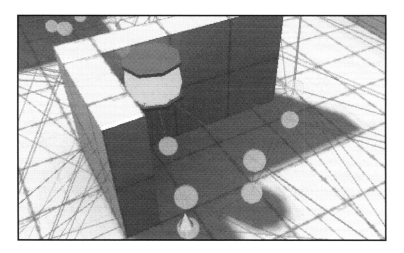

17. Since the **Rollerball** is able to jump, place the higher probes even higher so that they will sample the lighting above the shadowed areas of the scene:

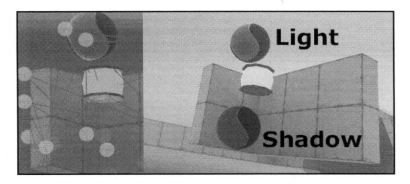

18. Placing too many **Light Probes** on a scene might be memory intensive. Try optimizing the **Light Probes Group** by removing the probes from the regions that the player won't have access to. Also, avoid overcrowding the regions of continuous lighting conditions by removing the probes that are too close to others in the same lighting condition:

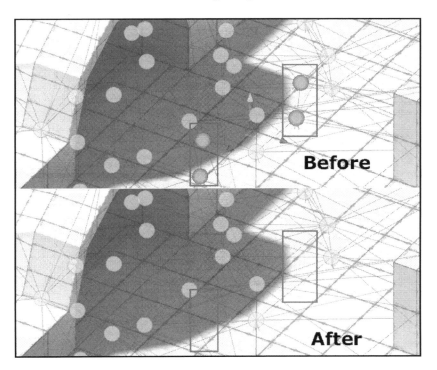

19. To check out which **Light Probes** are influencing the **Rollerball** at any place, move the **Rollerball** Game Object around the scene. A polyhedron will indicate which probes are being interpolated at that position, as follows:

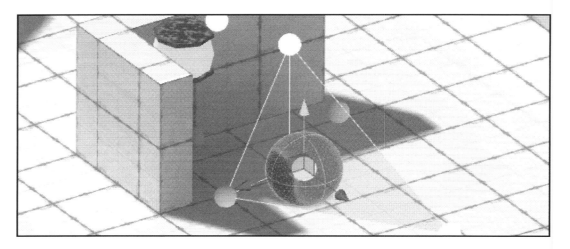

20. From the bottom of the **Lighting Settings** window, click on the **Generate Lighting** button and wait for the **Lightmaps** to be baked.
21. Test the scene. The **Rollerball** will be lit according to the **Light Probes**:

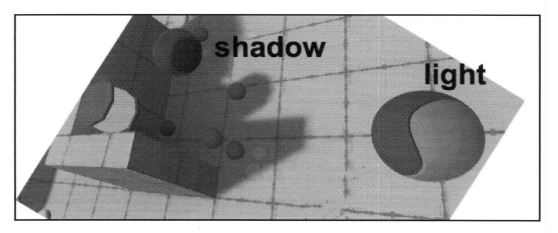

22. Keep adding probes until the level is completely covered.

How it works...

Light Probes work by sampling the scene's illumination at the point that they're placed at. A dynamic object that has Use **Light Probes** enabled has its lighting determined by the interpolation between the lighting values of the four **Light Probes**, defining a volume around it (or, in case there are no probes suited to define a volume around the dynamic object, a triangulation between the nearest probes is used).

More information on this subject can be found in the Unity's documentation at `http://docs.unity3d.com/Manual/LightProbes.html`.

There's more...

In case you can spare some processing power, you can exchange the use of Light probes for a Mixed light.

Do the following:

1. Delete the **Light Probe Group** from your scene.
2. Select the **Directional Light** and, from the **Light** component, change **Baking** to Mixed.
3. Set **Shadow** Type as **Soft Shadows** and **Strength** as 0.5, as shown in the following screenshot:

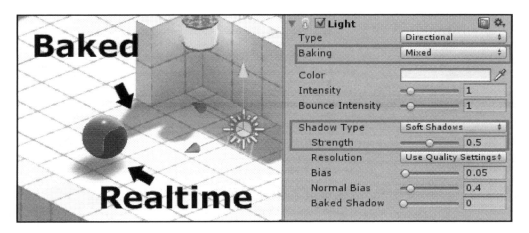

4. Finally, click on the **Generate Lighting** button and wait for the **Lightmaps** to be baked. The **Real-Time** light/shadows will be cast into/from the dynamic objects, such as **Rollerball**.

2D Animation 9

In this chapter, we will cover:

- Flipping a sprite horizontally—the Do-It-Yourself approach
- Flipping a sprite horizontally—using Animator State Chart and Transitions
- Animating body parts for character movement events
- Creating a 3-frame animation clip to make a platform continually animate
- Making a platform start falling once stepped-on using a Trigger to move animation from one state to another
- Creating animation clips from sprite sheet sequences
- Creating a platform game with Tiles and Tilemaps
- Creating a Scene with the 2D Gamekit

Introduction

Since Unity 4.6 in 2014, Unity has shipped with dedicated 2D features, and Unity 2018 continues to build on these. In this chapter, we present a range of recipes to introduce the basics of 2D animation in Unity 2018, and help you understand the relationships between the different animation elements.

The Big picture

In Unity 2D, animations can be created in several different ways—one way is to create many images, each slightly different, which frame-by-frame give the appearance of movement. A second way to create animations is by defining keyframe positions for individual parts of an object (for example, the arms, legs, feet, head, and eyes), and getting Unity to calculate all the in-between positions when the game is running:

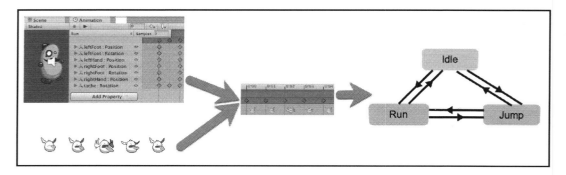

Both sources of animations become **Animation Clips** in the **Animation** panel. Each **Animation Clip** then becomes a **State** in the **Animator Controller State Machine**. We can also duplicate **States** based on **Animation Clips**, or create new **States**, and add scripted **Behaviors**.

We also can define sophisticated **Conditions**, under which GameObject will **Transition** from one animation **State** to another.

Grids, Tilemaps, and Tile Palettes

Unity has introduced a set of **Tile** features that makes creating **Tile**-based **Scenes** quick and easy. A **Tile Grid** GameObject acts as the parent to **Tilemaps**. **Tilemaps** are the GameObjects onto which **Tiles** are painted, from the **Tile Palette** panel. **Sprites** can be made into **Tile** assets, and a collection of **Tiles** can be added to form a **Tile Palette** from which to paint a Scene.

It also offers powerful, scripted **Rule Tiles** that enhance the **Tile** brush tools, automatically adding top, left, right, and bottom edge **Tiles** as more **Grid** elements are painted with Tiles. **Rule Tiles** can even randomly choose from a selection of **Tiles** under defined conditions. Learn more at `https://unity3d.com/learn/tutorials/topics/2d-game-creation/using-rule-tiles-tilemap`.

The 2D GameKit – bringing 2D tools together

Perhaps the most exciting 2D feature introduced by Unity is the **2D GameKit**. This brings together several powerful Unity features for constructing 2D games, including:

- **Tilemaps** and **Rule Tiles**
- **Character Controller 2D** (and Input **Mapper** and **Player Character** components)
- **Cinemachine** intelligent camera control
- The Unity event system
- Many prefabricated common 2D game components, including doors, teleporters, dialog panels, switches, inventory, melee, collectables and inventory, damageables, and enemies and much more

The final recipe in this chapter introduces the **2D GameKit**, and the other recipes in this chapter, and some others, introduce some of the components individually, so that you'll know enough to start taking your first steps with the **2D GameKit** and learning how to build Scenes that tightly combine core 2D game features.

Resources

In this chapter, we introduce recipes demonstrating the animation system for 2D game elements. The PotatoMan2D character is from the Unity 2D Platformer, which you can download yourself from the Unity asset store. That project is a good place to see lots more examples of 2D game and animation techniques:

Here are some links for useful resources and sources of information to explore these topics further:

- Overview of 2D features in Unity: `https://unity.com/solutions/2d`
- Unity's beginners walkthrough guide to 2D game development:
  `https://unity3d.com/learn/tutorials/topics/2d-game-creation/2d-ga
  me-development-walkthrough`

- Unity's 2D Rogue-like tutorial series:
  https://unity3d.com/learn/tutorials/s/2d-roguelike-tutorial
- Unity 2D Platformer (where the PotatoMan character comes from):
  https://www.assetstore.unity3d.com/en/#!/content/11228
- The platform sprites are from Daniel Cook's Planet Cute game resources:
  http://www.lostgarden.com/2007/05/dancs-miraculously-flexible-game.html
- Creating a basic 2D platformer game:
  https://www.unity3d.com/learn/tutorials/modules/beginner/live-training-archive/creating-a-basic-platformer-game
- Hat Catch 2D game tutorial:
  https://www.unity3d.com/learn/tutorials/modules/beginner/live-training-archive/2d-catch-game-pt1
- Unity games from a 2D perspective video:
  https://www.unity3d.com/learn/tutorials/modules/beginner/live-training-archive/introduction-to-unity-via-2d
- A fantastic set of modular 2D characters with a free Creative Commons license from Kenny. These assets would be perfect for animating body parts in a similar way to the potato-man example in this chapter and in the Unity 2D platformer demo:
  http://kenney.nl/assets/modular-characters
- Joe Strout's illuminating Gamasutra article on three approaches to 2D character animation with Unity's scripting and animation states:
  https://www.gamasutra.com/blogs/JoeStrout/20150807/250646/2D_Animation_Methods_in_Unity.php

Flipping a sprite horizontally – the DIY approach

Perhaps the simplest 2D animation is a simple flip, from facing left to facing right, or facing up to facing down, and so on. In this recipe, we'll add a cute bug sprite to the scene, and write a short script to flip its horizontal direction when the *Left* and *Right* arrow keys are pressed:

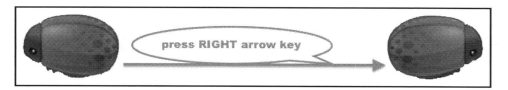

Getting ready

For this recipe, we have prepared the image you need in a folder named Sprites in folder 08_01.

How to do it...

To flip an object horizontally with arrow key presses, follow these steps:

1. Create a new Unity 2D project.

 If you are working in a project that was originally created in 3D, you can change the default project behavior (for example, new **Sprite Textures** and **Scene** mode) to 2D via menu: **Edit** | **Project Settings** | **Editor**, then choose 2D for the **Default Behavior Mode** in the **Inspector**.

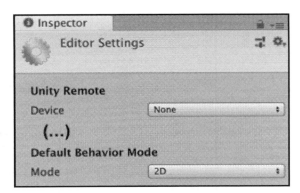

2. Import the provided image: **EnemyBug.png**.
3. Drag an instance of the red **Enemy Bug** image from the **Project** | **Sprites** folder into the **Scene**. Position this GameObject at (**0, 0, 0**) and scale to (**2, 2, 2**).
4. Create a C# script-class named **BugFlip**, and add an instance-object as a component to the **Enemy Bug**:

```
using UnityEngine;
using System.Collections;

public class BugFlip : MonoBehaviour {
  private bool facingRight = true;
```

```
void Update() {
    if (Input.GetKeyDown(KeyCode.LeftArrow) &&
facingRight)
        Flip ();
    if (Input.GetKeyDown(KeyCode.RightArrow) &&
!facingRight)
        Flip();
}

void Flip (){
    // Switch the way the player is labelled as facing.
    facingRight = !facingRight;

    // Multiply the player's x local scale by -1.
    Vector3 theScale = transform.localScale;
    theScale.x *= -1;
    transform.localScale = theScale;
}
}
```

5. When you run your scene, pressing the *Left* and *Right* arrow keys should make the bug face left or right.

How it works...

The C# class defines a **Boolean** variable, facingRight, that stores a **true/false** value corresponding to whether or not the bug is facing right. Since our bug sprite is initially facing right, we set the initial value of facingRight to true to match this.

Every frame, the Update() method, checks to see whether the *Left* or *Right* arrow keys have been pressed. If the *Left* arrow key is pressed and the bug is facing right, then the Flip() method is called, likewise if the *Right* arrow key is pressed and the bug is facing left (that is, facing right is false), again the Flip() method is called.

The Flip() method performs two actions; the first simply reverses the true/false value in variable facingRight. The second action changes the +/- sign of the X-value of the localScale property of the transform. Reversing the sign of the localScale results in the 2D flip that we desire. Look inside the PlayerControl script for the PotatoMan character in the next recipe – you'll see the same Flip() method being used.

Flipping a sprite horizontally – using Animator State Chart and Transitions

In this recipe, we'll use (in a simple way) the Unity animation system to create two states corresponding to two animation clips, and a script that changes localScale according to which animation state is active. We'll use a second script, which will map the arrow keys press **Horizontal** input axis values to a **Parameter** in the state chart, and which will drive the transition from one state to the other.

While it may seem like a lot of work, compared to the previous recipe, such an approach illustrates how we can map from input events (such as key presses or touch inputs), to **Parameters** and **Triggers** in a **State Chart**.

Getting ready

For this recipe, we have prepared the image you need in a folder named Sprites in folder 08_02.

How to do it...

To flip an object horizontally using **Animator State Chart** and **Transitions**, follow these steps:

1. Create a new Unity 2D project.
2. Import the provided image: **EnemyBug.png**.
3. Drag an instance of the red **Enemy Bug** image from the **Project | Sprites** folder into the scene. Position this GameObject at (**0, 0, 0**) and scale to (**2, 2, 2**).

4. With the **Enemy Bug** GameObject selected in **Hierarchy**, open the **Animation** panel (menu: **Window | Animation | Animation**), and click the **Create** button to create a new **Animation Clip** asset. Save the new **Animation Clip** asset as **beetle-right**. You will also see that an **Animator** component has been added to the **Enemy Bug** GameObject:

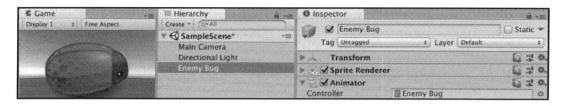

5. If you look at the **Project** panel, you'll see two new asset files have been created: the **beetle-right Animation Clip** and an **Animator Controller** named **Enemy Bug**:

6. Close the **Animation** panel, and double click the **Enemy Bug Animator Controller** to start editing it – it should appear in a new **Animator** panel. You should see four *states*, **Any State** and **Exit** are unlinked, and state **Entry** has a **Transition** arrow connecting to **Animation Clipbeetle-right**. This means that as soon as the **Animator Controller** starts to play, it will enter the **beetle-right** state. State **beetle-right** is tinted orange, to indicate that it is the **Default** state.

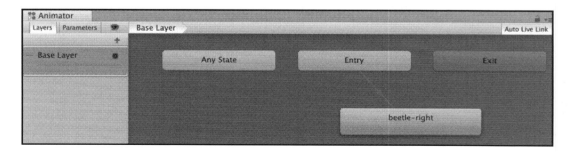

If there is only one **Animation Clip** state, that will be the **Default** state automatically. Once you have other states added to the state chart, you can right-click a different state and use the context menu to change which state is first entered.

7. Select the **beetle-right** state and make a copy of it, renaming the copy **beetle-left** (use can use the right-mouse menu, or the *Ctrl + C/V* keyboard shortcuts). It makes sense to position **beetle-left** to the **left** of **beetle-right**:

8. Move your mouse pointer over the **beetle-right** state, and then in the mouse right-click context menu, choose **Make Transition**, and drag the white arrow that appears into the **beetle-left** state:

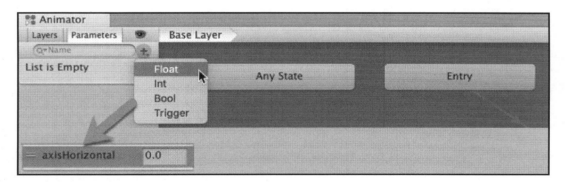

9. Repeat this step with **beetle-left**, to create a **Transition** back from **beetle-left** to **beetle-right**:

10. We want an instance **Transition** between left- and right-facing. So for **each Transition**, uncheck the **Has Exit Time** option. Click the **Transition** arrow to select it (it should turn blue), then uncheck this option in the **Inspector**:

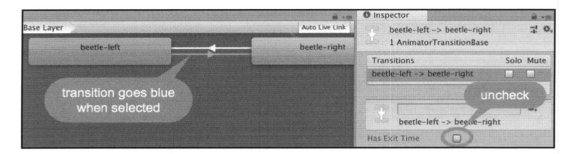

 To delete a **Transition**, first select it, then use the *Delete* key (**Windows**) or press *Fn + Backspace* (**macOS**).

11. For our condition to decide when to change the active state, we now need to create a **Parameter** indicating whether the *Left/Right* arrow keys have been clicked. *Left/Right* keys presses are indicated by the Unity input system's **Horizontal** axis value. Create a state chart float **Parameter** named **axisHorizontal** by selecting **Parameters** (rather than Layers) in the top-left of the **Animator** panel, clicking the plus-symbol "+" button, and choosing **Float**. Name your new **Parameter axisHorizontal**:

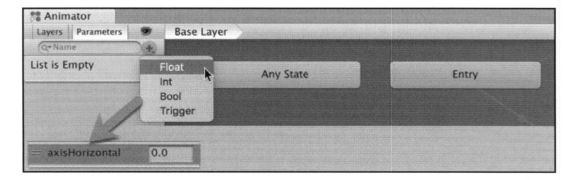

12. With our **Parameter**, we can define the conditions for changing between the left- and right-facing states. When the *Left* arrow key is pressed, the Unity input system's **Horizontal** axis value is negative, so select the **Transition** from **beetle-right** to **beetle-left**, and in the **Inspector** click the plus symbol in the **Conditions** section of the **Transition** properties. Since there is only one **Parameter**, this will automatically be suggested, with defaults of **Greater** than **zero**. Change the **Greater** to **Less**, and we have our desired condition:

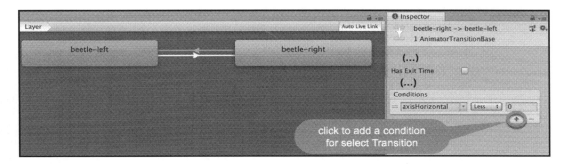

13. Now, select the **Transition** from **beetle-left** to **beetle-right**, and add a **Condition**. In this case, the defaults, **axisHorizontal Greater** than **zero**, are just what we want (since a positive value is returned by Unity's input system **Horizontal** axis when the *Right* arrow key is pressed).

14. We need a method to actually map from the Unity input system's **Horizontal** axis value (from the *Left*/*Right* array keys) to our **Animator** state chart **ParameteraxisHorizontal**. This we can do with a short script class, which we'll create in the next steps.

15. Create a C# script class named **InputMapper**, and add an instance object as a component to the **Enemy Bug** GameObject:

```
using UnityEngine;

public class InputMapper : MonoBehaviour {
    Animator animator;

    void Start() {
        animator = GetComponent<Animator>();
    }

    void Update() {
        animator.SetFloat("axisHorizontal",
Input.GetAxisRaw("Horizontal"));
```

```
        }
    }
```

16. Now we need to actually change the local scale property of the GameObject when we switch to the left or right facing state. Create a C# script class named **LocalScaleSetter**:

```
using UnityEngine;

public class LocalScaleSetter : StateMachineBehaviour  {
    public Vector3 scale = Vector3.one;

    override public void OnStateEnter(Animator animator,
AnimatorStateInfo stateInfo, int layerIndex) {
        animator.transform.localScale = scale;
    }

}
```

17. In the Animator panel, select the **beetle-right** state. In the **Inspector**, click the **AddBehaviour** button, and select **LocalScaleSetter**. The default public Vector three scale value of (**1,1,1**) is fine for this state.

18. In the Animator panel, select the **beetle-left** state. In the **Inspector**, click the **AddBehaviour** button, and select **LocalScaleSetter**. Change the public Vector three scale to a value of (**-1,1,1**) – that is, we need to swap the X-scaling to make our **Sprite** face to the left:

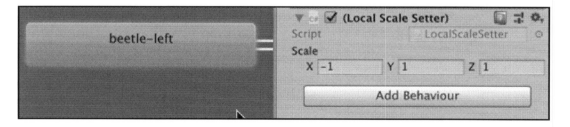

Adding instance objects of C# script classes to **Animator** states is a great way to link the logic for actions when entering into/exiting a state with the **Animator** states themselves.

19. In the **Animator** panel, select the **beetle-right** state. In the Inspector, click the **AddBehaviour** button, and select **InputMapper**.

20. When you run your **Scene**, pressing the *Left* and *Right* arrow keys should make the bug face left or right.

How it works...

Each frame the `Update()` method of the **InputMapper** C# script-class reads the Unity input system's **Horizontal** axis value each frame, and sets the **Animator** state chart **ParameteraxisHorizontal** to this value. If the value is less than (left arrow) or greater than (right arrow) zero, if appropriate, the **Animator** state system will switch to the other state.

The **LocalScaleSetter** C# script class actually changes the **localScale** property (initial value **1,1,1**, or reflect horizontally to make it face left **-1,1,1**). For each state the public **Vector3** variable can be customized to the appropriate values.

The `OnStateEnter(...)` method is involved each time you enter the state that an instance object of this C# class is attached to. You can read about the various event messages for the StateMachineBehaviour class at `https://docs.unity3d.com/ScriptReference/StateMachineBehaviour.html`.

When we press the *Left*-arrow key, the value of the Unity input system's **Horizontal** axis value is negative, and this is mapped to the **Animator** state chart, **Parameter axisHorizontal**, causing the system to **Transition** to the **beetle-left** state, and `OnStateEnter(...)` of the **LocalScaleSetter** script class instance to be executed, setting the local scale to **(-1, 1, 1)**, making the **Texture** flip **Horizontally**, so the beetle faces left.

There's more...

Here are some suggestions for enhancing this recipe.

Instantaneous swapping

You may have noticed a delay, even though we set **Exit Time** to **zero**. This is because there is a default blending when **Transitioning** from one state to another. However, this can be set to **zero**, so that the state machine switches instantaneously from one state to the next.

Do the following:

1. Select each **Transition** in the **Animator** panel.
2. Expand the **Settings** properties.
3. Zero both the **Transition Duration** and the **Transition Offset**:

Now when you run the **Scene**, the bug should immediately swith left and right as you press the corresponding arrow keys.

Animating body parts for character movement events

In this recipe, we'll learn to animate the **hat** of the Unity potato-man character in response to a jump event.

Getting ready

For this recipe, we have prepared the files you need in folder 08_03.

How to do it...

To animate body parts for character movement events, follow these steps:

1. Create a new Unity 2D project.
2. Import the provided **PotatoManAssets** package into your project.
3. Increase the size of the **Main Camera** to 10.
4. Set up the 2D gravity setting for this project – we'll use the same setting as from Unity's 2D platform tutorial, a setting of **Y= -30**. Set 2D gravity to this value by choosing menu: **Edit | Project Settings | Physics 2D**, and then at the top change the Y value to **-30**:

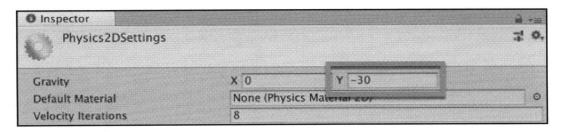

5. Drag an instance of the PotatoMan **hero** character2D from the **Project | Prefabs** folder into the **Scene**. Position this GameObject at (0, 3, 0).
6. Drag an instance of the sprite **platformWallBlocks** from the **Project | Sprites** folder into the **Scene**. Position this GameObject at (0, -4, 0).
7. Add a **Box Collider 2D** component to the **platformWallBlocks** GameObject by choosing menu: **Add Component | Physics 2D | Box Collider 2D**.
8. We now have a stationary platform that the player can land upon, and walk left and right on. Create a new **Layer** named **Ground**, and assign the **platformWallBlocks** GameObject to this new layer, as shown in the following screenshot. Pressing the *Space* key when the character is on the platform will now make him jump:

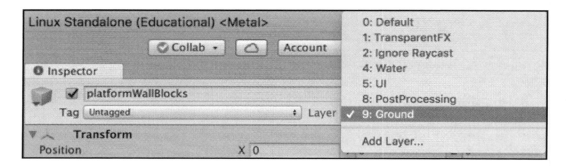

9. Currently the PotatoMan **hero** character is animated (arms and legs moving) when we make him jump. Let's remove the **Animation Clips** and **Animator Controller** and create our own from scratch. Delete the **Clips** and **Controllers** folders from **Project | Assets | PotatoMan2DAssets | Character2D | Animation**, as shown:

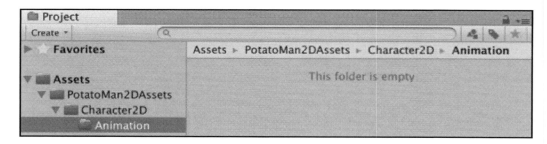

10. Let's create an **Animation Clip** (and its associated **Animator Controller**) for our **hero** character. In the **Hierarchy**, select GameObject **hero**. Ensuring GameObject **hero** character2D is selected in the **Hierarchy**, open the **Animation** panel, and ensure it is in **Dope Sheet** view (this is the default).

11. Click the **Animation** panel's **Create** button, and save the new clip in the **Character2D | Animation** folder, naming it as **character-potatoman-idle**. You've now created an **Animation Clip** for the **Idle** character state (which is not animated):

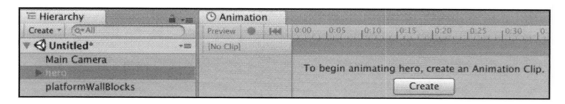

Your final game may end up with dozens, or even hundreds, of **Animation Clips**. Make things easy to search by prefixing the names of clips with object type, name, and then a description of the animation clip.

12. Looking at the **Character2D | Animation** folder in the **Project** panel, you should now see both the **Animation Clip** you have just created (**character-potatoman-idle**) and a new **Animator Controller**, which has defaulted to the name of your **hero** character2D GameObject:

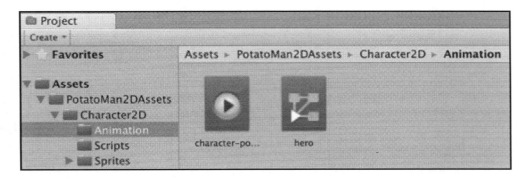

13. Ensuring the **hero** GameObject is selected in the **Hierarchy**, open the **Animator** panel and you'll see the **State Machine** for controlling the animation of our character. Since we only have one **Animation Clip** (**character-potatoman-idle**), upon entry, the **State Machine** immediately enters this state:

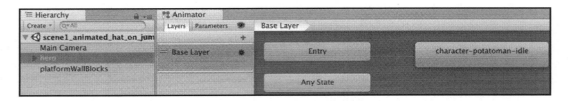

14. Run your **Scene**. Since the character is always in the 'idle' state, we see no animation yet when we make it jump.

15. Create a jump **AnimationClip** that animates the **hat**. Ensure that the **hero** GameObject is still selected in the **Hierarchy**. Click the empty drop-down menu in the **Animation** panel (next to the word **Samples**), and create a new clip in your **Animation** folder, naming it **character-potatoman-jump**:

16. Click the **Add Property** button, and chose **Transform | Position** of the **hat** child object, by clicking its + (plus-sign) button. We are now ready to record changes to the (X, Y, Z) position of the **hat** GameObject in this animation clip:

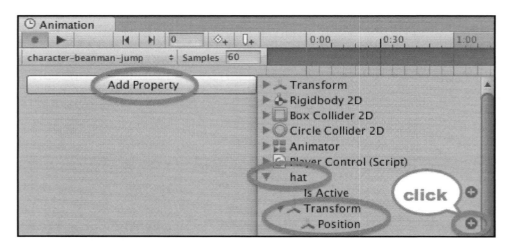

17. You should now see two keyframes at 0.0 and at 1.0. These are indicated by diamonds in the **Timeline** area in the right-hand section of the **Animation** panel.

18. Click to select the first keyframe (at time 0.0) – the diamond should turn blue to indicate it is selected.

19. Let's record a new position for the **hat** for this first frame. Click the red **Record** circle button once to start recording in the **Animation** panel. Now in the **Scene** panel, move the **hat** up and left a little, away from the head. You should see that all three X, Y, Z values have a red background in the **Inspector** – this is to inform you that the values of the **Transform** component are being recorded in the **Animation Clip**:

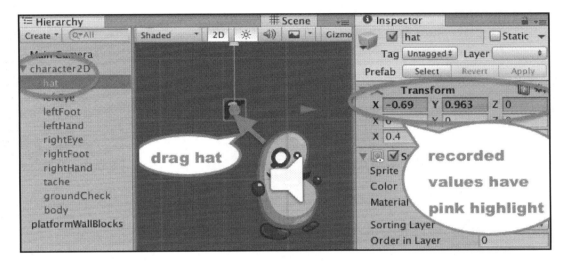

20. Click the red **Record** circle button again to stop recording in the **Animation** panel.
21. Since 1 second is perhaps too long for our jump animation, drag the second keyframe diamond to the left to a time of 0.5:

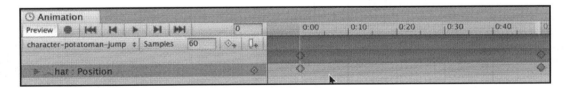

22. We need to define when the character should **Transition** from the **Idle** state to the **Jump** state. In the **Animator** panel, select the **character-potatoman-idle** state, and create a **Transition** to the **character-potatoman-jump** state by right-mouse-clicking and choosing the **Make Transition** menu, then drag the **Transition** arrow to the **character-potatoman-jump** state, as shown:

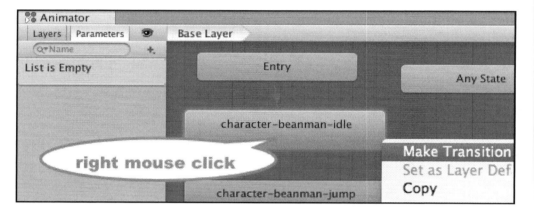

23. Let's add a **Trigger** parameter named **Jump**, by clicking on the add parameter plus-sign "+" button at the top-left of the **Animator** panel, choosing **Trigger**, and typing the name **Jump**:

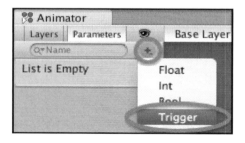

24. We can now define the properties for when our character should **Transition** from **idle** to **jump**. Click the **Transition** arrow to select it, set the following two properties, and add one condition in the **Inspector** panel:
    - **Has Exit Time**: Uncheck this option
    - **Transition Duration(s)**: Set to 0.01
    - **Conditions**: Add **Jump** (click + button at bottom):

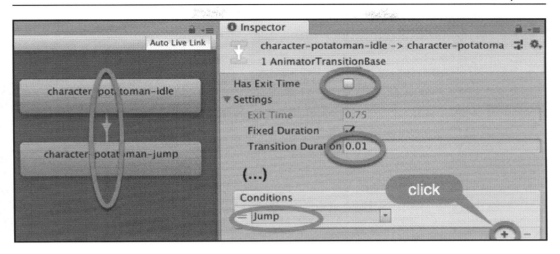

25. Save and run your **Scene**. Once the character has landed on the platform and you press the *Space* key to jump, you'll see the character's hat jump away from his head, and slowly move back. Since we haven't added any **Transition** to leave the **Jump** state, this **Animation Clip** will loop, so the **hat** keeps on moving even when the jump is completed.

26. In the **Animator** panel, select the **character-potatoman-jump** state and add a new **Transition** back to the **character-potatoman-idle** state. Select this **Transition** arrow, and in the **Inspector** panel sets its properties as follows:
    - **Has Exit Time**: (leave as checked)
    - **Exit Time**: 0.5 (this needs to be the same time value as the second keyfame of our Jump animation clip):

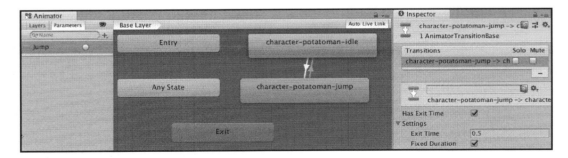

27. Save and run your **Scene**. Now when you jump, the **hat** should animate once, after which the character immediately returns to its **Idle** state.

How it works...

You have added an **Animation Controller State Machine** to the **hero** GameObject. The two **Animation Clips** you created (**idle** and **jump**) appear as **States** in the **Animator** panel. You created a **Transition** from **Idle** to **Jump** when the **JumpTrigger** parameter is received by the **State Machine**. You created a second **Transition**, which transitions back to the **Idle** state after waiting 0.5 seconds (the same duration between the 2 key-frames in our **Jump Animation Clip**).

The player makes the character jump by pressing the *Space* key. This causes code in the `PlayerControl` C#-scripted component of the **hero** GameObject to be invoked, that makes the sprite move upwards on screen, and also sends a `SetTrigger(...)` message to the Animator controller component, for the Trigger named Jump.

The difference between a **Boolean Parameter** and a **Trigger** is that a **Trigger** is temporality set to **True** and once the `SetTrigger(...)` event has been consumed by a state transition, it automatically returns to being **False**. So **Triggers** are useful for actions we wish to do once and then revert to a previous state. A **Boolean Parameter** is a variable, which can have its value set to **True** or **False** at different times during the game, and so different **Transitions** can be created to fire depending on the value of the variable at any time. Note that **Boolean Parameters** have to have their values explicitly set back to **False** with `SetBool(...)`.

The following screenshot highlights the line of code that sends the `SetTrigger(...)` message:

```
                 PlayerControl.cs              ○
No selection
    69          // If the player should jump...
    70⊟         if(jump)
    71          {
    72              // Set the Jump animator trigger parameter.
    73              anim.SetTrigger("Jump");
    74
    75              // Add a vertical force to the player.
```

State Machines for animations of a range of motions (running/walking/jumping/falling/dying) will have more **States** and **Transitions**. The Unity-provided potato-man **hero** character has a more complex **State Machine**, and more complex animations (of hands and feet, and eyes and hat, and so on, for each **Animation Clip**), which you may find useful to explore.

Learn more about the Animation view on the Unity Manual web pages at `http://docs.unity3d.com/Manual/AnimationEditorGuide.html`.

Creating a three-frame animation clip to make a platform continually animate

In this recipe, we'll make a wooden-looking platform continually animate, moving upwards and downwards. This can be achieved with a single three-frame **Animation Clip** (starting at top, position at bottom, top position again):

Getting ready

This recipe builds on the previous one, so make a copy of that project, and work on the copy for this recipe.

How to do it...

To create a continually-moving animated platform, follow these steps:

1. Drag an instance of the **platformWoodBlocks** sprite from the **Project |
   Sprites** folder into the **Scene**. Position this GameObject at **(-4, -5, 0)**, so that
   these wood blocks are neatly to the left, and slightly below, the wall blocks
   platform.

2. Add a **Box Collider 2D** component to
   the **platformWoodBlocks** GameObject so that the player's character can
   stand on this platform too. Choose menu: **Add Component | Physics 2D |
   Box Collider 2D**.

3. Create a new folder named **Animations**, in which to store the **Animation
   Clip** and controller we'll create next.

4. Ensuring the **platformWoodBlocks** GameObject is still selected in the
   Hierarchy, open an **Animation** panel, and ensure it is in **Dope Sheet** view
   (this is the default).

5. Click the **Animation** panel's **Create** button, and save the new clip in your
   new **Animation** folder, naming it **platform-wood-moving-up-down**.

6. Click the **Add Property** button, choose **Transform**, and the click the plus-
   sign by **Position**. We are now ready to record changes to the (X, Y, Z)
   position of the **platformWoodBlocks** GameObject in this **Animation Clip**:

7. You should now see 2 keyframes at 0.0 and at 1.0. These are indicated by
   diamonds in the **Timeline** area in the right-hand section of the **Animation**
   panel.

8. We need 3 keyframes, with the new one at 2:00 seconds. Click at 2:00 in
   the **Timeline** along the top of the **Animation** panel, so that the red line for
   the current playhead time is at time 2:00. Then click the diamond **+** button
   to create a new keyframe at the current playhead time:

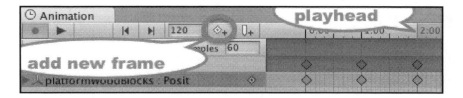

9. The first and third keyframes are fine – they record the current height of the wood platform at **Y= -5**. We need to make the middle keyframe record the height of the platform at the top of its motion, and Unity **in-betweening** will do all the rest of the animation work for us.

10. Select the middle keyframe (at time 1:00), by clicking on the diamond at time 1:00 (they should both turn blue, and the red playhead vertical line should move to 1:00, to indicate the middle keyframe is being edited).

11. Click the red **Record** cirle button to start recording changes.

12. In the **Inspector**, change the Y-position of the platform to 0. You should see that all three X, Y, and Z values have a red background in the **Inspector** – this is to inform you that the values of the **Transform** component are being recorded in the **Animation Clip**.

13. Click the red **Record** circle button again, to finish recording changes.

14. Save and run your **Scene**. The wooden platform should now be animating continuously, moving smoothly up and down the positions we set up.

 If you want the potatoman character to be able to jump when on the moving wooden block, you'll need to select the block GameObject and set its layer to **Ground**.

How it works...

You have added an animation to the **platformWoodBlocks** GameObject. This animation contains three keyframes. A keyframe represents the values of properties of the object at a point in time. The first keyframe stores a Y-value of -4, the second keyframe a Y-value of 0, and the final keyframe -4 again. Unity calculates all the **in-between** values for us, and the result is a smooth animation of the Y-position of the platform.

There's more...

Here are some suggestions for enhancing this recipe.

Copy animation relative to a new parent GameObject

If we wanted to duplicate the moving platform, simply duplicating the **platformWoodBlocks** GameObject in the **Hierarchy** and moving the copy won't work – since when you run the **Scene** each duplicate would be animated back to the location of the original animation frames (that is, all copies would be positioned and moving in the original location).

The solution is first to create a new, empty GameObject (named **movingBlockParent**), and then a **platformWoodBlocks** parent to this GameObject. Now we can duplicate the **movingBlockParent** GameObject (and its **platformWoodBlocks** child) to create more moving blocks in our scene that each move relative to where the parent GameObject is located at **Design-Time**.

Making a platform start falling once stepped on using a Trigger to move animation from one state to another

In many cases, we don't want an animation to begin until some condition has been met, or some event has occurred. In these cases, a good way to organize the **Animator Controller** is to have two animation states (clips) and a **Trigger** on the **Transition** between the clips. We use code to detect when we want the animation to start playing, and at that time we send the **Trigger** message to the **Animation Controller**, causing the **Transition** to start.

In this recipe, we'll create a water platform block in our 2D platform game; such blocks will begin to slowly fall down the screen as soon as they have been stepped on, and so the player must keep on moving otherwise they'll fall down the screen with the blocks too! It looks as follows:

Getting ready

This recipe builds on the previous one, so make a copy of that project, and work on the copy for this recipe.

How to do it...

To construct an animation that only plays once a **Trigger** has been received, follow these steps:

1. In the **Hierarchy**, create an Empty GameObject named **water-block-container**, positioned at (2.5, -4, 0). This empty GameObject will allow us to make duplicates of animated Water Blocks that will animate relative to their parent GameObject position.

2. Drag an instance of the **Water Block** sprite from the **Project | Sprites** folder into the scene and child it to the **water-block-container** GameObject. Ensure the position of your new child Water Block GameObject is (0, 0, 0), so that it appears neatly to right of the wall blocks platform:

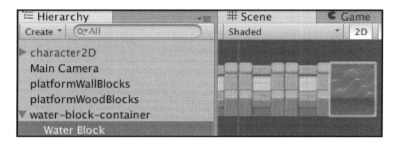

3. Add a **Box Collider 2D** component to the child **Water Block** GameObject, and set the layer of this GameObject to **Ground**, so that the player's character can stand and jump on this water block platform.

4. Ensuring the child **Water Block** GameObject is selected in the **Hierarchy**, open an **Animation** panel, then create a new clip named **platform-water-up,** saving it in your **Animations** folder.

5. Create a second **Animation Clip**, named **platform-water-down**. Again, click the **Add Property** button, chose **Transform** and **Position**, and delete the second keyframe at 1:00.

6. With the first keyframe at 0:00 selected, click the red **Record** button once to start recording changes, and set the Y-value of the GameObject's Transform Position to -5. Press the red **Record** button again to stop recording changes. You have now completed the creation of the water-block-down **Animation Clip**, so you can click the red **Record** button to stop recording.

7. You may have noticed that as well as the up/down **Animation Clips** that you created, another file was created in your **Animations** folder, an **Animator Controller** named **Water Block**. Select this file and open the **Animator** panel, to see and edit the **State Machine** diagram:

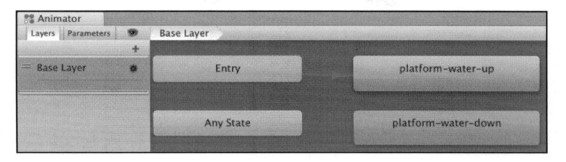

8. Currently, although we created 2 **Animation Clips** (states), only the **Up** state is ever active. This is because when the scene begins (Entry), the object will immediately go in the **platform-water-up** state, but since there are no **Transition** arrows from this state to **platform-water-down**, at present the **Water Block** GameObject will always be in its **Up** state.

9. Ensure the **platform-water-up** state is selected (it will have a blue border around it), and create a **Transition** (arrow) to the **platform-water-down** state by choosing **Make Transition** from the mouse-right-click menu.

10. If you run the **Scene** now, the default **Transition** settings are that after 0.75 seconds (default **Exit Time**), the **Water Block** will **Transition** into their **Down** state. We don't want this – we only want them to animate downwards after the player has walked onto them.

11. Create a **Trigger** named **Fall**, by choosing the **Parameters** tab in the **Animator** panel, clicking the + button and selecting **Trigger**, and then selecting **Fall**.

12. Do the following to create the transition to wait for our **Trigger**:
    - In the **Animator** panel, select the **Transition**
    - In the **Inspector** panel, uncheck the **Has Exit Time** option
    - Set **Transition Duration** to 3.0 (so the **Water Block** slowly **Transitions** to its **Down** state over a period of 2 seconds)

- In the **Inspector** panel, click the + button to add a **Condition**, which should automatically suggest the only possible **Condition Parameter**, which is our **Trigger Fall**:

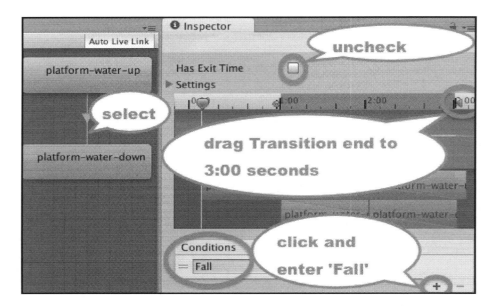

 An alternative to setting the **Transition Duration** numerically is to drag the **Transition** end time to 3:00 seconds in the **Animation Timeline** offered under the **Transition Settings** in the **Inspector**.

13. We need to add a **Collider** trigger just above the **Water Block**, and a C# script class behavior to send the **Animator Controller Trigger** when the player enters the collider.

14. Ensure the child **Water Block** GameObject is selected, add a (second) **2D Box Collider**, with a Y-Offset of 1, and tick its **Is Trigger** checkbox:

15. Create a C# script class named **WaterBlock**, and add an instance object as a component to the child **Water Block** GameObject:

```
using UnityEngine;
using System.Collections;

public class WaterBlock : MonoBehaviour {
    private Animator animatorController;

    void Start(){
        animatorController = GetComponent<Animator>();
    }

    void OnTriggerEnter2D(Collider2D hit){
        if(hit.CompareTag("Player")){
            animatorController.SetTrigger("Fall");
        }
    }
}
```

16. Make 6 more copies of **water-block-container** GameObject, with X positions increasing by 1 each time, that is, 3.5, 4.5, 5.5, and so on.

17. Run the **Scene**, and as the player's character runs across each water block they will start falling down, so he had better keep running!

How it works...

You created a two-state **Animator Controller** state machine. Each state was an **Animation Clip**. You created a **Transition** from the **Water Block Up** state to its **Down** state that will take place when the **Animator Controller** received a **Fall Trigger** message. You created a **Box Collider 2D** with a **Trigger**, so that the scripted **WaterBlock** component could be detected when the player (tagged **Player**) enters its collider, and at that point send the **Fall Trigger** message to make the **Water Block** GameObject start gently **Transitioning** into its **Down** state further down the screen.

Learn more about the **Animator Controllers** on the Unity Manual web pages at http://docs.unity3d.com/Manual/class-AnimatorController.html.

Creating animation clips from sprite sheet sequences

The traditional method of animation involved hand-drawing many images, each slightly different, which displayed quickly frame-by-frame to give the appearance of movement. For computer game animation, the term **Sprite Sheet** is given to the image file that contains one or more sequences of sprite frames. Unity provides tools to break up individual sprite images into large **Sprite Sheet** files, so that individual frames, or sub-sequences of frames, can be used to create **Animation Clips** that can become **States** in **Animator Controller State Machines**. In this recipe, we'll import and break up an open source monster sprite sheet into three animation clips for **Idle**, **Attack**, and **Death**, which looks as shown:

Getting ready

For all the recipes in this chapter, we have prepared the sprite images you need in folder 08_04. Many thanks to Rosswet Mobile for making these **Sprites** available as **Open Source** at http://www.rosswet.com/wp/?p=156.

How to do it...

To create an animation from a sprite sheet of frame-by-frame animation images, follow these steps:

1. Create a new Unity 2D project.
2. Import the provided image: **monster1**.
3. With the **monster1** image selected in the **Project** panel, change its **Sprite** mode to **Multiple** in the **Inspector**, the click the **Apply** button at the bottom of the panel:

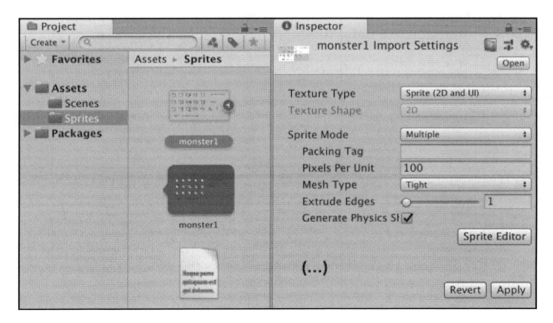

4. In the **Inspector,** open the **Sprite Editor** panel by clicking the **Sprite Editor** button.

5. In the **Sprite Editor,** open the **Slice** drop-down dialog, set the **Type** to **Grid,** set the grid **PixelSize** to **64x64,** and then click the **Slice** button. For **Type,** choose the drop-down option **Grid** by **CellSize,** and set X and Y to **64.** Click the **Slice** button, and then the **Apply** button in the bar at the top right of the **Sprite Editor** panel:

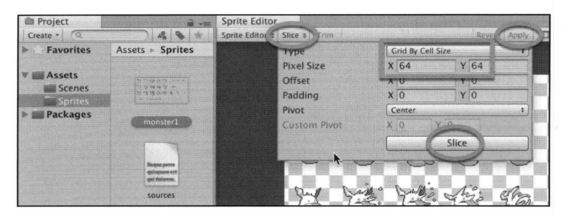

6. In the **Project** panel, you can now click the expand triangle button on the right-hand side of the sprite, and you'll see all the different child frames for this sprite (as highlighted in the following screenshot):

7. Create a folder named **Animations.**

8. In your new folder, create an **Animator Controller** asset file named **monster-animator,** choose **Project** panel menu: **Create | Animator Controller.**

9. In the scene, create a new Empty GameObject named **monster1** (at position 0, 0, 0), and drag your **monster-animator** into this GameObject.

10. With the **monster1** GameObject selected in the **Hierarchy**, open up the **Animation** panel, and create a new **Animation Clip** named **monster1-idle**.

11. Select the **monster1** image in the **Project** panel (in its expanded view), and select and drag the first 5 frames (frames **monster1_0 .. monster1_4**) into the **Animation** panel. Change the sample rate to 12 (since this animation was created to run at 12 frames per second):

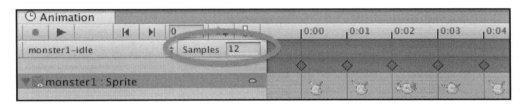

12. If you look at the **State Chart** for monster-animator, you'll see it has a default state (clip) named **monster-idle**.

13. When you run your **Scene**, you should now see the **monster1** GameObject animating in its **monster-idle** state. You may wish to make the **Main Camera** size a bit smaller (size 1), since these are quite small sprites:

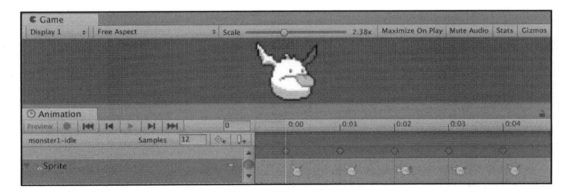

How it works...

Unity's **Sprite Editor** knows about **Sprite Sheets**, and once the correct grid size has been entered, it treats the items in each grid square inside the **Sprite Sheet** image as an individual image, or frame, of the animation. You selected sub-sequences of sprite animation frames and added them into several **Animation Clips**. You added an **Animation Controller** to your GameObject, and so each **Animation Clip** appears as a state in the **Animation Controller State Machine**.

You can now repeat the process, creating an **Animation Clipmonster-attack** with frames 8-12, and a third clip **monster-death** with frames 15-21. You would then create **Triggers** and **Transitions** to make the **monster** GameObject transition into the appropriate states as the game is played.

Learn more about the Unity Sprite Editor from the Unity video tutorials at https://unity3d.com/learn/tutorials/modules/beginner/2d/sprite-editor.

Learn more about 2D animation with **Sprite Sheets** in an article by John Horton on GameCodeOldSchool.com: http://gamecodeschool.com/unity/simple-2d-sprite-sheet-animations-in-unity/.

Creating a platform game with Tiles and Tilemaps

One of the powerful 2D tools introduced by Unity is the **Tilemapper**. In this recipe, we'll create a simple 2D platformer, building a grid-based **Scene** using some free **Tile Sprite** images:

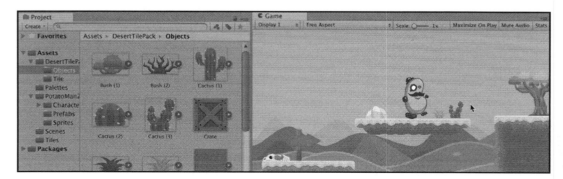

Getting ready

For this recipe, we have prepared the Unity package and images you need in folder 08_07.

Special thanks to GameArt2D.com for publishing the Desert image Sprites with the **Creative Commons Zero** licence: https://www.gameart2d.com/free-desert-platformer-tileset.html.

How to do it...

To create a platform game with **Tiles** and **Tilemaps**, follow these steps:

1. Create a new Unity 2D project.
2. Import the provided images.
3. The tile **Sprites** we've using for this recipe are **128 x 128** pixels. It's important to ensure that we set the pixels per unit to **128**, so that our **Sprite** images will map to a grid of 1 x 1 Unity units. Select all the **Sprites** in the **Project | DesertTilePack | Tile** folder, and in the **Inspector** set **Pixels per Unit** to **128**:

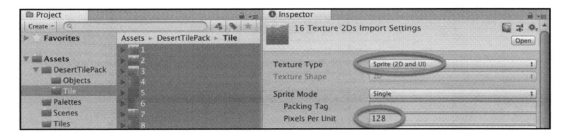

4. Display the **Tile Palette** panel, by choosing menu: **Window | 2D | Tile Palette**.
5. In the **Project** panel, create a new folder named **Palettes** (this is where you'll save your **TilePalette** assets).

6. Click the **Create New Palette** button in the **Tile Palette** panel, and create a new **Tile Palette** named **DesertPalette**:

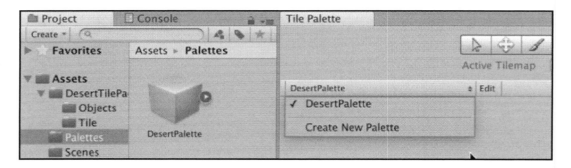

7. In the **Project** panel, create a new folder named **Tiles** (this is where to save your **Tile** assets).

8. Ensure **Tile Palette DesertPalette** is selected in the **Tile Palette** panel, select all the Sprites in the **Project | DesertTilePack | Tile** folder, and drag them into the **Tile Palette** panel. When asked where to save these new **Tile** asset files, select your new **Assets | Tiles** folder. You should now have 16 **Tile** assets in your **Tiles** folder, and these **Tiles** should be available to work with in your **DesertPalette** in the **Tile Palette** panel:

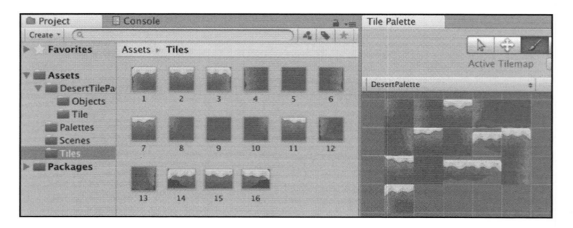

9. Drag **Sprite BG** from the **Project** panel, **DesertTilePack**, into the **Scene**. Resize the **Main Camera** (it should be **Orthographic** since this is a 2D project), so that the desert background fills the entire **Game** panel.

10. Add a **Tilemap** GameObject to the **Scene**, choose the create menu: **2D Object | Tilemap**. You'll see a **Grid** GameObject added, and as a child of that, you'll see a **Tilemap** GameObject. Rename the **Tilemap** GameObject to **Tilemap-platforms**:

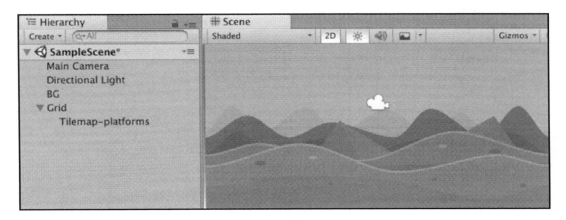

 Just as **UI** GameObjects are children of a **Canvas**, **Tilemap** GameObjects are children of a **Grid**.

11. We can now start *painting* **Tiles** onto our **Tilemap**. Ensure **Tilemap-platforms** is selected in the **Hierarchy**, and that you can see the **Tile Palette** panel. In the **Tile Palette** panel, select the **Paint with active brush** tool (the *paintbrush* icon). Now click on a **Tile** in the **Tile Palette** panel, and then in the **Scene** panel, each time you click the mouse button you'll be adding a **Tile** to **Tilemap-platforms**, automatically aligned with the grid:

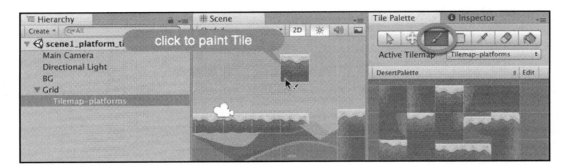

12. If you want to delete a **Tile**, use Shift-Click over that grid position.

13. Use the **Tile Palette** brush to paint two or three platforms.

14. Add a suitable **Collider** to the **Tilemap-platforms** GameObject. Select the **Tilemap-platforms** GameObject in the **Hierarchy**, and in the **Inspector** add a **Tilemap Collider 2D**. Click **Add Component** then choose **Tilemap | Tilemap Collider 2D**.

15. Create a new **Layer** named **Ground**, and set the **Tilemap-platforms** GameObject to be on this **Layer** (this will allow characters to jump when standing on a platform).

16. Let's test our platform **Scene** with a 2D character – we can reuse the potatoman character from Unity's free tutorials. Import the provided **PotatoManAssets** package into your project.

17. Let's set up the 2D gravity setting for this project since the size of the potatoman character is big with respect to the platforms. We'll make the character move slowly by having a heavy gravity setting of **Y= -60**. Set 2D gravity to this value by choosing menu: **Edit | Project Settings | Physics 2D**, and then at the top change the Y value to **-60**.

18. Drag an instance of the potatoman **hero** character2D from the **Project | Prefabs** folder into the **Scene**. Position him somewhere above one of your platforms.

19. Play the **Scene**. The 2D **hero** character should fall down and land on the platform. You should be able to move the character left and right, and make him jump using the *Space* key.

20. You may wish to decorate the scene by dragging some of the **Objects Sprites** onto the **Scene** (in the **Project** panel folder, **Project | DesertTilePack | Object**).

How it works...

By having a set of platform **Sprites** that are all a regular size (**128 x 128**), it is straightforward to create a **Tile Palette** from those **Sprites**, and then to add a **Grid** and **Tilemap** to the **Scene**, allowing the **Tile Palette** brush to paint **Tiles** into the **Scene**.

You had to set the **Sprite** pixels per unit to 128, so each **Tile** maps to a 1 x 1 Unity grid unit.

You added a **Tilemap Collider 2D** to the **Tilemap** GameObject, so that characters (such as the potatoman) can interact with the platforms. By adding a **Layer Ground**, and setting the **Tilemap** GameObject to this **Layer**, jumping code in the potatoman character-controller script can test the **Layer** of the object being stood above, so that the jump action will only be possible when standing on a platform **Tile**.

There's more...

Here are some suggestions for enhancing this recipe.

Tile Palettes for objects and walls

The object **Sprites** in the **Desert** free pack are all different sizes, and certainly not consistent with the **128 x 128** Sprite size for the platform Tiles.

However, if the **Sprites** for the objects and walls in your game *are* the same size as your platform **Sprites**, you can create a **Tile Palette** for your objects, and paint them into the **Scene** using the **Tile Palette** brush.

Rule Tiles for intelligent Tile selection

If you explore the **2D Extras Pack**, or the **2D GameKit** (see next recipe), you'll learn about **Rule Tiles**. These allow you to define rules about the choice of a **Tile** based on its neighbors. For example, you wouldn't put a platform top **Tile** immediately on top of another one, so **Rule Tiles** would place some kind of ground tile to be the **Tile** under the platform top tile. Rules can ensure the leftmost and rightmost tiles in a group select the **Tiles** with artwork for the edges, and so on.

A good introduction to **Rule Times** can be found in this Unity live training video session: `https://unity3d.com/learn/tutorials/topics/2d-game-creation/using-rule-tiles-tilemap`.

Learning more

Here are some learning resources about Tilemapping:

- Unity **TileMap** tutorial:
  `https://unity3d.com/learn/tutorials/topics/2d-game-creation/intro-2d-world-building-w-tilemap`
- Unity tutorial **TileMap** assets:
  `https://oc.unity3d.com/index.php/s/VzImolXrvp3K2Q5/download`
- Lots of 2D Extra resources, free from Unity Technologies:
  `https://github.com/Unity-Technologies/2d-extras`
- Sean Duffy's great tutorial on Tilemapping on the Ray Wenderlich site:
  `https://www.raywenderlich.com/188105/introduction-to-the-new-unity-2d-tilemap-system`

Creating a game with the 2D Gamekit

A collection of Unity 2D tools has been combined to become the Unity **2D GameKit**. In this recipe, we'll create a simple 2D-platformer to explore some of the features offered by the **2D GameKit**, including pressure plates, doors, and falling objects damaging enemies:

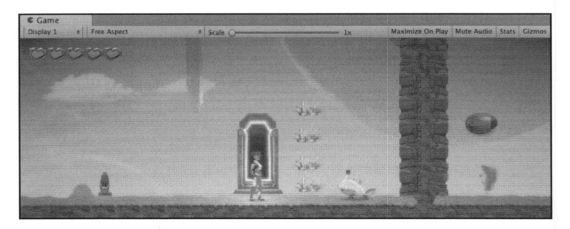

Getting ready

This recipe uses the free Unity **Asset Store** and **Package Manager** packages.

How to do it...

To create a game with the **2D GameKit**, follow these steps:

1. Create a new Unity 2D project.
2. Use the **Package Manager** to install the **Cinemachine** and **Post Processing** packages (if these are installed, you'll get errors when downloading the **2D GameKit**).
3. Import **2D GameKit** (free from Unity Technologies) from the **Asset Store**.
4. Close and then re-open the Unity Editor.
5. Create a new **2D GameKitScene**, by choosing menu: **Kit Tools | Create New Scene**. You'll then be asked to name the **Scene**, and a new **Scene** asset file will be created in your **Project | Assets** folder. You'll see there are quite a few special GameObjects in the **Hierarchy** of your new **Scene**:

6. As you can see, the new **Scene** starts off containing an animated 2D character (**Ellen**), and a small platform.

7. In the **Inspector**, select the **Tilemap** child of
   the **TilemapGrid** GameObject – we are getting ready to paint some **Tiles**
   onto this **Tilemap** GameObject.

8. Display the **Tile Palette**, choose menu: **Window | 2D | Tile Palette**. Select
   TilesetGameKit, and click on the green-topped grass platform **Tile**. Select
   the **Paint with active Brush** tool (the *paintbrush* icon).

9. Start painting grass-topped platforms onto the **Scene**. This is a **Rule Tile**,
   so it cleverly ensures that only the top **Tiles** in a touching group are
   painted with the grass-topped **Tile**. The other touching tiles
   (left/right/below) are painted with a brown, earthy **Tile**.

10. Create a wide, flat area, and then to the right of where **Ellen** starts, create a
    very tall wall of earth, too tall for **Ellen** to jump over.

11. Add four Spikes between **Ellen** and the earth wall, so she would get hurt
    trying to jump over them. Drag instances of the **Spikes Prefab** from
    the **2DGameKit | Prefabs | Environment** Project folder.

12. To make things even harder, add a **Chomper** enemy between the **Spikes**
    and the earth wall! Drag an instance of the **Chomper** Prefab from
    the **2DGameKit | Prefabs | Enemies** Project folder:

13. We have to give **Ellen** some way to get past the earth wall that avoids the
    Spikes and **Chomper** obstacles. Let's add a **Teleporter**, to the left of where
    Ellen starts. Drag an instance of the **Teleporter** Prefab from
    the **2DGameKit | Prefabs | Interactables** Project folder.

14. Let's create a destination point for the **Teleporter** using a custom **Sprite**.
    Import the **EnemyBug Sprite** into this project, and drag an instance from
    the **Project** panel into the **Scene** – somewhere to the right of the earth wall.

15. **Teleporters** require a **Transition Point** component in the GameObject that is to be the destination of the teleportation. Add a **Collider 2D** to **Enemy Bug**, choose **Add Component | Physics 2D | Box Collider 2D**. Check its **Is Trigger** option.

16. Add a **Transition Point** component to **Enemy Bug**, choose **Add Component**, search for **Transition**, and then add **Transition Point**.

17. We can now set up the **Teleporter**. With the **Teleporter** selected in the **Hierarchy**, in the **Inspector** for the **Transition Point (Script)** component, do the following:

    - **Transitioning Game Object**: Drag **Ellen** into this slot
    - **Transition Type**: Choose **Same Scene** from the drop-down menu
    - **Destination Transform**: Drag **Enemy Bug** into this **Transition Point** slot
    - **Transition When**: Choose **On Trigger Enter** from the drop-down menu:

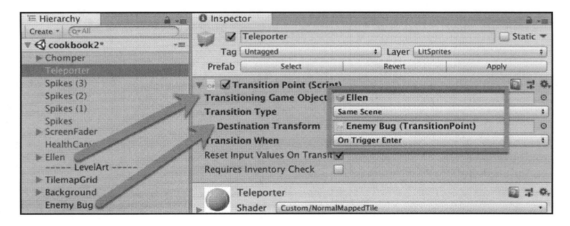

18. Run the **Scene**. Ellen can safely avoid the **Spikes** and **Chomper** by using the **Teleporter**.

19. Let's make it a bit more interesting – having the **Teleporter** GameObject initially inactive (not visible or able to be interacted with), and adding a switch that **Ellen** has to hit to make the **Teleporter** active.

20. Select the **Teleporter** GameObject in the **Hierarchy**, and uncheck its active box at the top-left of the **Inspector** – the GameObject should be invisible, and appear greyed out in the **Hierarchy**.

21. Add a single-use switch to the game, to the left of where **Ellen** starts. Drag an instance of the **Single Use Switch** from the **2DGameKit | Prefabs | Interactables** Project folder.

22. With the **Single Use Switch** selected in the **Hierarchy**, in the **Inspector** set the following:

   - **Layers:** Add **Layer Player** to the **Interactable Layers** (so the switch can be enabled by the Player colliding or firing a bullet)
   - **On Enter:** Drag **Teleporter** into a free **RunTime Only** GameObject Slot, and change the action drop-down menu from **No Function** to **GameObject | Set Active (bool)**, and then **check** the checkbox that appears.

23. Run the **Scene**. **Ellen** now has to travel over to the switch, to reveal the **Teleporter**, which then leads her to safely transport to the **Enemy Bug** location, beyond the earth wall and away from danger.

How it works...

We have dipped our toes into the wide range of features of the 2D GameKit. Hopefully this recipe gives you an idea of how to work with the provided Prefabs, and also how to explore how custom artwork can be used, with appropriately-added components to create your own GameObjects using the features of the 2D GameKit.

If you look at the Ellen 2D character, you'll see some scripted components that manage the character's interaction with the 2D GameKit. These include:

- **CharacterController 2D**: Movement and physics interactions
- **Player Input**: Keyboard/input control mapping, so you can change which keys/controller buttons control movement, jumping, and so on
- **Player Character**: How characters interact with the **2D GameKit**, including fighting (melee), damage, and bullet pool

Learn more about **Ellen** and her component in the reference guide: `https://unity3d.com/learn/tutorials/projects/2d-game-kit/ellen?playlist=49633`.

There's more...

Here are some learning resources about the Unity 2D GameKit:

- Unity's 2D GameKit online tutorials/Reference guide/Advanced topics:
  `https://unity3d.com/learn/tutorials/s/2d-game-kit`
- Unity 's official 2D GameKit forum:
  `https://forum.unity.com/threads/2d-game-kit-official-thread.51724`
  `9/`
- Asset Store 2D GameKit tutorial project:
  `https://assetstore.unity.com/packages/essentials/tutorial-project`
  `s/2d-game-kit-107098`
- Series of YouTube video tutorials from Unity Technologies entitled Getting Started with 2D Game Kits:
  - Overview and Goals [1/8]:
    `https://www.youtube.com/watch?v=cgqIOWu8W1c`
  - Ellen and Placing Hazards [2/8] Live 2018/2/21:
    `https://www.youtube.com/watch?v=V2_vj_bbB4M`
  - Adding Moving Platforms [3/8]:
    `https://www.youtube.com/watch?v=SfC3qYz4gAI`
  - Doors and Destructible Objects [4/8]:
    `https://www.youtube.com/watch?v=-hj6HnbI7PE`
  - Adding and Squishing Enemies [5/8]:
    `https://www.youtube.com/watch?v=WRKG_DDlUnQ`
  - Using The Inventory System [7/8]:
    `https://youtu.be/LYQz-mtr90U`
  - Teleporting and Dialog Boxes [8/8]:
    `https://www.youtube.com/watch?v=gZ_OZL57c0g`

10
3D Animation

In this chapter, we will cover the following:

- Configuring a character's Avatar and idle animation
- Moving your character with root motion and Blend Trees
- Mixing animations with Layers and Masks
- Organizing States into Sub-State Machines
- Transforming the Character Controller via script
- Adding rigid props to animated characters
- Using Animation Events to throw an object
- Applying Ragdoll physics to a character
- Rotating the character's torso to aim a weapon
- Creating geometry with Probuilder
- Creating a game with the 3D Gamekit
- Importing third-party 3D models and animations from Mixamo

Introduction

The **Mecanim** animation system has revolutionized how characters are animated and controlled within Unity. In this chapter, we will learn how to take advantage of its flexibility, power, and friendly and highly visual interface.

The big picture

Controlling a playable character with the **Mecanim** system might look like a complex task, but it is actually very straightforward:

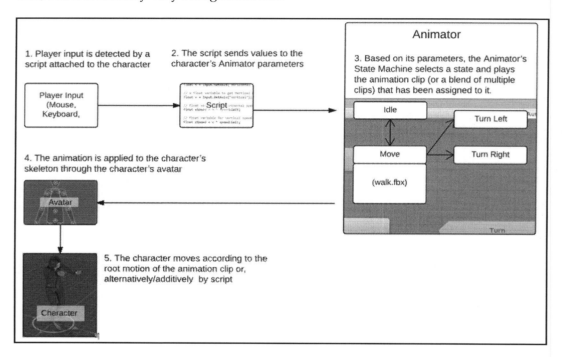

By the end of the chapter, you will have gained a basic understanding of the Mecanim system. For a more complete overview of the subject, consider taking a look at Jamie Dean's *Unity Character Animation with Mecanim*, also published by Packt Publishing.

All the recipes will make use of Mixamo motion packs. Mixamo is a complete solution for character production, rigging, and animation. In fact, the character used was designed with Mixamo's character creation software called Fuse and rigged with the Mixamo **Auto-Rigger**. You can find out more about Mixamo and their products at Unity's **Asset Store** or the Mixamo website:

```
https://assetstore.unity.com/packages/3d/animations/melee-a
xe-pack-35320
https://www.mixamo.com/
```

Please note that although Mixamo offers **Mecanim**-ready characters and animation clips, for the recipes in this chapter, we will use unprepared animation clips. The reason for this is to make you more confident when dealing with assets obtained by other methods and sources.

Configuring a character's Avatar and idle animation

One feature that makes **Mecanim** so flexible and powerful is the ability to quickly reassign **Animation Clips** from one character to another. This is made possible through the use of **Avatars**, which are basically a layer between your character's original rig and Unity's **Animator** system.

In this recipe, we will learn how to configure an **Avatar** skeleton on a rigged character.

Getting ready

For this recipe, you will need the **MsLaser@T-Pose.fbx** and **Swat@rifle_aiming_idle.fbx** files, which are provided in the 09_03 folder.

How to do it...

To configure an Avatar skeleton, follow these steps:

1. Import the **MsLaser@T-Pose.fbx** and **Swat@rifle_aiming_idle.fbx** files into your project.
2. Select the **MsLaser@T-Pose model** from the **Project** panel.
3. In the **Inspector**, under **MsLaser@T-Pose** Import Settings, activate the **Rig** section. Change **Animation Type** to **Humanoid**. Then, leave **Avatar Definition** as **Create From this Model**. Now, click **Apply** to apply these settings. Finally, click on the **Configure...** button:

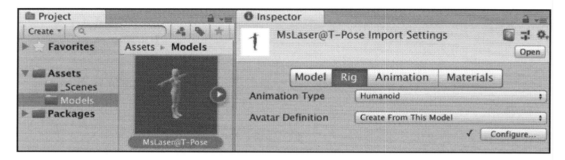

4. The **Inspector** will show the newly created **Avatar**. Observe how Unity correctly mapped the bones of our character to its structure, assigning, for instance, the **mixamoRig:LeftForeArm** bone as the **Avatar's Lower Arm**. We could, of course, reassign bones if needed. For now, just click on the **Done** button to close the view:

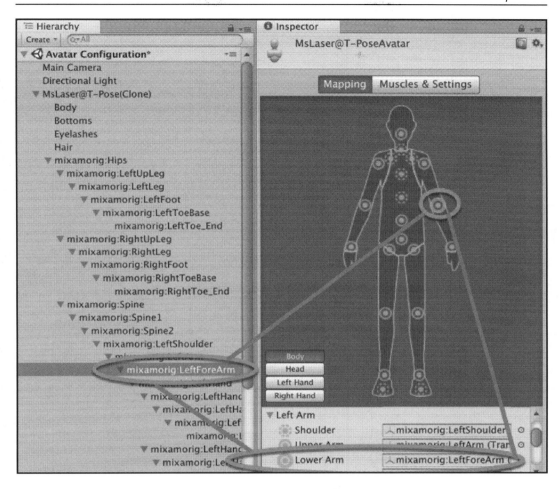

5. Now that we have our **Avatar** ready, let's configure our animation for the **Idle** state. From the **Project** panel, select the **Swat@rifle_aiming_idle** file.

6. Select the **Rig** section, change **Animation Type** to **Humanoid**, and leave **Avatar Definition** as **Create From this Model**. Confirm by clicking on **Apply**.

7. Select the **Animations** section (to the right of the Rig). The **rifle_aiming_idle** clip should be selected. Drag **MsLaser@T-Pose** to the **Preview** area at the bottom of the **Inspector**:

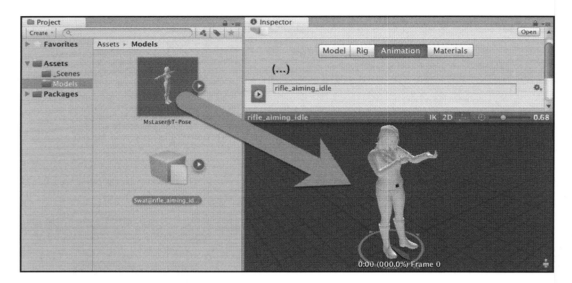

8. With **rifle_aiming_idle** selected from the **Clips** list, check the **Loop Time** and **Loop Pose** options. Also, click on the **Clamp Range** button to adjust the timeline to the actual time of the **Animation Clip**. Then, under **Root Transform Rotation**, check **Bake Into Pose** and select **Based Upon | Original**. Under **Root Transform Position (Y)**, check **Bake Into Pose** and select **Based upon Original**. Under **Root Transform Position (XZ)**, leave **Bake Into Pose** unchecked and select **Based Upon (at Start) | Center of Mass**. Finally, click on **Apply** to confirm the changes:

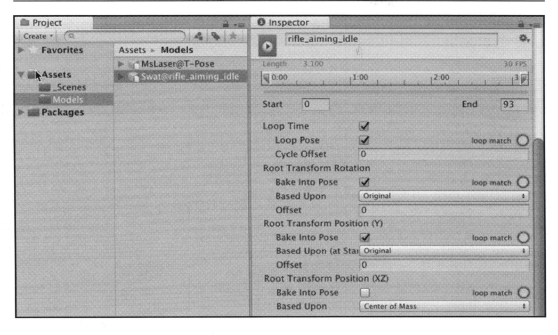

9. In order to access **Animation Clips** and play them, we need to create a **Controller**. Do this by choosing Project panel menu: **Create | Animator Controller**. Name it **MainCharacter**.

10. Double-click on the **Animator Controller** to open the **Animator** panel.

11. From the **Animator** panel, right-click on the grid to open a context menu. Then, select the **Create State | Empty** option. A new box named **New State** will appear. It will be in orange, indicating that it is the default state:

12. Select **New State** and, in the **Inspector**, change its name to **Idle**. Also, in the **Motion** field, choose **rifle_aiming_idle** by either selecting it from the list or dragging it from the **Project** panel:

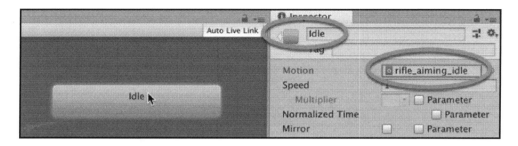

13. Drag the **MsLaser@T-Pose** model from the **Project** panel into the **Hierarchy** and place it in the **Scene**.

14. Select **MsLaser@T-Pose** from the **Hierarchy** and observe its **Animator** component in the **Inspector**. Then, assign the newly created **MainCharacter** controller to its **Controller** field:

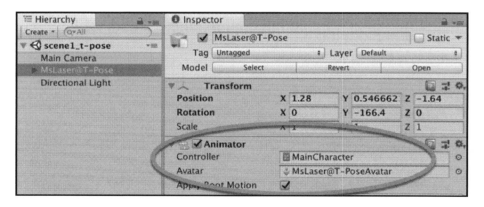

15. Play your **Scene** to see the character correctly animated.

How it works...

Preparing our character for animation took many steps. First, we created its **Avatar**, based on the character model's original bone structure. Then, we set up the **Animation Clip** (which, as the character mesh, is stored in an **.fbx** file), using its own **Avatar**.

After this, we adjusted the **Animation Clip**, clamping its size and making it a loop. We also baked its **Root Transform Rotation** to follow the original file's orientation. Finally, an **Animator Controller** was created, and the edited **Animation Clip** was made into its default **Animation State**.

The concept of the **Avatar** is what makes Mecanim so flexible. Once you have an **Animator Controller**, you can apply it to other humanoid characters, as long as they have an **Avatar** body mask.

There's more...

Here are some ways to go further with this recipe.

Use Controller with another 3D character Avatar

Let's swap **MsLaser** for a **Mascot 3D** character. Do the following:

1. Import the provided model, **mascot.fbx**.
2. The apply steps 3 and 4 for this character to create its **Avatar**.
3. Drag an instance of the model into the **Scene**.
4. In the Inspector for its **Animator Component**, set the **Controller** to the **MainCharacter Animator Controller** you created in this recipe.
5. Run the **Scene**; you should see the mascot playing the **rifle_aiming_idle** animation clip.

See also

To read more information about the Animator Controller, check out Unity's documentation
at http://docs.unity3d.com/Manual/class-AnimatorController.html.

Moving your character with root motion and Blend Trees

The Mecanim animation system is capable of applying **Root Motion** to characters. In other words, it actually moves the character according to the animation clip, as opposed to arbitrarily translating the character model while playing an in-place animation cycle. This makes most of the Mixamo animation clips perfect for use with Mecanim.

Another feature of the animation system is **Blend Trees**, which can blend **Animation Clips** smoothly and easily. In this recipe, we will take advantage of these features to make our character walk/run forward and backward, and also strafe right and left at different speeds.

Getting ready

For this recipe, we have prepared a Unity package named **Character_02**, containing a character and featuring a basic **Animator Controller**. The package can be found inside the `09_02` folder, along with the FBX files for the animation clips you need.

There are two ways to import animations in Unity. One approach involves having each animation as a separate file, named in the form `modelName@animation`, such as `MsLazer@idle`, `MsLazer@jumping`, and so on. The other approach is when a model has several animations all in a single take, in which case you can break the take into separate named animation clips in the Unity editor, specifying the start and end frame for each clip. In this chapter, we'll use the first approach, since it's more straightforward. Learn more from the Unity documentation at `https://docs.unity3d.com/Manual/Splittinganimations.html`.

How to do it...

To apply **Root Motion** to your character using **Blend Trees**, follow these steps:

1. Import **Character_02.unityPackage** into a new project. Also, import the following FBX files:
    - **Swat@rifle_run**
    - **Swat@run_backward**

- **Swat@strafe**
- **Swat@strafe_2**
- **Swat@strafe_left**
- **Swat@strafe_right**
- **Swat@walking**
- **Swat@walking_backward**

2. We need to configure our **Animation Clips**. From the Project panel, select **Swat@rifle_run**.

3. Activate the **Rig** section. Change **Animation Type** to **Humanoid** and **Avatar Definition** to **Create From this Model**. Confirm by clicking on **Apply**:

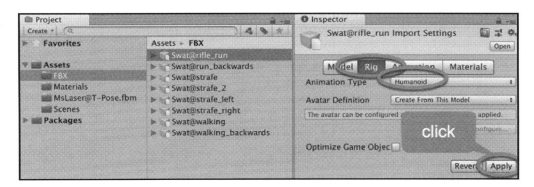

4. Now, activate the **Animations** section (to the right of **Rig**). Clip **rifle_run** should be selected. The **Preview** area (at the bottom of the **Inspector**) will display the message **No model is available** for preview. Drag **MsLaser@T-Pose** onto the **Preview** area.

5. With asset **Swat@rifle_run** still selected in the **Project** panel, in the **Inspector** check the **Loop Time** and **Loop Pose** options. Also, click on the **Clamp Range** button to adjust the timeline to the actual time of the animation clip. Click on **Apply** to confirm these changes:

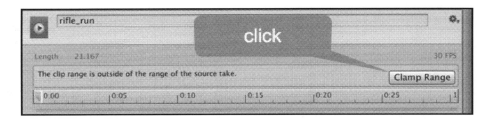

6. Then, under **Root Transform Rotation**, check **Bake Into Pose** and select **Based Upon | Original**. Under **Root Transform Position (Y)**, check **Bake Into Pose** and select **Based Upon (at Start) | Original**. Under **Root Transform Position (XZ)**, leave **Bake Into Pose** unchecked and select **Based Upon (at Start) | Center of Mass**. Finally, click on **Apply** to confirm the changes:

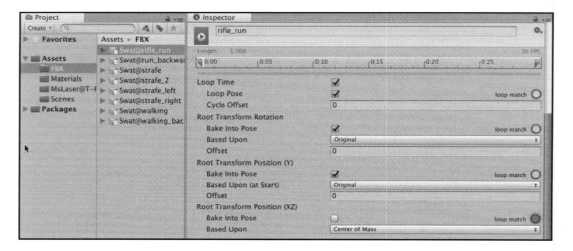

7. Repeat steps 3 to 6 for each one of the following animation clips: **Swat@run_backward**, **Swat@strafe**, **Swat@strafe_2**, **Swat@strafe_left**, **Swat@strafe_right**, **Swat@walking**, and **Swat@walking_backward**.

8. Add a 3D Plane to the **Scene**, choose menu: **Create | 3D Object | Plane**.

9. Drag an instance of the **MsLaser** prefab into the **Scene** and position it on the **3D Plane**.

10. From the **Hierarchy** panel, select the **MsLaser** GameObject. In the **Inspector**, add a **Character Controller** component to it (click **Add Component** and choose **Component | Physics | Character Controller**). Then, set its **Skin Width** to 0.0001 and its **Center** as (0, 0.9, 0); also, change its **Radius** to 0.34 and its **Height** to 1.79:

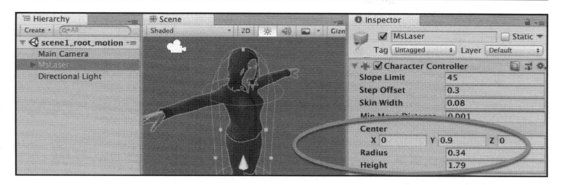

11. In the **Project** panel, double-click the **MainCharacter** controller asset file; it should open in the **Animator** panel.

12. In the top-left corner of the **Animator** panel, select the **Parameters** section and use the + sign to create three new **Parameters (Float)** named **xSpeed**, **zSpeed**, and **Speed**:

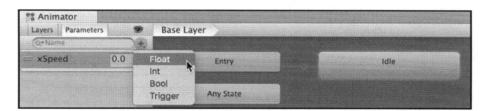

13. We do have an Idle state for our character, but we need new ones. Right-click on the grid area and, from the context menu, navigate to **Create State | From New Blend Tree**. In the **Inspector**, change its name from the **Default Blend Tree** to **Move**:

14. Double-click on the **Move** state. You will see the empty blend tree that you have created. Select it and in the **Inspector**, rename it **Move**. Then, change its **Blend Type** to **2D Freeform Directional**, also setting **xSpeed** and **zSpeed** in the **Parameters** tab. Finally, using the **+** sign from the bottom of the **Motion** list, add nine new **Motion Fields**:

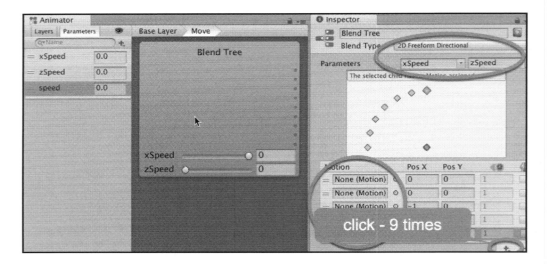

15. Now, populate the **Motion** list with the following motion clips and respective Pos X and Pos Y values: **Run_backwards**, 0, -1; **Walking_backwards**, 0,-0.5; **Rifle_aiming_idle**, 0, 0; **Walking**, 0, 0.5; **Rifle_run**, 0, 1; **Strafe**, -1, 0; **Strafe_left**, -0.5, 0; **Strafe_right**, 0.5, 0; **Strafe_2**, 1, 0. You can populate the **Motion** list by selecting it from the list or, if there is more than one clip with the same name, you can drag it from the **Project** panel onto the slot by expanding the appropriate model icon:

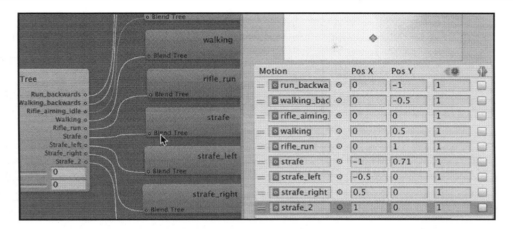

Motion		Pos X	Pos Y		
run_backwa	○	0	−1	1	
walking_bac	○	0	−0.5	1	
rifle_aiming	○	0	0	1	
walking	○	0	0.5	1	
rifle_run	○	0	1	1	
strafe	○	−1	0.71	1	
strafe_left	○	−0.5	0	1	
strafe_right	○	0.5	0	1	
strafe_2	○	1	0	1	

16. To return to the **Base Layer**, either double-click on the grid background of the **Animator** panel, or click the **Base Layer** button in the information bar along the top of the **Animator** panel:

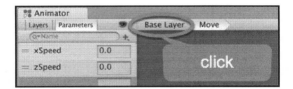

17. Since we have the **rifle_aiming_idle** Motion clip in our **Move** blend tree, we can get rid of the original **Idle** state. Right-click on the **Idle** state box and, from the menu, select **Delete**. The **Move** blend state will become the new default state, turning orange.

18. Now, we must create the script-class that will actually transform the player's input into those variables that are created to control the animation. Create a new C# script-class named **BasicController**, and add an instance-object as a component of the **MsLazer** GameObject:

```
using UnityEngine;
using System.Collections;

public class BasicController: MonoBehaviour {
    private Animator anim;
    private CharacterController controller;
    public float transitionTime = .25f;
    private float speedLimit = 1.0f;
    public bool moveDiagonally = true;
    public bool mouseRotate = true;
```

```
                    public bool keyboardRotate = false;

                    void Start () {
                      controller = GetComponent<CharacterController>();
                      anim = GetComponent<Animator>();
                    }

                    void Update () {
                      if(controller.isGrounded){
                        if (Input.GetKey (KeyCode.RightShift)
||Input.GetKey (KeyCode.LeftShift))
                            speedLimit = 0.5f;
                        else
                            speedLimit = 1.0f;

                        float h = Input.GetAxis("Horizontal");
                        float v = Input.GetAxis("Vertical");
                        float xSpeed = h * speedLimit;
                        float zSpeed = v * speedLimit;
                        float speed = Mathf.Sqrt(h*h+v*v);

                        if(v!=0 && !moveDiagonally)
                          xSpeed = 0;

                        if(v!=0 && keyboardRotate)
                            this.transform.Rotate(Vector3.up * h,
Space.World);

                        if(mouseRotate)
                            this.transform.Rotate(Vector3.up *
(Input.GetAxis("Mouse X")) * Mathf.Sign(v),
Space.World);

                        anim.SetFloat("zSpeed", zSpeed, transitionTime,
Time.deltaTime);
                        anim.SetFloat("xSpeed", xSpeed, transitionTime,
Time.deltaTime);
                        anim.SetFloat("Speed", speed, transitionTime,
Time.deltaTime);
                      }
                    }
                }
```

19. Play your **Scene** and test the game. You should be able to control your character with the arrow keys (or *WASD* keys). Keeping the *Shift* key pressed will slow it down.

How it works...

Whenever the **BasicController** script detects any directional keys in use, it sets the **Speed** variable of the **Animator** state to a value higher than 0, changing the **Animator** state from **Idle** to **Move**. The **Move** state, in turn, blends the motion clips that it was populated with, according to the input values for **xSpeed** (obtained from **Horizontal Axis** input, typically the *A* and *D* keys) and **zSpeed** (obtained from **Vertical Axis** input, typically the *W* and *S* keys). Since **Mecanim** is capable of applying root motion to the characters, our character will actually move in the resulting direction.

For instance, if the *W* and *D* keys are pressed, the **xSpeed** and **zSpeed** values will rise to 1.0. From the **Inspector**, it is possible to see that such a combination will result in a blend between the motion clips called **rifle_run** and **strafe_2**, making the character run diagonally (to the front and right):

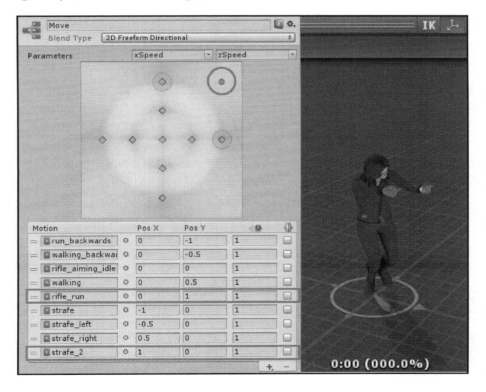

Our **BasicController** includes three checkboxes for more options: **Move Diagonally**, which is set as true by default and allows for blends between forward/backward and left/right clips; **Mouse Rotate**, which is set as true by default and allows for rotating the character with the mouse, changing their direction while moving; and **Keyboard Rotate**, which is set as false by default and allows for rotating the character through simultaneous use of the left/right and forward/backward directional keys.

There's more...

Here are some sources of further information about these topics.

Our blend tree used the **2D Freeform Directional Blend Type**. However, if we only had four **Animation Clips** (forward, backward, left, and right), **2D Simple Directional** would have been a better option.

Learn more about **Blend Trees** and 2D blending from Unity's Documentation:

- http://docs.unity3d.com/Manual/BlendTree-2DBlending.html

Also, if you want to learn more about the **Mecanim** Animation System, there are some links that you might want to check out, such as Unity's documentation:

- http://docs.unity3d.com/Manual/AnimationOverview.html

Mecanim Example Scenes are available from the Unity **Asset Store**:

- https://www.assetstore.unity3d.com/en/#!/content/5328

Mecanim Video Tutorial are available here:

- http://unity3d.com/pt/learn/tutorials/topics/animation

Mixing animations with Layers and Masks

Mixing animations is a great way of adding complexity to your animated characters without requiring a vast number of animated clips. Using **Layers** and **Masks**, we can combine different animations by playing specific clips for specific body parts of the character.

In this recipe, we will apply this technique to our animated character, triggering animation clips for firing a rifle and throwing a grenade with the character's upper body. We will do this while keeping the lower body moving or idle, according to the player's input.

Getting ready

For this recipe, we have prepared a Unity Package named **Mixing**, containing a basic **Scene** that features an animated character. We have also provided the FBX animation clips **Swat@firing_rifle.fbx** and **Swat@toss_grenade.fbx**. These files can be found in the 09_03 folder.

How to do it...

To mix animations using layers and masks, follow these steps:

1. Create a new 3D project and import the **Mixing** Unity Package, as well as the FBX files **Swat@firing_rifle.fbx** and **Swat@toss_grenade.fbx**.
2. Then, from the **Project** panel, open the **mecanimPlayground** level.
3. We need to configure the **Animation Clips**. Select the **Swat@firing_rifle** asset in the **Project** panel.
4. Select the **Rig** section. Change **Animation Type** to **Humanoid**, and **Avatar Definition** to **Create From this Model**. Confirm this by clicking on **Apply**:

5. Now, activate the **Animations** section. The firing_rifle clip should be selected; click on the **Clamp Range** button to adjust the timeline and check the **Loop Time** and **Loop Pose** options. Under **Root Transform Rotation**, check Bake Into Pose and select Based **Upon** | **Original**. Under **Root Transform Position (Y)**, check **Bake Into Pose** and select **Based Upon** (at Start) | Original. Under **Root Transform Position (XZ)**, leave **Bake** Into Pose unchecked. Click on **Apply** to confirm the changes:

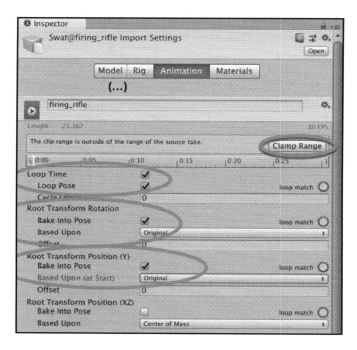

6. Select the Swat@toss_grenade animation clip. Select the Rig section. Then, change **Animation Type** to Humanoid and Avatar Definition to **Create From** this Model. Confirm it by clicking on Apply.

    1. Now, activate the **Animations** section. The toss_grenade animation clip should be selected. Click the Clamp Range button to adjust the timeline, and leave the **Loop Time** and **Loop Pose** options unchecked. Under Root **Transform Rotation,** check **Bake** Into **Pose** and select **Based Upon** | **Original.** Under **Root Transform Position (Y)**, check **Bake** Into **Pose** and select Based Upon (at Start) | Original. Under Root Transform Position (XZ), leave Bake Into Pose unchecked. Click on Apply to confirm the changes.

7. Let's create a Mask. From the Project panel, click on the Create button and add an Avatar Mask to the project. Name it BodyMask.

8. Select the **BodyMask** tab and, in the **Inspector,** expand the Humanoid section. Green body sections and IK spots are selected (all are by default), and red are unselected. Deselect the character's two legs, the circle base the feet are standing on, and the two feet IK spots (they should turn red):

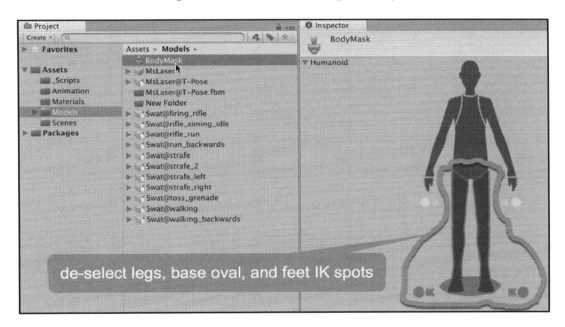

10. In the **Project** panel, double-click the `MainCharacter` controller asset file; it should open up in the Animator panel.

11. In the Animator panel, create a new layer by clicking on the + sign in the top-left **Layers** tab, above the Base Layer.

12. Name the new `layerUpperBody` and click on the gear icon for the settings. Then, change its **Weight** to 1 and select the **BodyMask** in the Mask slot. Also, change Blending to Additive:

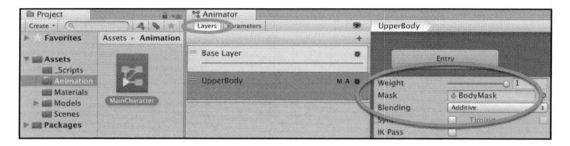

13. Now, in the Animator panel, with the `UpperBody` layer selected, create three new empty states (by right-clicking on the grid area and navigating to Create State | Empty from the menu). Name the default (orange) state null, and the other twoFire and Grenade.

14. Now, access the **Parameters** tab and add two new parameters of type Bool, Fire and Grenade:

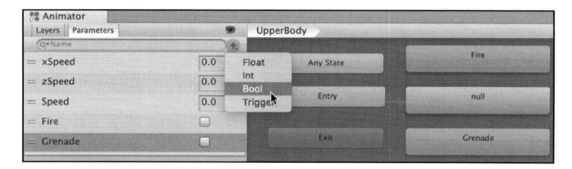

15. Select the Fire state and, in the **Inspector,** add the firing_rifle Animation Clip to the Motion field:

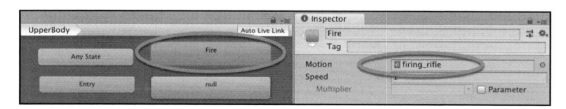

16. Now, select the **Grenade** state and, in the **Inspector,** add the `toss_grenade` animation clip to the Motion field.

17. Right-click on the null state box and, from the menu, select **Make Transition**. Then, drag the white arrow onto the Fire box.

18. Select the arrow (it will turn blue). From the **Inspector,** uncheck the Has **Exit Time** option. Then, access the Conditions list, click on the + sign to add a new condition, and set it as Fire and true:

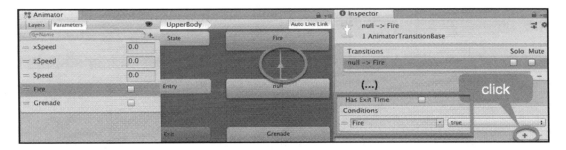

19. Now, make a **Transition** from null to Grenade. Select the arrow (it will turn blue). From the **Inspector,** uncheck the Has **Exit Time** option. Then, access the Conditions list, click on the + sign to add a new condition, and set it as Grenade and true.

20. Now, create transitions from Fire to null, and from **Grenade** to null. Then, select the arrow that goes from Fire to null and, in the Conditions box, select the Fire and false options. Leave the Has **Exit Time** option checked.

21. Finally, select the **Transition** arrow that goes from **Grenade** to null. In the **Conditions** box, select the options **Grenade**, false. Leave the Has **Exit Time** option checked. See the screenshot for these setting choices:

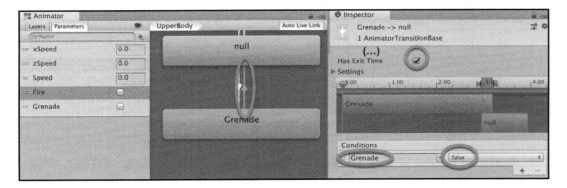

22. Open the `BasicController` C# script-class in your code editor (in Project folder `Scripts`). Immediately before the end of the `Update()` function, add the following code:

```
if(Input.GetKeyDown(KeyCode.F)){
    anim.SetBool("Grenade", true);
} else {
    anim.SetBool("Grenade", false);
}

if(Input.GetButtonDown("Fire1")){
    anim.SetBool("Fire", true);
}

if(Input.GetButtonUp("Fire1")){
    anim.SetBool("Fire", false);
}
```

23. Save the script and play your Scene. You will be able to trigger the `firing_rifle` and `toss_grenade` animations by clicking on the fire button and pressing the *F* key. Observe how the character's legs still respond to the Move animation state, so that the character can keep walking backward while throwing the grenade.

How it works...

Once the Avatar mask is created, it can be used as a way of filtering the body parts that would actually play the animation states of a particular layer. In our case, we have constrained our `fire_rifle` and `toss_grenade` animation clips to the upper body of our character, leaving the lower body free to play movement-related animation clips such as walking, running, and strafing.

There's more...

Here are some ways to go further with this recipe.

Override versus Additive blending

You might have noticed that the `UpperBody` layer has a parameter named Blending, which we have set to Additive. This means that animation states in this layer will be added to the ones from the lower layers.

If changed to Override, the animation from this would override animation states from the lower layers when played. In our case, Additive helps in keeping the aim stable when firing while running.

For more information on Animation Layers and Avatar Body Masks, check out Unity's documentation:

- `http://docs.unity3d.com/Manual/AnimationLayers.html`
- `http://docs.unity3d.com/Manual/class-AvatarMask.html`

Organizing States into Sub-state Machines

Whenever content in the **Animator** panel gets too cluttered, you can always consider organizing your **Animation States** into **Sub-State Machines**. In this recipe, we will use this technique to organize animation states for turning the character. Also, since the animation clips provided do not include Root Motion, we will use the opportunity to illustrate how to overcome the lack of Root Motion via a script, using it to turn the character 45 degrees to the left and right:

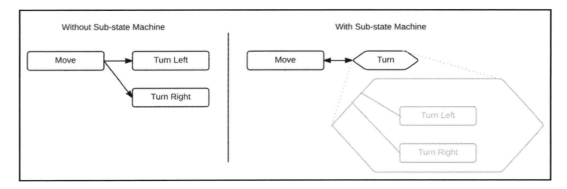

Getting ready

For this recipe, we have prepared a Unity Package named **Turning,** containing a basic scene that features an animated character. We have also provided the FBX animation clips `Swat@turn_right_45_degrees.fbx` and `Swat@turn_left.fbx`. These files can be found in the `09_04` folder.

How to do it...

To organize States into Sub-State Machines, please follow these steps:

1. Create a new 3D project and import the Mixing Unity Package, as well as the FBX files Swat@turn_right_45_degrees.fbx and Swat@turn_left.fbx.

2. Then, from the **Project** panel, open the mecanimPlayground level.

3. We need to configure the **Animation** Clips. Select the Swat@turn_left asset in the **Project** panel.

4. Choose the Rig section. Change **Animation Type** to **Humanoid** and **Avatar Definition** to Create From this Model. Confirm by clicking on **Apply**.

5. Now, choose the **Animations** section. The turn_left clip should be selected. Click the **Clamp Range** button to adjust the timeline and check the **Loop Time** option. **Under Root Transform Rotation**, check **Bake Into Pose** and navigate to Based Upon | Original. **Under Root Transform Position (Y)**, check **Bake Into Pose** and select **Based Upon (at Start)** | **Original**. **Under Root Transform Position (XZ)**, leave **Bake Into Pose** unchecked. Click on **Apply** to confirm the changes:

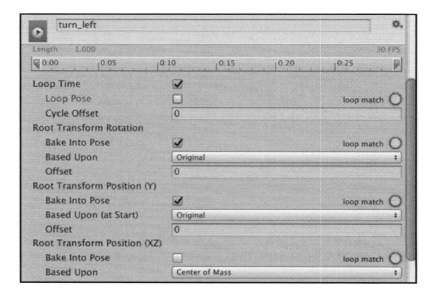

6. Repeat steps 4 and 5 for `Swat@turning_right_45_degrees`.

7. In the **Project** panel, double-click the `MainCharacter` controller asset file; it should open in the **Animator** panel.

8. From the top-left corner of the **Animator** panel, select the **Parameters** section and use the **+** sign to create the two new Parameters (Boolean) named `TurnLeft` and `TurnRight`.

9. Right-click on the grid area. From the context menu, select Create `Sub-State` Machine. In the Inspector, rename it Turn:

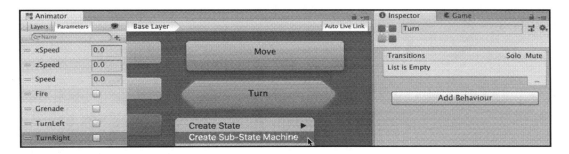

10. Double-click on the **Turn Sub-State Machine**. Right-click on the grid area, select **Create State | Empty,** and add a new state. Rename it to **Turn Left.** Then, add another state named **Turn Right**.

11. From the **Inspector,** populate Turn Left with the `turn_left` motion clip. Then, populate **Turn Right** with `turning_right_45_degrees`:

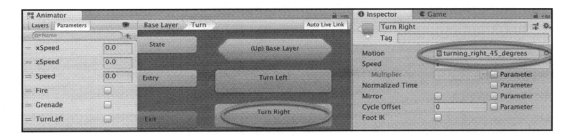

12. In the **Animator** panel, return to the **Base Layer** (click Base Layer in the information bar along the top of this panel).

13. Create two **Transitions** from **State Move**, one into the **Turn Left** sub-state, and one into the **Turn Right** sub-state:

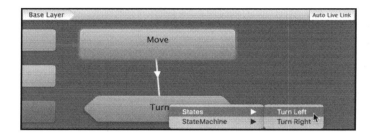

14. Create two return **Transitions,** from the Turn Left back to Move sub-state, and from the Turn Right sub-state back to Move. Do this by entering the Turn sub-state, dragging the **Transition** arrows from Turn Left and Turn Right into (Up) **Base Layer**, and choosing **State Move.**

15. Select the **Transition** arrow that goes from Turn Right to (Up) Base Layer. It will turn blue. From the **Inspector,** uncheck the **Has Exit Time** option. Then, access the Conditions list, click the + sign to add a new condition, and set it as **TurnRight** and **false:**

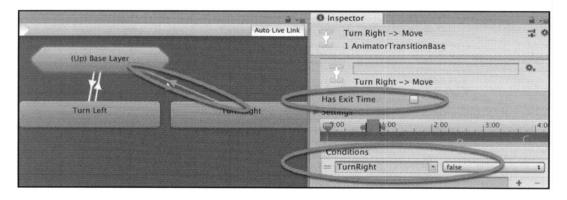

16. Select the arrow that goes from (Up) Base Layer to Turn Right. From the **Inspector,** uncheck the Has Exit Time option. Then, access the Conditions list, click the + sign to add a new condition, and set it as **TurnRight** and **true.**

17. Repeat steps 14 and 15 with the arrows that go between (Up) Base Layer and Turn Left, using TurnLeft as a condition this time.

18. Open the `BasicController` C# script-class in your code editor (**folder Project | Scripts**). Immediately after the `if(controller.isGrounded)` line, add this:

```
if(Input.GetKey(KeyCode.Q)){
    anim.SetBool("TurnLeft", true);
    transform.Rotate(Vector3.up * (Time.deltaTime * -45.0f),
Space.World);
} else {
    anim.SetBool("TurnLeft", false);
}

if(Input.GetKey(KeyCode.E)){
    anim.SetBool("TurnRight", true);
    transform.Rotate(Vector3.up * (Time.deltaTime * 45.0f),
Space.World);
} else {
    anim.SetBool("TurnRight", false);
}
```

19. Save your script-class. Then, select the `MsLaser` character and, from the **Inspector,** select the **Basic Controller** component. Leave the Move Diagonally and Mouse Rotate options unchecked. Also, leave the Keyboard Rotate option checked.

20. Play the **Scene.** You will be able to turn left and right by using the *Q* and *E* keys respectively.

How it works...

As should be clear from the recipe, Sub-State Machines work in a similar way to groups or folders, allowing you to encapsulate a series of state machines into a single entity for easier reference. States from the Sub-State Machines can be Transitioned from external states, in our case the Move state, or even from different sub-state machines.

Regarding character rotation, we have overcome the lack of root motion by using the `transform.Rotate(Vector3.up` * `(Time.deltaTime * -45.0f)`, Space.World) command to make the character actually turn around when the Q and E keys are held down.

This command was used in conjunction with `animator.SetBool("TurnLeft", true)`, which triggers the right animation clip:

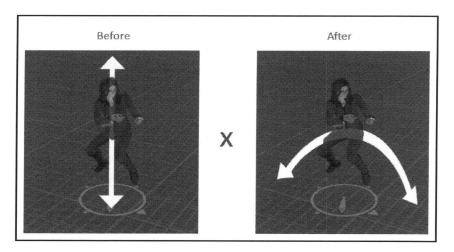

Transforming the Character Controller via scripts

Applying Root Motion to your character might be a very practical and accurate way to animate it. However, every now and then, you might need to manually control one or two aspects of the character's movement. Perhaps you only have an in-place animation to work with, or maybe you want the character's movement to be affected by other variables. In these cases, you will need to override **Root Motion** via a script.

To illustrate this issue, this recipe makes use of an animation clip for jumping, which originally moves the character only in the Y-axis. In order to make her move forward or backward while jumping, we will learn how to access the character's velocity to inform the jump direction via a script.

Getting ready

For this recipe, we have prepared a Unity Package named Jumping, containing a basic scene that features an animated character. We have also provided the FBX animation clip `Swat@rifle_jump`. These files can be found in the `09_05` folder.

How to do it...

To apply Root Motion via a script, please follow these steps:

1. Create a new 3D project and import the Jumping Unity Package, as well as the FBX `Swat@rifle_jump.fbx` file.

2. Then, from the Project panel, open the `mecanimPlayground` level.

3. We need to configure the **Animation** Clips. Select the `Swat@rifle_jump` asset in the **Project** panel.

4. Select the Rig section. Change Animation Type to Humanoid and Avatar Definition to Create From this Model. Confirm this by clicking on Apply.

5. Now, activate the **Animations** section. The `rifle_jump` clip should be selected. Click the Clamp Range button to adjust the timeline, and check the Loop Time and Loop Pose options. Under Root Transform Rotation, check Bake Into Pose and select Based Upon | Original. Under Root Transform Position (Y), leave Bake into Pose unchecked and select **Based Upon (at Start) | Original**. Under Root Transform Position (XZ), leave Bake Into Pose unchecked. Click on **Apply** to confirm the changes:

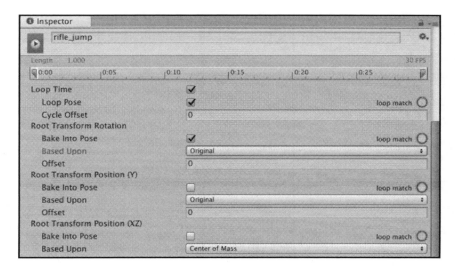

6. In the **Project** panel, double-click the `MainCharacter` controller asset file; it should open up in the Animator panel.

7. From the top-left corner of the Animator panel, select the Parameters section and use the + sign to create a new **Trigger** parameter named Jump:

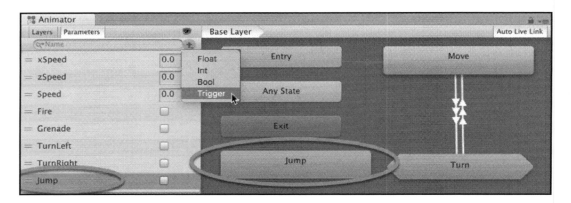

8. Add a new State named Jump. Do this by right-clicking the grid area and choosing **Create State | Empty**, then changing its name in the Inspector.

9. Select the **Jump** state. Then, from the **Inspector,** populate it with the `rifle_jump` motion clip:

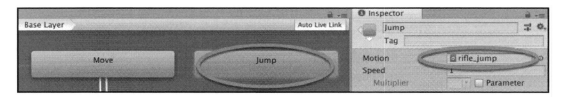

10. Create a **Transition** from Any State to Jump (using the Make Transition right-mouse-click menu). Select the **Transition,** uncheck Has Exit Time, and add a Condition for Trigger Jump:

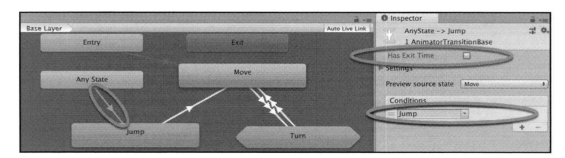

11. Now, create a **Transition** from Jump to Move. Ensure the Has Exit Time option is checked:

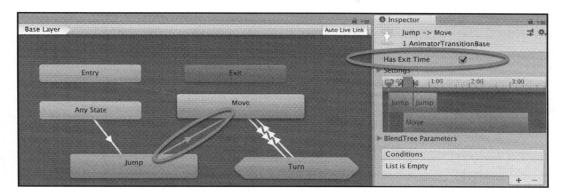

12. Open the `BasicController` C# script-class in your code editor (folder Project | Scripts).

13. Right before the `Start()` function, add the following code:

```
public float jumpHeight = 3f;
private float verticalSpeed = 0f;
private float xVelocity = 0f;
private float zVelocity = 0f;
```

14. Immediately after the `if(controller.isGrounded)` line, add this:

```
if (Input.GetKey (KeyCode.Space)) {
   anim.SetTrigger("Jump");
   verticalSpeed = jumpHeight;
}
```

15. Finally, add a new function at the end of the code for this script-class. So it is inserted immediately before the final brace (}) of the code:

```
void OnAnimatorMove(){
   Vector3 deltaPosition = anim.deltaPosition;
   if (controller.isGrounded) {
     xVelocity = controller.velocity.x;
     zVelocity = controller.velocity.z;
   } else {
     deltaPosition.x = xVelocity * Time.deltaTime;
     deltaPosition.z = zVelocity * Time.deltaTime;
     anim.SetBool ("Jump", false);
   }
   deltaPosition.y = verticalSpeed * Time.deltaTime;
```

```
            controller.Move (deltaPosition);
            verticalSpeed += Physics.gravity.y * Time.deltaTime;
            if ((controller.collisionFlags &
     CollisionFlags.Below) != 0) {
                verticalSpeed = 0;
            }
        }
    }
```

16. Save your script and play the Scene. You will be able to jump around using the spacebar. Observe how the character's velocity affects the direction of the jump.

How it works...

Observe that once this function is added to the script, the Apply Root Motion field in the Animator component changes from a checked box to Handled by Script:

The reason is that in order to override the animation clip's original movement, we have placed a series of commands inside Unity's OnAnimatorMove() function to move our character controller while jumping. The `controller.Move (deltaPosition)` line of code basically replaces the jump's direction from the original animation with the deltaPosition 3D Vector, which is made up of the character's velocity at the instant before the jump (x and z-axis) and the calculation between the jumpHeight variable and gravity over time (y-axis).

The Transition from Any State to Animation State Jump has the condition that the Jump Transition has fired (become true). In the code, we activate the Trigger Jump in the Animator Controller with the `SetTrigger("Jump")` statement. Triggers are like Bool Parameters, but when set become True for one instance, then automatically return to false again. This means there is no need to write extra code to set the Trigger to False.

Triggers are perfect for events that happen, and then you want things to return to normal afterwards. The Transition from the Jump Animation State back to Move does not need any condition, so after the Jump animation has played, the character returns to the Move state.

Adding rigid props to animated characters

If you haven't included a sufficient number of props for your character when modeling and animating it, you might want to give her the chance to collect new ones at runtime. In this recipe, we will learn how to instantiate a GameObject and assign it to a character while respecting the animation hierarchy.

Getting ready

For this recipe, we have prepared a Unity Package named Props, containing a basic Scene that features an animated character and a prefab named badge. There is also a Texture named `texture_pickupBadge.png`. The files can be found in the `09_06` folder.

How to do it...

To add a rigid prop at runtime to an animated character, follow these steps:

1. Create a new 3D project and import the Props Unity Package and the `texture_pickupBadge.png` Texture.
2. Then, from the **Project** panel, open the `mecanimPlayground` level.
3. From the **Project** panel, add the badge prop to the scene by dragging it into the Hierarchy.

4. Make the badge a child of the `mixamorig:Spine2` Transform (use the Hierarchy tree to navigate to MsLaser | `mixamorig:Hips` | `mixamorig:Spine` | `mixamorig:Spine1` | `mixamorig:Spine2`). Then, make the badge object visible above the character's chest by changing its Transform Position to (-0.08, 0, 0.15) and Rotation to (0.29, 0.14, -13.29):

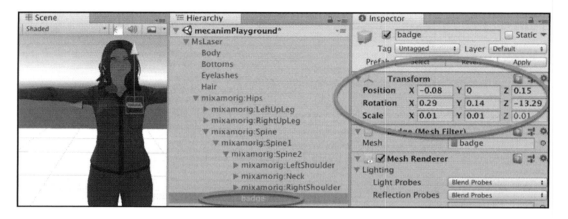

5. Make a note of the **Position** and **Rotation** values, and delete the badge object from the scene.

6. Add a 3D Cube named Cube-pickup to the Scene by choosing **Create | 3D Object | Cube**. In the **Inspector,** set its **Transform Position** to (0, 0.5, 2) and check the Is Trigger option for the Box Collider component.

7. Drag the `texture_pickupBadge.png` Texture from the **Project** panel onto the Cube-pickup GameObject. You should see the Pickup Badge text written on all sides of the Cube.

8. In the **Project** panel, create a new C# script-class named **AddProp** containing the following code, and add an instance-object as a component to the Cube-pickup GameObject:

```
using UnityEngine;
using System.Collections;

public class PropManager : MonoBehaviour  {
    public GameObject prop;
    public Transform targetBone;
    public Vector3 positionOffset;
    public Vector3 rotationOffset;
    public bool destroyTrigger = true;

    void OnTriggerEnter(Collider collision) {
```

```
                  bool addPropCondition =
targetBone.IsChildOf(collision.transform) &
!AlreadyHalreadyHasChildObject();

            if (addPropCondition)
                AddProp();
    }

    private void AddProp() {
        GameObject newprop;
        newprop = Instantiate(prop, targetBone.position,
        targetBone.rotation) as GameObject;
        newprop.name = prop.name;
        newprop.transform.parent = targetBone;
        newprop.transform.localPosition +=
positionOffset;
        newprop.transform.localEulerAngles +=
rotationOffset;

        if(destroyTrigger)
            Destroy(gameObject);
    }

    private bool AlreadyHalreadyHasChildObject() {
        string propName = prop.name;

        foreach(Transform child in targetBone){
            if (child.name == propName)
                return true;
        }

        return false;
    }
}
```

9. Select the Cube-pickup GameObject and look at the properties of the **Prop Manager (Script)** component in the Inspector. Populate the public variables as follows:

- Prop: the badge prefab
- Target Bone: the `mixamorig:Spine2` transform inside the `MsLaser` **Hierarchy** GameObject
- Position Offset: (-0.08, 0, 0.15)
- Rotation Offset: (0.29, 0.14, -13.29)

- Destroy Trigger: checked (true)

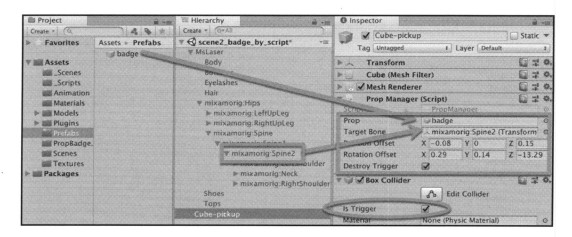

10. Run the **Scene.** Using the WASD keyboard control scheme, direct the character to the the Cube-pickup GameObject. Colliding with it will add a badge to the character the first time. If public variable **Destroy Trigger** was checked, then the **Cube-pickup** GameObject should be removed from the Scene after the first collision:

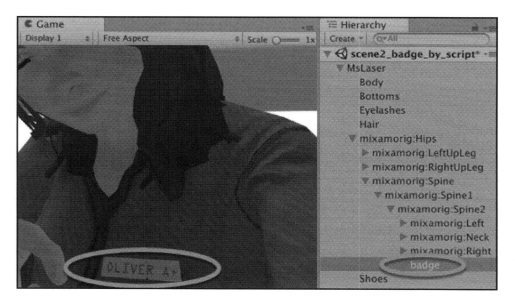

How it works...

Once it's been triggered by the character, the scripted instance-object attached to the Cube-pickup GameObject instantiates the assigned prefab, making it a child of the bones that they have been "placed into." The **Position Offset** and **Rotation Offset** can be used to fine-tune the exact position of the prop relative to its parent Transform. As the props become parented by the bones of the animated character, they will follow and respect the parent character GameObejct's hierarchy and animation.

The `AlreadyHalreadyHasChildObject()` method checks for preexisting props of the same name before actually instantiating a new one, so we don't attempt to instantiate the prop more than once as a new child of the target bone.

There's more...

Here are some ways to go further with this recipe.

Removing props with a script

You can make a similar script to remove props. In this case, the `OnTriggerEnter(...)` method would invoke the following `RemoveProp()` method:

```
private void RemoveProp() {
    string propName = prop.name;

    foreach(Transform child in targetBone){
        if (child.name == propName)
            Destroy (child.gameObject);
    }
}
```

Setting Active if there's only one type of Prop

If there will only be one prop, then rather than having the code Instantiate a new GameObject, you could have the prop always in the Hierarchy but initially not active, and then when the pickup Trigger object is hit, you change the prop GameObject to be active.

Although less flexible, it's a much simpler script. Do the following:

1. Drag the badge **Prefab** and make it a child of the `mixamorig:Spine2` Transform, then set **Position** and **Rotation** as you did in Step 4 of the previous recipe.

2. In the **Inspector,** uncheck the Active checkbox for the whole badge GameObject at the top.

3. Replace the content of the C# script-manager with the following code:

```
using UnityEngine;

public class PropManager : MonoBehaviour {
    public GameObject propObject;

    void OnTriggerEnter(Collider hit) {
        if (hit.CompareTag("Player")) {
            propObject.SetActive(true);
            Destroy(gameObject);
        }
    }
}
```

4. With the Cube-pickup GameObject selected in the **Hierarchy,** in the Inspector drag the badge child of mixamorig:Spine2 into the public slot for the Prop Object variable of the Prop Manager (Script) component.

Using Animation Events to throw an object

Now that your animated character is ready, you might want to coordinate some of her actions with her animation states. In this recipe, we will show this by making the character throw an object whenever the appropriate animation clip reaches a particular tie point in the animation. To do so, we will make use of **Animation** Events, which basically trigger a function from the animation clip's timeline. This feature, introduced in the Mecanism system, should feel familiar to those experienced with the Add Event feature of the classic **Animation** panel:

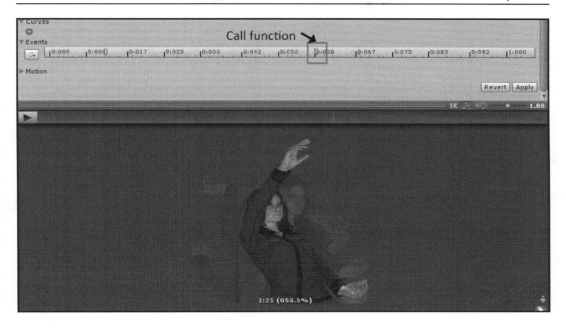

Getting ready

For this recipe, we have prepared a Unity Package named **Throwing,** containing a basic scene that features an animated character and a **prefab** named **EasterEgg.** The files can be found in the 09_07 folder.

How to do it...

To make an animated character throw an object, follow these steps:

1. Create a new 3D project and import the Props Unity Package and the EasterEgg Texture.
2. Open the mecanimPlayground level.
3. Play the level and press *F* on your keyboard. The character will move as if she is throwing something with her right hand.

4. Create a new C# script-class named `ThrowObject`, and add an instance-object as a component to the character's `MsLaser` GameObject:

```csharp
using UnityEngine;
using System.Collections;

public class ThrowObject : MonoBehaviour {
    public GameObject prop;
    private GameObject proj;
    public Vector3 posOffset;
    public Vector3 force;
    public Transform hand;
    public float compensationYAngle = 0f;

    public void Prepare () {

        proj = Instantiate(prop, hand.position, hand.rotation) as GameObject;
        if(proj.GetComponent<Rigidbody>())
          Destroy(proj.GetComponent<Rigidbody>());
        proj.GetComponent<SphereCollider>().enabled = false;
        proj.name = "projectile";
        proj.transform.parent = hand;
        proj.transform.localPosition = posOffset;
        proj.transform.localEulerAngles = Vector3.zero;
    }

    public void Throw () {

        Vector3 dir = transform.rotation.eulerAngles;
        dir.y += compensationYAngle;
        proj.transform.rotation = Quaternion.Euler(dir);
        proj.transform.parent = null;
        proj.GetComponent<SphereCollider>().enabled = true;
        Rigidbody rig = proj.AddComponent<Rigidbody>();
        Collider projCollider = proj.GetComponent<Collider> ();
        Collider col = GetComponent<Collider> ();
        Physics.IgnoreCollision(projCollider, col);
        rig.AddRelativeForce(force);
    }
}
```

5. In the **Hierarchy,** ensure the **MsLaser** GameObject is selected. In the **Inspector,** examine its **Throw Object (Script)** component. Populate the following:

- Prop: The `EasterEgg` prefab
- Hand: `mixamorig:RightHand`
- Pos Offset: Set to (0; 0.07, 0.04)
- Force: Set to (0; 200, 500)

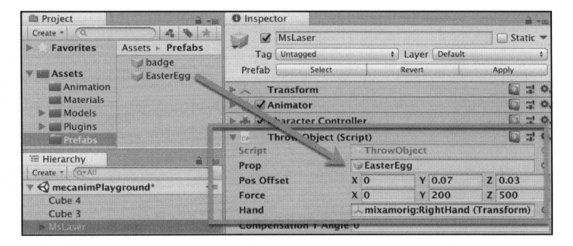

6. From the **Project** panel, select the `Swat@toss_grenade` asset file. In the **Inspector,** select the **Animation** section, scroll down to the **Events** section, and expand it.

7. Explore the **Animation** preview panel and see how, as you drag the preview playhead along the preview **Timeline,** the playhead also moves correspondingly in the **Events** timeline. At the bottom of the **Preview** panel, the time, percentage, and Frame properties are displayed. When you click the add event button, a new **Animation Event** will be added in the **Events Timeline** at the current playhead position, so ensure you have the playhead at the correct frame before creating a new **Animation** Event:

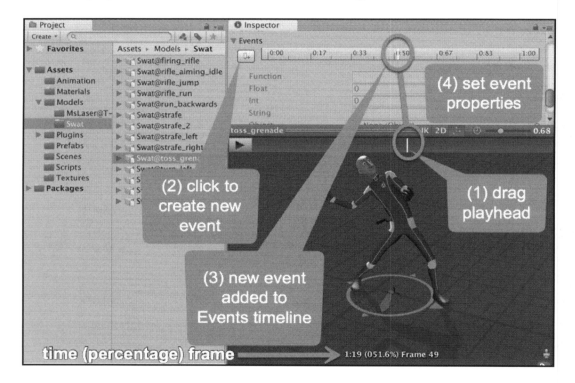

 You may view the contents of this panel by focussing on the avatar animation itself when moving the playhead, and visually choosing the appropriate frame when the character is the desired position for the event. Or, you may already know the time/percentage/frame number at which you wish the Animation Event to be created, and so be focussing on the numerical values at the bottom of the Preview panel.

9. Create two **Animation Events** in the Events section as follows:
   - 017.9%: Set Function to Prepare
   - 057.1%: Set Function to Throw
   - Then, click the Apply button:

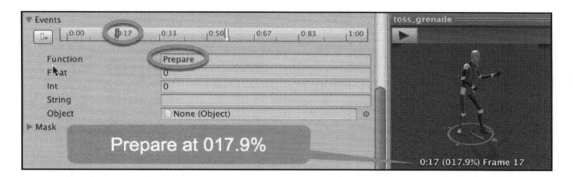

10. Play your **Scene.** Your character will now be able to throw an **Easter Egg** when you press the F key.

How it works...

Once the `toss_grenade` animation reaches the points to which we have set our **Events,** the `Prepare()` and `Throw()` methods are invoked.

The `Prepare()` method instantiates a prefab, now named projectile, in the character's hand (Projectile Offset values are used to fine-tune its position), also making it respect the character's hierarchy. Also, it disables the prefab's collider and destroys its Rigidbody component, provided it has one.

The `Throw()` method enables the projectile's collider and adds a Rigidbody component to it, making it independent from the character's hand. Finally, it adds a relative force to the projectile's Rigidbody component, so it will behave as if thrown by the character. The Compensation YAngle can be used to adjust the direction of the grenade, if necessary.

Applying Ragdoll physics to a character

Action games often make use of Ragdoll physics to simulate the character's body's reaction to being affected by a hit or explosion. In this recipe, we will learn how to set up and activate Ragdoll physics for our character whenever she touches a spiky object. We will also use the opportunity to reset the character's position and animations a number of seconds after that event has occurred:

Getting ready

For this recipe, we have prepared a Unity Package named Ragdoll, containing a basic scene that features an animated character, and a prefab already placed in the scene named Spawnpoint. The files can be found in the `09_08` folder.

How to do it...

To apply Ragdoll physics to your character, follow these steps:

1. Create a new 3D project and import the Ragdoll Unity Package.
2. Open the `mecanimPlayground` level.
3. You will see the animated MsLaser character and a disc, Spawnpoint.
4. First, let's create and set up our Ragdoll. Create a new 3D Ragdoll by choosing **Create I 3D Object I Ragdoll...**. The **Ragdoll** wizard should pop up.
5. Assign the transforms as follows:
   - Pelvis: `mixamorig:Hips`
   - Left Hips: `mixamorig:LeftUpLeg`
   - Left Knee: `mixamorig:LeftLeg`

- Left Foot: `mixamorig:LeftFoot`
- Right Hips: `mixamorig:RightUpLeg`
- Right Knee: `mixamorig:RightLeg`
- Right Foot: `mixamorig:RightFoot`
- Left Arm: `mixamorig:LeftArm`
- Left Elbow: `mixamorig:LeftForeArm`
- Right Arm: `mixamorig:RightArm`
- Right Elbow: `mixamorig:RightForeArm`
- Middle Spine: `mixamorig:Spine1`
- Head: mixamorig:Head
- Total Mass: 20
- Strength: 50

6. See the screenshot for these settings:

Create Ragdoll		
Make sure your character is in T-Stand. Make sure the blue axis faces in the same direction the chracter is looking. Use flipForward to flip the direction		
Pelvis	mixamorig:Hips (Transform)	○
Left Hips	mixamorig:LeftUpLeg (Transform)	○
Left Knee	mixamorig:LeftLeg (Transform)	○
Left Foot	mixamorig:LeftFoot (Transform)	○
Right Hips	mixamorig:RightUpLeg (Transform)	○
Right Knee	mixamorig:RightLeg (Transform)	○
Right Foot	mixamorig:RightFoot (Transform)	○
Left Arm	mixamorig:LeftArm (Transform)	○
Left Elbow	mixamorig:LeftForeArm (Transform)	○
Right Arm	mixamorig:RightArm (Transform)	○
Right Elbow	mixamorig:RightForeArm (Transform)	○
Middle Spine	mixamorig:Spine1 (Transform)	○
Head	mixamorig:Head (Transform)	○
Total Mass	20	
Strength	50	
Flip Forward	☐	

7. Select the **MsLaser** GameObject in the Hierarchy. In the **Inspector,** set its **Tag** to **Player.**

8. Create a new C# script-class named `RagdollCharacter` and add an instance-object as a component to the **MsLaser** GameObject:

```
using UnityEngine;
using System.Collections;
```

```
public class RagdollCharacter : MonoBehaviour {
    private Transform spawnPoint;

    void Start () {
        spawnPoint = GameObject.Find("Spawnpoint").transform;
        DeactivateRagdoll();
    }

    public void ActivateRagdoll() {
        gameObject.GetComponent<CharacterController> ().enabled = false;
        SetActiveRagdoll(true);
        StartCoroutine (Restore ());
    }

    public void DeactivateRagdoll() {
        SetActiveRagdoll(false);
        RespawnPlayer();
        gameObject.GetComponent<CharacterController>().enabled = true;
    }

    IEnumerator Restore() {
        yield return new WaitForSeconds(5);
        DeactivateRagdoll();
    }

    public void SetActiveRagdoll(bool isActive) {
        gameObject.GetComponent<CharacterController> ().enabled = !isActive;
        gameObject.GetComponent<BasicController> ().enabled = !isActive;
        gameObject.GetComponent<Animator> ().enabled = !isActive;

        foreach (Rigidbody bone in GetComponentsInChildren<Rigidbody>()) {
            bone.isKinematic = !isActive;
            bone.detectCollisions = isActive;
        }

        foreach (CharacterJoint joint in GetComponentsInChildren<CharacterJoint>()) {
            joint.enableProjection = isActive;
        }

        foreach (Collider col in GetComponentsInChildren<Collider>()) {
            col.enabled = isActive;
```

```
        }
    }

    private void RespawnPlayer() {
        transform.position = spawnPoint.position;
        transform.rotation = spawnPoint.rotation;
    }
}
```

9. This recipe needs something to collide with; create a GameObject named death-object. You could create a simple 3D Cube (menu: **Create | 3D Object | Cube).** However, any 3D object with a Physics Collider will be fine for the player's character to interact with.

 It's more fun to have a visually interesting 3D model to interact with. When creating the screenshots for this recipe, we used the high-quality, low-poly, free Stilized Crystal assets from LowlyPoly in the Unity Asset Store as example objects you might use to cause a Ragdoll collision in a game: https://assetstore.unity.com/packages/3d/props/stylized-crystal-77275

10. Create a new C# script-class named DeadlyObject, and attach an instance-object as a component to the death-object GameObject:

```
using UnityEngine;

public class DeadlyObject : MonoBehaviour {
    public float range = 2f;
    public float force = 2f;
    public float up = 4f;
```

```
        void OnTriggerEnter(Collider hit) {
            if (hit.CompareTag("Player")) {
                RagdollCharacter ragdollCharacter =
hit.gameObject.GetComponent<RagdollCharacter>();
                ExplodePlayer(ragdollCharacter);
                Destroy(gameObject);
            }
        }

        private void ExplodePlayer(RagdollCharacter ragdollCharacter)
{
            ragdollCharacter.ActivateRagdoll();
            Vector3 explosionPos = transform.position;
            Collider[] colliders =
Physics.OverlapSphere(explosionPos, range);

            foreach (Collider collider in colliders) {
                if (collider.GetComponent<Rigidbody>())
collider.GetComponent<Rigidbody>().AddExplosionForce(force,
explosionPos, range, up);
            }
        }
    }
```

11. Play the **Scene.** Using the WASD keyboard control scheme, direct the character to the death-object GameObject. Colliding with it will activate the character's Ragdoll physics and apply an explosion to it. As a result, the character will be thrown a considerable distance away and will no longer be in control of its body's movement, akin to a Ragdoll.

How it works...

Unity's Ragdoll Wizard assigns the Collider, Rigidbody, and Character Joint components to selected transforms. In conjunction, those components make Ragdoll physics possible. However, they must be disabled whenever we want our character to be animated and controlled by the player. In our case, we switch those components on and off using the RagdollCharacter script and its two functions: ActivateRagdoll() and DeactivateRagdoll(). The latter includes instructions to respawn our character in the appropriate place.

For testing purposes, we have also created the DeadlyObject script, which calls the RagdollCharacter script's function named ActivateRagdoll(). It also applies an explosion to our ragdoll character, throwing it outside the range of the explosion.

There's more...

Here are some ways to go further with this recipe.

Using a new player GameObject rather than deactivating and moving to a respawn point

Instead of resetting the character's transform settings, you could have destroyed its GameObject and instantiated a new one over the respawn point using Tags. For an example of how to do this, check out Unity's documentation:
`http://docs.unity3d.com/ScriptReference/GameObject.FindGameObjectsWithTag.html`

Rotating the character's torso to aim a weapon

When playing a Third-Person Character, you might want her to aim her weapon at a target that is not directly in front of her, without making her change direction. In this case, you will need to apply what is called a Procedural Animation, which does not rely on pre-made animation clips, but rather on the processing of other data, such as player input, to animate the character. In this recipe, we will use this technique to rotate the character's spine by moving the mouse, allowing for adjustments in the character's aim. We will also use this opportunity to cast a ray from the character's weapon and display a crosshair over the nearest target. Please note that this approach will only work with cameras standing behind the third-person controlled characters:

Getting ready

For this recipe, we have prepared a Unity Package named `AimPointer`, containing a basic scene that features an animated character. The package, which also includes the `crossAim` sprite to be used as a crosshair for aiming, can be found inside the `09_09` folder.

How to do it...

To rotate the character's torso to aim a weapon, do the following:

1. Create a new project and import the `AimPointer` Unity Package.
2. Open the `mecanimPlayground` level. In the **Inspector** and **Scene** panels, you will see an animated character named **MsLaser** holding the **pointerPrefab** object.
3. Create a new C# script-class named `MouseAim`, and add an instance-object as a component to the **MsLaser** GameObject:

```
using UnityEngine;
 using System.Collections;

 public class MouseAim: MonoBehaviour  {
     public Transform spine;
     public Transform weapon;
     public GameObject crosshairImage;
     public Vector2 xLimit = new Vector2(-30f, 30f);
     public Vector2 yLimit= new Vector2(-30f, 30f);
     private float xAxis = 0f;
     private float yAxis = 0f;

     public void LateUpdate() {
         RotateSpine();
         ShowCrosshairIfRaycastHit();
     }

     private void RotateSpine() {
         yAxis += Input.GetAxis("Mouse X");
         yAxis = Mathf.Clamp(yAxis, yLimit.x, yLimit.y);
         xAxis -= Input.GetAxis("Mouse Y");
         xAxis = Mathf.Clamp(xAxis, xLimit.x, xLimit.y);
         Vector3 newSpineRotation = new Vector3(xAxis,
yAxis, spine.localEulerAngles.z);
         spine.localEulerAngles = newSpineRotation;
     }
```

```
            private void ShowCrosshairIfRaycastHit() {
                  Vector3 weaponForwardDirection =
weapon.TransformDirection(Vector3.forward);
                  RaycastHit hit;
                  Vector3 fromPosition = weapon.position +
Vector3.one;
                  if (Physics.Raycast (fromPosition,
weaponForwardDirection, out hit)) {
                        Vector3 hitLocation =
Camera.main.WorldToScreenPoint(hit.point);
                        DisplayPointerImage(hitLocation);
                  } else
                        crosshairImage.SetActive(false);
            }

            private void DisplayPointerImage(Vector3 hitLocation)
{
                  crosshairImage.transform.position = hitLocation;
                  crosshairImage.SetActive(true);
            }
      }
```

4. In the **Hierarchy,** create a new UI Image named Image-crosshair by choosing **Create | UI | Image.**

5. In the **Inspector** for the Rect Transform component, set its Width and Height to 16 and populate the **Source Image** field with the `crossAim` sprite:

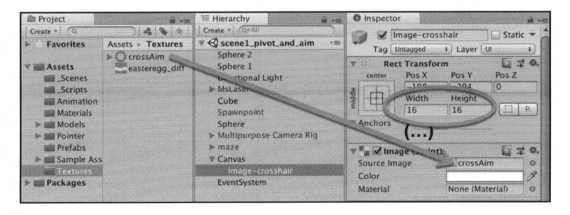

6. Select the **MsLaser** GameObject in the **Hierarchy,** and in the **Inspector** for the Mouse Aim component, populate the following:

- Spine: `mixamorig:Spine` (in **MsLaser | mixamorigHips)**
- Weapon: `pointerPrefab` (in **MsLaser|Hips|Spine|Spine1|Spine2|RightShoulder|Arm|Fo reArm|Hand)**
- Crosshair: Image-crosshair GameObject

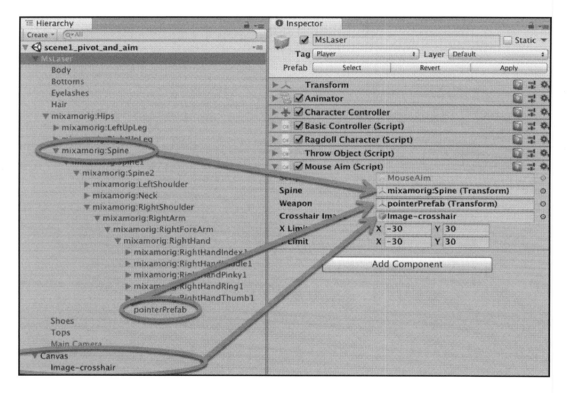

7. Play the Scene. You will now be able to rotate the character's torso by moving the mouse. Even better, the Image-crosshair UI image will be displayed at the top of the object that is being aimed at by the pointer.

How it works...

You might have noticed that all the code invoked for rotating the character's spine is inside the LateUpdate() method, as opposed to the more common Update() method. The reason for this is to make sure that all the transform manipulation will be executed after the original animation clip is played, overriding it.

Regarding the spine rotation, our script adds the horizontal and vertical speed of the mouse to the xAxis and yAxis float variables. These variables are then constrained within the specified limits, avoiding distortions to the character's model. Finally, the spine object transform rotations for the x and y axes are set to xAxis and yAxis respectively. The z axis is preserved from the original Animation Clip.

Additionally, our script uses a Raycast command to detect whether there is an object's collider in the direction of the weapon's aim, in which case, a crosshair will be drawn on the screen.

There's more...

Here are some ways to go further with this recipe.

Generic solution for Cameras other than the Main Camera

Since this recipe's script was tailored for cameras standing behind third-person-controlled characters, we have included a more generic solution to the problem - in fact, a similar approach to the one presented in *Unity 4.x Cookbook, Packt Publishing*.

An alternate script named MouseAimLookAt, which can be found inside the 09_09 folder, starts by converting our bi-dimensional mouse cursor screen's coordinates to three-dimensional world space coordinates (stored in a point variable). Then, it rotates the character's torso towards the point location, using the LookAt() command to do so. Additionally, it makes sure that the spine does not extrapolate minY and maxY angles, which would otherwise causing distortions to the character model.

Also, we have included a Compensation `YAngle` variable, which makes it possible for us to fine-tune the character's alignment with the mouse cursor. Another addition is the option to freeze the X-axis rotation, in case you just want the character to rotate their torso laterally but not look up or down. Again, this script uses a **Raycast** command to detect objects in front of the weapon, drawing a crosshair on the screen when they are present.

Creating geometry with Probuilder

A recent addition to the 3D Unity tools is **Probuilder,** which allows you to create and manipulate geometry inside the Unity Editor. Much more powerful than the existing **Terrain** editor, **Probuilder** allows you to create 3D Primitives and then manipulate them, such as by extruding or moving Vertices, Edges, or Faces, and then painting with colors or texturing with Materials.

In this recipe, we'll create some geometry that might be useful for an original game, or to add to a 3D Gamekit Scene (such as the Scene worked with in the following recipe).

If you've not used a 3D modeling package before (such as Blender, 3D Studio Max, or Maya), then it is well worth exploring the different features of **Probuilder.** You'll learn key concepts, including the following:

- Vertex: Point where lines touch—a corner where edges touch
- Edges: Straight line between two vertices
- Faces: Flat 2D surfaces, usually a rectangle or triangular

Getting ready

This recipe uses the free Unity Asset Store and Package Manager packages.

How to do it...

To create geometry with Probuilder, follow these steps:

1. Create a new Unity 3D project.
2. Use the **Package Manager** to install the **Probuilder** package.

3. Display the **Probuilder** panel with **Tools | Probuilder | Window.**

4. Dock the panel (next to the **Hierarchy** works well). Choose **Text Mode** or **Icon Mode**, as you prefer, via the right mouse button's context menu.

5. Create a new **Probuilder** Plane by clicking **New Shape** and choosing **Plane** from the **Shape Tool** window. Accept the default options and click the green **Build Plane** button.

6. With the new **Probuilder** Plane selected in the Hierarchy, you'll see the object selected in the Scene panel and its properties in the Inspector. We can see in the Inspector that, as well as its Transform, Mesh, and Mesh Renderer components, there are two special Probuilder components, Pb_mesh_nnnnn and Pb_Object (Script).

Pb_mesh_nnnnn is a special component that stores the data for the 3D object mesh of this GameObject; this data can be edited in the **Scene** panel at design time. At runtime, a Unity Mesh is created based on this data.

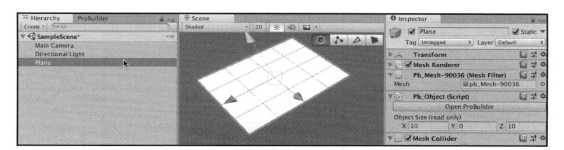

7. Note that when a **Probuilder** GameObject is selected, there is a small **Probuilder** tool icon bar displayed in the Scene panel, allowing the Object, Vertex, Edge, and Face detection modes:

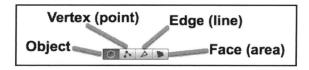

8. Let's make a depression in the middle of our Plane. Choose Face selection (the rightmost of the four **Probuilder** section icons), and using the Shift key for multiple section, select the four inner faces (selected faces turn Yellow). Then, use the Y-axis arrow to move these four selected faces downwards:

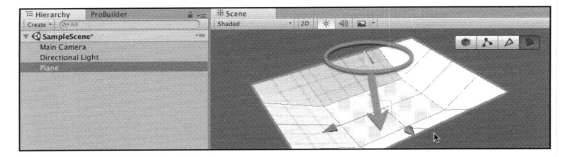

9. Let's Vertex Paint some color on the object. This is easier to do carefully when there are more faces. First, in the Probuilder panel, click the Subdivide tool.

10. Now, click Probuilder Vertex Colors +. The **Probuilder** Vertex Painter pop-up panel should be displayed. Click the red color and choose a darker red. Then, click the white square above your color to choose this dark red brush color. Make the brush size big (2 or 3), and paint all over the Plane to make it all dark red. Now, click the white square in the Vertex Painter panel to choose the yellow brush, and make the brush size smaller (say 1.5). Now, click on just the nine vertices in the middle of the depressed region of the Plane. Now, you should have a dark red Plane with yellow in the lower parts of it:

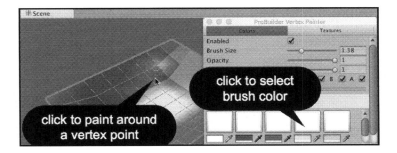

11. Save your Scene. Since the **Probuilder** Mesh data is stored in the Scene data, you'll lose all your Probuilder work if you forget to save your Scene.

How it works...

You've added the Probuilder package to a new 3D project and used the **Probuilder** tools panel to add a **Probuilder** mesh object to the Scene. You've used the face selection tool to allow you to select and then move some of the faces to create a depression. You then subdivided the object to give you more faces to work with for final detailed working. Finally, you learned to Vertex Paint with difference colors and brush sizes.

Probuilder offers many more features, including creating object by drawing a line-by-line polygon and Texturing surfaces rather than just simple **Vertex Painting**. Learn more about **Probuilder** here:

- Unity Technology **Probuilder** documentation manual:
  `https://docs.unity3d.com/Packages/com.unity.probuilder@3.0/manual/index.html`
- Unity Technology **Probuilder** videos:
  `https://www.youtube.com/user/Unity3D/search?query=Probuilder`

Creating a game with the 3D Gamekit

A collection of Unity 3D tools has been combined to become the Unity 3D **GameKit**. In this recipe, we'll create a new **Scene** and make use of some of the kit's Prefabs and Scripts to illustrate how characters can interact with objects such as doors and pickups:

Getting ready

This recipe uses the free **Unity Asset Store** and **Package Manager** packages.

How to do it...

To create a game with the 3D Gamekit, follow these steps:

1. Create a new **Unity 3D** project.
2. Use the **Package Manager** to install the following packages (required by the 3D GameKit):
     - **Cinemachine**
     - **Post Processing** (agree to the Quality Settings pop-up diaglog)
     - **Probuilder**
3. Import the **3D GameKit** (free from Unity Technologies) from the **Asset Store**:

4. Agree to the **Quality Settings** pop-up diaglog. After a few minutes (in which it is setting up a project with lots of assets), you'll see a new folder in the **Project** panel named **3DGamekit**.
5. Close and then reopen the Unity Editor.
6. First, open the example **Scene** provided and explore the 3D world by controlling the 3D **Ellen** character.

> Movement is standard *WASD-SPACE*/arrow keys. Camera control is via the mouse pointer. Click the left mouse button to use a weapon.

7. Create a new 3D **GameKit** Scene by choosing **Kit Tools | Create New Scene**. You'll then be asked to name the **Scene**, and a new **Scene** asset file will be created in your **Project | Assets** folder. You'll see there are quite a few special GameObjects in the **Hierarchy** of your new **Scene**:

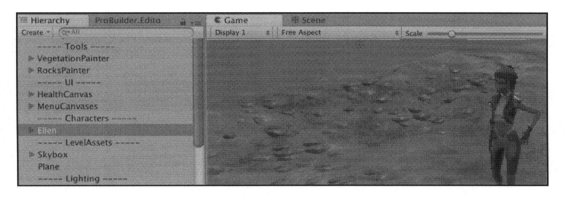

8. As you can see, the new **Scene** starts off containing an animated 3D character **(Ellen)** on a ProBuilder **3D Plane** that forms the ground she is standing on.

9. Add a small door in the **Scene**. Drag a clone of the **DoorSmall Prefab** from the Project panel (**Assets | 3DGamekit | Prefabs | Interactables**) into the middle of the 3D Plane **Scene**.

10. Add a **Crystal** in the **Scene**, on the opposite side of the door from where the **Ellen** character starts. Drag a clone of the **Crystal Prefab** from the **Project** panel (**Assets | 3DGamekit | Prefabs | Interactables**) into the **Scene** behind the door.

11. Now, add some walls on either side of the door, so the door must be opened in order for **Ellen** to reach the **Crystal**. Drag two clones of Prefab **Wall2x** from the **Project** panel (**Assets | 3DGamekit | Prefabs | Interactables**) into the **Scene**:

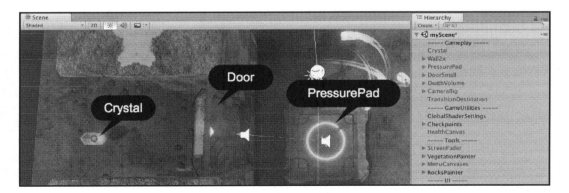

12. We now need to connect the **PressurePad** to the **Door**, so when **Ellen** steps on the **PressurePad** it sends a message to open the door. This is very straightforward, since the Door has a **GameCommandReceiver** component, which can be linked to the **PressurePad**'s Send on **Trigger Enter (Script)** component: Select the **PressurePad** GameObject in the **Hierarchy** and drag **DoorSmall** into the public **Interactive Object** slot of its **Send on Trigger Enter (Script)** component:

13. Run the **Scene**. When **Ellen** steps onto the **PressurePad**, the **Door** should open.

14. We now need to make the **Crystal** collidable by adding a **Box Collider**. Add a **Box Collider** component to GameObject **Crystal** and check its **On Trigger** option.

15. The **3D Gamekit** has inventory features. Let's make the **Crystal** collectable by the player by adding an **Inventory Item (Script)** component. In the **Inspector**, click **Add Component**, then type **inven** and choose the **Inventory Item** scripted component. For that component, type **Crystal** as the name of the **Inventory Key**:

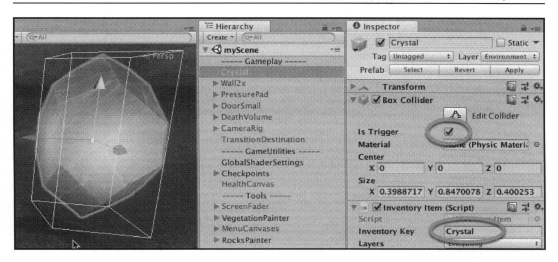

The **Inventory Key** names must match between the **Inventory Object** and the Inventory slot.

16. Now, we can add an **Inventory Controller (Script)** component to **Ellen**, with a slot for a **Crystal**. In the **Hierarchy**, select the **Ellen** GameObject. In the **Inspector**, click **Add Component**, then type **inven** and choose the **Inventory Item** scripted component.

17. In the **Inspector**, we now need to configure the properties of the **Inventory Controller (Script)** component as follows:

    - Change the **Size** from 0 to 1

    - For its **Key**, type **Crystal**

    - For the **On Add()** events, click the plus sign, +, to create a new event.

    - Drag **Ellen** into the **Object** slot for the new event (below **Runtime Only**).

- Change the function from **No Function** to **InventoryController Add Item**.
- Finally, type the name of this item in the **Inventory** as **Crystal**:

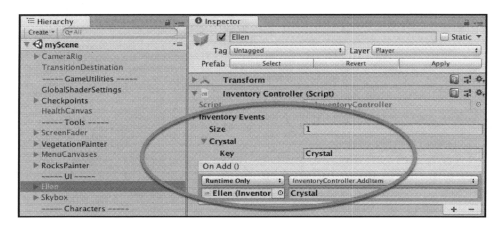

18. Run the **Scene**. **Ellen** can now open the **Door** via the **PressurePad** and walk into the **Crystal**, which is added to her inventory.

How it works...

We have dipped our toes into the wide range of features of the **3D GameKit**. Hopefully, this recipe gave you an idea of how to work with the provided **Prefabs**, and how **3D Gamekit** components could be added to custom GameObjects.

Check out these links to learn more:

- The 3DGamekit reference guide:
  `https://unity3d.com/learn/tutorials/projects/3d-game-kit/introduction-3d-reference-guide?playlist=51061`
- The Unity 3DGamekit walkthrough pages:
  `https://unity3d.com/learn/tutorials/projects/3d-game-kit/introduction-walkthrough?playlist=51061`
- Download the 3DGameKit, including a sample Scene, from the Asset Store:
  `https://assetstore.unity.com/packages/essentials/tutorial-projects/3d-game-kit-beta-115747?_ga=2.127077645.1823824032.1533576706-1834737598.1481552646`

Importing third-party 3D models and animations from Mixamo

While there are many **3D models** and animations available and ready to use in Unity from the **Asset Store**, there are many more sources of 3D assets from third-party organisations. **Mixamo** (now part of **Adobe**) offers a fantastic range of characters and animations via their web-based system.

In this recipe, we'll select and download a character and some animations, formatting them for use with Unity and controlling the animations with an **Animation Controller State Chart**:

Getting ready

This recipe uses the free **Adobe Mixamo** system, so you'll need to sign up for an account with them if you don't have one already.

How to do it...

To import third-party **3D models** and animations from **Mixamo**, follow these steps:

1. Open a web browser and visit `Mixamo.com`.
2. Sign up/log in with your **Mixamo/Adobe** account.
3. Select the **Characters** section (from navigation bar at top-left of web page)
4. Select your character, such as **Lola B Styperek**. You'll see this character appear in the right-hand preview panel.

5. Download your character, choosing **FBX For Unity (.fbx)** and **T-pose**:

6. Create a new 3D Unity project, and in the **Project** panel create a folder named `Models`.

7. Import the downloaded FBX file into the `Models` folder.

8. Select the asset file in the **Project** panel, and in the **Inspector** select the **Materials** section.

9. Click the **Extract Textures...** button and extract the model's **Textures** into your `Models` folder. If asked to fix an issue with a **Material** using a **Texture** as a **Normal Map**, choose **Fix Now**:

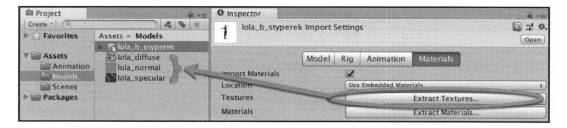

10. Drag the clone of the character from the **Project** panel into the **Scene**:

11. We need an **Animator Controller** to manage animations. Create a new **Animator Controller** file in the **Project** panel named **Lola-Animator-Controller**.

12. Select **Lola B Styperek** in the **Hierarchy**. In the **Inspector**, you'll see a **Controller** slot for the **Animator** component. Drag the **Lola-Animator-Controller** file from the **Project** panel into the **Animator | Controller** slot.

13. Now, let's animate this model. Go back to the Mixamo.com webpage and select an animation, such as **Golf Drive**. Click the **Download** button and choose these options:

    - **Format: FBX for Unity (.fbx)**
    - **Frames per second: 30**
    - **Skin: Without skin**
    - **Keyframe reduction: none**

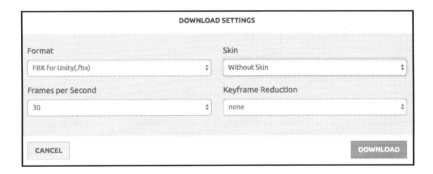

14. Import the **Animation Clip** FBX file (**lola_b_styperek@Golf Drive.fbx** in this case) into the **Animation** folder of your Unity project.

15. Double-click the **Lola-Animator-Controller** file to open the **Animator** (state machine) editor panel.

16. Drag the **Golf Drive Animation Clip** into the **Animator** panel; it should appear as an orange state, with a **Transition** from **Entry** to it (that is, this one state becomes the default state):

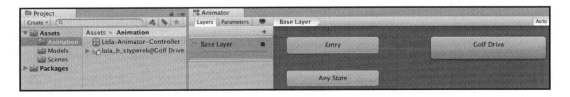

17. Run the **Scene**. You should now see **Lola** practicing her golf swing. If you have the character selected in the **Hierarchy** and can view the **Animator** panel, you'll see that the **Golf Swing Animation Clip (State)** is playing:

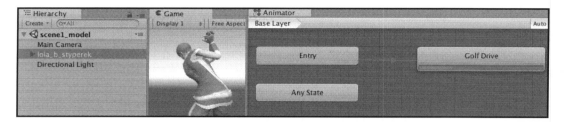

How it works...

Mixamo exports 3D rigged character models and **Animation Clips** in FBX format. The **Materials** for models are embedded in the FBX file, so we had to extract them once the model was imported into Unity.

Unity controls the animation of models with an **Animator Controller**, so we had to create one for our character model and then drag in the **Animation Clip** we wished to use to animate our model.

There's more...

Here are some ways to go further with this recipe.

Looping the animation

Select the **Animation Clip** in the **Project** panel, and in the **Inspector** check its **Loop Time** option, then click the **Apply** button to make the change to this asset file. When you run the **Scene**, **Lola** will now repeat the animation indefinitely.

Scripting events to control when Animation Clips are played

Additional **Animation Clips** can be added to the **State Chart** in the character's **Animator Controller**. You can then define variables and **Triggers**, to define when **Animations Transition** from one clip to another. Many of the recipes in this chapter illustrate ways to allow scripts to influence the **Transition** from one **Animation Clip (State)** to another.

Information sources about importing models and animations into Unity

Learn more about model and animation importing from the following:

- Unity docs on importing **3D Models**:
  https://docs.unity3d.com/Manual/HOWTO-importObject.html
- Unity docs about the **Model Import Settings** window:
  https://docs.unity3d.com/Manual/class-FBXImporter.html
- Unity docs about the **Model** tab:
  https://docs.unity3d.com/Manual/FBXImporter-Model.html
- Unity docs about **Model** file formats:
  https://docs.unity3d.com/Manual/3D-formats.html
- Samples of **Mixamo** free assets in the **Asset Store**:
  - https://assetstore.unity.com/packages/3d/animations/melee-axe-pack-35320
  - https://assetstore.unity.com/packages/3d/animations/magic-pack-36269

11
Webserver Communication and Online Version-Control

In this chapter, we will cover:

- Setting up a leaderboard using PHP and a database
- Unity game communication with a web-server leaderboard
- Creating and cloning a GitHub repository
- Adding a Unity project to a Git repository, and pushing it up to GitHub
- Unity project version-control using GitHub for Unity
- Preventing your game from running on unknown servers

Introduction

A **Server** waits for messages requesting something for a **Client**, and when one is received, it attempts to interpret and act upon the message, and send back an appropriate response to the **Client**. A **Client** is a computer program that can communicate with other **Clients** and/or Servers. **Clients** send **Requests**, and receive **Responses**.

It us useful to keep these concepts of **Client/Server/Request/Response** in mind when thinking about and working with **Client-Server** achitectures.

The Big Picture

The world is networked, which involves many different **Clients** communicating with other **Clients**, and also with **Servers**.

Each of the Unity deployment platforms illustrates an example of a **Client**:

- WebGL (running in a web browser)
- Windows and Mac applications
- Nintendo Switch
- Microsoft Xbox
- Sony Playstation

The **Servers** that these games can communicate with include dedicated multiplayer **Game Servers**, regular webservers, and online database servers. Multiplayer game development is the topic for a whole book of its own.

Web and database servers can play many roles with game development and Runtime interaction. One form of Unity game interaction with web servers involves a game communicating with an online **Server** for data, such as high scores, inventories, player profiles, and chat forums.

Another kind of **Client-Server** relationship is for **Distributed Version Control Systems (DVCS)**, where content on a local computer (laptop or desktop) can be synchronized with an online server, both for backup and historical change purposes, and also to allow the sharing, and collaborative authoring, of code projects with other people. Private repositories are used within commercial game companies, and public repositories are used for **Open Source** projects, allowing anyone access to the contents.

The recipes in this chapter explore a range of these **Client-Server** communication scenarios in relation to the Unity game development, online Run-Time communication, and cloud code version-control and sharing.

Setting up a leaderboard using PHP and a database

Games are more fun when there is a leaderboard of high scores that the players have achieved. Even single-player games can communicate with a shared web-based leaderboard. This recipe creates the web **Server-Side** (PHP) scripts to set and get player scores from a SQL database. The recipe after this one then creates a Unity game **Client** that can communicate with this web leaderboard **Server**.

Getting ready

This recipe assumes that you either have your own web hosting, or are running a local web server. You could use the built-in PHP web **Server**, or a web **Server** such as Apache or Nginx. For the database, you could use a SQL database Server such as MySQL or MariaDB, however, we've tried to keep things simple using SQLLite—a file-based database system. So all you actually need on your computer is PHP 7, since it has a built-in web **Server** and can talk to SQLite databases, which is the setup on which this recipe was tested.

All the PHP scripts for this recipe, and the SQLLite database file, can be found in the `12_01` folder.

If you do want to install a web server and database server application, a great choice is XAMPP. It is a free, cross-platform collection of everything you need to set up a database and web server on your local computer. The download page also contains FAQs and installation instructions for Windows, Mac, and Linux: `https://www.apachefriends.org/download.html`.

How to do it...

To set up a leaderboard using PHP and a database, do the following:

1. Copy the provided PHP project to where you will be running your webserver:
    - **Live website hosting**: Copy the files to the live web folder on your server (often `www` or `httdocs`)
    - **Running on local machine**: At the comment line, you can use the Composer script shortcut to run the PHP built-in web server by typing **composer run**:

2. Open a web browser to your website location:
   - **Live website hosting**: Visit the URL for your hosted domain
   - **Running on local machine**: Visit the `localhost:8000` URL:

3. Create/reset the database by clicking the last bulleted link: **reset database**. You should see a page with message **database has been reset**, and a link back to the **home** page (click that link).

4. To view the leaderboard scores as a web page in your web browser, click the second link: **list players (HTML):**

5. Try the fifth link – **list players (TXT)** – to retrieve the leaderboard data as a text file. Note how it looks different viewed in the web browser (which ignores line breaks), than when you view the actual source file returned from the server:

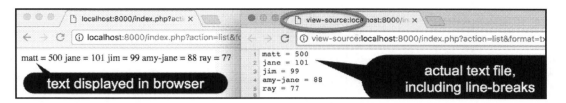

6. Do the same with the JSON and XML options – to see how our **Server** can return the contents of the database wrapped up as HTML, plain text (TXT), XML, or JSON.

7. Click the sixth link – **create (username = mattilda, score=800)**. When you next retrieve the contents, you'll see that there is a new database record for player mattilda with a score of 800. This shows that our server can receive data and change the contents of the database, as a well as just returning values from it.

How it works...

The player's scores are stored in a SQLLite database. Access to the database is facilitated through the PHP scripts provided. In our example, all the PHP scripts were placed in a folder on our local machine, from which we'll run the Server (it can be anywhere when using the PHP built-in server). So, the scripts are accessed via `http://localhost:8000`.

All the access is through the PHP filem called `index.php`. This is called a Front Controller, acting like a receptionist in a building, interpreting Requests and asking the appropriate function to execute some actions and return a result in **Response** to the **Request**.

There are five actions implemented, and each is indicated by adding the action name at the end of the URL (this is the GET HTTP method, which is sometimes used for web forms. Take a look at the address bar of your browser next time you search Google for example). The actions and their parameters (if any) are as follows:

- **action = list & format = HTML / TXT / XML / JSON**: This action asks for a listing all player scores to be returned. Depending on the value of second variable format (html/txt/xml/json), the list of users and their scores is returned in different text file formats.

- **action = reset**: This action asks for a set of default player names and score values to replace the current contents of the database table. This action takes no argument. It returns some HTML stating that the database has been reset, and a link to the homepage.

- **action = get & username = & format = HTML / TXT**: This action asks for the integer score of the named player that is to be found. It returns the score integer. There are two formats: HTML, for a webpage giving the player's score, and TXT, where the numeric value is the only content in the HTTP message returned.

- **action = update & username = <usermame> & score = <score>**: This action asks for the provided score of the named player to be stored in the database (but only if this new score is greater than the currently-stored score). It returns the word success (if the database update was successful), otherwise -1 (to indicate that no update took place).

There's more...

Here are some ways to go further with this recipe.

SQLite, PHP, and database servers

The PHP code in this recipe used the PDO data objects functions to communicate with a SQLite local file-based database. Learn more about PHP and SQLite at http://www.sqlitetutorial.net/sqlite-php/.

When SQLite isn't a solution (not suported by a web-hosting package), you may need to develop locally with a SQL Server, such as MySQL Community Edition or MariaDB, and then deploy with a live database **Server** from your hosting company.

A good solution to try things out on your local machine can be a combined web application collection, such as XAMP/WAMP/MAMP. Your web **Server** needs to support PHP, and you also need to be able to create the MySQL databases.

PHPLiteAdmin

When writing code that talks to database files and database **Servers**, it can be frustrating when things are not working to not be able to see inside the database. Therefore, database **Clients** exist to allow you to interact with database **Servers** without having to use code.

A lightweight (single file!) solution when using PHP and SQLLite is PHPLiteAdmin, which is free to use (although you may consider donating if you use it a lot). It is included in the `phpLiteAdmin` folder with this recipe's PHP scripts. It can be run using the Composer script shortcut command—**composer dbadmin**—and will run locally at `localhost:8001`. Once running, just click on the link for the players table to see the data for each player's score in the database file:

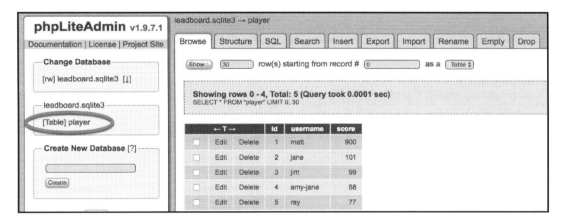

Learn more about PHPLiteAdmin at the project's GitHub repository and website:

- `https://github.com/phpLiteAdmin/pla`
- `https://www.phpliteadmin.org/`

Unity game communication with web-server leaderboard

In this recipe, we create a Unity game **Client** that can communicate, via UI buttons, with our web server leaderboard from the previous recipe:

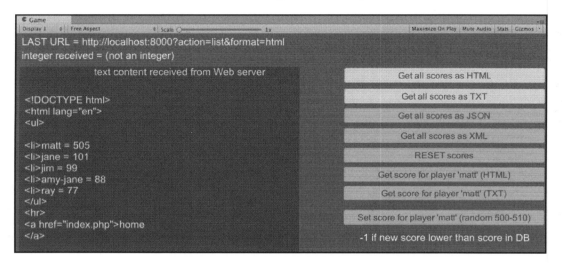

Getting ready

Since the scene contains several UI elements and the code of the recipe is the communication with the PHP scripts and SQL database, in the 12_02 folder, we have provided a Unity package called `UnityLeaderboardClient`, containing a scene with everything set up for the Unity project.

How to do it...

To create a Unity game that communicates with the web-server leaderboard, do the following:

1. Import the provided Unity package, `UnityLeaderboardClient`.
2. Run the provided **Scene**.
3. Ensure your PHP leaderboard is up and running.

4. If you are not running locally (`localhost:8000`), you'll need to update the URL by selecting the **Main Camera** in the Hierarchy, and then editing the **Leader Board URL** text for the **Web Leaderboard (Script)** component in the **Inspector**:

5. Click on the **UI Buttons** to make Unity communicate with the PHP scripts that have access to the highscore database.

How it works...

The player's scores are stored in an SQL database. Access to the database is facilitated through the PHP scripts provided by the web server project that was set up in the previous recipe.

In our example, all the PHP scripts were placed in a web **Server** folder for a local webserver. So, the scripts are accessed via `http://localhost:8000/`. However, since the URL is a public string variable, this can be set before running to the location of your Server and site code.

There are buttons in the Unity scene (corresponding to the actions the web leaderboard understands) that set up the corresponding action and the parameters to be added to the URL, for the next call to the web **Server**, via the `LoadWWW()` method. The `OnClick()` actions have been set up for each button to call the corresponding methods of the `WebLeaderBoard` C# script of the **Main Camera**.

There are also several **UI Text** objects. One displays the most recent URL string sent to the server. Another displays the integer value that was extracted from the response message that was received from the server (or a message as **not an integer** if some other data was received).

The third **UI Text** object is inside a **UI Panel**, and has been made large enough to display a full, multiline text string received from the Server (which is stored inside the textFileContents variable).

We can see that the contents of the HTTP text Reponse message are simply an integer when a random score is set for player Matt, when the Get score for player 'matt' (TXT) button is clicked, and a text file containing 505 is returned:

The **UI Text** objects have been assigned to public variables of the WebLeaderBoard C# script for the Main Camera. When any of the UI Buttons are clicked, the corresponding method of the WebLeaderBoard method is called, which builds the URL string with parameters, and then calls the LoadWWW() method. This method sends the Request to the URL, and waits (by virtue of being a coroutine) until a Response is received. It then stores the content, received in the textFileContents variable, and calls the UpdateUI() method. There is a prettification of the text received, inserting newline characters to make the JSON, HTML, and XML easier to read.

There's more...

Here are some ways to go further with this recipe.

Extracting the full leaderboard data for display within Unity

The XML/JSON text that can be retrieved from the PHP web server provides a useful method for allowing a Unity game to retrieve the full set of the leaderboard data from the database. Then, the leaderboard can be displayed to the user in the Unity game (perhaps, in a nice 3D fashion, or through a game-consistent UI).

See Chapter Working with Plain Text, XML, and JSON Text Files in this cookbook to learn how to process data in XML and JSON formats.

Using the secret game codes to secure your leaderboard scripts

The Unity and PHP code that is presented illustrates a simple, unsecured web-based leaderboard. To prevent players hacking into the board with false scores, we should encode some form of secret game code (or key) into the communications. Only update requests that include the correct code will actually cause a change to the database.

The Unity code will combine the secret key (in this example, the **harrypotter** string) with something related to the communication – for example, the same MySQL/PHP leaderboard may have different database records for different games that are identified with a game ID:

```
// Unity Csharp code
string key = "harrypotter"
string gameId = 21;
string gameCode = Utility.Md5Sum(key + gameId);
```

The server-side PHP code will receive both the encrypted game code, and the piece of game data that is used to create that encrypted code. In this example, it is the game ID and MD5 hashing function, which is available in both Unity and in PHP. You can learn more about MD5 hashing on Wikipedia: `https://en.wikipedia.org/wiki/MD5`.

The secret key (**harrypotter**) is used with the game ID to create an encrypted code that can be compared with the code received from the Unity game (or whatever user agent or browser is attempting to communicate with the leaderboard **Server** scripts). The database actions will only be executed if the game code created on the **Server** matches that sent along with the request for a database action:

```
// PHP - security code
$key = "harrypotter"
$game_id =  $_GET['game_id'];
$provided_game_code =  $_GET['game_code'];
$server_game_code = md5($key.$game_id);
if( $server_game_code == $provided_game_code ) {
  // codes match - do processing here
}
```

Creating and cloning a GitHub repository

Distributed Version Control Systems (DVCS) are becoming a bread-and-butter everyday tool for software developers. An issue with Unity projects can be the many binary files in each project. There are also many files in a local system's Unity project directory that are not needed for archiving/sharing, such as OS-specific thumbnail files and trash files. Finally, some Unity project folders themselves do not need to be archived, such as Temp and Library.

While Unity provides its own **Unity Teams** online collaboration, many small game developers chose not to pay for this extra feature. Also, Git and Mercurial (the most common DVCSs) are free, and work with any set of documents that are to be maintained (programs in any programming language, text-files, and so on). So, it makes sense to learn how to work with a third-party, industry-standard DVCS for the Unity projects. In fact, the documents for this very book were all archived and version-controlled using a private **GitHub** repository!

In this project, we'll create a new online project repository using the free **GitHub** server, and then clone (duplicate) a copy onto a local computer. The recipe that follows will then transfer a Unity project into the local project repository, and use the stored link from the cloning to push the changed files back up to the **GitHub** online server.

NOTE: **All** the projects from this Cookbook have been archived on **GitHub** in public repositories for you to read, download, edit, and run on your computer. Depsite a hard disk crash during the authoring of this book, no code was lost, since the steps of this recipe were being followed for every part of this book.

NOTE: **Git** is a version-control system, **GitHub** is one of several online systems that host projects archived in the **Git** format. A popular alternative to **GitHub** is **BitBucket**, which can host both **Git** and **Mercurial** version-control project formats.

Getting ready

Since this recipe illustrates hosting code on **GitHub**, you'll need to create a (free) **GitHub** account at GitHub.com if you do not already have one.

If not already installed, you'll need to install **Git** on your local computer as part of this recipe. Learn how, and download the client from the following links:

- `http://git-scm.com/book/en/Getting-Started-Installing-Git`
- `http://git-scm.com/downloads/guis`

 The screenshots for this recipe were created on a Mac. On Windows, you would use the Git BASH (see `https://gitforwindows.org/`) or Powershell (see `https://docs.microsoft.com/en-us/powershell/`) Terminal windows for command-line Git operations.

How to do it...

To create and clone a **GitHub** repository, do the following:

1. Install **Git** for the command line on your computer. As usual, it is good practice to do a system backup before installing any new application: `https://git-scm.com/book/en/v2/Getting-Started-Installing-Git`.

2. Test that you have **Git** installed, by typing **git** at the command line in a terminal window. You should see text help displayed, showing a list of possible command options:

```
Matthews-MacBook-Air-2:~ ma t$ git

usage: git [--version] [--help] [-C <path>] [-c name=value]
           [--exec-path[=<path>]] [--html-path] [--man-path] [-
           [-p | --paginate | --no-pager] [--no-replace-objects
           [--git-dir=<path>] [--work-tree=<path>] [--namespace
           <command> [<args>]

These are common Git commands used in various situations:

start a working area (see also: git help tutorial)
   clone      Clone a repository into a new directory
```

3. Open a web browser and nagivate to your **GitHub** repositories page:

4. Click the green button to start creating a new repository (such as my-github-demo):
    - Enter a name for the new repository, such as **my-github-demo**
    - Click the option to create a **README** (important, so you can clone the files to a local computer)
    - Add a `.gitignore` file – choose the Unity one:

The `.gitignore` file is a special file; it tells the version control system which files do not need to be archived. For example, we don't need to record the Windows or Mac image thumbnail files (`DS_STORE` or `Thumbs.db`).

5. With the options selected, click the green **Create Repository** button.
6. You should now be taken to the repository contents page. Click the green dropdown named **Clone or download**, and then click the URL copy-to-clipboard tool button. This has copied the special **GitHub** URL needed for connecting to GitHub and copying the files to your local computer:

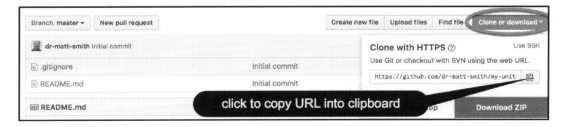

7. Open a command-line **Terminal** window, and navigate to the location where you wish to clone your **GitHub** project repository (such as Desktop or Unity-projects).

8. At the CLI (Command-Line Interface), type **git clone**, and then paste the URL from your clipboard, it will be something like `https://github.com/dr-matt-smith/my-unity-github-demo.git`:

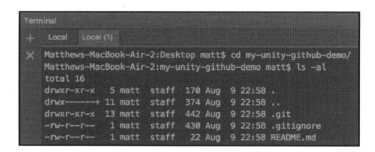

9. Change into your cloned directory, such as `cd my-unity-github-demo`.

10. List the files. You should see your README.md, and if you have the option to see hidden folders and files, you'll also see .git and .gitignore:

```
Terminal
  +   Local   Local (1)
  X   Matthews-MacBook-Air-2:Desktop matt$ cd my-unity-github-demo/
      Matthews-MacBook-Air-2:my-unity-github-demo matt$ ls -al
      total 16
      drwxr-xr-x    5 matt   staff   170 Aug  9 22:58 .
      drwx------+  11 matt   staff   374 Aug  9 22:58 ..
      drwxr-xr-x   13 matt   staff   442 Aug  9 22:58 .git
      -rw-r--r--    1 matt   staff   430 Aug  9 22:58 .gitignore
      -rw-r--r--    1 matt   staff    22 Aug  9 22:58 README.md
```

11. Use the `git remote -v` command to see the stored link from this copy of the project files on your computer, then back up to the GitHub online repository:

```
$ git remote -v
  origin
https://github.com/dr-matt-smith/my-unity-github-demo.git
(fetch)
  origin
https://github.com/dr-matt-smith/my-unity-github-demo.git
(push)
```

How it works...

You learned how to create a new empty repository on the **GitHub** web server. You then cloned it to your local computer.

You also checked to see that this clone had a link back to its remote origin.

 If you have simply downloaded and decompressed the ZIP file, you would not have the `.git` folder, nor would you have the remote links back to its GitHub origin.

The .git file actually contains the entire history of changes to the project repository files – and using different Git commands, you can update the folder to re-instance any of the committed snapshots for the project repository contents.

The special file called `.gitignore` lists all the files and directories that are **not** to be archived. At the time of writing, here are the contents of files that do not need to be archived (they are either unnecessary or can be regenerated when a project is loaded into Unity):

```
      [Ll]ibrary/
[Tt]emp/
[Oo]bj/
[Bb]uild/
[Bb]uilds/
Assets/AssetStoreTools*
# Visual Studio cache directory
.vs/
# Autogenerated VS/MD/Consulo solution and project files
ExportedObj/
.consulo/
*.csproj
*.unityproj
*.sln
*.suo
*.tmp
*.user
*.userprefs
*.pidb
*.booproj
*.svd
*.pdb
*.opendb
# Unity3D generated meta files
*.pidb.meta
```

```
*.pdb.meta
# Unity3D Generated File On Crash Reports
sysinfo.txt
# Builds
*.apk
*.unitypackage
```

As we can see, folders such as **Library** and **Temp** are not to be archived. Note that if you have a project with a lot of resources (such as those using the 2D or 3D Gamekits), rebuilding the **Library** may take some minutes depending on the speed of your computer.

Note that the recommended files to ignore for **Git** change from time to time as Unity changes its project folder structure. **GitHub** has a master recommended .gitignore for Unity, and it is recommended you review it from time to time, especially when upgrading to a new version of the Unity editor:
https://github.com/github/gitignore/blob/master/Unity.gitignore.

 If you are using an older (pre-2018) version of Unity, you may need to look up what the appropriate .gitignore contents should be. The details given in this recipe were up to date for the 2018.2 version of the Unity editor.

There's more...

Here are some ways to go further with this recipe.

Learn more about DVCS

Here is a short video introduction to DVCS: http://youtu.be/1BbK9o5fQD4.

Note that the Fogcreek Kiln "harmony" feature now allows seamless work between **Git** and **Mercurial** with the same Kiln repository:
http://blog.fogcreek.com/kiln-harmony-internals-the-basics/.

Learn more about Git at the command line

If you are new to working with a **CLI**, it is well worth following up some online resources to improve your skills. Any serious software development will probably involve some work at a command line at some point.

Since both **Git** and **Mercurial** are open source, there are lots of great, free online resources available. The following are some good sources to get you started:

- Learn all about Git, download free GUI clients, and even get free online access to The Pro Git book (by Scott Chacon), available through Creative Commons license: `http://git-scm.com/book`.
- You will find an online interactive Git command line to practice in: `https://try.github.io/levels/1/challenges/1`.

Using Bitbucket and SourceTree visual applications

Unity offers a good tutorial on version-control using the Bitbucket website and the SourceTree application:

- `https://unity3d.com/learn/tutorials/topics/cloud-build/creating-your-first-source-control-repository`

SourceTree is a free Mercurial and Git GUI client, available at:

- `http://www.sourcetreeapp.com/`

Learning about Mercurial rather than Git

The main Mercurial website, including free online access to *Mercurial: The Definitive Guide (by Bryan O'Sullivan)* is available through the Open Publication License at `http://mercurial.selenic.com/`.

Adding a Unity project to a local Git repository, and pushing files up to GitHub

In the previous recipe, you created a new online project repository using the free **GitHub Server**, and then cloned (duplicate) a copy onto a local computer.

In this recipe, we will transfer a Unity project into the local project repository, and use the stored link from the cloning to push the changed files back up to the Guthub online **Server**.

Getting ready

This recipe follows on from the previous one, so ensure you've completed that receipe before beginning this one.

How to do it...

To add a Unity project to a **Git** repository, and push it up to **GitHub**, do the following:

1. Create a new Unity project (or make use of an old one), save the **Scene**, and quit Unity. For example, we created a project named **project-for-version-control** that contains the default `SampleScene` and a Material named `m_red`. It is the asset files in the Project panel that are the files that are stored on disk, and are the ones you'll be version controlling with **Git** and **GitHub**.

 It is important that all work has been saved and the Unity application is not running when you are archiving your Unity project, since if Unity is open there may be unsaved changes that will not get correctly recorded.

2. On your computer, copy the following folders into the folder of your cloned **GitHub** repository:

```
/Assets
/Plugins (if this folder exists - it may not)
/ProjectSettings
/Packages
```

3. The folder after copying these contents is illustrated below:

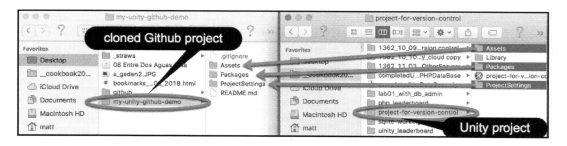

4. At the **CLI**, type git status to see a list of folders/files that have changed and need to be committed to the next snapshot of project contents for out **Git** version-control system.

5. Add all these files by typing `git add`.

6. Commit our new snapshot with the `git commit -m "files added to project"` command:

```
matt$ git commit -m "files added to project"

[master 1f415a3] files added to project
 23 files changed, 1932 insertions(+)
 create mode 100644 Assets/Scenes.meta
 create mode 100644 Assets/Scenes/SampleScene.unity
 ...
```

7. We have created a snapshop of the new files and folders, so now we can push this new committed snapshot up to the GitHub cloud servers. Type `git push origin master`:

```
matt$ git push origin master

Counting objects: 29, done.
Delta compression using up to 4 threads.
Compressing objects: 100% (27/27), done.
Writing objects: 100% (29/29), 15.37 KiB | 0 bytes/s,
done.
Total 29 (delta 0), reused 0 (delta 0)
To
https://github.com/dr-matt-smith/my-unity-github-demo.git
       1b27686..1f415a3  master -> master
matt$
```

NOTE: The first time you do this, you'll be asked for your **GitHub** username and password.

8. Visit **GitHub**, you should see that there is a new commit, and that your Unity files and folders have been uploaded to the **GitHub** online repository:

How it works...

In the previous recipe, you had created a project repository on the **GitHub** cloud **Server**, and then cloned it to your local machine. You then added the files from a (closed) Unity application to the cloned project repository folder. These new files were added and committed to a new **snapshot** of the folder, and the updated contents pushed up to the **GitHub Server**.

Due to the way Unity works, it creates a new folder when a new project is created. Therefore, we had to turn the contents of this the Unity project folder into a **Git** repository. There are two ways to do this:

1. Copy the files from the Unity project to a cloned **GitHub** repository (so it has remote links set up for pushing back to the **GitHub** server).
2. Make the Unity project folder into a **Git** repository, and then either link it to a remote **GitHub** repository, or push the folder contents to the **GitHub** server and create a new online repository at that point in time

For people new to Git and GitHub, the first procedure, which we followed in this recipe, is probably the simplest to understand. Also, it is the easiest to fix if something goes wrong – since a new GitHub repo can be created, cloned to the local machine, and the Unity project files copied there, and then pushed up to GitHub (and the old repo deleted), by pretty much following the same set of steps.

Interestingly, the second approach is recommended when using the **Open Source GitHub for Unity** package – which is explored in the next recipe.

Unity project version-control using GitHub for Unity

GitHub has released an **Open Source** tool integrating **Git** and **GitHub** into Unity, which we'll explore in this recipe.

Getting ready

You will need **Git** installed at the command line on your computer:

- https://git-scm.com/book/en/v2/Getting-Started-Installing-Git

You may need to install Git LFS (Large File Storage) for the GitHub for Unity package to work correctly:

- https://git-lfs.github.com/

You may wish to create a .gitattributes file to specify which files should be used with Git **Large File Storage (LFS)**. For some guidance, check out Rob Reilly's useful article, *How to Git With Unity*: https://robots.thoughtbot.com/how-to-git-with-unity.

How to do it...

To manage Unity project version-control using GitHUb for Unity, do the following:

1. Start a new Unity project.
2. Open the **Asset Store** panel, choose menu: **Window | General | Asset Store**.

3. In the **Asset Store**, search for **GitHub for Unity**, download and import this into your project:

4. If there is a popup about a newer version, accept it and download the newer version. This will download as a Unity package (probably in your **Downloads** folder), which you can then import into your Unity project.

5. Once imported, you should see a **Plugins | GitHub** folder in your **Project** panel. You will also now see two new items on your Window menu, for **GitHub** and **GitHub Command Line**:

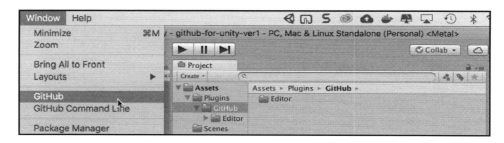

6. Choosing the **Window | GitHub Command Line** allows you to use the **Git** commands listed in the previous two recipes (it will open at the directory of your Unity project).

7. Choosing the **Window | GitHub** menu item will result in a **GitHub** panel being displayed. Initially this project is not a **Git** repository, so it will need to be initialized as a new **Git** project, which can be performed by clicking the **Initialize as a git repository for this project** button:

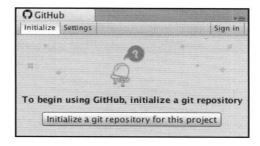

8. You will be able to see that there is one commit, for the snapshot for this initialization of the **Git** version-control-tracking for this project:

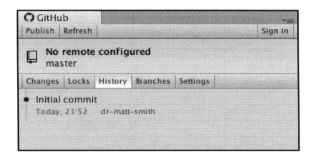

9. Sign in with your **GitHub** username and password:

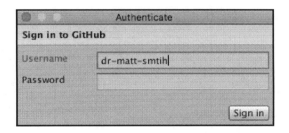

10. Open a web browser, log in to your **GitHub** account, and create a new empty repository (with no extra files, that is, no README, .gitignore, or Licence):

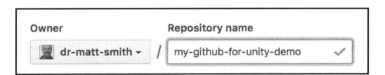

11. Copy the URL for the new repository onto your clipboard:

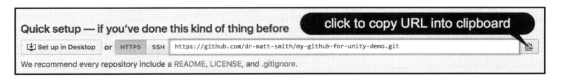

12. Back in Unity, for the **GitHub** panel, click the **Settings** button, paste the URL for the `Remote: origin` property, and click the **Save Repository** button to save this change. Your Unity project is now linked to the remote **GitHub** cloud repository:

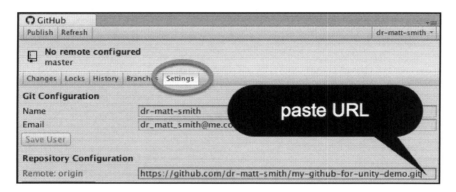

13. You may now commit and push changes from your Unity project up to **GitHub**.

14. Add some new assets (such as a new C# script and a **Material** named **m_red**). Click the **Changes** tab in the **GitHub** panel, ensure the complete `Assets` folder is checked (and all its contents), write a brief summary of the changes, and click the **Commit to [master]** button:

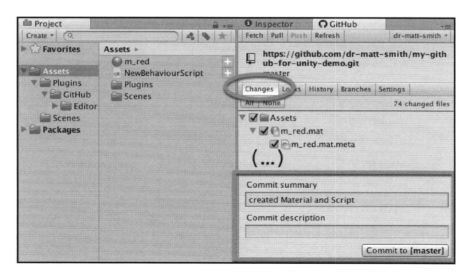

15. You now have a commited snapshot of the new Unity project contents on your computer. Push this new committed snapshot up to the **GitHub** server by clicking the **Push (1)** button. The (1) indicates that there is one new commited snapshot locally that has not yet been pushed, that is, the local machine is 1 commit ahead of the master on the **GitHub Server**:

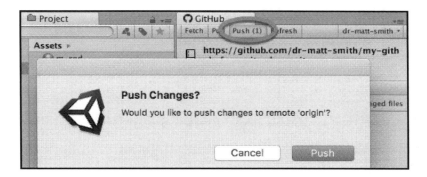

16. Visit the repository on **GitHub** in your web browser, and you'll see the new committed snapshot of the Unity project contents have been pushed up from your computer to the **GitHub** cloud **Servers**:

How it works...

The **GitHub for Unity** package adds a special panel with functionality for the following **Git/GitHub** actions:

- Initializing a new **Git** project repository for the current Unity Project
- Signing in with your **GitHub** username and password credentials

- Linking your Unity project's **Git** history to a remote **GitHub** online repository
- Committing a snapshot of the changes in the Unity project you wish to record
- Pushing committed changes to the remove **GitHub** online repository

There's more...

Here are some ways to go further with this recipe.

Further reading about GitHub for Unity

Check out the following links for more information:

- The project website: https://unity.github.com/
- The Quick Start guide: https://github.com/github-for-unity/Unity/blob/master/docs/using/quick-guide.md

Pulling down updates from other developers

The **GitHub** plugin also provides the feature of being able to pull down changes from the remote **GitHub** repository to your computer (useful if you are working on multiple computers, or a fellow game developer is helping add features to your game).

 If you are working with other game developers, it is very useful to learn about Git branches. Also, before starting work on a new feature, perform a pull to ensure you are then working with the most up-to-date version of the project.

Unity Collaborate from Unity Technologies

Although **Git** and **GitHub** are used for many Unity projects, they are general-purpose version-control technologies. Unity Technologies offers its own online system for developers and teams to collaboratively work on the same Unity projects, however this is a feature that is no longer in the free Unity licence plan.

Learn more about **Unity Collaborate** and **Unity Teams** on the Unity website:

- `https://unity3d.com/unity/features/collaborate`
- `https://unity3d.com/teams`

Preventing your game from running on unknown servers

After all the hard work you've had to go through to complete your web game project, it wouldn't be fair if it ended up generating traffic and income on someone else's website. In this recipe, we will create a script that prevents the main game menu from showing up unless it's hosted by an authorized **Server**.

Getting ready

For this recipe, you will need access to a webspace provider where you can host the game. However, you can test locally using a localhost web **Server**, such as the built-in PHP one, or an AMP Apache or Nginx web server.

You also will need to have installed the Unity **WebGL** build target.

NOTE: At the time of writing (summer 2018), for macOS computers, there is still an issue adding the **WebGL** package if it is not included at the time of original installation via Unity Hub. The macOS WebGL package requires the Unity application to be in the Applications | Unity folder. When installed via Unity Hub, it is actually in **Applications | Unity | Hub | Editor | 2018.2.2f1**. If you have multiple versions, they will each be in the Editor folder. The solution for installing WebGL for a particular Unity version is to temporarily move the **Applications | Unity | Hub** folder somewhere else (such as the desktop), and then to copy (or temporarily move) the contents of your Unity version folder (for me it was 2018 .2.2f1) into Applications | Unity. Then you can run the WebGL package installer successfully and it will add to the `PlaybackEngines` folder in Applications | Unity. Finally, you can move the Unity applications back where they were for **Unity Hub** to continue working.

How to do it...

To prevent your web game from being pirated, follow these steps:

1. From the **Hierarchy**, create a **UI Text** GameObject named **Text-loading-warning**, choosing menu: **Create | UI | Text**.
2. In the Inspector for the **Text** component enter **Loading...**
3. Set the properties for the **Text (Script)** component in the **Inspector** set the **Horizontal** and **Vertical Overflow** to **Overflow**, and use the Rect Transform to align the object in the center of the **Scene**. Make the font size nice and big (50).
4. Create a new C# script class named BlockAccess, and add an instance object as a component to the **Text-loading-warning** GameObject:

```
using UnityEngine;
using System.Collections;
using UnityEngine.UI;
using UnityEngine.SceneManagement;

public class BlockAccess : MonoBehaviour {
    public Text textUI;
    public string warning;
    public bool fullURL = true;
    public string[] domainList;

    private void Start() {
        Text scoreText = GetComponent<Text>();
        if (Application.platform ==
RuntimePlatform.WebGLPlayer)
        {
            string url = Application.absoluteURL;
            if (LegalCopy(url))
                LoadNextScene();
            else
                textUI.text = warning;
        }
    }

    private bool LegalCopy(string Url) {
        if (Application.isEditor)
        return true;

        for (int i = 0; i < domainList.Length; i++){
            if (Application.absoluteURL == domainList[i])
                return true;
```

```
                      if
(Application.absoluteURL.Contains(domainList[i]) && !fullURL)
                    return true;
            }

        return false;
    }

    private void LoadNextScene() {
        int currentSceneIndex =
SceneManager.GetActiveScene().buildIndex;
        int nextSceneIndex = currentSceneIndex + 1;
        SceneManager.LoadScene(nextSceneIndex);
    }
}
```

5. From the **Inspector**, leave the **Full URL** option checked, increase **Size** of **Domain List** to 1, and fill out Element 0 with the complete URL for your game. In the Warning field, type in "This is not a valid game copy":

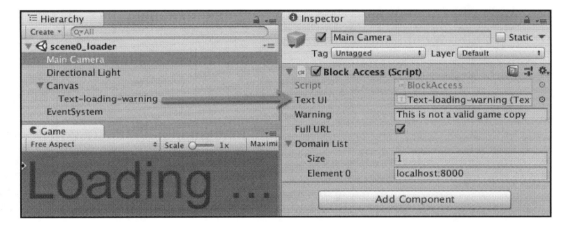

6. Save your **Scene** as scene0-loading. Add this **Scene** to the Build (menu: **File | Build Settings...**). It should be the first one, with index 0.

7. Create a new Scene, change its Main Camera background color to black, and add a UI Text message saying Game would play now.

8. Save this second **Scene** as scene1-gamePlaying. Add this Scene to the Build – it should be the second one, with index 1.

9. Let's build our **WebGL** files. Again, open the **Build Settings** panel, and this time ensure that the deployment platform is WebGL. Click the Build button, and choose the name and folder to be the location for your built files:

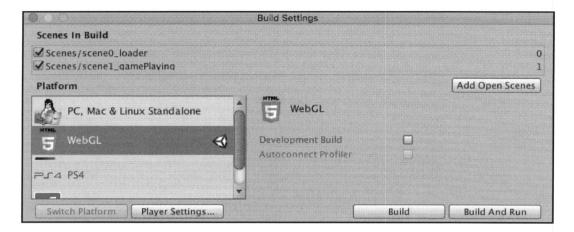

10. You should now have a folder containing an HTML file (index.html) and the Build and TemplateData folders:

11. Copy these folder contents to the public folder on your web **Server**, and use the browser to access the web page through the web **Server**.

12. If your URL is in the list, you'll see the game play (possible with a short view of the **Loading... Scene message**). If your URL is not in the list, you'll see the **This is not a valid game copy** message, and the game will not start playing.

 If you try to open the file using your web browser, you will probably get a WebGL not working error. You must be visiting the HTML page through a web server (such as localhost:8000 or from your publicly-hosted page).

How it works...

As soon as the **Scene** starts, the script compares the actual URL of the location of the running Unity-generated **WebGL** webpage to the ones listed in the **BlockAccess** scripted component. If they don't match, the next level in the build is not loaded and a message appears on the screen. If they do match, the next scene from the build list will be loaded.

There's more...

Here are some ways to go further with this recipe.

Enabling WebGL in Google Chrome

For this recipe, you'll need **WebGL** enabled in your web browser. At present, our test browser (Google Chrome) has WebGL disabled by default. To enabled **WebGL** in Google Chrome, do the following:

1. Open Google Chrome and enter the `chrome://flags` URL.
2. Locate the **Web GL Draft Extensions** (search for **WebGL**).
3. Use the drop-down menu to change from **Disabled** to **Enabled.**
4. Click the **RELAUNCH NOW** button to restart the application with the new settings as active:

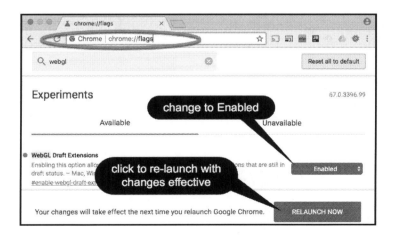

5. You should now be able to use web pages with embedded **WebGL** content.

Improving security by using full URLs in your domain list

Your game will be more secure if you fill out the domain list with complete URLs, such as `http://www.myDomain.com/unitygame/index.html`, rather than just the main domain, such as www.myDomain.com. In fact, it's recommended that you leave the Full URL option selected so that your game won't be stolen and published under a URL such as www.stolenGames.com/yourgame.html?www.myDomain.com.

12
Controlling and Choosing Positions

In this chapter, we will cover the following topics:

- Player control of a 2D GameObject (and limiting the movement within a rectangle)
- Player control of a 3D GameObject (and limiting the movement within a rectangle)
- Choosing destinations – finding a random spawn point
- Choosing destinations – finding the nearest spawn point
- Choosing destinations – respawning to the most recently passed checkpoint
- Moving objects by clicking on them
- Firing projectiles in the direction of movement

Introduction

Many **GameObjects** in games move! Movement can be controlled by the player, by the (simulated) laws of physics in the environment, or by the **Non-Player Character** (**NPC**) logic; for example, objects that follow a path of a waypoint, or seek (move toward) or flee (away) from the current position of a character. Unity provides several controllers for first and third-person characters, and for vehicles such as cars and airplanes. **GameObject** movement can also be controlled through the state machines of the Unity **Mecanim** animation system.

However, there may be times when you wish to tweak the Player character controllers from Unity, or write your own. You might wish to write directional logic—simple or sophisticated **Artificial Intelligence (AI)** to control the game's NPC and enemy characters. Such AI might involve your computer program making objects orient and move toward or away from characters or other game objects.

This chapter (and the chapter that follows) presents a range of such directional recipes, from which many games can benefit in terms of a richer and more exciting user experience.

Unity provides sophisticated classes and components, including the `Vector3` class and rigid body physics for modeling realistic movements, forces, and collisions in games. We make use of these game engine features to implement some sophisticated NPC and enemy character movements in the recipes of this chapter.

The big picture

For 3D games (and to some extent, 2D games as well), a fundamental class of object is the `Vector3` class objects that store and manipulate (**x, y, z**) values representing locations in a 3D space. If we draw an imaginary arrow from the origin (0, 0, 0) to a point on the space, then the direction and length of this arrow (vector) can represent a velocity or force (that is, a certain amount of magnitude in a certain direction).

If we ignore all the character controller components, colliders, and the physics system in Unity, we can write code that teleports objects directly to a particular (**x, y, z**) location in our scene. Sometimes, this is just what we want to do; for example, we may wish to spawn an object at a location. However, in most cases, if we want objects to move in more physically realistic ways, then we either apply a force to the object's **RigidBody**, or change its velocity component. Or, if it has a **Character Controller** component, then we can send it a `Move()` message.

Some important concepts in the NPC object movement and creation (instantiation) include the following:

- **Spawn points**: Specific locations in the scene where objects are to be created, or moved to
- **Checkpoints**: Locations (or colliders) that, once passed through, change what happens later in the game (for example, extra time, or if a Player's character gets killed, they respawn to the last crossed checkpoint, and so on)

- **Waypoints**: A sequence of locations to define a path for NPCs or, perhaps, the Player's character, to follow

In this chapter, we will introduce a few recipes and demonstrate a selection of approaches to character control, spawn points, and checkpoints. In the next chapter, we'll look at waypoints for AI controlled characters.

You can learn more about the Unity 2D character controllers at `http://unity3d.com/learn/tutorials/modules/beginner/2d/2d-controllers`.
You can learn about the Unity 3D character component and control at `http://docs.unity3d.com/Manual/class-CharacterController.html` and `http://unity3d.com/learn/tutorials/projects/survival-shooter/player-character`.

Every game needs textures. Here are some of the sources of free textures that are suitable for many games:

- CG Textures are available at `http://www.cgtextures.com/`
- Naldz Graphics blog, available at `http://naldzgraphics.net/textures/`

Player control of a 2D GameObject (and limiting the movement within a rectangle)

While the rest of the recipes in this chapter are demonstrated in 3D projects, basic character movement in 2D and also limiting the movement to a bounding rectangle, are core skills for many 2D games, and so this first recipe illustrates how to achieve these features for a 2D game.

Since in Chapter 3, *Inventory UIs*, we already created a basic 2D game, we'll adapt this game to restrict the movement to a bounding rectangle:

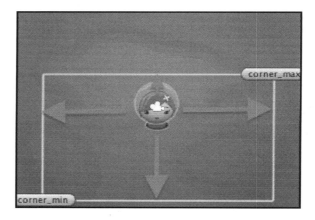

Getting ready

This recipe builds on a simple 2D game called the **Simple2DGame_SpaceGirl** mini game from the first recipe of Chapter 3, *Inventory UIs*. Start with a copy of this game, or use the provided completed recipe project as the basis for this recipe. You can download the completed project from https://github.com/dr-matt-smith/unity-cookbook-2018-ch03.

How to do it...

To create a 2D sprite controlled by the user with a movement that is limited to within a rectangle, follow these steps:

1. Create a new, empty **GameObject** named corner_max, and position it somewhere above and to the right of the **GameObject** called player_spaceGirl. With this **GameObject** selected in the **Hierarchy** view, choose the large yellow oblong icon, highlighted in the **Inspector** panel:

2. Duplicate the **corner_max GameObject** by naming the clone as corner_min, and position this clone somewhere below and to the left of the **player-spaceGirl GameObject**. The coordinates of these two **GameObjects** will determine the maximum and minimum bounds of movement, permitted for the player's character.

3. Modify the C# Script called PlayerMove to declare some new variables at the beginning of the class:

```
public Transform corner_max;
public Transform corner_min;
private float x_min;
private float y_min;
private float x_max;
private float y_max;
```

4. Modify the C# Script called PlayerMove so that the Awake() method now gets a reference to the SpriteRenderer, and uses this object to help set up the maximum and minimum X and Y movement limits:

```
void Awake(){
    rigidBody2D = GetComponent<Rigidbody2D>();
    x_max = corner_max.position.x;
    x_min = corner_min.position.x;
    y_max = corner_max.position.y;
    y_min = corner_min.position.y;
}
```

5. Modify the C# Script called PlayerMove to declare a new method called KeepWithinMinMaxRectangle():

```
private void KeepWithinMinMaxRectangle(){
    float x = transform.position.x;
    float y = transform.position.y;
    float z = transform.position.z;
    float clampedX = Mathf.Clamp(x, x_min, x_max);
    float clampedY = Mathf.Clamp(y, y_min, y_max);
```

```
      transform.position = new Vector3(clampedX, clampedY, z);
   }
```

6. Modify the C# Script called `PlayerMove` so that, after having updated the velocity in the `FixedUpdate()` method, a call will be made to the `KeepWithinMinMaxRectangle()` method:

```
void FixedUpdate(){
   rigidBody2D.velocity = newVelocity;

   // restrict player movement
   KeepWithinMinMaxRectangle();
}
```

7. With the **player-spaceGirl GameObject** in the **Hierarchy** view, drag the **corner_max** and **corner_min GameObjects** over the public variables called **corner_max** and **corner_min** in the Inspector.

Before running the scene in the **Scene** panel, try repositioning the **corner_max** and **corner_min GameObjects**. When you run the scene, the positions of these two **GameObjects** (max and min, and X and Y) will be used as the limits of movement for the Player's **player-spaceGirl** character.

How it works...

You added the empty **GameObjects** called **corner_max** and **corner_min** to the scene. The X and Y coordinates of these **GameObjects** will be used to determine the bounds of movement that we will permit for the character called **player-spaceGirl**. Since these are the empty **GameObjects**, they will not be seen by the player when in play-mode. However, we can see and move them in the **Scene** panel, and having added the yellow oblong icons, we can see their positions and names very easily.

Upon using the `Awake()` method on the `PlayerMoveWithLimits` object, inside the **player-spaceGirl GameObject**, the maximum and minimum X and Y values of the **GameObjects** called **corner_max** and **corner_min** are recorded. Each time the physics system is called via the `FixedUpdate()` method, the velocity of the **player-spaceGirl** character is updated to the value set in the `Update()` method,which is based on the horizontal and vertical keyboard/joystick inputs. However, the final action of the `FixedUpdate()` method is to call the `KeepWithinMinMaxRectangle()` method, which uses the `Math.Clamp(...)` function to move the character back inside the X and Y limits. This happens so that the player's character is not permitted to move outside the area defined by the **corner_max** and **corner_min GameObjects**.

We have kept to a good rule of thumb:

> *"Always listen for **input** in* Update().
> *Always apply **physics** in* FixedUpdate()."*

Learn more about why we should not check for inputs in FixedUpdate() in the Unity Answers thread (which is also the source for the preceding quote from user Tanoshimi) at https://answers.unity.com/questions/1279847/getaxis-being-missed-in-fixedupdate-work-around.html.

There's more...

There are some details that you don't want to miss out on.

Drawing a gizmo yellow rectangle to visually show bounding a rectangle

As developers, it is useful to *see* elements like bounding rectangles when run-testing our game. Let's make the rectangular bounds of the movement visually explicit in yellow lines in the **Scene** panel by having a yellow "gizmo" rectangle drawn. Add the following method to the C# script class called PlayerMove:

```
void OnDrawGizmos(){
    Vector3 top_right = Vector3.zero;
    Vector3 bottom_right = Vector3.zero;
    Vector3 bottom_left = Vector3.zero;
    Vector3 top_left = Vector3.zero;

    if(corner_max && corner_min){
      top_right = corner_max.position;
      bottom_left = corner_min.position;

      bottom_right = top_right;
      bottom_right.y = bottom_left.y;

      top_left = top_right;
      top_left.x = bottom_left.x;
    }

    //Set the following gizmo colors to YELLOW
    Gizmos.color = Color.yellow;

    //Draw 4 lines making a rectangle
```

```
    Gizmos.DrawLine(top_right, bottom_right);
    Gizmos.DrawLine(bottom_right, bottom_left);
    Gizmos.DrawLine(bottom_left, top_left);
    Gizmos.DrawLine(top_left, top_right);
}
```

The `OnDrawGizmos()` method tests that the references to the **corner_max** and **corner_min GameObjects** are not **null**, and then sets the positions of the four **Vector3** objects, representing the four corners defined by the rectangle, with **corner_max** and **corner_min** at the opposite corners. It then sets the **Gizmo** color to yellow, and draws lines, connecting the four corners in the **Scene** panel.

See also

- Refer to the following recipe for more information about limiting Player controlled character movements.

Player control of a 3D GameObject (and limiting the movement within a rectangle)

Many of the 3D recipes in this chapter are built on this basic project, which constructs a scene with a textured terrain, a **Main Camera**, and a red cube that can be moved around by the user with the four directional arrow keys. The bounds of movement of the cube are constrained using the same technique as in the previous 2D recipe:

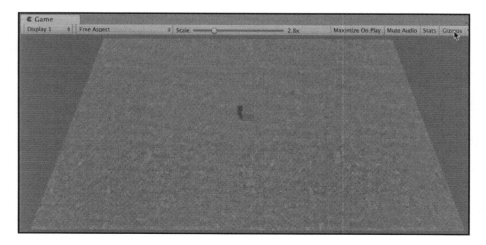

How to do it...

To create a basic 3D cube controlled game, follow these steps:

1. Create a new, empty 3D project.
2. Once the project has been created, import the single **Terrain Texture** named **SandAlbedo** by choosing menu: **Assets | Import Package | Environments**. Deselect everything, and then locate and tick the asset by going to `Assets/Environment/TerrainAssets/SurfaceTextures/SandAlbedo.psd`.

> You could have just added the **Environment Asset Package** when creating the project, but this would have imported hundreds of files, and we only needed this one. Starting a project in Unity and then selectively importing just what we need is the best approach to take if you want to keep the project's `Asset` folders to small sizes.

3. Create a new terrain by choosing menu: **Create | 3D Object | Terrain**. With this new terrain **GameObject** selected in **Hierarchy**, in its **Inspector** properties, set the size to **30 x 20**, and its position to **(-15, 0, -10)**:

   The transform position for the terrains relates to their corner and not their center.

> Since the **Transform** position of the terrains relates to the corner of the object, we center such objects at (0, 0, 0) by setting the X coordinate equal to (*-1width/2*), and the Z-coordinate equal to (*-1length/2*). In other words, we slide the object by half its width and half its height to ensure that its center is just where we want it.
>
> In this case, the width is 30 and the length is 20, hence we get **-15** for X (*-1 * 30/2*), and **-10** for Z (*-1 * 20/2*).

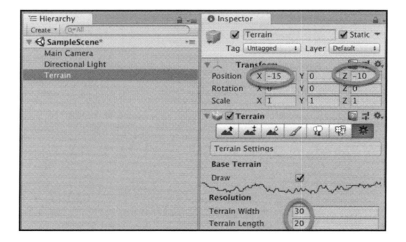

4. Texture paint this terrain with your texture called **SandAlbedo**.

5. Make the following changes to the **Main Camera**:
   - **Position**: (0, 20, -15)
   - **Rotation**: (60, 0, 0)

6. Change the **Aspect Ratio** of the **Game Panel** from **Free Aspect** to 4:3. You will now see the whole of the **Terrain** in the **Game Panel**.

7. Create a new empty **GameObject** named **corner_max**, and position it at **(14, 0, 9)**. With this **GameObject** selected in the **Hierarchy**, choose the large, yellow oblong icon, highlighted in the **Inspector** panel.

8. Duplicate the **corner_max GameObject**, naming the clone as **corner_min**, and position this clone at **(-14, 0, -9)**. The coordinates of these two **GameObjects** will determine the maximum and minimum bounds of the movement permitted for the player's character.

9. Create a new cube called **GameObject** by choosing menu: **Create | 3D Object | Cube**. Name this `Cube-player`, and set its position to **(0, 0.5, 0)**, and size as **(1, 1, 1)**.

10. Add a rigid body component to the **Cube-player GameObject** (**Physics | RigidBody**), and uncheck the **RigidBody** property **Use Gravity**.

11. Create a red **Material** named `m_red`, and apply this Material to **Cube-player**.

12. Create a C# Script class called `PlayerControl`, and add an instance object as a component to **GameObject Cube-player**:

```csharp
using UnityEngine;

public class PlayerControl : MonoBehaviour {
    public Transform corner_max;
        public Transform corner_min;
        public float speed = 40;
        private Rigidbody rigidBody;
        private float x_min;
        private float x_max;
        private float z_min;
        private float z_max;
        private Vector3 newVelocity;

    void Awake() {
        rigidBody = GetComponent<Rigidbody>();
        x_max = corner_max.position.x;
        x_min = corner_min.position.x;
        z_max = corner_max.position.z;
        z_min = corner_min.position.z;
    }

private void Update() {
    float xMove = Input.GetAxis("Horizontal") * speed *
Time.deltaTime;
    float zMove = Input.GetAxis("Vertical") * speed * Time.deltaTime;
    float xSpeed = xMove * speed;
    float zSpeed = zMove * speed;
    newVelocity = new Vector3(xSpeed, 0, zSpeed);
}

void FixedUpdate() {
    rigidBody.velocity = newVelocity;
    KeepWithinMinMaxRectangle();
}

 private void KeepWithinMinMaxRectangle() {
   float x = transform.position.x;
   float y = transform.position.y;
   float z = transform.position.z;
   float clampedX = Mathf.Clamp(x, x_min, x_max);
   float clampedZ = Mathf.Clamp(z, z_min, z_max);
   transform.position = new Vector3(clampedX, y, clampedZ);
 }
 }
```

13. With the **Cube-player GameObject** selected in **Hierarchy**, drag the **GameObjects** called **corner_max** and **corner_min** over the public variables called **corner_max** and **corner_min** in the **Inspector** panel.

When you run the scene, the positions of the **corner_max** and **corner_min GameObjects** will define the bounds of movement for the Player's **Cube-player** character.

How it works...

The scene contains a positioned terrain so that its center is **(0, 0, 0)**. The red cube is controlled by the user's arrow keys through the `PlayerControl` script.

Just as with the previous 2D recipe, a reference to the (3D) **RigidBody** component is stored when the `Awake()` method executes, and the maximum and minimum X and Z values are retrieved from the two corner **GameObjects**, and are stored in the `x_min`, `x_max`, `z_min`, and `z_max` variables. Note that for this basic 3D game, we won't allow any Y-movement, although such movement (and bounding limits by adding a third **max-height** corner **GameObject**) can be easily added by extending the code in this recipe.

The `KeyboardMovement()` method reads the horizontal and vertical input values (which the Unity default settings read from the four directional arrow keys). Based on these left-right and up-down values, the velocity of the cube is updated. The amount it will move depends on the speed variable.

The `KeepWithinMinMaxRectangle()` method uses the `Math.Clamp(...)` function to move the character back inside the X and Z limits so that the player's character is not permitted to move outside the area defined by the **corner_max** and **corner_min GameObjects**.

There's more...

There are some details that you don't want to miss out on.

Drawing a gizmo yellow rectangle to visually show bounding a rectangle

As developers, it is useful to *see* elements like bounding rectangles when test-running our game. Let's make the rectangular bounds of the movement visually explicit in yellow lines in the **Scene** panel by having a yellow "gizmo" rectangle drawn. Add the following method to the C# Script class called `PlayerMove`:

```
void OnDrawGizmos (){
        Vector3 top_right = Vector3.zero;
        Vector3 bottom_right = Vector3.zero;
        Vector3 bottom_left = Vector3.zero;
        Vector3 top_left = Vector3.zero;

        if(corner_max && corner_min){
          top_right = corner_max.position;
          bottom_left = corner_min.position;

          bottom_right = top_right;
          bottom_right.z = bottom_left.z;

          top_left = bottom_left;
          top_left.z = top_right.z;
        }

        //Set the following gizmo colors to YELLOW
        Gizmos.color = Color.yellow;

        //Draw 4 lines making a rectangle
        Gizmos.DrawLine(top_right, bottom_right);
        Gizmos.DrawLine(bottom_right, bottom_left);
        Gizmos.DrawLine(bottom_left, top_left);
        Gizmos.DrawLine(top_left, top_right);
    }
```

The `OnDrawGizmos()` method tests that the references to the **corner_max** and **corner_min GameObjects** are not null, and then sets the positions of the four **Vector3** objects, representing the four corners defined by the rectangle, with the **corner_max** and **corner_min GameObjects** at the opposite corners. It then sets the **Gizmo** color to yellow, and draws lines, connecting the four corners in the **Scene** panel.

Choosing destinations – finding a random spawn point

Many games make use of spawn points and waypoints. This recipe demonstrates choosing a random spawn point, and then the instantiation of an object at that chosen point.

Getting ready

This recipe builds upon the previous recipe. So, make a copy of this project, open it, and then follow the steps in the next section.

How to do it...

To find a random spawn point, follow these steps:

1. In the **Scene** panel, create a sphere (by navigating to **Create | 3D Object | Sphere**) sized as **(1, 1, 1)** at **(2, 2, 2)** position, and apply the **m_red Material**.

2. In the **Project** panel, create a new **Prefab** (by going to **Create | Prefab**) named `Prefab-ball`, and drag your sphere into it (and then delete the sphere from the **Hierarchy** panel).

3. In the **Scene** panel, create a new capsule (by navigating to **Create | 3D Object | Capsule**) named `Capsule-spawnPoint` at **(3, 0.5, 3)**, and give it a tag of **Respawn** (this is one of the default tags that Unity provides):

 For testing, we'll leave these **Respawn** points visible. For the final game, we'll then uncheck the **Mesh Rendered** of each **Respawn GameObject** so that they are not visible to the Player.

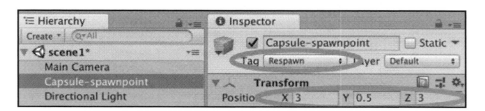

4. Make several copies of your **Capsule-spawnPoint** by moving them to different locations on the terrain.

5. Create a C# Script class called **SpawnBall**, and add an instance object as a component to the **Cube-player GameObject**:

```
using UnityEngine;

public class BallSpawner : MonoBehaviour {
    public GameObject prefabBall;
    private SpawnPointManager spawnPointManager;
    private float timeBetweenSpawns = 1;

    void Start () {
        spawnPointManager = GetComponent<SpawnPointManager> ();
        InvokeRepeating("CreateSphere", 0, timeBetweenSpawns);
    }

    private void CreateSphere() {
        GameObject spawnPoint =
        spawnPointManager.RandomSpawnPoint();

        GameObject newBall = (GameObject)Instantiate(
            prefabBall, spawnPoint.transform.position,
            Quaternion.identity);
        Destroy(newBall, timeBetweenSpawns/2);
    }
}
```

6. Create a C# Script class called `SpawnPointManager` and add an instance object as a component to the **Cube-player GameObject**:

```
using UnityEngine;

public class SpawnPointManager : MonoBehaviour {
    private GameObject[] spawnPoints;

    void Start() {
        spawnPoints =
GameObject.FindGameObjectsWithTag("Respawn");
    }

    public GameObject RandomSpawnPoint() {
        int r = Random.Range(0, spawnPoints.Length);
        return spawnPoints[r];
    }
}
```

7. Ensure that **Cube-player** is selected in the **Inspector** for the **SpawnBall** scripted component. Then, drag **Prefab-ball** over the public variable projectile called **Prefab Ball**.

8. Now, run your game. Every second, a red ball should be spawned and disappear after half a second. The location each ball is spawned at should be random.

How it works...

The `Capsule-spawnPoint` objects represent candidate locations, where we might wish to create an instance of our ball **Prefab**. When our `SpawnPointManager` object, inside the **Cube-player GameObject**, receives the `Start()` message, the respawned **GameObject** array is set to the array, which is returned from the call to `FindGameObjectsWithTag("Respawn")`. This creates an array of all the objects in the scene with the **Respawn** tag—that is, all our `Capsule-spawnPoint` objects.

When our `SpawnBall` object GameObject **Cube-player** receives the `Start()` message, it sets the `spawnPointManager` variable to be a reference to its sibling `SpawnPointManager` script component. Next, we use the `InvokeRepeating(...)` method to schedule the `CreateSphere()` method to be called every 1 second.

The `SpawnBall` method `CreateSphere()` assigns the `spawnPoint` variable to the **GameObject** returned by a call to the `RandomSpawnpoint(...)` method of our `spawnPointManager`. Then, it creates a new instance of `prefab_ball` (via the public variable) at the same position as the **spawnPoint GameObject**.

See also

The same techniques and code can be used for selecting spawn points or waypoints. Refer to the *NPC NavMeshAgent control to follow waypoints in sequence* recipe in the next chapter (`Navigation Meshes and Agents`) for more information about waypoints.

Choosing destinations – finding the nearest spawn point

Rather than just choosing a random spawn point or waypoint, sometimes, we want to select the one closest to some object (such as the player's **GameObject**). In this recipe, we will modify the previous one to find the nearest spawn point to the player's cube, and use that location to spawn a new red ball prefab.

Getting ready

This recipe builds upon the previous recipe. So, make a copy of this project, open it, and then follow the steps in the next section.

How to do it...

To find the nearest spawn point, follow these steps:

1. Add the following method to the C# Script class called `SpawnPointManager`:

```
public GameObject NearestSpawnpoint (Vector3 source){
    GameObject nearestSpawnPoint = spawnPoints[0];
    Vector3 spawnPointPos = spawnPoints[0].transform.position;
    float shortestDistance = Vector3.Distance(source,
spawnPointPos);

    for (int i = 1; i < spawnPoints.Length; i++){
      spawnPointPos = spawnPoints[i].transform.position;
      float newDist = Vector3.Distance(source, spawnPointPos);
      if (newDist < shortestDistance){
        shortestDistance = newDist;
        nearestSpawnPoint = spawnPoints[i];
      }
    }

    return nearestSpawnPoint;
  }
```

2. We now need to change the first line in the C# class called `SpawnBall` so that the `spawnPoint` variable is set by a call to our new method called `NearestSpawnpoint(...)`:

```
private void CreateSphere(){
   GameObject spawnPoint =
   spawnPointManager.NearestSpawnpoint(transform.position);

   GameObject newBall = (GameObject)Instantiate (prefabBall,
   spawnPoint.transform.position, Quaternion.identity);
   Destroy(newBall, timeBetweenSpawns/2);
}
```

3. Now, run your game. Every second, a red ball should be spawned, and disappear after half a second. Use the arrow keys to move the player's red cube around the terrain. Each time a new ball is spawned, it should be at the spawn point closest to the player.

How it works...

In the `NearestSpawnpoint(...)` method, we set nearestSpawnpoint to the first (array index 0) **GameObject** in the array as our default. We then loop through the rest of the array (array index 1 up to `spawnPoints.Length`). For each **GameObject** in the array, we test to see if its distance is less than the shortest distance so far, and if it is, then we update the shortest distance, and also set `nearestSpawnpoint` to the current element. When the array has been searched, we return the **GameObject** that the `nearestSpawnpoint` variable refers to.

There's more...

There are some details that you don't want to miss out on.

Avoiding errors due to an empty array

Let's make our code a little more robust so that it can cope with the issue of an empty `spawnPoints` array, that is, when there are no objects tagged as `Respawn` in the scene.

To cope with the no objects tagged as `Respawn`, we need to do the following:

1. Improve our `Start()` method in the C# Script class called `SpawnPointManager` so that an *error* is logged if the array of the objects tagged as `Respawn` is empty:

```
public GameObject NearestSpawnpoint (Vector3 source){
  void Start() {
    spawnPoints = GameObject.FindGameObjectsWithTag("Respawn");

    // logError if array empty
    if(spawnPoints.Length < 1)
      Debug.LogError ("SpawnPointManagaer - cannot find any objects
      tagged 'Respawn'!");
  }
```

2. Improve the `RandomSpawnPoint()` and `NearestSpawnpoint()` methods in the C# Script class called `SpawnPointManager` so that they still return a **GameObject**, even if the array is empty:

```
public GameObject RandomSpawnPoint (){
    // return current GameObject if array empty
    if(spawnPoints.Length < 1)
      return null;

  // the rest as before ...
```

3. Improve the `CreateSphere()` method in the C# class called `SpawnBall` so that we only attempt to instantiate a new **GameObject** if the `RandomSpawnPoint()` and `NearestSpawnpoint()` methods have returned a non-null object reference:

```
private void CreateSphere(){
    GameObject spawnPoint = spawnPointManager.RandomSpawnPoint ();

    if(spawnPoint){
      GameObject newBall = (GameObject)Instantiate (prefabBall,
      spawnPoint.transform.position, Quaternion.identity);
      Destroy(newBall, destroyAfterDelay);
    }
  }
```

See also

- The same techniques and code can be used for selecting spawn points or waypoints. Refer to the *NPC NavMeshAgent control to follow waypoints in sequence* recipe in the next chapter (Navigation Meshes and Agents)

Choosing destinations – respawning to the most recently passed checkpoint

A checkpoint usually represents a certain distance through the game (or perhaps a track) in which an agent (user or NPC) has succeeded reaching. Reaching (or passing) checkpoints often results in bonus awards, such as extra time, points, ammo, and so on. Also, if a player has multiple lives, then often a player will only be respawned back as far as the most recently passed checkpoint, rather than right to the beginning of the level.

This recipe demonstrates a simple approach to the checkpoints, whereby once the player's character has passed a checkpoint, if they die, they are moved back to the most recently passed checkpoint:

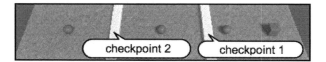

Getting ready

This recipe builds upon the player-controlled 3D cube Unity project that you created at the beginning of this chapter. So, make a copy of this project, open it, and then follow the steps for this recipe.

How to do it...

To have the respawn position change upon losing a life depending on the checkpoints passed, follow these steps:

1. Move the **Cube-player GameObject** to the **(12, 0.5, 0)** position.
2. Select **Cube-player** in the **Inspector** panel and add a **Character Controller** component by clicking on **Add Component | Physics | Character Controller** (this is to enable the **OnTriggerEnter** collision messages to be received).
3. Create a cube named **Cube-checkpoint**-1 at **(5, 0, 0)**, scaled to **(1, 1, 20)**.
4. With **Cube-checkpoint-1** selected, check the **Is Trigger** property of its **Box Collider** component in the **Inspector** panel.
5. Create a **CheckPoint** tag, and assign this tag to **Cube-checkpoint-1**.
6. Duplicate **Cube-checkpoint-1** and name the clone `Cube-checkpoint-2`, and position it at **(-5, 0, 0)**.
7. Create a sphere named `Sphere-Death` at **(7, 0.5, 0)**. Assign the **m_red** material to this sphere to make it red.
8. With **Sphere-Death** selected, check the **Is Trigger** property of its **Sphere Collider** component in the **Inspector** panel.
9. Create a `Death` tag, and assign this tag to **Sphere-Death**.
10. Duplicate **Sphere-Death**, and position this clone at **(0, 0.5, 0)**.
11. Duplicate **Sphere-Death** a second time, and position this second clone at **(-10, 0.5, 0)**.
12. Add an instance of the following C# Script class called `CheckPoints` to the **Cube-player GameObject**:

```
using UnityEngine;

public class CheckPoint : MonoBehaviour {
    private Vector3 respawnPosition;
    void Start () {
        respawnPosition = transform.position;
    }

    void OnTriggerEnter (Collider hit) {
        if(hit.CompareTag("Checkpoint"))
            respawnPosition = transform.position;

        if(hit.CompareTag("Death"))
```

```
                            transform.position = respawnPosition;
          }
     }
```

Run the scene. If the cube runs into a red sphere before crossing a checkpoint, it will be respawned back to its starting position. Once the red cube has passed a checkpoint, if a red sphere is hit, then the cube will be moved back to the location of the most recent checkpoint that it passed through.

How it works...

The C# script class called `CheckPoint` has one variable called `respawnPosition`, which is a **Vector3** that refers to the position the player's cube is to be moved to (respawned) if it collides with a `Death` tagged object. The default setting for this is the position of the player's cube when the scene begins, so in the `Start()` method, we set it to the player's position.

Each time an object tagged called `Checkpoint` is collided with, the value of `respawnPosition` is updated to the current position of the player's red cube at this point in time (that is, where it is when it touches the stretched cube tagged object called **CheckPoint**). The next time the object tagged `Death` is hit, the cube will be respawned back to where it last touched the object tagged called **CheckPoint**.

Moving objects by clicking on them

Sometimes, we want to allow the user to interact with objects through mouse pointer clicks. In this recipe, we will allow the user to move an object in a random direction by clicking on it.

Getting ready

This recipe builds upon the player-controlled 3D cube Unity project that you created at the beginning of this chapter. So, make a copy of this project, open it, and then follow the steps for this recipe. The result of following this recipe should look as follows:

How to do it...

To move objects by clicking on them, follow these steps:

1. Delete the **Cube-player GameObject**.
2. Set the **Main Camera** position to (**0, 3, -5**), and its rotation to (**25, 0, 0**).
3. Create a C# Script class called `ClickMove`:

```
using UnityEngine;

[RequireComponent(typeof(Rigidbody))]
public class ClickMove : MonoBehaviour {
    public float multiplier = 500f;
    private Rigidbody rigidBody;

    private void Awake() {
        rigidBody = GetComponent<Rigidbody>();
    }

    void OnMouseDown() {
        float x = RandomDirectionComponent();
        float y = RandomDirectionComponent();
        float z = RandomDirectionComponent();
        Vector3 randomDirection = new Vector3(x,y,z);
        rigidBody.AddForce(randomDirection);
    }

    private float RandomDirectionComponent() {
        return (Random.value - 0.5f) * multiplier;
    }
}
```

4. Create a Cube **GameObject** and add an instance object of the script class
   ClickMove as a component.

You should see that a **RigidBody** component is automatically added
to the new cube, since the script class has the directive
RequireComponent(typeof(Rigidbody)). This only works if the
directive is in the code before the script class is added to a
GameObject.

5. Make four more duplicates of the cube, and arrange the six objects into a
   pyramid by setting their positions to be the following:

   (0, 2.5, 0)
   (-0.75, 1.5, 0), (0.75, 1.5, 0)
   (-1, 0.5, 0), (0, 0.5, 0), (1.5, 0.5, 0)

6. Run the scene. Each time you use the mouse pointer to click on a cube, the
   clicked cube will have a random directional force applied to it. So, with a
   few clicks, you can knock down the pyramid!

How it works...

The public float variable multiplier allows you to change the maximum magnitude of
the force by changing the value in the ClickMove scripted component of each cube.

The ClickMove script class has a private variable called rigidBody set as a reference
to the **RigidBody** component in the Awake() method.

Each time the cube receives a MouseDown() message (such as when it has been
clicked with the user's mouse pointer), this method creates a random directional
Vector3, and applies this as a force to the object's rigidBody reference.

The RandomDirectionComponent() method returns a random value between –
multiplier and +multiplier.

Firing projectiles in the direction of movement

Another common use of force is to apply a force to a newly instantiated object, making it a projectile travelling in the direction the Player's **GameObject** is facing. That's what we'll create in this recipe. The result of following this recipe should look as follows:

Getting ready

This recipe builds upon the player-controlled 3D cube Unity project that you created at the beginning of this chapter. So, make a copy of this project, open it, and then follow the steps for this recipe.

How to do it...

To fire projectiles in the direction of movement, follow these steps:

1. Create a new Sphere **GameObject** (by navigating to **Create | 3D Object | Sphere**). Set its size as (**0.5, 0.5, 0.5**).

2. Add a **RigidBody** component to the Sphere (go to **Physics | RigidBody**).

3. In the **Project** panel, create a new blue **Material** named m_blue (go to **Create | Material**).

4. Apply the m_blue **Material** to your sphere.

5. In the **Project** panel, create a new **Prefab** named prefab_projectile.

6. Drag the sphere from the **Hierarchy** panel over your **prefab_projectile** (it should turn blue).

7. You can now delete the Sphere from the **Hierarchy**.

8. Ensure that **Cube-player** is located at **(0, 0.5, 0)**.

9. Create a new cube named `Cube-launcher`. Disable its **Box Collider** component, and set its transform as follows:
   - **Position (0, 1, 0.3)**
   - **Rotation (330, 0, 0)**
   - **Scale (0.1, 0.1, 0.5)**

10. In the **Hierarchy**, make **Cube-launcher** a child of **Cube-player** by dragging **Cube-launcher** onto **Cube-player**. This means that both objects will move together when the user presses the arrow keys.

11. Create a C# Script class called `FireProjectile` and add an instance object as a component to **Cube-launcher**:

```
using UnityEngine;

public class FireProjectile : MonoBehaviour {
    const float FIRE_DELAY = 0.25f;
    const float PROJECTILE_LIFE = 1.5f;


    public Rigidbody projectilePrefab;
    public float projectileSpeed = 500f;

    private float nextFireTime = 0;

    void Update() {
        if (Time.time > nextFireTime)
            CheckFireKey();
    }

    private void CheckFireKey() {
        if(Input.GetButton("Fire1")) {
            CreateProjectile();
            nextFireTime = Time.time + FIRE_DELAY;
        }
    }

    private void CreateProjectile() {
        Vector3 position = transform.position;
        Quaternion rotation = transform.rotation;

        Rigidbody projectileRigidBody =
            Instantiate(projectilePrefab, position, rotation);
        Vector3 projectileVelocity =
transform.TransformDirection(
            Vector3.forward * projectileSpeed);
```

```
      projectileRigidBody.AddForce(projectileVelocity);

      GameObject projectileGO = projectileRigidBody.gameObject;
      Destroy(projectileGO, PROJECTILE_LIFE);
   }
}
```

12. With **Cube-launcher** selected in the **Inspector**, from the **Project** panel, drag **prefab_projectile** into the public variable **Projectile Prefab** in the **Fire Projectile (Script)** component in the **Inspector**.

13. Run the scene. You can move around the terrain with the arrow keys, and each time you click the mouse button, you should see a blue sphere projectile launched in the direction that the player's cube is facing.

How it works...

You created a blue sphere as a **Prefab** (containing a **RigidBody**). You then created a scaled and rotated cube for the projectile launcher **Cube-launcher**, and childed this object to **Cube-player**.

The `FireProjectile` script class contains a constant `FIRE_DELAY`—this is the minimum time between the firing of new projectiles, set to `0.25` seconds. There is also a second constant called `PROJECTILE_LIFE`—this is how long each projectile will "live" until it is automatically destroyed, otherwise, the scene and memory would fill up quickly with lots of old projectiles!

There are also two public variables. One is for the reference to the sphere prefab, and the second is for the initial speed of newly instantiated prefabs.

There is also a private variable called `nextFireTime`—this is used to decide whether or not enough time has passed to allow a new projectile to be fired.

The `Update()` method tests the current time against the value of `nextFireTime`. If enough time has passed, then it will invoke the `CheckFireKey()` method.

The `CheckFireKey()` method tests to see if the **Fire1** button has been clicked. This is usually mapped to the left mouse button, but can be mapped to other input events through the **Project Settings** (navingate to **Edit | Project Settings | Input**). If the `Fire1` event is detected, then the next fire time is reset to be `FIRE_DELAY` seconds in the future, and a new projectile is created by invoking the `CreateProjectile()` method.

The `CreateProjectile()` method gets the current position and rotation of the parent **GameObject**. Remember that the instance object of this class has been added to **Cube-launcher**, so our scripted object can use the position and rotation of this launcher as the initial settings for each new projectile. A new instance of `projectilePrefab` is created with these position and rotation settings.

Next, a Vector3 called `projectileVelocity` is created by multiplying the `projectileSpeed` variable with the standard forward vector **(0, 0, 1)**. In Unity, for 3D objects, the Z-axis is generally the direction in which the object is facing.

The special method `TransformDirection(...)` is used to turn the local-space forward direction into a world-space direction so that we have a Vector representing a forward motion relative to the **Cube-launcher** object.

This world-space directional vector is then used to add a force to the projectile's **RigidBody**.

Finally, a reference is made to the parent **GameObject** of the projectile, and the `Destroy(...)` method is used so that the projectile will be destroyed after `1.5` seconds—the value of `PROJECTILE_LIFE`.

You can learn more about `Transform.TransformDirection()` at `https://docs.unity3d.com/ScriptReference/Transform.TransformDirection.html`.

13
Navigation Meshes and Agents

In this chapter, we will cover the following:

- NPC to travel to destination while avoiding obstacles
- NPC to seek or flee from a moving object
- Point-and-click move to object
- Point-and-click move to tile
- Point-and-click raycast with user-defined higher-cost Navigation Areas
- NPC to follow waypoints in sequence
- Controlling object group movement through flocking
- Creating a movable NavMesh Obstacle

Introduction

Unity provides **Navigation Meshes** and Artificial Intelligence (AI) Agents that can plan pathways and move objects along those calculated paths. **Pathfinding** is a classic AI task, and Unity has provided game developers with fast and efficient **Pathfinding** components that work out of the box.

Having objects that can automatically plot and follow paths from their current location to a desired destination point (or a moving object) provides the components to many different kinds of interactive game characters and mechanics. For example, we can create point-and-click games by clicking on a location or object, towards which we wish one or more characters to travel. Or, we can have enemies that "wake up" when our player's character is nearby, and move towards (seek) our player, perhaps then going into combat or dialogue mode once they are within a short distance of our player's character.

Or, objects can collectively flock together, moving as a swarm towards a common destination.

This chapter explores ways to exploit Unity's navigation-based AI components to control game character **Pathfinding** and movement.

The big picture

At the core of Unity's navigation system are two concepts/components:

- **Navigation Meshes**
- **Navigation Mesh Agents**

A Navigation **Mesh** defines the areas of the world that are navigable. It is usually represented as a set of polygons (2D shapes), so that a path to a destination is plotted as the most efficient sequence of adjacent polygons to follow, taking into account the need to avoid non-navigable obstacles.

The **Agent** is the object that needs to calculate (plot) a path through the mesh from its current position to its desired destination position. **NavMesh Agents** have properties such as a stopping distance, so they aim to arrive at a point a certain distance from the target coordinates, and auto braking, so they gradually slow down as they get close to their destination.

A **Navigation Mesh** can be made up of **Areas** that have different "costs." The default cost for an area is 1. However, to make a more realistic path calculation by AI Agent controlled characters, we might want to model the additional effort it takes to travel through water, or mud, or up a steep slope. Therefore, Unity allows us to define custom Areas, with names that we choose (such as Water or Mud), and associated costs, such as 2 (that is, water is twice as tiring to travel through).

Different navigable areas can be connected via **NavMesh Links**:

- `https://docs.unity3d.com/Manual/class-NavMeshLink.html`

Run-Time Nav Mesh Obstacles

The most efficient way for games to work with **Navigation Meshes** is to pre-calculate the costs of polygons in the game world; this is known as **Baking** and is performed at **Design-Time**, before we run the game.

However, sometimes there will be features in the game that we wish to use to influence navigation decisions and route planning differently at different times in the game, that is, dynamic Run-Time navigation obstacles. Unity provides a **NavMesh Obstacle** component, which can be added to GameObjects, and has features such as "carving out" (temporarily removing) areas of a **NavMesh** to force AI-Agents to recalculate paths that avoid areas blocked by GameObjects with **NavMesh Obstacle** components.

Source of further information about Unity and AI navigation

Some **NavMesh** features (such as **NavMesh Links** and dynamic mesh baking at **Run-Time**) are not part of the standard Unity installation and require additional installation. Learn more about these components, their APIs, and how to install them here:

- https://docs.unity3d.com/Manual/NavMesh-BuildingComponents.html
- https://docs.unity3d.com/Manual/NavMesh-BuildingComponents-API.html

Learn more about Unity **NavMeshes** from the Unity Technologies tutorial, which is available here:

- http://unity3d.com/learn/tutorials/modules/beginner/live-training-archive/navmeshes

Learn lots about computer-controlled moving GameObjects from the classic paper entitled **Steering Behaviors For Autonomous Characters** by Craig W. Reynolds, presented at the GDC-99 (Game Developer's Conference):

- http://www.red3d.com/cwr/steer/gdc99/

While the Unity development community have been asking for 2D **NavMeshes** for some years now, they've not yet been released as a core feature. There is a lot of online information about how to write your own **Pathfinding** system that would work in 2D. A good thread with plenty of links can be found at **TIGForums**:

- https://forums.tigsource.com/index.php?topic=46325.0

In this chapter, you'll learn how to add **NavMesh Agents** to control characters and how to work with your game environment to specify and bake **Navigation Meshes** for a scene. Some recipes explore how to create point-and-click style games, where you indicate where you want a character to navigate to by clicking on an object or point in the game world.

You'll create "swarms" of objects that move and flock together, and you'll also learn to add **NavMesh Obstacle** components to moving GameObjects, forcing AI agents to dynamically recalculate their paths at **Run-Time** due to objects moving in their way.

NPC to travel to destination while avoiding obstacles

The introduction of Unity's **NavMeshAgent** has greatly simplified the coding for NPC (Non-Player Character) and enemy agent behaviors. In this recipe, we'll add some wall obstacles (scaled cubes), and generate a **NavMesh** so that Unity knows not to try to walk through walls. We'll then add a **NavMeshAgent** component to our NPC GameObject, and tell it to head to a stated destination location by intelligently planning and following a path, while avoiding the wall obstacles.

When the **Navigation** panel is visible, then the **Scene** panel displays the blue-shaded walkable areas, as well as unshaded, non-walkable areas at the edge of the terrain and around each of the two wall objects:

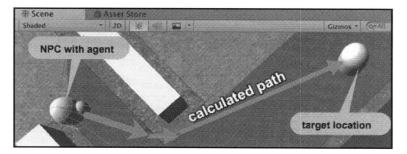

Getting ready

The required **Terrain TextureSandAlbedo** can be found in the 15_01 folder. Alternatively, you can go to **Assets | Import Package | Environments**, deselect everything, and then locate and tick this asset: **Assets/Environment/TerrainAssets/SurfaceTextures/SandAlbedo.psd**

How to do it...

To make an NPC to travel to a destination while avoiding obstacles, follow these steps:

1. Create a new, empty 3D project.
2. Create a new 3D **Terrain**, choose menu: **Create | 3D Object | Terrain**. With this new **Terrain** GameObject selected in the **Hierarchy**, in its **Inspector** properties set its size to **30 x 20**, and its position to **(-15, 0, -10)** so we have this GameObject centered at **(0,0,0)**.
3. Texture paint this terrain with the **SandAlbedo** texture.
4. Create a 3D **Capsule** named **Capsule-destination** at (-12, 0, 8). This will be the target destination for our NPC self-navigating GameObject.
5. Create a sphere named **Sphere-arrow** that is positioned at **(2, 0.5, 2)**. Scale it to **(1,1,1)**.
6. Create a second sphere named **Sphere-small**. Scale it to **(0.5, 0.5, 0.5)**.
7. In the **Hierarchy**, child **Sphere-small** to **Sphere-arrow** and position it at **(0, 0, 0.5)**:

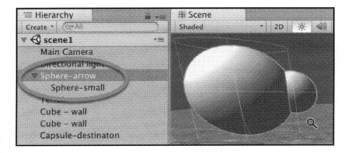

8. In the Inspector panel, add a new **NavMeshAgent** to **Sphere-arrow**. Do this by choosing menu: **Add Component | Navigation | Nav Mesh Agent**.

9. Set the **Stopping Distance** property of the **NavMeshAgent** component to **2**:

10. Create the `ArrowNPCMovement` C# script-class, and add an instance-object to the **Sphere-arrow** GameObject:

```
using UnityEngine;
using UnityEngine.AI;

public class ArrowNPCMovement : MonoBehaviour {
public GameObject targetGo;
private NavMeshAgent navMeshAgent;

void Start() {
navMeshAgent = GetComponent<NavMeshAgent>();
HeadForDestintation();
}

private void HeadForDestintation () {
Vector3 destination = targetGo.transform.position;
navMeshAgent.SetDestination (destination);
}
}
```

11. Ensure that **Sphere-arrow** is selected in the **Inspector** panel. For the **ArrowNPCMovement** scripted component, drag **Capsule-destination** over the **Target Go** variable.

12. Create a 3D **Cube** named **Cube-wall** at **(-6, 0, 0)**, and scale it to **(1, 2, 10)**.

13. Create another 3D **Cube** named **Cube-wall2** at **(-2, 0, 6)**, and scale it to **(1, 2, 7)**.

14. Display the **Navigation** panel by choosing menu: **Window | Navigation**.

> A great place to dock the **Navigation** panel is next to the **Inspector** panel since you will never be using the **Inspector** and **Navigation** panels at the same time.

15. In the **Hierarchy** panel, select both of the **Cube-wall** objects (we select the objects that are not supposed to be a part of the walkable parts of our scene), and then in the **Navigation** panel, click the **Object** button and check the **Navigation Static** checkbox:

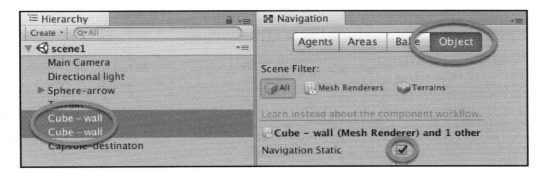

16. In the Inspector, click on the **Bake** button at the top for baking options. Then, click on the **Bake** button at the bottom-right to create your Navigation Mesh asset:

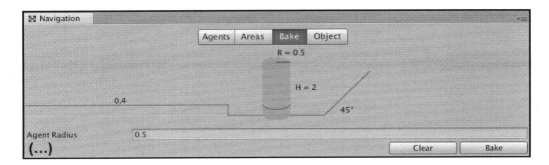

17. When the **Navigation** panel is displayed, you'll see a blue tint on the parts of the **Scene** that are areas for a **NavMeshAgent** to consider for its navigation paths.

18. Now, run your game. You will see the **Sphere-arrow** GameObject automatically move towards the **Capsule-destination** GameObject, following a path that avoids the two wall objects.

How it works...

The **NavMeshAgent** component that we added to **Sphere-arrow** GameObject does most of the work for us. **NavMeshAgents** need two things:

- A destination location to head towards
- ANavMesh component of the terrain with walkable/non-walkable areas, so that it can plan a path by avoiding obstacles

We created two obstacles (the **Cube-wall** objects), and these were selected when we created the **NavMesh** for this scene in the **Navigation** panel. When the **Navigation** panel is displayed, at the same time in the **Scene** panel (and the **Game** panel with **Gizmos** enabled), we see walkable areas forming a blue navigation mesh.

Note: The blue areas are the default **NavMesh Area**. See, later in this chapter, a recipe for different, custom named, costed, color-coded **NavMesh Areas**.

The location for our NPC object to travel towards is the position of the **Capsule-destination** GameObject at **(-12, 0, 8)**; but, of course we could just move this object in the **Scene** panel at **Design-Time**, and its new position would be the destination when we run the game.

The ArrowNPCMovement C# script class has two variables: one is a reference to the destination GameObject, and the second is a reference to the **NavMeshAgent** component of the GameObject, in which our instance of the ArrowNPCMovement class is also a component. When the scene starts, the **NavMeshAgent** sibling component is found via the Start() method, and the HeadForDestination() method is called, which sets the destination of the **NavMeshAgent** to the position of the destination GameObject.

Once the **NavMeshAgent** has a target to head towards, it will plan a path there and will keep moving until it arrives (or gets within the **Stopping Distance** if that parameter has been set to a distance greater than zero).

In the **Scene** panel, if you select the GameObject that contains the **NavMeshAgent** and choose the **Show Avoidance Gizmo**, then you can see the candidate local target positions the agent is considering. The lighter the squares are, the better a position ranks.

The darker red the squares are, the less desirable the position; so, dark red squares indicate positions to avoid, since they might, for instance, cause the agent to collide with a **NavMesh Static** obstacle:

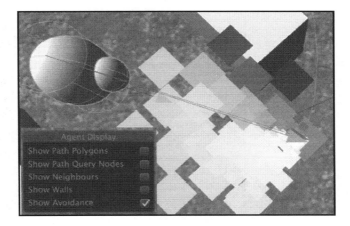

Ensure that the object with the **NavMeshAgent** component is selected in the **Hierarchy** panel at **Run-Time** to be able to see this navigation data in the **Scene** panel.

NPC to seek or flee from a moving object

Rather than a destination that is fixed when the scene starts, let's allow the **Capsule-destination** object to be moved by the player while the scene is running. In every frame, we'll get our NPC arrow to reset the **NavMeshAgent's** destination to wherever **Capsule-destination** has been moved to.

Getting ready

This recipe adds to the previous one, so make a copy of that project folder and do your work for this recipe with that copy.

How to do it...

To make an NPC seek or flee from a moving object, follow these steps:

1. In the **Inspector,** add a **Rigid Body Physics** component to **GameObject Capsule-destination**.

2. In the Inspector, for the **Capsule-destination** GameObject, check the **Freeze Position** constraint for the Y axis in the **Constraints** options of the **RigidBody** component. This will prevent the object moving in the Y-axis due to collisions when being moved.

3. Create the `SimplePlayerControl` C# script-class, and add an instance-object as a component to the **Capsule-destination** GameObject:

```
using UnityEngine;

public class SimplePlayerControl : MonoBehaviour {
public float speed = 1000;
private Rigidbody rigidBody;
private Vector3 newVelocity;

private void Start() {
rigidBody = GetComponent<Rigidbody>();
}

void Update() {
   float xMove = Input.GetAxis("Horizontal") * speed *
Time.deltaTime;
   float zMove = Input.GetAxis("Vertical") * speed *
Time.deltaTime;
   newVelocity = new Vector3(xMove, 0, zMove);
}

void FixedUpdate() {
   rigidBody.velocity = newVelocity;
}
}
```

4. Update the `ArrowNPCMovement` C# script-class so that we call the `HeadForDestintation()` method every frame, that is, from `Update()`, rather than just once in `Start()`:

```
void Start() {
    navMeshAgent = GetComponent<NavMeshAgent>();
}

private void Update() {
```

```
    HeadForDestintation();
}
```

How it works...

The `SimplePlayerControl` script-class detects arrow key presses and translates them into a force to apply to move the **Capsule-destination** GameObject in the desired direction.

The `Update()` method of the `ArrowNPCMovement` script-class makes the **NavMeshAgent** update its path **every** frame, based on the current position of the **Capsule-destination** GameObject. As the user moves **Capsule-destination**, so the **NavMeshAgent** calculates a new path to the object.

There's more

Here are some details that you don't want to miss.

Using a Debug Ray to show a source-to-destination line

It's useful to use a visual **Debug Ray** to show us the straight line from the NPC with the **NavMeshAgent** to the current destination it is trying to navigate towards. Since this is a common thing we may wish to do for many games, it's useful to create a static method in a general-purpose class, and then the ray can be drawn with a single statement.

To use a **Debug Ray** to draw a source-to-destination line, follow these steps:

1. Create a `UsefulFunctions.cs` C# script-class, containing the following:

```
using UnityEngine;

public class UsefulFunctions : MonoBehaviour {
 public static void DebugRay(Vector3 origin, Vector3
destination, Color c) {
 Vector3 direction = destination - origin;
 Debug.DrawRay(origin, direction, c);
 }
 }
```

2. Now, add a statement at the end of
   the HeadForDestination() method in the NPCMovement C# script-class:

```
private void HeadForDestintation () {
Vector3 destination = targetGo.transform.position;
navMeshAgent.SetDestination (destination);
// show yellow line from source to target
 UsefulFunctions.DebugRay(transform.position, destination,
Color.yellow);
 }
```

We can now see a yellow line in the **Scene** panel when the scene is running. We can also see this in the **Game** panel if the **Gizmos** option is selected (top-right of the **Game** panel title bar):

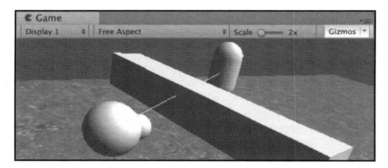

Constantly updating NavMeshAgent destination to flee from Player's current location

There are times when we want an AI-controlled NPC character to move **away** from another character, rather than go towards it. For example, an enemy with very low health might run away, and so gain time to regain its health before fighting again. Or, a wild animal might flee from any other character moving near it.

To instruct our **NavMeshAgent** to flee from the player's location, we need to replace the ArrowNPCMovement C# script class with the following:

```
using UnityEngine;
using UnityEngine.AI;

public class ArrowNPCMovement : MonoBehaviour {
public float runAwayDistance = 10;
public GameObject targetGO;
```

```
  private NavMeshAgent navMeshAgent;

void Start() {
 navMeshAgent = GetComponent<NavMeshAgent>();
 }

void Update() {
 Vector3 targetPosition = targetGO.transform.position;
 float distanceToTarget = Vector3.Distance(transform.position,
targetPosition);
 if (distanceToTarget < runAwayDistance)
 FleeFromTarget(targetPosition);
 }

private void FleeFromTarget(Vector3 targetPosition) {
 Vector3 destination = PositionToFleeTowards(targetPosition);
 HeadForDestintation(destination);
 }

private void HeadForDestintation (Vector3 destinationPosition) {
 navMeshAgent.SetDestination (destinationPosition);
 }

private Vector3 PositionToFleeTowards(Vector3 targetPosition) {
 transform.rotation = Quaternion.LookRotation(transform.position -
targetPosition);
 Vector3 runToPosition = targetPosition + (transform.forward *
runAwayDistance);
 return runToPosition;
 }
 }
```

There is a public variable, runAwayDistance. When the distance to the enemy is less than the value of this runAwayDistance variable, then we'll instruct the computer-controlled object to flee in the opposite direction.

The Start() method caches a reference to the **NavMeshAgent** component.

The Update() method calculates whether the distance to the enemy is within runAwayDistance, and if so, it calls the FleeFromTarget(...) method, which passes the location of the enemy as a parameter.

The FleeFromTarget(...) method calculates a point that is the runAwayDistance in Unity units away from the Player's cube, in a direction that is directly away from the computer-controlled object. This is achieved by subtracting the enemy position vector from the current transform's position.

Finally, the `HeadForDestintation(...)` method is called, passing the flee-to position, which results in the **NavMeshAgent** being told to set the location as its new destination.

Unity units are arbitrary, since they are just numbers on a computer. However, in most cases, it simplifies things to think of distances in terms of meters (1 Unity unit = 1 meter), and mass in terms of kilograms (1 Unity unit = 1 kilogram). Of course, if your game is based on a microscopic world, or pan-galactic space travel, then you need to decide what each Unity unit corresponds to for your game context. For further discussion of units in Unity, check out this post about Unity measurements: `http://forum.unity3d.com/threads/best-units-of-measurement-in-unity.284133/#post-1875487`.

The **Debug Ray** shows the point the NPC is aiming for, whether it be to flee away from the player's character, or to catch up and maintain a constant distance from it:

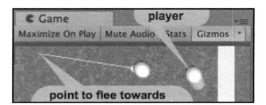

Maintain constant distance from target ("lurking" mode!)

It is simple to adapt the previous code to have an NPC try to maintain a constant distance from a target object. It involves always moving towards a point that is `runAwayDistance` away from the target, regardless of whether this point is towards or away from the target.

Just remove the `If` statement in the `Update()` method:

```
void Update() {
  Vector3 targetPosition = targetGO.transform.position;
  float distanceToTarget = Vector3.Distance(transform.position,
targetPosition);
  FleeFromTarget(targetPosition);
  }
```

However, with this variation, it might be better to have the method named something like `MoveTowardsConstantDistancePoint()` rather than `FleeFromTarget()`, since our NPC is sometimes fleeing and sometimes following.

Point-and-click move to object

Another way to choose the destination for our **Sphere-arrow** GameObject is by the user clicking on an object on the screen, and then the **Sphere-arrow** GameObject moving to the location of the clicked object:

Getting ready

This recipe adds to the first recipe in this chapter, so make a copy of that project folder and do your work for this recipe with that copy.

How to do it...

To create an object-based point-and-click mini-game, do the following:

1. In the **Inspector,** add the **Player** Tag to the **Sphere-arrow** GameObject.
2. Delete the two 3D **Cubes** and the 3D **Capsule-destination** from the scene.
3. Create a `ClickMeToSetDestination` C# script-class containing the following:

```
using UnityEngine;

public class ClickMeToSetDestination : MonoBehaviour
  {
  private UnityEngine.AI.NavMeshAgent playerNavMeshAgent;

void Start() {
  GameObject playerGO =
GameObject.FindGameObjectWithTag("Player");
```

```
  playerNavMeshAgent =
playerGO.GetComponent<UnityEngine.AI.NavMeshAgent>();
  }

  private void OnMouseDown() {
  playerNavMeshAgent.SetDestination(transform.position);
  }
  }
```

4. Add instance-objects of the `ClickMeToSetDestination` C# script-class as components to your 3D **Cube**, **Sphere,** and Cylinder.
5. Run the **Scene**. When you click on one of the 3D objects, the **Sphere-arrow** GameObject should navigate towards the clicked object.

How it works...

The `OnMouseDown()` method of the `ClickMeToSetDestination` C# script-class changes the destination of the **NavMeshAgent** in the **Sphere-arrow** GameObject to be the position of the clicked 3D object.

The `Start()` method of the `ClickMeToSetDestination` C# script-class gets a reference to the **NavMeshAgent** component of the GameObject tagged **Player** (that is, the **Sphere-arrow** GameObject).

Each time a different object is clicked, the **NavMeshAgent** inside the **Sphere-arrow** GameObject is updated to make the GameObject move towards the position of the clicked object.

There's more

There are some details that you don't want to miss.

Creating a mouse-over yellow highlight

A good UX (**User Experience**) feedback technique is to visually indicate to the user when an object can be interacted with via the mouse. A common way to do this is to present an audio or visual effect when the mouse is moved over an interactable object.

We can create a **Material** with a yellow color, which can make an object appear yellow while the mouse is over it, and then return to its original material when the mouse is moved away.

Create the `MouseOverHighlighter` C# script-class with the following contents. Then, add an instance-object as a component to each of the three 3D GameObjects:

```
using UnityEngine;

public class MouseOverHighlighter : MonoBehaviour
  {
  private MeshRenderer meshRenderer;
  private Material originalMaterial;

void Start() {
  meshRenderer = GetComponent<MeshRenderer>();
  originalMaterial = meshRenderer.sharedMaterial;
  }

void OnMouseOver() {
  meshRenderer.sharedMaterial = NewMaterialWithColor(Color.yellow);
  }

void OnMouseExit() {
  meshRenderer.sharedMaterial = originalMaterial;
  }

private Material NewMaterialWithColor(Color newColor) {
  Shader shaderSpecular = Shader.Find("Specular");
  Material material = new Material(shaderSpecular);
  material.color = newColor;

return material;
  }
  }
```

Now, when running the game, when your mouse is over one of the three objects, that object will be highlighted yellow. If you click on the mouse button when the object is highlighted, the **Sphere-arrow** GameObject will make its way up to (but stop just before) the clicked object.

Point-and-click move to tile

Rather than clicking specific objects to indicate the target for our AI-controlled agent, we can create a grid of 3D **Plane** (tile) objects to allow the player to click any tile to indicate a destination for the AI-controller character. So, any location can be clicked, rather than only one of a few specific objects:

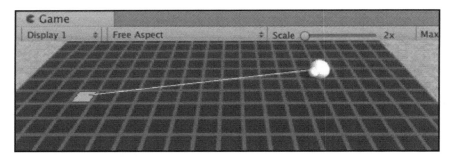

Getting ready

This recipe adds to the previous one, so make a copy of that project folder and do your work for this recipe with that copy.

For this recipe, we have prepared a red-outlined black square **Texture** image named **square_outline.png** in a folder named **Textures** in the 15_04 folder.

How to do it...

To create a point-and-click game making GameObjects to a selected tile, do the following:

1. Delete your 3D **Cube**, **Sphere**, and **Cylinder** GameObjects from the scene.
2. Create a new 3D **Plane** object, scaled to (**0.1, 0.1, 0.1**).
3. Create a new **Material** with the **Texture** image **square_outline.png** provided (black square with a red outline). Apply this **Material** to your 3D **Plane**.
4. Add an instance-object of the ClickMeToSetDestination script-class as a component to your 3D **Plane**.
5. In the **Project** panel, create a new empty Prefab named **tile**.

6. Populate your Prefab **tile** with the properties of your 3D **Plane** GameObject by dragging the plane GameObject over your Prefab **tile** (it should change from white to blue to indicate the Prefab now has the properties of your GameObject).

7. Delete your 3D **Plane** GameObject from the scene.

8. Create a new `TileManager` C# script-class containing the following, and add an instance-object as a component to the **Main Camera** GameObject:

```
using UnityEngine;

public class TileManager : MonoBehaviour {
 public int rows = 50;
 public int cols = 50;
 public GameObject prefabClickableTile;

void Start () {
 for (int r = 0; r < rows; r++) {
 for (int c = 0; c < cols; c++) {
 float y = 0.01f;
 Vector3 pos = new Vector3(r - rows/2, y, c - cols/2);
 Instantiate(prefabClickableTile, pos, Quaternion.identity);
 }
 }
 }
}
```

9. Select the **Main Camera** in the **Hierarchy**, and in the **Inspector** for the **Tile Manager (Script)** component, populate the **Prefab Clickable Tile** public property with your Prefab **tile** from the **Project** panel.

10. Run the scene. You should now be able to click on any of the small square tiles to set the destination of the **NavMeshAgent** controlled **Sphere-arrow** GameObject.

How it works...

You created a Prefab, containing the properties of a 3D **Plane** named **tile**, which contained a component instance-object of the `ClickMeToSetDestination` C# script-class.

The `TileManager` script class loops to create 50 x 50 instances of this **tile** Gameobject in the **Scene**.

When you run the game, if you click on the mouse button when the mouse pointer is over a tile, the NavMeshAgent inside the **Sphere-arrow** GameObject is set to that tile's position. So, the **Sphere-arrow** GameObject will move towards, but stop just before reaching, the clicked tile position.

The **Y** value of **0.01** means the plane will be just above the **Terrain**, so we avoid any kind of Moire interference pattern due to meshes at the same location. By subtracting rows/2 and cols/2 for the **X** and **Z** positions, we center our grid of tiles at (**0, Y, 0**).

There's more

There are some details that you don't want to miss.

Yellow debug-ray to show destination of AI-agent

We can show a debug ray from a moving object to its destination tile by creating the MouseOverHighlighter C# script-class with the following contents. We then add an instance-object as a component to the **NavMeshAgent** controlled **Sphere-arrow** GameObject:

```
using UnityEngine;
  using UnityEngine.AI;

public class DebugRaySourceDestination : MonoBehaviour {
  void Update() {
  Vector3 origin = transform.position;
  Vector3 destination = GetComponent<NavMeshAgent>().destination;
  Vector3 direction = destination - origin;
  Debug.DrawRay(origin, direction, Color.yellow);
  }
  }
```

Point-and-click Raycast with user-defined higher-cost Navigation Areas

Rather than indicating a desired destination by clicking an object or tile, we can use Unity's built-in Physics.Raycast(...) method to identify which Vector3 (x,y,z) position relates to the object surface in the game.

This involves translating from the 2D (x,y) screen position to an imagined 3D "ray" from the user's point of view, through the screen, into the game world, and identifying which object (polygon) it **hits** first.

This recipe uses `Physics.Raycast` to set the position of the location clicked on as the new destination for a **NavMeshAgent** controller object. The actual route followed can be influenced by defining **Navigation Mesh Areas** of different costs. For example, walking through mud or swimming through water can have a higher cost, since they would take longer, so the AI **NavMeshAgent** can calculate the lowest-cost route, which may not be the shortest distance route in the scene:

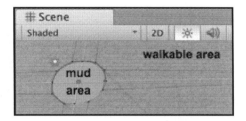

Getting ready

This recipe adds to the previous one, so make a copy of that project folder and do your work for this recipe with that copy.

How to do it...

To create a point-and-click game using a **Raycast**, do the following:

1. Remove the **Tile Manager (Script)** component from the **Main Camera** GameObject.
2. Create a new 3D **Sphere**, named **Sphere-destination**, scaled to (0.5, 0.5, 0.5).
3. Create a new **Material** that is red in color, and assign this material to the **Sphere-destination** GameObject.

4. Create a new `MoveToClickPoint` C# script-class containing the following, and add an instance-object as a component to the Sphere-arrow GameObject:

```
using UnityEngine;
using UnityEngine.AI;

public class MoveToClickPoint : MonoBehaviour {
  public GameObject sphereDestination;
  private NavMeshAgent navMeshAgent;
  private RaycastHit hit;

void Start() {
  navMeshAgent = GetComponent<NavMeshAgent>();
  sphereDestination.transform.position = transform.position;
  }

void Update() {
  Ray rayFromMouseClick =
Camera.main.ScreenPointToRay(Input.mousePosition);

if (FireRayCast(rayFromMouseClick)){
  Vector3 rayPoint = hit.point;
  ProcessRayHit(rayPoint);
  }
  }

private void ProcessRayHit(Vector3 rayPoint) {
  if(Input.GetMouseButtonDown(0)) {
  navMeshAgent.destination = rayPoint;
  sphereDestination.transform.position = rayPoint;
  }
  }

private bool FireRayCast(Ray rayFromMouseClick) {
  return Physics.Raycast(rayFromMouseClick, out hit, 100);
  }
  }
```

5. Select the Sphere-arrow GameObject in the **Hierarchy**, and in the **Inspector** for the **MoveToClickPoint (Script)** component, populate the **Sphere Destination** public property with your red **Sphere-destination** GameObject.

6. Run the scene. You should now be able to click anywhere on the **Terrain** to set the destination of the **NavMeshAgent** controlled **Sphere-arrow** GameObject. As you click, the red **Sphere-destination** GameObject should be positioned at this new destination point, towards which the **Sphere-arrow** GameObject will navigate.

How it works...

You created a small red 3D **Sphere** named **Sphere-destination**.

There is one public variable for the `MoveToClickPoint` scripted component of the Sphere-arrow GameObject. This public `sphereDestination` variable has been linked to the red **Sphere-destination** GameObject in the scene.

There are two private variables:

- `navMeshAgent`: This will be set to refer to the **NavMeshAgent** component of the Sphere-arrow GameObject, so its destination can be reset when appropriate.
- `hit`: This is a `RaycastHit` object, which is passed in as the object to be set by `Physics.Raycast(...)`. Various properties of this object are set after a **Raycast** has been created, including the position in the scene where the **Raycast** hit the surface of an object.

The `Start()` method caches a reference to the **NavMesh** component of the Sphere-arrow GameObject, and also moves the **Sphere-destination** GameObject to the current object's location.

Each frame, in the `Update()` method, a Ray is created based on the **Main Camera** and the (2,y) point clicked on the screen. This **Ray** is passed as a parameter to the `FireRayCast(...)` method. If that method returns true, then the position of the object hit is extracted and passed to the `ProcessRayHit(...)` method.

The `FireRayCast(...)` method receives a Ray object. It uses `Phyics.Raycast(...)` to determine whether the **Raycast** collides with part of an object in the scene. If the **Raycast** hits something, the properties of the `RaycastHit` `hit` object are updated. A true/false for whether `Physics.Raycast(...)` hit a surface is returned by this method.

Each time the user clicks on the screen, the corresponding object in the scene is identified with the **Raycast**, the red sphere is moved there, and the **NavMeshAgent** begins to navigate towards that location.

Learn more about the Unity **Raycast** C# script-class at `https://docs.unity3d.com/ScriptReference/RaycastHit.html`.

There's more

Here are some details that you won't want to miss.

More intelligent pathfinding by setting different costs for custom-defined navigation areas such as Mud and Water

We can create objects whose meshes are defined as more expensive for **NavMeshAgents** to travel across, helping AI-agent behavior be more realistic in terms of choosing faster paths that avoid Water, Mud, and so on.

To create a custom **NavMesh Area** (we'll pretend it's mud) with a higher travelling cost, do the following:

1. In the **Navigation** panel, reveal the areas by clicking the **Areas** button. Then, define a new area named **Mud** with a cost of **2**:

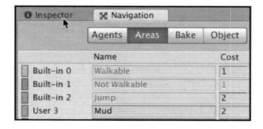

2. Create a new 3D **Cylinder** named **Cylinder-mud**, positioned at (0, -4.9, 0) and scaled to (5,5,5).
3. Ensure the **Cylinder-mud** GameObject is selected in the Hierarchy, and that the **Navigation** panel is displayed.

4. In the **Navigation** panel, click the **Object** button, check **Navigation Static**, and choose **Mud** from the **Navigation Area** drop-down list:

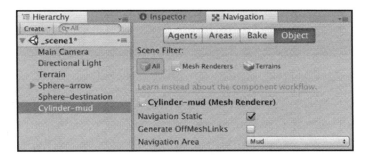

5. Now, click the **Bake** button to show the **NavigationBake** sub-panel, and then in this sub-panel click the **Bake** button to regenerate the **Navigation Mesh** with the new object.

Now, if you click to move the Sphere-arrow GameObject near the edge of the **Cylinder-mud** area, then, say, click on the opposite side, you'll see the **NavMeshAgent** make the Sphere-arrow GameObject follow a semi-circular (lowest cost) path around the edge of the **Cylinder-mud** area, rather than follow a direct line (as the crow flies) path *through* the higher cost mud area:

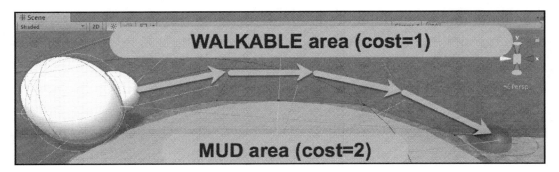

Improving UX by updating a "gaze" cursor each frame

It's nice to know where our destination will be set to **before** we click the mouse. So, let's add a yellow sphere to show the 'candidate' destination for where our **Raycast** is hitting a surface, updated each frame as we move the mouse.

So, we need to create a second, yellow sphere. We also need to create a **Layer** to ignore; otherwise, if we move the yellow sphere to the point where a **Raycast** hits a surface, then in the next frame our **Raycast** will hit the surface of our yellow sphere - moving it closer and closer to us each frame!

To improve UX by updating a "gaze" cursor each frame, do the following:

1. Create a new yellow **Material** named **m_yellow**.
2. Create a second 3D **Sphere**, named **Sphere-destination-candidate** and textured with **m_yellow**.
3. Create a new Layer, **UISpheres**.
4. Set the **Layer** for both **Sphere-destination** and **Sphere-destination-candidate** GameObjects to **LayerUISpheres**.
5. Modify the `MoveToClickPoint` C# script-class as follows to add a new public variable, `sphereDestinationCandidate`:

```
public class MoveToClickPoint : MonoBehaviour {
public GameObject sphereDestination;
public GameObject sphereDestinationCandidate;
```

6. Modify the `MoveToClickPoint` C# script-class as follows to add an **Else-clause to the logic in the** `ProcessRayHit(...)` **method, so that if the mouse is** not clicked, then the yellow **sphereDestinationCandidate** object is moved to where the **Raycast** hit a surface:

```
private void ProcessRayHit(Vector3 rayPoint) {
if(Input.GetMouseButtonDown(0)) {
navMeshAgent.destination = rayPoint;
sphereDestination.transform.position = rayPoint;
} else {
sphereDestinationCandidate.transform.position = rayPoint;
}
}
```

7. Modify the `MoveToClickPoint` C# script-class as follows, so that a `LayerMask` is created to ignore **Layer UISpheres**, and passed as a parameter when `Physics.Raycast(...)` is invoked:

```
private bool FireRayCast(Ray rayFromMouseClick) {
LayerMask layerMask = ~LayerMask.GetMask("UISpheres");
return Physics.Raycast(rayFromMouseClick, out hit, 100,
layerMask.value);
}
```

8. Select the Sphere-arrow GameObject in the **Hierarchy**, and in the **Inspector** for the **MoveToClickPoint (Script)** component, populate the **Sphere Destination Candidate** public property with your yellow **Sphere-destination-candidate** GameObject.

9. Run the scene. You should now be able to click anywhere on the **Terrain** to set the destination of the **NavMeshAgent** controlled **Sphere-arrow** GameObject. As you click, the red **Sphere-destination** GameObject should be positioned at this new destination point, towards which the **Sphere-arrow** GameObject will navigate.

We have set a `LayerMask` using the `~LayerMask.GetMask("UISpheres")` statement, which means every layer apart from the named one. This is passed to the `Raycast(...)` method, so that our red and yellow **Spheres** are ignored when casting the ray and looking to see which surface the ray hits first.

NPC NavMeshAgent to follow waypoints in a sequence

Waypoints are often used as a guide to make autonomously moving NPCs and enemies follow a path in a general way, but be able to respond with other directional behaviors, such as flee or seek, if friends/predators/prey are sensed nearby. The waypoints are arranged in a sequence, so that when the character reaches or gets close to a waypoint, it will then select the next waypoint in the sequence as the target location to move towards. This recipe demonstrates an arrow object moving towards a waypoint, and then when it gets close enough, it will choose the next waypoint in the sequence as the new target destination. When the last waypoint has been reached, it again starts heading towards the first waypoint.

Since Unity's **NavMeshAgent** has simplified coding NPC behavior, our work in this recipe basically becomes finding the position of the next waypoint and then telling the **NavMeshAgent** that this waypoint is its new destination:

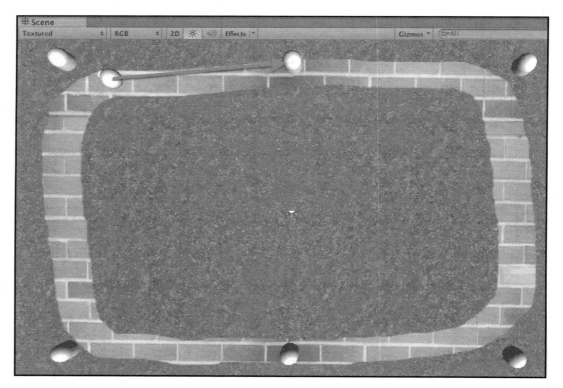

Getting ready

This recipe adds to the first recipe in this chapter, so make a copy of that project folder and do your work for this recipe with that copy.

For this recipe, we have prepared the yellow brick texture image that you need in a folder named **Textures** in the 1362_08_06 folder.

How to do it...

To instruct an object to follow a sequence of waypoints, follow these steps:

1. Replace the contents of the `ArrowNPCMovement` C# script class with the following:

```
using UnityEngine;
 using UnityEngine.AI;

public class ArrowNPCMovement : MonoBehaviour {
 private GameObject targetGo = null;
 private WaypointManager waypointManager;
 private NavMeshAgent navMeshAgent;

void Start () {
 navMeshAgent = GetComponent<NavMeshAgent>();
 waypointManager = GetComponent<WaypointManager>();
 HeadForNextWayPoint();
 }

void Update () {
 float closeToDestinaton = navMeshAgent.stoppingDistance * 2;
 if (navMeshAgent.remainingDistance < closeToDestinaton) {
 HeadForNextWayPoint ();
 }
 }

private void HeadForNextWayPoint () {
 targetGo = waypointManager.NextWaypoint (targetGo);
 navMeshAgent.SetDestination (targetGo.transform.position);
 }
 }
```

2. Create a new 3D **Capsule** object named **Capsule-waypoint-0** at **(-12, 0, 8)**.

3. Copy **Capsule-waypoint-0**, name the copy **Capsule-waypoint-3**, and position this copy at **(8, 0, -8)**.

 We are going to add some intermediate waypoints numbered 1 and 2 later on. This is why our second waypoint here is numbered 3, in case you were wondering.

4. Create the `WaypointManager` C# script class with the following contents, and add an instance-object as a component to the Sphere-arrow GameObject:

```
using UnityEngine;

public class WaypointManager : MonoBehaviour {
public GameObject wayPoint0;
public GameObject wayPoint3;

public GameObject NextWaypoint(GameObject current) {
if(current == wayPoint0)
return wayPoint3;

return wayPoint0;
}
}
```

5. Ensure that **Sphere-arrow** is selected in the Inspector for the `WaypointManager` scripted component. Drag **Capsule-waypoint-0** and **Capsule-waypoint-3** over the public variable projectiles called **Way Point 0** and **Way Point 3**, respectively.

6. Now, run your game. The arrow object will first move towards one of the waypoint capsules, then when it gets close to it, it will slow down, turn around, head towards the other waypoint capsule, and keep doing that continuously.

How it works...

The **NavMeshAgent** component that we added to the **Sphere-arrow** GameObject does most of the work for us. **NavMeshAgent** needs two things:

- A destination location to head towards
- A **NavMesh**, so that it can plan a path and avoid obstacles

We created two possible waypoints as the locations for our NPC to move towards: **Capsule-waypoint-0** and **Capsule-waypoint-3**.

The C# script class called `WaypointManager` has one job: to return a reference to the next waypoint that our NPC should head towards. There are two variables, `wayPoint0` and `wayPoint3`, which reference the two waypoint GameObjects in our scene. The `NextWaypoint(...)` method takes a single parameter named current, which is a reference to the current waypoint that the object is moving towards (or `null`). This method's task is to return a reference to the next waypoint that the NPC should travel towards. The logic for this method is simple: if current refers to waypoint0, then we'll return `waypoint3`; otherwise, we'll return `waypoint0`. Note that if we pass this method `null`, then we'll get `waypoint0` back (so, it is our default first waypoint).

The `ArrowNPCMovement` C# script class has three variables. One is a reference to the destination GameObject named `targetGo`. The second is a reference to the `NavMeshAgent` component of the GameObject in which our instance of the class called `ArrowNPCMovement` is also a component. The third variable, called `waypointManager`, is a reference to the sibling scripted component, an instance of our `WaypointManager` script class.

When the scene starts via the `Start()` method, the **NavMeshAgent** and **WaypointManager** sibling components are found, and the `HeadForDestination()` method is called.

The `HeadForDestination()` method first sets the variable called `targetGO` to refer to the GameObject that is returned by a call to the `NextWaypoint(...)` of the scripted component called **WaypointManager** (that is, `targetGo` is set to refer to either **Capsule-waypoint-0** or **Capsule-waypoint-3**). Next, it instructs the `NavMeshAgent` to make its destination the position of the `targetGO` GameObject.

Each frame method called `Update()` is called. A test is made to see whether the distance from the NPC arrow object is close to the destination waypoint. If the distance is smaller than twice the stopping distance set in our **NavMeshAgent**, then a call is made to `WaypointManager.NextWaypoint(...)` to update our target destination to be the next waypoint in the sequence.

There's more...

Here are some details that you won't want to miss.

Working with arrays of waypoints

Having a separate `WaypointManager` C# script-class to simply swap between **Capsule-waypoint-0** and **Capsule-waypoint-3** may have seemed to be a bit heavy duty and a case of over-engineering, but this was actually a very good move. An instance-object of the `WaypointManager` script-class has the job of returning the next waypoint. It is now very straightforward to add the more sophisticated approach of having an array of waypoints, without us having to change any code in the `ArrowNPCMovement` C# script-class. We can choose a random waypoint to be the next destination; for example, see the *Choosing destinations - find nearest (or a random) spawnpoint* recipe in `Chapter 14`, *Choosing and Controlling Positions*. Or, we can have an array of waypoints and choose the next one in the sequence.

To improve our game so that it works with an array of waypoints to be followed in sequence, we need to do the following:

1. Copy **Capsule-waypoint-0**, name the copy **Capsule-waypoint-1**, and position this copy at **(0, 0, 8)**.

2. Make four more copies (named **Capsule-waypoint-1, 2, 4, 5**), and position them as follows:
   - **Capsule-waypoint-1**: Position = **(-2, 0, 8)**
   - **Capsule-waypoint-2**: Position = **(8, 0, 8)**
   - **Capsule-waypoint-4**: Position = **(-2, 0, -8)**
   - **Capsule-waypoint-5**: Position = **(-12, 0, -8)**

3. Replace the `WaypointManager` C# script-class with the following code:

```
using UnityEngine;
using System;

public class WaypointManager : MonoBehaviour {
 public GameObject[] waypoints;

public GameObject NextWaypoint (GameObject current) {
 if( waypoints.Length < 1 )
 Debug.LogError ("WaypointManager:: ERROR - no waypoints have
been added to array!");

 int currentIndex = Array.IndexOf(waypoints, current);
 int nextIndex = (currentIndex + 1) % waypoints.Length;

return waypoints[nextIndex];
 }
 }
```

4. Ensure that **Sphere-arrow** is selected. In the **Inspector** panel for the `WaypointManager` scripted component, set the size of the Waypoints array to 6. Now, drag in all six capsule waypoint objects called **Capsule-waypoint-0/1/2/3/4/5**.

5. Run the game. Now, the **Sphere-arrow** GameObject will first move towards waypoint 0 (top left), and then follow the sequence around the terrain.

6. Finally, you can make it look as if the **Sphere** is following a yellow brick road. Import the provided yellow brick texture, add this to your terrain, and paint the texture to create an oval-shaped path between the waypoints. You may also uncheck the **Mesh Renderer** component for each waypoint capsule, so that the user does not see any of the waypoints, just the arrow object following the yellow brick road.

In the `NextWaypoint(...)` method, first we check in case the array is empty, in which case an error is logged. Next, the array index for the current `waypoint` GameObject is found (if present in the array). Finally, the array index for the next waypoint is calculated using a modulus operator to support a cyclic sequence, returning to the beginning of the array after the last element has been visited.

Increased flexibility with a WayPoint class

Rather than forcing a GameObject to follow a single rigid sequence of locations, we can make things more flexible by defining a `WayPoint` class where each waypoint GameObject has an array of possible destinations, and each of these has its own array. In this way, a digraph (directed graph) can be implemented, of which a linear sequence is just one possible instance.

To improve our game and make it work with a digraph of waypoints, do the following:

1. Remove the scripted `WayPointManager` component from the **Sphere-arrow** GameObject.

2. Replace the `ArrowNPCMovement` C# script-class with the following code:

```
using UnityEngine;
using System.Collections;

public class ArrowNPCMovement : MonoBehaviour {
public Waypoint waypoint;
private bool firstWayPoint = true;
private NavMeshAgent navMeshAgent;
```

```
void Start () {
navMeshAgent = GetComponent<NavMeshAgent>();
HeadForNextWayPoint();
}

void Update () {
float closeToDestinaton = navMeshAgent.stoppingDistance * 2;
if (navMeshAgent.remainingDistance < closeToDestinaton){
HeadForNextWayPoint ();
}
}

private void HeadForNextWayPoint (){
if(firstWayPoint)
firstWayPoint = false;
else
waypoint = waypoint.GetNextWaypoint();

Vector3 target = waypoint.transform.position;
navMeshAgent.SetDestination (target);
}
}
```

3. Create a new `WayPoint` C# script-class containing the following code:

```
using UnityEngine;
using System.Collections;

public class Waypoint: MonoBehaviour {
public Waypoint[] waypoints;

public Waypoint GetNextWaypoint () {
return waypoints[ Random.Range(0, waypoints.Length) ];
}
}
```

4. Select all six GameObjects called **Capsule-waypoint -0/1/2/3/4/5** and add to them an instance-object component of the `WayPoint` C# class.

5. Select the **Sphere-arrow** GameObject and add to it an instance-object component of the `WayPoint` C# class.

6. Ensure that the **Sphere-arrow** GameObject is selected. In the **Inspector** panel for the ArrowNPCMovement scripted component, drag **Capsule-waypoint-0** into the `Waypoint` public variable slot.

7. Now, we need to link **Capsule-waypoint-0** to **Capsule-waypoint-1**, **Capsule-waypoint-1** to **Capsule-waypoint -2**, and so on. Select **Capsule-waypoint-0**, set its **Waypoints** array size to **1**, and drag in **Capsule-waypoint-1**. Next, select **Capsule-waypoint-1**, set its **Waypoints** array size to **1**, and drag in **Capsule-waypoint-2**. Continue in this way until you finally link **Capsule-waypoint-5** back to **Capsule-waypoint-0**.

You now have a much more flexible game architecture, allowing GameObjects to randomly select one of several different paths at each waypoint reached. In this recipe variation, we have implemented a waypoint sequence, since each waypoint has an array of just one linked waypoint. However, if you change the array size to 2 or more, you will then be creating a graph of linked waypoints, adding random variations in the sequence of waypoints that a computer controlled character follows for any given run of your game.

Controlling object group movement through flocking

A realistic, natural-looking flocking behavior (for example birds, antelope, or bats) can be created through creating collections of objects with the following four simple rules:

- **Separation**: Avoid getting too close to neighbors
- **Avoid obstacles**: Turn away from an obstacle immediately ahead
- **Alignment**: Move in the general direction the flock is heading
- **Cohesion**: Move towards a location in the middle of the flock

Each member of the flock acts independently, but needs to know about the current heading and location of the members of its flock. This recipe shows you how to create a scene with two flocks of cubes: one flock of green cubes and one flock of yellow cubes.

To keep things simple, we'll not worry about separation in our recipe:

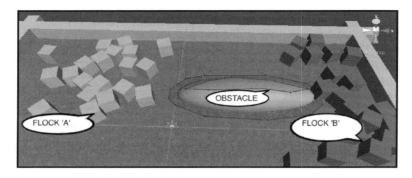

Getting ready

This recipe builds upon the player-controlled 3D cube Unity project that you created in the first recipe. So, make a copy of this project, open it, and then follow the steps for this recipe.

The required script to control movement of the red Cube (`PlayerControl.cs`) is provided in the `15_07` folder.

How to do it...

To make a group of objects flock together, please follow these steps:

1. Create a **Material** in the **Project** panel and name it **m_green** with the **Main Color** tinted green.
2. Create a **Material** in the **Project** panel and name it **m_yellow** with **Main Color** tinted yellow.
3. Create a 3D **Cube** GameObject named **Cube-drone** at (0,0,0). Drag the **m_yellow** Material into this object.
4. Add a **Navigation | NavMeshAgent** component to **Cube-drone**. Set the **Stopping Distance** property of the **NavMeshAgent** component to **2**.
5. Add a **Physics RigidBody** component to **Cube-drone** with the following properties:
    - **Mass** is 1
    - **Drag** is 0
    - **Angular Drag** is 0.05

- **Use Gravity** and **Is Kinematic** are both unchecked
- **Constraints Freeze Position:** check the Y-axis

6. Create the following `Drone` C# script-class, and add an instance-object as a component to the **Cube-drone** GameObject:

```
using UnityEngine;
using UnityEngine.AI;

public class Drone : MonoBehaviour {
private NavMeshAgent navMeshAgent;

void Start() {
navMeshAgent = GetComponent<NavMeshAgent>();
}

public void SetTargetPosition(Vector3 swarmCenterAverage,
Vector3 swarmMovementAverage) {
Vector3 destination = swarmCenterAverage +
swarmMovementAverage;
navMeshAgent.SetDestination(destination);
}
}
```

7. Create a new empty **Prefab** named **dronePrefabYellow**, and from the **Hierarchy** panel, drag your **Cube-boid** GameObject into this Prefab.

8. Now, drag the **m_green** Material into the **Cube-boid** GameObject.

9. Create a new empty **Prefab** named **dronePrefabGreen**, and from the **Hierarchy** panel, drag your **Cube-drone** GameObject into this Prefab.

10. Delete the **Cube-drone** GameObject from the **Scene** panel.

11. Create the following `Swarm` C# script-class, and add an instance-object as a component to the **Main Camera**:

```
using UnityEngine;
using System.Collections.Generic;

public class Swarm : MonoBehaviour {
public int droneCount = 20;
public GameObject dronePrefab;

private List<Drone> drones = new List<Drone>();

void Awake() {
for (int i = 0; i < droneCount; i++)
AddDrone();
}
```

```
void FixedUpdate() {
 Vector3 swarmCenter = SwarmCenterAverage();
 Vector3 swarmMovement = SwarmMovementAverage();

foreach(Drone drone in drones )
 drone.SetTargetPosition(swarmCenter, swarmMovement);
 }

private void AddDrone()
 {
 GameObject newDroneGo = Instantiate(dronePrefab);
 Drone newDrone = newDroneGo.GetComponent<Drone>();
 drones.Add(newDrone);
 }

private Vector3 SwarmCenterAverage() {
 Vector3 locationTotal = Vector3.zero;
 foreach(Drone drone in drones )
 locationTotal += drone.transform.position;

return (locationTotal / drones.Count);
 }

private Vector3 SwarmMovementAverage() {
 Vector3 velocityTotal = Vector3.zero;
 foreach(Drone drone in drones )
 velocityTotal +=
drone.GetComponent<Rigidbody>().velocity;

return (velocityTotal / drones.Count);
 }
 }
```

12. With **Main Camera** selected in the **Hierarchy** panel,
    drag **dronePrefabYellow** from the **Project** panel over the **Drone Prefab** public variable.

13. With **Main Camera** selected in the **Hierarchy** panel, add a second instance-object of the Swarm script-class to this GameObject, and then drag **dronePrefabGreen** from the **Project** panel over the **Drone Prefab** public variable.

14. Create a new 3D **Cube** named **wall-left** with the following properties:
    - **Position**: (-15, 0.5, 0)
    - **Scale**: (1, 1, 20)

15. Duplicate the **wall-left** object by naming the new object **wall-right**, and change the position of wall-right to (15, 0.5, 0).

16. Create a new 3D **Cube** named **wall-top** with the following properties:
    - **Position**: (0, 0.5, 10)
    - **Scale**: (31, 1, 1)

17. Duplicate the **wall-top** object by naming the new object **wall-bottom**, and change the position of wall-bottom to (0, 0.5, -10).

18. Create a new 3D **Sphere** named **Sphere-obstacle** with the following properties:
    - **Position**: (5, 0, 3)
    - **Scale**: (10, 3, 3)

19. In the **Hierarchy** panel, select the **Sphere-obstacle** GameObject. Then in the **Navigation** panel, check the **Navigation Static** checkbox. Then, click on the **Bake** button at the bottom of the **Navigation** panel.

20. Finally, create a red 3D **Cube** for the player to control, making it red by adding **Materialm_red** to it and making it large by setting its scale to (3,3,3). Now, add an instance-object of the `PlayerControl` C# script-class provided as a component to this GameObject.

How it works...

The Swarm class contains three variables:

1. `droneCount`: It is an integer referencing the number of the Swarm class members created

2. `dronePrefab`: It references the Prefab to be cloned to create swarm members

3. `drones`: A list of objects that reference drones; a list of all the scripted `Drone` components inside all the `Swarm` objects that have been created

Upon creation, as the scene starts, the Swarm script class's `Awake()` method loops to create `droneCount` swarm members by repeatedly calling the `AddDrone()` method. This method instantiates a new GameObject from the prefab, and then sets the `newDrone` variable to be a reference to the Drone scripted object inside the new `Swarm` class member. In each frame, the `FixedUpdate()` method loops through the list of `Drone` objects by calling their `SetTargetPosition(...)` method, and passes in the `Swarm` center location and the average of all the swarm member velocities.

The rest of this `Swarm` class is made up of two methods: one (`SwarmCenterAverage`) returns a `Vector3` object representing the average position of all the `Drone` objects, and the other (`SwarmMovementAverage`) returns a `Vector3` object representing the average velocity (movement force) of all the `Drone` objects:

1. `SwarmMovementAverage()`:
    1. What is the general direction that the swarm is moving in?
    2. This is known as alignment: a swarm member attempting to move in the same direction as the swarm average

2. `SwarmCenterAverage()`:
    1. What is the center position of the swarm?
    2. This is known as cohesion: a swarm member attempting to move towards the center of the swarm

The core work is undertaken by the `Drone` class. Each drone's `Start(...)` method finds and caches a reference to its **NavMeshAgent** component.

Each drone's `UpdateVelocity(...)` method takes as input two `Vector3` arguments: `swarmCenterAverage` and `swarmMovementAverage`. This method then calculates the desired new velocity for this `Drone` by simply adding the two vectors, and then uses the result (a `Vector3` location) to update the **NavMeshAgent's** target location.

Most of the flocking models in modern computing owe much to the work of Craig Reynolds in the 1980s. Learn more about Craig and his boids program at `http://en.wikipedia.org/wiki/Craig_Reynolds_(computer_graphics)`.

Creating a movable NavMesh Obstacle

Sometimes, we want a moving object to slow down or prevent an AI **NavMeshAgent** controlled character passing through an area of our game. Or, perhaps we want something like a door or drawbridge to sometimes permit travel, and not at other times. We can't "bake" these objects into the **NavMesh** at **Design-Time**, since we want to change them during **Run-Time**.

While computationally more expensive (that is, they slow down your game more that static non-navigable objects), **NavMesh Obstacles** are components that can be added to GameObjects, and these components can be enabled and disabled like any other component.

A special property of **NavMesh Obstacles** is that they can be set to "carve out" areas of the **NavMesh**, causing **NavMeshAgents** to then recalculate routes that avoid these carved out parts of the mesh.

In this recipe, you'll create a player-controlled red **Cube**, which you can move to obstruct an AI **NavMeshAgent** controlled character. Also, if your cube stays in one place for a half-second or longer, it will carve out part of the **NavMesh** around it, and so cause the **NavMeshAgent** to stop bumping into the obstacle, and calculate and follow a path that avoids it:

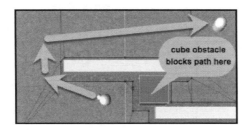

Getting ready

This recipe adds to the first recipe in this chapter, so make a copy of that project folder and do your work for this recipe with that copy.

The required script to control the movement of the red Cube (`PlayerControl.cs`) is provided in the `15_08` folder.

How to do it...

To create a movable **NavMesh Obstacle**, please follow these steps:

1. Create a **Material** in the **Project** panel, and name it **m_green** with the **Main Color** tinted green.

2. Create a red 3D **Cube** for the player to control, named **Cube-player**, making it red by added **Material m_red** to it and making it large by setting its scale to (3,3,3).

3. Add an instance of the provided `PlayerControl` C# script-class as a component to this GameObject.

4. In the **Inspector**, add a **Navigation | NavMesh Obstacle** component to **Cube-player** and check its **Carve** property.

5. Run the game. You can move the player-controlled red **Cube** to get in the way of the moving Sphere-arrow GameObject. After the **NavMesh Obstacles Time-to-stationary** time of half a second, if you have **Gizmos** displayed, you'll see the carving out of the **NavMesh**, so that the area occupied by **Cube-player**, and a little way around it, is removed from the **NavMesh**, and the Sphere-arrow GameObject will then recalculate a new route, avoiding the carved out area where **Cube-player** is located.

How it works...

At **Run-Time**, the AI **NavMeshAgent** controlled Sphere-arrow GameObject heads towards the destination point, but stops when the player-controlled red **Cube** is in its way. Once the **Cube** is stationary for 0.5 seconds or more, the **NavMesh** is carved out, so that the AI **NavMeshAgent** controlled **Sphere-arrow** GameObject no longer even attempts to plan a path through the space occupied by the cube, and recalculates a new path completely avoiding the obstacle, even if it means back-tracking and heading away from the target for part of its path.

14
Design Patterns

In this chapter, we will cover:

- State-driven behavior DIY states
- State-driven behavior State Design Pattern classes
- State-driven behavior with Unity Scriptable Objects
- Publisher-Subscriber pattern C# delegates and events
- Model-View-Controller (MVC) pattern

Introduction

In computer programming in general, some types of features and requirements occur commonly. For computer game programming, there are often features for new games that have things in common with existing games. Software **Design Patterns** are reusable, computer-language-independent templates for how to solve common problems.

Not all design patterns are needed for all languages (for example, some computer languages may have features that already provide an easy way to solve a common problem). In this chapter, we'll explore several common design patterns in the context of Unity game programming in the C# programming language.

The big picture

There is no need to reinvent the wheel, and there are many advantages for game programmers to adopt tried-and-tested approaches to solving common features for game projects. Design patterns have been designed by experience, and refined to encourage good programming practice and well-designed architectural software solutions. A common theme in design patterns is the independence of code components, and clearly-defined interfaces for when components do need to know about each other and the protocols for their interactions.

In this chapter, the recipes focus on three main design patterns, all of which are well known and found not only in game software designs but in the design of many interactive software systems, such as web applications and mobile phone programming. The design patterns explored in this chapter are:

- **The State pattern**: States and their transitions
- **The Publisher-Subscriber pattern**: Observers subscribing to event-publishing objects
- **The Model-View-Controller (MCV) pattern**: Separating internal workings from UI components and display representations

In this chapter, examples are presented in generic object-oriented designs, also there are C#-specific features (such as **delegates** and **events**), and some Unity-specific features (such as **scriptable objects**). While generic approaches have the advantage that programmers from other languages or domains will be instantly familiar with their Unity game implementations, the most significant game memory-speed improvements are found through exploiting language- and engine-specific features.

C# **Delegate** variables are like a container for a function (or collection of functions) that can be passed around and invoked. They have values assigned to them and can be changed at runtime. **Delegates** can multicast through the use of the += operator, multiple methods can be assigned a single delegate, and all will be invoked when the delegate is invoked. C# **events** are a special, more secure kind of delegate. By defining public static event variables, we restrict other script classes to only be allowed to:

- Subscribe one of their methods
- Unsubscribe one of their methods

Events ensure a good separation of our code logic, and mean that the script class publishing events does not need to know anything about, or how many, other script classes are subscribing to published events.

Here are some sources where you can learn more about **Design Patterns** and Unity:

- The Unity tutorial about **Scriptable Objects** for enemy state-driven AI:
  `https://unity3d.com/learn/tutorials/topics/navigation/finite-stat`
  `e-ai-delegate-pattern`
- The Unity tutorial about **delegates** and **events**:
  - `https://unity3d.com/learn/tutorials/topics/scripting`
    `/delegates?playlist=17117`
  - `https://unity3d.com/learn/tutorials/topics/scripting`
    `/events`
- Prime[31]'s video about Unity delegates and events (from 2011, but still a nice introduction): `http://www.youtube.com/watch?v=N2zdwKIsXJs`
- Eric Nordeus' tutorial on Unity and **Design Patterns**:
  `http://www.habrador.com/tutorials/programming-patterns/`
- Unity **Model-View-Controller** tutorials:
  - Gameasutra:
    `https://www.gamasutra.com/blogs/TabeaIseli/20160926/`
    `282062/MVC_in_Unity.php`
  - Eduardo Dias Da Costa:
    `https://www.toptal.com/unity-unity3d/unity-with-mvc-`
    `how-to-level-up-your-game-development`
  - Jackson Dunstan:
    `https://jacksondunstan.com/articles/3092`

State-driven behavior DIY states

Games as a whole, and individual objects or characters, can often be thought of (or modeled as) passing through different states or modes. Modeling states and changes of state (due to events or game conditions) is a very common way to manage the complexity of games and game components. In this recipe, we create a simple three-state game (game playing/game won/game lost) using a `GameManager` class. Buttons and a timer are provided to simulate the events that would allow a player to win or lose the game:

How to do it...

To use states to manage object behavior, follow these steps:

1. Create two UI Buttons at the top-middle of the screen. Name one `Button-win` and edit its text to read `Win Game`. Name the second `Button-lose` and edit its text to read `Lose Game`.

2. Create a UI Text object at the top left of the screen. Name this `Text-state-messages`, and set its **Rect Transform** height property to `300` and its **Text (Script) Paragraph Vertical Overflow** property to `Overflow`.

3. Create a new C# script class, `GameStates.cs`:

```
public class GameStates
{
    public enum GameStateType
    {
        GamePlaying,
        GameWon,
        GameLost,
    }
}
```

4. Create the `MyGameManager.cs` C# script class, and add an instance object as a component to the **Main Camera**:

```
using UnityEngine;
 using System;
 using UnityEngine.UI;

public class MyGameManager : MonoBehaviour
{
    public Text textStateMessages;
    public Button buttonWinGame;
    public Button buttonLoseGame;

    private GameStates.GameStateType currentState;
    private float timeGamePlayingStarted;
    private float timeToPressAButton = 5;

    void Start()
    {
        currentState = GameStates.GameStateType.GamePlaying;
    }

    //--------- Update[ S ] - state specific actions
    void Update()
```

```
        {
            switch (currentState)
            {
                case GameStates.GameStateType.GamePlaying:
                    UpdateStateGamePlaying();
                    break;
                case GameStates.GameStateType.GameWon:
                    // do nothing
                    break;
                case GameStates.GameStateType.GameLost:
                    // do nothing
                    break;
            }
        }

        public void NewGameState(GameStates.GameStateType
newState)
        {
            // (1) state EXIT actions
            OnMyStateExit(currentState);

            // (2) change current state
            currentState = newState;

            // (3) state ENTER actions
            OnMyStateEnter(currentState);

            PostMessageDivider();
        }

        public void PostMessageDivider()
        {
            string newLine = "\n";
            string divider = "--------------------------------";
            textStateMessages.text += newLine + divider;
        }

        public void PostMessage(string message)
        {
            string newLine = "\n";
            string timeTo2DecimalPlaces =
    String.Format("{0:0.00}", Time.time);
            textStateMessages.text += newLine +
    timeTo2DecimalPlaces + " :: " + message;
        }

        private void DestroyButtons()
        {
```

```
                    Destroy(buttonWinGame.gameObject);
                    Destroy(buttonLoseGame.gameObject);
            }

            //--------- OnMyStateEnter[ S ] - state specific actions
            private void OnMyStateEnter(GameStates.GameStateType
    state)
            {
                string enterMessage = "ENTER state: " +
                state.ToString();
                PostMessage(enterMessage);

                switch (state)
                {
                    case GameStates.GameStateType.GamePlaying:
                        OnMyStateEnterGamePlaying();
                        break;
                    case GameStates.GameStateType.GameWon:
                        // do nothing
                        break;
                    case GameStates.GameStateType.GameLost:
                        // do nothing
                        break;
                }
            }

            private void OnMyStateEnterGamePlaying()
            {
                // record time we enter state
                timeGamePlayingStarted = Time.time;
            }

            //--------- OnMyStateExit[ S ] - state specific actions
            private void OnMyStateExit(GameStates.GameStateType
    state)
            {
                string exitMessage = "EXIT state: " +
    state.ToString();
                PostMessage(exitMessage);

                switch (state)
                {
                    case GameStates.GameStateType.GamePlaying:
                        OnMyStateExitGamePlaying();
                        break;
                    case GameStates.GameStateType.GameWon:
                        // do nothing
                        break;
```

```
                case GameStates.GameStateType.GameLost:
                    // do nothing
                    break;
            }
        }

        private void OnMyStateExitGamePlaying()
        {
            // if leaving gamePlaying state then destroy the 2
buttons
            DestroyButtons();
        }


        private void UpdateStateGamePlaying()
        {
            float timeSinceGamePlayingStarted =
            Time.time - timeGamePlayingStarted;
            if (timeSinceGamePlayingStarted > timeToPressAButton)
            {
                string message = "User waited too long -
automatically
                going to Game LOST state";
                  PostMessage(message);
                NewGameState(GameStates.GameStateType.GameLost);
            }
        }
    }
```

5. Create the ButtonActions.cs C# script class, and add an instance object as a component to the **Main Camera**:

```
using UnityEngine;

public class ButtonActions : MonoBehaviour
{
    private MyGameManager myGameManager;

    private void Start()
    {
        myGameManager = GetComponent<MyGameManager>();
    }

    public void BUTTON_CLICK_ACTION_WIN_GAME()
    {
        string message = "Win Game BUTTON clicked";
        myGameManager.PostMessage(message);
        myGameManager.NewGameState
```

```
                        (GameStates.GameStateType.GameWon);
    }

    public void BUTTON_CLICK_ACTION_LOSE_GAME()
    {
        string message = "Lose Game BUTTON clicked";
        myGameManager.PostMessage(message);
        myGameManager.NewGameState
        (GameStates.GameStateType.GameLost);
    }

}
```

6. In the **Hierarchy**, select the **Button-win** button, and for its **Button (Script)** component, add an **OnClick** action to call the `BUTTON_CLICK_ACTION_WIN_GAME()` method from the **ButtonsActions** component in the **Main Camera** GameObject.

7. In the **Hierarchy**, select the **Button-lose** button, and for its **Button (Script)** component, add an **OnClick** action to call the `BUTTON_CLICK_ACTION_LOSE_GAME()` method from the **ButtonActions** component in the **Main Camera** GameObject.

8. In the **Hierarchy**, select the **Main Camera** GameObject. Drag this GameObject into the **Inspector** to ensure that all three **GameManager (Script)** public variables (**Text State Messages**, **Button Win Game**, and **Button Lose Game**) have the corresponding Canvas GameObjects dragged into them (the two buttons and the UI Text GameObject).

How it works...

As can be seen in the following state chart figure, this recipe models a simple game, which starts in the `GamePlaying` state; then, depending on the button clicked by the user, the game moves either into the `GameWon` state or the `GameLost` state. Also, if the user waits too long (five seconds) to click on a button, the game moves into the `GameLost` state.

The possible states of the system are defined using the enumerated `GameStateType` type in the `GameStates` class, and the current state of the system at any point in time is stored in the `currentState` variable of GameManager:

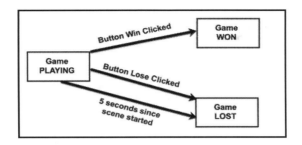

The initial state, GamePlaying, is set in the Start() method of MyGameManager.

GameManager seems to now be a special asset name in Unity, for that reason, we have named our game manager script classes MyGameManager to avoid any issues.

When the MyGameManager object receives messages (for example, every frame for Update()), its behavior must be appropriate for the current state. So, we see a Switch statement in the Update() method that calls state-specific methods. For example, if the current state is GamePlaying, when an Update() message is received, the UpdateStateGamePlaying() method will be called.

The NewGameState(...) method first calls the OnMyStateExit(...) method with the current state, since there may be actions to be performed when a particular state is exited; for example, when the GamePlaying state is exited, it destroys the two buttons. Next, the NewGameState(...) method sets the currentState variable to be assigned the new state. Next, the OnMyStateEnter(...) method is called, since there may be actions to be performed immediately when a new state is entered. Finally, a message divider is postedto the UI Text box, with a call to the PostMessageDivider() method.

The BUTTON_CLICK_ACTION_WIN_GAME() and BUTTON_CLICK_ACTION_LOSE_GAME() methods are executed if their corresponding buttons have been clicked. They move the game into the corresponding GameWon or GameLost state.

Logic has been written in the UpdateStateGamePlaying() method, so once MyGameManager has been in the GamePlaying state for more than a certain time (defined in the timeToPressAButton variable), the game will automatically change into the GameLost state.

So, for each state, we may need to write methods for state exit, state entry, and update events, and also a main method for each event with a Switch statement to determine which state method should be called (or not). As can be imagined, the size of our methods and the number of methods in our `MyGameManager` class will grow significantly as more states and a more complex game logic are needed for non-trivial games.

See also

- The next recipe takes a more sophisticated approach to state-driven games, where each state has its own class. The next recipe in this chapter illustrates how to manage the complexity of states with class inheritance and the State Design Pattern.

State-driven behavior using the State Design Pattern

The previous pattern illustrated not only the usefulness of modeling game states, but also how a game manager class can grow in size and become unmanageable. To manage the complexity of many states and complex behaviors of states, the State pattern has been proposed in the software-development community. Design patterns are general-purpose software component architectures that have been tried and tested and found to be good solutions to commonly-occurring software-system features. The key features of the State pattern are that each state is modeled by its own class and that all states inherit (are subclassed) from a single parent state class. The states need to know about each other in order to tell the game manager to change the current state. This is a small price to pay for the division of the complexity of the overall game behavior into separate state classes.

Note: Many thanks to the contribution from Bryan Griffiths, which has helped improve this recipe.

Getting ready

This recipe builds upon the previous recipe. So, make a copy of that project, open it, and then follow the steps for this recipe.

How to do it...

To manage an object's behavior using the State pattern architecture, perform the following steps:

1. Create a new C# script class called `GameState`:

    ```
    public class GameState
      {
          public enum EventType
          {
              ButtonWinGame,
              ButtonLoseGame
          }

          protected MyGameManager gameManager;
          public GameState(MyGameManager manager)
          {
              gameManager = manager;
          }

          public virtual void OnMyStateEntered() {}
          public virtual void OnMyStateExit() {}
          public virtual void StateUpdate() {}
          public virtual void OnEventReceived(EventType eventType)
    {}
      }
    ```

2. Create a new C# script class called `StateGamePlaying`:

    ```
    using UnityEngine;

    public class StateGamePlaying : GameState
    {
        public StateGamePlaying(MyGameManager manager) :
        base(manager) { }

        public override void OnMyStateEntered()
        {
            string stateEnteredMessage = "ENTER state:
            StateGamePlaying";
            gameManager.DisplayStateEnteredMessage
            (stateEnteredMessage);
            Debug.Log(stateEnteredMessage);
        }

        public override void OnEventReceived(EventType eventType)
        {
    ```

```
                switch(eventType){
                    case (EventType.ButtonWinGame):
gameManager.NewGameState(gameManager.stateGameWon);
                        break;
                    case (EventType.ButtonLoseGame):
                    case (EventType.TimerFinished):
                        gameManager.NewGameState
                        (gameManager.stateGameLost);
                        break;
                }
            }
        }
```

3. Create a new C# script class called StateGameWon:

```
using UnityEngine;

public class StateGameWon : GameState
{
    public StateGameWon(MyGameManager manager) :
base(manager) { }

    public override void OnMyStateEntered()
    {
        string stateEnteredMessage = "ENTER state:
StateGameWon";
        gameManager.DisplayStateEnteredMessage
        (stateEnteredMessage);
        Debug.Log(stateEnteredMessage);
    }
}
```

4. Create a new C# script class called StateGameLost:

```
using UnityEngine;

public class StateGameLost : GameState
{
    public StateGameLost(MyGameManager manager) :
base(manager) { }

    public override void OnMyStateEntered()
    {
        string stateEnteredMessage = "ENTER state:
StateGameLost";
        gameManager.DisplayStateEnteredMessage
        (stateEnteredMessage);
        Debug.Log(stateEnteredMessage);
```

```
                    }
              }
```

5. Replace the contents of the `MyGameManager` C# script class with the following:

```
using UnityEngine;
 using UnityEngine.UI;

public class MyGameManager : MonoBehaviour
{
     public Text textGameStateName;
     public Button buttonWinGame;
     public Button buttonLoseGame;

     [HideInInspector]
     public StateGamePlaying stateGamePlaying;

     [HideInInspector]
     public StateGameWon stateGameWon;

     [HideInInspector]
     public StateGameLost stateGameLost;

     private GameState currentState;

     private void Awake()
     {
         stateGamePlaying = new StateGamePlaying(this);
         stateGameWon = new StateGameWon(this);
         stateGameLost = new StateGameLost(this);
     }

     private void Start()
     {
         NewGameState(stateGamePlaying);
     }

     private void Update()
     {
         if (currentState != null)
             currentState.StateUpdate();
     }

     public void NewGameState(GameState newState)
     {
         if (null != currentState)
             currentState.OnMyStateExit();
```

```
            currentState = newState;
            currentState.OnMyStateEntered();
        }

        public void DisplayStateEnteredMessage(string
        stateEnteredMessage)
        {
            textGameStateName.text = stateEnteredMessage;
        }

        public void
  PublishEventToCurrentState(GameState.EventType
        eventType)
        {
            currentState.OnEventReceived(eventType);
            DestroyButtons();
        }

        private void DestroyButtons()
        {
            Destroy(buttonWinGame.gameObject);
            Destroy(buttonLoseGame.gameObject);
        }
    }
```

6. In the **Hierarchy**, select the **Button-win** button, and for its **Button (Script)** component, add an **OnClick** action to call the BUTTON_CLICK_ACTION_WIN_GAME() method from the **GameManager** component in the **Main Camera** GameObject.

7. In the **Hierarchy**, select the **Button-lose** button, and for its **Button (Script)** component, add an **OnClick** action to call the BUTTON_CLICK_ACTION_LOSE_GAME() method from the **GameManager** component in the **Main Camera** GameObject.

8. In the **Hierarchy**, select the **Main Camera** GameObject. Drag it into the **Inspector** to ensure that all three **GameManager (Script)** public variables (**Text State Messages**, **Button Win Game**, and **Button Lose Game**) have the corresponding Canvas GameObjects dragged into them (the two buttons and the **UI Text** GameObject).

How it works...

The scene is very straightforward for this recipe. There is the single **Main Camera** GameObject that has the MyGameManager script object component attached to it.

A C# scripted class is defined for each state that the game needs to manage—for this example, StateGamePlaying, StateGameWon, and StateGameLost. Each of these state classes is a subclass of GameState. GameState defines properties and methods that all subclass states will possess:

- An enumerated type EventType, which defines the two possible button click events that the game might generate: ButtonWinGame and ButtonLoseGame.
- The gameManager variable so that each state object has a link to the game manager.
- The constructor method that accepts a reference to MyGameManager, which automatically makes the gameManager variable refer to the passed-in MyGameManager object.
- The four methods with empty bodies: OnMyStateEntered(), OnMyStateExit(), OnEventRecieved(...), and StateUpdate(). Note that these methods are declared virtual so that they can be overridden by subclasses if necessary, but if not overridden then will do nothing.

When the MyGameManager class's Awake() method is executed, three state objects are created, one for each of the playing/win/lose classes. These state objects are stored in their corresponding variables: stateGamePlaying, stateGameWon, and stateGameLost.

The MyGameManager class has a variable called currentState, which is a reference to the current state object at any time while the game runs (initially, it will be null). Since it is of the GameState class (the parent of all state classes), it can refer to any of the different state objects.

After Awake(), GameManager will receive a Start() message. This method initializes currentState to be the stateGamePlaying object.

For each frame, GameManager will receive Update() messages. Upon receiving these messages, GameManager sends a StateUpdate() messages to currentState object. So, for each frame, the object for the current state of the game will execute those methods. For example, when currentState is set to game playing, for each frame, the gamePlayingObject will calls its (in this case, empty) StateUpdate() method.

The `StateGamePlaying` class implements statements in its `OnEventReceived()` method so that when the user clicks on a button, the `gamePlayingObject` will call the `GameManager` instance's `NewState(...)` method, passing it the object corresponding to the new state. So for example, if the user clicks on **Button-win**, the `NewState(...)` method is passed to `gameManager.stateGameWon`.

There's more...

There are some details that you don't want to miss.

Adding the Timer event to lose the game after five seconds

The state pattern solution makes it much simpler, and cleaner to add new features. For example, to add the five-second-timer feature to this recipe, do the following:

1. Create a new C# script class called `SimpleTimer`, and add an instance object as a component to the **Main Camera** GameObject:

```
using UnityEngine;

public class SimpleTimer : MonoBehaviour
{
    private float timeGamePlayingStarted;
    private float timeToPressAButton = 5;

    private MyGameManager myGameManager;

    private void Start()
    {
        myGameManager = GetComponent<MyGameManager>();
        timeGamePlayingStarted = Time.time;
    }

    void Update ()
    {
        float timeSinceGamePlayingStarted = Time.time -
        timeGamePlayingStarted;

        if (timeSinceGamePlayingStarted > timeToPressAButton)
        {
            myGameManager.PublishEventToCurrentState
            (GameState.EventType.TimerFinished);
```

```
        }
    }
}
```

2. Add a new event type of `TimerFinished` to the `GameState` script class:

```
public enum EventType
{
    ButtonWinGame,
    ButtonLoseGame,
    TimerFinished
}
```

3. Add a new case to the switch statement in `StateGamePlaying`, so that this `TimerFinished` event also causes the game to go into the `GameLost` state:

```
public override void OnEventReceived(EventType eventType)
{
    switch(eventType){
        case (EventType.ButtonWinGame):
gameManager.NewGameState(gameManager.stateGameWon);
            break;
        case (EventType.ButtonLoseGame):
        case (EventType.TimerFinished):
gameManager.NewGameState(gameManager.stateGameLost);
            break;
    }
}
```

See also

- In this recipe, some of the complexity of different types of events causing the `MyGameManager` to change its current state was implemented by other scripted objects (`ButtonActions` and `SimpleTimer` as scripted object components inside **Main Camera**) invoking the `PublishEventToCurrentState(...)` public method. A better was to implement events in games is provided later in this chapter in the *Publisher-Subscriber pattern C# delegates and events* recipe.

State-driven behavior with Unity Scriptable Objects

Unity has a feature called Scriptable Objects. Scriptable Objects are asset files stored in the `Assets` folder, like any other asset (such as Materials or Textures). In some ways, Scriptable Objects are like Monobehaviours, but they are not attached to GameObjects. Both logic (code) and data can be stored as asset files in the form of Scriptable Objects.

In this recipe, we implement a state-based game where the game starts in a game-playing state, and goes to a game-lost state when a timer runs out. If two stars are collected before the timer runs out, the game goes into the game-won state. A **UI Button** is offered to the user, which collects a star each time it is clicked.

As you'll see, Scriptable Object asset files are used to represent which decisions cause which state changes to take place.

How to do it...

To manage a game's state-driven behavior with Unity Scriptable Objects, perform the following steps:

1. Create a **UI Button** in the middle of the screen. Name it `Button-collect-star` and edit its text to read `Collect a star`.
2. Create a **UI Text** object at the top-right of the screen. Name this `Text-current-state`.
3. Create a **UI Text** object at the top-left of the screen. Name this `Text-stars-collected`.
4. Create a second UI Text object at the top-left of the screen, positioned below `Text-stars-collected`. Name this `Text-seconds-left`.
5. Create a new C# script class called `Decision`:

```
using UnityEngine;

public abstract class Decision : ScriptableObject
{
    public abstract bool Decide(StateController controller);
}
```

6. Create a new C# script class called `Transition`:

```
[System.Serializable]
 public class Transition
 {
     public Decision decision;
     public State trueState;
 }
```

7. Create a new C# script class called `State`:

```
using UnityEngine;

[CreateAssetMenu(menuName = "MyGame/State")]
public class State : ScriptableObject
{        public Transition[] transitions;

    public void UpdateState(StateController controller)
    {
        CheckTransitions(controller);
    }

    private void CheckTransitions(StateController controller)
    {
        for (int i = 0; i < transitions.Length; i++)
        {
            bool decisionSucceeded =
            transitions[i].decision.Decide(controller);

            if (decisionSucceeded)
            {
                controller.TransitionToState
                (transitions[i].trueState);
            }
        }
    }
}
```

8. Create a new C# script class called `StateController`:

```
using UnityEngine;

public class StateController : MonoBehaviour
{
    public State currentState;
    [HideInInspector] public MyGameManager gameManager;

    void Awake()
```

```
        {
            gameManager = GetComponent<MyGameManager>();
        }

        private void Update()
        {
            currentState.UpdateState(this);
            gameManager.DisplayCurrentState(currentState);
        }

        public void TransitionToState(State nextState)
        {
            currentState = nextState;
        }
    }
```

9. Create a new C# script class called `GameWonDecision`:

```
    using UnityEngine;

    [CreateAssetMenu(menuName =
 "MyGame/Decisions/GameWonDecision")]
    public class GameWonDecision : Decision
    {

        public override bool Decide(StateController controller)
        {
            return GameWonActionDetected(controller.gameManager);
        }

        private bool GameWonActionDetected(MyGameManager
 gameManager)
        {
            return gameManager.HasCollectedAllStars();
        }
    }
```

10. Create a new C# script class called `GameLostDecision`:

```
    using UnityEngine;

    [CreateAssetMenu(menuName =
 "MyGame/Decisions/GameLostDecision")]
    public class GameLostDecision : Decision
    {

        public override bool Decide(StateController controller)
        {
```

```
                  return
GameLostActionDetected(controller.gameManager);
        }

        private bool GameLostActionDetected(MyGameManager
gameManager)
        {
            return gameManager.GetTimeRemaining() <= 0;
        }
    }
```

11. Create a new C# script class called `MyGameManager`, and add an instance object as a component of the **Main Camera**:

```
using UnityEngine;
 using UnityEngine.UI;


public class MyGameManager : MonoBehaviour
{
    public Text textCurrentState;
    public Text textStarsCollected;
    public Text textSecondsLeft;

    public float secondsLeft = 10;
    public int totalStarsToBeCollected = 2;
    private int starsColleted = 0;

    void Update()
    {
        secondsLeft -= Time.deltaTime;
        UpdateDisplays();
    }

    public void DisplayCurrentState(State currentState)
    {
        textCurrentState.text = currentState.name;
    }

    public bool HasCollectedAllStars()
    {
        return (starsColleted == totalStarsToBeCollected);
    }

    public float GetTimeRemaining()
    {
        return secondsLeft;
    }
```

```
public void BUTTON_ACTION_PickupOneStar()
{
    starsColleted++;
}

private void UpdateDisplays()
{
    textStarsCollected.text = "stars = " + starsColleted;
    textSecondsLeft.text = "time left = " + secondsLeft;
}
}
```

12. In the **Hierarchy**, select the **Button-collect-star** button, and for its **Button (Script)** component, add an **OnClick** action to call the BUTTON_ACTION_PickupOneStar() method from the MyGameManager component in the **Main Camera** GameObject.

13. In the **Project** panel, create two new folders, named _Decisions and _States. These folders will contain the Scriptable Object asset files for this project.

14. In the _Decisions folder, create two new Decision Scriptable Objects named GameWonDecision and GameLostDecision. Do this by choosing menu: **Assets | Create | MyGame | Decisions**.

15. In the _States folder, create three new State Scriptable Objects named StateGamePlaying, StateGameWon, and StateGameLost. Do this by choosing menu: **Assets | Create | MyGame | State**.

16. In the **Project** panel folder _States, select the StateGamePlaying Scriptable Object, and in the **Inspector**, set the size of its **Transitions** property to 2.

   - For **Element 0**, set the **Decision** to **GameWonDecision** and the **True **state to **StateGameWon**
   - For **Element 1**, set the **Decision** to **GameLostDecision** and the **True **state to **StateGameLost**:

17. In the **Hierarchy**, select the **Main Camera** GameObject. Drag it into the **Inspector** to ensure that all three **GameManager (Script)** public variables (**Text Current State**, **Text Stars Collected**, and **Text Seconds Left**) have the corresponding Canvas **UI Text** GameObjects dragged into them.

18. Run the game. The game should start in StateGamePlaying. If the user does nothing, when the timer gets to zero, the game should go into StateGameLost. If the user clicks the button twice (simulating collecting two stars) before the timer hits zero, the game should go into StateGameWon.

How it works...

GameManager knows nothing about the state-based decisions going on in this game. It has a public method giving the number of seconds left in the timer: GetTimeRemaining(). It also has a public method that returns a Boolean (true/false) about whether or not all stars have been collected: HasCollectedAllStars(). It also has references to the three **UI Text** GameObjects, so it can keep the display updated with the time left and stars collected. A public DispayCurrentState(...) method also updates the name of current game state (that is, whatever was passed to this method).

The core game behavior is driven by the StateController script class. This maintains the current state, and has a reference to the instance object of the MyGameManager class that is its sibling component in the **Main Camera**. Its Awake() method gets the reference to the MyGameManager object. Its Update() method invokes the current state's UpdateState(...) method. It passes a reference to itself to the current state. It also has a third public method, TransitionToState(...), which allows a state to instruct the controller to change the current state.

The `Transition` class has no methods, it simply stores references to two objects: a decision and the state that the system will to change to if the decision is true.

The `Decision` class is abstract, which means there will never be any objects created from this class, but subclasses may be defined. It declares that any subclasses must implement a method named `Decide(...)`, which returns a Boolean (true/false) value.

The `State` class has an array of `Transition` objects, and its `UpdateState()` method simple invokes its `CheckTransitions(...)` method. `CheckTransitions(...)` loops through each transition, testing its `Decision`. If the decision is true, it tells `StateController` to make the current state the true state of the transition.

In this project, we have declared two subclasses of the `Decision` class:

- `GameWonDecision`: This class' `Decide(...)` method returns the value of its `GameWonActionDetected(...)` method. `GameWonActionDetected(...)` returns the value of the game manager's `HasCollectedAllStars()` method, that is, the game-won decision is true when the game manager says that all stars have been collected.
- `GameWonDecision`: This class's `Decide(...)` method returns the value of its `GameLostActionDetected(...)` method. `GameLostActionDetected(...)` returns true if the game manager's timer is zero or less (time has run out).

We have created five scriptable object assets:

- **Three states**: `StateGamePlaying`, `StateGameWon`, `StateGameLost`
- **Two decisions**: `GameWonDecision` and `GameLostDecision`

We were able to create these Scriptable Object assets via the **Create** menu through the statements immediately before the script-class declarations for `Decision` and `State` that declared that there should be a new sub-menu in the **Create Asset** menu named **MyGame**:

```
[CreateAssetMenu(menuName = "MyGame/Decisions/GameLostDecision")]
```

The only one of these Scriptable Objects that needed any customizing was `StateGamePlaying`. Two transitions were defined in this object:

- If `GameWonDecision` becomes true, the State Controller should set the current state to `StateGameWon`
- If `GameLostDecision` becomes true, the State Controller should set the current state to `StateGameLost`

While it may seem like there was a lot of work for this simple game, what this recipe illustrates is how some generic state-machine classes can be created (`State`, `Decision`, `Transition`, `StateController`), and that the actual game behavior is modelled through a set of Scriptable Object assets, and two classes to implement the decision-making for special game events (`GameWonDecision` and `GameLostDecision`).

Since Scriptable Object are asset files, there are only one of them. At times, we may want the same Scriptable Object to be used by different GameObjects when the game is running—for example, the state transitions for the AI of lots of different enemy characters may share the use of the same Scriptable Object. For this reason, a reference to a `StateController` object instance is passed when methods are invoked on `State` and `Decision` Scriptable Objects, so the logic in the methods of the Scriptable Object can work on whatever run-time controller object is provided with. This is an example of another design pattern known as the **Delegate** design pattern (not to be confused with a C# delegate!).

There's more...

There are some details that you don't want to miss.

Extending the game to model Player health

To further understand the power of this data-centric approach to state-based games, let's add the following behavior to the game:

- The player has a health value, starting at 100% (a float value of 1.0)
- In each frame, a random amount of health is added or subtracted
- The game is lost if the health of the player goes down to zero

To implement this feature, all we need to do is:

1. Add a test to the GameLostDecision script class to return true if time or health are zero:

```
private bool GameLostActionDetected(MyGameManager gameManager)
{
    return (gameManager.GetTimeRemaining() <= 0) ||
    (gameManager.GetHealth() <= 0);
}
```

2. Add the health feature to the GameManager script class:

```
private float health = 1;
 public float healthPlusMaximum = 0.03f;
 public float healthMinusMaximum = -0.03f;

void Update()
{
    // extra feature
    RandomlyChangeHealth();

    secondsLeft -= Time.deltaTime;
    UpdateDisplays();
}

// extra freature
public float GetHealth()
{
    return health;
}

// health can't go below 0 or above 1
private void RandomlyChangeHealth()
{
    float healthChange = Random.Range(healthMinusMaximum,
    healthPlusMaximum);
    health += healthChange;
    health = Mathf.Clamp(health, 0, 1);
}
```

We could also add another **UI Text** on screen to see the current value of health. If the public healthPlusMaximum variable is set smaller than the minus maximum (for example, 0.02), the health will go downwards since the random average will be less than zero.

To add another state, such as StatePauseGame, all that is needed are the following steps:

1. Create new GamePausedDecision script class, with the logic to detect whether the game is paused (for example, the game manager could have an isPaused boolean variable that gets set to true when the user presses the *P* key)
2. Create a new StateGamePaused Scriptable Object State
3. Create a new GamePausedDecision Scriptable Object State
4. Add a third transition to the StateGamePlaying Scriptable Object State (element 2), with GamePausedDecision and the true state of StateGamePaused

See also

- To see this approach to state-driven games using Scriptable Objects taken much further, including adding the feature for actions to be performed during each state, follow the online video Unity tutorial about Scriptable Objects for enemy state-driven AI: https://unity3d.com/learn/tutorials/topics/navigation/finite-state-ai-delegate-pattern.

Publisher-Subscriber pattern C# delegates and events

When events can be based on visibility, distance, or collisions, we can use such events as OnTriggerExit and OnBecomeInvisible. When events can be based on time periods, we can use coroutines. However, some events are unique to each game situation, and C# offers several methods of broadcasting user-defined event messages to scripted objects. One approach is the SendMessage(...) method, which, when sent to a GameObject, will check every Monobehaviour scripted component and execute the named method if its parameters match. However, this involves an inefficient technique known as reflection. C# offers another event message approach known as delegates and events, which we describe and implement in this recipe.

Delegates and events work in a similar way to SendMessage(...), but are much more efficient since Unity maintains a defined list of which objects are listening to the broadcast events. SendMessage(...) should be avoided if performance is important, since it means that Unity has to analyze each scripted object (reflect over the object) to see whether there is a public method corresponding to the message that has been sent; this is much slower than using delegates and events.

Delegates separate the code declaring the delegate from any of the codes (classes) that use the delegate. The script-class that declares the public delegate does not need to know anything about the object or objects that make use of its delegated functionality.

Delegates and events implement the **Publisher-Subscriber design pattern (pubsub)**. This is also known as the **Observer** design pattern. Objects can subscribe one of their methods to receive a particular type of event message from a particular publisher. In this recipe, we'll have a manager class that will publish new events when **UI Buttons** are clicked. We'll create some **UI objects**, some of which subscribe to the color-change events. Each time a color-change event is published, subscribed **UI objects** receive the event message and change their color accordingly.

We will also add a console event logger, to listen for and log messages about color-change events.

C# publisher objects don't have to worry about how many objects subscribe to them at any point in time (it could be none or 1,000!). This is known as **loose coupling**, since it allows different code components to be written (and maintained) independently and is a desirable feature of object-oriented code:

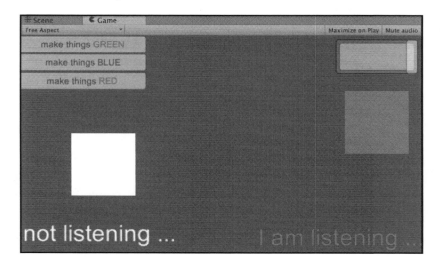

Getting ready

For this recipe, a Unity Package has been provided (colorChangeScene.unitypackage) in the 17_04 folder. This package contains a scene with **UI Buttons** and other objects for the recipe.

How to do it...

To implement the Publisher-Subscriber pattern using C# delegates and events, follow these steps:

1. Create a new Unity project, and delete the default Scenes folder.
2. Import the provided Unity package (colorChangeScene.unitypackage).
3. Add the following ColorManager C# script class to the **Main Camera**:

```
using UnityEngine;

public class ColorManager : MonoBehaviour
{
    private ColorModel colorModel;
    private ColorChangeListenerConsole
colorChangeListenerConsole;

    void Awake()
    {
        colorModel = new ColorModel();
        colorChangeListenerConsole = new
        ColorChangeListenerConsole();
    }

    public void BUTTON_ACTION_make_green()
    {
        colorModel.SetColor(Color.green);
    }

    public void BUTTON_ACTION_make_blue()
    {
        colorModel.SetColor(Color.blue);
    }

    public void BUTTON_ACTION_make_red()
    {
        colorModel.SetColor(Color.red);
    }
}
```

4. Create the ColorChangeListenerImage C# script class, and add an instance object as a component to the Image-listening and Slider-listening GameObjects (both children of **Canvas | listening-game-objects**):

```
using UnityEngine;
 using UnityEngine.UI;

public class ColorChangeListenerImage : MonoBehaviour
{
    void OnEnable() {
        ColorModel.OnChangeColor += ChangeColorEvent;
    }

    void OnDisable(){
        ColorModel.OnChangeColor -= ChangeColorEvent;
    }

    void ChangeColorEvent(Color newColor)
    {
        GetComponent<Image>().color = newColor;
    }
}
```

5. Create the ColorChangeListenerText C# script class, and add an instance object as a component to the Text-listening GameObject (a child of **Canvas | listening-game-objects**):

```
using UnityEngine;
 using UnityEngine.UI;

public class ColorChangeListenerText : MonoBehaviour
{
    void OnEnable() {
        ColorModel.OnChangeColor += ChangeColorEvent;
    }

    void OnDisable(){
        ColorModel.OnChangeColor -= ChangeColorEvent;
    }

    void ChangeColorEvent(Color newColor)
    {
        GetComponent<Text>().color = newColor;
    }
}
```

6. Create the `ColorChangeListenerConsole` C# script class:

```
using UnityEngine;

public class ColorChangeListenerConsole
{
    public ColorChangeListenerConsole()
    {
        ColorModel.OnChangeColor += ChangeColorEvent;
    }

    ~ColorChangeListenerConsole()
    {
        ColorModel.OnChangeColor -= ChangeColorEvent;
    }

    void ChangeColorEvent(Color newColor){
        Debug.Log("new color = " + newColor);
    }
}
```

7. Create the `ColorModel` C# script class:

```
using UnityEngine;

public class ColorModel
{
    private Color color;

    public delegate void ColorChangeHandler(Color newColor);
    public static event ColorChangeHandler OnChangeColor;

    private void PublishColorEvent()
    {
        // if there is at least one listener to this delegate
        if (OnChangeColor != null)
            // broadcast change colour event
            OnChangeColor(this.color);
    }

    public void SetColor(Color newColor)
    {
        this.color = newColor;
        PublishColorEvent();
    }
}
```

8. With **button-GREEN** selected in the **Hierarchy**, add a new **OnClick()** event for this button, dragging the **Main Camera** as the target GameObject and selecting the **BUTTON_ACTION_make_green()** public function. Do the same for the **button-BLUE** and **button-RED** buttons with the **BUTTON_ACTION_make_blue()** and **BUTTON_ACTION_make_red()** functions, respectively.

9. Run the game. When you click a **change-color** button, the three **UI objects** on the right of the screen show all changes to the corresponding color, while the two **UI objects** at the bottom-left of the screen remain in the default white color. You should also see `Debug.Log` messages in the Console panel, showing the RBG color corresponding to the button that was clicked.

How it works...

We have added an instance object of `ColorManager` to the Main Camera. This class does three main things:

- Creates an instance object of the `ColorChangeListenerConsole` script class
- Creates an instance object of the `ColorModel` script class
- Offers three public methods that can be invoked by clicking the red/green/blue UI Buttons

Each time a button is clicked, the `colorModel` object is told to `SetColor(...)` to the corresponding color.

The `ColorModel` script class has a private variable of the current color. This value can be changed by invoking its `SetColor(...)` method (from the `ColorManager` when a button is clicked). As well as changing the value of color, the `SetColor(...)` method also invokes the `PublishColorEvent()` method. The `PublishColorEvent()` method publishes the `OnChangeColor(this.color)` event, so that all registered listeners to this event will be invoked with the new color value.

On the right-hand side of the screen, we have three GameObjects: **Image-listening, Slider-listening,** and **Text-listening**. Each of these objects has a scripted component of either `ColorChangeListenerImage` or `ColorChangeListenerText`. These components register their respective `OnChangeColor(...)` methods to listen for `OnChangeColor(this.color)` events. The `ColorChangeListenerImage` and `ColorChangeListenerText` script classes both register their `ChangeColor(...)` methods to the `OnChangeColor(...)` event of the `ColorModel` script class.

The `ColorChangeListenerConsole` script class also registers its `ChangeColor(...)` methods to the `OnChangeColor(...)` event of the `ColorModel` script class.

Since our scripted objects may be disabled and enabled at different times, each time a scripted `ColorChangeListener` object is enabled (such as when its GameObject parent is instantiated), its `OnChangeColor()` method is added (+=) to the list of those subscribed to listen for color-change events, likewise, each time `ColorChangeListenerImage` or `Text` objects are disabled, those methods are removed (−=) from the list of event subscribers.

 It is very important that methods are removed from the list of subscribers to an event when they are no longer required. Failure to do this can lead to significant problems, such as memory leaks.

When `ColorChangeListenerImage` or a `Text` object receives a color-change message, its subscribed `OnChangeColor()` method is executed and the color of the appropriate component is changed to the received color value (green/red/blue).

The `ColorManager` class declares a **Delegate** named `ColorChangeHandler`. Delegates define the return type (in this case, `void`) and argument signature of methods that can be delegated (subscribed) to an event. In this case, methods must have the argument signature of a single parameter of the `Color` type. Our `OnChangeColor()` method in the `ColorChangeListenerImage`, `Text`, and `Console` classes matches this argument signature and so is permitted to subscribe to `changeColorEvent` in the `ColorManager` class.

You may notice that `ColorChangeListenerConsole` does not have `OnEnable` or `OnDisable` methods. This is because it is not a MonoBehaviour, and so does not receive Unity runtime events such as `Awake()`, `Update()`, or `OnEnable()`. However, being a simple class, it can have a constructor method invoked when a new object instance is created with the new keyword, and a destructor method invoked when the object is no longer referenced. So it is in those methods that these objects register and deregister to listen to `ColorModel.OnChangeColor` events.

Model-View-Controller (MVC) pattern

The **Model-View-Controller** (**MVC**) pattern is a software architecture that tries to separate the data (Model) from the displays (Views) and actions that change that data (Controller).

In this recipe, we use the MVC pattern to implement a feature of many games—a visual health bar representing the Player's numeric health value (in this case, a float number from 0.0 - 1.0). As the user presses the Up/Down arrow keys (simulating healing and damage), the value of the player's heath changes. With the health-change events, the visual display and a **Console** log are updated to present the new health values to the user:

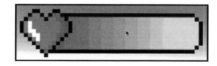

Getting ready

For this recipe, two images been provided in the `17_05` folder:

- `health_bar_outline.png`: A red heart image and outline for the health filler
- `health_bar_fill_blue_to_green.png`: A graduated (blue left to green right) filler image, indicating how much health is left

Thanks to Pixel Art Maker for the health bar image:

- http://pixelartmaker.com/art/49e2498a414f221

How to do it...

To implement the MVC pattern in Unity, follow these steps:

1. Import the two provided images.
2. Create a **UI Image** named `Image-health-bar-outline`, and populate it with the `health_bar_outline` image asset.
3. Create a **UI Image** named `Image-health-bar-filler`, and populate it with the `health_bar_fill_blue_to_green` image asset. In the **Inspector** for the **Image (Script)** component, set the **Image Type** to **Filled**, and the **Fill Type** to **Horizontal**.
4. Arrange your **Canvas** so that **Image-health-bar-filler** is before **Image-health-bar** in the **Hierarchy** (the filler appears behind the outline).
5. Create a new C# script class, Player:

```
public class Player
  {
      public delegate void HealthChangeAction(float health);
      public static event HealthChangeAction OnHealthChange;

      private float health;
      const float MIN_HEALTH = 0;
      const float MAX_HEALTH = 1;

      public Player(float health = 1)
      {
          this.health = health;

          // ensure initial value published
          PublishHealthChangeEvent();
      }


      public float GetHealth()
      {
          return this.health;
      }

      public void AddHealth(float amount)
      {
          this.health += amount;
          if (this.health > MAX_HEALTH)
          {
              this.health = MAX_HEALTH;
          }
```

```
            PublishHealthChangeEvent();
    }

    public void ReduceHealth(float amount)
    {
        this.health -= amount;
        if (this.health < MIN_HEALTH)
        {
            this.health = MIN_HEALTH;
        }
        PublishHealthChangeEvent();
    }

    // event
    private void PublishHealthChangeEvent()
    {
        if (null != OnHealthChange)
            OnHealthChange(this.health);
    }
}
```

6. **Create a new C# script class, **PlayerController:

```
using UnityEngine;

public class PlayerController
{
    private Player player;

    public PlayerController()
    {
        player = new Player();
    }

    public void AddToHealth()
    {
        player.AddHealth(0.5f);
    }

    public void ReduceHealth()
    {
        player.ReduceHealth(0.1f);
    }
}
```

7. Create a new C# script class, HealthBarDisplay, and add an instance object as a component to Image-health-bar-filler:

```
using UnityEngine;
using UnityEngine.UI;

public class HealthBarDisplay : MonoBehaviour
{
    private Image healthMeterFiller;

    private void Start()
    {
        healthMeterFiller = GetComponent<Image>();
    }

    private void OnEnable()
    {
        Player.OnHealthChange += UpdateHealthBar;
    }

    private void OnDisable()
    {
        Player.OnHealthChange -= UpdateHealthBar;
    }

    public void UpdateHealthBar(float health)
    {
        healthMeterFiller.fillAmount = health;
    }
}
```

8. Create a new C# script class, HealthChangeLogger:

```
using UnityEngine;

public class HealthChangeLogger
{
    public HealthChangeLogger()
    {
        Player.OnHealthChange += LogNewHealth;
    }

    ~HealthChangeLogger()
    {
        Player.OnHealthChange -= LogNewHealth;
    }

    public void LogNewHealth(float health)
```

```
        {
            // 1 decimal place
            string healthAsString = health.ToString("0.0");
            Debug.Log("health = " + healthAsString);
        }
    }
```

9. Add the following `PlayerManager` C# script class to the **Main Camera**:

```
using UnityEngine;

public class PlayerManager : MonoBehaviour
{
    private PlayerController playerController;
    private HealthChangeLogger healthChangeLogger;

    void Start()
    {
        playerController = new PlayerController();
        healthChangeLogger = new HealthChangeLogger();
    }

    void Update()
    {
        if (Input.GetKeyDown("up"))
            playerController.AddToHealth();

        if (Input.GetKeyDown("down"))
            playerController.ReduceHealth();
    }
}
```

10. Run the game. Pressing the Up/Down arrow keys should raise/lower the player's health, which should be confimed by the meter fill image, and in the `Debug.Log()` messages in the **Console**.

How it works...

You were provided with two **UI Images:** one is a health bar outline (red heart and a black outline), the second is the filler image—to show dark blue to light blue to green, for weak to strong health values.

You set the **Image Type** of **Image-health-bar-filler** to be **Filled**, and that it is to be filled **Horizontally** (left to right). Therefore, the **fillAmount** property of a UI Image determines how much of this filler image is displayed to the user (from 0.0 to 1.0).

The PlayerManager script class is a manager script that initializes the PlayerController and HealthChangeLogger objects, and also allows the user to change the health of the Player by pressing the Up and Down arrow keys (simulating healing/damage during a game). Via the Update() method, each Up/Down arrow key press invokes the PlayerController methods: AddToHealth() and ReducedHealth().

The PlayerController script class creates a PlayerModel object in its constructor. It has two other methods, AddToHealth() and ReducedHealth(), that add to/reduce the health of the PlayerModel object by +0.5 and -0.1, respectively.

The PlayerModel script class manages values for Player health, and uses delegates and events to publish health changes to any listening **View** classes. When a new object is created, the health property is initialized, and a health-change event is published to all listening objects. Likewise, when the AddHealth(...) and ReduceHealth(...) methods are invoked with a value, the value of the health is changed, and the health-change event is published to all listening objects. The OnHealthChange event is visible to other objects as a static public event. The PublishHealthChangeEvent() method publishes the new value of health by invoking all listening OnHealthChange(...) methods.

There are two View classes that register to listen for Player.OnHealthChange(...) events:

- HealthBarDisplay: Updates fillAmount for a UI Image for each new health value received
- HealthChangeLogger: Prints messages about the new Player health value received to the Debug.Log file

As can be seen, each of the Model/View/Controller classes is quite small and simple, and each has their own, well-defined responsibilities. It would be easy to add another kind of health-change event listener, perhaps to play a sound, without having to change any code in any of these existing classes. Likewise, it would be straightforward to add a new property to our PlayerModel (perhaps a score or inventory value of stars collected, and then add another public static event for score/inventory changes to be published to subscribed listening views).

See also

- Only PlayerManager is a MonoBehaviour. One of the advantages of this MVC architecture is that each of these components becomes much easier to unit-test in isolation. A version of this recipe is used as an example in the *State Design Pattern PlayMode and Unit Testing a health bar with events, logging, and exceptions* recipe in Chapter 19, *Automated Testing* .

15
Editor Extensions and Immediate Mode GUI (IMGUI)

In this chapter, we will cover the following topics:

- Menu items to log messages and clear the console
- Displaying a panel with text data
- An interactive panel and persistent storage
- Creating GameObjects, parenting and registering Undo actions
- Working with selected objects and deactivating menu items
- Menu item to create 100 randomly positioned prefab clones
- A progress bar to display proportion completed of Editor extension processing
- An editor extension to allow pickup type (and parameters) to be changed at design time via a custom Inspector UI
- An editor extension to have an object-creator GameObject, with buttons to instantiate different pickups at cross-hair object's location in scene
- Extensible class-based code architecture to manage complex IMGUIs

Introduction

One aspect of game development in general (and inventories as our particular examples in this chapter) is the distinction about when we undertake an activity. Runtime is when the game is running (and when all our software and UI choices take effect). However, design-time is the time when different members of our game design team work on constructing a wide range of game components, including the scripts, audio and visual assets, and the process of constructing each game level (or scene in Unity-speak).

Unity's Editor extensions are scripting and multimedia components that enable a game software engineer to make design-time work easier and less likely to introduce errors. Editor extensions allow workflow improvements, thus allowing designers to achieve their goals quicker and more easily; for example, removing the need for any scripting knowledge when generating many randomly located inventory pickups in a scene via a menu choice or editing the type or properties of pickups being hand-placed in different locations in a level.

The Big picture

Apart from plain text, there are four sections below will give you an idea of what this chapter is about.

Unity Immediate Mode GUI (IMGUI)

In the early versions of Unity, all **UI** components were created through code - there was no **Canvas**, or **Rect** Transform, or drag-and-drop **UI** control layout and so on. A few years ago (Unity 4.6), Unity introduced what we now know as the **UI** system. The new (play-mode) UI system is an example of a **Retained Mode UI**; the **UI** items we created are remembered frame-to-frame and don't need to be re-created/displayed by us as developers. However, the code-based GUI system still has an important role to play for Editor Extensions. The **IMGUI** system is called **Immediate Mode**, since its code executes one more times each frame. Therefore, there is no need to clear previous GUI displays, since that it automatic.

Identifying and saving changes

The concept of serialization is raised in the Editor extension recipes, whereby we need to remember that, when we are editing item properties in the Inspector, each change needs to be saved to disk, so that the updated property is correct when we next use or edit that item. This is achieved in the OnInspectorGUI() method by first calling the serializedObject.Update() method and, after all changes have been made in the Inspector, finally calling the serializedObject.ApplyModifiedProperties() method.

We can detect when the user has made a change to a GUI control by interrogating Unity's special public bool value: GUI.changed. This is set to true if a GUI control has changed input data (for example, if the user has been typing or clicking GUI controls). Here is a simple example of using GUI.changed to log a message when the content of a text input field has been updated:

```
stringToEdit = GUILayout.TextField(stringToEdit, 25);

if (GUI.changed)
    Debug.Log("new contents of 'stringToEdit' = " + stringToEdit);
```

Unity's EditorGUI class provides Begin-End ChangeCheck() methods that will set GUI.changed to true if the user has changed one or more interactive GUI components in a block of statements delimited by these methods:

```
EditorGUI.BeginChangeCheck();
stringToEdit = GUILayout.TextField(stringToEdit, 25);
... other interactive GUI statements here
EditorGUI.EndChangeCheck();

// logic if any have changed
if(GUI.changed)
    ... do actions since user has changed at least one GUI control
```

If they have, we can save a statement, since `EditorGUI.EndChangeCheck()`, as well as declaring the end of the block of statements for GUI.change. This also returns the bool value of GUI.changed. So, we can actually use this method call in our if-statement instead of GUI.changed. In essence:

```
EditorGUI.BeginChangeCheck();
 stringToEdit = GUILayout.TextField(stringToEdit, 25);
 ... other interactive GUI statements here

 // logic if any have changed
 if(EditorGUI.EndChangeCheck())
     ... do actions since user has changed at least one GUI control
```

Memory - EditorPrefs persistent storage

An issue with Immediate Mode systems is that everything is temporary and forgotten. Unity provides **EditorPrefs,** similar to **PlayerPrefs,** a facility for storing data that is remembered between the closing of a panel and its reopening. Just as with **PlayerPrefs,** different **types** of values can be stored and retrieved using `Get<>()` and `Set<>()` methods, including:

- `SetString(<key>, <value>)`
- `GetString(<key>)`
- And so on

Also provided are methods to delete all stored EditorPrefs data (`DeleteAll()`), to delete just one item for a given key (`DeleteKey(<key>)`), and to check if an item exists for a given key (`HasKey(<key>)`).

 Of course, `DeleteAll()` isn't something to be used without careful consideration. There is an example of `DeleteAll()` in the Unity documentation that ensures the game developer is first asked if they are sure they really want to delete all stored values: `https://docs.unity3d.com/ScriptReference/EditorPrefs.DeleteAll.html`

Typically, values are **loaded** from **EditorPrefs** using getters (if the `<key>`s exist) each time the panel gets the focus. For example:

```
private void OnFocus()
 {
     if (EditorPrefs.HasKey("PlayerName"))
         playerName = EditorPrefs.GetString("PlayerName");
 }
```

Likewise, when panels lose focus (`OnLostFocus()`) or are closed (`OnDestroy()`) we may wish to automatically save any values to EditorPrefs using setters.

Conclusions and further resources

While Editor extensions are quite an advanced topic, having someone on your team who can write custom editor components, such as those we illustrate, can greatly increase the productivity of a small team with only one or two members who are confident at scripting.

In this chapter, we introduce recipes demonstrating some Unity Editor extension scripts, illustrating how we can make things easier, less-script based, and less prone to errors, by limiting and controlling the properties of objects and how they are selected or changed via the Inspector.

There is a lot to working with Editor Extensions and the IMGUI. Here is a list of resources to learn more about these topics:

- Learn more about EditorPrefs in the Unity Documentation: `https://docs.unity3d.com/ScriptReference/EditorPrefs.html`
- Unity blog post about IMGUI: `https://blogs.unity3d.com/2015/12/22/going-deep-with-imgui-and-editor-customization/`
- Video about IMGUI by Casey Muratori: `https://caseymuratori.com/blog_0001`
- the Unity Immediate Mode GUI reference pages: `https://docs.unity3d.com/Manual/GUIScriptingGuide.html`
- The Unity GUI event scripting reference page: `https://docs.unity3d.com/ScriptReference/Event.html`
- Unity scripting OnGUI reference page: `https://docs.unity3d.com/ScriptReference/MonoBehaviour.OnGUI.html`
- Ryan Meier's blog: `http://www.ryan-meier.com/blog/?p=72`
- Tutsplus tutorials and custom scripts (including grids and color pickers): `http://code.tutsplus.com/tutorials/how-to-add-your-own-tools-to-unitys-editor--active-10047`
- Gamasutra getting starting Editor Extensions article: `https://www.gamasutra.com/blogs/ElmarTalibzade/20160418/270604/Getting_Started_Creating_Editor_Extensions_in_Unity.php`

- Menu
  items: https://docs.unity3d.com/ScriptReference/MenuItem.html
- EditorGUI.BeingChangeCheck: https://docs.unity3d.com/ScriptRefere
  nce/EditorGUI.BeginChangeCheck.html

Menu items to log messages and clear the console

Custom menus are a great way to offer game developers easy access to your Editor Extension features. Logging actions is a good way to display and keep a record of actions performance and object properties that have been changed. In this recipe, we'll create a new menu for the Unity Editor application and a menu item that when selected logs a simple message:

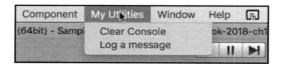

How to do it...

To create a menu with a menu item to log messages to console, follow these steps:

1. In the **Project** panel, create a new folder, Editor.
2. In your new **Editor** folder, create a new C# script-class named ConsoleUtilities.cs, containing the following:

```
using UnityEditor;
 using UnityEngine;
 using System.Reflection;

public class ConsoleUtilities : EditorWindow
 {
     [MenuItem("My Utilities/Clear Console")]
     public static void ClearLogConsole()
     {
         var assembly =
Assembly.GetAssembly(typeof(SceneView));
         var type =
assembly.GetType("UnityEditor.LogEntries");
```

```
        var method = type.GetMethod("Clear");
        method.Invoke(new object(), null);
    }

    [MenuItem("My Utilities/Log a message")]
    public static void LogHello()
    {
        Debug.Log("Hello from my console utilties");
    }
}
```

3. After a few seconds, you should now see a menu named **My Utilities** appear with two items **Clear Console** and **Log a message**.

4. You should now be able to clear the console and generate Log messages with these menu items.

How it works...

You created an editor extension script-class in a folder **Editor** that extends the EditorWindow class. You defined two methods; each method was immediately preceded by an attribute to add a menu item to a menu named **My Utilities**.

The ClearLogConsole() method was immediately preceded by an attribute declaring a new menu, My Utilities, and its single menu item Clear Console:

```
    [MenuItem("My Utilities/Clear Console")]
```

The **MenuItem attribute** immediately precedes a **static** method, that implements the actions to be executed if the menu item is selected by the user. The menu path is in the form:

- **MenuName/MenuItemName** or
- **MenuName/SubMenuName/MenuItemName** and so on for submenus

The LogHello() method creates a new Log message each time it is invoked.

The ClearLogConsole() method gets a reference to the Unity logs and clears them.

You can learn more about Editor Extensions for menus in the Unity tutorial on this topic:
https://unity3d.com/learn/tutorials/topics/interface-essentials/unity-edit
or-extensions-menu-items

It should be noted that using Reflection is very slow and so generally only used for Editor scripts or scripts that are only executed once and a short delay will not impact upon the user's or game developer's quality of experience.

There's more

There are some details that you don't want to miss.

Keyboard shortcuts

Special characters in the Menu Item string can be used to specify a keyboard shortcut for the menu item:

- % indicates the CTRL-key (Windows) or CMD-key (Mac)
- # indicate the SHIFT-key
- <c> then the (lowercase) letter or character shortcut key (e.g. 'k' for the K-key)

When keyboard shortcut has been defined, Unity also indicates this to the right of the menu item:

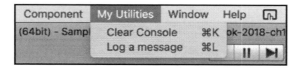

So, let's add shortcuts so that *CTRL/CMD-L* logs a message and *CTRL/CMD-K* clears the log (keys *L* and *K* are next to each other on the keyboard):

```
[MenuItem("My Utilities/Log a message %l")] // CMD + L
public static void LogHello()
{
    Debug.Log("Hello from my console utilties");
}

[MenuItem("My Utilities/Clear Console %k")] // CMD + K
public static void ClearLogConsole()
{
    var assembly = Assembly.GetAssembly(typeof(SceneView));
    var type = assembly.GetType("UnityEditor.LogEntries");
    var method = type.GetMethod("Clear");
```

```
        method.Invoke(new object(), null);
    }
```

Learn more about Unity Menu Item Keyboard Shortcuts at
`https://docs.unity3d.com/ScriptReference/MenuItem.html`.

Sub-menus

You can create sub-menus by adding a third text item between forward slashes, in the
following form:

```
Menu Name/Sub-menu name/menu item
```

So, to have a menu **Utilities** with a sub-menu **Console** and two items for that
submenu, you could write the following:

```
[MenuItem("Utilities/Console/Clear Console")]
 public static void ClearLogConsole() {
     // code here
 }

 [MenuItem("Utilities/Console/Log a message")]
 public static void LogHello() {
     // code here
 }
```

Displaying a panel with text data

Sometimes, we want to create and display a new panel as part of an Editor Extension.
In this recipe, we create a menu item that creates and displays a new panel,
displaying some text information:

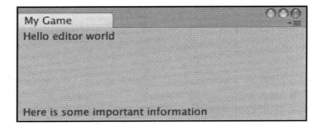

How to do it...

To display a panel with text data, follow these steps:

1. In the **Project** panel, create a new folder, **Editor**.
2. In your new **Editor** folder, create a new C# script-class named
   InformationPanel.cs, containing the following:

```
using UnityEditor;
 using UnityEngine;

public class InformationPanel : EditorWindow
{
    [MenuItem("My Game/Info Panel")]
    public static void ShowWindow()
    {
        GetWindow<InformationPanel>("My Game", true);
    }

    private void OnGUI()
    {
        GUILayout.Label("Hello editor world");
        GUILayout.FlexibleSpace();
        GUILayout.Label("Here is some important
information");
    }
}
```

3. After a few seconds, you should now see a menu named **My Game** appear,
   with menu item **Info Panel**.
4. Select menu item **Info Panel** - you should now see a new panel appear,
   entitled **My Game** and containing the two text messages.

How it works...

You preceded the ShowWindow() method with an attribute to add a menu item Info
Panel to a menu named My Game. The GetWindow() statement gets a reference to an
InformationPanel object - if no such window-panel exists, it creates one. It searches
for a window-panel of type (that is, for this script-class). The first argument is the title
of the panel My Game. The true for the second argument tells Unity to make the
window-panel have the focus (if a window panel already existed).

If a new window panel has been created it will always be given the focus.

The `OnGUI()` method, which executes a least once every frame, uses `GUILayout` to display two text labels. Since `GUILayout` begins adding items at the top-left, the first message Hello editor world appears in the top-left of the panel. Then there is a `FlexibleSpace()` statement. This tells the GUI layout manager to fill up as much (default - vertical) space as it can, while allowing space in the panel for any other content. The third statement displays a second text label. The result is that the second text label is pushed to the bottom of the panel by the `FlexibleSpace()`.

Try resizing the panel; you'll see the second text label is always at the bottom.

There's more

Here are some details that you won't want to miss throughout.

Vertical centering

If we wanted to vertically center some text, we can have a `FlexibleSpace()` statement both before and after the content. For example, the following code would vertically center text Here is some important information:

```
GUILayout.Label("Hello editor world");

GUILayout.FlexibleSpace();
GUILayout.Label("Here is some important information");
GUILayout.FlexibleSpace();
```

Vertical and horizontal centering (middle of an area)

To center horizontally, we need to change from the default vertical layout by starting (and ending) a horizontal layout, in the following form:

```
GUILayout.BeginHorizontal();
// content here is laid out horiztonally
GUILayout.EndHorizontal();
```

By the having `FlexibleSpace()` before and after the content in the horizontal layout, we can center content horizontally as well.

To center both vertically and horizontally, we use `FlexibleSpace()` before and after the horizontal layout, and also before and after the content inside the horizontal layout. For example:

```
private void OnGUI() {
    GUILayout.Label("Hello editor world");
    GUILayout.FlexibleSpace();

    GUILayout.BeginHorizontal();
    GUILayout.FlexibleSpace();

        GUILayout.Label("I am in the center !!!");

    GUILayout.FlexibleSpace();
    GUILayout.EndHorizontal();

    GUILayout.FlexibleSpace();
}
```

This use of flexible spacing is illustrated in the following screenshot:

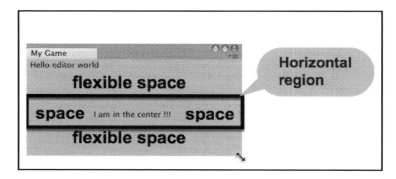

An interactive panel with persistent storage

With Immediate Mode, we have to store the values of interactive controls like buttons and text inputs at the time we display them. Also, we need to decide if, and when, to persistently store values to be remembered when the panel is out of focus or closed.

In this recipe, we display a text label saying hello to the player and using their name if it has been found in the **EditorPrefs** storage. We also offer a text input and a button and, when the button is clicked, we update the name being greeted:

How to do it...

To offer an interactive panel with persistent storage, follow these steps:

1. In the **Project** panel, create a new **Editor** folder.
2. In your new **Editor** folder, create a new C# script-class named `Welcome.cs` containing the following:

```
using UnityEditor;
 using UnityEngine;

public class Welcome : EditorWindow
 {
     private string playerName = "";
     private string tempName = "";

     [MenuItem("Welcome/Hello Player")]
     public static void ShowWindow()
     {
         GetWindow<Welcome>("Welcome", true);
     }

     private void OnGUI()
```

```
        {
            // hello
            string helloMessage = "Hello (no name)";
            if (playerName.Length > 0){
                helloMessage = "Hello " + playerName;
            }

            GUILayout.Label(helloMessage);
            GUILayout.FlexibleSpace();

            // text input
            tempName = EditorGUILayout.TextField("Player name:",
tempName);

            // button
            if (GUILayout.Button("Update")){
                playerName = tempName;
            }
        }
    }
```

3. After a few seconds, you should now see a menu named **Welcome** appear with menu item **Hello Player**.
4. Select the menu item **Hello Player**. You should now see a new panel appear, entitled **Welcome**, displaying a hello message, a text input box, and a button labeled **Update**.
5. Enter your name in the text box and, when you press the button, you should see a message greeting you by name.

How it works...

You preceded the ShowWindow() method with an attribute to add a menu item, **Hello Player**, to a menu named Welcome. The GetWindow() statement gets a reference to an EditorWindow object of type (that is, for this script-class), creating a new one if no existing window-panel of this type can be found.

The OnGUI() method, which executes every frame, uses GUILayout to display the following:

- A text label in the form **Hello**
- A text input with the prompt **Player name**
- An **Update** button

There is some `FlexibleSpace()` between the first item (greeting label) and the input box and button, so the input box and button appear at the bottom of the panel.

There are two private string variables:

- `playerName`
- `tempName`

The `playerName` variable is used to decide what greeting to display. If the length of this string is greater than zero (in essence, it's not an empty string), then the hello message will be Hello. If `playerName` was empty, then the message will be Hello (no name).

The second variable, `tempName`, is set to the value in the text box. This has to be re-assigned every frame (in `OnGUI()`), since the text box is redisplayed every frame. Each time the user types different text in the text box, the new text is immediately stored in the `tempName` variable.

Finally, there is an `if` statement that displays the Update button. If, during a frame, the button is clicked by the user, then the `if`-statement will be executed, which copies the `tempName` from the text box into the `playerName` variable. The very next frame, we'll see the greeting change to reflect the new value inside `playerName`.

We have used `EditorGUILayout.TextField(...)` for the text field entry, whereas the other methods are GUILayout methods. The `EditorGUILayout` methods make interactive controls easier, while the GUILayout methods make layout easier. For window-panels like this you can mix-and-match these GUI methods.

There's more

There are some details that you don't want to miss.

Persistent storage with EditorPrefs

At present, if the panel is closed (for example, due to a new panel layout being invoked), then any name that was being shown will be lost. However, we can add some code that uses the **EditorPrefs** system to store the new name each time the **Update** button is clicked. Additional code can then check for an **EditorPrefs** value when the panel is newly displayed and initialize `playerName` to the stored value.

First, when the panel is created/gets the focus, let's attempt to read an **EditorPrefs** item with the key `"PlayerName"`. If found, we'll retrieve that string and assign the `playerName` variable to the stored value:

```
private void OnFocus() {
 if (EditorPrefs.HasKey("PlayerName"))
 playerName = EditorPrefs.GetString("PlayerName");
 }
```

Now, let's create a method that will save the value in `playerName` into **EditorPrefs**, again using the key `"PlayerName"`:

```
private void SavePrefs() {
    EditorPrefs.SetString("PlayerName", playerName);
 }
```

There are two times we may wish to ensure the value is saved, when the panel loses focus and when it is closed (destroyed). So, for both these events, we'll write methods that will invoke our `SavePrefs()` method:

```
// automatic save when panel loses focus
 private void OnLostFocus() {
    SavePrefs();
 }

 // automatic save when panel closed/destroyed
 private void OnDestroy() {
    SavePrefs();
 }
```

GUILayout versus EditorGUILayout

You may have noticed there were two different `GUILayout` different method calls in this recipe:

```
GUILayout.Label(helloMessage);
 GUILayout.FlexibleSpace();
 tempName = EditorGUILayout.TextField("Player name:", tempName);
```

`GUILayout` and `EditorGUILayout` both perform very similar roles, in that they provide UI controls with some automated layout - that is, we don't have to specify exact (x,y) values or rectangles for the window-panel size and position of each item. `GUILayout` offers some of the more flexible layout options, like `FlexibleSpace` and horizontal and vertical groups, which with `FlexibleSpace` can vertically and horizontally align items. However, `EditorGUILayout` offers easier and more powerful numeric and text input fields, as well as color selection widgets, foldout groups, and so on.

DM Gregory, in a StackExchange post in 2017, lists many of the extra methods available when using `EditorGUILayout`:
https://gamedev.stackexchange.com/questions/139192/difference-between-guilayout-and-editorguilayout

Creating GameObjects, parenting, and registering Undo actions

Whether from a menu item, or an **Inspector** view, there are times when we want to create a new **GameObject** in the scene from an Editor Extension. In this recipe, we'll create a new **GameObject** and set its position and color randomly:

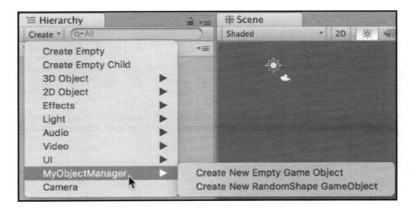

How to do it...

To create an object and change its value follow these steps:

1. In the **Project** panel, create a new folder, **Editor**.
2. In your new **Editor** folder create a new C# script-class named `ObjectManager.cs`, containing the following:

```
using UnityEditor;
 using UnityEngine;

 public class ObjectManager : EditorWindow
 {
     [MenuItem("GameObject/MyObjectManager/Create New Empty
Game Object")]
     static void CreateCustomEmptyGameObject(MenuCommand
menuCommand)
     {
         GameObject go = new GameObject("GameObject - custom -
Empty");
         go.transform.position = RandomPosition(5);

         // Ensure it gets reparented if this was a context
click (otherwise does nothing)
         GameObjectUtility.SetParentAndAlign(go,
menuCommand.context as GameObject);

         // Register the creation in the undo system
         Undo.RegisterCreatedObjectUndo(go, "Create " +
go.name);
         Selection.activeObject = go;
     }

     private static Vector3 RandomPosition(float limit)
     {
         float x = Random.Range(-limit, limit);
         float y = Random.Range(-limit, limit);
         float z = Random.Range(-limit, limit);
         return new Vector3(x,y,z);
     }
 }
```

3. After a few seconds, you'll see added to the GameObject menu a new sub-menu named **MyObjectManager** appear, with menu item Create New Empty Game Object.

4. Choose menu: **GameObject | MyObjectManager | Create New Empty Game Object**.

5. You should now see a new GameObject named **GameObject - custom - Empty** created in the Hierarchy panel. If you select this object, it's position (x,y,z) values should be random, in the range -0.5 ... 0.5.

6. You can Undo this create **GameObject** from the **Edit** menu (or *CTRL/CMD-Z*).

7. With the new empty GameObject selected in the Hierarchy, right-mouse click to get the context menu for this object. Now, choose **menu: Create | MyObjectManager | Create New Empty Game Object**.

8. You should now see a second empty GameObject created as a child of the first one;

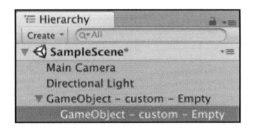

How it works...

You preceded the `CreateCustomEmptyGameObject(...)` method with an attribute to add to existing menu GameObject a sub-menu MyObjectManager with menu item **Create New Empty Game Object**.

The `CreateCustomEmptyGameObject(...)` method creates a new, empty GameObject with the name **GameObject - custom - Empty**. It then sets the position property to a Vector3 random location, returned from method `RandomPosition(...)`.

The `CreateCustomEmptyGameObject(...)` method then uses the `GameObjectUtility.SetParentAndAlign(...)` method to parent the new GameObject to the object selected in the Hierarchy, if the menu was invoked in the contents of a selected GameObject. Otherwise, the new GameObject will have no parent in the Hierarchy.

The `RandomPosition(...)` method takes as input a float parameter <limit>, and generates three values (x,y,z) in the random range from negative to positive <limit>. It then creates and returns a new Vector3 object with these three values.

Because we chose to add our action to the special GameObject menu, our sub-menu item appears in the Hierarchy panel's content Create menu as: **Create | MyObjectManager | Create New Empty Game Object**.

There's more

There are some details that you don't want to miss.

Registering object changes to allow Undo'ing of actions

When we performance an object creation/deletion/change action in the Unity Editor, we should offer the user the change to Undo the action. Unity makes it very easy for us to facilitate this, through registration of the changed object by providing an Undo class.

We can add to `CreateCustomEmptyGameObject(...)` a call to the `Undo.RegisterCreatedObjectUndo(...)` method. This registers the GameObject creation in the Unity system Undo register so that the action can be undone if the uses wishes to do so:

```
[MenuItem("GameObject/MyObjectManager/Create New Empty Game Object")]
 static void CreateCustomEmptyGameObject(MenuCommand menuCommand)
 {
     GameObject go = new GameObject("GameObject - custom - Empty");
     go.transform.position = RandomPosition(5);

     // Ensure it gets reparented if this was a context click
(otherwise does nothing)
     GameObjectUtility.SetParentAndAlign(go, menuCommand.context as
GameObject);
```

```
    // Register the creation in the undo system
    Undo.RegisterCreatedObjectUndo(go, "Create " + go.name);
    Selection.activeObject = go;
}
```

Learn more about the Undo features in the Unity documentation pages: `https://docs.unity3d.com/ScriptReference/Undo.html`

Creating primitive 3D GameObjects with random colors

Rather than creating empty GameObjects, we can create new GameObjects that are 3D primitives like cubes and spheres etc. We can do this using the `GameObject.CreatePrimitive(...)` method. By adding the following three methods, we'll be able to create randomly positioned, randomly colored, random 3D GameObjects from a second menu item in our **MyObjectManager** sub-menu:

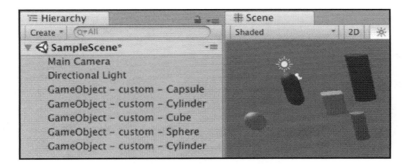

Let's write a method to add a second menu item, which offers to create random GameObjects with 3D primitives:

```
[MenuItem("GameObject/MyObjectManager/Create New RandomShape
GameObject")]
  static void CreateCustomPrimitiveGameObject(MenuCommand menuCommand){
      // Create a custom game object
      GameObject go = BuildGameObjectRandomPrimitive();
      go.transform.position = RandomPosition(5);
      go.GetComponent<Renderer>().sharedMaterial =
RandomMaterialColor();
  }
```

We can choose a random integer from 0..3 to choose between
Cube/Sphere/Capsule/Cylinder 3D primitives for our new GameObject:

```
private static GameObject BuildGameObjectRandomPrimitive() {
    GameObject go;
    PrimitiveType primitiveType = PrimitiveType.Cube;
    int type = Random.Range(0, 4);

    switch (type) {
        case 0:
            primitiveType = PrimitiveType.Sphere;
            break;

        case 1:
            primitiveType = PrimitiveType.Capsule;
            break;

        case 2:
            primitiveType = PrimitiveType.Cylinder;
            break;
    }

    go = GameObject.CreatePrimitive(primitiveType);
    go.name = "GameObject - custom - " + primitiveType.ToString();
    return go;
}
```

Here is the final method we need to create a new **Material** with a random color, that
can be assigned to the new primitives **sharedMaterial** property:

```
private static Material RandomMaterialColor() {
    Shader shaderSpecular = Shader.Find("Specular");
    Material material = new Material(shaderSpecular);
    material.color = Random.ColorHSV();

    return material;
}
```

Working with selected objects and deactivating menu items

Sometimes, we only want to execute some statements if an object is currently selected, related to those actions. In this recipe, we learn how to disable a menu item if nothing is selected. If a GameObject is selected, we'll get a reference to that object and move it back to the origin (0,0,0):

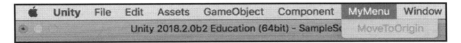

How to do it...

To work with selected objects and deactivate menu items follow these steps:

1. In the **Project** panel, create a new folder, **Editor**.
2. In your new **Editor** folder create a new C# script-class named `SelectedObjectManager.cs`, containing the following:

```
using UnityEditor;
 using UnityEngine;

public class SelectedObjectManager : EditorWindow
{
    [MenuItem("MyMenu/Move To Origin")]
    static void ZeroPosition()
    {
        GameObject selectedGameObject =
Selection.activeTransform.gameObject;

        Undo.RecordObject (selectedGameObject.transform,
"Zero Transform Position");
        selectedGameObject.transform.position = Vector3.zero;
    }

    [MenuItem("MyMenu/Move To Origin", true)]
    static bool ValidateZeroPosition()
    {
        // Return false if no transform is selected.
        return Selection.activeTransform != null;
    }
}
```

3. After a few seconds, you'll see a new menu MyMenu created, with menu item **Move To Origin**.
4. If no GameObject is selected in the **Hierarchy**, then the **Move To Origin** menu item should be greyed out (inactive).
5. Create a new, empty GameObject and set its transform position to (5,6,7).
6. With this new GameObject selected in the Hierarchy, choose **menu: MyMenu | Move To Origin**. The menu item should be active, and once chosen the position of the GameObject should be zeroed to (0,0,0).

How it works...

You preceded the `ZeroPosition()` method with a MenuItem attribute to create a new menu MyMenu with menu item Move To Origin. This method gets a reference to the currently selected GameObject using the `Selection.activeTransform.gameObject` property. The object is registered to the Undo systems property change record, and then its transform position is set to (0,0,0).

There is a second method, `ValidateZeroPosition()`. This method is preceded by a **MenuItem** attribute with the same **menu path** as method `ZeroPosition()`. The **MenuItem** attribute is passed true to indicate this is a validation method:

```
[MenuItem("MyMenu/MoveToOrigin", true)]
```

Validation methods must be static methods, marked with the same **MenuItem** attribute as the item they are validating, and pass true to the validation argument. The method must return a bool true/false, to indicate whether the condition has been met for the menu item to be active.

`ValidateZeroPosition()` returns the bool true/false value of the expression `Selection.activeTransform != null`. In other words, it returns true if there is a selected GameObject, and false if there is not.

Learn more about Editor Extension menu items in the Unity tutorial: https://unity3d.com/learn/tutorials/topics/interface-essentials/unity-editor-extensions-menu-items

Menu item to create 100 randomly positioned prefab clones

Sometimes we want to create *lots* of pickups, randomly in our scene. Rather than doing this by hand, it is possible to add a custom menu and item to the Unity editor, which, when selected, will execute a script. In this recipe, we create a menu item that calls a script to create 100 randomly positioned star pickup prefabs in the **Scene**:

Getting ready

This recipe assumes you are starting with the project Simple2Dgame_SpaceGirl setup from the first recipe in Chapter 3, *Inventory UI*.

How to do it...

To create an editor extension to add 100 randomly located copies of a prefab with one menu click, follow these steps:

1. Start with a new copy of mini-game Simple2Dgame_SpaceGirl.
2. In the **Project** panel, create a new folder named **Prefabs**. Inside this new folder, create a new empty prefab named prefab_star. Populate this prefab by dragging GameObject star from the Hierarchy panel over prefab_star in the Project panel. The prefab should now turn blue and have a copy of all of GameObject star's properties and components.

3. Delete GameObject star from the **Hierarchy**.

4. In the **Project** panel, create a new folder named **Editor**. Inside this new folder, create a new C# script class named `MyGreatGameEditor`, with the following code:

```
using UnityEngine;
 using UnityEditor;

 public class MyGreatGameEditor : MonoBehaviour {
     const float X_MAX = 10f;
     const float Y_MAX = 10f;

     static GameObject starPrefab;

     [MenuItem("My-Great-Game/Make 100 stars")]
     static void PlacePrefabs() {
         string assetPath =
"Assets/Prefabs/prefab_star.prefab";
         starPrefab =
(GameObject)AssetDatabase.LoadMainAssetAtPath(assetPath);

         int total = 100;
         for(int i = 0; i < total; i++){
             CreateRandomInstance();
         }
     }

     static void CreateRandomInstance() {
         Vector3 randomPosition = RandomPosition();
         Instantiate(starPrefab, randomPosition,
Quaternion.identity);
     }

     private static Vector3 RandomPosition() {
         float x = Random.Range(-X_MAX, X_MAX);
         float y = Random.Range(-Y_MAX, Y_MAX);
         float z = 0;
         return new Vector3(x,y,z);
     }
  }
```

5. After a few seconds, depending on the speed of your computer, you should see a new menu appear, My Great Game, with a single menu item, Make 100 stars.

6. Choose this menu item and, as if by magic, you should now see 100 new `prefab_star(Clone)` GameObjects appear in the scene!

How it works...

The core aim of this recipe is to add a new menu, containing a single menu item that will execute the action we desire. C# attribute `[MenuItem("<menuName>/<menuItemName>")]` declares the menu name and the menu item name, and Unity will execute the static method that follows in the code listing, each time the menu item is selected by the user.

In this recipe, the `[MenuItem("My-Great-Game/Make 100 stars")]` statement declares the menu name as **My-Great-Game** and the menu item as Make 100 stars. The method immediately following this attribute is the `PlacePrefabs()` method. When this method is executed, it makes the `starPrefab` variable become a reference to the prefab found via the `Assets/Prefabs/prefab_star.prefab` path. Then, a For-loop is executed 100 times, each time calling the `CreateRandomInstance()` method.

The `RandomPosition()` method returns a Vector3 variable that is a random position, making use of `X_MAX` and `Y_MAX` constants (z is always zero).

The `CreateRandomInstance()` method get a Vector3 randomPosition by calling the `RandomPosition()` method. The `Instantiate(...)` built-in method is then used to create a new GameObject in the scene, making a clone of the prefab and locating it at the position defined by randomPosition.

There's more...

Some details you don't want to miss:

Childing each new GameObject to a single parent, to avoid filling up the Hierarchy with 100s of new objects

Rather than having hundreds of new object clones fill up our Hierarchy panel, a good way to keep things tidy is to have an empty "parent" GameObject and child a collection of related GameObjects to it. Let's have a GameObject in the Hierarchy named **Star-container** and child all the new stars to this object:

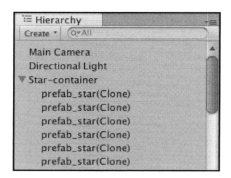

We need a variable that will be a reference to our container object, starContainerGO. We also need a new method, `CreateStarContainerGO()`, which will find a reference to GameObject star-container, if such an object already exists it is deleted, and then the method will create a new empty GameObject and give it this name. Add the following variable and method to our script class:

```
static GameObject starContainerGo;

static void CreateStarContainerGo() {
    string containerName = "Star-container";
    starContainerGo = GameObject.Find(containerName);
    if (null != starContainerGO)
        DestroyImmediate(starContainerGO);

    starContainerGo = new GameObject(containerName);
}
```

Before we create the prefab clones, we need to first ensure we have created our star container GameObject. So, we need to call our new method as the first thing we do when the `PlacePrefabs()` method is executed, so add a statement to call this method at the beginning of the `PlacePrefabs()` method:

```
static void PlacePrefabs(){
    CreateStarContainerGo();

    // rest of method as before ...
}
```

Now, we need to modify the `CreateRandomInstance()` method so that it gets a reference to the new GameObject it has just created and can then child this new object to our star-container GameObject variable starContainerGO. Modify the `CreateRandomInstance()` method so that it looks as follows:

```
static void CreateRandomInstance() {
    float x = UnityEngine.Random.Range(-X_MAX, X_MAX);
    float y = UnityEngine.Random.Range(-Y_MAX, Y_MAX);
    float z = 0;
    Vector3 randomPosition = new Vector3(x,y,z);

    GameObject newStarGo = (GameObject)Instantiate(starPrefab,
randomPosition, Quaternion.identity);
    newStarGo.transform.parent = starContainerGO.transform;
}
```

A progress bar to display proportion completed of Editor extension processing

If an **Editor** task is going to take more than half a second or so, then we should indicate progress complete/remaining to the user via a progress bar so that they understand that something is actually happening and the application has not crashed and frozen:

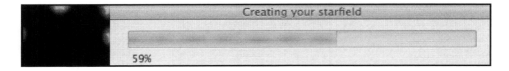

Getting ready

This recipe adds to the previous one, so make a copy of that project folder and do your work for this recipe with that copy.

How to do it...

To add a progress bar during the loop (and then remove it after the loop is complete), replace the `PlacePrefabs()` method with the following code:

```
static void PlacePrefabs(){

    string assetPath = "Assets/Prefabs/prefab_star.prefab";

    starPrefab =
(GameObject)AssetDatabase.LoadMainAssetAtPath(assetPath);

    int total = 100;

        for(int i = 0; i < total; i++){

            CreateRandomInstance();

            EditorUtility.DisplayProgressBar("Creating your starfield", i
+ "%", i/100f);

        }

        EditorUtility.ClearProgressBar();

    }
```

How it works...

As can be seen, inside the for loop, we call the `EditorUtility.DisplayProgressBar(...)` method, passing three parameters. The first is a string title for the progress bar dialog window, the second is a string to show below the bar itself (usually a percentage is sufficient), and the final parameter is a value between 0.0 and 1.0, indicating the percentage complete to be displayed.

Since we have loop variable i that is a number from 1 to 100, we can display this integer followed by a percentage sign for our second parameter and just divide this number by 100 to get the decimal value needed to specify how much of the progress bar should be shown as completed. If the loop were running for some other number, we'd just divide the loop counter by the loop total to get our decimal progress value.

Finally, after the loop has finished, we remove the progress bar with the `EditorUtility.ClearProgressBar()` statement. If we don't have this step, the progress bar window-panel will be left floating around - annoying the user!

An editor extension to allow pickup type (and parameters) to be changed at design time via a custom Inspector UI

The use of **enums** and corresponding drop-down menus in the Inspector panel to restrict changes to one of a limited set often works fine (for example, pickup types for a pickup object). However, the trouble with this approach is, when two or more properties are related and need to be changed together, there is a danger of changing one property, for example, pickup type from **Heart** to **Key**, but forgetting to change corresponding properties; for example, leaving the Sprite Renderer component still showing a **Heart** sprite. Such mismatches cause problems both in terms of messing up intended level design and, of course, the frustration for the player when they collide with something showing one pickup image, but a different kind of pickup type is added to the inventory!

If a class of GameObject has several related properties or components, which all need to be changed together, then a good strategy is to use Unity Editor extensions to do all the associated changes each time a different choice is made from a drop-down menu showing the defined set of enumerated choices.

In this recipe, we introduce an **Editor** extension for `PickUp` components of GameObjects:

Getting ready

This recipe assumes you are starting with the `Simple2Dgame_SpaceGirl` project setup from the first recipe in *Chapter 3, Inventory UI*.

How to do it...

To create an editor extension to allow pickup type (and parameters) to be changed at Design Time via a custom Inspector UI, follow these steps:

1. Start with a new copy of mini-game `Simple2Dgame_SpaceGirl`.

2. In the **Project** panel, create a new folder named **EditorSprites**. Move the following images from folder Sprites into this new folder: **star**, **healthheart**, **icon_key_green_100**, **icon_key_green_32**, **icon_star_32**, and **icon_heart_32**:

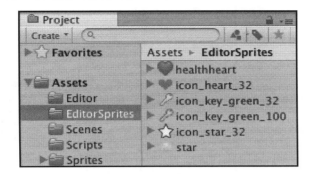

3. In the **Hierarchy** panel, rename GameObject star to be named **pickup**.
4. Edit the tags, changing tag **Star** to **Pickup**. Ensure the pickup GameObject now has the tag Pickup.
5. Create C# script-class `PickUp` and add an instance-object as a component to GameObject pickup in the Hierarchy:

```
using UnityEngine;
using System;
using System.Collections;

public class PickUp : MonoBehaviour {
   public enum PickUpType {
      Star, Health, Key
   }

   [SerializeField]
   public PickUpType type;

   public void SetSprite(Sprite newSprite){
      SpriteRenderer spriteRenderer =
GetComponent<SpriteRenderer>();
      spriteRenderer.sprite = newSprite;
   }
}
```

6. In the **Project** panel, create a new folder named **Editor**.
7. Inside this new **Editor** folder, create a new C# script class named `PickUpEditor`, with the following code:

```
using UnityEngine;
using System.Collections;
using System;
using UnityEditor;
using System.Collections.Generic;
```

```
[CanEditMultipleObjects]
[CustomEditor(typeof(PickUp))]
public class PickUpEditor : Editor
{
  public Texture iconHealth;
  public Texture iconKey;
  public Texture iconStar;

  public Sprite spriteHealth100;
  public Sprite spriteKey100;
  public Sprite spriteStar100;

  UnityEditor.SerializedProperty pickUpType;

  private Sprite sprite;
  private PickUp pickupObject;

  void OnEnable () {
    iconHealth =
AssetDatabase.LoadAssetAtPath("Assets/EditorSprites/icon_heart
_32.png", typeof(Texture)) as Texture;
    iconKey =
AssetDatabase.LoadAssetAtPath("Assets/EditorSprites/icon_key_3
2.png", typeof(Texture)) as Texture;
    iconStar =
AssetDatabase.LoadAssetAtPath("Assets/EditorSprites/icon_star_
32.png", typeof(Texture)) as Texture;

    spriteHealth100 =
AssetDatabase.LoadAssetAtPath("Assets/EditorSprites/healthhear
t.png", typeof(Sprite)) as Sprite;
    spriteKey100 =
AssetDatabase.LoadAssetAtPath("Assets/EditorSprites/icon_key_1
00.png", typeof(Sprite)) as Sprite;
    spriteStar100 =
AssetDatabase.LoadAssetAtPath("Assets/EditorSprites/star.png",
typeof(Sprite)) as Sprite;

    pickupObject = (PickUp)target;
    pickUpType = serializedObject.FindProperty ("type");
  }


  public override void OnInspectorGUI()
  {
    serializedObject.Update ();

    string[] pickUpCategories = TypesToStringArray();
```

```
      pickUpType.enumValueIndex = EditorGUILayout.Popup("PickUp
TYPE: ", pickUpType.enumValueIndex, pickUpCategories);

    PickUp.PickUpType type =
(PickUp.PickUpType)pickUpType.enumValueIndex;
    switch(type)
    {
    case PickUp.PickUpType.Health:
      InspectorGUI_HEALTH();
      break;

    case PickUp.PickUpType.Key:
      InspectorGUI_KEY();
      break;

    case PickUp.PickUpType.Star:
    default:
      InspectorGUI_STAR();
      break;
    }

    serializedObject.ApplyModifiedProperties ();
  }

  private void InspectorGUI_HEALTH()
  {
    GUILayout.BeginHorizontal();
    GUILayout.FlexibleSpace();
    GUILayout.Label(iconHealth);
    GUILayout.Label("HEALTH");
    GUILayout.Label(iconHealth);
    GUILayout.Label("HEALTH");
    GUILayout.Label(iconHealth);
    GUILayout.FlexibleSpace();
    GUILayout.EndHorizontal();

    pickupObject.SetSprite(spriteHealth100);
  }

  private void InspectorGUI_KEY()
  {
    GUILayout.BeginHorizontal();
    GUILayout.FlexibleSpace();
    GUILayout.Label(iconKey);
    GUILayout.Label("KEY");
    GUILayout.Label(iconKey);
    GUILayout.Label("KEY");
    GUILayout.Label(iconKey);
```

```
        GUILayout.FlexibleSpace();
        GUILayout.EndHorizontal();

        pickupObject.SetSprite(spriteKey100);
    }

    private void InspectorGUI_STAR()
    {
      GUILayout.BeginHorizontal();
      GUILayout.FlexibleSpace();
      GUILayout.Label(iconStar);
      GUILayout.Label("STAR");
      GUILayout.Label(iconStar);
      GUILayout.Label("STAR");
      GUILayout.Label(iconStar);
      GUILayout.FlexibleSpace();
      GUILayout.EndHorizontal();

      pickupObject.SetSprite(spriteStar100);
    }
    private string[] TypesToStringArray(){
      var pickupValues =
(PickUp.PickUpType[])Enum.GetValues(typeof(PickUp.PickUpType))
;

        List<string> stringList = new List<string>();

        foreach(PickUp.PickUpType pickupValue in pickupValues){
          string stringName = pickupValue.ToString();
          stringList.Add(stringName);
        }

        return stringList.ToArray();
    }
  }
```

8. In the Inspector panel, select GameObject pickup and choose different values of the drop-down menu **PickUp Type**. You should see corresponding changes in the image and icons in the Inspector for the **Pick Up (Script)** component (three icons with the name of the type in between). The **Sprite** property of the **Sprite Renderer** component for this GameObject should change. Also, in the Scene panel, you'll see the image in the scene change to the appropriate image for the pickup type you have chosen.

How it works...

Our script class `PickUp` has the enum `PickUpType` with the three values: `Star`, **Health**, and `Key`. Also, there is the variable type, storing the type of the parent GameObject. Finally, there is a `SetSprite(...)` method that sets the **Sprite Renderer** component of the parent GameObject to be set to the provided **Sprite** parameter. It is this method that is called from the editor script each time the pickup type is changed from the drop-down menu (with the corresponding sprite for the new type being passed).

The vast majority of the work for this recipe is the responsibility of the script class `PickUpEditor`. While there is a lot in this script, its work is relatively straightforward: for each frame, via method `OnInspectorGUI()`, a dropdown list of PickUpType values is presented to the user. Based on the value selected from this drop-down list, one of three methods is executed: `InspectorGUI_HEALTH()`, `InspectorGUI_KEY()`, or `InspectorGUI_STAR()`. Each of these methods displays three icons and the name of the type in the Inspector beneath the drop-down menu and ends by calling the `SetSprite(...)` method of the GameObject being edited in the Inspector to update the Sprite Renderer component of the parent GameObject with the appropriate sprite.

The C# attribute `[CustomEditor(typeof(PickUp))]` appearing before our class is declared, tells Unity to use this special editor script to display component properties in the Inspector panel for **Pick Up (Script)** components of GameObjects, rather than Unity's default Inspector which displays public variables of such scripted components.

Before and after its main work, the `OnInspectorGUI()` method first ensures that any variables relating to the object being edited in the Inspector have been updated - `serializedObject.Update()`. The last statement of this method correspondingly ensures that any changes to variables in the editor script have been copied back to the GameObject being edited - `serializedObject.ApplyModifiedProperties()`.

The `OnEnable()` method of script class PickUpEditor loads the three small icons (for display in the Inspector) and the three larger sprite images (to update the Sprite Renderer for display in the Scene/Game panels). The `pickupObject` variable is set to be a reference to the PickUp scripted component, allowing us to call the `SetSprite(...)` method. The `pickUpType` variable is set to be linked to the type variable of the PickUp scripted component whose special Inspector editor view makes this script possible - `serializedObject.FindProperty ("type")`.

There's more...

Here are some details you don't want to miss.

Offer the custom editing of pickup parameters via Inspector

Many pickups have additional properties, rather than simply being an item being carried. For example, a health pickup may add health points to the player's character, a coin pickup may add money points to the character's bank balance, and so on. So, let's add an integer points variable to our PickUp class and offer the user the ability to easily edit this points value via a **GUI slider** in our customer **Inspector** editor:

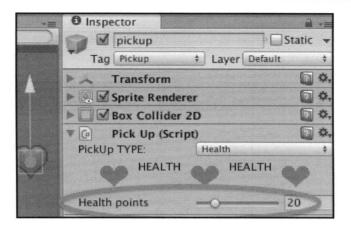

To add an editable points property to our PickUp objects, follow these steps:

1. Add the following extra line into C# script PickUp to create our new integer points variable:

   ```
   public int points;
   ```

2. Add the following extra line into C# script PickUpEditor to work with our new integer points variable:

   ```
   UnityEditor.SerializedProperty points;
   ```

3. Add the following extra line into the OnEnable() method in C# script PickUpEditor to associate our new points variable with its corresponding value in the PickUp scripted component of the GameObject being edited:

   ```
   csharp void OnEnable () {

   points = serializedObject.FindProperty ("points");

   pickUpType = serializedObject.FindProperty ("type");

   // rest of method as before...
   ```

4. Now, we can add an extra line into each GUI method for the different `PickUp` types. For example, we can add a statement to display an `IntSlider` to the user to be able to see and modify the points value for a Health PickUp object. We add a new statement at the end of the `InspectorGUI_HEALTH()` method in C# script `PickUpEditor` to display a modifiable `IntSlider` representing our new points variable as follows:

```
private void InspectorGUI_HEALTH(){
    // beginning of method just as before...

    pickupObject.SetSprite(spriteHealth100);

 // now display Int Slider for points
    points.intValue = EditorGUILayout.IntSlider ("Health
points", points.intValue, 0, 100);
  }
```

We provide four parameters to the `IntSlider(...)` method. The first is the text label the user will see next to the slider. The second is the initial value the slider displays. The last two are the maximum and minimum values. In our example, we are permitting values from 0 to 100, but if health pickups only offer one, two, or three health points, then we'd just call with `EditorGUILayout.IntSlider ("Health points, points.intValue, 1, 5")`. This method returns a new integer value based on where the slider has been positioned, and this new value is stored back into the integer value part of our `SerializedProperty` variable points.

Note that the loading and saving of values from the scripted component in the GameObject and our editor script is all part of the work undertaken by our calls to the `Update()` method and the `ApplyModifiedProperties()` method on the serialized object in the `OnInspectorGUI()` method.

Note that, since points may not have any meaning for some pickups, for example, keys, then we simply would not display any slider for the GUI Inspector editor when the user is editing `PickUp` objects of that type.

Offer a drop-down list of tags for key-pickup to fit via Inspector

While the concept of points may have no meaning for a key pickup, the concept of the type of lock that a given key fits is certainly something we may wish to implement in a game. Since Unity offers us a defined (and editable) list of string tags for any GameObject, often it is sufficient, and straightforward, to represent the type of lock or door corresponding to a key via its tag. For example, a green key might fit all objects tagged **LockGreen** and so on:

Therefore, it is very useful to be able to offer a custom Inspector editor for a string property of key pickups that stores the tag of the lock(s) the key can open. This task combines several actions, including using C# to retrieve an array of tags from the Unity editor, then the building and offering of a drop-down list of these tags to the user, with the current value already selected in this list.

To add a selectable list of strings for the tag for lock(s) that a key fits, follow these steps:

1. Add the following extra line into C# Script `PickUp` to create our new integer `fitsLockTag` variable:

```
public string fitsLockTag;
```

2. Add the following extra line into C# script `PickUpEditor` to work with our new integer `fitsLockTag` variable:

```
UnityEditor.SerializedProperty fitsLockTag;
```

3. Add the following extra line into the `OnEnable()` method in C# script `PickUpEditor` to associate our new `fitsLockTag` variable with its corresponding value in the `PickUp` scripted component of the GameObject being edited:

```
csharp void OnEnable () {

fitsLockTag = serializedObject.FindProperty ("fitsLockTag");
points = serializedObject.FindProperty ("points");

pickUpType = serializedObject.FindProperty ("type");

// rest of method as before...
```

4. Now, we need to add some extra lines of code into the GUI method for key PickUps. We need to add several statements to the end of method `InspectorGUI_KEY()` in C# script PickUpEditor to set up and display a selectable popup drop-down list representing our new `fitsLockTag` variable as follows. Replace the `InspectorGUI_KEY()` method with the following code:

```
private void InspectorGUI_KEY() {
    GUILayout.BeginHorizontal();
    GUILayout.FlexibleSpace();
    GUILayout.Label(iconKey);
    GUILayout.Label("KEY");
    GUILayout.Label(iconKey);
    GUILayout.Label("KEY");
    GUILayout.Label(iconKey);
    GUILayout.FlexibleSpace();
    GUILayout.EndHorizontal();

    pickupObject.SetSprite(spriteKey100);
```

```
        string[] tags =
UnityEditorInternal.InternalEditorUtility.tags;
        Array.Sort(tags);
        int selectedTagIndex = Array.BinarySearch(tags,
fitsLockTag.stringValue);
        if(selectedTagIndex < 0)
            selectedTagIndex = 0;

        selectedTagIndex = EditorGUILayout.Popup("Tag of door key
fits: ", selectedTagIndex, tags);

        fitsLockTag.stringValue = tags[selectedTagIndex];
    }
```

We've added several statements to the end of this method. First tags, an array of strings, is created (and sorted), containing the list of tags currently available in the Unity editor for the current game. We then attempt to find the location in this array of the current value of fitsLockTag - we can use the BinarySearch(...) method of built-in script class Array because we have alphabetically sorted our array (which also makes it easier for the user to navigate). If the string in fitsLockTag cannot be found in array tags, then the first item will be selected by default (index 0).

The user is then shown the drop-down list via the GUILayout method EditorGUILayout.Popup(...) and this method returns the index of whichever item is selected. The selected index is stored into selectedTagIndex and the last statement in the method extracts the corresponding string and stores that string into the fitsLockTag variable.

Note: Rather than displaying all possible tags, a further refinement might remove all items from array tags that do not have the prefix Lock. So the user is only presented with tags such as LockBlue and LockGreen, and so on.

Logic to open doors with keys based on fitsLockTag

In our player collision logic, we can now search through our inventory to see if any key items fit the lock we have collided with. For example, if a green door was collided with, and the player was carrying a key that could open such doors, then that item should be removed from the inventory List<> and the door should be opened.

To implement this, you would need to add an if test inside the `OnTriggerEnter()` method to detected collision with the item tagged `Door`, and then logic to attempt to open the door, and, if unsuccessful, do the appropriate action (for example, play sound) to inform the player they cannot open the door yet (we'll assume we have written a door animation controller that plays the appropriate animation and sounds and when a door is to be opened):

```
if("Door" == hitCollider.tag){
    if(!OpenDoor(hitCollider.gameObject))
        DoorNotOpenedAction();
}
```

The `OpenDoor()` method would need to identify which item (if any) in the inventory can open such a door, and, if found, then that item should be removed from the `List<>` and the door should be opened by the appropriate method:

```
private bool OpenDoor(GameObject doorGO){
    // search for key to open the tag of doorGO
    int colorKeyIndex = FindItemIndex(doorGO.tag);
    if( colorKeyIndex > -1 ){
        // remove key item from inventory List<>
        inventory.RemoveAt( colorKeyIndex );

        // now open the door...
        DoorAnimationController doorAnimationController =
doorGO.GetComponent<>(DoorAnimationController);
        doorAnimationController.OpenDoor();

        return true;
    }

    return false;
}
```

The following is the code for a method to find the inventory list key item fitting a door tag:

```
private int FindItemIndex(string doorTag){
    for (int i = 0; i < inventory.Count; i++){
        PickUp item = inventory[i];
        if( (PickUp.PickUpType.Key == item.type) &&
(item.fitsLockTag == doorTag))
            return i;
    }

    // not found
    return -1;
}
```

The need to add [SerializeField] for private properties

Note that, if we wished to create editor extensions to work with private variables, then we'd need to explicitly add [SerializeField] in the line immediately before the variable to be changed by the editor script. Public variables are serialized by default in Unity, so this was not required for our public type variable in script class PickUp, although it's good practice to flag ALL variables that are changeable via an Editor Extension in this way.

Learn more from the Unity editor scripts documentation pages: http://docs. unity3d.com/ScriptReference/Editor.html

An editor extension to have an object-creator GameObject, with buttons to instantiate different pickups at cross-hair object location in scene

If a level designer wishes to place each pickup carefully "by hand", we can still make this easier than having to drag copies of prefabs manually from the Projects panel. In this recipe, we provide a "cross-hairs" GameObject, with buttons in the Inspector allowing the game designer to create instances of three different kinds of prefab at precise locations by clicking the appropriate button when the center of the cross-hairs is at the desired location.

A **Unity Editor** extension is at the heart of this recipe and illustrates how such extensions can allow less technical members of a game development team to take an active role in level creation within the Unity Editor.

Getting ready

This recipe assumes you are starting with the Simple2Dgame_SpaceGirl project setup from the first recipe in Chapter 3, *Inventory UI*.

For this recipe, we have prepared the cross-hairs image you need in a folder named **Sprites** in the 18_09 folder.

How to do it...

To create an object-creator GameObject, follow these steps:

1. Start with a new copy of mini-game Simple2Dgame_SpaceGirl.

2. In the **Project** panel, rename GameObject star as **pickup**.

3. In the **Project** panel, create a new folder named **Prefabs**. Inside this new folder, create three new empty prefabs named **star**, **heart**, and **key**.

4. Populate the star prefab by dragging GameObject **pickup** from the **Hierarchy** panel over star in the **Project** panel. The prefab should now turn blue and have a copy of all of the star GameObject's properties and components.

5. Add a new tag **Heart** in the **Inspector**. Select GameObject **pickup** in the **Hierarchy** panel and assign it the tag **Heart**. Also, drag from the **Project** panel (folder Sprites) the **healthheart** image into the **Sprite** property of GameObject **pickup** so that the player sees the heart image on screen for this pickup item.

1. Populate the heart prefab by dragging GameObject pickup from the **Hierarchy** panel over heart in the **Prefabs** folder in the **Project** panel. The prefab should now turn blue and have a copy of all of the pickup GameObject's properties and components.

2. Add a new tag **Key** in the **Inspector**. Select GameObject's pickup in the Hierarchy panel and assign it this tag **Key**. Also, drag from the Project panel (folder Sprites) image **icon_key_green_100** into the Sprite property of GameObject's pickup so that the player sees the key image on screen for this pickup item.

3. Populate the key prefab by dragging GameObject pickup from the **Hierarchy** panel over key in the **Prefabs** folder in the **Project** panel. The prefab should now turn blue and have a copy of all of the pickup GameObject's properties and components.

4. Delete GameObject **pickup** from the Hierarchy.

5. In the **Project** panel, create a new folder named Editor. Inside this new folder, create a new C# script class named `ObjectBuilderEditor`, with the following code:

```
using UnityEngine;
using UnityEditor;

[CustomEditor(typeof(ObjectBuilderScript))]
public class ObjectBuilderEditor : Editor{
    private Texture iconStar;
    private Texture iconHeart;
    private Texture iconKey;
    private GameObject prefabHeart;
    private GameObject prefabStar;
    private GameObject prefabKey;
    void OnEnable () {
        iconStar =
AssetDatabase.LoadAssetAtPath("Assets/EditorSprites/icon_star_
32.png", typeof(Texture)) as Texture;
        iconHeart =
AssetDatabase.LoadAssetAtPath("Assets/EditorSprites/icon_heart
_32.png", typeof(Texture)) as Texture;
        iconKey =
AssetDatabase.LoadAssetAtPath("Assets/EditorSprites/icon_key_g
reen_32.png", typeof(Texture)) as Texture;
        prefabStar =
AssetDatabase.LoadAssetAtPath("Assets/Prefabs/star.prefab",
typeof(GameObject)) as GameObject;
        prefabHeart =
AssetDatabase.LoadAssetAtPath("Assets/Prefabs/heart.prefab",
```

```
typeof(GameObject)) as GameObject;
        prefabKey =
AssetDatabase.LoadAssetAtPath("Assets/Prefabs/key.prefab",
typeof(GameObject)) as GameObject;
    }
    public override void OnInspectorGUI() {
        GUILayout.Label("");
        GUILayout.BeginHorizontal();
        GUILayout.FlexibleSpace();
        GUILayout.Label("Click button to create instance of
prefab");
        GUILayout.FlexibleSpace();
        GUILayout.EndHorizontal();
        GUILayout.Label("");
        GUILayout.BeginHorizontal();
        GUILayout.FlexibleSpace();
        if(GUILayout.Button(iconStar))
AddObjectToScene(prefabStar);
        GUILayout.FlexibleSpace();
        if(GUILayout.Button(iconHeart))
AddObjectToScene(prefabHeart);
        GUILayout.FlexibleSpace();
        if(GUILayout.Button(iconKey))
AddObjectToScene(prefabKey);
        GUILayout.FlexibleSpace();
        GUILayout.EndHorizontal();
    }
    private void AddObjectToScene(GameObject
prefabToCreateInScene) {
        ObjectBuilderScript myScript =
(ObjectBuilderScript)target;
        GameObject newGo = Instantiate(prefabToCreateInScene,
myScript.gameObject.transform.position, Quaternion.identity);
        newGo.name = prefabToCreateInScene.name;
    }
}
```

11. Our **Editor** script is expecting to find the three icons in a folder named **EditorSprites**, so let's do this. First, create a new folder named **EditorSprites**. Next, drag the three 32 x 32 pixel icons from the Sprites folder into this new **EditorSprites** folder. Our **Editor** script should now be able to load these icons for image-based buttons that it will be drawing in the **Inspector**, from which the user chooses which pickup prefab object to clone into the scene.

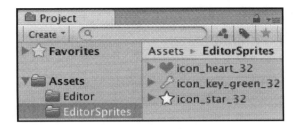

12. From the **Project** panel, drag `sprite cross_hairs.fw` into the Scene. Rename this GameObject **object-creator-cross-hairs**, and in its **Sprite Renderer** component in the Inspector, set **Sorting Layer** to **Foreground**.

13. Attach the following C# script to GameObject **object-creator-cross-hairs**:

```
using UnityEngine;

public class ObjectBuilderScript : MonoBehaviour {
  void Awake(){
    gameObject.SetActive(false);
  }
}
```

14. Select the **Rect Tool** (shortcut key T), and as you drag gameObject **object-creator-cross-hairs** and click on the desired icon in the **Inspector**, new **pickup** GameObjects will be added to the scene's Hierarchy.

How it works...

The script class `ObjectBuilderScript` has just two methods, one of which has just one statement - the `Awake()` method simply makes this GameObject become inactive when the game is running (since we don't want the user to see our cross-hairs created tool during gameplay). The `AddObjectToScene(...)` method receives a reference to a prefab as a parameter and instantiates a new clone of the prefab in the scene at the location of GameObject object-creator-cross-hairs at that point in time.

Script class `ObjectBuilderEditor` has a C# attribute `[CustomEditor(typeof(ObjectBuilderScript))]` immediately before the class is declared, telling Unity to use this class to control how `ObjectBuilderScript` GameObject properties and components are shown to the user in the Inspector.

There are six variables, three textures for the icons to form the buttons in the Inspector, and three GameObject references to the prefabs of which instances will be created. The `OnEnable()` method assigns values to these six variables using the built-in method `AssetDatabase.LoadAssetAtPath()`, retrieving the icons from the Project folder EditorSprites and getting references to the prefabs in the Project folder Prefabs.

The `OnInspectorGUI()` method has a variable myScript, which is set to be a reference to the instance of scripted component `ObjectBuilderScript` in GameObject **object-creator-cross-hairs** (so we can call its method when a prefab has been chosen). The method then displays a mixture of empty text `Labels` (to get some vertical spacing) and `FlexibleSpace` (to get some horizontal spacing and centering) and displays three buttons to the user, with icons of star, heart, and key. The scripted GUI technique for Unity custom **Inspector** GUIs wraps an `if` statement around each button, and on the frame the user clicks the button, the statement block of the if statement will be executed. When any of the three buttons is clicked, a call is made to `AddObjectToScene(...)` of the scripted component `ObjectBuilderScript`, passing the prefab corresponding to the button that was clicked.

Extensible class-based code architecture to manage complex IMGUIs

For complex objects and editor interactions, you may find the number of GUI statements gets high, and code can quickly get hard to manage with very long `OnGUI()` methods. One approach to organise complex GUIs involves a list of items, and each item being an object-instance of a wrapper-class for a GUI control object. Each wrapper class will implement its own `OnGUI()` method.

In this recipe, we'll use this approach to create a complex GUI with well-organised code. This recipe is adapted from an example posted by **Statement** on answers.unity.com in 2013 to a question about the different IMGUI libraries: `https://answers.unity.com/questions/601131/editorgui-editorguilayout-gui-guilayout-pshhh-when.html`

We'll create IMGUI static labels, interactive text boxes and a button, and illustrate some flexible space and centering using `BeginHorizontal()` and `EndHorizontal()`, where the fiddly GUILayout statements are put into their own classes.

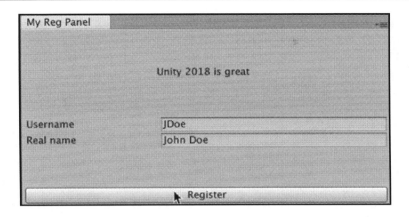

How to do it...

To create an extensible class-based code architecture to manage complex IMGUIs, follow these steps:

1. First let's create an **interface**, that is, a template script-class that defines a method all implementing-classes must have. Create a folder **Editor**. Inside that create a folder **MyGUI**. Inside that create a new C# script-class named IMyGUI containing the following:

    ```
    public interface IMyGUI
    {
        void OnGUI();
    }
    ```

2. Now, let's define a **FlexibleSpace** class for our GUI library. Create a C# script class named MyGUIFlexibleSpace containing the following:

    ```
    using UnityEngine;

    public class MyGUIFlexibleSpace : IMyGUI
    {
        public void OnGUI()
        {
            GUILayout.FlexibleSpace();
        }
    }
    ```

3. Now, we'll create a button class. Create a C# script class named `MyGUIButton` containing the following:

```
using UnityEngine;

public class MyGUIButton : IMyGUI
{
    public GUIContent label = new GUIContent();
    public event System.Action OnClick;

    public void OnGUI() {
        // if button clicked, invoke methods registed with
'OnClick' event
        if (GUILayout.Button (label) && OnClick != null)
            OnClick ();
    }
}
```

4. Now, we'll create an input Text Field class. Create a C# script class named `MyGUITextField` containing the following:

```
using UnityEngine;
using UnityEditor;

public class MyGUITextField : IMyGUI
{
    public string text = "";
    public GUIContent label = new GUIContent();

    public void OnGUI() {
        text = EditorGUILayout.TextField (label, text);
    }
}
```

5. Now, we'll create a non-interactive text label class. Create a C# script class named `MyGUILabel` containing the following:

```
using UnityEngine;

public class MyGUILabel : IMyGUI {
    private string text;
    private bool centerFully;

    public MyGUILabel(string text, bool centerFully = false)
{
        this.text = text;
        this.centerFully = centerFully;
    }
```

```
public void OnGUI() {
    if (centerFully) {
        GUILayout.BeginVertical();
        GUILayout.FlexibleSpace();
        GUILayout.BeginHorizontal();
        GUILayout.FlexibleSpace();
    }

    GUILayout.Label(text);
    if (centerFully) {
        GUILayout.FlexibleSpace();
        GUILayout.EndHorizontal();
        GUILayout.FlexibleSpace();
        GUILayout.EndVertical();
    }
}
}
```

6. In **Editor** folder, we'll now create a class to display an interactive custom panel, making use of our MyGUI classes above. Create C# script-class MyEditorWindow containing the following to start with:

```
using UnityEngine;
using UnityEditor;
using System.Collections.Generic;

// adapted from answers.unity.com sample code posted by
'Statememt' (Dec 2013)
// 
https://answers.unity.com/questions/601131/editorgui-editorgui
layout-gui-guilayout-pshhh-when.html
public class MyEditorWindow : EditorWindow
{
    MyGUITextField username;
    MyGUITextField realname;
    MyGUIButton registerButton;
    MyGUIFlexibleSpace flexibleSpace;

    // Optional, but may be convenient.
    List<IMyGUI> gui = new List<IMyGUI>();

    [MenuItem("Example/Show Window")]
    public static void ShowWindow () {
        GetWindow<MyEditorWindow>("My Reg Panel", true);
    }
}
```

7. We'll now add the method to display a menu item to open our window-panel. Add the following to C# `script-class MyEditorWindow`:

```
[MenuItem("Example/Show Window")]
 public static void ShowWindow () {
  GetWindow<MyEditorWindow>("My Reg Panel", true);
 }
```

8. We'll now add a method to setup our `MyGUI` objects and add them to our GUI list of objects. Add the following to C# script-class `MyEditorWindow`:

```
void OnEnable()
 {
      username = new MyGUITextField ();
      username.label.text = "Username";
      username.text = "JDoe";

      realname = new MyGUITextField ();
      realname.label.text = "Real name";
      realname.text = "John Doe";

      registerButton = new MyGUIButton ();
      registerButton.label.text = "Register";
       // add RegisterUser() to button's OnClick event
broadcaster
      registerButton.OnClick += LogUser;

      bool centerFully = true;
      gui.Add(new MyGUILabel("Unity 2018 is great",
centerFully));

      gui.Add (username);
      gui.Add (realname);
      gui.Add(new MyGUIFlexibleSpace());
      gui.Add (registerButton);
 }
```

9. We'll now add a method loop through and display all our GUI objects each frame. Add the following to C# script-class `MyEditorWindow`:

```
void OnGUI() {
  foreach (var item in gui)
      item.OnGUI();
 }
```

Chapter 15

10. Finally, we need to add a method to respond to the button clicks (`LogUser`). Also a method to ensure we re-register this method when the window is disabled (to avoid memory leaks). Add these two methods to C# script-class `MyEditorWindow`:

```
private void OnDisable()
  {
   registerButton.OnClick -= LogUser;
  }

void LogUser()
  {
   var msg = "Registering " + realname.text + " as " +
username.text;
   Debug.Log (msg);
  }
```

11. After a few seconds, you should now see a menu named **Example** appear with a **Show Window** item.

12. You should now be able to display our custom registration panel by choosing this menu item.

How it works...

Since there are several C# script-classes, each shall be separately described in the following.

Script-class MyEditorWindow

In C# script-class `MyEditorWindow`, you preceded the `ShowWindow()` method with an attribute to add a menu item **Show Window** to a menu named Example. The `GetWindow()` statement gets a reference to an `MyEditorWindow` object - if no such window-panel exists, it creates one. The first argument is the title of the panel **My Reg Panel**. The true for the second argument tells Unity to make the window-panel have the focus (if a window panel already existed).

The OnEnable() method is executed when the window-panel first becomes enabled (active). It creates 2 MyGUITextField objects for username and real name, and a register MyGUIButton. Each of these objects are based on the MyGUI component script-classes in folder MyGUI. Then GUI objects are added in the sequence we wish, to the list variable guiCompoennts. The first GUI component added to the list is a new object-instance of an non-interactive MyGUILabel (passing the text string Unity 2018 is great and a true for full centering). Then, we add the two text input components (username and real name), then a new MyGUIFlexible space object-instance, and finally a MyGUIButton with the label Register, whose OnClick event will cause the invocation of the LogUser() method.

The LogUser() method logs the names in the two text fields to the Debug.Log.

The OnDisable() method ensures that when the window-panel is being disabled/closed we de-register the LogUser() method from the OnClick event of the button object.

The OnGUI() method, which executes every frame, simply loops through each GUI compoennt in list guiComponents, invoking the components' OnGUI() method. So each frame, our GUI is redisplayed.

Script-class IMyGUI

This C# script-class declares an **interface named** IMyGUI. An interface is a template script-class that defines method(s) all implementing classes must implement. Our interface class is very simple, it simply requires all implementing classes must defined an OnGUI() method. There is a naming convention that recommends all interface classes have a capital letter I, before the upper-camel case class name.

By declaring this interface, we can now implement lots of different IMyGUI classes, which can all be treated the same way - that is, they can have their OnGUI() method invoked each frame.

Script-class MyGUIFlexibleSpace

This simple script-class adds a GUILayout.FlexibleSpace() to the IMGUI system when its OnGUI() method is invoked.

Script-class MyGUITextField

This class declares two public items: a public string (for the text the user can see and edit), and a public label. Its OnGUI() method displays the labelled text field, and stores its value back into variable text.

So our custom editor classes can set the initial text value and label, and also read any new value of the text from an object-instance of this class.

Script-class MyGUILabel

This class has two private values: the text to be displayed, and a bool, defining whether or not to fully center the text. Its OnGUI() method will add a GUILayout.Lable() to the GUI, and if the bool is true, it will add other GUILayout components before and after the label to ensure the label is both vertically and horizontally centered when displayed.

This is an example of how some of the complexity of an interface can be delegated to its own class like this. By setting a single bool to true, several Begin/End/Vertical/Horizontal statements and FlexibleSpace statements are added to the GUI that is output.

The screenshot illustrates how the flexible space and vertical/horizonal groups result in the desired alignment and spacing in the window-panel the user sees:

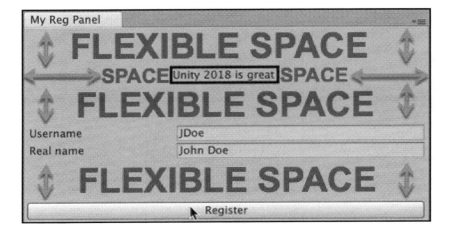

Script-class MyGUIButton

This class declares a public label, and also a public `OnClick` event. During the execution of its `OnGUI()` method, if the button has been clicked any methods that have been registered to listen for, `OnClick` events will be invoked.

There is a condition in the `OnGUI()` method, to ensure that if no methods are registered to list for `OnClick` events, then no statement is executed.

We can see the `LogUser` method of the `MyEditorWindow` the window-panel object being registered for the `OnClick` event of the `registerButton` object, in its `OnEnable()` method:

```
registerButton = new MyGUIButton ();
registerButton.label.text = "Register";
// add RegisterUser() to button's OnClick event broadcaster
registerButton.OnClick += LogUser;
```

While perhaps overkill for this simple window-panel, this recipe illusrtates how the use of an Interface and a list of GUI component objects, allows for an extensible system of custom GUI component classes to be created, while allowing the complexity of the `EditorWindow` classes to be maintained.

NOTE: An alternative to C# events would be to use Unity Events and in some cases lambda expressions. You can read a discussion of such topics in these online articles:

- http://www.blockypixel.com/2012/09/c-in-unity3d-dynamic-methods-with-lambda-expressions/
- https://forum.unity.com/threads/how-to-use-an-action.339952/

Bonus Chapters

Working with External Resource Files and Devices

This chapter helps you explore and choose between the different locations at which data for games can be stored. This chapter explores a range of locations and strategies for separating your game data from the logic, and for loading the data when needed. It also explores ways to save runtime data between Scenes, through static variables and the Unity PlayerPrefs system. A method of saving screenshots when the game is running is presented. Two recipes illustrate how to load and save game components as Unity Asset Bundles.

You can read the chapter here: https://www.packtpub.com/sites/default/files/downloads/WorkingwithExternalResourceFilesandDevices.pdf

Working with Plain Text, XML, and JSON Text Files

This chapter presents different ways for using text files in games to represent and communicate data. Creating, reading, and writing to text files can be performed in many ways, and apart from generic plain text files, there are the common data interchange text file formats of JSON and XML. This chapter presents a range of recipes for creating, reading, and writing to text files with different types of text content. These are useful for games that save data locally to the device they are running on, and also when communicating with online clients.

You can read the chapter here: https://www.packtpub.com/sites/default/files/downloads/WorkingwithPlainTextXMLandJSONTextFiles.pdf

Virtual Reality and Extra Features

This chapter presents some of the additional features of Unity 2018 not covered elsewhere in the book. In this chapter, we will present a range of additional Unity features that we wanted to include, such as slow motion, gizmos, and a pause-game recipe. With VR, such an up-and-coming feature of games, we also include a set of recipes illustrating VR game development in Unity.

You can read the chapter here: `https://www.packtpub.com/sites/default/files/downloads/VirtualRealityandExtraFeatures.pdf`

Automated Testing

This chapter introduces ways in Unity to automate the testing of code and GameObjects. Having a set of automated tests that can be executed quickly means that when programmers and game designers make changes to a game, they can quickly check that no unintended consequences have been created, which either give rise to errors or make GameObjects behave in ways they are not meant to. In this chapter, we will introduce the Unity Test Runner, and we will present recipes illustrating how to automate isolated testing of code (unit tests), and runtime testing of the interaction of code and the Unity system (such as physics and animation) in play-mode tests. The recipe concludes with both play-mode and unit testing of a health bar game component, illustrating logging and exceptions.

You can read the chapter here: `https://www.packtpub.com/sites/default/files/downloads/AutomatedTesting.pdf`

Other Books You May Enjoy

If you enjoyed this book, you may be interested in these other books by Packt:

Unity 2018 By Example - Second Edition
Alan Thorn

ISBN: 978-1-78839-870-1

- Understand core Unity concepts, such as game objects, components, and scenes
- Study level-design techniques for building immersive and interesting worlds
- Make functional games with C# scripting
- Use the toolset creatively to build games with different themes and styles
- Handle player controls and input functionality
- Work with terrains and world-creation tools
- Get to grips with making both 2D and 3D games

Unity 2018 Augmented Reality Projects

Jesse Glover

ISBN: 978-1-78883-876-4

- Build and run AR applications for specific headsets, including HoloLens and Daydream
- Create 3D scenes with Unity and other 3D tools while learning about world space and scale
- Move around your AR scenes using locomotion and teleportation
- Create filters or overlays that work in tandem with facial recognition software
- Use GPS, geolocation services, and the camera feed to create a fitness application
- Integrate AR and VR concepts together in a single application

Leave a review - let other readers know what you think

Please share your thoughts on this book with others by leaving a review on the site that you bought it from. If you purchased the book from Amazon, please leave us an honest review on this book's Amazon page. This is vital so that other potential readers can see and use your unbiased opinion to make purchasing decisions, we can understand what our customers think about our products, and our authors can see your feedback on the title that they have worked with Packt to create. It will only take a few minutes of your time, but is valuable to other potential customers, our authors, and Packt. Thank you!

Index